Garde Manger

COLD KITCHEN FUNDAMENTALS

American Culinary Federation

Garde Manger

COLD KITCHEN FUNDAMENTALS

Contributing Authors

Chef Edward G. Leonard
CMC, GMC, FSP, AAC

Brenda R. Carlos

Chef Tina Powers
CEC, CEPC, CCE, CMB

Special thanks to Arno Schmidt

Prentice Hall

Boston   Columbus   Indianapolis   New York   San Francisco   Upper Saddle River
Amsterdam   Cape Town   Dubai   London   Madrid   Milan   Munich   Paris   Montreal   Toronto
Delhi   Mexico City   São Paulo   Sydney   Hong Kong   Seoul   Singapore   Taipei   Tokyo

Editorial Director: Vernon R. Anthony
Senior Acquisitions Editor: William Lawrensen
Editorial Assistant: Lara Dimmick
Director of Marketing: David Gesell
Senior Marketing Manager: Thomas Hayward
Senior Marketing Coordinator: Alicia Wozniak
Marketing Assistant: Les Roberts
Associate Managing Editor: Alexandrina
 Benedicto Wolf
Project Manager: Kris Roach
Senior Operations Supervisor: Pat Tonneman

Operations Specialist: Deidra Skahill
Senior Art Director: Diane Y. Ernsberger
Text and Cover Designer: Wanda Espana
Cover Art: Istock
Art Editor: Janet Portisch
Media Director: Michelle Churma
Full-Service Project Management: S4Carlisle Publishing Services
Composition: S4Carlisle Publishing Services
Printer/Binder: LSC Communications
Cover Printer: LSC Communications
Text Font: 11/13, Adobe Garamond Pro

Photos, unless otherwise noted, are by Richard Embery/owned and copyrighted by Pearson. Credits and acknowledgments borrowed from other sources and reproduced, with permission, in this textbook appear on pages 886–890.

Library of Congress Cataloging-in-Publication Data

Leonard, Edward G.
  Garde manger : cold kitchen fundamentals / Edward G. Leonard, Brenda R. Carlos, and Tina Powers.
    p. cm.
  Includes bibliographical references and index.
  ISBN 978-0-13-118219-6
  1. Cookery (Cold dishes) 2. Quantity cookery. I. Carlos, Brenda R. II. Title.

TX830.P693 2010
641.7'9—dc22   2010005190

Prentice Hall
is an crimson imprint of

www.pearsonhighered.com

ISBN 10:   0-13-118219-6
ISBN 13: 978-0-13-118219-6

Contents

Preface

>> To the Student

Cold Kitchen Fundamentals has been written for the new student who is just starting to learn the basics of knife skills, emulsification, and fabrication as well as for the advanced student who is gearing up for the competitive arena such as an ACF Culinary Salon. It is a text for the garde manger and the pantry work that is a foundational skill needed for successful chefs and culinarians. When coupled with the ACF's *Culinary Fundamentals* and *Baking Fundamentals,* these texts provide students with the necessary skills to begin a professional journey.

This textbook focuses on techniques. It is also a good source of recipes to add to any professional repertoire. We hope that the information contained in this book will open your eyes to the possibilities of working with diverse ingredients and inspire you to develop your artistic and creative talents so that you can eventually create your own signature sauces, salads, and cold soups.

>> To the Instructor

Thank you for selecting this text for your students. This book has been written in response to the need for a comprehensive, yet basic, cold kitchen book. It is the companion to the ACF's *Culinary Fundamentals* and *Baking Fundamentals* textbooks, but can also stand alone, if needed. It covers all aspects of the garde manger, from simple salad prep, dressings, and sauce making, to the more challenging tasks of creating appetizers, soups, and sandwiches as well as charcuterie, cheese making, ice carving, and competition.

This book is not just a recipe book, although it does contain lots of beautiful recipes. The recipes are easy-to-teach recipes that have been tested in working kitchens and culinary classrooms. Above and beyond the recipes, this book focuses on teaching the processes and procedures chefs need to know to work in the cold kitchen, In addition, we hope that the learning activities will stimulate a student's curiosity and creativity. We have focused on presenting the topics in a timely manner, appealing to the visual learner with over 600 illustrative photographs so that students can see the processes discussed. In many cases, we've included photos of the finished dish to serve as a template to the desired outcome.

The Chef's Tips provide additional information from chefs with over 30 years of experience. The unit summaries and review questions will help students to review the material and test their comprehension.

The supplements provide added support to educators.

>> Key Features and Benefits of the Book

This book lives up to its name, *Cold Kitchen Fundamentals,* as it focuses on giving the culinary student a fundamental understanding of garde-manger work.

This book is organized into sections, and within each section are teaching units. As students progress from one section to another, they will build a strong foundation of knowledge and experience.

>> The Organization of the Text

Section 1 covers the history of the cold kitchen, from its earliest prehistoric foundations, on up through the Roman Empire, into the Dark Ages, and into the light of the Renaissance and Reformation, through the age of the Guilds and into the Gilded Age when Escoffier was king and the beauty and pageantry of the cold kitchen was in full bloom. Section 1 also covers the most important aspect of the cold kitchen—sanitation and safety. By its very nature, food prepared hot and served cold has special needs and considerations when it comes to sanitation, and this is covered extensively. Equipment is covered as well in this section, from the smallest of Parisian scoops to the largest of blast chillers, and every mold and cutting device in between.

Section 2 focuses on the ingredients used in the cold kitchen. Spices, herbs, fruits and vegetables, nuts, cheese, and proteins including fish, fowl, and meat are covered in depth as they apply to the use in the pantry and in the production of cold items. When we understand the uses and the flavors of the many ingredients used, and when we utilize all types of cuts and products, the cold kitchen then becomes a center of efficiency as well as profit.

Section 3 showcases the starters or beginnings of the meals. Every type of small finger food is covered in these units, from canapés, hors d'oeuvre, and amuse bouche to appetizers.

Section 4 covers the basics or benchmarks of making and serving sandwiches and cold soups. From the simplest to the most elegant, sandwiches and soups tease or make the meal, from breakfast items to soups served for dessert.

Section 5 is about salads in all their green and glistening glory. We start off by presenting the basic pre-prep and identification of the greens and other salad ingredients. We then take you to the other types of salads—bound salads, fruit salads, and composed salads, from the simplest to the most exotic.

Section 6 covers dips, dressings, cold sauces, salsas, relishes, chutney, and every type of cold sauce used for salads, accents, and accompaniments.

Section 7 begins with a change from the lighter fare to the fabrication, processes, and production of charcuterie. We explore the systems of preserving from salting, smoking, and curing, taking you through the step-by-step procedures necessary to master these important cold kitchen skills.

Section 8 covers the backbone of most large-scale professional kitchens—the buffet and catering businesses. The cold kitchen chef is generally actively involved in both buffet preparation and in catering. We cover the logistics of on- and off-premise catering including mass production, plating, and box lunches.

Section 9 finishes up our text with decorations and competition. It is important that beginning students master the hand–eye coordination that decorative work develops. Taking this to a higher level, competition fast-tracks the culinarian by pushing competitors toward mastery over their craft. By competing, the student or novice cooks alongside more experienced chefs and gleans precious knowledge not only from the chance to win a medal, but by the interaction and direction of the accomplished judges. These hard-won skills push anyone who participates into a higher level of learning.

>> Special Features in This Book

BENCHMARK RECIPES

Reading about a skill is not as valuable to a student as performing that skill. The Benchmark Recipes presented in this book expose students to a foundational method or basic recipe. Each Benchmark Recipe was chosen to teach a specific lesson about an important ingredient.

PHOTOGRAPHS

The words in this text are supported with over 600 photographs. Each recipe includes a photo of one of the important ingredients, steps, or finished product. The Benchmark Recipes are supported with additional photographs showing each of the basic steps. There is truth in the saying that "a picture is worth a thousand words."

LEARNING ACTIVITIES

The Learning Activities were created to support the theories and information presented in each unit. The activities are simple to execute and teach an important concept. Instructors and students alike will appreciate the learning activities.

CHEF'S TIPS

Our writing team has years and years of culinary experience. The tips sprinkled throughout this book provide added information. It is as if a chef is standing behind the student in the kitchen sharing his or her experience.

LEARNING OBJECTIVES AND KEY TERMS

Learning Objectives provide a preview of each unit as well as a benchmark to judge the students' competencies once they finish the unit. The Learning Objectives tell what students should learn in each unit if they read it and work to create the assigned recipes. The Key Terms give the students a "heads-up" to know when important words are being introduced or emphasized within that unit.

SUMMARIES AND UNIT REVIEWS

The unit ends with a Summary that reminds students of the important steps included in that unit and points out the key elements. The Review Questions provide a method to test the students' knowledge and to review the material presented.

APPENDICES

Appendices containing the charts provided within the book appear at the end of the book. They provide students with easy access to the charts found within the text.

BIBLIOGRAPHY

No one book has all of the answers, and it is important to keep learning. We have provided a good list of books, magazines, blogs and websites, links, and printed materials for further research. Our business changes daily, and the professional chef has to be aware of nutritional trends, new flavors, and cultural diversity. In order to keep sharp, one needs to keep on top of what is happening in the world of food and flavors. Using the listed resources is a good starting place.

GLOSSARY

The Glossary covers not only key terms listed in the units, but additional terms and words used in the cold kitchen. These words and terms are the language of our business. "Kitchenese" is critical if you are to be considered a professional. Knowing the words and their correct meaning ensures accuracy in menus, as well as respect for our craft and those who developed the classical cuisine.

Supplements include the following:

Companion Website
Study Guide
Instructor's Manual with Test Item File
PowerPoint presentations
Testgen

>> An Explanation on Units of Measure

U.S. customary units of measure are used throughout this textbook as the principal system of measurement. The instructions and recipes were first developed using this system of liquid volume and dry weight measurement. There are many people, however, who use the metric system, and for this reason we have included metric units of measurement. Many people use scientific equipment and scales, and purchase ingredients and other items in metric quantities. For this reason, we list ingredients in both the U.S. and Metric system.

Although it is very common practice to round up when using metric conversion, we have not done so, as accuracy in a teaching textbook is important. We have included conversion charts in the appendices, however, for your benefit; we include a few common examples that will help with your conversions. Weight is different from volume in most, but not all, foods and liquids, and this also applies to the Metric system. For example, 1 solid ounce weighs in at 28.35 grams; 1 fluid ounce measures at 29.57 milliliters. You can convert using these by rounding up to 30 grams or 30 milliliters; in small quantities, it will not be a problem. When you start making larger quantities, however, especially when factoring any costing, it is up to the discretion of the chef as to whether to round up or not.

It is our hope that you will enjoy using this text as a teaching tool, and that your students will expand their knowledge and heighten their curiosity and passion for the art and science of the cold kitchen processes. This side of the kitchen can be a tremendous outlet for the artistic side of each student, and will bring much satisfaction and pleasure in the accomplishment of these tasks. There are many opportunities to advance in our profession with just some of the many skills provided in this text. By acquiring these cold kitchen skills, developing signature items, saving underutilized products and materials, and turning the cold kitchen into a cost-saving center, your opportunities within this field will make for a rich and rewarding career in the culinary industry!

Acknowledgments

I dedicate this book to the cooks, chefs, and bakers who made this all possible. To Frank Schellings and Pierre Bosman, the first "real" certified chefs that I ever met: Their sense of devotion and dedication to cooking and, more importantly, to teaching and inspiring their students put me on the path that I now travel. To Jack Barnett, a consummate hospitality professional that dedicated his life to the good service of others and showed me that teamwork is the real key to success in our profession, and to my husband, Edward, my sons, Benjamin Thomas and Edward Martin, and my daughter, Jennifer Jean-Marie, the center of my success and the reason for my passion, family.

—Tina Powers

>> From Tina Powers

I want to first thank the ACF for the opportunity to work on this textbook. As an educator, it is a privilege to work with such an outstanding organization. The support for all cooks, chefs, bakers, pastry chefs, and foodservice professionals is invaluable, and the ACF has been there every step of the way.

I would also like to acknowledge the help, input, critique, and support of the many dozens of ACF chefs and educators who had a hand in the production of this book. This book, like any good dish, needs quality ingredients to produce quality on the plate, and their comments have added to the seasoning of this "dish."

I want to thank the tremendous students, Junior ACF team members, culinary instructors, and the administration of Le Cordon Bleu in Portland, Oregon, and the Oregon Coast Culinary Institute in Coos Bay, Oregon. Special thanks to Chefs Shawn Hanlin, CEC; Woojay Poynter, CSC; Tom Roberts, CEC; and Nilda DoVale, CCE. I want to thank and acknowledge my 2004/2005 ACF Junior Team Nebraska, and our sponsor, Chef Gary Hoffman, CEC for his continuing support to all culinary student competitors, both at the high school and college levels. Without their help, kindness, willingness to test recipes and techniques, and unwavering cooperation, this book would not have been possible. I want to especially thank Chefs Russ Langstadt, Brian Harper, Dean Murray, Kenneth Narcavage, Steve Watson, Susie Wilcox, Kevin Monti, Peter Edris, Wendy Bennett, Jennifer White, Mariko Wilkinson, Shermichael Williams, Christina Chambers, Jennifer Black, Peggy Alter, Shannon Wheeler, Mavricio Tomasino, and Edward Powers for their invaluable assistance.

I acknowledge Richard Embery for his outstanding photography throughout the text. He put into pictures what we tried to convey and his work is truly art. I want to thank Mark Huth for keeping the project going smoothly and burnishing the rough edges where needed. Lastly, I want to thank Brenda Carlos, the most wonderful wordsmith and friend, for helping me find the right words at the right time.

Finally, I want to thank my dear husband, Ed Powers, who continually supports me in all of my activities.

>> From Brenda R. Carlos

There are many individuals who greatly contributed to this text. First I would like to thank Vern Anthony from Prentice-Hall, who invited me to become part of the writing team for this book. I also wish to acknowledge William Lawrensen, our editor, who continually showed his support, as well as Mark Huth, who was responsible for editorial development and reviews. His help was truly appreciated.

From the beginning, Ed Leonard and Arno Schmidt provided their insights and shared recipes. Their years of experience and passion for this topic helped to breathe life into this text. Richard Embery provided most of the photography for this book, and his amazing talent certainly enhanced this text.

I loved working with Tina Powers, who jumped into the project and provided hours of dedicated guidance and support. She is an amazing chef and culinary instructor and it has been a privilege to work with her on almost a daily basis as we've completed this book. Chef Powers's students should be commended, as many helped out during our photo shoot. The administration and staff at Le Cordon Bleu, Portland, were the perfect hosts for our photo shoot and I thank them.

A special thank you goes to our many reviewers whose comments and suggestions helped to improve this book. They are Michael Baskette, CEC, CCE, AAC; Wilfred Beriau, Southern Main Tech College; Keith Buerker, SUNY Cobleskill; Chef Ray Duey, Anne Arundel Community College; Sally Frey; Keith Gardiner, Guilford Technical Community College; Richard Kimball, Fox Valley Technical College; Gerard J. Murphy, Southern Westchester Board of Cooperative Educational Services; John Reiss, Milwaukee Area Technical College; Hans Schadler; Cory Shute, Kansas Area Technical School; James R. Taylor, MBA, CEC, AAC, Columbus State Community College; and Louis R. Woods, Jr., CEC, CCA, Anne Arundel Community College.

Kristi Begley and her team at the American Culinary Federation provided guidance and suggestions that were also greatly appreciated.

And I can't close without thanking my family, who continually support me and encourage me. Thanks, Rudy, you have truly been my best friend and helpmate for over 30 years. I love and appreciate my two sons, Chad and Clint, and daughters-in-law, Melissa and Amie. I also acknowledge my parents, Jean and Perry Langer, who always taught me that I could do anything I wanted, as long as I was willing to work hard enough.

Students and staff from Western Culinary Institute who helped with the photo shoot.

About the Authors

>> Edward G. Leonard CMC, GMC, FSP, AAC

Chef Edward G. Leonard is the vice president and corporate chef for the Le Cordon Bleu Schools in North America. He is a past president of the American Culinary Federation (ACF) and former executive chef of The Westchester Country Club and the vice president of the World Cooks Societies.

He is one of only 72 Certified Master Chefs in the United States and a member of the World Master Chef Society, along with being a certified WACS master chef. He received an honorary full doctorate in culinary arts from Johnson and Wales University and from HMIF. Chef Leonard has extensive experience as an educator, speaker, manager, cook, restaurant owner, and executive chef. He maintains a strong reputation as a speaker and motivator. Chef Leonard was the team chef and leader of the ACF Culinary Team USA from 1998 to 2008 leading a team of chefs from America that cook on an international stage every four years in Germany in the culinary Olympics. His team in 2004 finished with one of only four gold medals earned out of 32 national teams from around the globe in the hot kitchen, finishing third overall. He led the national team to three golds and one silver and his regional team to the world championship in 2008. He has led the Culinary Team USA to five championships and more than 34 gold medals in the international arena. Chef Leonard has won more than 50 gold medals in competitions and having gold in every category including pastry and centerpiece work.

He is one of the top chefs in the country and a leader for the industry and is invited to speak all over the world in regard to the profession and American cuisine.

>> Brenda R. Carlos

Brenda Carlos has served as publisher and managing editor for the Hospitality News Group, publishers of *Hospitality News for the Western U.S.* as well as the *International Education Guide.* She has authored countless articles focusing on all aspects of the foodservice industry, event management, and running a business. She also was a contributing editor to *Service at Its Best, Waiter-Waitress Training* (Prentice-Hall). She is the co-author of three previously published textbooks: *Event Management for Tourism, Cultural, Business and Sporting Events* (Prentice Hall); *The American Culinary Federation's Baking Fundamentals* (Prentice Hall); and *Knife Skills for Chefs* (Prentice Hall). She is a regular contributor to the American Culinary Federation's *National Culinary Review.* She is the founder of BC Editorial Services and works with a number of hospitality clients. Ms. Carlos is an enthusiastic and dynamic speaker; she loves to speak to students and business owners about the culinary, hospitality, and event management industries. She is a former member of the International Foodservice Editorial Council and a current member of Toastmasters, International.

>> Chef Tina Powers, CEC, CCE, CEPC, CMB

Tina Powers is currently a full-time culinary instructor at the Oregon Coast Culinary Institute, at Southwestern Oregon Community College in Coos Bay, Oregon, where she teaches both baking and culinary classes. She is the owner of a restaurant and bakery consulting business that serves both the culinary and baking industries in the United States, as well as in Eastern Europe and Russia. She was formerly affiliated with a community college in the Midwest where she was the department representative and one of the senior instructors as well as the first coach for the school's ACF Junior team. In 2005, she became a Certified Master Baker. She received an ACF Presidential Gold Medal in 2005; an ACF Steady Eddie Award, Central Region, in 2004; and she was awarded the ConAgra Excellence in Education Award in 2003, as well as the National Institute for Staff & Organizational Development Excellence Award for Community College Instructors. She was the vice president of the ACF Chefs and Culinarians of the Heartland Chapter, as well as the education and certification chairperson during her tenure. In 2000, she was awarded the Phi Theta Kappa Instructor of the Year. From 1993 to 1997, she was the program director and senior instructor for both culinary and baking at the Emily Griffith Opportunity School in Denver, Colorado. During that time, she was the certification chairperson for the ACF Colorado Chefs De Cuisine as well as team coach for her school's Junior ACF team. Chef Powers became a Certified Culinary Educator and a Certified Executive Chef in 1992 and continued on with additional Certification as a Certified Executive Pastry Chef in 2009.

Chef Powers was a founding member of the ACF Eastbay Chefs Association and, in 1983, became an executive chef working in Northern California, Texas, and Colorado, where she continued until 1993. She then became a full-time culinary and bakery arts instructor.

Authors Brenda R. Carlos with Tina Powers, CEC, CCE, CEPC, CMB.

History of the Cold Kitchen and Basic Food Safety, Sanitation, and Equipment

>> **Unit 1**

Introduction to the Cold Kitchen

>> **Unit 2**

Sanitation and Safety

>> **Unit 3**

Basic Equipment

Section 1 offers a brief overview of the historical evolution of cooking, specifically concerning the history of storing food, preserving food, and preparing cold dishes. The history of the cold kitchen tells fascinating stories about legendary Roman feasts, how the early guilds were formed and then established guidelines for sausage makers during medieval time, and why many of today's kitchen terms came from the French. It explains the French term "garde manger" as well as other duties and responsibilities of the chefs working in the "garde manger" and how these responsibilities evolved into the cold kitchen work of today's pantry.

This section also discusses safe food handling and storage as well as proper sanitation practices. Kitchen safety is also reviewed. After working through these two introductory units, students should have a good understanding of the cold kitchen and a basic review of food safety and sanitation.

Using the right tool for the job is as important to a chef as it is to a craftsman. Unit 3 gives a brief overview of the basic equipment used in the cold kitchen.

Introduction to the Cold Kitchen

>> Learning Objectives

After you have finished reading this unit, you should be able to:

- Define "garde manger."
- Describe the role of the charcutier.
- Explain the culinary contributions made by Apicius, Carême, and Escoffier.
- List some of the main duties of the chef garde manger in the past.
- List some of the main duties of the chef garde manger of today.

>> Key Terms

Apicius	chaud froid (*shoh-*	garde manger (*gahr*	Marie-Antoine Carême
Auguste Escoffier	*FRWAH*)	*mohn-zahj*)	pantry
charcuterie (*shahr-coo-*	chef garde manger	intermezzo	pemmican
tuhr-EE)	chefs de partie	IQF	

This unit touches on the evolution of cold kitchen design, how the open hearth—the common cooking place for thousands of years—was no longer adequate when many elaborate dishes had to be prepared and served at the same time. Consequently, open-hearth cooking evolved with the invention of the iron stove, and in Europe these new stoves were moved to the center of the kitchen, enabling many cooks to work from all sides at the same time. In America, the stoves were moved against the wall in large hotels for better workspace flow, which ultimately provided better service for customers. This unit describes how the kitchens were organized into stations or brigades, a practice that began in large establishments such as the grand hotels and steamships where many complicated meals were prepared at the same time. It also goes on to describe the modern cold kitchens of today and how form meets function.

The most common definition for the term **"garde manger"** stems from the French phrase, "to protect or guard" the "manger," a place where the animals were kept in ancient times. It literally translates to guarding or keeping edibles. Modern large production kitchens refer to this area as the pantry section, cold kitchen, or garde manger. This is the area in the kitchen where all cold foods are prepared and stored. It can be as small as a one-person station with a sandwich board and reach-in refrigerator or as large as a separate kitchen the size of half a football field with its own designated walk-in refrigerators and freezers. Salad ingredients, produce, and cheese are commonly found in these areas.

The task of producing items from the cold kitchen is also called garde manger. So the term "garde manger" is both a noun and a verb, depending on how it is used in the sentence. The cook or chef in charge of the cold kitchen is referred to as **chef garde manger.** He or she is responsible for all cold food preparations including **chaud froid** (dishes prepared hot and served cold), some **charcuterie** (the production of sausages, pâtés, terrines, galatines, and other similar foods), cold salads, sauces, dressings, sandwiches, appetizers, hors d'oeuvre, cold soups, and other cold kitchen items. A position with fewer responsibilities, but in the same area of the kitchen, would be titled pantry chef or cook.

>> A Brief History

Dining with others is nothing new. Prehistoric cave paintings discovered in Grotte Cosquer, near Marseille, France, and dating from about 25,000 years ago recorded early tribal hunting feasts. These ancient paintings depict images of bison, deer, auk (a type of bird), and other big game being roasted by fires and feeding large amounts of people. These paintings demonstrated that in earlier prehistoric times, communal feeding was an important part of the human experience. The fact that these early feasts were recorded places importance to the act of eating. Embellishing food can be traced back in history many millennia.

PRESERVATION

While we were still hunters and gatherers, methods of preservation were developed to keep as much of the hunt as possible for the tribe's or clan's use. Smoking, salting, and drying were the chief methods of this earliest preservation system (Figure 1-1). Methods developed centuries ago

Figure 1-1 An illustration by Theodore de Bry depicts two Native Americans standing beside a spit covered with many pieces of meat and various animals as a smoking fire cooks the food from below.
Harper Collins Publishers/Picture Desk, Inc./Kobal Collection

are as popular today due, in part, to the savory flavors that these techniques provided as well as the means to safely keep food for long periods. When we evolved from a hunter/gatherer society and moved to an agrarian society, growing our own food, the supply became more abundant. With the fear of hunger diminished, people started to attach importance not only to food for sustenance and nutrition, but also to its flavor and the way it looked on the table.

FOOD IS REVERED

Aesthetics was first expressed in cave paintings and later on by decorating the vessels, platters, and table utensils used for serving (Figure 1-2). Food was elevated to ceremonial and religious significance. Both as sacrifices to the gods or for the gods and as representatives of gods, food has played an important role in the spiritual side of the human experience (Figure 1-3). Examples of highly decorated and ornamented bread loaves were found in the tombs of the Egyptians. Decorated food molds were found in the deserts of modern-day Iraq and Syria. Tombs, burial sites, and other ancient remains from Aztec, Incan, and other ancient civilizations of Central and South America all have long chapters of celebratory and sacrificial foods. These foods were produced by bakers, cooks, and, in some cases, the priests. Little is recorded in history about the organization and location of cold kitchens, but it can be assumed that the division of labor in kitchen work was broken down by talent and experience. Talented chefs and bakers were much admired and well paid. The beautiful Egyptian Princess Cleopatra gave a dinner of incredible lavishness for her Roman lover Marcus Antonius, and he rewarded her chef with a whole city including all inhabitants and their taxes.

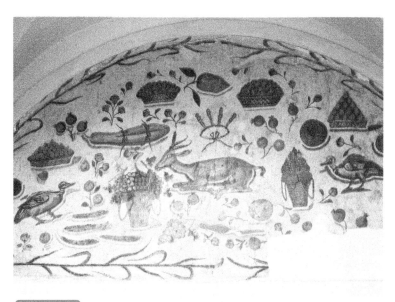

Figure 1-2 A semi-circular ancient Roman banquet platter features several types of food and culinary dishes including plates of vegetables and a cooked duck and gazelle.

Figure 1-3 Eighteenth Dynasty mural depicting Ancient Egyptian servants bringing offerings of food, located at the Valley of the Nobles at Qurna. *The Art Archive / Dagli Orti*

Figure 1-4 An ancient Roman mosaic depicts a male slave carrying a platter of food near his head at a banquet. *Dagli Orti/Picture Desk, Inc./Kobal Collection*

THE ROMAN EMPIRE

During the golden age of the Roman Empire, early documents and stone tablets record massive banquets and luxurious meals often lasting for days. Wealthy Romans encouraged, compelled, and cajoled their chef into creating more elaborately decorated dishes (Figure 1-4). Lucius Licinius Lucullus, 114–57 BC, was a Roman general and epicure with incredible wealth. His name is still synonymous with luxurious and, at times, outlandish dinners. He moved a small mountain to create a fishpond fed by water from the Adriatic Sea; and when his fortune was exhausted, he committed suicide rather than face the embarrassment of not being able to afford entertaining at that scale.

Trimalchio, a Roman aristocrat, spent his fortune on lavish meals; and historic records mention gilded birds and huge pies, baked and cut open, revealing live birds flying out and roast peacocks resting on thrones decorated with their feathers. Huge fish were presented whole, filled with crayfish and oysters, each containing a pearl; and rump of lion was roasted, spread with honey, and dusted with almonds. The feasts lasted for days, and the diners were refreshed by ice-cold drinks made with snow from nearby Mt. Vesuvius. These ice-cold drinks were flavored with spices and herbs. This custom gave birth to the **intermezzo,** used as a way to cleanse the palate in between courses.

Intermezzo is traditionally a short and inexpensive course used to refresh the palate. It is usually a cold, acidic sorbet or granite used to clear the palate after heavier courses in preparation for the entrée to come. Intermezzo sorbets can be made from fruit juices such as ruby red grapefruit, blood orange, Meyer lemon, and dark red berries, or a lighter sparkling wine such as a bubbly rose, sparkling Prosecco, and, for special occasions, French Champagne. Sometimes, champagne is poured over the sorbet for an extra touch of glamour.

Chefs today are circumventing traditions and putting a modern twist on the intermezzo. Occasionally using cold soups such as a deep red cassis served in a demi bowl, with a dollop of lemon sorbet on the top for garnish, would be such an example.

Intermezzo should be simple (just one to two bites at most) and should be effortless to serve. Using a hollowed out lemon or lime shell with your citrus sorbet is a most effective means to display citrus sorbet. Flatten the bottom of the citrus shell by slicing a small piece off of the bottom to level. Scoop or fill the shell and freeze till needed. Decorate with any appropriate garnish and serve.

Serving exotic animals attested to the wealth of the host and included swans, sturgeon, lions, and elephant. Leftovers were often shared with the servants. First-century **Apicius** was a Roman gourmand of incredible wealth. He or one of his ancestors named Apicius left recipes and is credited with writing the first cookbook. His notes were compiled and published about three centuries later. His book describes in detail liquamen or garum, a fermented condiment used in Roman cooking, consisting of salted fish fermented in open vats for two or three months. The condiment was popular and manufactured in large factories. The sauce is not unlike the modern fish sauce popular in Viet Nam and Indonesia.

THE DARK AGES

The age of overindulgence and excess disappeared when the Roman Empire disintegrated, but even during the Dark Ages, the attention to the eye appeal of food was not completely lost (Figure 1-5). The custodians of culture and refinement shifted to the Catholic monasteries spreading over Europe. The average per-

Figure 1-5 The Bayeux tapestry depicts a banquet of Norman dignitaries during the Dark Ages.

son subsisted on a grain-based diet, supplemented with gathered greens and the occasional bit of game. Church regulations at times discouraged extravagant dinners, but gastronomy continued on a subdued level. Cultivating vineyards, growing herbs and vegetables, making cheese, collecting honey, and raising fish in ponds continued in monasteries. Medieval paintings document platters heaped with food and decorated with fruit and flower garlands alongside beautifully crafted beverage pitchers. In the castles of feudal lords, whole, roasted animals—often wild boar or venison—were heralded and paraded around the refectory, then served on wooden boards, or "trenchour." The boards were eventually replaced by large loaves of bread in rectangular shapes. These bread plates, called trenchers, were used to sop up the juices and sauces from the dripping meats. The trenchers were given, along with any leftovers, to the servants and lower classes. This unsanitary habit helped to spread the great plagues of the day.

DEVELOPMENT OF THE GARDE MANGER

During the thirteenth and fourteenth centuries, the trade routes opened up, and with trade came a developing merchant or middle class. By the 1500s, dining tables set with elaborate table cloths, along with pewter and precious china, came back into fashion (Figure 1-6). The emphasis was placed on the use of exotic spices such as saffron, pepper, and the sweet spices of clove, cinnamon, mace, and nutmeg. They were expensive, but early written records note the abundant use of these strong spices. During this time period, the term "garde manger" came into use. This name was given to the area in the kitchen that was the coldest. Before mechanical refrigeration was invented, the coolest place, which was usually the cellar, was used to store food. Fresh meat and fish were stored in troughs on wooden slats on top of ice cut from lakes the previous winter. Furred and feathered game was hung from the ceiling rafters to age; smoked and cured meats were

Figure 1-6   This painting shows King Philip II (1527–1598) banqueting with his Courtiers. Notice the linens and fine dishes and goblets.

Figure 1-7   A larder outfitted with hanging meats, fresh breads, pottery, and candles.

suspended from meat hooks; and wire mesh cages dangling from the ceiling stored cheese, keeping rodents and flies away (Figure 1-7). This was where the scullery maids or cooks pickled, salted, and cured foods. Sometimes this storage area was located in a spring house, a structure that was built over a natural cold spring. Preserved foods were often stored there as the temperature rarely went above 40°F.

The person in charge of this area of the kitchen was called the chef garde manger. Some of the duties of the chef garde manger were decorating all food platters and trays, curing and smoking meats, and sausage making. Preserving meat from slaughtered animals was a challenge considering the lack of refrigeration; so this was a position of great responsibility. During this time the craft of preserving whole hams and sides of bacon was developed; some were salted and air-dried like the famous Proscuitto ham from Parma, Italy, and the Serrano ham from Spain; others were heavily smoked like the Westphalian ham from Germany.

The art of curing hams was passed on through many generations and ultimately was brought by settlers to Virginia; and the Smithfield ham, made from peanut and acorn fed hogs, became famous. The technique of preserving meat with salt is ancient, with corned beef dating back to the late ninth century (Figure 1-8). Large grains of sand called "corns" were rubbed into the beef or pork. The resultant liquid pulled from the meat, plus the salt, preserved the meat for months. Corning meat in salt brine was a method for preserving large pieces of beef and pork, which was important during the age of exploration as it served as a provision on ships that often sailed for many months without touching land.

CHARCUTERIE

Although sausage making has been around since the Greeks and Romans, sausage making came of age during the Middle Ages. The familiar sausages of today, such as bologna and frankfurters, actually took their names from the cities that produced them: Bologna, Italy, and Frankfurt, Germany.

Figure 1-8   The process of curing hams has been used since the ninth century.

Sausage making provided an opportunity for utilizing and preserving smaller cuts of meat and innards (Figure 1-9). The knowledge and practice of sausage making was already known by the Romans and described in the cookbook of Apicius. Different versions of sausages were developed in many other cultures. The Scots stuffed lamb stomachs with barley, suet, and chopped innards and called it Haggis; the Irish stuffed blood and fatback into sausage casings and called it Black Pudding; and Germans used the pork livers for Leberwurst.

GUILDS

During Medieval times, the French and other European royalty established strict guild systems to keep rival food guilds from fighting. Each guild focused on certain food products, and jealously guarded their domain. Charcutiers, for example, were only permitted to process and sell cooked pork products. Les bouchers, or the butchers, were only permitted to slaughter and dress the hogs. There were guilds for cattle as well as horseflesh. Charcutiers established a monopoly for making hure (stuffed pig heads), terrines, and pâtés. Molds were lined with dough and filled with forcemeats. Bakers established a powerful guild for making the dough; and for a while another guild reserved the right to stoke the bake-ovens with firewood. The bakers jealously watched other guilds and prevented the charcutiers from lining the pâtés molds with dough. To get around this prohibition, ceramic molds resembling pâté en croûte were manufactured and called terrines.

By the mid-1700s, guilds in many parts of Europe controlled and protected sausage making and often imposed restrictions on the type and variety of sausages their members could produce. Germanwurstmacher and charcutiers in France created many different sausages and often guarded the recipes jealously to keep them from being duplicated elsewhere. There was also a certain amount of unsavory practices with the use of questionable ingredients in sausage and forcemeats. Once the sausage was stuffed, it was difficult to ascertain what meats were used, and food poisoning resulted frequently from eating insufficiently cured or smoked sausages. The authorities tried to impose cruel punishment on cheaters, but this was spotty at best.

To avoid these problems, the guilds imposed a strict apprentice system and tried with varying success to impose sanitation guidelines on their members. The production methods were primitive. Before knowledge of bacterial hazards and before the invention of modern meat grinders and processing equipment, the sausage meat was chopped on hardwood slabs, blended with spices by hand in troughs, and stuffed with funnels into cleaned intestines. Sausages were often boiled before smoking or heavily salted, smoked, and then allowed to air dry.

PRESERVATION IN THE AMERICAN COLONIES

It did not take long before the technique of sausage making found its way to the American colonies. Dried meats and sausage were found on many a dining table in the 1600s. Beef jerky was an early American treat. Long strips of beef were air dried, salted, and smoked (Figure 1-10). Trappers used beef jerky as a main provision. **Pemmican** was a mixture of fatty game or buffalo meat pounded into a paste and flavored with dried wild berries. It was made by the indigenous tribes of the North American continent and quickly adopted by the early settlers. In the Cree language, the word *pemmican* means "the least food with the

Figure 1-9 Sausage makers stuff ground pork sausage filling into casings.

Figure 1-10 Strips of beef hang on a line over a fire as they are smoked and made into jerky.

most nourishment." Dried and smoked salmon was a favorite of the tribes that inhabited the Pacific Northwest (Figure 1-11). Again, local settlers adopted these local favorites.

THE MODERN BUFFET

During the eighteenth century and at the beginning of the nineteenth century, elaborate edible buffet and table centerpieces called "pièces montées" came back into fashion (Figure 1-12). It fell into the realm of the chef garde manger or the chef patissier to create these decorations. Chefs with artistic talents and skills were much in demand. The illustrious French chef, **Marie-Antoine Carême** (1783–1833), was the most famous author and culinary artist of this age. He was known for his complex architectural centerpieces. He worked for captains of industry as well as for kings, including the French diplomat Talleyrand, where he ran the kitchen for 12 years. Carême was also the chef of the future King George the IV and served the court of Russian Tsar Alexander I in St. Petersburg as well as for Prince Metternich in Vienna. In his later years, he worked for the Baron de Rothschild. Carême died at the relatively young age of 50, to quote his obit by Laurent Tailhade, "Burnt out by the flames of his genius and the charcoal of the roasting spit." He can be considered the benchmark of all future chef garde manger. He is considered "the father of haute or grand cuisine." The practice of using elegant and beautifully designed buffet tables continues on in our time (Figure 1-13).

BIRTH OF THE HOTEL INDUSTRY

Toward the end of the nineteenth century, with the advancement of the railroads and the changing social customs, many large hotels and restaurants were built. In London, the Savoy Hotel; in Monaco, The Grand Hôtel; and in Lucerne, Switzerland, the Hôtel National became famous. In New York City, The Waldorf-Astoria Hotel was built, and high-class restaurants such as Delmonico's Restaurant and the Café Martin attracted many customers (Figure 1-14).

The Edwardian Period, beginning in 1901, saw the launching of many grand ocean liners such as the Britannia, the Kaiser Wilhelm der Grosse, the Campania, and the Maureta-

Figure 1-11 Pacific Northwest tribes continue to preserve salmon today using some of the same smoking methods practiced for generations.

Figure 1-12 This 1840 painting by Mathilde shows a dining room's elaborate table settings.

nia. These grand floating hotels had state-of-the-art kitchens on board, and each kitchen had to be organized to quickly produce the thousands of meals needed in the dining rooms and banquet halls for each class.

To handle the workload efficiently, these grand kitchens were formed into separate departments. Each recipe was broken down into many components and prepared and cooked by specialized cooks called **"chefs de partie."** Foremost in the development of these systems or batteries was the French Chef **Auguste Escoffier** (1846–1935), who organized kitchens into clearly defined stations (Figure 1-15). He had worked in many of the great passenger ships and hotels in Europe. Under the system refined by Escoffier, the chef saucier made all sauces and sauté dishes, the chef rôtisseur made all roasts, and the chef poissonier cooked all poached fish dishes. Escoffier is considered the "Father of Modern French Cuisine," and his pioneering work is considered the foundation of much of our modern technique and terminology. Up until the 1950s, most menus in luxury hotels and fine restaurants throughout the world were written in French.

The garde manger became a commissary, supplying all stations with products that could be cooked and served quickly, including portioned meats and fish. The garde manger department stuffed chicken and fish, breaded veal cutlets and fish fillets, made mayonnaise and other dressings, and prepared all cold appetizers. In addition, the chef garde manger was still in charge of making culinary showpieces—albeit less elaborate than at the beginning of the century—and also platters for buffets and canapés for receptions. It was a busy place.

By the mid-twentieth century, many menu components previously made by the chef garde manger became commercially available. Eating habits also changed; customers ordered more salads as main courses and sandwiches in place of whole meals. Food decorations changed from ostentatious and detailed designs to simple, clean, and appetizing presentations. Efficiency, sanitation awareness, and recognitions of customer preferences changed the food industry. The duties of the chef garde manger changed accordingly.

The term **"pantry"** entered the industry vocabulary and is derived from *paneterie,* "bread room," a storage place for bread and condiments and for tableware between the kitchen and the dining room. In restaurant kitchens, pantries became service stations where a wide array of

Figure 1-13 Various entrées and side dishes are displayed in chaffing dishes on an elaborate buffet table. This tradition dates back to the 1800s.

Figure 1-14 A ladies' luncheon held in the dining room of Delmonico's Restaurant at the northeast corner of Fifth Avenue and 44th Street, New York City, in 1904.

Figure 1-15 Auguste Escoffier (1846–1935), the French chef otherwise known as "King of the Kitchen" and the "Father of Modern French Cuisine."

cold dishes, sandwiches, hot beverages, and often desserts were prepared. The heavy preparation work in large hotels, country clubs, and banquet halls is still done in the garde manger, but now much of the cold kitchen action takes place at the busy and vital pantry station. In many smaller operations where buffets and cold reception foods are not on the menu, the pantry is the only place in the kitchen where cold food is prepared. Menu components, formerly prepared in the garde manger, are seldom made from scratch. Items such as mayonnaise and many dressings are purchased. Meat is usually bought pretrimmed and portion cut. Appetizers may be purchased **IQF** (individually quick frozen) for immediate use.

Today, complete prepared meals and all conceivable menu components are purchased in a dazzling variety of quality and price points. However, professional chefs must know how these products are prepared and if they meet the quality expectations of the customers. Chefs must also be able to determine whether they are cost effective.

Many of the trend-setting restaurants are going back to the older methods of garde manger for their signature items. Being able to cure salmon, make a special sausage or pâté, and prepare a signature dressing or soup gives chefs the culinary edge that sets their food apart. The perception of quality is always associated with handmade items, and by taking the time to learn the techniques in the following chapters, you will be able to have a unique niche.

People still eat with their eyes first. Beautiful-looking, well-prepared, and flavorful food will always be in demand. Great chefs are skilled craftspersons with business savvy. They may also be culinary artists. Culinary art is constantly evolving; customers are better informed about food and nutrition and are more demanding and appreciative of culinary excellence. Mastering the art and duties of the chef garde manger is essential to becoming an accomplished chef (Figure 1-16). This book teaches the basic fundamentals and also the finer points of working in the cold kitchen or garde manger. Whether the kitchen is big or small, luxurious or budget oriented, excellence in garde manger work is the basis of good cooking.

Figure 1-16   A chef presents a tossed salad.

>> Summary

As the human race became more sophisticated so did the kitchen. The open hearth was the original food preparation area. However, as food dishes became more complicated and with the invention of stoves, things changed. In large commercial kitchens there was a designated space for preparing and storing all cold foods, known as the garde manger. The act of preparing foods in the cold kitchen is also called garde manger, so the term can be both a noun and a verb, depending on how it is used. The chef in charge of the cold kitchen is known as the chef garde manger.

Common cold preparations include chaud froid, which are dishes that are prepared hot and served cold, charcuterie (production of sausages, terrines, and other similar meat-based foods), cold salads, sauces, dressings, sandwiches, appetizers, hors d'oeuvre, cold soups, and other cold kitchen items.

>> Review Questions

TRUE/FALSE

1. Charcutier is the German name for sausage maker.
2. Terrines are metal baking molds.
3. Pantry is another name for pastry shop.
4. Marie-Antoine Carême worked in Paris for Prince Metternich.
5. Pemmican is a French sausage.
6. Today, the chef garde manger is in charge of the fish station.
7. Many hotels and restaurants were built toward the end of the nineteenth century.
8. Pantry is the place in the kitchen where most of the cold food is prepared.
9. Apicius wrote the first cookbook.
10. Auguste Escoffier was known as "King of the Kitchen."

MULTIPLE CHOICE

11. Define the term "intermezzo."
    a. ice cream dessert
    b. Roman flavoring sauce
    c. technique invented by Chef Escoffier
    d. palate cleanser
12. What is liquamen or garum?
    a. condiment
    b. French beverage
    c. salad dressing
    d. fish sauce similar to those found in Southeast Asia
13. When did Marie-Antoine Carême live?
    a. from 1846 to 1935
    b. during the twentieth century
    c. during the nineteenth century
    d. from 1783 to 1833
14. Charcutiers make
    a. sausages.
    b. sauces.
    c. bread.
    d. poached fish dishes.
15. Chef garde manger is responsible for
    a. dining room supervision.
    b. providing edible dinner plates.
    c. organization of medieval dinner.
    d. preparing cold food.
16. The term "garde manger" literally means
    a. cold buffets.
    b. stove.
    c. canapés.
    d. to guard or protect edibles.
17. Parma is famous for hams and is located in
    a. Spain.
    b. Virginia during colonial times.
    c. Italy.
    d. Black forest.
18. The term "pantry" is derived from
    a. cold kitchen.
    b. sandwich station.
    c. bread room.
    d. coffee station.
19. Who is known as the "Father of Modern French Cuisine"?
    a. Marie-Antoine Carême
    b. Lucius Licinius Lucullus
    c. Apicius
    d. Auguste Escoffier
20. "Chef de partie" is the French word for
    a. banquet chef.
    b. station chef.
    c. sous chef.
    d. party chef.

FILL IN THE ANSWERS

21. Garde manger refers to the _____ department.
22. _____, _____, and _____ were chief methods of this earliest preservation system.
23. According to the text, Roman gourmand Lucullus spent his fortune on _____.
24. The chef saucier was in charge of sauces and _____.
25. August Escoffier is credited with developing clearly defined _____.
26. The Waldorf-Astoria Hotel is located in _____.
27. The chef poissonier cooked _____ dishes.
28. Corning meat in salt brine was a method for _____.
29. List some of the products supplied by the garde manger.
    _____
    _____
30. Virginia's Smithfield Ham is made from what ingredients?
    _____

Sanitation and Safety

>> Learning Objectives

After you have finished reading this unit, you should be able to:

- Demonstrate proper handwashing methods.
- Explain the difference between cleaning and sanitizing.
- List three ways to help prevent a pest infestation.
- Discuss ways to purchase wholesome food, store it, and prepare it in a safe environment.
- Describe the ideal conditions for bacterial growth (FAT TOM).
- Describe the need to maintain Material Safety Data Sheets (MSDS).
- Discuss the principles of HACCP.
- Identify what to do in emergency situations in the cold kitchen that might include fire, bleeding, and choking.
- Demonstrate the proper method for avoiding back injuries while moving heavy objects.

>> Key Terms

biological contaminants	critical control points	Heimlich maneuver	sanitizing agent
chemical contaminants	FAT TOM	MSDS	temperature danger zone
	FIFO	MSDS book	
	HACCP	physical contaminants	

Unit 2 discusses sanitation and safety principles. Most culinary schools have at least one course devoted solely to food safety and sanitation. It is within that course that a student will gain the most knowledge of this important topic. Because the threat of transmitting food-borne illness cannot be overemphasized to all food professionals, this unit will again review these important principles as they apply to the cold kitchen. Many of the foods served from the cold kitchen receive no further cooking before service, so a strong sanitation and food safety program is imperative to the health of the guests. For additional information on safety and sanitation issues, please refer to the list of sanitation information in the Appendix.

On any given day, 132 million Americans dine out. In one year, foodservice operators will provide 70 million meal and snack occasions (National Restaurant Association, 2007). In most instances, these diners enjoy a positive, safe experience. Unfortunately there are times when careless

Figure 2-1 A clean and tidy uniform should be maintained throughout the work day.

methods have been employed at some level of the food chain and food safety is compromised. The Atlanta-based Centers for Disease Control (CDC) estimates that about 70 percent of all food-borne illness outbreaks occur in food service operations, whereas 20 percent are traced to private homes. It is the responsibility of all food professionals to see that the foods they produce are safe to eat. By applying common sense and learning the best practices for sanitation and safety, food professionals can dramatically decrease the risks and liabilities.

As in every other field, new information in the foodservice industry is constantly being discovered and new methods are replacing old ones. For this reason, it is important to continually update and study sanitation. By making sanitation a continuous focus, foodservice professionals can provide safe food for guests to eat. In the cold kitchen, we place a heavy emphasis on proper handling of food because many of the foods produced are handled after cooking or processing. Many of the foods that are central to the cold kitchen do not receive further cooking, so it is paramount that knowledge in safe food processing and storing procedures be followed to the letter. Proper handwashing, the correct use of gloves, as well as time and temperature controls are stressed throughout this unit.

>> It Starts with You

PERSONAL HYGIENE

The ancient Greeks worshiped the goddess of health, Hygea. The word "hygiene" is a derivative of this word. As in ancient times, we continue to place a high value on good health and hygiene. Coming to work clean and staying clean is a good start to keeping the cold kitchen a sanitary environment (Figure 2-1). The following list highlights the important points of personal hygiene:

- Bathe or shower and shampoo daily.
- Brush teeth daily.
    - Wear clean clothing.
    - Wear clean hat or hair restraint.
    - Wear clean socks and shoes.
    - Remove jewelry from hands and wrists (a plain ring such as a simple wedding band is permissible). Remove any visible piercings or other dangling jewelry.
    - Wash hands, especially after using the restroom, smoking, taking out garbage, eating, handling dirty dishes or equipment, touching face or hair, sneezing into your hands, and any time hands come in contact with contaminants. In general, wash hands whenever you switch jobs. Use plenty of soap and hot water. Wash hands for at least 20 or more seconds, using vigorous scrubbing. Use a nail brush to remove any dirt from the fingertips or nails. Rinse in hot water and air dry or use disposable one-time-use paper toweling to dry the hands off (Figure 2-2).
    - Always wash hands when handling raw meat, poultry, or seafood (before and after).
    - Use gloves where and when required. Change often—they can become contaminated.

Figure 2-2 Proper handwashing is an important step in maintaining a sanitary kitchen.

ADDITIONAL PRECAUTIONS

- If ill, report to your manager. Stay home if your illness is contagious.
- If injured with an open cut or wound, clean, cover with a clean bandage, and wear a finger cot and rubber or vinyl gloves. Change often.
- No one should wear make-up, heavy aftershave, or perfume in the kitchen.
- Wear gloves when preparing or dishing out food that is not cooked or was previously cooked before eating, such as sandwiches, salads, and cold cuts (Figure 2-3).

- Avoid touching your hair, face, or any exposed skin. Do not pick or scratch at any sores or cuts. If you do so, immediately wash your hands.
- Never put your hands into dressings, salads, and other cold foods. Use the proper serving utensils such as ladles, spoons, and scoops.
- Always use "one use" tasting spoons to taste the food. Never use your fingers to taste any food.

>> Keep Equipment and Work Areas Clean

Always clean as you go. Wash and sanitize equipment and surfaces before moving onto another task (Figure 2-4).

- Wash with soap and water to remove soil and food particles. Scrub if necessary.
- Sanitize with moist heat, 171°F (77°C) or above, for 30 seconds or use a chemical **sanitizing agent.**
- Always sanitize surfaces before switching to another task.
- Use cloths rinsed in sanitizing solution to wipe down work surfaces and equipment that cannot be immersed in a sink.
- Air dry tools, equipment, and surfaces completely.

Figure 2-3 Wear gloves when preparing foods that won't be cooked before they are eaten.

PEST CONTROL

Pests can ruin valuable commodities. In addition, they can carry contaminants and become a source of cross-contamination. Always hire a professional, licensed exterminator if a problem arises and for regular preventative visits.

- Keep your eyes open for evidence of pests, such as droppings, torn bags, and so on.
- Always clean up spills and crumbs.
- Inspect all deliveries for evidence of contamination. Refuse any suspect commodities.
- Store goods off the floor (Figure 2-5).

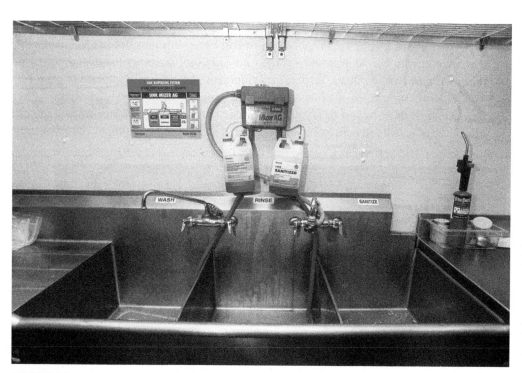

Figure 2-4 A commercial three-bay sink with compartments for washing, rinsing, and sanitizing.

Figure 2-5 Food should not be stored directly on the floor.

Figure 2-6 Trash cans should be lined and the liners dumped at regular intervals throughout the day.

Figure 2-7 Foods should be covered and labeled properly.

- Keep kitchen trash covered and don't allow it to stack up. Remove it regularly throughout the day (Figure 2-6).
- Keep all foods covered or refrigerated (Figure 2-7).

>> Providing for a Safe Dining Experience

It is important that you understand the dangers of food-borne illnesses and learn how to avoid them so that you can keep food safe. Food safety begins when you know the types of contaminants—and how to contain or remove them. The Centers for Disease Control (CDC) identifies several steps for keeping food safe:

1. **Obtain food from safe sources.** Always purchase food from a reputable source. This is the first defense when you are working with food. Purchase all meat, poultry, and fish products from a recognized and reputable purveyor. How can you tell if your purveyor is reputable? Contact your local health department, Better Business Bureau, or Chamber of Commerce, who will let you know if there are any complaints against the company. Inspect the purveyor's facilities. Inspect each shipment of food as it is received (Figure 2-8). Most will welcome an on-site inspection. If you have first-hand knowledge about the best practices of your purveyors or if you deal with a nationally known company, you increase the safety of your food supply. Never deal with a back-door, fly-by-night purveyor, espe-

Figure 2-8 Chefs or coworkers should inspect each delivery to ensure the quality of food purchased.

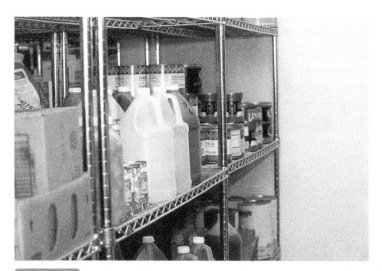

Figure 2-9   Store all dry goods in a dry, cool environment, up off the floor.

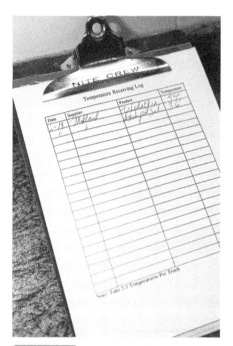

Figure 2-10   Temperature Receiving Logs help ensure that foods are kept within acceptable temperature ranges.

cially when it comes to fish and game. The fines and health risks far outweigh any perceived money-saving prospects if the discounted food makes even one person ill.

2. **Store the products according to the local health department rules.** Dry goods should be stored in a cool, dry environment (Figure 2-9). Items that must be kept cold must be refrigerated immediately and not be allowed to sit outside the refrigerators. Too many times, chefs and cooks get busy and forget that food is sitting on a back dock or in receiving; and the temperature of the food becomes unacceptable. Quality as well as safety are compromised. Put frozen foods in the freezer and refrigerated foods in the reach-ins or walk-ins. Label and date all foods to keep track for rotation and freshness (Figure 2-10).

3. **Cook food properly.** Undercooked food can harbor potentially hazardous bacteria and eating it can have lethal consequences. Know the temperature danger zone and heat foods to their correct, safe temperature (Figure 2-11).

4. **Hold foods at correct holding temperatures.** Bacteria can grow at a rapid rate. Food needs to be stored below 41°F (5°C) or colder or kept hot at 135°F (57°C) or higher. The zone between 41°F and 135°F, known as the danger zone, is the ideal temperature for growth in organisms. It is, therefore, important to keep foods out of those temperatures (Figure 2-12).

5. **Follow sanitation rules to avoid cross-contamination.** Use tools for one job only. Each sauce or soup on a buffet should have its own serving piece. Utilize color-coded cutting

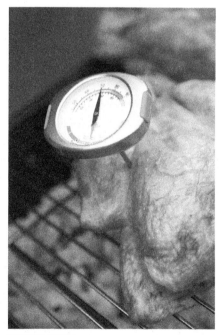

Figure 2-11   Use a meat thermometer for safely cooking different meats and poultry to their correct, safe temperatures.

Figure 2-12   Worker checks for proper temperature of potato salad in a salad bar.

Figure 2-13 Color-coded cutting boards can be used to visually help to prevent cross-contamination.

Figure 2-14 Keep tools and equipment clean at all times.

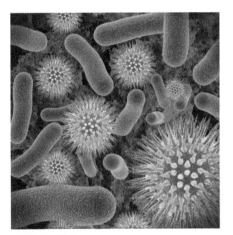

Figure 2-15 A microscopic view of bacteria growing on a scrub pad.

boards: green for produce, yellow for poultry, red for meat, and so on (Figure 2-13). Wash, rinse, and sanitize utensils, cutting boards, and equipment after each use.

6. **Practice proper personal hygiene.** Wash your hands as described earlier. Always keep your tools, equipment, and work space areas clean (Figure 2-14). Maintain a professional appearance with a clean uniform throughout the work day.

CONTAMINATIONS

There are three types of hazards commonly found in food that can cause contamination:

- **Biological contamination. Biological contaminants** include molds, fungi, bacteria, viruses, parasites, certain plant and mushroom products that contain poisons and alkaloids, as well as seafoods that contain neurotoxins (Figure 2-15).
- **Chemical contamination. Chemical contaminants** include heavy metals, alkaloids, acids, insecticides, bactericides, herbicides, cleaning materials, and petroleum-based products along with cookware that can leach poisonous minerals into the food such as lead, copper sulfate, and, in some cases, radioactive material from some glazed pottery serving dishes (Figure 2-16).

Figure 2-16 Keep all cleaning materials and insecticides away from food.

- **Physical Contamination. Physical contaminants** include shards of glass, staples from lettuce boxes, dirt, bugs, bandages, fingernails, bones, and hair. All can get lost in food products (Figure 2-17).

BIOLOGICAL CONTAMINATION

Bacteria

Due to the highly perishable nature of cold foods such as dressings, salads, forcemeat, or cured products, it is important for the food professional to be aware of some of the more common bacteria found in or on food. Certain bacteria are particularly hazardous to cold foods. When making forcemeats or sausage, for example, many steps are needed to make the finished product. There can be many hands involved with each step, and at each step or critical control point, bacteria can get a toehold and become a real sanitation problem. The following list represents some of the more common bacterial infections that plague the cold kitchen.

- **Campylobacteriosis.** Infection caused by *Campylobacter jejuni*, a bacterium found in chicken and other poultry products and processing water. It causes diarrhea, cramps, fever, and headache. Always cook chicken and other poultry products to 165°F. Avoid cross-contamination with raw product.
- **Salmonellosis.** Infection caused by *Salmonella* strains, bacteria found in chicken, poultry products, beef, raw egg products, and produce such as spinach and green onions. It can cause diarrhea, cramps, fever, and vomiting. Always cook chicken and other poultry products, beef, and eggs to required minimum internal temperatures. Avoid cross-contamination between raw and cooked product.

Figure 2-17 Physical contaminants can come from a host of sources, including a shattered wine glass.

- **Shigellosis.** Infection caused by *Shigella*, a bacterium found in human feces and transferred to food by way of human hand contact or water contaminated by human feces. Flies can also transfer this type of bacteria. Foods such as salads are one of the chief culprits as they contain foods most readily contaminated by water or hand contact. *Shigella* infection can cause bloody diarrhea, cramps, and fever. Workers should be excluded from working around food if they have diarrhea and/or if they have been diagnosed with shigellosis. Control flies both inside and outside of the establishment.
- **Listeriosis.** Infection caused by *Listeria monocytogenes*, a bacterium found in cool, moist environments such as walk-in and reach-in refrigerators. This bacterium is most commonly associated with cured meats and ready-to-eat products, and, though not as common, it is particularly dangerous to pregnant women, sometimes causing spontaneous abortions in pregnant women and sepsis and meningitis in newborns. Discard any past-dated products and avoid using unpasteurized dairy products. Cook all raw products to required minimum temperatures and avoid cross-contamination.
- *Vibrio* **Gastroenteritis.** Infection caused by two related bacteria, *Vibrio parahaemolyticus* and *Vibrio vulnificus*, bacteria found in uncooked or partially cooked oysters. They cause diarrhea, nausea, and vomiting, along with fever. *Vibrio vulnificus* is the more lethal of the two: it is capable of causing septicemia in people with diabetes or liver disease. The best way to avoid this nasty illness is to purchase oysters only from reputable sources and always serve the oysters thoroughly cooked. Make sure that the inspection tags are present when the oysters are delivered to you. By law, you must retain these tags for a minimum of 90 days.
- **Staphylococcal Gastroenteritis.** Infection caused by the most common food-borne illness bacterium, *Staphylococcus aureus*. This bacterium is found primarily in humans. It is primarily found in the hair, nose, throats, and sores of humans. This fast-acting disease is caused by the by-products of the bacterium, which cannot be killed by heating the food.

The most effective way of removing this bacterium from food is to avoid it in the first place by washing hands after touching the face, nose, hair, or open wounds, such as a cut finger. Foods most susceptible are prepared salads and cold cuts.

- ***Clostridium perfringens* Gastroenteritis.** Infection caused by *Clostridium perfringens*, a spore-producing bacterium. This bacterium causes one of the more common and fast-acting food-borne illnesses, resulting in diarrhea and abdominal pain. It is a toxin-producing bacterium whose growth is slowed by cold environments. It grows rapidly in the food danger zone, so to avoid it, keep food below the danger zone temperature of 41°F. Cool and reheat food properly.

- **Botulism.** Infection caused by *Clostridium botulinum* that is usually fatal. This anaerobic bacterium does not grow well in refrigeration. It is found in produce associated with soil such as potatoes, onions, garlic, and other root vegetables. It was common in early sausages due to the high fat content and lack of oxygen, but with the addition of sodium nitrates and sodium nitrites, this threat was reduced. Care must be taken when making

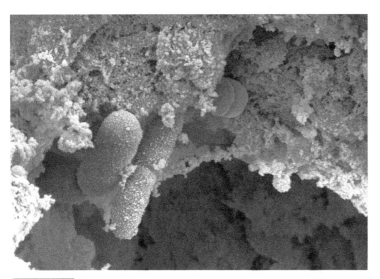

Figure 2-18   *E. coli* bacteria thriving on raw ground beef.

or using oils that have cooked vegetables stored in them, such as garlic oils or onions cooked in butter. Without proper refrigeration, botulism can grow undetected with tragic results.

- ***E. coli*/Hemorrhagic Colitis.** Dangerous food-borne illnesses caused by *E.coli* bacteria, which are found in the intestines. Over the past 60 years, super bugs that combined the relatively benign *E.coli* with the more potent strain of *Shiga* toxin-producing bacteria have developed, resulting in the very deadly strain called *Escherichia coli* 0157. This toxic bacterium has been associated with undercooked ground beef products and most recently with raw celery, spinach, and lettuce (Figure 2-18). Symptoms include diarrhea that eventually becomes bloody. Severe cases result in total system shutdown in the form of hemolytic uremic syndrome, with fatal results. To keep deadly bacteria at bay, meat must be cooked to proper temperatures, especially ground meat. Produce must be washed and cooked to safe temperatures. Avoid cross-contamination with raw meat and ready-to-eat products.

Viruses

Viruses are small microbial contaminants that need a host to survive and reproduce. They can survive freezing, and can be easily transmitted from food to people, from people to people, and from food surfaces to people. Viruses can contaminate water, food, and air. They usually get to food by way of unsafe food handling. Washing hands and using proper hygiene is the way to help safeguard against viruses. Viruses cause infections. There are two main viruses that impact the food industry:

- **Norovirus.** This particularly fast-acting food-borne illness, sometimes called the Norwalk Flu, is readily spread through contact with human feces by way of unwashed hands. It is also possible to get the illness by eating shellfish that were contaminated by sewage. Some symptoms include vomiting, diarrhea, nausea, and abdominal cramps.

- **Hepatitis A.** This illness is caused by the hepatitis A virus, which is found in the feces of people infected by the virus. This virus is spread through unwashed hands into ready-to-eat foods such as salads and sandwiches (Figure 2-19). Large outbreaks of hepatitis A have been reported in people with

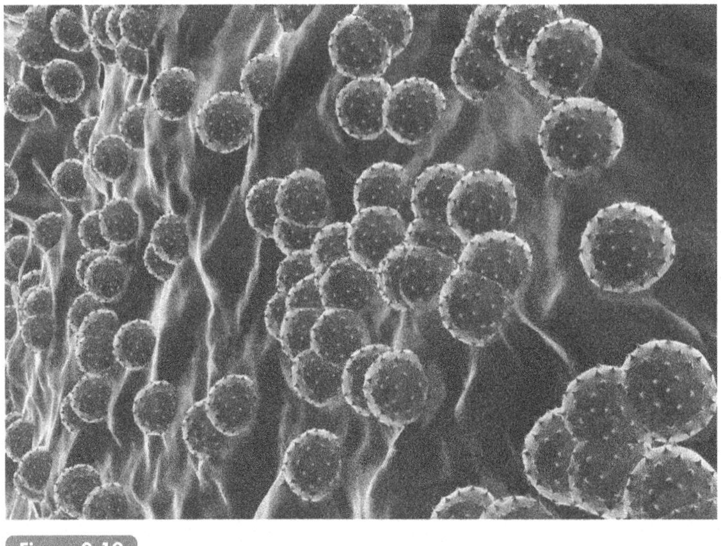

Figure 2-19   Hepatitis A is transmitted by water or food contaminated with infected feces. Using correct handwashing techniques can eliminate its spread.

weakened immune systems. The disease has been known to cause severe liver damage, which is sometimes fatal. Hepatitis A has been transmitted to people consuming contaminated shellfish. It is important to always purchase seafood and shellfish from reputable purveyors. Symptoms include fever, weakness, nausea, abdominal pain and swelling, and jaundice. Employees who have been diagnosed with hepatitis A should be prohibited from handling food.

Other Biological Contaminants

There are other biological contaminants that cause food-borne illnesses. Some of these affect the cold kitchen. The parasite *Anisakis simplex* is a worm-like parasite found in raw and undercooked fish such as halibut, cod, mackerel, and Pacific salmon. Purchasing fish through reputable purveyors is the safest bet. Two other parasites, *Cryptosporidium parvum* and *Cyclospora cayetanensis*, are found in untreated or improperly treated water and produce that has been soaked or sprayed with water contaminated by the parasites. Always purchase produce through a reputable purveyor.

CONDITIONS FOR BACTERIAL GROWTH

The acronym **FAT TOM** is an easy way to remember how to keep bacteria away. F = food; A = acidity; T = temperature; T = time; O = oxygen; and M = moisture.

- **Food.** Bacteria are attracted to high-protein foods and carbohydrates. High concentrations of sugar and salt deter most bacteria.
- **Acidity/Neutral pH.** Bacteria thrive in a neutral pH to a slightly acidic environment.
- **Temperature.** Bacteria love the same environments that most humans enjoy. The warmer the environment, the faster the bacteria multiply.
- **Time.** Bacteria multiply rapidly under favorable conditions, sometimes in only a few minutes to 2 hours in the danger zone. Keeping your food out of the danger zone is the best policy. Keep hot food at 135°F (57°C) and above and cold food at 41°F (5°C) and below.
- **Oxygen.** Aerobic bacteria need oxygen to grow, and anaerobic bacteria grow only in the absence of oxygen. Some types can grow with or without oxygen.
- **Moisture.** Bacteria need water to grow, just like more complex creatures.

PREVENTION OF BIOLOGICAL CONTAMINATION

This section offers ways to prevent food-borne illnesses due to biological contaminants:

- Avoid cross-contamination by using clean utensils and cutting boards with each job.
- Keep cold food cold and hot food hot. Check for proper holding temperatures.
- Clean as you go, wash, sanitize, and sterilize.
- Keep refrigerators and other cold storage areas clean and dry. Rotate products and remove any out-of-date products. Practice **FIFO,** which stands for "first in, first out." Keep products wrapped, labeled, and dated and rotate them properly. This applies to refrigerated foods as well as dry goods.
- Keep dry products 6 inches from the floor.
- Wash hands often. Use gloves when appropriate. Change gloves often as hands are contaminated. Remember, gloves do not protect you—proper handwashing does.
- Use only designated cutting boards to cut raw poultry. Most poultry carries salmonella bacteria. Wash, rinse, and sanitize the boards after each use.
- Wash hands vigorously with soap and water for at least 20 seconds after handling raw poultry.
- Never place kitchen towels on cutting boards or use the towel to dry equipment. Kitchen and side towels are loaded with bacteria after short use.

Figure 2-20 A fly is crawling on the surface of a piece of raw beefsteak left exposed in the kitchen.

- Air-dry equipment after cleaning and sanitizing. If needed immediately, use "single use" paper towels to wipe equipment or knives dry.
- Keep walk-in, reach-in refrigerator and freezer doors closed at all times. Never prop the door open for any reason. Check for proper temperatures. Refrigerators should be 41°F (5°C) or lower and freezers at 0°F (-17°C) or lower.
- Remove from refrigeration only food that can be processed within a reasonable time.
- Do not stick hot tools or equipment into cold soups or dressings, as the temperature can become elevated and bring food into the danger zone.
- If something falls on the floor, toss it out.
- Do not eat and drink in your kitchen station. This habit will contaminate the food you are working with by direct contact with germs or if you spill into or onto the food.
- Keep flies and other disease-carrying vectors out of the kitchen (Figure 2-20). Screens and other physical barriers need to be used to keep out mice, rats, and pests.

Store Food Properly

Food that is stored must be covered to prevent foreign objects from falling into the food. Label and date all food. When cooling food, it is important to note that food must be cooled from 135° to 70°F within 2 hours and from 70°F to 41°F or lower within the next 4 hours. Many chefs choose to reduce the overall temperature from 135°F to 4°F in 2 hours to ensure little room for error when it comes to the safety of their guests.

Large operations, especially hospitals, have blast chillers. These machines generate very cold air streams, and food placed inside will chill rapidly. Smaller kitchens usually do not have these devices.

To chill food in a safe manner, follow these guidelines:

1. Spread out hot soups, sauces, and dressings in shallow, 2-inch deep hotel pans to chill as rapidly as possible; stir frequently until evenly chilled (Figure 2-21).
2. Hot liquids can be chilled a number of ways. If possible, put the container in an ice bath or chilling tank, or put the container in a sink with an overflow device and let a small stream of cold water swirl around the pot. Stir frequently. If available, use "ice sticks."
3. Never put the pot in the cooler on a rack. This common but outdated practice can lead to food-borne illness by raising the temperature in the walk-in or reach-in. It can also damage the refrigeration unit by over-stressing the equipment.

The Importance of Proper Temperatures

All food comes from either plant or animal sources. That crunchy salad on a plate was originally a head of lettuce growing in the ground. The burger you may have had for lunch was, at one time, cattle munching somewhere in a field. The point is, food gets broken down into smaller molecules either by human intervention or by natural causes. Through bacterial action, all raw food is eventually returned to the soil from where it came. This process of decomposition is sped up by heat and moisture. When decomposition occurs in a compost pit, it is acceptable. When it occurs in a walk-in or in our food, problems arise. Chefs must understand that the clock is ticking the second that a burger is removed from the

Figure 2-21 Spread hot substances in a shallow pan to chill quickly.

broiler or when the salad is removed from the reach-in (Figure 2-22). Bacterial growth starts to immediately speed up whenever food is placed in the **temperature danger zone.** This is the temperature zone at which foodborne illness microorganisms grow at a rapid rate. Some foods, such as raw poultry, should be cooked to a higher temperature (165°F). Leftover foods that are to be reheated must be reheated to 165°F for 15 seconds. In foods such as potato salad, each component should be chilled first, then combined, to avoid certain types of bacteria. When storing food in a freezer, the food should be stored at 0°F or cooler.

When you are working on a salad, the clock starts when the ingredients are removed from the cold, not from the time the salad is complete. It is important to keep the food iced down, covered, and, whenever possible, under refrigeration.

CHEMICAL CONTAMINATION

Chemical contamination is another hazard that can affect the cold kitchen. Over-spray from cleaners and insect repellants, along with pesticides that may remain on certain vegetables, is a constant concern. By observing a few simple rules in the cold kitchen, you can easily avoid in-house chemical contamination. Get to know the **MSDS** (Material Safety Data Sheets) book, which is the book that gives you all of the information on chemical products that your establishment is using (Figure 2-23). It is usually provided by the chemical or sanitation service that is contracted to supply these substances to the kitchen. The MSDS includes a description of what is in the chemical product, the safety instructions, and any important information regarding usage and how to deal with accidents concerning the products. It is a good source of information to keep you working safe.

Figure 2-22 Foods must either be eaten immediately or held at proper temperatures to prevent bacterial growth. The clock starts ticking the moment the hamburger comes off the grill.

LEARNING ACTIVITY 2-1

Locate the **MSDS book** in your school or in any commercial kitchen. Select two cleaning products, look them up in the MSDS book, and find the following information. Record your findings in the space below.

Safe use and handling procedures for each product:

Product 1:

Product 2:

Note any precautions that are mentioned:

Product 1:

Product 2:

Emergency first aid information:

Product 1:

Product 2:

Material Safety Data Sheet

May be used to comply with
OSHA's Hazard Communication Standard,
29 CFR 1910.1200. Standard must be
consulted for specific requirements.

U.S. Department of Labor

Occupational Safety and Health Administration
(Non-Mandatory Form)
Form Approved
OMB No. 1218-0072

IDENTITY (As Used on Label and List)	Note: Blank spaces are not permitted. If any item is not applicable, or no information is available, the space must be marked to indicate that.

Section I

Manufacturer's Name	Emergency Telephone Number
Address (Number, Street, City, State, and ZIP Code)	Telephone Number for Information
	Date Prepared
	Signature of Preparer (optional)

Section II — Hazardous Ingredients/Identity Information

Hazardous Components (Specific Chemical Identity; Common Name(s))	OSHA PEL	ACGIH TLV	Other Limits Recommended	% (optional)

Section III — Physical/Chemical Characteristics

Boiling Point		Specific Gravity (H_2O = 1)	
Vapor Pressure (mm Hg.)		Melting Point	
Vapor Density (AIR = 1)		Evaporation Rate (Butyl Acetate = 1)	

Solubility in Water

Appearance and Odor

Section IV — Fire and Explosion Hazard Data

Flash Point (Method Used)	Flammable Limits	LEL	UEL

Extinguishing Media

Special Fire Fighting Procedures

Unusual Fire and Explosion Hazards

(Reproduce locally)   OSHA 174, Sept. 1985

Figure 2-23 The U.S. Department of Labor has created the MSDS sheets. One sheet should be created for each in-house chemical.

Chemical Contamination Prevention

This list of tips will help you to prevent chemical contamination:

- Keep all cleaning, sanitizing, and pesticide-type chemicals stored away from any foodstuffs in a separate storage area or locker.
- Use only cleaning and sanitizing chemicals that are provided by a reputable purveyor.
- Understand the safety sheets that are provided by the manufacturer.
- Follow instructions explicitly. Never mix chemicals.
- Use only trained pesticide specialists to apply pesticides. (Foodservice employees should not handle these chemicals.)
- Install a fly-catching device, if needed (Figure 2-24).
- Remove any lead-based products from foodservice, including dishware, glassware, and service pieces. If in doubt, purchase a testing kit.
- Watch out for any copper-based pans. Copper sulfate is a strong and potentially fatal poison. If using copper pots, make sure that the lining is not worn through. Have pots relined if they show any wear whatsoever. If using copper pots without lining, be sure to clean first with approved cleaner.
- Never use zinc or any glazed pot or pan that has chips in the enamel. Many of the glazed metal or cast iron pots have potentially poisonous underlayers and can leach toxic metal into whatever you may be cooking in the pot. Remove these pans from the kitchen.

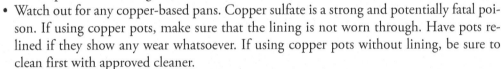 **Figure 2-24** This fly-catching machine attracts flies with its glowing blue lights.

PHYSICAL HAZARDS

Physical hazards are common types of hazards. They are generally more cosmetic than life threatening but can still be extremely dangerous. Always be on the alert for physical hazards.

- Keep glassware away from food. Drinking from a glass while working on a line is against all health codes. Never use a glass to get ice from an ice machine. One break and sanitation and safety are compromised. The machine will need to be emptied, inspected for broken glass, and washed, rinsed, and sanitized.
- Be careful when breaking down boxes. Large copper staples can find their way into the food preparation area.
- Make sure that if you are wearing a bandage, you are also wearing a latex glove to cover the bandage.
- Be careful when removing bones from shredded meat products. It can be fatal if a bone finds its way into an unsuspecting customer's throat. When working with mousse and other forcemeats, remove bones by putting the product through a food mill or tamis screen. This is not just for smoothing out a meat paste but is very practical for removing bones from the finished product.

UNDERSTANDING HACCP

The acronym **HACCP** stands for Hazard Analysis Critical Control Point. The Pillsbury Company developed the system for the NASA space program and, over the years, the federal government defined it through a national advisory committee. HACCP has since been adopted for use in foodservice operations around the country. This system uses a scientific approach that follows the flow of food through the foodservice operation and identifies each step, known as **critical control points,** in the process where contamination might occur.

When the food arrives in the cold kitchen, it should have already gone through a series of control points. Once in the kitchen, it is now up to the kitchen management to make sure that the food remains safe and avoids contamination during the preparation steps and service. The following list shows the seven steps used in the HACCP system to identify biological hazards and to monitor them through the food chain.

HACCP's Seven Steps

1. Assessing hazards.
2. Identifying critical control points.
3. Setting up procedures for those critical control points.
4. Monitoring the critical control points.
5. Taking corrective actions.
6. Setting up a record-keeping system.
7. Verifying that the system is working.

Learning to think through all the potential hazards is imperative when using the HACCP system. This is a team effort that requires training and cooperation from all employees. It is every employee's job to serve food that is wholesome and safe.

LEARNING ACTIVITY 2-2

The first step in HACCP is assessing hazards. This activity will help you think through each step of a recipe and look for possible hazards.

Choose two recipes from your class, personal collection, or work. Determine which steps during the preparation and service are most vulnerable. Prepare a flowchart of the steps or critical control points. Remember that hazards can be biological, chemical, or physical in nature.

Record the flowchart in the space provided below:

Recipe #1 _____

Recipe #2 _____

FOOD SAFETY REVIEW

This is a list of possible food safety hazards and remedies that chefs might face on a common basis. These are general suggestions—some food items will require a different remedy.

Hazards	Remedies
Holding cold food on buffet lines	Chefs or employees should use a hand-held, insta-read thermometer and check the temperature on a regular basis every half to one hour.
Food displays	Food displays should include sneeze guards, which provide a protective barrier between the customer and the food.
Pre-set banquet main-course salads	Avoid pre-setting this type of salad. If it must be done, ensure that the food is out of the refrigerator no more than half an hour before guests consume it.
Presentation dessert trays	Use dummy trays and keep the real dessert tray under refrigeration at all times.
Canapé trays	This type of tray can sit out at room temperature for up to 2 hours. Keep back-up trays in the refrigerator. Only replenish from these trays. Discard any canapés that have been sitting out for longer than 2 hours.
Flatware storage	To avoid dust and dirt, keep all flatware and dishes in covered conditions until needed for service.
Glassware storage	To prevent dust, smoke, fumes, and germs, avoid storing in overhead racks; instead, keep all glassware in covered conditions until needed for service.
Food holding	Hold cold food at 41°F or below and hot food at 135°F or above.
Service utensils	Always use clean serving utensils or handle with clean gloves.
Food storage	Always store food in clean and sanitized containers that are in good repair. Discard containers with pits, scratches, and chips. Store food only in proper refrigeration units or dry storage areas that are free from any vector contamination. Do routine temperature checks on all refrigeration and freezer units. Never store food in a malfunctioning unit.
Storing chemicals	Store chemicals away from any foodservice activity.
Mixing of foods	Never mix previously cooked or leftover foods into newly cooked or raw foods.
Sick employees	Ill workers should stay home until they are well.

>> Workplace Safety

In any professional kitchen setting, there is the significant risk of cuts, burns, shocks, slips, and falls. It is up to you, the individual, to take responsibility for your own safety.

KNIFE SAFETY

- Always keep your eye on your knife as you work.
- When transporting a knife, hold it next to your side and pointed toward the floor.
- Select the correct knife for the job.
- When possible, use color-coded cutting boards for the correct job.

Figure 2-26 Make sure that the guard is in place when using an electric meat slicer.

- Keep knives sharp and clean (Figure 2-25).
- Store properly after use.
- Never put a knife in a dish station where an unsuspecting coworker may not see it. Always clean your own knife immediately and put it away properly.
- Cut away from the body; hold and cut away from fingers, never toward the hand.
- Let a falling knife fall; don't try to catch the knife with your hand or foot.
- Put moist towels under cutting boards to prevent the board from sliding around.

ELECTRICAL SAFETY

- Unplug any electric machine or tool before attempting to clean or to perform maintenance.
- Keep your eyes on the work; do not get distracted.
- Report any defective equipment immediately to your supervisor or maintenance department.
- Make sure the floor and your hands are dry when working with any electrical equipment.
- Note any frayed or damaged electrical equipment or plug to your supervisor or maintenance personnel.
- Only use equipment that you have been trained and authorized to use.
- Never use the electric meat slicer without its guard (Figure 2-26).

BURN PREVENTION

- Wear uniform correctly; avoid sleeves that drag. Remove any dangling strings.
- Always use dry pot holders or towels. (Wet ones can cause steam burns.)
- Assume all metal surfaces are hot.
- Turn pot handles away from the front of the stove to avoid catching a sleeve (Figure 2-27).
- Be careful around a steamer; always open slowly with face and hands away from the door to avoid a facial steam burn.
- Avoid spilling hot liquids from heavy pots. If it is heavy, use the buddy system.
- Protect eyes and skin from harsh chemicals and odors.
- Alert coworkers about hot pans or pots.
- Communicate to others when walking through the kitchen with hot pans or pots.

Figure 2-27 Keep hot handles away from the front of the stove.

FIRE SAFETY

- Keep water away from hot grease.
- Keep cooking equipment, stoves, ovens, and broilers clean and free from grease build-up.
- Keep overhead grease filters and grease traps clean and free from grease build-up (Figure 2-28).
- Keep grease or fat below ignition temperature in deep-frying equipment; use equipment correctly according to manufacturer's instructions.

Handling Minor Cooking Fires

- If a pan or deep-frying unit flashes over, cover with a pan lid or sheet pan to smother the flames. Do not remove until fire is out and unit is cooled down.
- Use baking soda or salt to smother a fire. Never use flour or other combustible material.
- Never put water on a grease fire—it will explode and spray hot steam and grease, causing the fire to spread.
- Never put water on an electrical fire as the chance of shock is far too great.
- If necessary, use a hand-held fire extinguisher and be sure to use the appropriately marked fire extinguisher for each type of fire. Class A is for ordinary combustible materials such as paper, wood, or plastic. Class B is for flammable or combustible liquids such as gasoline, grease, or oil. Class C is for electrical equipment such as appliances, wiring, and electrical outlets (Figure 2-29).

Handling Small Oven Fires

- Keep equipment clean to avoid fires.
- If a fire starts, close the oven door; the fire will be contained. Smother it.

If a fire gets out of hand, call 911 and give precise location instructions including address, floor, back door, or area where the fire is located. Evacuate customers, employees, and yourself.

STEPS TO PROPER LIFTING

The correct way to lift a heavy object is to squat close to the load, keeping the back straight. Never stoop over the load to get a grip and then pick it up. Lift using your knees and legs, not your back, as leverage.

1. Examine object to determine if it is over-sized or too heavy; if so, ask for help.
2. Hold object close to body.
3. Bend at the knees, not straight back, and use legs to lift (Figure 2-30).
4. Keep your back straight, not bent forward or backward.

FLOOR SAFETY

The National Safety Council reports that slips and falls are the leading cause of death in the workplace and the cause of more than 20 percent of all disabling workplace accidents. Follow these procedures to avoid floor hazards:

- Clean up spills and grease with absorbent material first, alert others that there is grease or liquid on the floor, then wash the area properly. Do not salt

Figure 2-28 Fire suppression systems should be kept clean and receive regular professional cleaning and inspection.

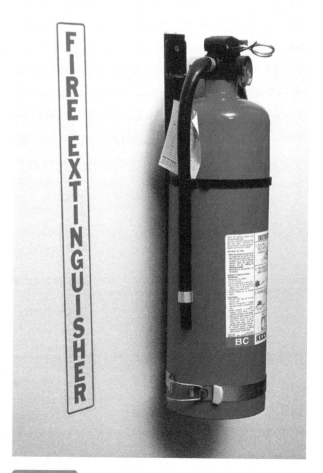

Figure 2-29 Know where the fire extinguishers are located in your facility and make sure that you use the right fire extinguisher for each type of fire.

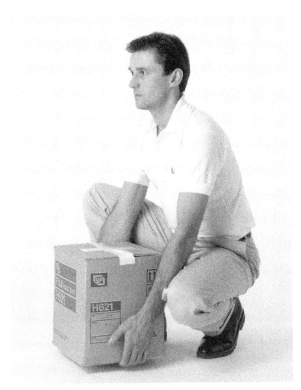

Figure 2-30 To lift a heavy load, start by bending your knees. Use your legs, not your back, to lift.

Figure 2-31 Use wet-floor signage when mopping the floor.

the floor. This common habit is not very safe or efficient. Salt can make an already wet or slick floor even more slippery.
- Keep floors dry and clean. Always alert others and post "wet floor" signs when mopping floors (Figure 2-31).
- Keep walkways clear of obstructions.
- Do not run in a kitchen . . . ever!
- Wear nonskid shoes, and closed-toe work shoes or boots.
- Know where your coworkers are at all times; look where you are going!
- Carry tools correctly; knives should be pointed toward the floor and held straight down next to your hip.
- Alert others of your presence behind them.

IN CASE OF AN EMERGENCY

Every foodservice operation has specific guidelines about how kitchen employees should behave when an accident happens and in case of fire. It is your responsibility to read these instructions carefully and remember them.

What should be done if there is an accident or emergency situation? The four most serious injuries or situations in any kitchen are bleeding, breathing, burns, and shock. These need to be dealt with immediately. Time is critical.

If you are experiencing an emergency, follow these steps:

1. Notify your immediate supervisor and/or call 911.
2. Do not attempt to render first aid unless you are specifically trained.
3. Without moving the victim, make him or her as comfortable as possible.
4. Try to stop heavy bleeding until aid arrives.
5. Do not administer any medication.

Insurance companies have become weary when accident victims received well-meaning first aid and then sued the company for inappropriate medical help. Many operations forbid their employees to give even an aspirin to a customer or an employee.

CHOKING VICTIMS

Choking on a physical hazard is a very real and dangerous thing to happen in a restaurant (Figure 2-32). The **Heimlich maneuver** is the approved method of helping choking victims. The law requires every operation to display, in a conspicuous place accessible to all employees, a poster outlining the steps of the Heimlich maneuver; such a poster is available through the National Restaurant Association in collaboration with the Red Cross. As a kitchen employee, you probably will not be required to practice the Heimlich maneuver, but you should know about it. As with any emergency, the staff should always call 911 if a guest is choking.

Figure 2-32 A choking diner grabs for his throat while eating in a restaurant.

BASIC FIRST AID

Always keep a list of emergency numbers near each telephone extension for police, fire, and ambulance service, and the local poison control center. When in doubt, call for emergency assistance. For minor injuries, knowing what to do is important knowledge, and again you are encouraged to attend a first aid class.

Injury	Action to Take
Minor cut	Clean with soap and hot water. Apply antibiotic cream (if your employer permits it) and a bandage. Use a finger cot and glove for finger cuts. Keep cut or wound clean and dry.
Serious cut	Call 911. Apply pressure to the wound with a thick, clean cloth. Elevate it above the victim's heart. Get immediate medical help.
Minor burn	Run cool water over the burn area or use indirect application of ice. Wash with mild soap; apply antibiotic cream. Never use grease, ointment, or butter.
Serious burn	Call 911. Wrap the injured area in large wet, clean towels. Get immediate medical help.
Poisoning	Call local poison control and be prepared to describe the product and the amount that was swallowed.
Electrical shock	Look but don't touch. The current may pass to you. Turn off any electrical power if possible. Otherwise move the source away from the victim with an object made of wood, plastic, or cardboard. Look for signs of breathing. Call 911 if victim is experiencing heart rhythm problems, respiratory failure, muscle pain and contractions, seizures, numbness and tingling, or unconsciousness.
Falls	Never try to move someone who has fallen unless he or she is certain that there are no breaks. If serious, call 911.

>> Summary

Preparing food is an awesome responsibility. Customers come to your establishment and expect that the food is safe, wholesome, good tasting, and consistent. The restaurant business, by nature, is a business with wide swings of activity. In the dining room, customers expect their meals to arrive within a reasonable time frame. The pressure of the dinner or lunch rush is great, and the temptation is always there to cut corners and disregard sanitary and safe practices. Cutting corners that place the food in dangerous temperatures or using bad practices that put employees' or customers' well-being in jeopardy should never be allowed in the food business.

The cold kitchen has special challenges. Foods prepared hot but served cold must be chilled properly and handled without contamination. Salads can be a source of food-borne illness.

They are subject to both biological contamination and physical contamination. Cleaning greens, making sure dressings are properly chilled and stored, and cooking and chilling high-protein items used in the cold kitchen will help to avoid problems. Always use proper handwashing technique, use gloves where appropriate and frequently change gloves, and use clean serving and storing equipment. Keep cold foods cold and out of the danger zone. Never take a chance with safety!

You provide the highest sanitary standards when you purchase foods from a reputable and safe source; when you store the foods in the appropriate manner and keep them rotated; when you cook, chill, and store the products utilizing a HACCP-type of system; and when you hold all staff responsible and accountable for practicing safe habits.

>> Review Questions

TRUE/FALSE

1. About 70 percent of all food-borne illness occurs in food-service operations; 20 percent of these illnesses occur in private homes.
2. Foodservice workers should always wash their hands for 20 seconds or more.
3. When sanitizing with moist heat, the water should be at least 200°F (93°C) or above.
4. In the color-coded cutting board system, the red cutting board should only be used for cutting fruits.

5. An insecticide is a type of physical contaminant.
6. Hepatitis A is caused by a virus.
7. FIFO stands for a method used to rotate food properly.
8. MSDS is a type of biological contaminant.
9. HACCP was first designed for the NASA space program.
10. Flour can be used to smother a fire.

MULTIPLE CHOICE

11. Sanitizing can be done with either moist heat or
    a. air.
    b. soapy water.
    c. chemical sanitizing agents.
    d. all of the above.
12. There are three types of hazards found in food; they are
    a. bacteria, virus, and poisons.
    b. biological, chemical, and physical.
    c. alkaloids, neurotoxins, and poisons.
    d. bacterial, chemical, and polluted.
13. The two main viruses that impact the food industry are
    a. hepatitis B and C.
    b. botulism and *E.coli*.

    c. Staphylococcal gastroenteritis and *E. coli*.
    d. norovirus and hepatitis A.
14. Hot food should be held at what temperatures?
    a. 120°F (48°C) and above
    b. 90°F (32°C) and above
    c. 110°F (43°C) and above
    d. 135°F (57°C) and above
15. Where can a restaurant employee find out the safety instructions for using a specific type of chemical cleaner?
    a. Look at the MSDS.
    b. Look on the back of the bottle.
    c. Consult the FAT TOM manual.
    d. Check out the FIFO files.

16. Which is *not* one of HACCP's Seven Steps?
    a. assessing possible hazards
    b. setting up a record-keeping system
    c. first in, first out
    d. monitoring the critical control
17. Which class of fire extinguisher should be used on a mixer that has caught fire?
    a. Class A
    b. Class C
    c. Class B
    d. Never use a fire extinguisher on an electric appliance.
18. When lifting a heavy box, never use your _____ as leverage.
    a. back
    b. legs
    c. elbows
    d. wrists
19. If someone ingests a poisonous substance, you should call
    a. the local poison control center.
    b. 911.
    c. an ambulance service.
    d. a physician.

FILL IN THE ANSWERS

20. What is the range of temperatures known as the danger zone?
    _____
    _____

21. Explain the acronym FAT TOM. _____

22. Describe three safe ways to chill hot food.
    _____
    _____
    _____

23. List the seven steps in the HACCP program.
    _____
    _____
    _____
    _____
    _____
    _____
    _____

24. Describe the correct way to transport a knife.
    _____
    _____

25. List the four most serious injuries or situations in any kitchen.
    _____
    _____
    _____
    _____

Basic Equipment

>> Learning Objectives

After you have finished reading this unit, you should be able to:

- Identify equipment used in the cold kitchen, including those items used for refrigeration, preparation, and storage.
- Identify tools used in the preparation of foods common to the cold kitchen.
- Discuss the safe methods for using and cleaning tools and equipment used in the cold kitchen.

>> Key Terms

blast chiller	buffalo chopper	NSF	vertical cutting
blender stick	immersion circulator	sous vide (*soo-VEED*)	machine (VCM)

U nit 3 covers the equipment and tools found in the cold kitchen. The first consideration in designing a cold kitchen space is sanitation and safety. Because many of the
foods served from the cold kitchen have no further cooking before service, the way they
are handled and stored is a major concern. With modern refrigeration and innovative technology, such as sous vide, blast chillers, chill plates, and food processors that freeze and foam, the
cold kitchen is becoming the center of creativity and profit in many restaurants and hotels.

>> Equipment and Tool Standards

When purchasing equipment or tools for the cold kitchen, it is important to consider, first of
all, sanitation. Ask the following questions:

- Will this equipment help make the food in a sanitary manner?
- Is it easy to clean, service, and maintain?
- Is the design of the equipment functional and practical?
- Can it easily be repaired if necessary?

By purchasing quality equipment and tools, you ensure a safe and sanitary work environment. It is important to note that home-use tools and equipment are not built to withstand the
constant usage that occurs in professional food production.

Figure 3-1 Look for the NSF seal of approval on all equipment.

Professional style does not mean professional standards unless the equipment is stamped with the familiar round symbol known as the National Sanitation Federation seal of approval **(NSF)** (Figure 3-1). This group, known formerly as the National Sanitation Foundation, sets standards for all professional foodservice equipment and tools. This standard is accepted nationwide and in foreign countries as the benchmark for use in professional kitchens. Many states and local governments require this certification before they allow certain equipment and tools in commercial kitchens.

The NSF seal ensures that the equipment you purchase has met certain standards. Equipment and tools with the NSF stamp must be low maintenance and easy to clean. These tools must have smooth surfaces and must be made from non-reactive, nontoxic, and nonabsorbent materials such as stainless steel or lexan. They must be corrosion resistant. All internal corners and edges must be smooth with no sharp angles. External edges and corners must be smooth with no sharp edges and, if welded, sealed to keep out any potential contaminants. Coating materials must be nontoxic and easy to clean and maintain, and external coatings must be chip and crack resistant.

LEARNING ACTIVITY 3-1

Work in small groups or individually to locate the NSF seal of approval on at least eight pieces of equipment found in your school's culinary lab. Make a list of the eight that you find. Also note any pieces of equipment, if any, that don't bear the seal.

Figure 3-2 Walk-in freezers are needed to hold large volumes of food.

>> Cold and Hot Heavy Equipment

REFRIGERATION

Having proper refrigeration is key. Whether your needs are for a tiny, single reach-in refrigerator unit in a sandwich cart or multiple walk-in refrigerator and freezer units at a large convention center or hotel, it is important that you understand the function of each piece of equipment and know how best to utilize it.

When designing a kitchen area where the primary products are cold, refrigeration becomes the most important aspect of the plan. It is imperative that the cold kitchen is equipped with adequate refrigerated cold space. Refrigeration can be a built-in or free-standing walk-in refrigerator or freezer or a free-standing unit such as a reach-in refrigerator or freezer with pass-through or glass doors or solid stainless steel doors. Walk-ins are used for keeping large amounts of foods cold or frozen and are larger, heavily insulated, room-size units with internal or external compressors (Figure 3-2). They are capable of holding hundreds and, in some cases, thousands of pounds of food. Storage shelves or racks usually line the walls. Some walk-in units have humidity controls for keeping produce and other products that require humidity. Other units are used for extended frozen storage and can be adjusted to −50°F (10°C) or colder.

Reach-in refrigerators are found throughout the cold kitchen (Figure 3-3). In smaller facilities, they may be the only source of refrigeration. There are many types of reach-ins, from upright units with glass doors or pass-through windows to stainless steel table models. There are also under-counter reach-ins or chilled drawer units, locker-style reach-ins, and reach-ins with sandwich prep tops for drop-in storage for the pantry, salad, or sandwich bar stations. These units usually have built-in or adjustable shelving to accommodate hotel or sheet pans.

Figure 3-3 Reach-in refrigerators should provide adequate space in the cold kitchen.

Some reach-in units display foods for customers and can have carousels or dispenser doors for ease of service.

No matter what type of refrigeration units are needed, they must adhere to the applicable health-code standards and be easy to clean and maintain. There are important questions to ask when purchasing cold storage equipment, including the following:

- Are the seals easy to clean?
- Can your sheet pans or hotel pans fit inside the doors without moving shelves and product around?
- What is the energy consumption and life span of the equipment?

BLAST CHILLERS OR SHOCKERS

Blast chillers are relatively new to retail foodservice and are designed to chill food in a matter of minutes instead of hours (Figure 3-4). While blast chillers have been used heavily in commercial food preparation for many years, smaller stand-alone blast or shock chillers are coming into their own in restaurants and other foodservice operations. Food is broken down into smaller unit sizes, placed inside the blast chiller or shocker, and within minutes chilled below the danger zone or even to freezing, depending upon the need.

For freezing items, the blast chiller is ideal. Ice crystals are miniscule, and foods such as mousses or creams can be chilled, set, or frozen in minutes. Blast chillers work by convection, using fans to circulate super cold air. Some units are self-cleaning and can be equipped with ultraviolet lights to kill bacteria.

Figure 3-4 Blast chillers can reduce the temperature of food in a few minutes by using fans to circulate chilled air.

Figure 3-5 Ice cream makers are used in the cold kitchen to make not only ice cream and sorbet but also mousse products.

ICE CREAM FREEZERS/MAKERS

Ice cream freezers or makers are used for many tasks in the cold kitchen (Figure 3-5). The primary function of this type of equipment is to make ice cream, sorbet, granitas, glacees, and gelato. With the advent of many of the savory ice creams or mousse products, ice cream makers or freezers play an important role in the cold kitchen.

FROZEN FOOD PROCESSORS

Frozen food processors and freezers are used for processing fruits, meats, and other products in a frozen state using a high-speed blade that shaves the foods into extremely fine layers. This device is able to produce single-serving portions of ice creams, sorbets, or savory mousse in a few seconds and large batches in less than 5 minutes.

ICE MACHINES

Ice machines make small pieces of ice chips or cubes (Figure 3-6). In the cold kitchen, ice cubes are used as an emulsification stabilizer in mousse-lines. They are also used to chill foods quickly in ice or water baths. Ice cubes are used as a display base for seafood dishes and other cold salads and sauces.

Figure 3-6 Ice machines produce ice cubes that have a number of important uses in the cold kitchen.

ICE BLOCK MACHINES

Specialized machines used for making high-quality, crystal-clear ice blocks suitable for carving are finding their way into large hotels and banquet facilities (Figure 3-7). The blocks are formed in a horizontal freezing pan. Ice blocks formed using this type of technology lack the internal hazing marks traditionally found in older, upright conventional ice block machines.

STOVES

While there is less need for hot equipment in the standard cold kitchen, stoves and other heating equipment are just as important as any other large piece of equipment. Whether stoves are used for cooking up pots of stock for consommé or for melting gelatin over a bain-marie, they are an important part of the cold kitchen. Many foods need to be heated and processed first before chilling.

Stoves can have a single- or multiple-burner top and generally are powered by electricity or gas (Figure 3-8). They can also be an induction-type stove top. Butane stoves are popular for catered events where the fuel must be transported.

Some stoves or ranges have flat tops for grilling or griddling items. Some have French tops with rings. They all heat by conduction through the metal pots placed on their surfaces. They should be easy to light, clean, and maintain.

OVENS

An oven is an enclosed space for the purpose of cooking or heating foods (Figure 3-9). Food is cooked by the hot air surrounding it. The heating unit is usually placed at the bottom or underneath the deck of the oven. Some ovens heat with infrared lamps that cook the product with radiant heat. In the cold kitchen, we use ovens to bake foods such as roast beef, chicken, and turkey. We also use ovens to slowly cook terrines and pâtés.

Conventional ovens cook the food with only hot air. When hot air is pushed around the food by a fan contained in the oven, this is called a convection oven.

Figure 3-7 Crystal-clear ice, made with an ice block machine, is essential when carving an ice sculpture.

Figure 3-8 A variety of stove options work in a commercial kitchen.

Figure 3-9 Traditional ovens cook with hot air.

This type of oven works faster due to the evaporative effects of the convecting hot air and the uniformity of the heat. Some ovens use heat, convection, and steam to cook or oven-braise food in a shorter amount of time. This type of oven, called a combi-oven, has been used in Europe for many years and only recently found its way into U.S. kitchens. Combi-ovens have a variety of cooking modes including hot air, steam, combination, steam that cycles, and a holding mode. With combi-ovens, you can bake, roast, grill, steam, braise, blanch, poach, and hold foods all in a single unit. Whole racks of plated food can be rethermed for large banquets. The cook and hold is useful for hotels and large banquet facilities, and smaller units are ideal for use with sous vide products for reheating.

Ovens come in all sizes and shapes, from free-standing convection ovens, stackable deck ovens, and roll-in rack ovens to built-in, room-sized reel ovens.

MICROWAVE OVENS

The microwave oven dates back to World War II when *radar* ("*ra*dio *d*etecting *a*nd *r*anging") was invented to locate enemy planes. The first ovens to use this technology were called radar ranges. Microwave ovens are used in kitchens to warm food.

STEAM-JACKETED KETTLES

The steam-jacketed kettle is a large stock pot used to make stocks and larger portions of soups and sauces (Figure 3-10). Unlike standard stockpots, steam kettles have two-layer construction with steam sandwiched in between. Because of the unique construction and use of steam, steam kettles heat foods faster and more uniformly than many other methods do. Steam-jacketed kettles can be stationary or set on gimbals for tilting. They come in a range of sizes from small, 2-gallon countertop models on up to several-hundred-gallon-sized units for commercial production. Some models have bottom spigots for draining.

Figure 3-10 Steam-jacketed kettles use steam to heat food.

BROILERS AND GRILLS

Broilers and grills are used to cook meat, poultry, fish, and vegetables on a rack or grill under or over a radiant heat source such as live coals, gas jets, or electric elements (Figure 3-11). Foods cooked this way have a smokier, more caramelized flavor. The grill marks serve the dual purpose of flavoring via caramelization of sugars and visual presentation from the hash marks of the hot grill bars.

SALAMANDER OR SANDWICH TOASTER

This device has an overhead heat source and is used to heat and melt cheese sandwiches. The larger models are called *salamanders*.

PANINI PRESS OR DOUBLE GRIDDLE

Griddles with heated lids, sometimes call *sandwich presses*, have been around for many years. A sandwich placed between the griddle and top will toast and brown on both sides. The panini press has grooves and grills that make an attractive pattern on the sandwich.

Figure 3-11 Broilers use radiant heat to cook food.

GRIDDLE

A griddle is simply a flat, stainless steel plate with a heat source underneath. It is the ubiquitous cooking apparatus in coffee shops and diners. Griddles can be gas or electrically heated and are used for preparing grilled closed sandwiches.

TOASTER

Most sandwich stations are equipped with toasters because many customers order the bread toasted. The most basic toaster is a pop-up model, usually with four compartments. Larger toasters are called *conveyor toasters* and are equipped with continuous running chain sections. The chains are horizontal on some models and vertical on others. Conveyor toasters are fully automatic and can handle bread of different thicknesses.

There are many other types of hot, large kitchen equipment such as deep-fry units and rotisseries, but they do not fall under the scope of this book. For more information, check out our companion books: *Culinary Fundamentals*, for a complete list of hot kitchen equipment and *Baking Fundamentals* for baking equipment.

>> Processing Equipment

Processing equipment and machines, such as grinders, food processors, slicers, blenders, and choppers, are required to prepare a myriad of forcemeats and sausages. Machines that pump brine into hams, tenderize pieces of meat, and dry or dehydrate jerky are just some of the other smaller pieces of equipment that you might find in an average cold kitchen.

Years ago, food had to be blended or chopped by hand or puréed in a heavy stone mortar and pounded with a pestle. As recently as a hundred years ago, commercial kitchens were equipped with large granite mortars and the heavy wooden pestles resting inside an iron ring above. Today, most kitchens have a number of electric devices to blend, purée, or chop food.

Before we can cook and chill foods in the cold kitchen, we must prepare these foods by grinding, chopping, and processing. When using these types of machines and equipment, safety and sanitation are key. Always practice good habits.

SAFETY STANDARDS

- Always keep your eyes on your work. Do not be distracted.
- Always unplug a machine when cleaning, maintaining. or servicing.
- Never use a machine without the required safety guards in place.
- When applicable, use safety glasses.
- Make sure blades are sharp and the tension is adjusted properly.
- Operate electrical equipment with dry hands to avoid shocks or slipping. Wear protective gloves when necessary.
- Be conscious of loose clothing that could get caught on or in a machine.
- Unplug and zero out slicer blades to protect your hands from accidental slicing when cleaning. (When the dial is turned to zero, the blade fits snugly against the machine in a safe position.)
- Disassemble the machine under supervision. Most machine parts can be cleaned in the dishwasher but not the electric motor and cable. Wash, rinse, and sanitize each part of the machine.
- For machines with a stationary base, use a soap and sanitizer on the machine itself. Use the raising device on most machines to lift up and clean under the machine where food particles can collect.
- Reassemble the machine when parts have been properly cleaned and sanitized.

ELECTRIC MEAT SLICER

The electric meat slicer is a device commonly found in most kitchens. It ranges in size from small to large machines that slice and can automatically stack the slices (Figure 3-12). It has a round blade that spins at a high rate of speed. Food is placed on a deck or carrier and

Figure 3-12 Meat slicers use a fast, spinning blade to slice meat.

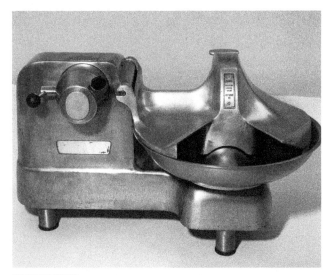

Figure 3-13 Food choppers can chop or grind food in a short period of time.

Figure 3-14 Meat grinders are used for forcemeats and sausage making in the cold kitchen.

pressed against the spinning blade with a safety guard. Meat slice thickness is adjustable, from paper thin to thick. This type of equipment is preferred for slicing large quantities of foods such as roast beef, ham, or cheese. It is also used in banquets for slicing large quantities of prime rib.

BREAD-SLICING MACHINE

Operations that specialize in hot sandwiches sometimes slice bread to make sure it is as fresh as possible. Bread-slicing machines are great for large-volume facilities. Some machines slice bread horizontally for catering and for finger sandwiches whereas most machines use a gravity feed to slice vertically.

FOOD CHOPPER

The food chopper is sometimes called a **buffalo chopper** or a "blitz" for the German word for "lightning" and is considered the workhorse machine in medium to large kitchens (Figure 3-13). Food choppers are used to chop foods to a uniform size or grind meats or other foods to a medium to fine paste. It is very useful when making large quantities of forcemeats, breadcrumbs, or chopped vegetables. This machine consists of a side motor with an attached rotating bowl and a vertical knife rotating under a protective cowling or cover. The bowl turns when the machine is in use. The heavy bowl can be lifted off the base and washed. This machine has adapters for attachments to grind and stuff sausage and shred or slice cheese.

MEAT GRINDER

The meat grinder is a device for grinding small to large quantities of meat, poultry, seafood, vegetables, and other items (Figure 3-14). It is unsurpassed for making ground beef and is the piece of equipment most used for forcemeats and sausage making in the cold kitchen.

Meat grinders have attachments for stuffing sausage casings and for grinding and slicing cheese.

Follow these steps when cleaning a meat grinder:

- Unplug the machine first.
- Loosen the grinder head by turning counter-clockwise while the machine is still attached but not running. The grinder head might become difficult to loosen when no longer attached to the machine.
- Remove the grinder head by turning counter-clockwise. Be careful—it is a heavy piece of equipment!
- Disassemble the parts. Remove all food pieces and residue still in the machine.
- Wash, rinse, and sanitize all parts except the blade and plate die in the dish machine or three-sink dish station.
- Wash, rinse, and sanitize the plate die and blade in the dish sink, not the dish machine. To clean the plate die (round metal plate with various-sized holes through which the product is forced), run a wire or skewer through the holes to remove stubborn pieces of sinew or meat. They are not rust proof and will corrode by commercial dish machine chemicals.
- Store all parts in cold dry storage until needed. To use, place all parts of the meat grinder in the freezer for several hours before use. The plate and knife will rust, so dry well or oil lightly. If the grinder is used infrequently, mineral oil should be used.

FOOD PROCESSORS

Food processors are the next generation of food choppers. The blade is inside a large bowl with straight sides. The motor base is underneath, and the blade spins on a vertical shaft. The food processor comes with multi-task shredding blades and a separate, removable housing.

Food processors are useful for grinding nuts to a paste, chopping and puréeing vegetables and fruits, making smooth meat pastes and mousselines, and preparing salad dressings and emulsified products such as mayonnaise.

VERTICAL CUTTING MACHINES (VCMS)

A **vertical cutting machine (VCM)** is used for large-quantity sauce or chopping jobs in the cold kitchen. It consists of a large bowl that can hold several gallons of food. Each unit has an S-shaped blade in the base. A VCM is useful for making gallons of salad dressings, salsas, and chopped fruits and vegetables.

BLENDERS

Blenders are similar to food processors in that they chop, blend, and purée (Figure 3-15). Blenders, however, are taller, with a narrow bowl; and, unlike the processor's S-shaped blade, they have a three- or four-pronged blade used primarily for liquefying foods such as fruit or vegetables into purées, smoothies, and other beverages or liquid sauces. Some models can chop ice as well. Blenders are primarily found in beverage stations.

Figure 3-15 Blenders can chop, blend, and purée food.

STICK OR IMMERSION BLENDERS

Stick, or immersion, blenders, also known as **blender sticks** or portable electric devices, are used to blend sauces and dressings (Figure 3-16). They are available in many sizes and consist of a long handle with a small propeller at the end that turns at several thousand revolutions per minute. When the stick is placed in the bottom of a container, it will blend, puree, or pulverize material in a very short time.

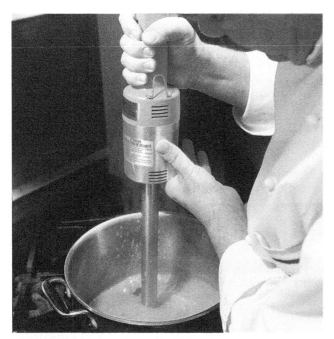

Figure 3-16 Blender, or immersion, sticks can quickly blend, purée, or pulverize food.

MIXERS

Mixers are not just for the bakery department (Figure 3-17). A standard 20-quart mixer is used in the production of many items found in the cold kitchen. Mixers are used to knead bread dough, mix cake and other batters, and whip a variety of sauces and fillings. In the cold kitchen, the mixer can blend ground meat mixtures, whip sauces and mousse, and, with attachments, shred cheese, grind forcemeats, and stuff sausage.

LEARNING ACTIVITY 3-2

Make a list of all the different equipment found in your school's culinary lab that can slice, grind, chop, or process food. Understand how to operate and clean each piece of equipment on your list.

JUICERS

Juicers are machines that extract juice from fruits and vegetables. There are three types of juicers: reamers, centrifugal extractors, and blender juicers.

Reamers press out the juices primarily in citrus fruits. They can be as simple as a hand-held reamer or a hand-pressed table model reamer juicer (Figure 3-18).

The extractor type of juicer uses centrifugal force to extract the juice and remove the pulp at the same time. Horizontal and vertical extractors work in similar ways. Both do an exceptional job of rendering pulp-free juices for many kitchen applications.

Another type of juicer is a blender type of machine capable of pulverizing all of the fruit and vegetables. This type of machine retains all of the fiber for health benefits. The speed of this type of juicer can generate heat and is also used as a multi-task machine for cooking the resulting vegetable or fruit juice and pulp into a soup or sauce.

DEHYDRATORS

A new device that is cropping up in cold kitchens uses ancient technology. In the quest for new ideas, innovative chefs have happened on the idea of concentrating flavors through dehydration. Dehydrators are being used to dehydrate fruits and vegetables to concentrate flavors, develop new textures in old stand-bys, and expand flavors in foods. New mediums such as foams, airs, powders, and gels become the carriers for these new and exciting flavor applications. A dish can be enhanced with the layering of flavors and textures. An example would be to incorporate a smooth berry sauce with a touch of dehydrated, crunchy berry topping.

>> Charcuterie Equipment

The process of preserving meat, poultry, fish, and vegetable protein by smoking or curing, as well as production of forcemeats, pâtés, terrines, and sausages, is within the realm of the cold kitchen. Along with the standard kitchen equipment and tools, there are specialized pieces of equipment used for these products.

SMOKERS

There are two types of smoking units found in the cold kitchen—cold smokers and hot smokers. In addition, pan smoking has found popularity in smaller kitchens.

Cold Smokers

Cold smokers are used to primarily give flavor to dry cured meats such as ham or salmon. The products hang inside the cabinet, which circulates cold smoke. This flavors and colors

Figure 3-17 Mixers can be used for a variety of jobs in the cold kitchen.

Figure 3-18 Reamer juicers press out the juice.

the meat and gives it a delicious aroma. Cold smoking does not cook the product because the temperatures used only vary between 70° and 120°F (20° and 50°C). Some products will need further cooking.

Hot Smokers

Hot smokers are used to not only flavor the items, but cook them as well. The heat source is directly in the smoking cabinet (Figure 3-19). Hot smoking is still done at a relatively low temperature, so it is important to monitor the heat carefully. Hot smoking cooks the outer layer of the sausage or meat, thus preventing molds from forming on the skin. Flavors can be adjusted according to temperature, time in the smoke, and the types of wood or items used to impart the fragrant smoke such as apple wood or hazelnut chips.

Pan Smoking

Pan smoking has found favor in kitchens without larger commercial-style smokers. For small items such as scallops, shrimp, and small pieces of poultry or firm tofu, stovetop pan smoking is easy and quick. Standard kitchen equipment such as hotel pans, cake cooling racks, and pie tins are used. It is important to remember to delegate one set of pans just for this purpose—the smoking process tends to stain the equipment.

>> Sausage-Making Equipment

To make sausages, we use various grinding devices that were discussed earlier in this unit. Along with grinding the meats into chunky mixtures or even smooth pastes, we need devices that stuff the forcemeat into casings to make link-style sausages. These machines can be as simple as a mechanical stuffer used to hand stuff each sausage. These devices are meant for small batches of 10 pounds or less. They come in a variety of shapes and sizes, but the most popular are the horizontal unit and the vertical unit that uses gravity to assist in the stuffing process. Some units use a worm gear or screw to move the forcemeat into the casing. Others use a pressure system. Product is loaded into the can or large tube container. A press attached to a handle is used to squeeze the product through a feed tube into the casing.

ELECTRIC SAUSAGE STUFFERS

For the more serious commercial sausage production, an electrical unit may be the answer (Figure 3-20). This type of stuffer can produce from 5 pounds of sausage up to 300 pounds or more. These units are electrical and hydraulic in nature. The motor turns the worm gear or screw and forces the ground meat into the casings.

BRINING AND CURING EQUIPMENT

Brining equipment consists of a brine tub or barrel used for mixing the curing or brine solution. The solution is then pumped into the product via long, hollow needles attached to the brine pump. The cure flows into the arteries, veins, and capillaries of the meat to cure and preserve it.

Brine Pump

Brine pumps can either be single- or multi-head units. A tub with a handle and a plunger is attached to a hollow needle. These units resemble a hypodermic needle in appearance. The

Figure 3-19 Salmon fillets are placed on racks above the heat source in this hot smoker.

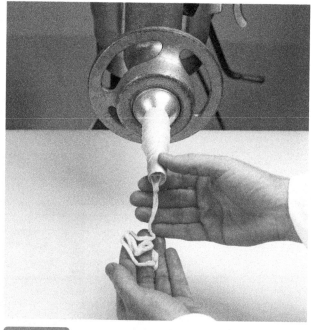

Figure 3-20 The chef is sliding the casing onto the sausage stuffer before adding the forcemeat.

handle is pulled out to suction or siphon off the curing liquid. It is then inserted into the artery or large muscle area and injected into the deepest parts of the flesh.

SOUS VIDE

Sous vide, the French word for "under vacuum," is a process that cooks food in a vacuum environment (Figure 3-21). It is a method of cooking foods for long periods of time at low temperatures under a vacuum seal. Foods cooked by this method are usually simmered well below the boiling point, around 140°F (60°C). The food is sealed in plastic bags or vacuum jars. This technique was developed in the 1970s by George Pralus for the Troigros Brothers and was adopted by many trend-setting French chefs. It came to the United States and initially had limited appeal. Throughout the years, it has become widely used throughout Europe and is now showing up in trendy kitchens of high-end chefs, as the systems have become better regulated and new equipment has been developed to minimize food-borne dangers.

Sous vide can be used for vacuum-packing both raw and cooked food and then regenerating or reheating these foods. It is also a method of cooking foods for the table. Its benefits are many: Foods cooked under vacuum pack can be cooked at much lower temperatures for over longer periods of times. Meats cooked in this manner retain much of the color and texture of rare meat as the muscle fibers do not contract in the same manner as foods cooked at higher temperatures. The myoglobin is not reacted upon by other proteins in the cooking process, resulting in bright red or pink meat that is typical of rare meats, but these foods are well done. Braised meats benefit from slow cooking. Vacuum-packing foods such as foie gras and galantines retains their shapes and maintains their emulsions. Certain foods may also be packed with nitrogen or other inert gases to maintain sanitation.

The major drawback of sous vide is the possibility of infection by *Botulinum* bacteria. In the hands of inexperienced or untrained amateurs or even professional cooks and chefs, it can be dangerous to produce foods in this manner, if sanitation is not maintained during all steps in the process.

When working with sous vide technology, it is vitally important to maintain sanitation standards, keep an eye on temperature controls, and utilize TCM when working with sausages and certain other meat mixtures. (TCM is discussed in detail in Unit 17.) Keeping foods out of the temperature danger zone, and cooking and utilizing foods such as seafood in a quick manner, are some of the ways to be effective with sous vide technology. To cook foods in a safe manner, trained chefs use water bath machines or **immersion circulators,** which

Figure 3-21 Preparing chicken in a sous vide.

are machines that maintain the temperature of the water surrounding the sealed foods. These machines are capable of circulating and holding temperatures at precise increments. The difference of even a few degrees can affect the end product in regard to safety and palatability, so care must be taken to do the research before using this method of cooking.

Sous vide has many applications in the cold kitchen. Marinating under vacuum speeds up the flavoring process and enables food to retain its bright colors and flavors. This is especially helpful when preparing a roulade or other layered product made with whole flesh. By vacuum-packing the product and then using slow emersion cooking, the resultant terrine or roulade will have a smooth yet tender consistency and a brighter, more natural color. Tighter layering is possible, and this also aids in transporting products for off-site catering.

> **CHEF'S NOTE**
> *Always check to make sure that your local health department approves this process.*

>> Kitchen Wares

Smaller kitchen wares or tools such as knives, cutters, and other hand tools are also discussed in this unit along with kitchen tools used to shape and mold cold foods such as mousse, terrines, and pâtés. Tools used for decorating and carving vegetable, tallow, and ice sculptures are discussed in this unit and again in specific units where they are presented.

KNIVES

Knives are an important part of the cold kitchen (Figure 3-22). A properly constructed knife should have a stainless steel blade, full tang, nonreactive and slip-resistant handle, and should be balanced in weight. It should be razor sharp and maintained in that condition at all times.

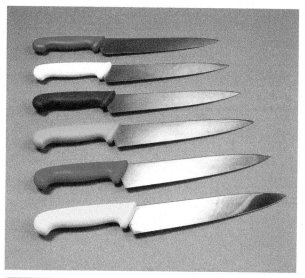

Figure 3-22 There are many types of knives found in the cold kitchen.

Chef's Knives

The chef's knife is used for many applications throughout the kitchen such as slicing, chopping, dicing, and mincing. The most common size used in the kitchen is a 10-inch knife.

Slicers

A slicing knive is used to cut roasts or cured salmon into paper-thin slices. It has a long and narrow, very thin blade. It can have granton grooves ground into the blade or it can be smooth with a round or pointed tip. Blades measuring 10 to 14 inches are standard lengths of these types of knives.

Paring Knives

Paring knives trim fruits and vegetables for service or make tournéed vegetables for salads. Generally, the blade is approximately 2 to 4 inches in length with a thin blade.

Tournée Knives

This knife is a curved version of a paring knife, and is 2 to 4 inches in length with a curved, thin blade (Figure 3-23). It is used to primarily carve potatoes or other root vegetables into tournées.

Utility Knives

The utility knife is an all-purpose knife with a rigid, 8-inch blade. It is used for trimming meats, fruits, and vegetables and can do the work of many types of knives.

Figure 3-23 A tournée knife is also called a bird's beak knife because of the shape of the blade.

Clam Knives

The clam knife is used to pry open clams (Figure 3-24). The blade is 3 inches long, and is rigid and thin with a slightly rounded tip. The edge is sharp for slicing through the adductor muscle of the clam.

Oyster Knives

The oyster knife is similar to a clam knife but is thicker. It is used to pry open oysters. The blade is 3 inches long and rigid. It has a blunt end and no edge. It is used to wedge open the end of the oyster to pry out the meat.

>> Additional Cutting Tools

PARISIAN SCOOPS

The Parisian scoop is a single- or double-ended, half-ball-shaped device with a sharpened edge attached to a handle (Figure 3-25). It is used to cut out round balls of melon or potatoes for the classical dish Pommes Parisiane.

Figure 3-24 The clam knife is used to release the clam from the bottom shell.

OLIVETTO KNIVES

The olivetto knife is a small knife that is similar to the Parisian scoop except that the bowl is more oblong and pointed at the end in the shape of a crescent. It is used to cut olive-shaped vegetables and potatoes.

PINEAPPLE CORERS

A pineapple core remover is a round device with a 10-inch-long cylindrical, serrated cutter with an outer ring. It is attached to a handle and is used to remove the core of a pineapple and the skin at the same time.

APPLE CORERS

An apple corer is used to cut the core out of apples and pears (Figure 3-26). It is a round, short, serrated ring attached to a 6-inch metal stick with a handle.

Figure 3-25 A Parisian scoop can cut round balls of cheese, butter, melons, and potatoes.

Figure 3-26 A chef uses an apple corer to remove the central core of an apple.

ZESTER

A zester has wedges of flat stainless steel with holes or grooves attached to a handle (Figure 3-27). By placing it next to the skin of an orange or other citrus fruit and dragging it across, thin shards of zest are stripped off. Zesters are used to flavor sauces, salads, desserts, and many other foods.

GARNISHING TOOL KITS

Garnishing tool kits are sets of assorted carving knives. Similar to wood-carving tools, this set is designed primarily for vegetable and fruit carving. It contains a carrot shaver for making flowers, and assorted small and delicate paring-style knives with super thin blades for fine detail work on melons and other fruits. It also contains stencils and templates along with stamping tools for specific designs such as hearts, diamonds, and animals, such as fish and crab. There is a set of round and V-shaped assorted knives that are used to cut grooves into fruit and vegetables.

Figure 3-27 Making a coarse lemon zest using a citrus zester.

>> Mixing Bowls, Colanders, Sieves, Strainers, and Scales

There is a wide variety of mixing bowls, colanders, sieves, and strainers in the average cold kitchen. Each has a specific job within this kitchen.

Mixing bowls come in many sizes. They are usually made of stainless steel or an inert type of plastic such as lexan.

Colanders are large strainers made from steel or aluminum (Figure 3-28). They are used to strain pasta, cleaned lettuce, and any other product needing liquid removed.

Strainers are used to remove large particles from food products such as soups. Sieves are fine-mesh wire strainers used to remove bits of bone or sinew from ground forcemeat mixtures such as mousseline (Figure 3-29). They are also used to sift flour or other finely ground substance.

Figure 3-28 A chef emptying steaming penne pasta into a metal colander.

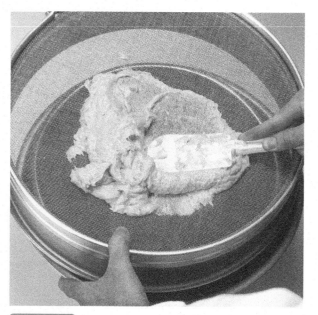

Figure 3-29 A chef uses a drum sieve to pass through forcemeat to ensure a smooth finished product.

Figure 3-30 The China cap is being used to juice whole tomatoes for tomato sauce.

Figure 3-31 A cheesecloth-lined chinoise is used to strain the brown juice.

China caps are conical-shaped, perforated metal devices used to strain water or liquids from foods such as pasta, rice, and other grains (Figure 3-30).

A chinoise is a conical-shaped, fine-wire meshed device used to strain fine liquids such as stocks and soups for a smooth finish (Figure 3-31).

PORTION SCALES

Portion scales are indispensable in most sandwich stations. Meats and other ingredients are measured out or weighed carefully so that consistency is maintained and all orders contain the same amount of product. Salads can also be measured out by weighing or with portion scoops.

>> Ladles, Serving Spoons, Scoops

These serving pieces are used for portion control of cold salads and sauces. They come in an assortment of sizes and shapes, each one designed specifically for the type of product being served.

Ladles are numbered according to the number of volume or fluid ounces they hold, such as a 2 oz., 3 oz., and so forth. Scoops are sized according to how many scoops fill a 32-quart volume measure. It will take 12 #12 scoops to fill a 32-quart measure. The following chart gives the size of common scoops.

Type of Scoop	Amount It Holds
#12	2.7 fl ounces
#16	2 fl ounces
#20	1.6 fl ounces
#30	1.1 fl ounces

>> Cutters, Molds, and Other Containers

Cutters are strips of steel, often coated with tin, that have a sharp cutting edge and a rolled edge to protect the hand. These bands are welded into specific shapes such as circles, squares, and triangles, as well as many other unique shapes. They come in a variety of diameters and depths from 1/4 inch across and 1 inch high, to 6 inches across and 3 inches deep. They are used to cut out shapes from a variety of food materials. These shapes are then used to decorate food.

Molds are containers for food to be baked or shaped in (Figure 3-32). Terrines, pâté molds, custard cups, timbales, and derrioles are a few examples. They are made from tinned steel, ceramic, clay, aluminum, and other heat-resistant materials.

>> Preventive Maintenance

Every piece of equipment in a professional kitchen has come with great expense and should be treated with respect and care. One of the most important steps in keeping equipment in tip-top shape is to use it only for its intended purpose. Become familiar with the manufacturer's recommended uses for each piece of equipment.

Next, adhere to the manufacturer's preventive maintenance steps. Equipment must be cleaned after each use with certain steps taken on a regular basis. Refrigeration fins and louvers, and hood filters, for example, must be cleaned at certain intervals. Some pieces of equipment need to be oiled, and others must be sharpened and calibrated. No business can afford to pay constant repair bills for equipment that has not been properly maintained. Every member of the culinary team must take part in the process.

Figure 3-32 Molds come in a variety of shapes and sizes and are made from a lot of different materials.

>> Summary

Using the right piece of equipment for the job is always an important consideration, as well as understanding the function of each piece of equipment and knowing how to best utilize it. When deciding which equipment is best, always consider the sanitation applications. Equipment that is applicable for the commercial kitchen should bear the NSF seal of approval, which ensures that it has met certain standards. Many of the same pieces of equipment used in all aspects of the kitchen are also used in the cold kitchen. Particular attention is paid to having the proper refrigeration. In certain operations, the cold kitchen is apart from the regular kitchen and has its own specialized equipment. Never try to operate any equipment or to clean or service it unless you have been fully trained.

Careful attention must be paid to safety procedures with processing equipment that has sharp blades, such as grinders, meat slicers, and food processors. Always make sure that the safety guards are in place.

Equipment will last longer if it is used solely for its intended purpose. Additionally, it will provide service longer if it is thoroughly cleaned and stored properly when not in use.

>> Review Questions

TRUE/FALSE

1. NSF stands for the National Safety Foundation.
2. Blast chillers can chill food in minutes instead of hours.
3. Blast chillers work by convection.
4. Frozen food processors use a high-speed blade that shaves frozen foods into fine layers.
5. Ice blocks made in ice block machines are formed in vertical freezing pans.
6. Conventional ovens cook food with circulating hot air.
7. The food chopper is considered the workhorse machine in medium to large kitchens.
8. Reamers use centrifugal force to extract juice.
9. A chinoise is used to cut out round balls of melon.
10. Molds are containers used for baking or shaping food.

MULTIPLE CHOICE

11. Equipment and tools with the NSF stamp must be
    a. low maintenance.
    b. easy to clean.
    c. corrosion resistant.
    d. all of the above.
12. Which piece of equipment can be used to chill below the danger zone or even to freezing within minutes?
    a. blast chiller
    b. extended frozen storage
    c. chilled drawer units
    d. none of the above
13. Grill marks add the visual presentation from the hash marks of the hot grill bars and
    a. flavor the food via caramelization of sugars.
    b. speed up the cooking process.
    c. tenderize pieces of meat.
    d. none of the above.
14. Always zero out the blade when using a
    a. VCM.
    b. meat grinder.
    c. meat slicer.
    d. all of the above.
15. "Blitz" is the nickname given to a
    a. meat slicer.
    b. food processor.
    c. food chopper.
    d. meat grinder.

16. This piece of equipment is the most used for forcemeats and sausage making in the cold kitchen.
    a. electric meat slicer
    b. VCM
    c. meat grinder
    d. food processor
17. This knife is most often used to trim fruit and vegetables.
    a. paring knife
    b. slicer
    c. utility knife
    d. olivetto knife
18. This knife is considered an all-purpose knife; is used for trimming meats, fruits, and vegetables; and can do the work of many types of knives.
    a. slicer
    b. utility knife
    c. bird's beak knife
    d. paring knife
19. This tool is used to remove bits of bone or sinew from ground forcemeat and to sift flour.
    a. colander
    b. sieve
    c. zester
    d. none of the above

FILL IN THE ANSWERS

20. List three questions to consider when determining what type of refrigeration is needed for a specific operation. _____

21. Why is an ice machine an important piece of equipment for the cold kitchen? _____

22. Describe the uses for a food chopper. _____

23. Describe the uses for a blender stick. _____

24. List the features of a properly constructed knife. _____

25. Describe a zester and explain its use. _____

Ingredients

>> **Unit 4**

Flavorings

>> **Unit 5**

Produce, Legumes, and Grains

>> **Unit 6**

Proteins in the Cold Kitchen

The cooking process releases flavor, and when ingredients are combined, a synergy of flavor results. Foods that are served and produced cold are at a flavor disadvantage—not only does the cooking process release flavors, but the taste bud receptors on the tongue are numbed when cold. Thus, it is imperative that only the freshest ingredients available are used in foods that are served cold. Researchers from Katholieke Universiteit, Leuven, Belgium, have determined that the sweet taste of ice cream is only perceived when it melts and heats up in the mouth—that's because the taste buds are highly sensitive to temperatures. They are hardly open at temperatures of 59°F or below. At 98°F the flavor receptors' sensitivity is increased by 100 percent.

Professional chefs have a leading role by using foods produced or grown locally when possible, by purchasing ingredients from reputable suppliers, by selecting only the freshest products affordable, and by observing strict food safety standards. Section 2 covers most of the staple ingredients found in the cold kitchen, from flavorings such as spices and herbs, oils, vinegars, and flavoring sauces in Unit 4, to produce in Unit 5, and proteins in Unit 6. It is important for the student to become familiar with these ingredients.

Flavorings

>> Learning Objectives

After you have finished reading this unit, you should be able to:

- Describe the difference between herbs and spices.
- Identify common herbs and spices.
- Discuss the many forms of salts and their culinary uses.
- Explain the difference between good fats and bad fats.
- Describe common varieties of olive oil and vinegar.
- Identify common flavoring sauces.

>> Key Terms

Fleur de Sel	Herbes de Provence	monounsaturated fats	saturated fats
green peppercorns	(AIRBS duh proh-	pink peppercorns	Sel Gris de Guerande
herb	VAWNS)	polyunsaturated fats	spice
	infused oils	rhizome	trans fats

Picture a little roadside stand in New Mexico, where the food is served from the back end of a truck. Not much décor, but oh, the locally produced tamale is like you never thought imaginable. The flavors of the chilies, the smokiness of the sauce, along with the intense smell of the pinion trees all work together to provide a taste sensation with melt-in-your-mouth consistency. In this example, the ingredients of the tamales clicked; they worked together to create a memorable taste experience. Flavorings are those ingredients that are capable of creating such a synergy. Without flavorings, food would be bland and certainly wouldn't create memorable taste sensations.

Flavorings are herbs, spices, oils, vinegars, and other condiments that add a new flavor to food and alter its natural taste or enhance its own characteristics. An example of this would be when the chef adds a pinch of sugar to a simple tomato sauce to cover up the flavor of the bitter herb oregano or to balance the sauce's tartness. The flavors "melt together" after cooking to complement each other. Choosing the proper flavoring materials is critical. In the cold kitchen, a chef or cook may have to decide whether to add a salty product like soy sauce, a sweet spice like cinnamon, or an acidic lime juice to balance out the flavor. It is important for the student to gain an understanding of the basic flavor ingredients found in the cold kitchen.

>> Herbs and Spices

It has been said that "Variety is the spice of life." But some chefs might prefer to change the saying to read, "Spices are the variety of life." Herbs and spices add flavor, variety, and aroma to food. In many cases, they enhance the basic dish and "bring it to life" when used properly. Many dishes would be bland and flavorless without these added seasonings. Herbs and spices should always be used with good judgment and in carefully measured proportions.

> From the hieroglyphics on the walls of the pyramids to the scriptures of the Bible, we find mention of the important part herbs and spices played in the lives of the ancients. So costly that only the wealthy could afford them, spices nevertheless were used in every conceivable way.

> From the American Spice Trade Association

Certainly herbs and spices have earned an important spot in the history of man. Cultures have been changed, battles waged, and many thousands of lives have been lost over these minute but critical commodities. Today, we take for granted the common use of herbs and spices that are readily available and affordable to most individuals.

Oftentimes the words herbs and spices are used interchangeably with beginning culinarians, but in reality, they are two very different types of flavorings. Both herbs and spices are garnered from plants, but that is where their similarities end.

OVERVIEW OF HERBS

Herbs come from the leaves of herbaceous plants (those plants with stalks that are soft and green compared to plants with woody stems) and are usually associated with savory foods. They hail from temperate climates. Culinary herbs are those herbaceous plants whose fresh or dried leaves are used in cooking. Drying can change the flavor and the potency, so fresh herbs are generally preferred (Figure 4-1). Many chefs grow fresh herbs outside their kitchen door and snip off what they need when they are cooking. Most food distributors carry a wide array of fresh herbs year round. Frozen herbs are now available and are an acceptable alternative to fresh herbs when fresh herbs are not available and when dried herbs are unacceptable for a certain dish.

Figure 4-1 This photo shows a collage of fresh herbs including basil, sage, fennel, chives, mint, and rosemary.

> **CHEF'S TIP**
> Fresh herbs are more effective when added at or near the end of the cooking process.

It is sometimes necessary to use dried and stored herbs. The drying method changes the volume of the herb, so adjustments must be made when substituting dried herbs for fresh herbs or vice versa. As a general rule, use three parts fresh herb to one part dried herb (the ratio is 3:1). There are exceptions: Fresh basil, tarragon, and rosemary are much more potent and powerful than their dried counterparts, so adjustments must be made accordingly. Always use whole-leaf dried herbs with good color that are no more than 6 months old. If you are not sure of the freshness of the dried herbs, contact your purveyor for pack dates. Purchase only the amount that you can use in a few months' time because the oils oxidize and change the flavor profiles of the herbs. (For more information on oxidation see storage information to follow in this unit.) If ground herbs are required, use a spice grinder to make your own fresh-tasting ground herbs and spices.

Place 1 tablespoon of ground sage and 1 cup of water into a saucepan and bring it to boil. Cool. Do the same using chopped, fresh sage leaves. Taste both. Which is more effective? (Repeat the experiment with two or three additional herbs including chives.)

OVERVIEW OF SPICES

Spices are obtained from the roots, flowers, seeds, pods, and bark of plants (Figure 4-2). Spices are commonly associated with baked goods and many international cuisines. Most spices are grown in tropical climates and are almost always used in a dried form, either whole or ground. Spice flavors tend to be stronger due to the higher oil content, and generally smaller amounts of spices are needed compared with herbs.

POTENCY

Herbs and spices are products of nature and develop a varying degree of flavor potency depending on:

- Plant variety
- Where cultivated or gathered
- How harvested or cut
- How processed after harvesting
- How shipped and the length of storage at the vendor
- Shape—whether whole or ground
- How stored in the kitchen

STORAGE

The flavor of herbs and spices is carried in the volatile oils in the leaves, stems, blossoms, seeds, and roots. As these oils evaporate, the flavor diminishes. The rate of evaporation is governed by temperature, moisture, shape, and oxidation. Oxidation is a chemical reaction that takes place in the herb or spice as it is exposed to oxygen. It can be detrimental to the life of the product. When spices and herbs are ground, they are exposed to heat, and the finer-ground particles have more contact with air; this causes oxidation and flavor loss. A good example is pepper. Ground pepper loses its flavor much faster than do whole peppercorns, and for this reason, many chefs prefer to use pepper freshly ground in pepper mills (Figure 4-3). Dried herbs and spices should be stored in closed containers in a cool and dry, dark place to avoid oxidation. Fresh herbs can be refrigerated for several days.

HERBS

Basil Ocimum, O. basilicum

Basil is synonymous with Asian food, and when used, it is said to bring "a touch of sunshine" to the dish. It is a member of the mint family and comes from Southeast Asia, where it has been in use for over 3,000 years (Figure 4-4). There are a number of other common varieties of basil including Purple Basil, Thai Basil, and Cinnamon Basil, which is grown in Mexico.

CHEF'S TIP
Unlike herbs, which should be added near the end of the cooking process, spices are best used at the beginning of the cooking process because the oils need time to blend the flavors. There are a few plants that are both herbs and spices. Dill is an example—the seeds are a spice and the stem and leaves are herbs. Another example is the Coriandrum sativum plant, whose leaves are the herb known as cilantro and the seeds are the spice called coriander. In the case of fennel, both the herb (leaves and stalk) and the spice (seeds) use the same name.

Figure 4-2 Assorted spices display a beautiful palate of rich colors and textures.

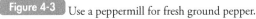

Figure 4-3 Use a peppermill for fresh ground pepper.

Figure 4-4 Basil.

Basil leaves are wonderfully aromatic and are used in the pantry on salads, specifically with sliced tomatoes. The leaves wilt rapidly. Basil is commonly used in sauces such as Pesto Genoese and in basil vinaigrette and basil oil.

Bay Leaves *Laurus nobilis*

Bay leaves come from the bay laurel plant, which is native to Eastern Mediterranean countries and is cultivated in Europe and the Americas (Figure 4-5). This herb is a long, pointed, leathery, dark green, aromatic leaf from an evergreen tree. Bay leaves add an impressionable flavor to soups, stews, and sauces and are essential ingredients in bouquet garnis.

Bay leaves are also used in many meat, poultry, and fish dishes. The leaf is placed on uncooked terrines and pâté to add additional flavor. Always remove bay leaves before serving—whole bay leaves are not edible.

Capers

Capers are actually the fruit of the *Capparis* plant, a shrub growing in Mediterranean regions, usually wild in full sun and poor soil (Figure 4-6). Because it is used as a garnish for added flavor in savory dishes, we have included it in this section. Large producers are Italy, especially Sicily, and France, Morocco, and Israel. Capers are sold packed in vinegar, dried, or salted. The smallest are

Figure 4-5 Bay leaves.

Figure 4-6 Capers.

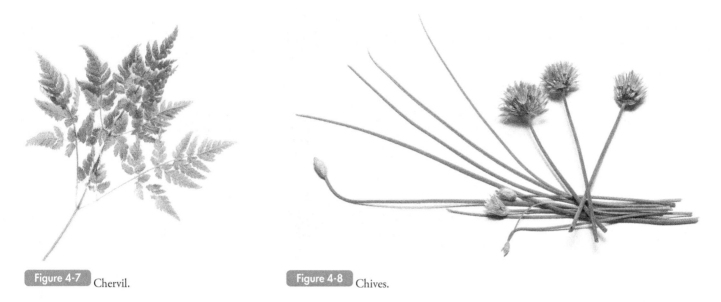

Figure 4-7 Chervil.

Figure 4-8 Chives.

called nonpareilles (nonparelles in Italian); then graduated by size: superfine, fine, capuchin, and capot (or gruesas in Italian). In the cold kitchen capers are used in caponata, tapenade, vitello tonnato, and are traditionally served with smoked salmon.

Chervil *Anthriscus cerefolium*

Chervil is a leafy herb that comes up in early spring (Figure 4-7). It is a native of Russia and southeast Europe. Chervil is used as a garnish and can be sprinkled on salads or used in very mild dressings. It is also used as an ingredient in soups. Its fragile leaves resemble parsley and offer a subtle scent of anise, caraway, and parsley.

Chives *Allium schoenoprasum, A. tuberosum*

Chives are in the onion family and are rather sturdy with a delicate flavor (Figure 4-8). They are green, slender, round, reed-like, and somewhat similar to scallions in appearance, but chives are thinner. They grow wild in most parts of the world and are popular worldwide. Round chives have an onion note, whereas the thin, reed-like Chinese chive has a hint of garlic.

Figure 4-9 Cilantro.

   The pantry is usually responsible for providing cut chives and sour cream for baked potatoes. Chives also are available in other forms such as freeze-dried or frozen for culinary use. Many operations use the freeze-dried and frozen forms for convenience. Fresh chives are inexpensive, easy to handle, and readily available.

Cilantro *Coriandrum sativum*

Cilantro looks similar to parsley, but its flavor is altogether different (Figure 4-9). It has a light ginger, lemon, and anise flavor. The leafy part of the cilantro plant is used in cooking. This herb is indispensable in both Mexican and Asian cooking. It will easily wilt and requires rinsing because of the possibility of sand being in the leaves.

Dill *Anethum graveolens*

Dill has feathery leaves with a strong anise and lemon flavor (Figure 4-10). It is native to cool-weather European countries and is popular in Scandinavian, Central and Eastern European, and Russian cuisines. Dill is often used in dips or cold sauces and, of course, in dill pickles and other cures and marinades.

Figure 4-10 Dill.

Figure 4-11 Fennel.

Figure 4-12 Lemon balm.

Figure 4-13 Marjoram.

Figure 4-14 Mint.

Fennel *Foeniculum vulgare*

Fennel is related to both dill and anise (Figure 4-11). Its feathery leaves are used with pork, veal, and fish. Fennel leaves are also good in fish stock, in sauces and stuffing, and in mayonnaise, flavored butters, and salad dressings. Fennel bulbs and stalks are used in soups and sauces and are handled similarly to celery.

Lemon Balm/Melissa *Melissa officinalis*

Lemon balm is a perennial and a member of the mint family (Figure 4-12). This herb has a strong lemon aroma and is used in sauces, especially dessert sauces, tisanes, and infusions.

Marjoram *Origanum majorana*

Marjoram and oregano are related plants, from the mint family, with similar flavor notes (Figure 4-13). Marjoram has delicate leaves and is softer in flavor than oregano. It has many applications in cooked dishes and is especially popular with lamb and beef dishes and in soups, stews, and sausages. In the pantry, it is used as a garnish or an ingredient in herb vinaigrette dressings.

Mint *Mentha species*

Mint is one of the most universal and popular flavors in the world (Figure 4-14). It is grown in temperate climates. Through hybridization and cross breeding by growers, there are hundreds of flavored mints such as chocolate mint, apple mint, and pineapple mint available on the market. The two most common varieties of mints are peppermint and spearmint; each has its own unique, strong aromas and flavors.

Mint complements lamb, poultry, pork, fruits, cold fruit soups, and drinks. It is very affordable and will keep up to a week in the refrigerator.

Oregano *Origanum vulgare*

Oregano is a popular herb originally found in the coastal regions of the Mediterranean (Figure 4-15). Its slightly bitter flavor note is a favorite on pizza, in sausages, and in many Italian, Greek, Northern African, and Mexican dishes.

Parsley *Petroselinum crispu, P. neapolitanum*

There are two basic varieties of parsley: curly or flat-leaf (Italian) parsley. Both varieties are inexpensive and readily available. Curly parsley requires careful washing because

Figure 4-15 Oregano.

Figure 4-16 Curly parsley, *P. crispum.*

grits of sand often cling to the leaves (Figure 4-16). Italian parsley is less likely to carry much sand but still needs washing (Figure 4-17). It is much more pungent than other types of parsley.

Usually the pantry is in charge of chopping parsley, often done with a chef's knife, mezzaluna, or a food chopper. Like most vegetables, parsley contains a lot of water, and chopped parsley sticks together. Common kitchen practice is to put the chopped parsley in a towel and squeeze out all the green juice under running water. The towel is then squeezed until no liquid is expressed, leaving the parsley dry and sand-like. Unfortunately, most of the flavor and vitamins are lost in this method. Today some kitchens do not chop parsley but instead sprinkle some whole leaves over the food.

Rosemary Rosmarinus officinalis

Rosemary looks like and has an aroma similar to small pine trees, and its needle-like leaves are used in both the cold and hot kitchen (Figure 4-18). It is a perennial that is grown in mild climates. Rosemary skewers are now in markets and can be used as a

Figure 4-17 Italian parsley, *P. neapolitanum.*

Figure 4-18 Rosemary.

Figure 4-19 Sage.

fragrant substitute for bamboo sticks for skewered items. Chefs are also using rosemary fronds for basting, similar to using a basting brush, but the fronds add a hint of rosemary. It is used in many herb blends such as **Herbes de Provence,** which is a blend of dried herbs of marjoram, thyme, sage, basil, rosemary, summer savory, fennel seeds, and lavender. It is associated with the cuisine of Southern France in the Provence region. Rosemary is best used in lamb, beef, and poultry dishes.

Sage *Salvia officinalis, S. purpurascens*

Sage is native to the Mediterranean region (Figure 4-19). It has an important place in both ancient and modern history as a medicinal herb as well as a culinary flavoring. Sage leaves are oval-shaped with a gray-green color and velvety texture. It is used in cooking, especially with pork and poultry and is an essential ingredient in stuffing and dressing. The blossoms are lilac, blue, and red in color and are used as an edible garnish. Sage is also used as a tea.

Savory *Satureja hortenis, S. montana*

Summer and winter savory is indigenous to Europe (Figure 4-20). Its primary uses are for flavoring meat mixtures, stuffing, and braised dishes. Savory has a flavor profile similar to that of thyme and marjoram. Small amounts may be used in vinaigrettes and dressings.

Sorrel (Sour Grass) *Rumex acetosa, R. scutatus*

Sorrel grows wild in meadows in Europe and Asia (Figure 4-21). It has a delicate texture and a refreshing, light lemon taste. Sorrel is a member of the dock family, which is the group of broad-leaf wayside weeds, and is high in vitamin C and A, as well as oxalic acid.

Sorrel greens are used for flavoring soups, salads, and sauces. It is also added to salad blends for additional flavor and texture but should be used in small quantities. Sorrel contains oxalic acids, and it can cause gastric upset when consumed in large quantities. Small amounts are harmless. Shredded sorrel leaves are often cooked and used in soups and sauces.

Figure 4-20 Savory.

Figure 4-21 Sorrel.

Figure 4-22 Tarragon.

Tarragon Artemisia dracunculus

Tarragon is native to Siberia and Western Arabia (Figure 4-22). The Arabs introduced it to European countries in the fifteenth century. The French cultivated it, and over time, French tarragon became the stronger-flavored herb. Today there are two common varieties: French tarragon has a strong and true flavor; Russian tarragon has very little taste, rendering it useless for most culinary applications.

Tarragon has slender, aromatic leaves that are used in dressings and sauces. The flavor is similar to that of licorice, basil, and anise. When preserved in vinegar, tarragon is useful as a flavor component. It is not uncommon to see tarragon vinegar listed as an ingredient in recipes.

Thyme Thymus vugaris, T. citriodorus, T. serpyllum, T. golden queen

Thyme, a perennial woody herb, is one of the most popular of culinary herbs (Figure 4-23). It is used in many meat applications such as marinades and seasoning blends as well as dressings. It has an affinity to poultry products as well as beef and lamb. The oil of thyme, thymol, is used in many culinary applications as well as perfumery. It has an added benefit of having antibacterial properties and is used in some medications and antibacterial cleaners.

Figure 4-23 Thyme.

LEARNING ACTIVITY 4-2

Gather as many fresh and corresponding dried herbs as possible; remove them from their containers so that they are not labeled. Conduct the following experiments and record your findings in the following chart.

- Match the fresh herbs with the dried herbs.
- Commit their names and properties to memory.
- Remember their shape and texture. Soft? Crisp? Curly? Flat?
- Sample and notice the tastes of each herb. Taste both the fresh and dried varieties.
- Compare the flavor intensity.

FRESH VS. DRIED HERB COMPARISON CHART

Name of Herb	Describe the Shape		Describe the Texture		Describe the Flavor	
	Fresh	Dried	Fresh	Dried	Fresh	Dried

SPICES

Allspice Pimenta diocia

Allspice is native to the West Indies and is the dried berry of a tree found in the myrtle family (Figure 4-24). It is the only spice that is grown exclusively in the Caribbean. It is called "allspice" because the flavor resembles a combination of clove, cinnamon, and nutmeg.

Allspice is used whole in pickling and curing blends. These blends are used as a food additive in processed foods such as pickles, meats, and fish and in sausage making. Allspice is usually ground in charcuterie, sausages and forcemeats, and baking. It is used in combination with other spices to make jerk spice mix and is also found in some pepper blends.

Figure 4-24   Allspice.

Anise *Pimpenella anisum*

Anise is a small, fragrant, pear-shaped, gray-green seed (Figure 4-25). It comes from a plant that is similar to fennel and is grown in pods that are shaped like a star. The spice comes from the ground seeds that come out of the pod. Anise has a slight licorice flavor and is used for dressings and in the manufacture of liqueur. It is also used in baking and in spice blends as well as in sausage making.

Annatto/Achiote Seeds *Bixa orellana*

These reddish, hard seeds, also known as achiote, are often used in Spanish, Mexican, and South American cooking (Figure 4-26). When the seeds are heated in oil they release a strong, yellow color, which is often used in cheese manufacturing to add color to naturally white cheese. In some cases, it is also used to add color to butter.

Figure 4-25 Anise.

Caraway Seeds *Carum carvi*

These sickle-shaped seeds come from a plant related to dill (Figure 4-27). They are popular in northern European countries for use in rye bread, kilbasa sausages, pork and lamb dishes, and as a key ingredient in alcoholic beverages including the Scandinavian drink known as aquavit. Caraway has a sweet, yet strong flavor similar to anise. Some say it tastes like cumin.

Cardamom *Eletarria cardamomum*

Cardamom seeds grow in three-cell, ovate triangular pods enclosing a number of small, dark, wrinkled seeds (Figure 4-28). The most common type has a pale grey-green exterior. It is also available in black or white varieties. Cardamom provides a pungent, woody aroma reminiscent of turpentine. Cardamom tastes spicy and sweet. The seeds are used in Indian dishes, and they are added to coffee in Arabic countries. Cardamom is also ground and used in baking.

Figure 4-26 Annatto.

Figure 4-27 Caraway.

Figure 4-28 Cardamom.

Figure 4-29 Cayenne pepper.

Cayenne Pepper Capsicum frutescens L., C. annuum L., C. microcarpum D.

This powerful spice comes from the finely ground pods and seeds of the dried hot peppers of the genus *Capsicum* (Figure 4-29). All chilies and peppers originated in Central and South America. Cayenne pepper is named after the city and province in Guyana, South America. The spice has a very hot, zesty flavor and is used sparingly and with caution. It is usually added toward the end of the cooking process to retain its potency. Liquefied cayenne is also known as Tabasco sauce, a brand used in wet applications. Some chefs prefer to use a pinch of cayenne for Hollandaise sauce and others prefer to use a drop of liquefied cayenne.

Chili Peppers Capsicum species

Explorers visiting South America brought chili peppers to all parts of the world and, consequently, most cuisines have embraced chili peppers as a way to liven up local dishes (Figure 4-30). In Africa, you find bird pepper, used in thick stews, called burgoos, made with meat or game and vegetables, and cooked outdoors. In Mexico, the list of peppers is endless with jalapeno, chipotle, habanero, and ancho leading the way in both flavor and heat. In Latin America and in the Caribbean, you might find Scotch bonnet, tabasco, aji amarillo, and malagueta. In Asia, you might use Thai, Kashmir, and Korean chilies.

Cassia Cinnamonum cassia

Cassia is a spice that closely resembles cinnamon (Figure 4-31). In fact, it is considered a less expensive and inferior version of true cinnamon. In the fifteenth century, cinnamon was reserved for the noble class, while cassia was used by the common people. Today, Chinese and Vietnamese cassia is a respectable substitute for true cinnamon. Cassia quills and buds are used in many types of spice blends.

Figure 4-30 Chili peppers.

Figure 4-31 Cassia.

Cinnamon *Cinnamomum verum*

True cinnamon is the dried bark of a tropical evergreen tree indigenous to Sri Lanka (Figure 4-32). In the United States, cassia is an allowable substitute for cinnamon; however, in England and in Europe, only the product of this variety is acceptable. The main flavor elements of cinnamon come from cinnamaldehyde and eugenol, which impart the characteristic scent and flavor of true cinnamon. It is available in whole sticks (quills) or ground. The West Indian variety of cinnamon is called *canela.* In the cold kitchen, cinnamon is used in spice blends for pâtés and other forcemeats.

Cloves *Eugenia caryophyllu, Syzygitum aromaticum*

Cloves, the dried, nail-shaped, unopened flower buds of an evergreen tree, have many culinary and medicinal uses (Figure 4-33). They are used as a powerful pain reliever for toothaches and as a culinary spice. Cloves are also used moderately in soups, hot cider, stocks, sauces, studding for onions, and baking. They are available whole and ground and are part of the traditional quatre épices, or Four Spices, that are used in pâtés and forcemeat mixtures.

Figure 4-32 Cinnamon.

Coriander Seeds *Coriandrum sativum*

Coriander seeds are the seed part of the cilantro family; they are also related to the other umbelliferae, whose flowers are produced in parasol-shaped clusters, such as dill and parsley (Figure 4-34). These round seeds resemble white peppercorns. Coriander has a strong musky aroma but a mild flavor. The seeds are used in stews, breads, curries, pastrami, and garam masala, which is a spice blend used in South Asia. They are usually added at the end of the cooking process and used with restraint so as not to overpower the dish. Garam masala is made with cardamom, cloves, mace, cumin, fennel seeds, black peppercorns, fenugreek seeds (native to India), and coriander.

Figure 4-33 Cloves.

Figure 4-34 Coriander.

Figure 4-35 Cumin.

Figure 4-36 Fennel.

Cumin *Cumina cyminum*

Cumin comes from the seeds of another member of the umbelliferae family (Figure 4-35). It is popular in Mexican cuisine and is a main component in chili powder mixes. The dried seeds are used in South American, Central Asian, and Indian cooking. Cumin is one of the major spices used in Indian curry and masala mixtures.

Fennel Seeds *Foeniculum vulgare*

Fennel is also a member of the umbelliferae family (Figure 4-36). It has feathery leaves and lantern-shaped seed pods that grow on tall, reed-like stalks. Fennel seeds have a strong licorice or anise-like aroma and a sweet anise flavor. They are used in sausage making and in many spice mixtures as well as in the baking industry. It is one of the spices used to make Chinese Five Spice powder (see spice blends later on in this unit).

Galangal *Alpinia galangal, A. officinarum*

Galangal is a dried **rhizome** found in India and Asia (Figure 4-37). It is a member of the ginger family and has the flavor of ginger and black pepper—pungent and aromatic. It is used in Thai and Indonesian cooking in stews and curry-style dishes as well as Southeast Asian-style marinades.

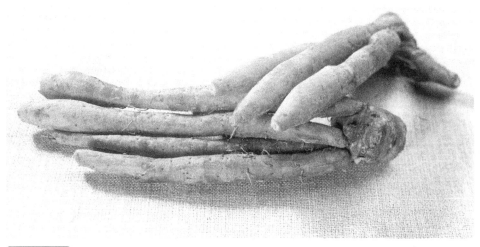

Figure 4-37 Galangal.

Figure 4-38 Ginger.

Figure 4-39 Grains of Paradise.

Ginger *Zingiber officinale, Z. mioga*

Ginger is an aromatic rhizome of a lily-like plant now cultivated in the United States, China, Jamaica, Hawaii, and Fiji (Figure 4-38). Its flavor is spicy, hot, and pungent. Ginger has medicinal and culinary uses such as pickling and canning, and is used in Asian cooking. It is also the key ingredient in some beverages. Ginger is available fresh, candied, or in powdered form.

Grains of Paradise, or Selim *Xylopia aethiopica*

Grains of Paradise, or selim, is also known as Guinea pepper, African pepper, or Ethiopian pepper (Figure 4-39). The seeds have a slightly musty, pepper note and are used as a pepper substitute. It is used in marinades and with game and poultry and is one of the spices used in Tunisian Five Spice.

Hibiscus *Hibiscus sabdariffa*

The beautiful bloom of the hibiscus is edible and offers a mild, sweet taste (Figure 4-40). The flowers are used raw in salads. The buds can be pickled or boiled as a vegetable or stuffed and deep fried. Hibiscus also makes a nice tea or tisane, which is an herbal infusion made by pouring boiling water over the flowers.

Horseradish *Armoracia rusticana*

Horseradish is a member of the crucifer family. Only the root of the plant is used, and it has a strong, acrid, mustard-like taste (Figure 4-41).

Figure 4-40 Hibiscus.

Horseradish is used as a condiment for beef, game, pork, fish, and egg dishes. It can be mixed with cream and bread panade or grated with apples or beets. The pungent, eye-watering effect of horseradish comes from the chemical sinigrin, a potent enzyme that contains sulfur. When

Figure 4-41 Horseradish.

Figure 4-42 Juniper berries.

Figure 4-43 Mace.

horseradish is grated, this volatile oil is released. Horseradish is available fresh, refrigerated in jars, or pickled. It is primarily used as a garnish—a little taste goes a long way.

Juniper Berries *Juniperus communis*

Junipers are bluish-black-colored fruit from an evergreen shrub or tree found throughout Europe and North America (Figure 4-42). They are twice the size of peppercorns. Juniper berries are crushed and used as a flavoring for gin, game dishes, pickling, and brining. They are also traditionally served with Bavarian-style hot sauerkraut.

Mace *Myristica fragrans*

Mace is one of two spices produced by the nutmeg tree (Figure 4-43). The orange-red outer "aril," or cage surrounding the nutmeg, is the mace. It is available ground or in slivers called *blades*. Mace's flavor is similar to that of nutmeg with a more refined flavor profile. The spice is used for pickling, in fish dishes, and in sausages.

Mustard Seeds *Sinapis alba, Brassica nigra, Brassica juncea*

There are three types of mustard plants used for their seeds (Figure 4-44). The seeds can be white, yellow or tan, brown, and black. Mustard seeds have a sharp taste and pungent aroma due to the glycoside sinigrin and sulphur compounds that are released when they are ground. Ground mustard commonly goes by the name of English mustard. When mustard powder is blended with spices and acidic liquids, the sharpness is tempered and changed. This wet mixture is the base used for numerous types of prepared mustard. Mustard seeds are used for marinades, cures, pickles, spice blends, curries, and fruit relishes. Prepared mustard is used as a condiment for beef, pork products, fish, and poultry dishes.

Nutmeg *Myristica fragrans*

Nutmeg is the inner seed of the edible nutmeg fruit (Figure 4-45). It is one of two spices from the nutmeg tree. It is round in shape and is available whole or ground. Nutmeg is used in curries, sweet spice blends, custards, milk products, cookies, vegetables such as spinach and potatoes, and in sauces. It is one of the spices used in the Quatre Spice and Tunisian Five Spice.

Figure 4-44 Mustard seeds.

Figure 4-45 Nutmeg.

Figure 4-46 Paprika.

Paprika *Capsicum annuum L.*

Paprika consists of ground ripe *Capsicum* peppers, which are in the same family as chili peppers (Figure 4-46). Major producing countries are Spain and Hungary. Spanish paprika is mild with a bright red color. Spanish paprika can also be smoked for added flavor. Hungarian paprika is more intense in flavor and is available in three levels ranging from the mild, sweet Red Rose to fiery hot. Hungarian food is most identified with paprika. Most Americans use the less-expensive Spanish paprika, mainly for color.

Peppercorns *Piper nigrum*

Figure 4-47 Peppercorns.

Pepper from ground peppercorns has become one of the world's favorite condiments (Figure 4-47). Pepper has been used for more than 3,000 years. During the Middle Ages it was worth more than gold by weight, and individual peppercorns were accepted as a form of legal currency. Pepper currently represents more than 25 percent of the world trade in spices, making it the most widely traded spice worldwide.

Ground pepper oxidizes and loses flavor rapidly, which is a solid reason for using only freshly ground pepper in all food preparation and service applications. A large variety of peppercorns is available, each with its own distinctive flavor and aroma.

Peppercorns in the shape of small berries grow on vines in tropical countries within 15° of the equator. India is the largest producer of pepper; Sri Lanka, Malaysia, Indonesia, and Brazil are also major exporters. The ripe berries are harvested, boiled briefly, and then allowed to ferment and dry in the sun or by forced-air heating. They turn black after drying.

When ground, peppercorns produce black pepper that is hot, pungent, and aromatic. Most black pepper consists of a variety of sources. The least-expensive grades come from Brazil and are less flavorful than others. Malibar, a popular variety from India, has a robust flavor. Tellicherry also comes from India and is considered one of the finest black peppers available. It provides a complex spicy flavor and aroma. Sarawak peppercorn comes from Malaysia and has a milder flavor and aroma that is often described as fruity. Lampong comes from Indonesia and is hotter than most other varieties of peppercorns. Talamanca Del Caribe has a robust flavor and pungent aroma. It is hotter than most other varieties and is considered rare. Only small batches are organically grown in Ecuador.

Figure 4-48 Green peppercorns.

The inside of peppercorns is white, and white pepper is made when the black outside shell has been removed. White pepper is hotter but less pungent than black pepper. It is generally used for visual reasons to avoid black specks in light-colored sauces, soups, potatoes, and beverages. The additional processing makes white pepper more expensive than black. The most common variety of white pepper is Muntok, which comes from Indonesia. Talamanca Del Caribe comes from Ecuador. It is hot and considered to be of premium quality, which explains its high price tag. Sarawak peppercorns are large and have a robust flavor. They are grown in Malaysia.

Varieties of Peppercorns

Green and pink peppercorns are unripe peppercorns and are available pickled in vinegar or dried.

Green peppercorns are berries that are picked before they are ripe and either air dried, freeze dried, or pickled in a brine to prevent fermentation (Figure 4-48). They are used dried in French, Creole, and Thai cooking. This is the pepper that is traditionally used in "pepper steak" sauce. Brazil is the chief exporter of green peppercorns. Because of the extra processing required and smaller yields, this type of pepper garners a premium price.

Pink peppercorns are expensive little berries that are cousins to the ragweed and cashew families and are not considered a true pepper (Figure 4-49). They can cause allergies; in fact, one in 10 people will have a slight to moderate reaction. They are bright pink to red in color and are used for their added color. Pink peppercorns have a light, sweet aroma similar to that of juniper berries. The Brazilian pink peppercorns, which are more commonly used and milder, are found predominantly in multi-colored peppercorn mixes.

LEARNING ACTIVITY 4-3

Pepper comes in many colors and flavors. In this activity, you will observe, smell, and taste a variety of ground pepper. Use a toothpick and sample a very small amount. Drink water between samples.

Type	Texture	Color	Aroma	Taste	Overall Impression
Black					
Green					
White					

Figure 4-49 Pink peppercorns.

Poppy Seeds Papaver somniferum

Poppy seeds are a notorious spice. They come from the plant that produces opium (Figure 4-50). When ripe, the seeds lose their narcotic substances and are transformed into a common spice.

Poppy seeds are grown in Europe, especially Holland and Austria. They are used in baking or as the filling of poppy seed strudel. Poppy seeds are also used as a popular topping for buttered noodles and as a key ingredient in salad dressings. Poppy seeds can produce a false positive on a drug screen test.

Figure 4-50 Poppy seeds.

Figure 4-51 Saffron.

Saffron Crocus sativus

The world's costliest spice, saffron comes from the dried stigmas of the autumn crocus plant originally cultivated in Greece and Persia (Figure 4-51). Enclosed in each blossom are three frail, thread-like stigmas. To obtain just 1 ounce (30 g) of saffron requires about 4,500 blossoms, vast acreage, and intense labor. In the past, Spain was a leading producer, but now most saffron is cultivated in Iran and Turkey. A lesser quality of saffron comes from the safflower plant and is used as a cheap substitute. "Indian saffron" is normally ground turmeric and is used as a less-expensive colorant. Saffron is used in soups, sauces, breads and bouillabaisse, and Milanese risotto.

Star Anise Illicium verum

Star anise is the star-shaped dried fruit of an evergreen tree thought to be originally from China (Figure 4-52). Although it is not related to anise, it shares the essential oil, anethole. This fragrant spice is used to flavor beverages and confections and is used in spice blends such as Chinese Five Spice. It goes well with duck, chicken, and pork dishes.

Figure 4-52 Star anise.

Figure 4-53 Sumac.

Figure 4-54 Tamarind.

Sumac *Rhus coriara*

The Sicilian or elm-leafed sumac is used in Middle Eastern and Central Asian cooking (Figure 4-53). It has a dark red to maroon color, an acidic sour flavor, and very little aroma. It is used as a substitute for lemon flavor and is found in areas where lemon is scarce. Sumac is used in marinades, zaatar, kebab, and shashlik spice blends. In the United States, local sumac has been used in the past as a lemonade-like beverage.

Tamarind *Tamarindus indica*

The tamarind originated in Africa but spread to the Middle East and Asia in prehistoric times (Figure 4-54). Today, Tamarind pods are used as an acidifying product in marinades, sauces, and beverages. They are used with the addition of sugar as syrup for soft drinks, and the pulp, paste, and syrup are used to flavor poultry, fish, and jams. Tamarind is often used as a component of Worcestershire sauce.

Turmeric *Curcuma longa*

Turmeric originated in Southeast Asia (Figure 4-55). India now produces 80 percent of the world's crop. Turmeric is a rhizome with strong yellow colors and a medicinal, earthy aroma. The yellow American mustard gets its color from ground turmeric. It is used in mustards, curry mixtures, curry powder, and rice dishes.

Figure 4-55 Turmeric.

Vanilla Beans *Vanilla planifolia*

Vanilla beans are actually the pods of a climbing orchid (Figure 4-56). They were native to Central America and vital to Mayan and Aztec cultures in conjunction with chocolate, where it was a key ingredient in the revered "drink of the Gods." Vanilla plants were taken in 1822 by the French and replanted in the Bourbon Islands, which are located in the Indian Ocean

Figure 4-56 Vanilla bean.

Figure 4-57 Wasabi.

(Madagascar, Reunion, and the Cormoros Islands) and in Tahiti. They thrive in countries with a hot, humid, tropical climate. Vanilla pods are fermented and dried in the sun for a month.

Vanilla is the most popular flavor in the world. Most of the vanilla consumed in the United States is from synthetic sources of vanillin from by-products of the wood pulp industry. Vanilla is used in many different applications from sweet cakes and cookies, ice cream, and chocolates to sauces, soups, and savory dishes.

Wasabi

This bright green rhizome provides a pungent flavor and color contrast to many Japanese dishes (Figure 4-57). Wasabi, also known as Japanese horseradish, is a favorite condiment with sushi and sashimi and Asian noodle dishes. It grows naturally in mountain streambeds in Japan. Today, it is commercially grown in parts of Japan as well as several other countries. Oregon is the only state that grows enough wasabi to export it. Because of its high cost and lack of availability, an imitation made with horseradish, mustard, and food coloring is often substituted for the real thing.

Figure 4-58 Chili powder.

SPICE BLENDS

Chili Powder

Chili powder is made from a blend of various chilies such as the New Mexican and Pasilla as well as from spices and herbs such as cumin, garlic, and oregano (Figure 4-58). It is used in Mexican and Southwestern dishes such as chili con carne, enchilada sauce, and many other marinades and dressings.

Chinese Five Spice Powder

The flavors of Chinese Five Spice powder come from a blend of equal parts of the following spices: ground cinnamon, cloves, star anise, fennel seed, and Szechuan peppercorns. It produces a unique and robust seasoning (Figure 4-59). Chinese Five Spice powder is often used as a meat marinade and a BBQ spice. Mixed with ground salt, it makes a dip for deep-fried Chinese foods. This blend can give a kick to spice cookies or pumpkin bread by substituting it for the called-for cinnamon in the recipe.

Figure 4-59 Chinese Five Spice powder.

Curry Powder

Curry powder, as is commonly available in the United States, is a spice blend of English origin made to remind the colonial British soldiers of their time in India (Figure 4-60). Each blend was made from a collection of spices from India to capture the flavors and colors of the foods. It is available in many different versions depending on local preferences. Typically, curry powder is a blend of coriander, turmeric, chilies, cumin, pepper, ginger, cinnamon, and cloves. Genuine Indian curry is a blend of vegetables and spices that are cooked briefly in fat to develop flavors before they are mixed. Curry is also available as a paste. Masala is similar to curry but is used after the cooking process to add additional bursts of flavor to the dish. Masala is also available as a dry spice blend. Curry should usually be cooked lightly in a little oil or butter to develop its flavor.

Figure 4-60 Curry powder.

Pâté Spices

Spice blends specifically manufactured for pâté are available (Figure 4-61). They usually contain pepper, nutmeg, ginger, thyme, and other spices. Each blend is unique to the manufacturer.

Pickling Spice

Pickling spice is a combination of coriander, mace, red pepper flakes, mustard seeds, bay leaves, and peppercorns (Figure 4-62). Various manufacturers may utilize different ingredients. This spice blend is used to pickle vegetables.

Quatre Epices

Quatre epices is a French term meaning "four spices." The basic blend centers around pepper, usually white, and a number of different spices (Figure 4-63). There is no set recipe but

Figure 4-61 Pâté spices.

Figure 4-62 Pickling spice.

Figure 4-63 Quatre epices.

this spice blend often includes nutmeg, ginger, cloves, cinnamon, and/or allspice along with the pepper. Quatre epices is used to enhance soups, stews, vegetables, and pâté.

Tunisian Five Spice/Qalat Daqqa

Tunisian Five Spice is a spicy blend used for lamb and poultry dishes and in marinades (Figure 4-64). It is a combination of freshly ground black pepper, Grains of Paradise, nutmeg, cinnamon, and cloves ground together for a fragrant combination.

Zaatar

Zaatar is a spice mixture that comes to us from the Middle East (Figure 4-65). Traditionally, it is said to give strength and clear thoughts. It is comprised of thyme, sumac, sesame seeds, and sea salt. Mixed with extra virgin olive oil, it is used as a flavorful dipping oil. It is also used in dressings, marinades, and salads.

Figure 4-64 Tunisian Five Spice/qalat daqqa.

Figure 4-65 Zaatar.

LEARNING ACTIVITY 4-4

Each spice has its own distinctive smell. Gather up a variety of spices. Smell each one and commit the smell to memory. Students may want to work in pairs so that one student blindfolds the other. A spice is named, and the blindfolded student must use his/her nose to find and identify the spice.

Figure 4-66 Salt.

>> Salt (sodium chloride)

The early Greeks worshipped salt no less than the sun, and they had a saying that "no one should trust a man without first eating a peck of salt with him" (Figure 4-66). The moral was that by the time one had shared a peck of salt with another person, the two would no longer be strangers.

Without salt, food would be lacking in flavor. Salt triggers the brain to intensify the flavors of food. Salt is also a necessary mineral for general good health and has been called "the essence of life." Salt holds the moisture that makes tissue and cells healthy. Some of Napoleon's troops died during the retreat from Moscow due to lack of salt in their diet, which prevented their ability to heal from their wounds.

Throughout history, salt was as valuable as gold. There are more than 30 references to salt in the Bible. The word "salary" comes from the Romans. They paid their soldiers in salt or "salrium argentums." In early Greece, salt was traded for slaves, which led to the saying "not worth his salt." Salt has played an equally prominent role in more recent history. The first patent issued by the British to an American settler was to Samuel Winslow of the Massachusetts Bay Colony for his method of making salt. In 1777, British troops tried to capture General George Washington's stock of salt. As the Erie Canal opened in 1825, it became known as "the ditch that salt built" due to the fact that is was used by ships transporting goods, especially salt. In many countries, taxes were imposed on salt but not in the United States, partly due to the abundance of this natural resource in this country. The United States is the world's largest salt producer—mining over 45 million tons a year (Figure 4-67).

Figure 4-67 Mining salt at the Great Salt Lake just outside of Salt Lake City, Utah.

Salt was used in ancient times to preserve food from spoilage. Food that was salted and dried out lasted for a long time in storage. This method is still used worldwide as one of the most common forms of modern food preservation.

Flavor and preservation are the two main uses for salt in the cold kitchen. Salt is used in brines, marinades, rubs, and many other preservative processes in cooking. It is used in the process of preserving hams, bacon, and other dry-cured meats. Salt acts on the moisture of the meat to draw out the water. Less water activity equals less chance for bacterial contamination. The presence of salt changes the water pressure in the cells, and, through osmosis, the water purges out of the meat. Salt is also a flavor carrier.

In the next section, we will discuss the many forms of salt and their uses in food preservation and cold kitchen items.

WHAT IS SALT?

Salt is the mineral *halite (sodium chloride)*. Halite is deep- or surface-mined or produced by evaporation of ocean water in large collection ponds. Salt is used to enhance the natural flavor of the food, unlike herbs or spices, which change the flavor profile. According to the Salt Institute, "Salt accents the flavor of meat, brings out individuality of vegetables, puts oomph into bland starches, deepens the flavor of delicate desserts, and develops flavor of melons and certain other fruits. No other seasoning has been found that can satisfactorily take the place of salt."

TYPES OF SALT FOR CULINARY USES

Basic table salt contains a small amount of silicon dioxide to prevent caking by humidity (Figure 4-68). It is available plain or with iodine added to prevent goiters, a disorder of the thyroid gland. In the early 1900s, many Americans were suffering from this condition. The U.S. government's goal was to find a way to get iodine to people. The solution was to mandate that salt companies add iodine to their product (Figure 4-69). Therefore, salt became the first fortified food product. Basic table salt is used in baking, cooking, and at-the-table seasoning.

Figure 4-68 Table salt.

Figure 4-69 Iodized salt.

Figure 4-70 Rock salt.

Figure 4-71 Kosher salt.

Figure 4-72 Fleur de Sel.

Rock salt is used to melt ice and to reduce the temperature of brine in old-fashioned ice cream machines (Figure 4-70). It can also be used to sprinkle over ice in a cooler to quickly chill canned or bottled beverages.

Kosher salt has fewer additives and is considered basically the same salt in a flake form (Figure 4-71). It has fewer additives and is considered purer compared to standard table salt. It is used in place of table salt in the same basic manner. It is also used to kasher or kosher meat, according to strict Orthodox Jewish dietary laws. Many chefs prefer it over table salt because it disperses more readily.

Sea salt has a rustic or earthy flavor preferred by many chefs. It is much more expensive than table salt. Whether the slight flavor differences warrant higher prices is a judgment call. Sea salt is made by evaporating ocean water; in some cases, the labels even identify the exact location from which it was derived.

Fleur de Sel is also known as the Flower of the Sea and is considered the premier quality of grey sea salt from France (Figure 4-72). Before the evaporation process is complete, a light film of salt flowers, or crystals, forms. This is harvested and sold as Fleur de Sel. There are many other sea salts available for the cold kitchen.

Sel Gris de Guerande is "moist," unrefined, and comes in coarse or stoneground fine grain. It is light grey to light purple in color because of the color of clay from the salt flats where it is collected in the Celtic Sea. This salt is hand collected and is considered by many as the best quality of salt available.

OTHER SALTS

Popcorn salt is a super-fine salt designed especially to adhere to popcorn and other snack items. It can also be used for French fries and corn-on-the-cob. Pickling salt is fine-grained and doesn't contain iodine or anti-caking preservatives, which can cause cloudy brine and dark pickles. Pretzel salt is a large-grained salt that doesn't melt easily. It is used for pretzels and bread sticks. Blended salts are blends of table salt with ground spices and/or artificial flavors. Brands vary greatly and most culinarians will try a number of blends before selecting their favorites. Some of the more popular blended salts include the following:

Celery salt: a blend of celery flavor and table salt usually purchased ready prepared (Figure 4-73).

Garlic salt: a blend of granulated garlic and table salt purchased ready prepared. It can be used for all dishes instead of fresh garlic or to enhance the garlic flavor in dishes along with fresh garlic. Some brands are lightly garnished with parsley and onion.

Seasoned salt: a unique blend of selected herbs and spices. It can include the rich taste of tomato and Worcestershire. Seasoned salt adds flavor to meats, fish, vegetables, eggs, salads, casseroles, stews, and more.

Smoked salt: has been either naturally smoked with a flavorful agent such as alderwood, oak, applewood, or hickory smoke or liquid smoke was added to the salt. This salt is useful in marinades and sauces where a smoky flavor note is required.

There are other variations of gourmet salts on the market, such as lavender, fennel, sour (citric acid), or vanilla salt, that can add different flavor profiles to dishes (Figure 4-74).

Figure 4-73 Celery salt.

Figure 4-74 Six different kinds of gourmet salt crystals.

LEARNING ACTIVITY 4-5

Salts from around the world have different textures, flavors, and, in some cases, aromas. Students should take a minute to look at each type of salt, smell it, and taste the samples before recording their impressions in the chart below. Don't overload; taste just a few granules and drink some water between tastings. Determine which salt is your favorite and least favorite.

Type	Texture	Color	Aroma	Taste	Overall Impression
Table					
Kosher					
Hawaiian					
Fleur de sel					
Pretzel					
Pickling					

Figure 4-75 Collage of fats and oils.

>> Oils

Fats and oils are a concentrated source of energy. Many types of fats and oils are used in the cold kitchen (Figure 4-75). Fats are solid at room temperature, whereas oils stay liquid at room temperature.

Fats are usually saturated; the most common are butter, shortening, and lard as well as duck, geese, and chicken fat. Rendered fats are used for flavor and to preserve foods such as duck confit.

Oils have hundreds of uses in the cold kitchen including cooking, marinating, and flavoring. Oils come from many sources, but we will be talking about two types of common cooking oils: seed oils and nut oils. Both are generally unsaturated fat. Seed oils come from the seeds of grasses and legumes such as corn, rapeseed or canola, sunflower, safflower, peanut, or soy. Peanuts are not true nuts, but legumes, and are therefore listed under the seed category. Nut oils come from the seeds of nut trees such as walnut, almond, hazelnut, and avocado oils.

FAT AND OIL HEALTH FACTS

There is a lot of confusion about the health benefits and hazards associated with fats and cooking oil. Let's take a look at the following facts about "good fats" and "bad fats" based on their heart-smart values—their ability to raise or lower total and LDL cholesterol.

The Bad Fats	
Saturated fats	Saturated fats raise total blood cholesterol as well as LDL cholesterol (the bad cholesterol). Saturated fats are mainly found in animal products such as meat, dairy, eggs, and seafood. Some plant foods such as coconut, palm oil, and palm kernel oil are also high in saturated fats.
Trans fats	Trans fats were invented as scientists began to "hydrogenate" liquid oils so that they could better withstand food production processes and provide a better shelf-life. As a result of hydrogenation, trans fatty acids are formed. Trans fatty acids are found in many commercially packaged goods such as cookies and crackers, commercially fried food such as French fries from some fast food chains, other packaged snacks such as microwave popcorn, as well as vegetable shortening and hard stick margarine.
The Good Fats	
Monounsaturated fats	**Monounsaturated fats** lower total cholesterol and LDL cholesterol (the bad cholesterol) and increase the HDL cholesterol (the good cholesterol). Nut, canola, and olive oils are high in monounsaturated fats.
Polyunsaturated fats	**Polyunsaturated fats** also lower total cholesterol and LDL cholesterol. Seafood like salmon and fish oil, as well as corn, soy, safflower, and sunflower oils, are high in polyunsaturated fats. Omega 3 fatty acids belong to this group.

Information provided by Healthcastle.com, "Which cooking oil is the best?" Written by: Gloria Tsang, RD.

Based on the above classifications, the ideal cooking oil should contain higher amounts of monounsaturated and polyunsaturated fats and have minimal or no saturated fats and trans fats. Oils that are considered good cooking oils include canola oil, flaxseed oil, peanut oil, olive oil, nonhydrogenated soft margarine, safflower oil, sunflower oil, and corn oil.

The following oils contain high percentages of **trans fat** or **saturated fats:** vegetable shortening; hard margarine, butter, palm oil, palm kernel oil, and coconut oil.

Fats in one form or another are necessary to our diets, providing vitamins A and E, minerals, amino acids, essential fatty acids, and antioxidants. They are also an important part of our culinary traditions. The key factor is to use them in moderation.

Oil is extracted by using pressure or with chemical solvents. In most cases, it is the oil from the seeds that is extracted for commercial use. Oils used in foodservice are often manufactured for specific purposes such as oil for frying and special salad oil blends (Figure 4-76). Vegetable oils are cholesterol free; they are generally odorless and have no flavor. Oils from nuts provide distinct nutty flavors and have a low smoke point.

Flavoring oils are used to add a touch of flavor to specific foods and are more expensive than regular oils. Their flavor profiles vary greatly, and some oils would be too strong or too expensive for general use and are added in small amounts. Other oils are more neutral, and their flavors are accepted by most customers. **Infused oils** have flavor components, which are usually added herbs or vegetables.

Oils can be flavored by combining with aromatic ingredients such as fresh herbs, peppers, chilies, and so forth, in the oil. Care must be taken, however, with some oils that contain solid cooked vegetable matter such as garlic and onions. There have been some cases of botulism from oil that contained these ingredients. In an anaerobic environment, botulism spores can multiply, contaminating the oils. These flavored oils have a short shelf-life and should be used fresh. Leftovers should be frozen. This type of flavored oil can be kept in the refrigerator for up to 10 days.

Figure 4-76 Oils collage.

Figure 4-77 Canola oil.

Figure 4-78 Corn oil.

Figure 4-79 Cottonseed oil.

Storing Oils

All oils are sensitive to heat, light, and oxygen. Oils can become rancid, which is an adverse reaction to air, light, and heat exposure. Rancid oil has an unpleasant taste and sharp aroma. It is best to store oil in the refrigerator or in a cool, dry place. Monounsaturated fats can be kept up to a year. Polyunsaturated fats should only be kept for about half of that time.

Seed Oils

Annatto oil is made from the annatto seed and has a distinctive flavor. It will add a reddish color to the food.

Canola oil is also called rapeseed oil or lear oil (Figure 4-77). It is made from pressing rapeseeds. Canola oil is a neutral-tasting oil that can be used in most cooking and cold kitchen applications. Canola oil is high in omega-3 fatty acids and relatively low in saturated fats. It is low in cost and is a popular oil for cooking and for baking, as well as in salad dressings.

Corn oil won't burn quickly and is therefore a good choice of oil to use when frying. It is light golden in color, tasteless, and is commonly used in baking and as an oil of choice for salad dressings (Figure 4-78). Corn oil is also used in the manufacture of margarine. It is very high in polyunsaturated fat.

Cottonseed oil is another one of those neutral-flavored oils that is often blended with other oils to create vegetable oil (Figure 4-79). It is a good oil to use when you want flavorless oil that will disappear into the finished dish. It is clear in color and economical to use. (It is also the oil with the largest amounts of trace pesticides due to the cotton plant being the most pesticide-sprayed agricultural product in the U.S. today.)

Flax seed is a rich source of omega-3 fatty acids. It has a rich, buttery taste that makes it a good oil for topping steamed vegetables and for use in salad dressings.

Grape seed is a by-product of the wine-making industry. It has little flavor and can be used in salad dressings, cooking, frying, and baking. Refined grape seed oil has a very high smoke point, making it ideal for frying or sautéing.

Mustard seed oil is extracted from the type of mustard seeds grown in India. It is hot and spicy and should be used sparingly as flavoring oil. It mellows as it heats, and the mustard flavor is more pronounced. It is a popular cooking oil in India and the Middle East. Mustard seed oil is used in salad dressings, stir fries, and marinades for fish and meat.

Palm kernel oil, which is also called dende oil, comes from the palm kernel rather than the fruit of the palm, as in palm oil. It is very high in saturated fat. It is light yellow and has a mild flavor. Palm kernel oil is used in some instances as an ingredient in margarine.

Peanut is a popular type of oil (Figure 4-80). It comes in varying strengths. The lighter oils are used for frying or sautéing and the fuller-bodied oils are best for salads and cold sauces. Refined peanut oil has a high smoke point and does well in sautéing and frying applications. It is also commonly used in sauces and dressings. Peanut oil is high in both monounsaturated and polyunsaturated fats. Because many individuals have allergies to peanuts, their use should be identified in commercial applications.

Poppy seed oil is almost clear. It has a pleasant flavor and is used as a condiment for bread dipping as well as in some salad dressings.

Pumpkin seed oil is dark brownish-green pungent oil imported from Austria. It can be used on salads in small quantities or combined with other oils or used as a flavoring on fish or vegetables. Pumpkin seed oil has a nutty flavor with a touch of pumpkin.

Figure 4-80 Peanut oil.

Safflower oil has a high heat point and is good for frying or sautéing (Figure 4-81). It is higher in polyunsaturated fats than any other cooking oil. It is golden yellow and has a strong, pleasant flavor.

Sunflower is a popular oil used for cooking and as an ingredient in salad dressings (Figure 4-82). It is pale yellow and flavorless. It is high in polyunsaturated fats and has a high smoke point, making it a good oil for sautéing and frying. It is also used in the production of margarine and shortening.

Figure 4-81 Safflower oil.

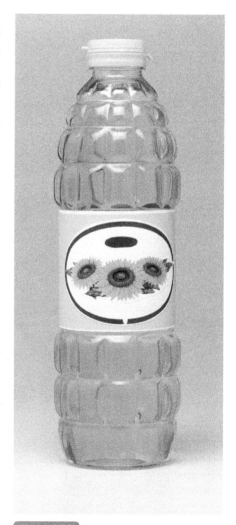

Figure 4-82 Sunflower oil.

Figure 4-83 Soybean oil.

Figure 4-84 Sesame seed oil.

Soybean oil is a good choice for frying and sautéing because it doesn't burn quickly (Figure 4-83). It is used more often than any other oil to make shortening and margarine because it has excellent emulsification properties. Soybean oil is high in polyunsaturated and monounsaturated fats and contains significant amounts of omega-3 fatty acid. It is colorless, tasteless, and inexpensive.

Sesame seed oil is used in Oriental cooking and can range from light to dark and from very hot to mild (Figure 4-84). It should be used only in very small quantities as a flavor enhancer. Sesame oil is flavoring oil with a pronounced taste. The thicker, darker versions from China and Japan have the most intense flavor. It goes rancid quickly and should be kept in the refrigerator after opening. Sesame oil, which comes from sesame seeds, is available very hot and pungent and is used as a condiment. Sesame oil is popular in Mexico, the Middle East, and India.

Tea oil is extracted from tea seeds, resulting in yellowish-green oil that has a sweet flavor and herbal aroma. It is used in Asian cooking, particularly in stir fries; as an ingredient in salad dressings; and as a base for sauces. It has a high smoke point, which makes it a good choice for frying and sautéing. Tea oil is high in vitamin E and contains no trans-fatty acids.

Nut Oils

Almond oil is extracted by pressing roasted almonds (Figure 4-85). Its flavor suggests a slight hint of almond. It is often used for dipping bread or is drizzled over vegetables; it is also used in baking. Many bakers consider almond oil to be the best oil for oiling baking tins. This type of oil is high in monounsaturated fats and has a low smoke point. This oil provides a significant source of vitamins A and E. It is very expensive but worth the price.

Figure 4-85 Almond oil.

Figure 4-86 Avocado oil.

Avocado oil has a high smoke point and can be used for high-heat cooking (Figure 4-86). It has a light, distinctive taste and is often used for salad dressings. It is a good source of vitamin E and is a monounsaturated fat.

Hazelnut oil should be stored in the refrigerator. This oil has a strong nutty flavor and fragrance. A little will go a long way. It is ideal for cold applications such as salads or bread dipping sauce. Heat will diminish its flavor; even so, it is often used in baking. Hazelnut oil is high in monounsaturated fats. It is a good source of vitamin E. It is a relatively expensive oil and is found at most gourmet shops. It is often used in conjunction with other oils for salad dressing.

Macadamia oil will enhance a fish or vegetable dish with a light, nutty flavor. It loses its flavor when heated, so it is best to add the oil prior to serving. It is high in monounsaturated fats.

Pecan oil is pleasant but expensive. The pecan flavor is evident. It is a great addition to a favorite salad dressing or when drizzled on vegetables. It is high in monounsaturated fats.

Pistachio oil is a beautiful, deep green color and tastes just like pistachio nuts. It is a great addition to any salad, as bread dipping sauce, or when drizzled over fish or vegetables prior to serving. This type of nut oil is high in monounsaturated fats.

Walnut oil is often imported from France and is a delicate, expensive salad oil (Figure 4-87). It has a rich, nutty, and flavorful taste. It is often used in combination with olive oil as a salad dressing. Even though it loses some of its flavor when heated, it is still used in sauces and baked goods. Walnut oil is rich in polyunsaturates as well as omega-3 polyunsaturated fatty acids.

Figure 4-87 Walnut oil.

Other Oils

Some chefs make flavored oils in the kitchen by adding herbs or other flavor components (Figure 4-88). Herbs should be blanched in boiling water for 15 seconds to sterilize before adding them to oil to prevent possible spoilage or fermentation.

Palm oil is often combined with other oils to create frying oils that are very heat stable. It is high in saturated fat. Palm oil comes from the pulp of the African palm's fruit. Used

Figure 4-88 Infused oils.

Figure 4-89 Vegetable oil.

alone, it has a reddish-orange color and a strong flavor. It is used with West African and Brazilian cooking.

Rice bran oil comes from the rice bran and is rich in vitamins, minerals, amino acids, fatty acids, and antioxidants. It has a nutty taste, making it a viable flavoring for many foods. It can also be used to sauté foods.

Truffle oil is a high-quality, pricey oil that has been infused with truffle flavor. It has a strong taste and should be used sparingly to flavor meat, fish, pasta, sauces, and salads. Always refrigerate truffle oil after opening.

Vegetable oil is usually made with a blend of various oils, commonly soybean, corn, and sunflower (Figure 4-89). Once in a while a single oil will be labeled as vegetable. The oil or oils used are not always disclosed on the label. Vegetable oil ranges in color from clear to golden yellow. The refining process gives it a high smoke point, so it is a good oil to use to fry and sauté. It is also a commonly used oil for salad dressings or in baking.

Wasabi oil has been described as being both sweet and spicy. It is made by combining wasabi with oil. Wasabi oil is used in many cooking applications and is especially nice for fish and seafoods or as an ingredient in marinades or salad dressing.

Olive Oil

Olive trees thrive in a Mediterranean climate, where winters are mild and summers are hot (Figure 4-90). They are cultivated in all countries around the Mediterranean and also in California. The trees grow slowly but can live and bear fruit for hundreds of years. Some countries boast of olive tree orchards that are 1,000 years old.

Like wine, there are countless olive varieties, and their flavors, which can range from peppery to nutty to fruity, are influenced by soil, climate, care in harvesting, and method of manufacturing. The color is also influenced by soil conditions and the country of origin. Olive oils can range from pale yellow to deep green. Spain is the largest producer of olive oil and classifies the oil by regions and olive varieties.

In Mediterranean countries, olive oil is selected according to its intended use. Some oils are used as all-purpose oils for cooking and frying; other oils are selected for salads or for eating with bread. The overriding quality yardstick is acidity level, not color.

Olive oil provides a great taste and aroma. It is a monosaturated oil and is considered to contribute to heart health. According to data provided by INDO (Instituto Nacional de Denominaciones de Origin), a division of the Spanish Ministry of Agriculture, "This type of oil is easily digested and completely absorbed. The circulatory system is aided by a diet which includes olive oil, reducing the risk of arteriolosclerosis and other circulatory ailments. This type of fat is not only cholesterol free but has been shown to reduce cholesterol levels."

Olive oils are graded with its degree of acidity.

Figure 4-90 Olive oil.

- **Extra virgin.** Comes from the first pressing of the olives (Figure 4-91). The olives are squeezed at room temperature, which results in a completely natural product. Extra virgin oil has a full, fruity flavor and the lowest acidity level (less than 1 percent). For extra-virgin oil, the fruit is picked (the finest are hand-picked) before fully maturing; only the best of the crop is used and crushed immediately at room temperatures no higher than 75°F. Olives crushed at higher temperatures will yield more oil, but quality will suffer. The best grades of oil are greenish to green in color; the lesser grades are more yellow. Fine oil should be smooth but not greasy and should have a distinctive, fruity flavor. Young oil might have a slightly bitter taste that will mellow as it ages. Extra-virgin oil accounts for about 5 percent of American consumption of olive oil. Extra-virgin oil is further graded. Premium extra-virgin olive oil is grown on small estates at very high altitudes from 1,000 to 2,000 feet above sea level, usually on limey soil in places such as Tuscany and Umbria in central Italy.
- **Virgin.** Comes from the first pressing of the olives. The best of the batch is marked *extra virgin*. The rest is labeled *virgin olive oil*. Virgin olive oil has up to 1.5 percent acidity. Virgin olive oil accounts for only about 2 percent of American consumption.
- **Pure olive oil.** This type of oil also comes from the first pressing, but it is made from Grade B olives. It has a lighter, less fruity taste and higher acidity level. Pure olive oil has up to 3 percent acidity and is sometimes called *olio di oliva, huile d'olive,* or just olive oil. Pure olive oil accounts for about 93 percent of American consumption, by far the most.
- **Olive pomace oil.** This is lower-grade oil. It is made from pressed olives with the aid of solvents. There are additional lower grades that are not exported to the United States, such as Italy's *olio di sansa di oliva rettificato*, which is extracted with solvents from the residue of previously pressed olives.

Cooking with Olive Oil

Olive oil isn't reserved for salad dressing; it can be used to replace butter or vegetable oil in most cooking applications.

Baking

Try splashing olive oil over fish or vegetables, including potatoes, prior to baking. It will brown nicely and offers the perfect flavor combination. Brush some on garlic bread or bruschetta before broiling.

Bread Dipping

Forget the butter. Serve a high grade of olive oil, such as extra virgin or virgin, in a small platter as a bread dipper. It's great plain or mixed with balsamic vinegar or herbs and spices.

Figure 4-91 Extra-virgin olive oil.

Sauces

Drizzle olive oil over steamed vegetables prior to serving. Use it as a key component in sauce recipes.

Salads

Olive oil is the perfect ingredient in salad dressings. Try making a simple dressing out of olive oil and vinegar or lemon juice.

LEARNING ACTIVITY 4-6

Taste Test Exercise

Place a small amount of each type of the following oils on its own plate (for a total of six plates). Provide bread pieces for students to dip into the oils. Students should try to correctly identify each type of oil. Ask students to record their impressions in the chart provided below. There is extra space at the end of the chart so that students can work with other oils.

- Extra-virgin olive oil
- Pure olive oil
- Grapeseed oil
- Corn
- Peanut oil
- Walnut oil

Type of Oil	Visual Characteristics	Taste Impressions	Odor
Extra virgin			
Pure olive			
Grapeseed			
Corn			
Peanut			
Walnut			

>> Vinegars

According to the Vinegar Institute, vinegar has been used for more than 10,000 years. It came about quite by accident when a cask of wine past its time had turned into another product. In French, "vinaigre" translates to *sour wine*, but in reality, vinegar can be made from many different ingredients including molasses, sorghum, fruits, berries, melons, coconut, honey, beer, maple syrup, potatoes, beets, malt, grains, and whey (Figure 4-92). The process includes fermentation, which turns the natural sugars first to alcohol, and then a secondary fermentation changes it to an acid form. The Babylonians were the first to use vinegar as a preservative and also as a condiment. They were also the first group to flavor vinegar with herbs. Roman legion members used it as a beverage called posca. During Hippocrates's time, it was used as one of the first known remedies. It is mentioned in the Bible for its healing abilities. Today we use vinegar to relieve the itch from rashes, bites, and other minor ailments.

Plain white vinegar is a liquid with about 5 percent acidity strength manufactured from distilled grain alcohol and even from wood. It is inexpensive and tastes acidic without any special flavors. Vinegar can be made at home by adding vinegar mother, a sticky, flabby mass, to wine or cider. The vinegar mother, Mère de vinaigre in French, converts the liquid into

Figure 4-92 Corked bottles of rich red wine vinegar, white vinegar, and Balsamic vinegar are popular liquid ingredients in a variety of dishes.

vinegar by bacterial action. Homemade vinegar is good for salad dressings and general use, but it may not have enough acidity for safe use in pickling and canning. Unless you are certain that the acidity level is at least 4 percent, do not pickle or can with it.

The Vinegar Institute conducted studies to find out how long vinegar will last. It confirmed that its shelf-life is almost indefinite. Because of its acidic nature, vinegar is self-preserving and does not need refrigeration. White vinegar will remain virtually unchanged over an extended period of time. And, while some changes can be observed in other types of vinegars, such as color changes or the development of a haze or sediment, this is only an aesthetic change. The product can still be used with confidence.

There are many other types of vinegar. We will talk about some of the more prevalent types:

- *Balsamic* vinegar is wine vinegar aged in small kegs with unfermented grape juice called *must* (Figure 4-93). The vinegar changes flavor and mellows in the porous barrels. Depending on the desired quality, the aging process can last for years in different-sized barrels made with different woods including chestnut, cherry, and juniper. Additional *must* is added every year. The best balsamic vinegar is aged for at least 12 years and is aromatic, mellow, almost sweet, and can be dribbled as a condiment over food. Very old balsamic vinegar is quite expensive. Its production is centered on the city of Modena in Italy and is highly controlled to ensure quality. Originally only the upper class in Italy had access to this type of vinegar. It spread throughout the rest of the world in the late twentieth century. Inexpensive balsamic vinegar is made with little aging, with the addition of grape sugar and caramel coloring. The foodservice operator must decide what quality level balsamic vinegar is appropriate for his or her operation.
- *Distilled white* vinegar is clear, not white (Figure 4-94). It is a very common type of vinegar and is used for both culinary and cleaning purposes.
- *Cider vinegars* can be made with any kind of fermented cider (Figure 4-95). Popular varieties include apple and pear. It is brownish yellow in color and is used for chutneys or marinades.
- *Coconut* vinegar is made from the sap of the coconut palm tree. It is popular in Southeast Asian cuisine, especially in Thailand, the Philippines, and India. It is cloudy and has a sharp acidic taste.
- *Cane* vinegar is made from sugar cane juice and is popular in the Philippines for pickle making and in mustards and vinaigrettes.

Figure 4-93 Balsamic vinegar.

Figure 4-94 White vinegar.

Figure 4-95 Cider vinegar.

Figure 4-96 Strawberry vinegar.

- *Fruit-flavored vinegars* are made when fruits, especially berries, are steeped in vinegar so that some flavor will transfer (Figure 4-96). Popular fruit vinegars are raspberry, strawberry, currants, quince, pineapple, and many other fruits. Fruit vinegar is gaining popularity and, as a result, the prices are going up. Most of the fruit vinegars on the market are made in Europe.
- *Herb vinegars are made when herbs are added* to flavor the vinegar. The best known are tarragon vinegar, followed by basil, thyme, rosemary, and lavender vinegars. The herbs are steeped in vinegar to transfer the flavor.
- *Malt* vinegar is made with fermented malt and is usually brown and mild (Figure 4-97). Malt vinegar is a favorite in Britain and the United States with fish and chips.
- *Rice* vinegar is used in Asian cooking and is available in white, red, black, and brown varieties (Figure 4-98). China and Japan manufacture most of the world's rice vinegar. Rice vinegar has a mellow and distinctive flavor compared to that of distilled vinegar.
- *Mirin* is a mild-flavored alcoholic rice liquid often used with rice vinegar as a flavoring component (Figure 4-99). The term *rice wine vinegar* is wrong—there is no *rice wine*. The vinegar is brewed.
- *Sherry vinegar* is a delicious addition to salad dressing or sauces. *Sherry* is a wine from southwest Spain and can range from very sweet to dry. The vinegar usually has a nutty flavor and is light brown in color.
- *Umeboshi vinegar* is made from the brine used to pickle Japanese plums. It is a deep cherry color and has a fruity, tangy taste. It contains salt and is not technically a true salt, but it is used as a substitute for vinegar in salad dressings and to flavor steamed vegetables.
- *Wine* vinegar is made from both red and white wine (Figure 4-100). Wine makers are extremely careful to keep unwanted vinegar bacteria away from the wine cellar to avoid contamination. Wine vinegar is made by specialized companies but never in wineries. The highest quality is aged in wooden barrels for several years and has a complex, mellow flavor.

Figure 4-98 Rice vinegar.

Figure 4-99 Mirin.

Figure 4-97 Malt vinegar.

Figure 4-100 Wine vinegar.

LEARNING ACTIVITY 4-7

Place a small amount of each type of the following vinegars on its own plate (for a total of six plates). Provide bread and let the students taste and identify the vinegars. Students should record their observations in the chart below.

- Tarragon vinegar
- White vinegar
- Balsamic vinegar
- Apple cider vinegar
- Red wine vinegar
- Malt vinegar

Type of Vinegar	Visual Characteristics	Taste Impressions	Odor
Tarragon			
White			
Balsamic			
Apple cider			
Red wine			
Malt			

>> Additional Flavorings

SOY SAUCE (SHOYU)

Soy sauce is the universal seasoning condiment of Asia, having many versions throughout China, Japan, Korea, Vietnam, and Southeast Asia (Figure 4-101). With a strong salty flavor, it is more common than salt in Asian cuisines. Soy sauce has a strong, tangy flavor with meaty umami overtones. Soy sauce is produced by pressure cooking soybeans, mixed with equal amounts of roasted wheat kernels and a starter culture of the molds *Aspergillus oryzae* and *A.souae*. It has been used for over 2,500 years, having been developed during the Zhou Dynasty (1134–246 B.C.) and is considered one of the world's oldest condiments. In the seventeenth century, Dutch traders brought soy sauce to Europe. In spite of the expense, this thick savory sauce spread in popularity. Unlike some other condiments that add to food, soy sauce is said to enhance the flavors of the foods it accompanies. The flavor elements of soy are composed of salts, amino acids, lactic acid, acetic acids, sugars, and volatile substances such as vanillin.

Chinese Buddhist monks discovered fermented grain mash (shih) as a flavoring agent. Zen Buddhist monks introduced the sauce to Japan because they were vegetarians. Low-sodium sauce and flavored soy sauce are available today. Tamari is a darker, wheat-free type of soy sauce that is popular with people who have wheat allergies.

Heavy, or black, soy sauce is sweeter and thick. Japanese-style soy sauce is lighter than Chinese soy sauce and is the most common type used in the United States. Soy sauce is used in marinades, sauces, soups, and anywhere that salt can have a savory application.

Figure 4-101 Soy sauce.

WORCESTERSHIRE SAUCE

There are several legends as to how this worcestershire sauce was discovered (Figure 4-102). According to *The Raj at the Table: A Culinary History of the British in India,* by David Burton (1994), Worcestershire sauce was originally an Indian recipe brought to Britain by Lord Marcus Sandys, ex-Governor of Bengal, India. In 1835, he brought the recipe for his favorite Indian sauce to John Lea and William Perrins, who ran a chemist's emporium on Broad Street in Worcester. Sandys asked the two to make a batch of the sauce. The chemist complied but the result was a "fiery mixture that almost blew the heads off Mssrs. Lea and Perrins, and a barrel they had made for themselves was consigned to the cellars." Several years later they came across the barrel and decided to taste it again before discarding it. This time it had fermented and mellowed into a phenomenal sauce. The chemists bought the recipe from Lord Sandys; and in 1838, it was launched commercially. Some of the duo's first customers were British passenger ships. Soon the sauce found its way onto many of the fleet's dining tables. It didn't take long before it was a favorite with the British, who used it primarily as a condiment for steaks.

Worcestershire sauce is made of water, vinegar, molasses, corn syrup, anchovies, spices, and flavorings. Today it is used as a popular meat and poultry marinade and as an ingredient in casseroles, soups, and cheese dishes. It is also used to make party Chex Mix and Bloody Marys.

HOISIN SAUCE

Hoisin sauce is also known as Peking duck sauce or plum sauce (Figure 4-103). There are no plums in the sauce, but it has a light, fruity taste and is the color of some varieties of plum. Hoisin is a thick, reddish-brown sauce made from fermented soy beans, red beans, ginger, vinegar, garlic, sugar, chili peppers, and numerous spices. It has been described as being both sweet and spicy with a pungent, garlic-like aroma. Hoisin is often used in Chinese cooking and as a table condiment. It is the ingredient that gives Chinese barbecued meat its reddish glaze. It is often used as a dipping sauce or added to stir-fried dishes and is a key ingredient in many Asian-inspired marinades and sauces.

FISH SAUCE

Fish sauces are essential ingredients in the cuisines of Southeast Asia (Figure 4-104). These fragrant, brown liquids are made by fermenting whole fish in a salty brine. The liquid from this

Figure 4-102 Worcestershire sauce.

Figure 4-103 Hoisin sauce.

Figure 4-104 Fish sauce.

process is drawn off and matured in the sun before bottling. Fish sauce is called *nuoc mam* in Vietnam and *nam pla* in Thailand. It is also used throughout Southeast Asia in Laos, Cambodia, Vietnam, Burma, and the Philippines. This product's high protein content has made it an essential part of the diet of people of Southeast Asia. Fish sauce is used as is or in combination with other seasonings and spices to make sauces, marinades, dressings, soups, and stews.

OYSTER SAUCE

Oyster sauce is similar to fish sauce in composition (Figure 4-105). This richly flavored, dark brown sauce is made from oysters that are brined. The resulting rich liquid is drawn off, fermented, and combined with sugar, soy beans, wheat flour, and starch. Oyster sauce is used to enhance many foods. It is a common, all-purpose seasoning for many Asian dishes, especially in stir fry and with noodles.

MISO

Miso is the Japanese name for a thick, soybean-based paste (Figure 4-106). It originated in China about 200 B.C. and made its way to Japan where it was first noted in AD 701. The Japanese use miso for soups and dressings and in simmered dishes. It is widely used throughout the rest of Asia to flavor soups, sauces, dressings, and marinades. Miso has a high protein content and is considered very nutritious. It is high in sodium, so only a little is needed. Miso soup is served at most Japanese meals, including breakfast. Miso comes in several varieties, depending on what grains have been mixed with the soybeans prior to fermentation. For example, red miso comes from a combination of soybeans and barley. Yellow miso is made with soybeans and rice. The fermented mixture is infused with yeast and left to age. The length of aging affects the flavor, texture, color, and aroma of the miso.

Figure 4-105 Oyster sauce.

DASHI

Dashi, a soup stock, is an essential flavoring in Japanese foods. It is the key ingredient in miso soup and many other Japanese noodle soups and sauces (Figure 4-107). Dashi is made from kelp and bonito, Skipjack tuna, or sardine flakes. It is available in granulated, powdered, or liquid pre-made forms. Vegetarian varieties are made with shiitake mushrooms. Some say that dashi has the smell of the sea and provides a very distinctive delicate flavor.

Figure 4-106 Miso.

Figure 4-107 Dashi.

>> Summary

Foods that are served in the cold kitchen have a flavor disadvantage compared with foods that are cooked. Not only does the cold numb the flavor receptors on the tongue, but, in addition, the cooking process releases flavors. It is imperative that chefs select the freshest products. This unit focused on major flavorings used in the cold kitchen. Herbs and spices add flavor variety and aroma to food. Herbs come from the leaves of herbaceous plants and are generally associated with savory food. Spices come from the roots, flowers, seeds, or bark of the plant and are commonly associated with baked goods and international cuisines.

Salt is the most common flavoring agent in the Western world. It has a rich history and has been a valuable commodity throughout the ages. Salt enhances the flavors of food and is used in brines, marinades, rubs, and many other preservative processes in cooking.

Fats and oils are a concentrated source of energy. Fats are solid at room temperature whereas oils remain liquid. Fats and oils have hundreds of uses in the cold kitchen including cooking, marinating, and flavoring. Common fats are butter, shortening, and lard. Oils come from a variety of sources including seeds and nuts.

Vinegars have been used for more than 10,000 years. It is an important ingredient in the cold kitchen for use in salad dressings and for pickling.

A host of additional flavoring sauces are used in cold kitchens around the globe. This unit focused on soy sauce, Worcestershire sauce, hoisin, and fish sauce, as well as oyster sauce, miso, and dashi.

Flavorings provide variety to foods. In many cases, they enhance the basic dish and "bring it to life" when used properly.

>> Review Questions

SHORT ANSWER

1. What adjustments should be made when substituting dried herbs for fresh herbs or vice versa?
2. Describe the differences between black and white pepper.
3. How does salt work as a preservative?
4. Describe the characteristics of a polyunsaturated fat.
5. Write a short description of the following types of olive oil: extra virgin, virgin, pure olive oil. Use the information presented in this text as well as additional sources from the library or Internet.

MATCHING

6. Match the herb to its description.

   a. chervil
   b. savory
   c. thyme
   d. sorrel
   e. chives

   1. has an onion note
   2. offers a subtle scent of anise, caraway, and parsley
   3. has a light lemon taste
   4. similar flavor to thyme or marjoram
   5. complements poultry, beef, and lamb

7. Match the spice to its description.

   a. cardamom
   b. fennel
   c. mace
   d. saffron
   e. tamarind

   1. used with sugar as a syrup for soft drinks
   2. tastes spicy and sweet; seeds are used in Indian dishes
   3. comes from the nutmeg tree
   4. has a strong licorice or anise-like aroma and flavor
   5. the world's costliest spice

8. Match the type of salt to its description.

   a. table salt
   b. rock salt
   c. kosher salt
   d. sea salt

   1. has a rustic or earthy flavor
   2. is available plain or with iodine added
   3. is considered purer than table salt
   4. is used to quickly chill canned or bottled beverages

9. Identify whether the oil is a seed oil or a nut oil.

   a. almond (seed or nut?)
   b. avocado (seed or nut?)
   c. safflower (seed or nut?)
   d. corn (seed or nut?)
   e. peanut (seed or nut?)
   f. canola (seed or nut?)

10. Match the vinegar to its description.

   a. balsamic
   b. white
   c. cider
   d. malt
   e. rice
   f. wine

   1. available in white, red, black, and brown varieties
   2. highest quality; aged in wooden barrels for several years
   3. always aged in small kegs with unfermented grape juice
   4. sometimes used for cleaning purposes
   5. varieties include apple and pear
   6. favorite in Britain

11. Match the sauce to its description.

   a. soy
   b. Worcestershire
   c. hoisin
   d. fish
   e. oyster
   f. miso
   g. dashi

   1. thick paste that is high in sodium
   2. important ingredient in Chex Mix
   3. considered one of the world's oldest condiments
   4. also known as plum sauce, but contains no plums
   5. vegetarian varieties are made with shiitake mushrooms
   6. high protein content is essential to Southeast Asian diets
   7. common seasoning for stir fries with noodles

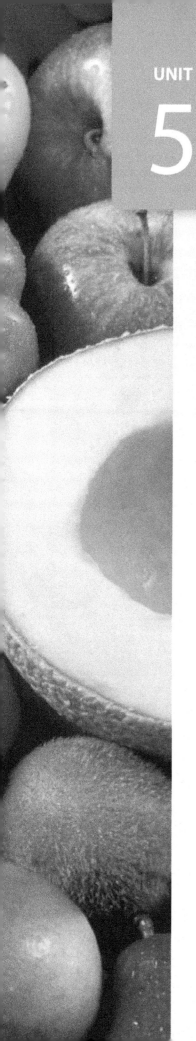

Produce, Legumes, and Grains

>> Learning Objectives

After you have finished reading this unit, you should be able to:

- Describe the difference between fruits and vegetables.
- Identify common fruits and vegetables.
- Discuss the major culinary uses for each fruit and vegetable.
- Identify common fruits that are used as vegetables.
- Explain why tropical fruits are being used more in today's recipes.
- Demonstrate the two most common methods for cooking dried beans or peas.
- Describe the process used to harvest truffles.

>> Key Terms

allium	drupes	oxidation	tuber
brassica	fruit	pomes	vegetable
cucurbitaceae	legume	produce	

The noun "produce" is the general term used to describe agricultural products, particularly fruits and vegetables. The cold kitchen is responsible for much of the preparation work with these products. It is important to become familiar with basic produce. This unit is not a comprehensive guide but rather a brief introduction to the major produce, legumes, and grains products used in the cold kitchen.

Legumes are the edible fruit from the legume family, including beans and peas. Legumes are gaining in popularity due to their healthy attributes and the fact that they are low in fat. They are also tasty and delicious and offer a break from traditional salad and side dish ingredients.

Grains provide the staff of life for most of the Western world in the form of wheat products such as bread and pasta, and rice in much of the rest of the world. Cooked whole grains such as quinoa and cracked wheat are also being used in the cold kitchen in a variety of applications, including salads.

As discussed in the introduction to this unit, **produce** is a general term for farm-produced goods, generally fruits and vegetables. Fresh, seasonal produce is preferred, and many culinarians go to great lengths to secure the best in their regions. This is accomplished by working

closely with purveyors or, in some cases, establishing a rapport with local growers and ordering directly from the farm or shopping at local farmer's markets (Figure 5-1).

Bob Welch summed up the benefits of using seasonal produce in an article titled, "Lazy days full of anticipation," that ran in *The Register Guard*, Eugene, Oregon, in 2002.

> "But what makes seasonal fruit so scrumptious is that it is part of a rhythm, a rhythm that allows you access to it only once a year. And, let's face it, it's the 11 months of not having fresh strawberries that make fresh strawberries so inviting,"

While using local, seasonal produce is a plus, it is not always feasible. With the global economy and improvements in transportation, it is possible to serve most produce throughout the year. Now crisp apples from New Zealand are available in the spring and summer months when U.S., Washington-grown apples are about gone for the season and berries come from South America in the middle of North America's most bitter winter months. Produce that was considered seasonal is now priced affordably and obtainable throughout the year in reasonably good shape.

>> Fruit or Vegetable?

It is usually easy to tell if something is a fruit or vegetable—but that's not always the case. Take the tomato, for instance. We use it much like we do other vegetables in salads or cooked in sauces. But tomatoes are actually fruits. Here's how Texas A&M University's Cooperative Extension service defines the difference between fruits and vegetables. "Botanically the **fruit** is the developed ovary of a seed plant with its contents and accessory parts, as the pea pod, nut, tomato, pineapple, etc. or the edible part of a plant developed from a flower with any accessory tissues, as the peach, mulberry, banana, etc. A **vegetable** is described as 'any herbaceous (non-woody) plant or plant part that is eaten with the main course rather than as a dessert.' It usually has a bland taste." The confusion arises because the "vegetable" can have "fruit," which is the reproductive parts. The tomato is probably the only legally declared vegetable based on a Supreme Court ruling in the early 1900s.

Still, there are exceptions to the above definition. Rhubarb, for one, is a vegetable that is used as a dessert. Eggplant, squash, peppers, cucumbers, chilies, olives, and tomatoes are fruits but they are used in a vegetable application. They will be covered in the vegetable section.

>> Fruits

Fruits offer taste, texture, and color to many dishes (Figure 5-2). The following section is filled with thumbnail sketches of many of the common fruits used in the cold kitchen.

BERRIES

Berries grow on bushes, vines, and runners (Figure 5-3). They must be handled with great care. Always inspect berries before accepting them. Reject soft, moldy berries—they are past their prime. Berries must be refrigerated until use. Never wash berries until they are to be used—

Figure 5-1 Farmer's Market, Chicago, Illinois.

Figure 5-2 Fruits come in a variety of flavors, textures, and colors.

washing will speed up the deterioration process. Berries add color and value to many dishes.

Blackberries *Rubus laciniatus/ulmifolius*

Blackberries are the fruit of a small, rambling cane-type bush found wild in temperate climates (Figure 5-4). They are used in sauces such as glazes and gastriques, fresh in salads and fruit trays, and in vinaigrettes. Because of their larger seeds, straining is often recommended when using blackberries to make sauces.

Blueberries *Vaccinium angustifolium*

In the early 1900s, Elizabeth White and Dr. Frederick Coville domesticated the wild high bush blueberry, resulting in today's cultivated blueberry industry (Figure 5-5). Blueberries come in two types: the smaller, and in the opinion of

Figure 5-3 Berries are colorful, delicious, and nutritious.

Figure 5-4 Blackberries.

Figure 5-5 Blueberries.

Figure 5-6   Boysenberries.

Figure 5-7   Cranberries.

some people, the better of the two, is the wild blueberry. The larger, cultivated blueberry is harvested in several states. Blueberries come in various retail packs including 1/2 pints, pints, quarts, 6-pint packs, and 5- and 10-pound bulk consumer packages as well as frozen IQF (individually quick frozen) and freeze-dried. Compared with other berries, blueberries are sturdy. They can be used in cake and muffin batters, fresh in salads, or as a topper for yogurt or cereal.

Boysenberries *Rubus deliciosus*

This berry is a cross between a blackberry and a raspberry, or a blackberry and a loganberry (Figure 5-6). Boysenberries can be used in the same applications as blackberries.

Cranberries *Vaccinium macrocarpon* or *Oxycoccus macrocarpus*

Cranberries are often associated with the fall and winter months and with both Thanksgiving and Christmas feasts. They are very tart berries used to make sauces and garnishes (Figure 5-7).

Currants *Ribes nigrum*

Currants are very tart and not practical for fresh applications. They are available in red, as well as sweeter white and black varieties (Figure 5-8). Currants provide a unique and delicious flavor when used to make syrups, sauces, or preserves. Black currants cultivated in France are called *cassis* and are used in syrups and liqueur.

Gooseberries *Ribes hirtellum/grossularia*

Gooseberries are a summer berry with a short growing season, lasting only a few weeks in June and July (Figure 5-9). Sweet varieties are eaten raw, whereas the tart varieties are

Figure 5-8   Currants.

Figure 5-9 Gooseberries.

Figure 5-10 Grapes.

used for jellies, jams, chutneys, and preserves. Gooseberries have a grape-green color with striated skin. The flesh is slightly pale green. Some varieties have a pale pink blush, and these tend to taste less tart. Other varieties are fuzzy skinned. Gooseberries are available fresh, frozen, and canned.

Grapes *Vitis vinifera*

Grapes are the most widely cultivated fruit in the world. We don't typically think of grapes as berries, but they do fit the classification because they grow in bunches or clusters on grape vines (Figure 5-10). Grapes have a long history of human consumption in the form of wine, vinegar, and fruit dating back to 6000 B.C. They are classified as seedless or seeded and by their color: black, red, pink, green, or purple. Most operations use only seedless grapes. Grapes should always be washed before use. The most efficient way to wash grapes is to fill the sink and dip the clusters in water. Drain grapes on a drain board. Avoid stacking wet grapes on top of each other. Select the best clusters for fruit baskets and use loose berries in fruit salads.

Loganberries *Rubus loganobaccus*

The loganberry is a hybrid (Figure 5-11) created by crossing a red raspberry with a blackberry. Loganberries are served fresh in salads and cooked in jams, sauces, and syrups.

Figure 5-11 Loganberries.

Marionberries *Rubus rosaceaer*

The marionberry is a hybrid berry created in Marion County, Oregon (Figure 5-12). It is the cross between two varieties of blackberries and has an intense blackberry flavor. Like any variety of blackberry, the marionberry can be served fresh or made into jams and sauces.

Raspberries *Rubus idaeus*

Raspberries are one of the most popular varieties of pantry berry (Figure 5-13). They are cultivated on perennial shrubs in temperate climates. The delicate berries vary in color from red

Figure 5-12 Marionberries.

Figure 5-13 Raspberries.

to nearly purple. Raspberries are highly perishable. They are sold in half-pint containers and should be handled as little as possible. Raspberries are popular as jam and also as syrup or as a garnish for entries and salads.

Strawberries *Fragaria ananassa*

Strawberries are the most popular berry variety used in the cold kitchen and are available year round (Figure 5-14). The size and shape does not determine the sweetness. There are more than 20 market varieties of strawberries. The size, color, flavor, and juiciness of the berry de-

Figure 5-14 Strawberries.

pend on the variety as well as the growing conditions. Strawberries have a high vitamin C content and are low in calories. They are sturdier than some of the other berries and are often used in salads. Strawberries are also excellent for jams and jellies.

Hulling should be done with a small paring knife, and only the leaves and any unripe segment should be removed. Strawberries should be washed when needed, never beforehand, because they tend to get mushy after hulling and washing.

CITRUS FRUITS

All citrus fruits have thick rinds that surround the pulp (Figure 5-15). In most cases, the fruit is peeled, divided into sections, and eaten fresh. The fruit can also be squeezed to make juice. The juice of all citrus fruit contains citric acid. The zest contains fragrant oils and is often used to flavor foods. From Sunkist, the nation's largest cooperative of citrus fruit growers,

> "There's something about fresh citrus fruit that makes people feel energized! From that zesty aroma when you sink your fingers into the skin of a fresh orange to the way your mouth waters when you slice a lemon in half, citrus exudes the essence of good health."

Citrus fruit is an important component of salads, a key ingredient in sauces, and is used fresh as a garnish.

Grapefruits *Citrus paradisi*

The tropical or semi-tropical evergreen grapefruit trees are cultivated for their edible fruit (Figure 5-16). Grapefruit is a round fruit with yellow to dark pink rind and juicy, somewhat acidic pulp. Quality grapefruits should be firm and heavy for their size, tangy

Figure 5-15 Citrus fruits are juicy and flavorful.

sweet with a clean finish, with medium to thick skin, depending upon the variety. The flesh can be pink to ruby red or white. The thicker the skin of the grapefruit, the less juice the fruit will contain. Grapefruits are picked when ripe and do not ripen any further once off the tree. They are sold by count per case—with sizes ranging from 36, 46, 54, 63, 70, 80, 96, and smalls are 126. Grapefruits are in season during the winter and spring. The cold kitchen is often responsible for preparing grapefruits for breakfast service. They are also used in salads, sauces, or as a palate cleanser when used in sorbet or granité, the French name for tart fruit ice. For breakfast, grapefruit is generally cut in half, segmented in the pantry, and eaten out of the skin with a spoon. Grapefruit juice is available frozen, bottled, and in concentrate form. Both sweetened and non-sweetened varieties are available and used as a beverage, mixer, and sauce ingredient.

Kumquat *Fortunella*

The kumquat is a tiny (grape-sized) citrus fruit with a bitter, sour taste (Figure 5-17). They are hardly ever eaten raw. Canned or candied kumquats are served as a component in fruit dishes. Kumquats are often served during Chinese celebrations, such as the Chinese New Year, to symbolize plenty. Kumquat sauce can be used in place of orange or lemon sauce.

Lemon *Citrus limon*

Lemons are among the most versatile fruits used in the cold kitchen (Figure 5-18). The juice, rind, and zest are important ingredients in all kinds of applications. Most lemons used in the United States and Japan are cultivated in California, with smaller quantities in Florida, Texas, and Arizona. The Eureka lemon is the most common variety on the market.

Figure 5-16 Grapefruits.

Figure 5-17 Kumquats.

Figure 5-18 Lemons.

Figure 5-19 Limes.

Meyer lemons are harder to find, but are sweeter and very flavorful. Lemons are purchased by the count from 75, 95, 115, 165, 200, and 235 per 38-pound carton; the most common sizes run between the 115 and 165 counts. A typical lemon will produce 2 ounces of juice. Lemon wedges are often served with shellfish cocktails or with fish. Lemon juice is used for dressings and marinades. Freshly squeezed juice is always best for flavor and quality; however, for convenience and consistency, many foodservice operations purchase bottled lemon juice, especially when used in salad dressings. The bottled juice has preservatives added and lacks fresh juice flavor. Lemon slices are used in many mixed drinks. The lemon's tart and clean flavor adds a refreshing taste. Lemon leaves are used for garnishing.

Lime *Citrus rutaceae spp.*

The lime is a tangy citrus fruit that resembles a lemon but has its own unique flavor. Limes are smaller than lemons and have a dark green peel (Figure 5-19). Like the lemon, limes are not generally eaten alone but are used as a flavoring ingredient. They have a strong acidic character, thus making them useful for dressings, sauces, and as palate cleansers. Most limes on the market are the Persian variety, which are green and tart. Lime juice is used extensively in bar drinks and in baking and sauce making. The Key West lime is rather sweet and yellow when ripe. Key limes are actually grown in commercial quantities in Mexico. The Florida Key lime industry was destroyed by bad weather and disease decades ago. Small organic farmers do produce a small cottage industry of Key West limes today, but Mexico has become a leading producer. The kaffir lime is the small lime used in Thai cooking. This type of lime does not have a lot of juice; it is the zest and leaves that are more typically used.

Figure 5-20 There are two major varieties of oranges: Valencia and Navel.

Limequat Citrus × Fortunella

A limequat is a cross between a lime and a kumquat. It looks more like a kumquat in size and shape but has a greenish-yellow skin. It tastes more like a lime than a kumquat and can be substituted for limes.

Orange Citrus sinenis

Sweet oranges are used in pantries for slicing and for cutting into skinless sections (Figure 5-20). They are used as a salad component or to brighten up and add a little flavor to foods. Orange zest is the outer, bright-colored layer of peel. It is grated thin with a zester tool and used in sauces and desserts. Underneath the zest is the pith—the white, fleshy, inner layer, which is usually discarded. Orange juice is manufactured from concentrates or from fresh oranges. Most operations purchase orange juice in 1/2-gallon (1.9 l) plastic jugs or frozen concentrate. The public is generally willing to pay a premium price for freshly squeezed orange juice, which is sometimes produced in-house using a commercial juicer.

Valencia Oranges

More Valencia oranges are grown than any other variety of oranges. Valencias have a smooth, thin skin and have seeds. They are used for eating and for making juice. Oranges are harvested when fully ripe and do not mature further off the tree.

Navel Oranges

Navel oranges get their name from the protrusion at the opposite end of the stem (the blossom end). Navels have thick skin and are seedless. They segment easily and have a very sweet flavor.

Other Varieties

Blood oranges/moro have red flesh and red juice. The outer skin is orange to dark red and looks like a Valencia at a quick glance. It is a less common variety. Clementines are tiny, sweet oranges. They have a stronger flavor than other domestic varieties. Mandarins seem to have a cushion of air between the segments and the thin skin, making them easier to peel than most other citrus fruits. They are primarily eaten out-of-hand, or the fresh sections are used in fruit

Figure 5-21 Pummelo.

Figure 5-22 Tangerines.

Figure 5-23 Tangelo.

salads. Mandarin oranges are the most commonly canned oranges. Seville oranges are bitter oranges used for marmalade and the juice is used as an ingredient in Mexican dishes. The sour juice is often used as an ingredient in mixed drinks.

Pummelo *C. maxima*

This citrus fruit is also known as the Chinese grapefruit (Figure 5-21). It has a thick peel with a pulp that tastes sweeter and milder than the grapefruit. The pummelo can be used in salads or made into preserves.

Tangerines *Citrus reticulata*

The tangerine is a type of mandarin orange with a reddish-orange peel (Figure 5-22). They have a unique deep flavor and are easy to peel. Tangerines are used in salads, main dishes, and in desserts. Tangerine juice is used to flavor beverages.

Tangelos *Citrus reticulata x Citrus maxima*

The tangelo is a cross between a mandarin orange and a grapefruit (Figure 5-23). This juicy fruit is easy to peel and provides a unique citrus flavor.

MELONS *Cucumis melo, Cucumis citrullus, Cucumis melo L. Inodorus*

Melons are one of the more common fruits used in the pantry (Figure 5-24). There are three groups of melons defined by skin color and form. Some have netting with a pattern on their skin, some have a smooth skin, and others have a warty or bumpy exterior.

Melons are eaten in their natural state, either as an appetizer, a breakfast fruit, or as a salad ingredient. One advantage of using melons in foodservice is that they can be prepared well in advance without turning brown. For sanitation, it is important to always peel melons that will be used for foodservice to cut down on cross-contamination. Once peeled, melons are seeded and cut into wedges or dices.

There are many melon varieties on the market, and thanks to efficient transportation, most varieties are available year-round.

The following is a list of common summer season melons:

Figure 5-24 Many varieties of melons are available year-round.

Canary Melons

Canary melons, also called Juan Canary melons, are summer melons (Figure 5-25). This type of melon is canary yellow when ripe and is used in fruit salads or fruit platters.

Cantaloupes

Cantaloupes belong to the broad group of muskmelons (Figure 5-26). A ripe cantaloupe should be firm except at the stem end, which should be slightly soft.

The most common count is 45 or 36 pieces in 85-pound crates. The peak season is June to August. The flesh is rather sturdy and is often used for melon balls, in fruit salads, or for fruit plates.

Casabas

Casabas are a melon with soft, white, juicy flesh (Figure 5-27). Casabas have rich, yellow skin and are fairly large melons. Casabas make a tasty addition to fruit salads or fruit platters.

Crenshaws

Crenshaws are a dependable melon with sweet, tender flesh that is salmon colored (Figure 5-28). Their skin is rough without webbing. They are used in fruit salads and platters.

Figure 5-25 Canary melon.

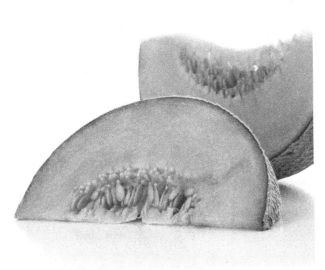

Figure 5-26 Canteloupe.

Figure 5-27 Casaba.

Honeydew Melon

Honeydews are a popular melon with light green, sweet, and delicate flesh (Figure 5-29). They have a smooth, greenish white rind. Honeydews are delicious in fruit salads or can be made into a refreshing sorbet.

Santa Claus Melons

Santa Claus melons are similar to the canary melon (Figure 5-30). The melons come on the market around Christmas and have long-keeping qualities. They are used in fruit salads and fruit platters.

Figure 5-28 Crenshaw melon.

Figure 5-29 Honeydew melon.

Figure 5-30 Santa Claus melon.

Figure 5-31 Watermelon.

Watermelons

Watermelons are large melons with bright red or orange-yellow flesh (Figure 5-31). They come with or without seeds and are often used in fruit trays and salads. They can also be used to make salsa, smoothies, or sorbet. Watermelons are usually sweet and juicy and are one of the most popular types of melons. The rind can be carved into showcase bowls, baskets, or centerpieces.

POMES

The **pomes** family consists of fruits with small seeds or pits that are found in the center of the fruit (Figure 5-32). When the fruit is sliced horizontally, the seeds form a star configuration. Apples and pears are the most common members of the pomes family.

Figure 5-32 Members of the pomes family.

Apples *Malus communis*

Fresh, raw apples are often used in fruit salads, as a decorative component on salad plates, and as ingredients in sauces such as chutney (Figure 5-33). Apples can be dried and used diced or in slices for sweet sauces. There are many apple varieties on the market. Some have a limited season while others have a limited distribution, and some apples lend themselves better for pantry work than others. *Golden Delicious* and *Red Delicious* apples are excellent in salads and are available year-round, and *Golden Delicious* oxidize (turn brown when cut) the least. Cut apples can be kept a limited time in water acidulated with lemon juice, grapefruit juice, or commercial ascorbic acid to prevent oxidation. Pasteurized apple cider will also prevent oxidation and can be added to cut apples as a means of preventing oxidation.

Apples are purchased by count in different packs. Apples come in various grades: Extra Fancy, Fancy, and No.1. The top two grades of apples are based on exterior appearance and size. Tray packs of 80 to 88 count are considered Fancy foodservice sizes. Apples should be stored at 31° to 32°F (−5° to 0°C) at 85 to 90 percent relative humidity. They should be kept in their boxes as they can absorb odors, and they give off ethylene gas, which can hasten ripening in other fruits and vegetables. Apple juice is available canned, in glass bottles, and as frozen concentrate.

Figure 5-33 Apples.

Pears *Pyrus communis*

Often pears are issued to the pantry while they are still hard and green, and the pantry personnel are responsible for ripening them (Figure 5-34). Pears do not ripen while on the trees but do ripen at room temperature. Bartlett pears turn yellow when ripe, but most pears do not change color as they ripen. Pears ripen from the inside out and are slightly soft to the touch when ripe. They should be stored in the refrigerator. Pears oxidize when cut open. Pears are often used on fruit salad plates or in fruit baskets.

Asian Pears *Ficus carica*

The Asian pear is a round fruit with thin, pale yellow to russet skin and an apple-like, crisp texture (Figure 5-35). Most of the U.S. supply is grown around the Sacramento River Valley in California, as well as in Oregon and Washington. The peak season is winter. Its unique taste is lightly sweet, and its aftertaste is perceived by some people to have an almost salty quality. The Asian pear is also known as aka nashi, or apple pear.

Figure 5-34 Pears.

Figure 5-35 Asian pear.

LEARNING ACTIVITY 5-1

Oxidation is a chemical reaction between a substance and oxygen. Enzymes in light-colored fruits such as apples, pears, and peaches can cause oxidative browning as soon as the fruit is peeled or cut. There are a variety of ways to counteract the reaction. In this activity, we will test some of the methods.

Peel, core, and slice an apple. Try one or two slices in each of the following solutions and see which you prefer. Judge each slice according to its taste and appearance. Let the slice rest in the solution for 2 minutes. Check each slice and record your findings in the chart below. Check them again in 10 minutes and record those results. Repeat the activity using a banana. Compare the results.

APPLE

	After 2 Minutes		After 10 Minutes	
Type of Solution	Taste	Appearance	Taste	Appearance
Water				
Pasteurized apple cider				
1/2 tsp ascorbic acid powder to 3 tbsp water				
Lemon juice				

BANANA

	After 2 Minutes		After 10 Minutes	
Type of Solution	Taste	Appearance	Taste	Appearance
Water				
Pasteurized apple cider				
1/2 tsp ascorbic acid powder to 3 tbsp water				
Lemon juice				

STONE FRUITS (DRUPES)

Stone fruits, also called **drupes,** are those fruits that have a single, large seed encased in a hard shell (Figure 5-36). The shell is called the pit or stone. The fleshy part of the fruit totally surrounds the pit.

Apricots *Prunus armeniaca*

Apricots can be difficult to ship when perfectly ripe and are often sold hard and relatively flavorless (Figure 5-37). They are in season June through August. They are hard to handle and seldom used fresh in the pantry, except in fruit baskets. Apricots will ripen off the tree but will become soft quickly. When apricots are used in salads, they are usually cut in half, the pit removed, and served as is with the skins on. Canned and dried apricots are used often in cold kitchens in sauces, compotes, and as a flavorful accompaniment to pork dishes.

Avocados *Persea spp.*

There are several dozen varieties of avocados, but the two main varieties used in cold kitchens are the Hass and the Fuerte.

Figure 5-36 Apricots, peaches, and nectarines are popular stone fruits.

Avocados were called *alligator pears* because the Hass variety has dark, maroon to black, crinkled skin similar to alligator's skin. The other common variety, the Fuerte, has smooth, green skin (Figure 5-38). Both of these common varieties are tropical fruits growing on trees and are cultivated extensively in California, Florida, and Mexico as well as other tropical countries. Avocados must be ripe when used. Once open, the flesh will oxidize rapidly and turn brown, so it is important to acidulate the fruit with lemon juice or ascorbic acid. Avocados are mostly used in salads and dips.

Figure 5-37 Apricots.

Figure 5-38 Avocados.

 Sweet cherries.

Figure 5-40 Sour cherries.

Cherries, Sweet (Bing) *Prunus spp.*

The bing cherry is the most popular eating cherry (Figure 5-39). The stone is relatively small while the fruit itself is crisp, firm, and juicy. This type of cherry has a dark red/burgundy color. They are mainly served fresh, but care must be taken when using fresh cherries in the pantry as there is always a hazard with the pits. Some kitchens do not use fresh cherries for this reason. Cherries do not continue to ripen once off the tree and decay quickly, so always store them in the refrigerator.

Sour Cherries/Montmorency Cherries *Prunus spp.*

Sour cherries, sometimes called pie cherries or tart cherries, are seldom sold fresh; they usually come canned or frozen as pastry filling and are available throughout the year (Figure 5-40). The cherry season is short, basically from mid-May to mid-July.

Nectarines *Prunus persica nectarina*

Figure 5-41 Nectarines.

Nectarines are peaches with a recessive gene that prevents the fruit from forming fuzz, and they have a flavor similar to that of the peach (Figure 5-41). They are a member of the rose family and are closely related to the almond. Nectarines are available in both clingstone and freestone varieties and with yellow or white flesh. Nectarines are a summer fruit common in desserts, sauces, and fruit displays and trays.

Peaches *Prunus persica*

Peaches are a popular fruit that can be basically divided between clingstone and freestone. The pit clings to the flesh in clingstone peaches; the pit can easily be removed in freestone peaches. Both clingstones and freestones have varieties with white or yellow flesh. Peaches are juicy and sweet with low acidity and have a fuzzy skin, which is usually removed before serving (Figure 5-42). Peaches should be acidulated with lemon juice or ascorbic acid to keep the flesh from turning brown once the peach is peeled. To peel peaches, blanch them in boiling water for 30 seconds, shock in ice water, and then remove the peels, which will slip right off. Peaches can also be peeled with a paring knife.

Figure 5-42 Peaches.

Figure 5-43 Red plums.

Plums Prunus americana

Like its cousins, the peach and nectarine, the plum is available in both cling-stone and freestone varieties (Figure 5-43). Typically, the clingstone variety is marketed as a fresh plum for eating, the freestone variety as a fresh prune. There are red, purple, yellow, and green plums. Most plums are sweet and juicy. Plums are eaten raw or used to make sauce, syrup, or jam. Plums are cut in half, the pit removed, and quartered as a fruit plate component.

TROPICAL FRUITS

Many Americans are just becoming acquainted with some of the varieties of tropical fruits, but these fruits have been staples throughout the world for many generations. With improved transportation systems, they are now available in most corners of the country. Tropical fruits are those fruits grown in equatorial areas (Figure 5-44). They are exciting and delicious and add a touch of class to any salad or fruit platter. Many tropical fruits have found their way into entrée recipes or as the base for sauces.

Bananas Musa nana

Bananas are ranked at the top as the workhorse of the fruit world and for eating out of hand (Figure 5-45). They are available year-round. Bananas are shipped green and are ripened with ethylene gas. A bunch of bananas is referred to as a "hand." Bananas are tricky to handle and should never be stored under refrigeration. Purchase what is needed for a few days, as they ripen rapidly at room temperature. Bananas are peeled as needed and will oxidize rapidly. The peeled fruit can be sliced or cut into large chunks. Although bananas may be used in fruit salads, care must be taken because they quickly become dark and mushy. Over-ripe bananas can be used for sauces.

Figure 5-44 Tropical fruit is exciting and delicious.

 Bananas.

Figure 5-46 Coconut.

Coconuts *Cocos nucifera*

The coconut is the fruit of the coconut palm tree (Figure 5-46). Coconuts are covered with a husk. The nut itself contains a creamy, watery substance and white flesh. The coconut water is easily drained by piercing the three soft "eyes" on the top of the nut. The meat inside the coconut will be covered with a brown skin that must be peeled off. The flesh is used fresh or dried in many culinary applications, including desserts and sweets as well as in savory dishes. The "milk" is used in flavoring entrées and sauces and is available canned.

LEARNING ACTIVITY 5-2

Opening a Coconut

Use one of the following methods to open up a coconut:

1. **Drain the coconut "milk."** Find the three "eyes" located on the end of the nut. One will be softer than the other two. Use an ice pick, skewer, or the pointed end of a pair of pointed utility scissors and open up the hole (Figure 5-47). You can also use a large nail that has been cleaned and sanitized. Position the nail over the hole and hit it with a hammer. Drain out the milk. (Make sure that it smells and tastes sweet and fresh. If not, there's no need to proceed—the nut is rancid.) You can drink the water or throw it away.

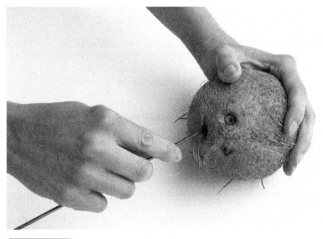

Figure 5-47 Experienced chef uses a skewer to drain the coconut.

2. **Open the nut.** Wrap the drained coconut in a kitchen towel. Place the wrapped coconut on the floor or on a counter. You can also put the wrapped coconut in a metal bowl on a counter. If you have a vise available, hold the coconut in place with a vise. Use a hammer to whack the coconut. Break it into several large pieces (Figure 5-48) . (Some chefs bake the coconut in a 400°F (200°C) oven, which will cause it to crack. Be careful not to damage the freshness of the meat inside by heating it too long.)

Figure 5-48 Crack the coconut to reveal the white flesh inside.

3. **Remove the meat.** To remove the meat from the shell, simply insert a kitchen knife between the meat and the shell (Figure 5-49). Twist the knife and the meat should pop right off. There will be a brown, thin layer at the base of the meat. This can be removed with a paring or chef's knife. The meat can be refrigerated as is or grated for use in a salad or recipe.

Figure 5-49 Use a sharp knife to cut the meat away from the shell. The coconut meat is now ready for use in salads, desserts, and other uses in the kitchen.

Dates *Phoenix dactylifera*

Dates are the fruit of the date palm tree and are about the size of a man's thumb (Figure 5-50). Dates have a single pit. Both fresh and dried dates are used in culinary applications. They can be seeded and stuffed or chopped and used in appetizers or main entrées. Dates have a high sugar content, a sweet taste, and a sticky texture.

Figure 5-50 Dates.   **Figure 5-51** Figs.

Figs Ficus carica

Figs are rounded fruits that are pointed at the stem end (Figure 5-51). Ripe figs vary in color from bright green to deep purple, depending on the variety. There are several varieties in the market such as Black Mission, Celeste, Kadota, and Brown Turkey. All figs have a soft, sweet, aromatic flesh. Fresh figs are very perishable and should be used within a day or two of purchase. Dried figs are readily available and have many culinary uses in both sweet and savory sauce applications. Figs are also used to make chutneys and compotes.

Guavas Psidium guajava L.

Depending on the variety, guavas are round or pear-shaped. Guavas are soft when ripe and creamy in texture and have a rind that softens to be fully edible (Figure 5-52). The flesh can be white, pink, yellow, or red. The seeds are numerous but small and, in good varieties, fully

Figure 5-52 Guava.

Figure 5-53 Kiwis.

edible. Guavas can be eaten raw in salads; however, they have a strong, musky smell. Cooking guava eliminates the odor. They are used in jam, butter, marmalade, chutney, relish, catsup, and other products.

Kiwis *Actinidia sinensis*

Kiwis, also called *Chinese Gooseberries,* are green fruits with a fuzzy skin. They have become very popular as a pantry fruit (Figure 5-53). The small, oval fruit has a thick brownish-green skin with a hairy surface. The flesh is bright green, with tiny purplish seeds surrounding a white core. Kiwis can be eaten raw in salads or garnish or cooked into a sauce for savory and sweet applications. It tastes like a cross between strawberries and pineapple and has a banana-like texture. Kiwis are ripe when they give slightly under light pressure and will ripen at room temperatures. Kiwis should be peeled before they are eaten and are usually sliced or cut into quarters.

Lychees *Litchi chinensis*

Lychees have an inedible, rough, leathery, reddish rind. From a distance the fruit resembles a large raspberry (Figure 5-54). The rind is easily removed. The fruit itself is only 1 to 2 inches long and has an inedible single seed. The fruit is white and firm. Its juice has a sweet, fragrant flavor. Lychees are used in salads or eaten out of hand. Canned lychees are available and used when fresh ones are out of season.

Mangos *Mangifera indica*

The mango is an intensely flavored, succulent tropical fruit that has a slightly acidic, sweet taste (Figure 5-55). The mango is considered one of the most popular tropical fruits. The fruit is elongated with a thin skin that is green when unripe and yellowish red when ripe. It comes fresh or canned. Mango is used in sauces, chutneys, and relishes, beverages, and salads.

Papayas *Carica papaya L.*

There are two types of papaya: the smaller Hawaiian and the larger Mexican. The Hawaiian varieties are pear-shaped and yellow when ripe (Figure 5-56). The flesh is orangish-yellow with a cluster of shiny,

Figure 5-54 Lychees.

Figure 5-55 Mango.

Figure 5-56 Papaya.

round, black seeds in the middle of the fruit. Mexican papayas are milder in taste but still very pleasant with yellow, orange, or pink flesh. Papayas can weigh as much as 20 pounds and are often called *tree melons*. They bruise easily and must be handled carefully.

Papayas have a buttery texture and a sweet, musky taste. The seeds are edible and taste almost like peppercorns. The papaya is associated with breakfast in many countries and is also used in salads, palate cleansers, sauces, juices, and baked goods.

Passion Fruit *Passiflora edulis*

Passion fruit is round and grows up to 3 inches wide (Figure 5-57). It has a tough rind that is smooth and waxy and ranges in hue from dark purple with faint, fine, white specks to light yellow or pumpkin color. The flesh is orange-colored with numerous small, dark brown seeds. Passion fruit has a unique musky, guava-like flavor that is sweet and tart at the same time. To prepare, cut the fruit in half and scoop out the seeds. Passion fruit juice is used for sauces, cold fruit soup, or in cocktails. Its juice is a popular addition to many tropical beverage blends.

Figure 5-57 Passion fruit.

Figure 5-58 Pineapple.

Figure 5-59 Starfruit.

Pineapples *Ananas comosus*

The pineapple is said to look like a large pine cone (Figure 5-58). It is juicy and fleshy with a fibrous core running through the fruit. Pineapples will not ripen once picked; they will only get softer, but not sweeter. Ripe pineapple will give off a sweet smell if held up to the nose. Most pineapples reaching the markets are, by necessity, picked unripe and do not develop the same flavor intensity as one that is vine ripened. Pineapples are purchased by count: 5's for salads, 14's for appetizer baskets. Pineapple is a popular ingredient in fruit salads or as a garnish to ham and other meat dishes.

Starfruit *Damasonium alisma*

The starfruit is also known as the carambola (Figure 5-59). The starfruit's texture is crunchy—similar to an apple. The skin and flesh are yellow, and the flavor is sweet with a hint of tart resembling a lemon. When the fruit is cut across, the slices resemble stars, adding a visual appeal for any salad.

EXOTICS

The final category of fruit is exotics—unique fruits that do not fall into any of the other categories previously discussed.

Loquats *Eriobotrya japonica*

Loquats grow in clusters that are between 1 and 2 inches long (Figure 5-60). The skin of the loquat is yellow, orange, or reddish. The fruit has been described as succulent and tangy. The loquat can be eaten fresh or in salads, after it has been peeled and seeded. It makes a delicious filling for pies and tarts, and because of its high pectin content, it is often used for jams and jellies or sauces. Loquats are also used to make wine.

Pomegranates *Punica granatum*

Pomegranates grow to the size of a baseball (Figure 5-61). They are covered with a rough, red rind. Once peeled, a white, bitter, spongy membrane separates hundreds of juicy nodules, called arils. Each aril contains a tiny, hard seed that is surrounded by a tangy, brilliant, burgundy-colored, juicy pulp. Pomegranate sauces are used in both savory and sweet applications.

Figure 5-60 Loquat.

Figure 5-61 Pomegranate.

Figure 5-62 Prickly pear cactus.

Prickly Pear (Cactus) Opuntia lasiacanta

Each cactus bears numerous flat pads or branches that resemble leaves about the size of a man's palm (Figure 5-62). Prickly pears are the fruits of the cactus plant. They can also be peeled, chopped, and eaten raw or used in salads and are also used to make jellies and sweet sauces.

Dragon Fruit (Pitaya) Hylocereus undatus (pink skinned); Selenicereus (yellow skinned)

Dragon fruit is the edible fruit of warm-climate cacti (Figure 5-63). The thin skin has large, exaggerated scales located randomly around the fruit. It is the flesh or pulp that is consumed. The flesh is full of tiny, crunchy seeds that are eaten. Dragon Fruit is said to be sweet, resembling the taste of kiwi. It is used in salads and is sometimes used to make juice.

Figure 5-63 Dragon fruit.

The instructor will provide an array of tropical and exotic fruits. Each student should have the opportunity to look at, taste, and smell each fruit. Once each fruit has been sampled, see if you can identify each fruit visually. Next, place fruit pieces into paper portion cups and cover with cheesecloth. Use your sense of smell to identify each fruit. Finally, sample each fruit and identify it from its taste.

>> Vegetables

Vegetables are important foods that are highly beneficial for the maintenance of health and prevention of disease (Figure 5-64). They add variety in color, texture, and taste. The following section is filled with thumbnail sketches of many of the common vegetables used in the cold kitchen.

BULBS/ALLIUMS

Members of the **allium** family have a strong "oniony" odor; these perennial bulbous plants are indigenous to northern temperate climates (Figure 5-65). Onions, shallots, leeks, and herbs such as garlic and chives (chives, which are considered an herb, are discussed in Unit 4) are the edible members of the allium family and provide important flavor components to recipes.

Garlic Allium sativum

Garlic is an important flavoring ingredient (Figure 5-66). It is a bulb vegetable and consists of small toes or cloves encased in papery skin; there are a number of varieties. Elephant garlic, as the name implies, has the largest bulbs. Red-skinned garlic has the strongest flavor.

Figure 5-64   An array of fresh vegetables.

Figure 5-65   Members of the allium family.

Figure 5-66 Garlic.

Figure 5-67 Leeks.

Peeling garlic is labor intensive; therefore, most foodservice operations purchase peeled garlic in gallon containers or they buy chopped garlic. Both products must be stored in the refrigerator. Granulated garlic is available as a convenient product to add flavor to dressings and sauces. The granules dissolve easily.

Leeks *Allium porrum*

Leeks look like giant green onions (Figure 5-67). Leeks are related to the onion but have a milder flavor. They are used in soups, in casseroles, or to season sauces. Leeks are also used as a side vegetable. Marinated leeks are often served as a component of French appetizers. Leeks are one of the main ingredients in vichyssoise, a rich, creamy potato and leek soup that is served cold. Leeks are often sandy inside and must be split, the leaves separated, and carefully washed.

Onions *Allium cepa*

Onions are classified as either summer or winter onions (Figure 5-68). Summer onions are generally sweeter than winter onions. They are available in yellow, red, and white and are primarily available from March through August. Sweet and mild onion varieties include Vidalia onions from a designated area in Georgia and Walla Walla Sweets, which are cultivated in Oregon and Washington. Green onions, sometimes called scallions, are harvested when the plant is young and tender before a large bulb forms and are used fresh in salads and sauces, in Asian stir fries, or as a garnish to top entrées. They are also cooked and used in stews or casseroles.

Winter onions are harvested in late fall, and in some regions of the country they are left in the ground through the winter months and harvested in early spring. They are also available in yellow, red, and white varieties. Red onions are milder than yellow onions and often have a sweet flavor. Red onions are used in salads, to top sandwiches, grilled, or cooked to flavor sauces, stews, and soups. White onions are milder than yellow onions and are often considered sweet. They are eaten raw in salads or sandwiches or baked, boiled, or cooked to flavor sauces, stews, and soups. Yellow onions are the most commonly used variety and are one of the most used vegetables in any kitchen. Yellow onions turn

Figure 5-68 Onions.

Figure 5-69 Shallots.

a rich dark brown color when cooked. There are no nutritional differences between the different types of onions.

Winter onions with firm flesh, and dry, crackly outer skins can be stored and will stay fresh for up to 2 months if stored in a cool, dry, and dark place.

Granulated onions are available as convenient products to add flavor to dressings and sauces. They dissolve easily and store well for long periods of time if kept in a cool, dark, and dry place.

Shallots Allium ascalonicum

There is a lot of confusion surrounding the shallot. Many people think that shallots are a variety of onion, but they are actually a species of their own. Similar to garlic, shallots grow in clusters with separate bulbs, reddish-brown skins, and a tapered shape (Figure 5-69). Shallots taste like mild onions and are considered by many to be the "gourmet" member of the onion family. Shallots are used primarily in sauces and marinades.

BRASSICA

The **brassica** family is comprised of a large variety of leafy and flowering plants ranging from mustard and cabbage, grown for their edible foliage, to cauliflower and broccoli, grown for their edible flower stalks.

Broccoli Brassica olerace, spp.

Figure 5-70 Broccoli.

Broccoli is made of a tight cluster of florets on top of an edible, wide stalk (Figure 5-70). Fresh broccoli can be kept under refrigeration for up to a week if left unwashed and kept in a covered container. This vegetable is used raw as a salad component and occasionally as garnish. It is also a popular component of stir fries and numerous entrées and can be steamed, boiled, or baked. Broccoli rabe (pronounced "rob") is one variety that has a tender texture, smaller heads, and a slightly bitter flavor.

Brussels Sprouts Brassica oleracea gemmifera

Brussels sprouts grow on a stalk that can grow up to 2 or 3 feet in height. We eat the swollen buds or sprouts (Figure 5-71). Each stem usually has between 20 and 40, 1-inch in diameter, sprouts. Brussels sprouts are usually cooked whole and used as a side dish. Tender Brussels sprouts can be served raw as a delicious addition to salads.

Figure 5-71 Brussels sprouts.

Figure 5-72 Cabbage.

Figure 5-73 Cauliflower.

Cabbage *Brassica oleracea*

Green and red cabbage heads are available year-round and are inexpensive (Figure 5-72). Red cabbage is often added to salads as a color component but can be made into cole slaw. Savoy, or curly, cabbage cannot be eaten raw and is used as a cooked vegetable. It is mild flavored and needs less cooking than other cabbages.

Cole slaw is a cold cabbage salad of Dutch origin that is made with shredded cabbage and sometimes onions, shredded carrots, sweet peppers, and pickles. It can have a mayonnaise base or a vinaigrette dressing. In Germany, hot cabbage slaw, made with caraway seeds, is a popular side dish.

Early varieties of cabbage store well refrigerated for up to 2 weeks. Late varieties can be kept refrigerated up to 3 months.

Cauliflower *Brassica spp.*

Cauliflower, also in the cabbage family, can be used in salads (Figure 5-73). Because it is white and does not contain any chlorophyll, it does not change color when blended with an acidic dressing. Cauliflower salad is perfect for buffets, as relish, and as garnish. It can also be cooked in soups or in vegetable side dishes. Be careful not to overcook it, which will cause the cauliflower to develop "off" flavors due to its sulfur compounds.

Fresh cauliflower can be kept up to 2 weeks if refrigerated.

Kale *Brassica oleracea*

Kale has deeply crinkled leaves and a dark grayish-green color (Figure 5-74). It looks similar to collard greens but tastes more like strong cabbage. The smaller leaves are more tender and have a milder flavor. The stems are tough, so the leaves should be pulled away from the stems. The stems should then be discarded. Wrap unwashed greens in damp paper towels, place in a plastic bag, and keep refrigerated for up to 2 weeks.

Kale can be boiled, steamed, and microwaved (cook until just wilted). Sauté cooked kale with onions and garlic, season with ham or smoked turkey, and serve as a tasty side dish. Add kale to soups or use chopped, cooked kale in stuffing. Chilled, cooked kale can be served cold with olive oil and lemon juice.

Figure 5-74 Kale.

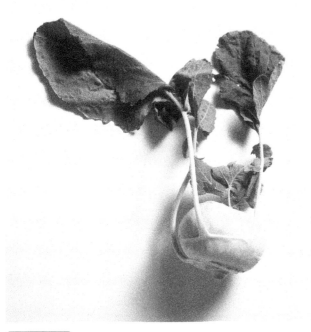

Figure 5-75 Kohlrabi.

Kohlrabi Brassica oleracea L. var. gongylodes

Kohlrabi is a close relative to broccoli even though it doesn't look much like it (Figure 5-75). The part we eat is the enlarged stem from which the leaves extend. It is best if harvested when the enlarged stem is around 2 or 3 inches in diameter. Any larger, and the vegetable will become woody and tough. Kohlrabi can be white, green, or purple in color.

The leaves of the kohlrabi are actually edible if the plants are young. Use them like you would use spinach or mustard greens. Peel kohlrabi before using raw in salads or as part of a relish tray. It tastes similar to a raw turnip. (Small kohlrabi may not require peeling.) It can also be steamed and used in any vegetable medley.

Mustard Greens Brassica juncea

The peppery leaves of the mustard plant have a pungent, mustard flavor (Figure 5-76). They are oval-shaped, have a dark green color, and have scalloped edges. Always rinse leaves in cool water to remove sand and dirt. Strip off the stems and discard. Young, tender leaves can be added to salads. Slow cooking mellows the flavor. Blanch them first when using in soups, creamy purées, or sautés.

CUCURBITACEAE

The **cucurbitaceae,** or cucurbit, family consists of the cucumber, gourd, melon (discussed earlier in the fruit section), and pumpkins. They grow on vines with large flowers primarily in warmer regions of the world.

Cucumbers Cucumis sativa

Salad cucumbers are available as slicing cucumbers and as more expensive seedless, "English" greenhouse cucumbers (Figure 5-77). Both varieties are available year-round. Cucumbers

Figure 5-76 Mustard greens.

Figure 5-77 Cucumbers.

PRODUCE, LEGUMES, AND GRAINS

Figure 5-79 Summer squash.

Figure 5-78 Pumpkin.

should be peeled because they are sometimes covered with wax to retain moisture. In some operations, cucumbers are split after peeling and the seeds removed with a tablespoon. Cucumbers are then sliced thin and, in some cases, slightly salted to remove excess moisture. Hydroponically grown cucumbers are usually very straight and seedless.

Pumpkin *Cucurbita pepo*

Pumpkins are large winter squash more suitable for purée, soup, and pie than for salads (Figure 5-78). The shell is hard and requires considerable force to cut open. After the numerous seeds are removed, the pumpkin must be boiled, baked, or steamed. The seeds of the pumpkin are edible and are used as a garnish for salads and soups.

SQUASH

There are two classifications of squash—those harvested in the summer and called summer squash and those with tougher skins and harvested in early fall, called winter squash, which can be stored in a cool, dark place for several months.

Summer Squash *Cucurbita pepo*

Zucchini, pattypan, and yellow crookneck squashes are all considered summer squash (Figure 5-79). They have tender skin and grow smaller than their winter squash counterparts. Summer squash can be eaten raw, lightly steamed, pan fried, stir fried, grilled, or baked. Summer squash is fragile, compared with winter squash, and should be used within a few days of purchase.

Winter Squash *Cucurbita maxima, moschata, pepo*

Butternut, buttercup, hubbard, acorn, turban, and spaghetti squash are all common varieties of what is known as winter squash (Figure 5-80). They have tough skins and require longer cooking times than summer squash.

Figure 5-80 Winter squash.

Beets.

Figure 5-82 Carrots.

ROOT VEGETABLES

Root vegetables include a variety of fleshy underground roots that are eaten as vegetables. This category does not include tubers, which we will discuss later in this chapter. Today, root vegetables are available year-round, but it wasn't long ago that they were harvested in late fall and used as the staple vegetables throughout the winter months. Root vegetables typically store well and are full of vitamins and minerals as well as hearty flavor, which is perfect for cold weather days.

Beet *Beta vulgaris*

Beets are usually a deep red color, though some varieties can be white or gold (Figure 5-81). They can be served cooked or raw. When beets are cooked, they should be boiled or roasted in their skins to prevent color loss. The color in beets can quickly alter any food they touch. Beets are used mostly for salads but can also be served as a side vegetable. Vibrant beet juice is used as a dye and to flavor horseradish. Beets are also an ingredient in borscht, a Russian beet soup. Beets can be boiled, steamed, or pan roasted.

Carrot *Daucus carota*

Carrots are members of the parsley family and are related to the parsnip, celery, and fennel (Figure 5-82). They have a strong, sweet flavor and are a good source of vitamin A, beta carotene, and potassium. They are delicious raw in salads or steamed and cooked as a side vegetable or a component in soups or stews. Carrots provide the key ingredient in carrot pudding and carrot cake. Carrot juice is widely marketed. Carrots are typically bright orange (there are white, yellow, red, and purple varieties) and add a vibrant punch of color to any dish.

Celeriac *Apium graveolens*

The vegetable is also known as knob celery and consists of a firm knob growing below ground and bushy leaves that grow above the ground (Figure 5-83). The solid knob can

Figure 5-83 Celeriac.

Figure 5-84 Daikon.

Figure 5-85 Jicama.

be braised as a vegetable or it can be shredded and used raw as a salad ingredient. It will oxidize when peeled and should be kept in acidic water. The hard knobs are rather sandy and must be peeled. The vegetable is usually shredded or cut into fine julienne.

Daikon *Raphanus R. sativus*

The most common variety of daikon is known as the Japanese white radish. It is served raw or cooked (Figure 5-84). It is often grated and served as a garnish for Japanese soups. A daikon looks like a large white carrot. This vegetable is an essential ingredient in Japanese, Chinese, and Korean recipes.

Jícama/Mexican Potato *Pachyrhizus P. erosus*

Jícama is a large, gourd-shaped tuber, about 4 to 6 inches in length and 2 or more inches in diameter (Figure 5-85). The thin, brown skin is inedible. Jícama can be used raw in salads and in relishes. The white, crunchy flesh resembles water chestnuts in both texture and flavor. In Mexico, jícama is usually served raw, chilled, sliced thin, sprinkled with lime juice, and as salad.

Figure 5-86 Parsnips.

Parsnips *Pastinaca sativa*

The parsnip is a member of the parsley family. The root resembles an off-white carrot in appearance but is stronger in taste than the carrot (Figure 5-86). Parsnips can be boiled or roasted and used in soups, stews, and casseroles.

Radish *Raphanus sativa*

Radishes come in many shapes, such as small, round, or oval and as tap root (Figure 5-87). Most radishes are red, but radishes used in Asian cooking can be white or black. In Germany, black radishes—peeled, spiral cut, and salted—are sold in beer gardens. Radishes are often shredded or sliced and sprinkled over salads. The red color is water soluble, and radishes should be stored only briefly in cold water. Radishes require little cleaning except cutting off the top and tap root. Radishes sold in bunches are sometimes sandy and must be washed carefully. Cello-packed radishes have been cleaned.

Figure 5-87 Radishes.

Salsify Tragopogon porrifolius

Salsify is a root vegetable that is also called the oyster plant. It consists of slender, brown roots (Figure 5-88). When peeled and cooked, the stalks are white, tender, and rather bland, making this vegetable suitable for many salad and dressing combinations.

Turnip Brassica rapa

The turnip is a cool-weather crop (Figure 5-89). The best-eating turnips are of medium size. They can be cooked in stews, baked as a side dish, or peeled and eaten raw in salads. Turnips can be served as crudités with or without dip. They have a tangy taste and similar texture to the carrot.

TUBERS

A **tuber** is an enlarged stem, also known as the rhizome, that stores food. They are usually found underground, as in the potato. Tubers are important sources of carbohydrates in many cultures.

Potato Solanum tuberosum

Potatoes are grouped into waxy potatoes and mealy potatoes (Figure 5-90). Waxy potatoes stay firm after cooking and are best known as Maine potatoes, Chefs' potatoes, and a variety with red skin, are known as Red Bliss. The mealy potatoes are the russet type. In between is the Yukon Gold potato, which is mealy yet firm. Waxy potatoes are generally preferred for potato salad. Mealy potatoes are the best for baking.

Figure 5-88 Salsify.

Figure 5-89 Turnip.

Figure 5-90 Potatoes.

LEARNING ACTIVITY 5-4

Talk to a produce manager or foodservice company and find out how many types of potatoes they sell. Write a brief description of each variety. Share your findings with your class members.

Sweet Potato *Ipomoea batatas*

The sweet potato, which is a cousin to the morning glory, has smooth skin (Figure 5-91). It ranges in color from white, red, or purple, to brown. The flesh is generally white, yellow, orange, or purple. Sweet potatoes are particularly popular in the Southern United States as well as in the East Indies, India, China, and Japan. They can be boiled, fried, baked, or sliced and fried and served as sweet potato chips.

Yam *Dioscorea cayenensis*

Some people interchange the term "yam" with "sweet potato," but the two are not even related botanically (Figure 5-92). Yams can be boiled, roasted, grilled, fried, mashed, made into chips, or pounded into a paste. Unlike the smooth-skinned sweet potato, yams have rough skin and are difficult to peel. The peel colors run from brown to light pink. The flesh ranges from white to orange in color. True yams are generally only found in specialty markets.

Jerusalem Artichoke or Sunchoke *Helianthus tuberosus*

The Jerusalem artichoke is nothing like its namesake, the globe artichoke, with its edible, globular flower (Figure 5-93). The Jerusalem artichoke is a tuber. It is sometimes called the sunchoke because its flowers resemble the sunflower. The Jerusalem artichoke resembles the potato but tastes more like a water chestnut. It can be cooked like potatoes—baked, boiled, mashed, or fried. Jerusalem artichokes can be served raw in salads but need a little vinegar or lemon juice to prevent them from darkening. They are also pickled.

Figure 5-91 Sweet potatoes.

LETTUCE AND GREENS

Lettuce is the backbone of most salads. It is always served fresh, and when not starring as a key ingredient in a salad, it is served as a garnish to brighten up a plate or as a sandwich layer. For many years, most Americans only saw iceberg or Boston Bibb (butterhead) lettuce in most groceries or restaurants. But that has changed. Today consumers can choose from a wide variety of types of lettuce. There are four basic types of lettuce based on the shape and type of leaf and whether it is a head lettuce or a loose-leaf lettuce: iceberg, leaf, butterhead, and romaine. Lettuce comes in many shades as well, from a pale almost cream color to a dark red bronze. It can also come in variegated shades of green and red.

Figure 5-92 Yams.

Figure 5-93 Jerusalem artichoke.

Figure 5-94 Arugula.

Figure 5-95 Belgian endive.

Greens can be used along with lettuce for salad mixes and can be cooked. In this section we will describe a host of greens and the four basic types of lettuce.

Arugula (Rocket) *Eruca sativa, Diplotaxis tenuifolia, Diplotaxis muralis*

Arugula is a green leafy vegetable with a bitter, pungent taste (Figure 5-94). It is usually blended into salads because it is too bitter to eat alone. The leaves, not the stems, are edible. Arugula is not a type of lettuce but is an herb and related to the mustard family. It is very popular with Italian cuisines. Arugula can be used in salads, as an ingredient in pestos, or cooked and served as a vegetable.

Belgian Endive *Cichorium intybus*

Belgian endive is an expensive winter vegetable often imported from Belgium but also cultivated in the United States (Figure 5-95). It is related to the chicory plant and has a slightly bitter taste. Producers keep the slender leaves white by covering them during the growing process. A purple-tipped variety has recently come on the market. Belgian endive can be used as a salad component or to make hors d'oeuvre. It can also be braised and served as a side dish.

Figure 5-96 Bibb lettuce.

Bibb Lettuce *Lactuca sativa*

Bibb is a delicate lettuce with green or slightly red leaves (Figure 5-96). It is related to Boston lettuce and is considered a butterhead lettuce. It has loose leaves and lots of mild flavor.

Many restaurants serve a whole head split as an individual salad. It works nicely as a component in a salad blend. There is little cleaning waste with Bibb lettuce.

Boston Lettuce *Lactuca sativa*

Boston lettuce is also a type of butterhead lettuce (Figure 5-97). It has soft, small, round heads and does not form a firm ball. The outer leaves are green, and the inner heart is yellowish green. The leaves are delicate and will wilt rapidly. The lettuce is usually sold in cartons with 24 heads. Boston lettuce is great in salads, on sandwiches, or as a garnish.

Figure 5-97 Boston lettuce.

Figure 5-98 Chicory.

Figure 5-99 Dandelion greens.

Chicory, Curly Endive *Cichorium intybus*

Chicory, also called curly endive or frisée, is known for its feathery leaves that are green on top and yellow in the center (Figure 5-98). When served as a salad, it is often spread out like a daisy blossom and requires careful washing. The center leaves are slightly bitter. This type of lettuce wilts quickly but can add a unique flavor to any salad blend.

Dandelion Greens *Taraxacum*

This generally despised spring garden weed is available as a salad blend ingredient (Figure 5-99). It is often rather sandy or muddy and requires repeated washing. Dandelion greens are said to taste like chicory and endive and are a welcome addition to salads or served steamed or sautéed as a side dish.

Escarole *Cichorium endivia*

This lettuce is related to chicory and is bitter (Figure 5-100). Its curly leaves are dark green and are used as a component in some salad mixes. It contrasts well with sweeter, milder lettuces and adds a zip to any salad.

Figure 5-100 Escarole.

Frisée

See Chicory, Curley Endive.

Iceberg Lettuce *Lactuca sativa*

Iceberg is the faithful standby lettuce that is often the backbone of salads (Figure 5-101). Iceberg can take much abuse, including the silly custom of smashing the dense heads on the kitchen table to loosen the trunk or core. The salad is bland, can take on any dressing, and does not wilt quickly. Many operations purchase the lettuce shredded or pre-cut in salad-sized bites.

Mache/Lamb's Quarter *Chenopodium album*

Many people think that this lettuce is a common weed (Figure 5-102). It tastes similar to spinach or chard with an earthy flavor. Lamb's quarters has delicate little leaves on short stems that require tedious cleaning. It is delicious in salads but will wilt almost immediately when blended with dressing. Lamb's quarters can also be steamed and served as a side dish.

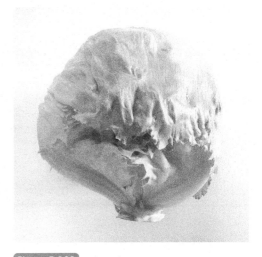

Figure 5-101 Iceberg lettuce.

Figure 5-102 Lamb's quarter.

Mesclun Greens

Mesclun isn't a type of lettuce but a salad mixture popularized in the mid-1980s by *Alice Waters*, owner of *Chez Panisse* restaurant in Berkeley, California (Figure 5-103). The assortment contains tender greens, such as delicate baby lettuce, peppery wild greens, herbs, and tangy greens.

Radicchio *Cichorium intybus*

Radicchio has small, compact, purple heads that can be used as salad and as vegetable (Figure 5-104). It was originally from Italy and continues to be a favorite ingredient in Italian dishes and salads. The expensive salad requires little cleaning and adds texture, a flavorful zip. and color to salad blends.

Figure 5-103 Mesclun greens.

Figure 5-104 Radicchio.

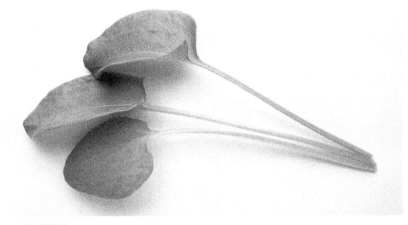

Figure 5-106 Sorrel.

Figure 5-105 Romaine lettuce.

Romaine Lettuce *Lactuca sativa*

Romaine is a head lettuce that grows in a loaf shape with long, closely packed green leaves and white ribs (Figure 5-105). It is often called Cos after the Mediterranean island of the same name. Romaine is a mild tasting, sturdy salad green and adds bulk to salad blends. It is the lettuce of choice for Caesar salad. It is sold in crates with 24 heads but also as fully trimmed hearts.

Sorrel *Rumex acetosa*

This perennial herb produces long, tender, succulent leaves that have a tangy, acidic flavor (Figure 5-106). It blends well with other salad greens and is excellent cooked and served with fish; puréed; or used in soups, stews, or sauces.

Figure 5-107 Spinach.

Spinach *Spinacia oleracea*

Spinach is a vegetable that is rich in nutrients (Figure 5-107). It is considered one of the healthiest foods on Earth. There are two basic varieties: curly leaf and flat leaf spinach. When purchased in whole bushels, the stems must be ripped off and the salad washed various times because sand is often lodged between the ridges of the leaves. Many operations purchase spinach washed in cello packs. Spinach is delicious fresh, in salads, or cooked in a casserole. It is also delicious steamed or creamed and served as a side dish. Baby spinach has become a favorite ingredient in many expensive salad blends.

Swiss Chard *Beta vulgaris var. cicla*

Swiss chard is known for its tender, vitamin-enriched leaves (Figure 5-108). It is a close relative to beets and spinach and has a similar taste profile. The leaves can be simmered in salted water and served with a little butter and vinegar or wine, or used as greens in any salad mix. The stalk can be cooked and served like asparagus.

Figure 5-108 Swiss chard.

Figure 5-109 Turnip greens.

Figure 5-110 Watercress.

Figure 5-111 Asparagus.

Turnip Greens *Brassica rapa*

Turnip greens tend to be sandy and may require numerous washings before they can be served (Figure 5-109). They have long been associated with Southern cooking and have an interesting flavor and high nutritional value. Traditional Southern turnip greens are boiled, usually with bacon or salt pork, and served with corn bread. Turnip greens are also delicious in soups.

Watercress *Nasturtium nasturtium-aquaticum, N. microphyllum*

Watercress has peppery, small leaves on long stems and is sold in bunches (Figure 5-110). Watercress is strictly a blending ingredient. For many years, watercress was used as a popular garnish on steaks.

VEGETABLES WITH AN EDIBLE PLANT STEM

This category focuses on those vegetables whose primary edible part is the above-ground stem or stalk. Because stems carry nutrients and water up and down the plant, these vegetables are packed with flavor and nutrients.

Asparagus *Asparagaceae officinalis*

Green or white asparagus is often used as salad and must be boiled or steamed (Figure 5-111). After cooking, asparagus should be plunged into cold water to arrest the cooking process and thereby keep the vegetable green. It should be drained quickly and never stored in water to prevent it from becoming soft and soggy. Raw, slender green asparagus spears are often served with dips as appetizers.

Anise *Pimpinella anisum*

The seeds of this plant are considered a spice and are used in cakes, cheese, and entrées (Figure 5-112). All above-ground parts of the young anise plant are also eaten as a vegetable. The bulb and stems resemble those of celery in texture. The flavor is slightly licorice. The vegetable is sometimes confused with the vegetable fennel, but fennel does not form a bulb. Anise can be diced and used in stews, soups, or for stuffing. The bulbs can be steamed and served as a side dish. Anise is also sliced thin and served raw in salads.

Artichokes *Cynara cardunculus L.*

Artichokes are the edible parts of a perennial thistle plant, which will grow up to 5 feet tall (Figure 5-113). The unopened flower of the plant is eaten. Small artichoke flowers can be

Figure 5-112 Anise.

Figure 5-113 Artichokes.

Figure 5-114 Prickly pear cactus leaves.

trimmed, split, cleaned, and served cooked as salad or breaded and deep fried as an appetizer. Many operations purchase pickled artichoke hearts in jars or cans because the preparation is labor intensive. Canned artichoke hearts (not pickled) are used in salads and as an ingredient in main dishes. Pickled artichokes are used in antipasto plates.

Cactus Leaves/Nopales *Cactaceae*

The paddle-shaped cactus leaves are known as nopales or nopalitos in Mexico (Figure 5-114). Once the stickers are removed, the pads can be squeezed for juice or boiled until tender, or used raw in salads with tomatoes, onions, oil, and vinegar. Some say this cactus resembles okra in taste. Nopales are also sold canned.

Celery *Apium graveolens dulce*

Celery is used in many salads, especially in protein salads as filler and for adding crispness (Figure 5-115). It is also an important ingredient in many soups, stews, casseroles. and other main dishes. Pascal celery is a popular variety of celery because the strings are soft and do not have to be removed.

Fennel *Foeniculum vulgare*

This vegetable is related to anise and similarly has a slight licorice taste (Figure 5-116). Most purveyors call the vegetable *anise* although there is a slight difference between the two plants. Like anise, fennel can be used in stews, soups, or for stuffing or sliced thin and served raw in salads.

> **CHEF'S TIP**
> *Some health departments suggest that when diced celery is used raw as a salad component, it should be dipped briefly in boiling water to kill any harmful pathogens.*

Figure 5-115 Celery.

Figure 5-116 Fennel.

Figure 5-117 Hearts of palm.

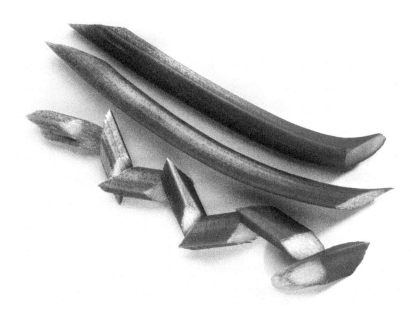

Figure 5-118 Rhubarb.

Hearts of Palm *Cocos nucifera*

The young, tender seedlings of a number of species of palm trees are harvested and consumed as hearts of palm (Figure 5-117). The trees die after the hearts are removed. The most frequently used variety is the coconut palm tree. Hearts of palm is a popular ingredient for appetizers and is also used in salads. This product is almost always canned and consists of white stalks in acidic brine. The tree dies after the heart has been cut out. The product is expensive.

Rhubarb *Rheum rhabarbarum*

Rhubarb is technically a vegetable, but has been classified as a fruit by the U.S. Customs Service since 1947 (Figure 5-118). The stalks must be cooked with sugar to make them edible. The leaves are poisonous; only the stalk is totally safe to eat. Rhubarb can be used to flavor chutney, relish, and gastriques.

SPROUTS

Sprouts have long been associated with health foods. They are tiny but packed with nutrients. There are numerous sprout varieties on the market. Sprouts are often added to salads or to sandwich toppings. They are very perishable and should be washed at the last moment and never stored in water. Some sprouts have been known to carry *Salmonella* bacillus, so keeping them properly stored and cleaned is imperative.

Alfalfa Sprouts *Medicago sativa*

Alfalfa sprouts have small, tender leaves and are often purchased still growing in containers (Figure 5-119). The mild flavor complements most salads and sandwich ingredients. Alfalfa sprouts add a slight crunch and are nutritious.

Bean Sprouts *Vigna radiata*

Bean sprouts are the most widely consumed of all the sprouts (Figure 5-120). The sprouts from mung beans are rather robust and are used more in cooking Chinese dishes than in salads, but in recent years it is not uncommon to see bean sprouts offered raw in salad bars. These sprouts are rich in vitamins and low in carbohydrates.

Figure 5-119 Alfalfa sprouts.

Figure 5-120 Bean sprouts.

Figure 5-121 Bell peppers.

FRUITS USED AS VEGETABLES

A number of fruits are consumed as vegetables. Remember that a fruit is defined as the developed ovary of a seed plant with its contents and accessory parts. The following fruits meet that description but are used as a vegetable or as salad components.

Bell Pepper *Capsicum annuum*

Bell peppers belong to the same family as the fiery chilies but are sweet to the taste (Figure 5-121). They are usually split, the seeds are scraped out, and then they are washed to remove any remaining seeds. It is easier to cut the peppers from the inside, the skin side facing the cutting board. Peppers are green when unripe and become red when ripe. Because green peppers are not ripe, they are less sweet and slightly bitter compared to other bell peppers. Yellow-, orange-, and purple-colored peppers have been developed and have a rather sweet taste. The different colors do not have a discernable difference in flavor. The various colors are pretty as salad ingredients but lose some of their color intensity when cooked.

Chili Pepper *Capsicum solanaceae*

"No other vegetable—or food for that matter—has made such a dramatic impact in the culinary world. Although garlic and chocolate have attained celebrity status (and cult followings), chilies have emerged as the superstar of the Über foods. And there's a good reason for this: Chilies not only seduce your palate with flavor, they thrill it with heat," says Heidi Allison in her book, *The Chili Pepper Diet*. (Über foods are considered super foods.)

There are many chili varieties, ranging from mild jalapeños to the fiercely hot cayenne peppers. Following is an abbreviated list of common chili peppers.

Aji

Aji is a general term for small chilies; they are used green, red, and yellow when fully ripe (Figure 5-122). They are very hot and they are used sparingly as a seasoning ingredient in a variety of dishes.

Figure 5-122 Aji chilies.

Figure 5-123 Ancho chilies.

Figure 5-124 Habanero chilies.

Figure 5-125 Jalapeños.

Figure 5-126 Pimentos.

Ancho/Poblano

Anchos is the common green chili (Figure 5-123). *Ancho* means wide in Spanish and refers to the dried poblano. The chilies are mild, and poblano is often stuffed with cheese and deep fried.

Habanero/Scotch Bonnet

Habaneros, also called Scotch Bonnet, resemble the shape of small bell peppers and can be red or yellow (Figure 5-124). They are considered the hottest chili pepper variety and are used in salsas, in table sauces, and with seafood.

Jalapeño

Jalapeño is a small green or red chili (Figure 5-125). Jalapeños are available in many ethnic markets and even in most supermarkets fresh, canned, or pickled. Jalapeños are relatively mild. Red jalapeños are sweeter than the green variety. Jalapeños are used in salsas, soups, sauces, and breads.

Pimentos

Pimentos (also spelled pimiento), also called cherry peppers, are ripe red mild peppers that are sold peeled and seeded in cans or jars (Figure 5-126). Spain is a major producer. Pimentos are the red stuffing in green olives, and they are also a popular ingredient in cheese spreads.

Serrano

Serranos are oblong red chili peppers that are spiced medium hot (Figure 5-127). Serranos are often roasted and used in sauces. Fresh serranos provide a hot zing to any tomato-based salsas.

Eggplant *Solanum melongena*

Purple eggplants are most common in the United States, but they also come in a wide variety of shapes (Figure 5-128). Most U.S. eggplants are large, but small Asian baby eggplants can also be found. Eggplants tend to be bitter. The bitterness and excess water can be leached out by slicing it and salting the eggplant with salt for a half hour or so before cooking.

Olive *Olea europaea*

The fruit of olive trees has been used as food and a source of oil since antiquity. Olive trees have been cultivated around the Mediterranean Sea for thousands of years. Raw olives must be cured to become edible. They can be salted, pickled, canned, and dried. Imported olives

Figure 5-128 Eggplant.

Figure 5-127 Serrano chilies.

are available at international markets and now in many supermarkets in a large variety of sizes and flavors (Figure 5-129). It is important to remember that olives used in salads must be pitted to prevent customers from biting into them.

Most of the olives grown in the United States are used for canning. The canned black olives are harvested green and undergo a lengthy process to make them black and rather bland tasting. Green pitted olives are often stuffed with slivers of pimento, garlic, almond, or anchovy. There are hundreds of varieties ranging in color from green to purple to dark brown. The most common varieties are listed below.

Amphissas

Amphissas are Greek, large, dark purple, juicy, and soft textured. Ionian green are Greek mild-tasting olives.

Bella di Cerignola

Bella di Cerignolas are Italian olives that are crisp, large, and sweet. They are usually bright green in color and delicious served with martinis.

Gaeta

Gaeta olives are small black olives from Italy. They are usually dry cured or brine cured.

Black Olives

Black olives are those olives left to ripen on the trees. The Mission olive is the most common black olive in the United States.

Kalamata

Kalamata are Greek, oval, smooth, and dark purple olives renowned for their meatiness, juiciness, and pungent, salty flavor.

Manzanilla

Manzanilla are Spanish olives often sold green, with and without a pit, sometimes stuffed with pimentos or almonds. In Spain, Manzanilla olives are sold in different degrees of ripeness and can range in color from light green to purple.

Figure 5-129 Olives.

Mission Olives

Mission olives are grown in California. They are the common black olives served on pizza or in salad bars.

Niçoise

Niçoise are French, small, dark olives popular in salads and other dishes. They are sour and a key ingredient in a salad Niçoise.

Picholines

Picholines have a small stone, and subtle, firm, and tasty meat. They pickle well and are often used in martinis.

Sicilian Olives

Sicilians are large, green, and acidic. They are sometimes pitted and stuffed.

Tomatillo Physalis philadelphica

These small fruits resemble small, green tomatoes but have a loose, papery husk (Figure 5-130). Technically, they are not tomatoes, and their flavor is a little different. They are usually sold green but get yellow when ripe. Tomatillos are the main ingredients in salsa verde.

Tomato Lycopersicon esculentum

The tomato is one of the most commonly used foods and is grown worldwide (Figure 5-131). Tomatoes are eaten raw in salads and cooked into a host of products such as ketchup, tomato paste, gazpacho, pizza, spaghetti sauce, purée, juice, and soup bases.

The trade delivers tomatoes graded in precise shapes and sizes indicated by the number of tomato layers in a variety of packs. These tomatoes are cultivated for shipping and are relatively flavorless but sturdy and can be cut on the electric meat-slicing machine. Local tomatoes harvested when mature have much better flavor. Beefsteak tomatoes are huge and used for slicing. Yellow tomatoes have come back on the market. Vine-ripe tomatoes are shipped still attached to the stems but are not necessarily riper than others. Cherry and grape tomatoes are small tomatoes and are served whole in salads. Plum or Roma tomatoes are egg-shaped with solid flesh and often used for cooking.

Large tomatoes should be cut with a serrated knife because the skin is tough.

Figure 5-130 Tomatillos.

CHEF'S TIP
Never store tomatoes in the refrigerator. The decrease in temperature speeds up flavor loss and changes the texture to a more starchy and grainy product. Tomatoes also give off ethylene gas and should never be stored near green leafy vegetables because the gas will speed up the ripening process, causing the greens to decay quicker.

Figure 5-131 Tomatoes.

PODS, SEEDS, AND LEGUMES

This category of vegetables includes corn, beans, peas, and lentils. **Legume,** also known as a pulse, is a generic, catchall name for the pods or seeds of starchy, leguminous plants. Legumes are usually sold dried and require lengthy cooking. Many operations avoid the cooking process and purchase legumes for salad fully cooked and canned.

Corn *Zea mays*

The kernel, or seed, of sweet corn is a popular starchy vegetable (Figure 5-132). There are varieties of sweet corn ranging from sweet to sweeter to super sweet. The kernels can be yellow or white (known as Shoe Peg) or a combination of yellow and white. Corn is used in salads, salsas, and as a side dish or main entrée ingredient. The kernels can be dried and ground into meal and used to make baked goods, including corn bread. Many operations purchase canned corn, although frozen corn and fresh corn on the cob are also available.

Figure 5-132 Corn.

Dried Peas, Lentils, and Beans

Most peas contain all the essential amino acids, and when combined with cereals or grains, they create a complete protein, which is the foundation of a balanced diet. Dried peas, like other legumes, are low in fat and high in protein and fiber. Most dried beans and peas need to be soaked prior to cooking. The exceptions are lentils and split peas, which don't require soaking.

Follow these simple directions for cooking beans:

Look through the beans/peas and discard the stems, stones, and broken beans. Rinse the beans/peas to clean. Use one of the following soak methods:

Overnight Soak Method
1. Place beans/peas in a large kettle or saucepot and cover with cold water.
2. Let soak in the water overnight (8 to 12 hours).
3. Prior to cooking, drain the beans and cover with cold water. Have at least 2 inches of water above the beans/peas. Bring to a boil. Reduce heat to low, cover, and simmer. (Don't continue to boil or the beans/peas may burst.) Stir occasionally and make sure that there is still ample water. Add more boiling water if needed.
4. The length of cooking time required will depend on the type of bean or pea. Cook until they are fork tender.
5. Drain cooked beans/peas.

Quick-Soak Method
1. Place beans/peas in a large kettle or saucepot and cover with cold water.
2. Bring pot to a boil and boil for 2 minutes.
3. Remove from the heat, cover, and let stand for at least 1 hour before continuing.
4. Drain the beans/peas and cover with cold water. Have at least 2 inches of water above the beans/peas. Bring to a boil. Reduce heat to low, cover, and simmer. (Don't continue to boil or the beans/peas may burst.) Gently stir occasionally and make sure that there is still ample water. Add more boiling water if needed.
5. The length of cooking time required will depend on the type of bean or pea. Cook until they are fork tender. Drain.

LEARNING ACTIVITY 5-5

Measure 2 cups of beans. Prepare 1 cup with the Overnight Soak Method and another with the Quick-Soak Method. Once the beans have soaked, go ahead and cook them as described above. Compare the two batches. Is there any difference in the taste or texture?

Figure 5-133 Black-eyed peas.

Figure 5-134 Chick peas.

Figure 5-135 Pigeon peas.

Figure 5-136 Split peas.

Dried Peas

Dried peas are dried in the fields by the late summer sun. Some varieties are split, which eliminates the need for soaking. Dried peas are packed with protein and fiber, complex carbohydrates, iron, and folic acid. They have little or no fat or cholesterol.

Black-Eyed Peas *Vigna unguiculata*

Black-eyed peas are a popular ingredient in Southern cooking (Figure 5-133). They are traditionally eaten on New Year's Day. Black-eyed peas, also known as cowpeas, get their name from the dark "eye-like" markings found on each white pea. Like split peas, black-eyed peas do not require soaking.

Chick Peas *Cicer arietinum*

Chick peas, also known as garbanzo beans, are a popular ingredient with Mediterranean and Middle Eastern cuisine (Figure 5-134). They have a firm texture and a nutty flavor. Chick peas are the key ingredient in hummus, falafel, and minestrone soup. Chick peas are also used in casseroles and salads and are often found in salad bars. The dried peas take a long time to soak, so many foodservice operators prefer to use canned product.

Pigeon Peas *Cajanus cajan*

Pigeon peas are associated with Caribbean, Indian, and Southern dishes (Figure 5-135). They are also known as the goongoo or Congo pea. Pigeon peas look like black-eyed peas without the "eye." They have a strong flavor compared with most other peas.

Split Peas *Pisum sativum*

Split peas are dried peas that have been split in two (Figure 5-136). They cook quickly compared to other dried peas and beans. Split peas are available in green and yellow varieties and are primarily used to make soup. The British use the yellow variety to make pease pudding.

Lentils *Lens culinaris*

Lentils provide all the health benefits of other legumes, but they are cooked much faster and don't require soaking (Figure 5-137). Lentils will get soft and mushy if overcooked. They come in a variety of colors, including the standard brownish green, red, yellow, and the masoor or salmon-colored lentil. French green lentils are especially good in salads because they remain firm after cooking and have a rich flavor. Black and shiny Beluga lentils are named after the high-quality beluga caviar, which they resemble. Lentils are good in salads and soups.

Dried Beans

Dried beans are inexpensive and nutritious. Because they need soaking, they aren't convenient for last-minute preparation. Most varieties of dried beans should be soaked a minimum of 6 hours and preferably overnight for 8 to 12 hours. Use either the Overnight Soak Method or the Quick-Soak Method as described under the header Dried Peas, Lentils, and Beans.

Butter Beans *Phaseolus lunatus*

Butter beans are small varieties of the lima bean (Figure 5-138). They are available dried as well as fresh, frozen, or canned. Butter beans taste creamier and are less starchy than the lima bean. Dried butter beans should be soaked at least 6 hours, but overnight is preferred. This type of bean mixes well with other vegetables for soups, stews, or casseroles.

Figure 5-137 Lentils.

Black Beans *Phaseolus vulgaris*

Black beans are popular in Latin America. They are sometimes called turtle beans or frijoles negros (Figure 5-139). Black beans are available dried or canned. They are used in soups, stews, and chilies as well as in salads, and instead of the traditional refried beans.

Canellini Bean *Phaseolus vulgaris*

The creamy white canellini bean is a popular bean in Italy. It is fairly large, about the same size as a kidney bean (Figure 5-140). Because it maintains its shape well when cooked and has a mellow flavor, the canellini bean is excellent in many dishes and can be used interchangeably with other white beans in many recipes.

Figure 5-138 Butter beans.

Figure 5-139 Black beans.

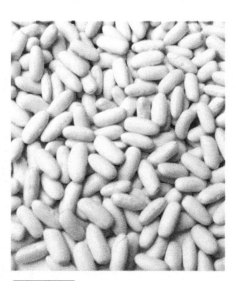

Figure 5-140 Canellini beans.

Figure 5-141 Kidney beans.

Figure 5-142 Mung beans.

Great Northern Bean

Great Northern beans are similar to the Navy bean, but larger; see description under Navy Bean.

Kidney Bean *Phaseolus vulgaris L.*

Kidney beans are shaped like kidneys, which obviously contributed to their name (Figure 5-141). Kidney beans are available both dried and canned. They are used in three-bean salads, soups, stews, chili, and vegetable dishes. They are solid and stay intact when cooked. Kidney beans take on the flavors of the foods they are cooked with, which makes them an important ingredient in many stews and as a blend in baked beans.

Mung Bean *Phaseolus aureus Roxb.*

The mung bean is a small, round, bright green bean (Figure 5-142) that can be cooked whole or split. Mung beans resemble split peas in looks and taste a lot like lentils. They are used in many Indian and Filipino dishes and are combined with rice. Mung beans are the base for a porridge drink that is popular in Malaysia. They also work well in soups or ground into flour for breads. Because they have a thin shell, they don't require the pre-soaking that most other beans must have.

Figure 5-143 Navy beans.

Navy Bean *Phaseolus vulgaris*

The navy bean is the smallest of the white beans and is sometimes called a Boston bean or white pea bean (Figure 5-143). Navy beans have a creamy taste. These dried or canned beans are used to make soups such as navy bean, in salads or chili, and as a key ingredient in traditional baked beans.

Pinto Bean

"Pinto bean" in Spanish means painted bean, referring to its spotted skin (Figure 5-144). Once cooked, the pinto bean loses its spots and is light pink in color. Pinto beans are associated with Mexican and Southwestern cooking. They are eaten whole, mashed, or refried and are the main ingredient in burritos. Pinto beans are used in soups, salads, main dishes, and breads.

Figure 5-144 Pinto beans.

Figure 5-145 Red beans.

Red Bean

Red beans and rice is a quintessential New Orleans dish that is traditionally served on Mondays. While kidney beans are sometimes used, it is the smaller, rounder, red bean that is most often associated with this Creole favorite (Figure 5-145). In the Southwest, red beans are sometimes used in place of pinto beans for refried beans or chili.

Soybean *Glycine max*

The soybean is a versatile bean used to make tofu, soy sauce, soy flour, soybean oil, and soy sauce (Figure 5-146). Fresh soybeans, called edamame, are eaten steamed. They are usually served in the pod, and the beans are popped out of the shell and eaten. Tofu is made from coagulated soymilk that is pressed into blocks.

FRESH BEANS AND PEAS

Broad Bean *Vicia faba L.*

Broad beans are usually eaten when they are young and tender (Figure 5-147). In Asia they are fried and eaten as a popular crunchy snack.

Green Bean *P. vulgaris*

The green bean is also known as the string bean or snap bean (Figure 5-148). Fresh beans should snap when broken in half. This type of bean is eaten within the pod. Fresh green

Figure 5-146 Soybeans.

Figure 5-147 Broad beans.

Figure 5-148 Green beans.

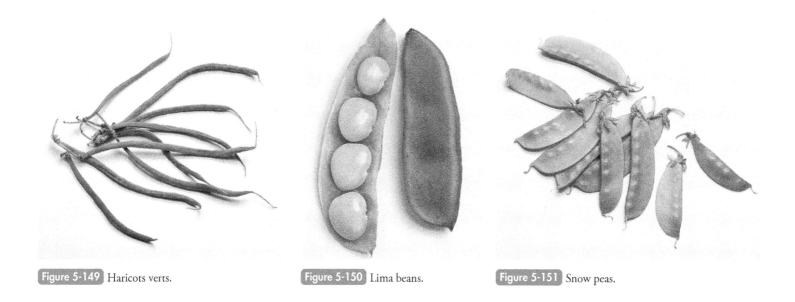

Figure 5-149 Haricots verts.

Figure 5-150 Lima beans.

Figure 5-151 Snow peas.

beans add color and variety to meals. Cook green beans just until they are tender. Be careful not to overcook them or they will become mushy and lose their bright green color.

Haricots Verts *Phaseolus vulgaris*

Haricots verts is French and refers to very slender string beans (Figure 5-149). They are expensive and often used for decorations rather than as salad. The spelling of this vegetable confuses many menu writers. Both words are plural because always more than one bean is served.

Lima Bean *Phaseolus lunatus*

Lima beans are available fresh, dried, frozen, and canned (Figure 5-150). Fresh lima beans can be difficult to find. Sometimes called "butter beans" because of their starchy yet buttery texture, lima beans have a delicate flavor that complements a wide variety of dishes.

Snow Pea *Pisum sativum var. macrocarpon*

Snow peas, eaten whole, are popular in Chinese cooking and are sometimes used in salads (Figure 5-151). They are very delicate, overcook easily, and lose color quickly when blended with dressing.

Wax Beans *Phaseolus vulgaris*

Wax beans are just one of the 2,500 varieties of beans (Figure 5-152). They are yellow and not affected by acidity. Many operations use wax beans in salads or in salad blends.

Figure 5-152 Wax beans.

PRODUCE, LEGUMES, AND GRAINS **153**

EDIBLE PODS

Okra *Abelmoschus esculentus*

Okra is related to the hollyhock or hibiscus (Figure 5-153). Its immature pods are used in soups and stews, or they can be used fried or
boiled as a side dish. It is a very popular ingredient in Southern dishes
such as gumbo. Okra contains a sticky substance that naturally thickens any broth. It can be eaten raw or in salads, and it can be pickled.

Sugar Snap *Sativum var. macrocarpon*

Sugar snap peas, also called sugar peas (Figure 5-154), are a cross between the English pea and the snow pea. They resemble snow peas
in looks and taste but are a little more robust in flavor. They can be
served raw or cooked briefly for stir fry and offer color, texture, and
a pleasant, sweet taste to salads or entrées. Some varieties of sugar
snap peas have a tough string that should be removed. To do so, simply locate the string at the tip of the pod and pull down to the bottom of the pod.

Snow Peas *Pisum sativum L.*

Snow peas are sometimes called Chinese pea pods (Figure 5-155).
Young peas are eaten whole as the pod is very tender. Fibers run
along the edges of pods, and the fiber should be removed before eating larger pods. Snow peas are delicious in salads or stir fries.

FUNGI

Mushrooms

There are many mushroom varieties available, but only the common white mushrooms, also called champignons, a generic French
term, are edible raw. Mushrooms will oxidize when cut and will soak
up water. They should always be cut at the last moment and never
left sitting in water.

Buttons *Agaricus bisporus*

Buttons are the most common type of mushroom cultivated
and used in cooking (Figure 5-156). They are white in color
and harvested before the caps open and the gills are exposed.
Button mushrooms are readily available fresh and canned.
They are popular raw in salads or cooked and used as a topping
for pizza, as stuffed mushrooms, or as an ingredient in many
main dish recipes.

Chanterelles *Cantharellus cibarius*

Attempts to commercially cultivate chanterelles have been futile.
They are only found in the wild, making them one of the world's
most beloved wild mushrooms (Figure 5-157). They are known
to cause some gastric discomfort when undercooked—it is important to cook them for at least 15 minutes. Chanterelles enhance soups, stews, and other main course entrées. They make a
nice side dish to chicken, pork, or beef dishes when sautéed in
olive oil or butter with onion and garlic.

Figure 5-153 Okra.

Figure 5-154 Sugar snap.

Figure 5-155 Snow peas.

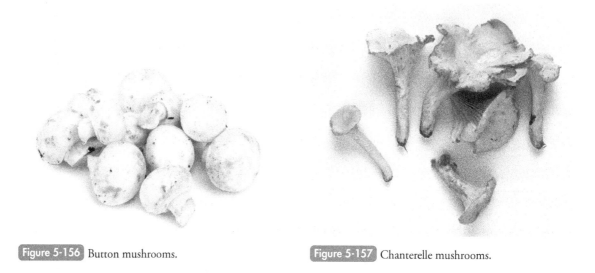

Figure 5-156 Button mushrooms.

Figure 5-157 Chanterelle mushrooms.

Crimini *A. bisporus*

Crimini mushrooms are very similar to button mushrooms. The only difference is that they are brown in color. Crimini are actually immature Portobello mushrooms. Criminis are harvested before reaching maturity and before the cap opens and the gills are exposed (Figure 5-158).

Shiitake *Lentinula edodes*

Fresh shiitakes are available throughout the United States (Figure 5-159). Dried shiitakes are also readily available and must be rehydrated before use. Many prefer the dried product as the drying process concentrates the flavor. Because the stem is tough, most chefs use only the tender cap. Shiitakes are an important ingredient in miso soup, stir fries, and other main dishes.

Figure 5-158 Crimini mushrooms.

Figure 5-159 Shiitake mushrooms.

Figure 5-160 Oyster mushrooms.

Figure 5-161 Enoki mushrooms.

Figure 5-162 Portabello mushrooms.

Oyster *Pleurotus ostreatus*

Oyster mushrooms are larger than button mushrooms and have a characteristic gray-brown cap (Figure 5-160). These mushrooms have a subtle oyster-like flavor.

Enoki *Flammulina velutipes*

Enokis are small, delicate mushrooms (Figure 5-161). They have a yellowish cap and a thin, tall stalk (compared with most other mushrooms). This type of mushroom is often associated with Japanese cuisine.

Portabello *Agaricus bisporus*

The portabello is a large version of the crimini mushroom (Figure 5-162). Like the crimini, portabellos are brown in color. Portabellos are left to grow large and are not harvested until the cap has opened and the brown gills are exposed.

Porcini *Boletus edulis*

Porcini mushrooms are delicious raw or cooked (Figure 5-163). They have a meaty, nutty, creamy taste. The word "porcini" means "piglet" in Italian, and porcini mushrooms are considered the king of the mushrooms in that part of the world. Many Americans have only tasted dried porcinis— fresh ones are hard to find. Both dried and fresh porcinis can be used in pastas, sauces, soups, and many other dishes.

Figure 5-163 Porcini mushrooms.

Morel *Morchella deliciosa*

Morels are highly prized (Figure 5-164). They are flavorful and add a unique, nutlike taste to any recipe. Unlike other mushrooms, morels are brittle and will crumble easily. They are known to cause gastric problems if eaten raw. Morels are particularly useful in sauces, soups, and stews.

> **CHEF'S TIP**
> Mushrooms can be hard to digest. Roast them quickly in a very hot sauté pan to make them easier to digest.

Truffle *Black: Tuber melanosporum; White: Tuber magnatum pico*

Truffles are a fungus growing underground along the roots of certain hardwood trees (Figure 5-165). Truffles are not yet successfully cultivated, and trained animals are needed to find them by smell because they cannot be seen. White or ivory-colored truffles are harvested in northern Italy and Croatia from October to December. Black truffles are harvested from November through December in Southern France around the town Perigourd. Truffles are the most prized and expensive mushrooms. Prices range up to $1,000 a pound. Many truffle products have come on the market, such as canned truffles in different sizes and shapes and

Figure 5-164 Morel mushrooms.

Figure 5-165 Truffles.

even truffle oil, truffle honey, and truffle paste. There are many varieties of truffles, many of them not edible and others of poor quality. Summer truffles are less aromatic and much less expensive.

> **CHEF'S TIP**
> *Not all flowers are edible. Only serve flowers purchased from reputable sources or from farmers who grow them solely for culinary applications—free of pesticides and chemicals.*

EDIBLE FLOWERS

It has become chic in recent years to use edible flowers in recipes and as a garnish, but it's certainly not a new tradition. Flowers have been used in cooking since the Roman era and have garnered particular favor in Middle Eastern, Indian, and Chinese cuisines. They add flavor, color, fragrance, and a "touch of class" to many dishes. In general, most flowers taste like the leaf, but spicier. Edible flowers can be added to green salads and used as an ingredient in flavored oils or jelly. Some varieties add a sweet flavor to desserts or as an ingredient in stir fries. Flowers can also be used along with other ingredients to make teas, wines, marinades, and salad dressings. A number of popular teas or wines are made with the blossoms of edible tea. Crystallized blossoms are used to decorate cakes, fine desserts, and candies.

When using flowers as a garnish, be careful to use varieties that complement the dish you are preparing. We will introduce students to a few of the basic blossoms that are used in professional kitchens.

Apple Blossom *Malus spp.*

Apple blossoms have a sweet, light, delicate taste (Figure 5-166). They are perfect with any fruit-based dessert and can be candied and used as a garnish.

Borage *Borago officinalis*

Borage blossoms are blue and star shaped (Figure 5-167). They taste like cucumbers and can be used in salads or as garnishes. They are beautiful and refreshing when floated in drinks. Use candied blossoms to decorate cakes and pastries.

Figure 5-166 Apple blossoms.

Borage.

Figure 5-168 Chive blossoms.

Chive Blossoms *Allium schoeonoprasum*

It's no surprise that chive blossoms have an onion flavor (Figure 5-168). They can be quite overwhelming and should be used sparingly.

Chrysanthemum *Chrysanthemum spp.*

Chrysanthemum petals are used in salads and stir fries to add a slight peppery flavor (Figure 5-169). Blanch the petals first before using in salads.

Citrus Blossoms

Citrus blossoms from lemon, lime, orange, grapefruit, and kumquat can be eaten sparingly (Figure 5-170). They have a strong citrus flavor and aroma.

Dandelions *Taraxacum officinale*

The sunny dandelion closes once it is picked (Figure 5-171). Young, tender blossoms are preferred and taste like honey. Older flowers are bitter. Dandelion blossoms are used fresh in salads, sprinkled on top of main dishes, or steamed as a side dish.

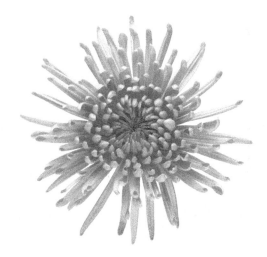

Figure 5-169 Chrysanthemum.

Figure 5-170 Citrus blossoms.

Figure 5-171 Dandelions.

Figure 5-172 Geranium.

Figure 5-173 Hibiscus.

Geranium Pelargonium spp.

Certain types of geraniums smell like familiar fruits or spices (Figure 5-172). Generally, the taste will match the smell, so a lemon-scented geranium will have a citrus flavor. Geranium petals can be sprinkled over desserts or in punches to add a hint of flavor and a splash of color.

Hibiscus Hibiscus rosasinensi

Hibiscus blossoms can add a touch of drama to any salad or as a garnish for desserts (Figure 5-173). This flower has a mildly citrus flavor.

Lavender Lavendula spp.

Lavender blossoms impart a unique fragrance and flavor to sorbets, ice creams, jellies, grilled meats, sauces, stews, as well as bakery goods (Figure 5-174).

Nasturtiums Tropaeolum majus

Nasturtium is a pretty annual summer plant that has sharp-tasting peppery blossoms and edible leaves (Figure 5-175). They can add a little pizzazz and novelty to any green salad blend.

Figure 5-174 Lavender.

Figure 5-175 Nasturtiums.

Figure 5-176 Pansies.

Figure 5-177 Roses.

Figure 5-178 Safflower.

Pansy *Viola x wittrockiana*

Pansies have a minty, vegetal flavor. They come in a variety of colors, and can add the right punch of color to a host of dishes (Figure 5-176). Use pansies in soups, salads, and desserts or as a garnish for plated pastries or on cakes.

Rose *Rosa spp.*

Each rose variety has a unique taste (Figure 5-177). Some have a spicy flavor; others taste fruity or minty. The flavor intensifies with the darker blossoms. Miniature roses are used whole to garnish desserts, and rose petals can be used in salads and desserts. They make a pretty addition to any punch bowl.

Safflower *Carthamus lanatus*

Safflower is known as Mexican saffron, and, like true saffron, cooked safflowers will turn any dish yellow (Figure 5-178). The flavor is subtle.

Figure 5-179 Sage blossom.

Sage Blossom *Salvia elegans*

The blossoms of the sage plant leaves offer a hint of pineapple (Figure 5-179). Pineapple sage blossoms are deep red and offer a tangy, citrus-mint flavor. They work well with creamy leek or potato soup. Sprinkle them on salads and in tea for a flavorful and eye-catching garnish. The fresh leaves have a distinctly pineapple taste.

Squash Blossom *Curcubita pepo*

Squash blossom can be used fresh as a garnish for many savory dishes (Figure 5-180). They can be stuffed with various fillings and fried. They provide a mild squash flavor.

Tuberous Begonia *Begonia tuberhybrida*

Tuberous begonias make quite a statement in any salad (Figure 5-181). These flowers provide lemonade tanginess, and their brilliant red and magenta blossoms will surely add a splash of color.

Violet *Viola odorata*

Violets are sweet and can be used to enhance fruit salads (Figure 5-182). They are often used as an accoutrement on cakes or to top an individual serving of sorbet or ice cream. Violets can be candied or crystallized.

Figure 5-180 Squash blossoms.

Figure 5-181 Begonias.

Figure 5-182 Violets.

Figure 5-183 Barley.

>> Grains

There are many types of grains, but for our purpose we will examine a few of the basic grains used in cold kitchen applications, primarily as ingredients in salads.

Barley *Hordeum Vulgare*

Barley has a nutlike flavor (Figure 5-183). Its high gluten content makes it chewy, similar to the texture of pasta. Barley resembles wheat berries in appearance but is lighter in color. It can replace wheat berries or other grains in most salad recipes.

Millet *Pennisetum glaucum*

Millet is a tasty grain with a nutty flavor and texture (Figure 5-184). It can be sprouted or cooked and used as a salad ingredient.

Quinoa *Chenopodium quinoa*

Unlike most other grains, quinoa contains all the essential amino acids, making it a complete protein (Figure 5-185). The United Nations has named quinoa as a super crop due to its high protein content. It has a similar taste and texture to rice and couscous and can therefore be used in their place in most salad recipes.

Figure 5-184 Millet.

Figure 5-185 Quinoa.

Figure 5-186 Brown and white rice.

Rice

There are over 40,000 varieties of rice (Figure 5-186). We will examine the types most commonly used in salads. Short-grained rice is typically not used in salads.

Brown Rice (Medium and Long Grain)

Brown rice has a firm texture. It is chewy and has a nut-like taste. Brown rice is golden brown when cooked.

White Rice (Medium and Long Grain)

White rice has a bland flavor but will blend with the flavors of the salad. Long grain is drier than the shorter varieties. Some varieties such as Basmati and Jasmine are aromatic.

Wheat Bulgur

Bulgur is a form of wheat that has been cleaned, parboiled, and dried (Figure 5-187). Because it was already cooked, it can be prepared quickly. It has a nut-like flavor and can be used in place of rice or alongside rice to add a variety of color and texture to any salad.

Figure 5-187 Wheat bulgur.

Wild Rice *Zizania palustris*

Wild rice really isn't rice but a grass seed (Figure 5-188). It has a distinctive, nutty flavor and texture. The dark brown kernels add visual variety to salads.

>> Pastas

Pasta salads are the perfect accompaniment to all kinds of meals and can also be used as a stand-alone meal (Figure 5-189). Pastas are versatile and will blend with the flavors of salad ingredients, making them the perfect base for salads. Pasta lends itself to experimentation, and chefs enjoy creating their own signature pasta salads by simply varying the shape and type of pasta.

There are more than 600 pasta shapes produced worldwide, but not all are used in the cold kitchen. The National Pasta Association recommends the following pastas for salads:

Figure 5-188 Wild rice.

- Rotini, also called spirals or twists. The twisted shape holds bits of meat, cheese, and vegetables, so it works well with salads.
- Angel hair and capellini are thin strands that can be used in salads that have a thin, delicate dressing.

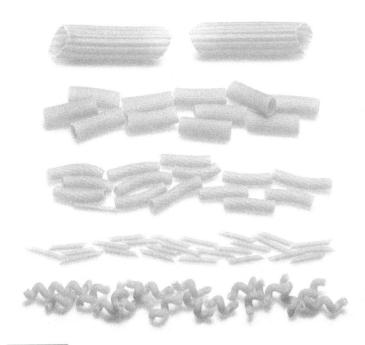

Figure 5-189 There are countless types of pastas that can be used in cold kitchen applications.

CHEF'S TIP

Be careful not to overcook pasta for pasta salads. As the salad marinates in the sauce, it will fall apart or become soft and mushy if it has been overcooked. Cook until al dente and then drain in cold water to stop the cooking process. Pasta has the ability to blend with other ingredients, so it's better if the salad has time to sit before serving.

- Couscous is a tiny type of pasta that tastes and looks like a grain. In Northern Africa it is considered a staple. Couscous is used as a side dish but can also be used in salads.
- Fettuccine can be broken in half and used for any pasta salad recipe.
- Penne and mostaccioli are tubular pastas that go well with cream- or mayonnaise-based salads.
- Wagon wheel pasta makes interesting salads that will especially appeal to children.
- Radiatore is a ruffled, ridged shape that can add an elegant touch to any salad.
- Ziti is a medium-sized, tubular pasta shape that is perfect with salads containing chunky ingredients.
- Shells are often associated with cold salads. Sauces can easily cling to the cupping shape.
- Macaroni is the most common type of pasta used in salads. The size is just right and the shape makes it easy to eat.
- Linguine is a great shape that is a good choice for salads.
- Bowtie or farfalle cooked al dente and mixed with a variety of vegetables makes for a memorable pasta salad.
- Ancini di pepe looks like grains of rice. It is actually a tiny pasta and is used in both sweet and savory pasta salad recipes.

There are also a number of flavored pastas such as spinach (green), tomato (red), or squid ink (black). The beautiful, vibrant colors and added flavor will add a unique touch to any salad.

LEARNING ACTIVITY 5-6

Select a basic pasta salad recipe, something from your files or one that is found in Unit 14. Make it according to directions. Then make a second batch, using flavored pasta. Try choosing a different shape of pasta and see if that affects the taste. Rate each salad for visual appeal, taste, and texture. Which pasta did you prefer?

>> Summary

Produce is generally farm-produced goods. Fruits are generally defined as the edible part of the plant developed from a flower. A vegetable is the nonwoody part of the plant that is eaten, generally with the main course rather than as part of the dessert. There are some fruits that are used in vegetable applications.

Some fruits are affected by the condition known as oxidation. Enzymes from the flesh of a fruit turn brown when exposed to oxygen, making it undesirable to eat. There are a number of ways to reduce or eliminate oxidation, including making a solution with ascorbic acid.

The use of edible flowers as a garnish or ingredient has become popular in the past few years, but this is not a new tradition. Flowers can add flavor, color, and fragrance to many dishes.

There are many fruits, vegetables, grains, and pastas that are used regularly in the cold kitchen. Budding chefs must take the time to become familiar with the most common ingredients.

>> Review Questions

SHORT ANSWER

1. Describe the difference between a fruit and a vegetable.
2. Is a tomato considered a fruit or a vegetable?
3. Identify the following mushrooms. Write the mushroom's name next to the photograph.

    a. _____

    b. _____

    c. _____

d. _____

e. _____

MATCHING

Match the ingredient to its description.

4. peach
5. squash
6. apple
7. daikon
8. cauliflower
9. banana
10. escarole
11. kumquat
12. leek
13. loquat
14. currant
15. Santa Claus
16. Jerusalem artichoke
17. chick pea
18. asparagus

a. allium
b. berry
c. exotic fruit
d. brassica
e. plant with edible stem
f. melon
g. citrus fruit
h. pomes
i. root vegetable
j. drupe
k. cucurbitaceae
l. tropical fruit
m. legume
n. tuber
o. lettuce

UNIT

6

Proteins in the Cold Kitchen

>> **Learning Objectives**

After you have finished reading this unit, you should be able to:

- Discuss the history of dairy and cheese products.
- Identify an assortment of dairy and cheese products commonly used in the cold kitchen.
- Describe quality in cheese products.
- Demonstrate how to make a variety of fresh cheeses.
- Describe how cheeses are used in the cold kitchen.
- Discuss HACCP in regard to cheese and dairy products.
- Explain how to serve cheese for banquet service.
- Identify an assortment of seafood, poultry, game, and meats commonly used in the cold kitchen.
- Describe quality in seafood, poultry, game, and meat.
- Explain the uses of seafood, poultry, game, and meat used in the cold kitchen.
- Discuss the importance of serving sustainable and renewable sources of seafood, poultry, game, and meat.
- Discuss HACCP in regards to seafood, poultry, game, and meat.
- Demonstrate how to carve large pieces of meat, poultry, and fish for banquet service.

>> **Key Terms**

blue-veined cheese	flatfish	primal cuts	subprimal cuts
casein	fresh cheese	ratite	waxed-rind cheese
cephalopod	hard cheese	rennet	whey
crustaceans	magret	round fish	
depurations	mollusk	semi-soft cheese	
fabricated cuts	pasta filata	soft-ripened cheese	

Proteins are among the most important, and most expensive, ingredients found in the cold kitchen. Proteins are what most individuals crave. They nourish us and sustain us; and while many plant-based proteins can supply all the required nutrients, most of us get our proteins from dairy and flesh-based sources. Protein is also found in grains, legumes, and nuts.

Milk- or dairy-based products such as kefir, quark, yogurt, and cheese can be found in nearly every corner of the world today and are just a few of the hundreds of products that a cold kitchen chef is able to use.

In the following pages, we will learn about the many dairy products used in the cold kitchen, including cheese based on texture, processing methods, and, in some cases, locations. We will learn to make some of these cheeses and evaluate them for taste and texture.

We will also explore the most popular seafood, poultry, and meat proteins used in the cold kitchen. Students should learn how to identify and purchase these items, how to use them, and how to properly store each type of shellfish, finfish, poultry, and red meat protein.

The cold kitchen is the last stop for usable food scraps and leftovers. In large hotels or catering venues, as an example, the cold kitchen chef is the magician who can take the trim and usable scraps from fish, poultry, and meat and can turn these edible products into delicious mousselines and fillings. Small chunks of cheese can be turned into cheese logs or balls used for catering or entertaining. When chefs learn how to use the otherwise discarded but very edible and usable pieces of fin, fowl, or flesh, the cold kitchen can become a profit center.

>> Dairy Products

Dairy products are foods that are derived from milk. These products include milk itself, buttermilk, cream, sour cream, and cheese, as well as frozen treats such as ice cream, custard, and yogurt (Figure 6-1).

We experience our first taste of protein in the form of mother's milk. Many of us have a taste for milk, and unlike other mammals, some of us never outgrow the desire for dairy products. Unfortunately, many humans lose the ability to digest the lactose, or milk sugar, at around 3 or 4 years of age and become lactose intolerant. Others have evolved digestive systems that are able to tolerate milk and dairy-based foods.

Somewhere in the distant past, the discovery was made that when milk was soured or cultured, it changed into a more digestible and portable source of protein-based food. While the science was unknown, the techniques were not, and through the ages, thousands of dairy-based products came to be.

Dairy products are high in protein and calcium and offer a host of vitamins and minerals. The fat content depends on the product.

Milk is mostly water, containing between 80 percent for sheep milk and up to 87 percent water and trace minerals for cow's milk. The remainder is small amounts of **casein,** which is milk protein, albumin, butterfat, naturally occurring salts, and lactose (milk sugar). In the culturing process, the dairy protein is exposed to some type of acidification from lactic, acetic, citric, and/or tartaric acids, causing the proteins to coalesce and clump up into soft curds. These acids come by way of the naturally occurring friendly bacteria such as a lactic acid-producing organism or by the addition of acidic products such as cider vinegar, lemon juice, or tartaric acid. When these curds are cut, the watery liquid called **whey** separates out of the curds, carrying the residual sugars that are released into the whey (Figure 6-2). By heating these curds, more whey is released, and the curds become firmer. These resulting curds are the tasty and digestible food we call cheese. Other cultured products such as sour cream, sour milk, butter-

Figure 6-1 A host of foodstuffs are made from milk.

milk, crème fraiche, kefir, and yogurt are made in similar ways, with friendly bacterial cultures to reduce and break down the lactose via bacterial action or by acidification using tartaric acid, citric acid in the form of lemon juice, acetic acid in the form of vinegar, and other acidic liquids. Some of these wonderful dairy products are easily duplicated in the cold kitchen.

Our focus in this segment is on the cultured, concentrated dairy product that we call cheese. This is a nutrient-dense form of milk product that is one of the major players in any cold kitchen.

CHEESE DEFINED

Cheese is a concentrated food product made from fresh milk that is separated into curds and the liquid substance called "whey." The curds are mostly solid milk protein called "casein," as well as small quantities of butterfat. The whey consists of water, slight amounts of sugar, and residual liquid protein. It takes 1 gallon of milk to produce approximately 1 pound of cheese. The type of milk used has a huge impact on the end product. The amount of fat, the type of milk (such as cow, sheep, or goat milk), and the feed that the animal ate all influence the flavors and aromas of the cheese. Milking time is also a factor. Milk that is collected in the evening is richer in butterfat than morning milk. Milk that is collected in the summer months has a sweeter flavor than milk that is collected in the winter when the cows are on silage versus fresh grass. All of these differences are what make up the hundreds of complex flavor notes found in a variety of cheeses.

CHEESE HISTORY

Cheese making has a history that is over 9,000 years old, dating back to the domestication of mammals. More recent records show that Sumerian herders stored milk in the dried stomach sacks of sheep as far back as 4,000 years ago. The enzyme rennin was present inside the stomach lining in sufficient quantities to curdle the milk. While the Sumarians didn't understand the science behind

Figure 6-2 A cheese maker scoops out a handful of whey during the cheese-making process.

this, they enjoyed the favorable and flavorful results. The Romans discovered that certain flowers and vegetables such as artichokes, thistles, and cardoons or the bark of certain fruit trees would cause milk to separate into curds and thus into cheese (Figure 6-3). Cheese (or a cheese-like substance) was also found in the tombs of the pharaohs dating from as far back as 2200 B.C.

The Greeks wrote about goat cheese, and Homer mentioned it in the *Odyssey* (Figure 6-4). During the Middle Ages, cheese making was done on a larger scale in the monasteries and

Figure 6-3 This Roman artifact is a terra cotta sculpture of a mule laden down with small packages of cheese.

Figure 6-4 A sixth century B.C. Archaic Greek sculpture depicts a seated man grating cheese. *Dagli Orti/Picture Desk, Inc./Kobal Collection*

convents. The processes have not changed throughout the years with many of these same monasteries still producing cheese with centuries-old formulas. Up until the mid-eighteenth century, cheese making was a cottage industry. In areas where there were sufficient goats, sheep, or dairy cattle available, cheese was commonly produced. In Switzerland and elsewhere in Europe, cheese making became industrialized, as the science behind the cheese-making process became known. Large-scale cheese production did not occur until the Industrial Age, approximately mid- to late eighteenth century.

The first known American cheese factory was established in Rome, New York, in 1851. This factory's cheese was so popular that hundreds of other cheese-making facilities opened in the surrounding areas. With the advent of scientific methods, controlled cultures, and mass production, cheese making spread throughout the United States. Many Europeans migrated to the United States during this period of time and brought their cheese-making formulas and methods with them. The Dutch and Scandinavians settled in Wisconsin, finding lush, green pastures for their dairy cattle. Wisconsin became known as a leading cheese-making state. Oregon, Iowa, and California, along with New York and Vermont, also became leading cheese producers.

As with many other foods that became mass produced, there has been a recent rebirth of the slower methods of cheese making. Artisan cheese making is becoming a cottage industry today. In any cheese shop, farmers' market, or grocery store, the standard yellow slice is being replaced by dozens of new and taste-tempting varieties that are locally farmed and produced.

Cheese is a complex, living food. It contains harmless living bacteria. During aging, it constantly changes and evolves in textures, aromas, and flavors.

To make cheese requires a series of steps that transform the liquid milk into a solid, concentrated form. In the United States, milk must first be rendered safe for human consumption by removing harmful bacteria through pasteurizing or heat treating.

The milk is then acidified, either by souring it with bacterial cultures that turn some of the lactose into lactic acid or by using an enzyme such as rennet that contains rennin to trigger the clumping up or curdling action. The rennin removes the little bumper-like tags from each protein molecule, thus allowing the molecules to attach to each other and clump up. In the United States, most of today's modern cheese making relies on an enzyme that is genetically engineered. The pure version of calves' enzyme is called "chymosin," and it is engineered to team up with a bacterium, yeast, or mold. In Europe, the traditional method of using calf stomach is still the norm, whereas only a quarter of the cheese produced in the United States is made from the traditional animal-based rennet. **Rennet** comes from the inner lining of the fourth, or true, stomach of milk-fed calves.

Either method raises the acid content and lowers the pH. This, in turn, causes the casein to clump up and precipitate out of the solution to form curds. What follows during the cheese-making process is the cutting of the curds, heating or cooking the curds to speed up the process, salting, and adding cultures for flavor and additional dehydration. The curds are then drained to remove the whey and pressed to release more water and whey. The cheese curds are pressed into rounds, blocks, or other shapes. At this stage, depending upon the type of cheese, it can be eaten fresh or stored in temperature- and humidity-controlled environments to be aged. Cheeses can be brined, salted, buried in ashes, the rind washed in friendly bacteria, injected with cultures, and treated in dozens of different ways to produce the hundreds of varieties of cheese that we enjoy today.

Usually, acids produce fresh style cheese only. For most hard cheeses, rennet is the preferred enzyme used to coagulate the proteins in the cheese.

Acids cause curdling, but some of the protein and calcium are lost in the whey. With rennet, the proteins firm up and bond with each other in a more cohesive manner, thus producing a firmer cheese.

In Europe, raw milk is often used to produce cheese, although this, too, is changing, and more European cheese is being made with pasteurized milk. If cheese is made from raw milk,

CHEF'S TIP
Do not attempt to make cheese from ultra-pasteurized milk or milk that is in aseptic packages. This type of product has already been cooked.

it is required to be aged a certain amount of time before it can be sold in the United States. Raw milk cheese must be made from certified disease-free herds.

Chefs must always be concerned about the health risks associated with certain foods.

A Note About Listeria

Any focus on dairy products would be incomplete without a quick discussion of *Listeria*. Listeriosis, a serious infection caused by eating food contaminated with the bacterium *Listeria monocytogenes*, has recently been recognized as an important public health problem in the United States. The disease affects primarily pregnant women, newborns, and adults with weakened immune systems. *Listeria* is sometimes found in cold, damp environments such as processing plants, refrigerators, and other cool places. It has also been found in unpasteurized (raw) milk or foods made from unpasteurized milk, raw vegetables, processed meat and poultry products, and processed seafood products. It has recently been found in prepared and chilled ready-to-eat foods such as bologna, hot dogs, sliced deli meats, soft cheeses, and paté.

To avoid *Listeria,* use only pasteurized milk and dairy products. Always cook foods to required minimum internal temperatures to destroy this pathogen. Thoroughly wash vegetables. Make sure to clean, rinse, and sanitize all work surfaces to avoid cross contamination. It is important to purchase cold cuts and meats from reputable purveyors. Keeping walk-ins and reach-in coolers cleaned and sanitized, along with a regular cleaning and maintainace schedule, is the way to protect your customers from this illness. Chefs should read industry news sources and perhaps the USDA website for any bulletins and alerts warning customers of product recalls or for any pertinent information about contaminated or dangerous food products.

TYPES OF CHEESE

Our list of cheeses is just a partial list of the thousands of cheeses that are available worldwide. There are many good sources for cheese information. A good starting point is your local and state dairy boards. If you are lucky enough to live in a dairy-producing state such as Wisconsin, New York, Vermont, California, or Oregon, you will likely find some terrific locally produced cheeses. If not, check the Internet for cheese boards and other dairy and cheese resources. Many of the cheeses listed here are available through your local purveyors or by mail order.

> **CHEF'S TIP**
> Cheese can also be made from goat, rice, soy, and nut milks. Chefs who desire to use these products in cheese making must do the research needed to understand the challenges of working with each ingredient.

Fresh Cheese

Fresh cheese is cheese that has not been aged. These cheeses are ready for consumption shortly after they are made. They rely solely on some type of acidification for their character. Tartaric acid, citric acid, and other acids are used to precipitate the formation of curds and bring about a change in texture and flavors. Fresh cheese can be made from the milk of cows, goats, and sheep. It can also be made with rennet and heated to start curd formation. The excess whey is then drained off and the curds are shaped, molded, or whipped to a smooth texture. Fresh cheese is easy to make. Its tart and tangy flavor and moist texture are refreshing in dressings, dips, and sauces, or it can be eaten fresh as a spread with berries or conserves.

Soft fresh cheeses have a high moisture content compared to harder cheeses with lower moisture content. Because of its high moisture content, fresh cheese deteriorates quickly and cannot be aged. Soft fresh cheese has at most a 2-week shelf-life.

Farmer's or Pot Cheese

Farmer's, or pot, cheese is a mild white cheese with a moist, soft curd (Figure 6-5). This type of cheese is usually eaten alone or is used in salads. When sweetened, it can be used for pastry fillings. It takes well to many flavors, both

Figure 6-5 Farmer's cheese.

savory and sweet. Chives, garlic, thyme, orange zest, and lavender can be used to flavor this mild soft cheese. This type of cheese can be used as a filling or stuffing for cooked foods and blended with herbs and spices for a tasty dip.

Cream Cheese

Cream cheese is a fresh cheese that has a soft, spreadable texture and mild, creamy flavor (Figure 6-6). It is a work horse in the cold kitchen. Cream cheese has a relatively high moisture content of 50 percent and is mildly acidic, which gives it a slight tanginess that goes with many foods. It is often combined with herbs and spices such as dill, chives, and garlic. Cream cheese is used in spreads, dips, and is a major component of both sweet and savory cheesecakes. It is spread on toast and most typically bagels. It contains at least 33 percent butterfat. It is sold in a brick-like shape of 8 ounces for retail and 3-pound blocks for commercial and wholesale use.

Cream cheese is also available in a whipped version. It is sold in tubs, either plain or flavored with other ingredients such as smoked salmon, lox, sundried tomato, dill, and herbs and garlic.

Figure 6-6 Cream cheese block and a golden bagel with cream cheese.

Mascarpone

Mascarpone is an Italian-style cream cheese similar to ricotta but with a creamier texture. It is primarily used in desserts both as an ingredient and as a spread or dip for fruit. It is white in color and has a smooth, butter-like consistency. When made fresh, it is ready to use and eat in 24 hours. It is one of the main ingredients for tiramisu (Figure 6-7).

Figure 6-7 Mascarpone is a key ingredient in traditional Italian tiramisu.

mascarpone cheese *Yield: 2 quarts (1.89 l) 32 each 2 oz servings*

Ingredients	Amounts U.S.	Metric	Procedures
Heavy cream	1 gallon	3.78 l	In a nonreactive pan, heat the cream to 180°F (82°C), stirring often with a clean wooden spoon or heatproof spatula to prevent the protein and lactose in the cream from burning on the bottom of the pan.
Tartaric acid	1 tsp	5 g	When the milk reaches 180°F (82°C), turn off the heat, gently stir in the tartaric acid, then allow the mixture to clump up and form soft coagulated curds. When the mixture is cooled to 90°F (32°C), place mixture in a strainer or large china cap lined with several layers of cheesecloth or a large coffee filter. Allow this mixture to drain 24 hours in the refrigerator. Keep away from strongly aromatic foods. This mixture will continue to thicken and may be stored for up to 5 days under refrigeration.

NUTRITIONAL INFORMATION PER 2 OZ SERVING: 410 Calories; 44 g Fat (94.5% calories from fat); 2 g Protein; 3 g Carbohydrate; 0 g Dietary Fiber; 163 mg Cholesterol; 45 mg Sodium. Exchanges: 1/2 Nonfat Milk; 9 Fat; 0 Other Carbohydrates.

Fromage Blanc

Fromage blanc is a white cheese with a slightly tangy flavor and soft, creamy texture (Figure 6-8). This cheese is a smooth-textured cheese made from uncooked and unripened curd. It goes well as a spread with berries.

Ricotta

Ricotta means "twice cooked," and so it is. It has a sweet flavor and a cottage cheese-type of texture (Figure 6-9). In Italy, it is made from the by-product of Romano cheese, sheep's whey, which is then additionally cooked to precipitate out additional curds.

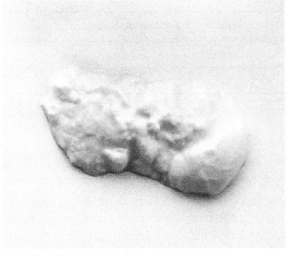

Figure 6-8 Fromage blanc.

Figure 6-9 Ricotta cheese.

In the United States, ricotta is made with either skim or whole cow's milk. It is unsalted and low in fat. It is used in fillings for ravioli, cannoli, and other savory or sweet Italian favorites. It can be enhanced with additional flavorings such as candied orange zest, toasted pistachios, and chocolate.

ricotta cheese
Yield: 8 to 12 oz of cheese (227 g to 340 g)
4 each 2 oz (57 g) servings

Ingredients	Amounts U.S.	Metric	Procedures
Whole or skim milk	1 gallon	3.78 l	In a nonreactive pan, heat the milk and salt to 185°F (85°C), stirring often to prevent scorching. Stir using a clean wooden spoon or heatproof spatula. Skim away the scum as it rises to the top of the milk mixture.
Lemon juice	6 fl oz	177 ml	When the milk reaches 185°F (85°C), turn off the heat, gently stir in the lemon juice, then allow the mixture to set for 10 minutes.
Salt	4 tsp	20 g	Once the curd has formed, ladle mixture into a cheesecloth-lined china cap and allow 1 to 3 hours for whey to drain from the curd. Make sure to do this under refrigeration. Hang the cheese-filled cloth from a rack and have it drain into a stainless steel pot or bowl.

NUTRITIONAL INFORMATION PER SERVING: 489 Calories; 26 g Fat (47.3% calories from fat); 26 g Protein; 40 g Carbohydrate; trace Dietary Fiber; 106 mg Cholesterol; 2,088 mg Sodium. Exchanges: 0 Fruit; 3 Nonfat Milk; 4 1/2 Fat.

LEARNING ACTIVITY 6-1

Make two batches of ricotta cheese: one with whole milk and one with skim milk. Compare the two in terms of texture, taste, and appearance. Record your findings in the chart below.

Ingredients	Texture	Taste	Appearance
Whole milk			
Skim			

Figure 6-10 Cottage cheese.

Cottage Cheese

Large or small curd cottage cheese is made from pasteurized cow's milk. This is a moist curd cheese created by souring the milk with rennet. The large curds are drained and rinsed (Figure 6-10). It has a bland flavor profile with a slightly acidic milky finish. Cream is often added back to the cheese to enhance the creamy texture of the curds. Cottage cheese is also sold as a dry curd pack.

cottage cheese *Yield: 16 oz (454 g)*

Ingredients	Amounts U.S.	Metric	Procedures
Whole milk	1 gallon	3.78 l	In a nonreactive pan, heat the milk until tepid, 99°F (37°C).
Rennet tablets, crushed	4 each	4 each	Add the crushed rennet tablets dissolved in 1 oz water and stir until thoroughly blended. Remove from heat and place in warm area for 2 hours to allow curds to form. Once the curds have formed, cut through the curds making 1-inch wide cuts through the mixture. Cut 90° into 1-inch squares.
Water	1 oz	30 ml	
Salt	2 to 3 tsp	10 to 15 g	Place this mixture in a nonreactive pan and heat to 110°F (43°C), stirring gently; then remove from heat. Let the mixture sit for 30 minutes. Turn out mixture into a triple cheesecloth-lined china cap or strainer and let drain for 4 hours refrigerated. When the whey has drained off the curds, salt the curds lightly and mix in a little Half & Half or heavy cream for added moisture. The cottage cheese will keep covered for up to 1 week refrigerated.
Half & Half or heavy cream	2 oz	59 ml	

NUTRITIONAL INFORMATION PER SERVING: 90 Calories; 4 g Fat (25.0% calories from fat); 13 g Protein; 4 g Carbohydrate; 0 g Dietary Fiber; 15 mg Cholesterol; 410 mg Sodium. Exchanges: 0 Grain (Starch); 1 Lean Meat; 0 Vegetable; 0 Fruit; 1/2 Fat.

Fresh Mozzarella

Mozzarella is one of the Italian pasta filata, or threadlike, spun-curd cheeses. It has a mild, creamy flavor and a creamy, white color (Figure 6-11). Originally made from water buffalo's milk, it is made with cows' milk in the United States. To make this cheese, curds are heated in water until they become elastic and form strands. These strands are stretched and shaped into oval balls. Some are stretched into logs that can be twisted or braded. Fresh mozzarella is good for use in cooked dishes as it has binding qualities. It is used in traditional Italian pizzas and in the classical Caprese salad of sliced tomatoes and mozzarella balls, drizzled with extra virgin olive oil and served with a dusting of fresh basil chiffonade.

Figure 6-11 Fresh mozzarella.

fresh mozzarella cheese   *Yield: 1 1/2 pounds (681 g) balls or twists*
12 each 2 oz (57 g) servings

Ingredients	Amounts		Procedures
	U.S.	Metric	
Rennet tablet	1 each	1 each	Dissolve the rennet tablet in cold water by smashing the rennet to a powder and stirring in.
Water, chlorine free	2 fl oz	59 ml	
Milk	2 gallons	7.571	Place milk in a large, nonreactive, stainless steel, heavy-bottomed pot. Sprinkle citric acid over the top of the milk. Heat this mixture to 90°F (32°C).
Citric acid	4 tsp	20 g	
			The milk will begin to coagulate. At this stage, add the rennet mixture and continue to stir slowly using a wooden spoon or heat-resistant rubber spatula until the milk reaches110°F (32°C). Remove from the heat and you will begin to see larger curds forming. The liquid will be somewhat clear. This is the whey. Remove the curds from the liquid and place in a stainless steel colander lined with cheesecloth. Drain to remove as much whey as possible. Store in refrigerator over a large bowl to collect the whey. Whey can be saved for other purposes or discarded. Refrigerate for 2 hours. When the curds have drained, you are ready to make some homemade pasta filata cheese or fresh mozzarella. Break up the curded mass into small curds.
Salt	To taste	To taste	In a stainless steel pot, heat water to 165°F. Add the salt, 1 to 2 tsp per quart. Heat cheese curds and knead them with gloved hands until they get stretchy. You should begin to see large strings form. Pull these stringy curds into a rope until you can knead it. It should have the consistency of taffy or bubble gum. Stretch and smooth it until it is shiny. Do not overheat it at this point. When you can make a medium-sized rope, twist or shape into balls. Place twists or balls into 1 pint cold water with 1 tsp salt. You can add 1/2 tsp. Liquid Smoke to it for extra flavor. Let this cheese firm up and set. Serve with salads or use for appetizers.

NUTRITIONAL INFORMATION PER SERVING: 402 Calories; 22 g Fat (48.3% calories from fat); 21 g Protein; 31 g Carbohydrate; 0 g Dietary Fiber; 88 mg Cholesterol; 320 mg Sodium. Exchanges: 2 1/2 Nonfat Milk; 4 Fat; 0 Other Carbohydrates.

Feta

Originally from Greece, feta is a popular cheese made from sheep's milk, cow's milk, and/or occasionally from goat's milk. It is white in color, has a crumbly, soft texture, and has a strong, sharp, salty flavor (Figure 6-12). European versions are more creamy and tender whereas the feta varieties made in the United States are drier and grainier. Usually, feta is kept in a brine solution to keep it from dehydrating. It comes packed in tins or in buckets. Feta is popular used fresh in salads, fillings, and blended into dips.

Queso Blanco

Queso blanco is a white, crumbly cheese made in Mexico and Latin America. It is mild and bland with a slight saltiness (Figure 6-13). The term "queso blanco" is Spanish for "white cheese." It is the cheese used for many Mexican and Latin American cooking applications

Figure 6-12 Feta cheese.

Figure 6-13 Queso blanco.

queso blanco *Yield: 1 pound (454 g) 8 each 2 oz (57 g) servings*

Ingredients	Amounts U.S.	Metric	Procedures
Whole milk	1 gallon		In a nonreactive pan, heat the milk to 190°F (88°C). Slowly sprinkle the vinegar over the milk and stir in gently. Remove from heat and let sit for 10 minutes.
Apple cider vinegar	2 oz		
Kosher salt	2 tbsp		Add the salt and stir gently. Pour curds into a cheesecloth-lined colander or china cap and tie into a bundle. Hang this over a bowl to drain the curds. Refrigerate for several hours or overnight.

NUTRITIONAL INFORMATION PER 2 OZ SERVING: 301 Calories; 16 g Fat (48.3% calories from fat); 16 g Protein; 23 g Carbohydrate; 0 g Dietary Fiber; 66 mg Cholesterol; 1,649 mg Sodium. Exchanges: 0 Fruit; 2 Nonfat Milk; 3 Fat.

such as making chile rellenos, chiliquiles, enchiladas, and other dishes that require a cheese that has cooking properties similar to those of cheddar.

Cotija

Cotija is a salty, pungent cheese that is white in color and has a semi-firm to firm, crumbly texture. It is a Hispanic-style cheese similar to feta to crumble and sprinkle over cooked dishes, soups, beans, and salads.

Soft-Ripened Cheese

Soft-ripened cheeses are similar to fresh cheese in that they are typically soft in nature but are allowed to mature and ripen under controlled environments to produce cheeses that have complex flavors and soft to almost liquid textures. Most have some sort of velvety rind, and, when allowed to ripen, go from a creamy white interior to a golden interior with stronger, pungent aromas. They are dusted or sprayed with a mold, then left to ripen from the outside in. When young, they are slightly firm and chalky. As they mature, the interior becomes softer to the point of being runny and the flavor intensifies. Overly ripe cheese can take on an ammonia aroma.

Figure 6-14 Brie cheese.

Figure 6-15 Camembert cheese.

The two most popular soft-ripened cheeses are brie and camembert. Both cheeses originated in France and today can be found in many other countries as well. Because the names "brie" and "camembert" were not protected by law, quality varies. so be sure to select them with care.

Brie

High-quality brie should have a slightly golden cream to rust red exterior with a few traces of white (Figure 6-14). It should have a slightly firm and chalky interior when young and a nice, creamy, golden interior when ripe. It comes in flat disk forms of varying thicknesses ranging in diameter from 8 inches across up to 16 inches. When fully ripe, brie can be slightly runny and pale yellow in color. It goes well with pears, apples, grapes, walnuts, and almonds, as well as pâté. Serve with crisp baguette slices or crackers.

Camembert

Camembert originated in the Normandy province of France. While there are many camembert cheese producers around the world, none can match the original, which relies on the salty richness of Normandy milk for its unique character. Smaller than a brie, camembert has a hearty, fruity flavor of great complexity (Figure 6-15). High-quality camembert is made from whole milk and is made mainly in the winter by a process very similar to that used in the manufacture of brie. The bacterial cultures are slightly different from those used for brie and give camembert a slightly bitter flavor profile. This may be due to the oat straw used to wrap the cheese during the curing process. Camembert goes well with guava paste, mango, pears, and other full-flavored fruits and is often served on toasted baguette slices.

Other Soft-Ripened Cheeses

There are many other artisan cheese makers that produce single, double, and triple cream cheeses. They are called this because of the high butterfat content that can range from 50 to 70 percent butterfat, respectively.

All soft-ripened cheeses should be eaten when properly ripened. Too young, and the cheese lacks flavor and is chalky. Too ripe, and the cheese picks up ammonia overtones and is liquefied.

To achieve peak flavor, soft-ripened cheeses should be served at room temperature as dessert cheese or as appetizers. Bring them out a half hour to an hour before service for optimum flavor and aroma.

A nice way to serve these cheeses is to wrap them in puff paste or fillo dough and bake until the crust is golden and the cheese is melted through (Figure 6-16). They can also be topped with toasted almonds or walnuts, brown sugar, and sun-dried tomatoes and warmed in an oven. These types of cheeses are served with the rind on. It is perfectly safe to eat and enjoy the rind; however, it is a matter of taste—some people do not enjoy the texture or the flavor of the rind.

Semi-Soft Cheese

Semi-soft cheese includes cheese that has been washed with brine, salt, and acids. In this category, we include some of the more pungent and aromatic cheeses. They have a wide variety of flavor profiles that include buttery and nutty to strong and nose-ripping,

Figure 6-16 Savory fillo triangles are filled with soft cheese and baked to golden brown.

eye-wateringly pungent. This category of cheese ripens in several ways from a dry rind finish to a washed rind that is edible to a waxed rind cheese that needs to be peeled. This group of cheese covers hundreds of tasty cheeses from around the world.

Washed-Rind Cheese

Washed-rind cheeses are mainly soft to semi-soft in texture. They are washed while in the curing stage with salt brine, acidic liquids such as wine, alcoholic beverages such as beer, hard apple cider, and brandy, or with aromatic oils during the ripening period.

Keeping these types of cheese moist encourages friendly bacterial growth, called *Brevibacterium* linens. This bacterium lives best in an environment that is very salty. A smear or paste is used to apply this bacterium and it works mainly on the outside of the cheese. These bacteria add strong, aggressive flavors and enhance the ripening of the cheese, which can take place in a dry or moist environment depending upon the cheese type. These types of cheese ripen from the outside in. Their rinds can be vividly colored with the degree of shading determined by the frequency of washing and duration of soak or amount of coating. The cheese itself does not sustain this mold growth, but it is the sticky surfaces that attract the friendly bacteria that assist in developing the flavors. For the most part, these cheeses tend to be very aromatic and pungent. When allowed to come to room temperature, they can become almost excessively pungent. The rind is the part that smells and, for this reason, is usually discarded.

Dauphin

This is a cow's milk cheese with a washed rind. This cheese comes in crescent, shield, or heart shapes. It is flavored with cracked pepper and tarragon. It has a smooth brown rind, creamy interior, and strong odor.

Figure 6-17 Limburger cheese.

Figure 6-18 Munster cheese.

Limburger

Limburger originated in Limburg, Belgium. It is a wash-rind cheese with a soft texture and full flavor (Figure 6-17). It is a highly aromatic cheese that tastes much better than it smells. It goes well with rye bread, water crackers, and beer.

Munster

Munster cheese originated in Muenster, Germany. Today, in the United States, most Munster comes from Wisconsin. It is a semi-soft cheese with a straw-yellow interior and a bright orange to apricot-colored rind. It has a buttery mild to slightly nutty and sometimes spicy flavor (Figure 6-18). It is popular sliced and served with roast beef for sandwiches. It comes packaged as sliced, chunk, round, or brick-shaped rectangles.

Port Salut or Esrom

Port salut is made from cow's milk. It is one of the milder cheeses of this style; it has a light yellow interior, a fairly firm texture with tiny holes, and an apricot orange exterior (Figure 6-19). Port salut is similar to gouda and edam in taste and appearance. Serve it with wine or fruit as a dessert cheese.

Dry-Rind Cheese

Dry-rind cheeses are semi-soft cheeses that develop a dry rind during the ripening process. They do not receive any washing down, so the skin dehydrates and protects the interior. Because stronger-flavored bacteria do not attach themselves to the rind, these cheeses tend to be much less pungent. Most have a buttery flavor and a slightly firm but tender texture.

Bel Paese

Originated in Italy, bel paese was imported and introduced to the United States in 1929. Its name means "beautiful country." Bel paese has a buttery, mild flavor and firm yet tender texture. It is good for slicing or cubing for cheese boards.

Figure 6-19 Port Salut cheese.

Figure 6-20 Havarti cheese.

Figure 6-21 Gouda cheese.

Havarti

Danish havarti is a popular dry-rind cheese, with a buttery flavor that is often enhanced with herbs or spices such as caraway, dill weed or seed, and basil (Figure 6-20). Mild, slightly tangy, pale yellow, semi-firm havarti is a mild cheese similar to gouda and edam. This cheese is used for out-of-hand snacking, is shredded and used cooked in foods, and is diced in salads.

Waxed-Rind Cheese

Waxed-rind cheeses are semi-soft cheeses that are sealed in wax prior to the aging process. Gouda and edam are the most famous of these cheeses. Both cheeses got their names from the two towns in Holland where they were first produced. While these two cheeses have been around for several centuries, today much of the gouda and edam used in the United States comes from Wisconsin. In the late 1800s, many immigrants who came from Holland settled in Wisconsin and started dairy farms. They found Wisconsin to be like their homeland. With an abundance of milk came cheese production in the form of domestic gouda and edam.

Gouda

Gouda originated in Holland eight centuries ago. It has a distinctive button shape with a round body, flattened on the top and the bottom (Figure 6-21). This type of cheese has a mild, nut-like flavor profile that becomes more pronounced with age. When aged for over 3 years, it becomes similar in texture to a good grana or grating cheese like parmesiano reggiano. The interior of the cheese is pale gold to cream, and it has a smooth, semi-soft to hard texture that is soft and sliceable. It is excellent for use on a cheese tray as its stunning red wax outer shell makes a dramatic appearance. Gouda has a higher fat content than edam.

Edam

Edam originated in Holland and today is processed in several European countries as well as in the United States. It is made from partly skimmed milk that forms curds quickly due to the large amount of rennet used to process the cheese (Figure 6-22). It is lightly colored with annatto to give it a more golden color. Fermentation for edam is slow and continues until the rind is hard and nonporous. When the cheese is fully fermented and the skin of the cheese is hard, it is coated with a thin layer of linseed oil. It is then covered with a creamy yellow coating of wax or, in some cases, silver-colored wax. It has a semi-soft to firm texture when ripe and has a mild, milky-like, nut flavor.

Figure 6-22 Edam cheese.

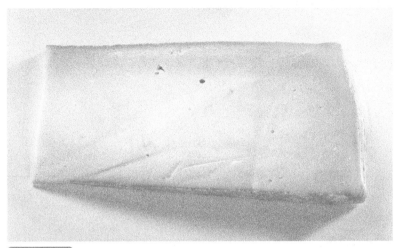

Figure 6-23 Figure 6-23 Fontina cheese.

Figure 6-24 Brick cheese.

Figure 6-25 French roquefort.

Fontina

This is a mild, nutty cheese with a creamy yellow interior and a firm texture (Figure 6-23). Fontina is a mild, pleasant cheese used for sandwiches, salads, cheese trays, and displays as well as for snacking.

Brick Cheese

Brick cheese originated in the United States. It has a creamy yellow interior and is semi-soft to firm in texture with small, numerous holes (Figure 6-24). It has a slightly salty flavor with nutty overtones. It is a great cheese for snacking, sandwiches, appetizers, and cubed for cheese trays.

Beer Kaese Cheese

This cheese is similar in texture to brick cheese with the pungent nose of a Limburger. It slices well and goes well with roast beef sandwiches, pretzels, and beer.

Blue-Veined Cheese

Blue-veined cheese (sometimes spelled *bleu*) has veins of greenish-blue, edible mold. Blues are some of the oldest styles of cheese around. Theory has it that a piece of cheese was left next to some bread in a moist cave. When the cave dweller returned to his bread, he noticed that both the bread and the cheese had become moldy. He gave this cheese a bite, and it proved to be tasty with perhaps better keeping qualities than the fresh cheese, so a new idea was born. There is no way of knowing for sure what happened in the sands of time, but caves were the early storage places of cheese, so this theory has possibilities. Today in France cheeses are stored in caves to age them in temperature-controlled environments. The blue veining comes from a form of penicillin mold that occurs naturally in these caves. Modern production methods of blue-veined style cheese include the use of stainless steel needles or rods to puncture the cheese, thus allowing fermentation gases to escape along with oxygen to enter and support the penicillin mold growth inside of the cheese. The cheese is salted or soaked in brine for a short period and then placed in temperature- and humidity-controlled storage rooms to duplicate what happened in the original natural caves.

French Roquefort

One of the world's finest cheeses, roquefort is a sheep's milk cheese that is blue-veined, semi-soft with a mellow to very sharp flavor profile (Figure 6-25). The unique feature of this cheese is that the curds are mixed with rye bread crumbs that have been inoculated with *Penicillium* roquefort mold. This special type of bread is dried first, then ground into fine powder. This mold is not cultured in laboratories unlike the other blue cheeses made. This makes it unique among all blue-style cheese.

The cheese is stored in cool, damp caves found in Southern France for 3 months to develop its unique character. French roqueforts are stored for an additional 3 to 12 months as the market allows. After this time, French roquefort is available for sale, but ideally it is aged for several months longer for the best flavor to develop.

It has a grey green exterior and a slightly yellowish interior color streaked with blue veins when properly aged. If it is pale white and chalky, it is not completely fermented and is a very young cheese.

French roquefort is an excellent cheese for the dessert tray or cheese course. It is fantastic for salads, both as an ingredient in dressing or crumbled on a salad, in dips and spreads, enjoyed with robust wine, spread generously on dark rye, and has many other uses. The Roquefort Association, Inc., ensures that quality standards and name integrity are protected.

Italian Gorgonzola

Italian gorgonzola is made from cow's milk, unlike the French roquefort made from sheep's milk. Gorgonzola comes in a dolce form that is sweet, soft, and mild or in a sharper, creamier, and aggressively aromatic version. Both styles are elegant for the cheese service tray (Figure 6-26). The exteriors of both types are washed with salt brine during the ripening process. They are then pierced with stainless steel or copper needles, and the resulting holes allow oxygen to enter and nourish a commercially manufactured *Penicillium*. Gorgonzola is then aged for 6 months. It has a pale yellow to white interior, streaked with a greenish blue. Dolce, or sweet gorgonzola, is aged for 3 months whereas the stronger, sharp gorgonzola is aged much longer for a robust flavor. Gorgonzola goes well with fruit, wine, and breads; as a spread or dip; and mixed in sauces for a rich, creamy flavor.

Figure 6-26 Gorgonzola.

English Stilton

Stilton is made from cow's milk with additional cream. Because of its unique color and flavor, it is often referred to as the "King of blue-veined cheeses." It was first produced in England. Stilton is made initially like cheddar and has a similar texture. It has deep blue grey to green streaks throughout (Figure 6-27). It is dense and crumbly with a very sharp, yet buttery-rich flavor. It ripens for several months before being ready for service. With its tangy flavor and firmer, cheddar-like texture, it is perfect on a cheese board or tray, and goes with strong fruit flavors such as grapes, apples, and pears along with walnuts. It is also served with a fine dessert or fortified wine such as Madeira, port, or sherry. Stilton cheese is not sliced but usually scooped out of the center of the wheel with a blunt cheese knife and served with slices of bread, water biscuits, or crackers. It is a great addition to hearty beef or pork sandwiches and is also used in hot dips, sauces, and salad dressings for assertive greens.

Figure 6-27 Stilton cheese.

Danablu

Danablu cheese is a Danish cheese made from cow's milk. It is a tart, yet milky, sweet cheese with a pale, creamy interior (Figure 6-28). It is best used in dressings, cheese trays, and sauces. Danablu has a thin crust or rind that is edible. It can be stored for over 6 months if kept under proper refrigeration and turned every week. This type of cheese becomes sharper as it ages. It can also be preserved in oil with herbs and is used as a spread.

Spanish Blue Cabrales

Blue cabrales is a very pungent variety of blue cheese from Spain. It is made with a combination of milk usually from cows, sheep, and goats. When well aged, it has a strong, acidic note. This cheese goes well with port, sherry, and oil-roasted Spanish almonds. It has a soft and creamy texture.

American Maytag Blue

American Maytag blue cheese comes from the same family that invented the Maytag washing machine in Newton, Iowa. This blue-veined cheese is made from cow's

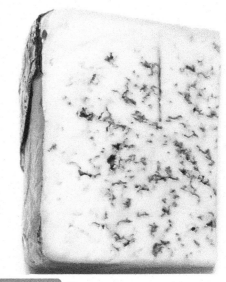

Figure 6-28 Danablu cheese.

Figure 6-29 Maytag blue cheese.

milk (Figure 6-29). During the Great Depression family members wanted to expand the profits from their herd of dairy cattle. They collaborated with food scientists from Iowa State University to develop a blue cheese. Maytag blue cheese continues to be popular today. It has a rich, creamy interior with blue veins. This cheese is moist and has a sharp, spicy taste. To obtain the best flavor, serve it at room temperature.

Other American Blues

Rogue River blue, Point Reyes blue, and Tolibia blue are just a few of the dozens of American-based farmstead or Artisan blue cheeses being produced in the United States.

Most are tangy and share similar flavor notes with the Danish-style blue cheese. Others are creamy like Italian gorgonzola, and still others are made from sheep's milk and come close to the tangy French-style blues.

Pasta Filata Cheese

Pasta filata literally means "spun curds" or "spun paste." There are many different types of pasta filata-style cheeses. After the initial curds are developed, the curds are then placed in hot water, which slightly melts them. The cheese maker takes the curds from the hot water and stretches or spins them until the desired shape and texture is achieved. Different textures can be achieved by how they are handled and aged. Some are smoked whereas others are braided and seasoned. The following is a partial list of some of the more famous pasta filata cheeses.

Mozzarella

Mozzarella is originally from Italy, but it is now one of the most produced cheeses in the United States. Most known for its use as a "pizza" cheese, it is a white, sweet, milky-flavored cheese with a semi-soft to firm texture (Figure 6-30). It has a creamy smoothness and becomes elastic when heated. In any given year, it is estimated that over 2 billion pounds of mozzarella are produced. Two types of mozzarella are available: fresh, which we have already discussed, and low-moisture mozzarella, which has a longer shelf-life than fresh mozzarella. Low-moisture mozzarella has a firmer texture and is ideal shredded for topping pizzas, for use in lasagnas, and for cutting into blocks or cubes for cheese trays and displays.

Provolone

Provolone is a cow's milk cheese made in the pasta filata style, like mozzarella, with a slightly different culture for a richer flavor (Figure 6-31). The curd is stretched, kneaded, and tied into a long, tube-shaped cheese. It is rubbed with salt brine, tied into a long, log-shaped

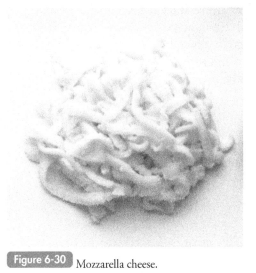

Figure 6-30 Mozzarella cheese.

Figure 6-31 Provolone cheese.

cheese, and hung to dry. Provolone comes in many sizes and shapes weighing from 9 ounces up to 200 pounds. It can be shaped like balls, pears, and salami. A smoked version is also available.

Smoked Scamorza

Scamorza has a mild flavor with a smooth, dense texture (Figure 6-32). It is lightly smoked over pecan hulls. Scamorza is hand-formed and dipped in wax to preserve it. As with provolone, it is shaped into a horseshoe-shaped knot.

Hard Cheese

Hard cheese has a firm, slightly crumbly interior texture. It can be sliced easily as well as grated. Cheddar cheese is one of the most famous types of hard cheese and is the most popular cheese in the United States. Cheddar was originally produced in England, but over time we have come to think of cheddar as an American product. Swiss cheese is also considered a hard cheese and is the most popular cheese for sandwiches worldwide.

Figure 6-32 Scamorza cheese.

Monterey Jack is a distinctly American cheese made with the cheddaring method. It is light in color and has a rich, nutty flavor. It is also dried and used as a grating cheese. The majority of cheeses produced in the United States are made by this layering, or "cheddaring," method.

Cheddar

The English Pilgrims first brought cheddar cheese to the New World. It gets the name "cheddar" from the process of manufacture. The "cheddaring" process involves turning the drained curds and stacking them in slab form in the troughs to drain off the whey. This stacking process compacts the curds and removes more whey. The soft protein curds gradually stick together to form solid loaves. These loaves are then placed into large square or round containers lined with cheesecloth. Weights are placed on the top of the cheese, and the cheese is further compacted down into the familiar blocks and rounds that we see today. This method gives the cheese its characteristic, slightly crumbly texture (Figure 6-33).

The bright yellow to gold color that we associate with some varieties of cheddar cheese is achieved by dyeing it with a natural colorant made from the achiote seed. The paste is called "annatto," and it is the same natural dye used to color butter. Once all the whey is removed, it is

Figure 6-33 Cheddar cheese.

wrapped in cheesecloth and painted or dipped in wax and cured or ripened in temperature- and humidity-controlled storage. The cheese is turned weekly or bi-weekly. Cheddar is characterized by age. When the cheddar is aged, it goes from a mild, creamy flavor to a bold, assertive, tangy flavor with a crumbly, dry texture. Cheddar is somewhat granular, and as it ages, this becomes more pronounced. The following chart explains the characterization of cheddar depending on the length of time it is aged.

Length of Time Aged	Description
Newly processed, aged for 30 days	Mild
1 to 3 months	Mild
3 to 6 months	Medium
6 to 9 months	Sharp
9 months to 2 years or more	Extra sharp

Cheddar comes in various sizes; the largest commercial size is approximately 90 pounds. However, cheddars up to 500 pounds have been produced for special functions and purposes. The smallest commercial size is the 8-ounce stick. Cheddars come in different shapes such as wedges, rounds, or blocks.

Colby

Colby is an American-made cheese that was developed in the town of Colby, Wisconsin, in 1874. It is a mild, pleasant cheese similar to cheddar in texture and flavor profile and is a pale yellow to burnt orange color depending upon the amount of annatto used to color it (Figure 6-34). Cojack is a blend of Colby and Jack cheese curds pressed and formed into a solid block of two-toned and dual-flavored cheese. This blend is cut into cubes for snacking and is used in sandwiches and on cheese boards or trays. When Colby slabs are cut in half, they are known as longhorns. Longhorn Colby has a mild to sharp flavor, depending upon age, and a firm, sliceable texture. The longhorn's size and shape make it easy to slice for cheese trays.

Swiss

Swiss cheese is a cow's milk cheese originally from Switzerland. This type of cheese is characterized by holes, sometimes called eyes, which range in size from tiny pinholes to the size of a quarter (Figure 6-35). To produce such holes, the Swiss use a bacterium called *Propionibactera*. This bacterium consumes the lactic acid during the ripening process and produces organic acids, which flavor the cheese and carbon dioxide gas that forms the characteristic bubbles or holes in the cheese.

Swiss cheese varieties with larger holes are called "big-eye Swiss." In general, Swiss cheese is mellow in flavor and has excellent melting properties. Some of the better-known varieties of Swiss cheese include the following.

Emmentaler

Emmentaler is an original Swiss cheese that is white, smooth, and has large holes. It has a medium to sharp, nutty-rich flavor. Emmentaler is great served with fruit desserts, on sandwiches, grated in sauces, and in casseroles (Figure 6-36).

Gruyère

Gruyère is a cream-colored, smooth-textured Swiss cheese with small holes and a nutty, medium-sharp flavor that goes well with fruits, chutneys, and relishes (Figure 6-37). It is most commonly used for sandwiches and in salads.

Figure 6-34 Colby cheese.

Figure 6-35 Swiss cheese.

Figure 6-36 Emmentaler cheese.

Figure 6-37 Gruyère cheese.

Jarlsberg

Jarlsberg is a Norwegian made, Swiss-style cheese that has a creamy, white interior and smooth texture with small holes (Figure 6-38). It has a mild, slightly nutty, buttery flavor and is often served with fruits and relishes.

Monterey Jack

Monterey Jack is an American original cheese that is produced with the cheddaring method (Figure 6-39). It was first made by David Jacks in Monterey, California, in 1849 and has remained popular throughout the years. It is a favorite for Mexican-style dishes, and it has great melting qualities.

Grana or Grating Cheese

Grana, or grating, cheeses are the driest of the cheeses. They have an extremely low moisture content and a dry, almost crystalline texture. In Italy, these dry cheeses are known as granas,

Figure 6-38 Jarlsberg cheese.

Figure 6-39 Monterey Jack cheese.

Figure 6-40 Parmigiano-Reggiano cheese.

Figure 6-41 Parmesan cheese.

a granular grainy textured cheese commonly grated for service. This crystalline substance is calcium lactate or tyrosine, an amino acid produced when protein breaks down during the aging process. Some of the more famous of these grana cheeses are the Parmigiano-Reggiano and Pecarino Romano; and for a domestic variety, we have the California Dry Jack, which was described previously.

Parmigiano-Reggiano

The recipe for this cheese has not changed in centuries, and it dates back perhaps a thousand years. It is manufactured under strict government controls and is aged for no less than 14 months. Most that are available in the United States are aged for 2 years or longer. Parmigiano Reggiano has been described as a nutty, spicy, dry cheese with strong umami tones (Figure 6-40). A good substitute for Parmigiano would be Grana Padano, a slightly higher-fat cheese with a buttery, nutty flavor, Asiago (saltier), or Sapsago, a cheese made from whey.

Parmesan

Parmesan is a domestic style, dry, grating cheese made in the United States and Canada. It is pale yellow in color and has a granular, hard-grating texture with a sharp flavor (Figure 6-41). Parmesan is used as a garnish on casseroles, soups, and pasta dishes or used in salads and sauces.

Pecorino Romano

Pecorino Romano is another of the Italian grana cheeses and is characterized by its sharper, tangier flavor (Figure 6-42). It is a sheep's milk cheese that is good for grating. This type of cheese was named after the city of Rome. Pecorino Romano is most often grated or shaved but is also traditionally eaten in chunks broken off with a special knife.

Romano

Domestic romanos (those made in the United States) aren't as well regarded as the Italian varieties. Many domestic romanos are made with cow's milk. Romano is pale yellow in color, with a grainy texture and very sharp flavor (Figure 6-43).

Figure 6-42 Pecorino Romano cheese.

Figure 6-43 Romano cheese.

Asiago

Asiago is a piquant cheese with sharp flavor (Figure 6-44). It is light yellow in color. Its texture is hard to very hard, depending on age. This Italian-style cheese is similar to parmesan. It is typically grated over cooked foods or salads.

Dry Jack

Dry Jack is a specialty version of Monterey Jack cheese from Sonoma, California. This excellent grating cheese has a mild, nutty flavor. Its color is pale yellow, and its texture is hard to very hard, depending on its age. Dry Jack is eaten as is, in cooked foods, or grated onto pasta or salads.

Manchego (Aged)

Aged manchego cheese is yellow and is a terrific grating cheese. Don't confuse it with unaged manchego cheese, which is almost white, semi-firm, and typically used as a melting cheese. The aged variety is a great substitute for pecorino romano.

Figure 6-44 Asiago cheese.

Goat Cheese

There are many styles of goat and sheep cheeses on the market today. With the renewed interest in artisanal and farmstead cheese, goat cheese is being made into many types of cheese.

Chevre

The most familiar goat cheese we use in the cold kitchen is chevre. Originally from France, it is the most popular goat cheese in the United States and is found in many shapes and sizes. This type of cheese is often covered with leaves or herbs (Figure 6-45). Young chevre is mild and creamy. As it ages, its texture dries out, and its taste becomes sharper and more acidic.

Montrachet

Montrachet is a cylindrical, log-shaped, goat cheese from the Burgundy region of France. It is soft and slightly acidic. It goes well with tossed green salads and toasted nuts.

Figure 6-45 Chevre cheese.

Pyramide

As its name implies, pyramide is a pyramid-shaped, aged goat cheese. It has a richer, tangier note than most other goat cheeses.

Boucheron

Boucheron is a larger (2 kilogram), log-shaped goat cheese. It is a strong and creamy chevre and makes a good addition to any cheese course.

LEARNING ACTIVITY 6-2

Conduct a cheese tasting by selecting two cheeses from each category. After you have tasted the cheese, record your findings for the aroma, texture, and flavor notes in the chart below.

Type of Cheese	Aroma	Texture	Flavor Notes
Fresh 1. 2.			
Soft-Ripened 1. 2.			
Washed-Rind 1. 2.			
Dry-Ring 1. 2.			
Waxed-Rind 1. 2.			
Blue-Veined 1. 2.			

Type of Cheese	Aroma	Texture	Flavor Notes
Pasta Filata 1. 2.			
Hard Cheese 1. 2.			
Swiss 1. 2.			
Grating 1. 2.			
Goat 1. 2.			

CHEESE SERVICE

Cheese service in a restaurant is an exciting challenge. Whether creating a cheese tray for a buffet or as individual appetizer or dessert servings, the cold kitchen is often responsible for the selection and design (Figure 6-46). Most cheeses, specifically soft and delicate cheeses, have a ripening period and, once ripe, deteriorate quickly. Ripening is retarded by cold temperature; ripening is encouraged by room temperature and can happen rather rapidly if the cheese is almost ripe. Exposing cheese to the standard kitchen temperature changes the texture of the cheese dramatically. During the ripening process, aromas become more pronounced. The aromas vary by cheese variety and can be mild and subtle to acrid and unpleasant. In the kitchen, these smells are less noticeable due to the ventilation systems, but in a dining room or banquet hall, the smells might be overwhelming to the guests.

Cheeses suitable for cheese service, whether it be served on a platter or butler style, include the following:

- Bel Paese
- Cheddar varieties

Figure 6-46 Cheese trays usually showcase a number of cheeses with accompanying crackers and fruit.

- Fontina
- Swiss cheese
- Gruyère, a cheese in the Swiss cheese family
- Manchego
- Camembert
- Brie
- Gorgonzola
- Pont l'Eveque
- Neufchatel

ADDITIONAL DAIRY PRODUCTS

Cheese is the most common dairy product used in the cold kitchen, but other major dairy foods are used in that arena. The following sections include some of those foods.

Milk

Milk is a liquid dairy product that contains 3 1/2 percent fat, 8 1/2 percent nonfat milk solids, and 88 percent water when it comes straight from the cow (Figure 6-47).

There are several forms of milk available, including the following:

- UHT stands for "ultra-high temperature" pasteurization, which is done at temperatures between 280° to 300°F (138° to 149°C) for 2 to 4 seconds, packed in sterile containers, and aseptically sealed. This type of milk is widely available in Europe and is becoming more available in the United States.

Figure 6-47 Milk is available in a number of varieties.

- Pasteurized milk/ultra-pasteurized milk is heated to 161°F (72°C) for pasteurized and 275°F (135°C) for ultra-pasteurized for 15 seconds, then brought down to a cool temperature of below 40°F (4°C). This process kills bacteria and disease-producing pathogens and ensures that the milk is safe for consumption. However, it does alter the flavor slightly.
- Raw milk is a nonpasteurized product. It is illegal to sell unless state certified. Raw milk is found in healthfood stores and is available to foodservice through specialty purveyors. Raw milk has a fresh taste and desirable consistency.
- Homogenized milk is milk that has been forced under pressure through stainless steel plates with infinitely microscopic holes. The process breaks up fat into tiny particles so small that they stay distributed.
- Skim or nonfat milk contains 0.5 or less percent fat milk. It has most or all fat removed.
- Low-fat milk has a fat content of 0.5 to 3 percent. This product is what is usually called 2 percent milk.
- Fortified nonfat milk is milk in which vitamins such as vitamin D and A and extra nonfat milk solids like calcium have been added for health enhancement.
- Flavored milk has added flavors such as chocolate, strawberry, or other fruit flavors.
- Acidophilus milk is milk with added *Lactobaccilius* and *Acidophilous* for promotion of healthy flora and fauna in the intestinal tract. These additions make milk palatable for most lactose-intolerant folks by breaking down the lactaise.
- Canned milk products include evaporated milk and condensed sweetened milk. In these products, 60 percent of the water is removed by heat, which leaves the milk with a rich, cooked taste. Condensed sweetened milk has added sugar.
- Dry milk products include dry whole milk, freeze-dried buttermilk, dried goat's milk, and nonfat dry milk. These products are freeze dried and sprayed or heat sprayed to remove all of the water. Dry milk products are convenient for cooking, baking, and storing.

Cultured Dairy Products

Cultured dairy products start out as milk or cream. The addition of specific bacterial cultures and acidifiers produces cultured products (Figure 6-48). Yogurt, buttermilk, sour cream, kefir, and crème fraiche are some of the many products produced by these dairy cultures. The specific lactobacilli convert milk sugar or "lactose" into lactic acid. This acidification gives these products their characteristic body, texture, and tangy as well as unique flavors. The acid content also retards the growth of lethal and dangerous microorganisms; thus, these cultures have been used for centuries to preserve milk.

The following is a list of cultured dairy products and their characteristics.

- Yogurt is made from milk that is cultured with special bacteria that cause the milk to thicken to custard-like consistency. It usually has additional nonfat milk solids.
- Buttermilk was originally a by-product from butter churning; today it is made from fresh liquid milk—usually skim milk—that has been slightly heated and then cultured. Real buttermilk is delicious and nutritious.
- Sour cream/sour milk is made with cream or milk that has been cultured with lactic acid and bacteria, giving it a thick consistency and tangy taste.
- Kefir is a more liquid form of yogurt that is usually flavored and served as a beverage. It is very popular in the Middle East and in Russia.
- Crème fraiche is slightly aged, cultured heavy cream used for sauce making. Adding buttermilk to cream and keeping it at or slightly above room temperature for 24 to 48 hours makes an acceptable mock version of crème fraiche. This thickens the product and helps prevent it from curdling and separating during the cooking process.

Figure 6-48 Sour cream is a cultured dairy product.

Butter

Butter is made by agitating or churning cream to separate out the fatty substance from the whey and water. Butter consists of approximately 80 percent milk fat, not more than 16 percent water, and 2 to 4 percent milk solids. It may contain annatto, a natural-based coloring agent derived from the seed of the achiote plant. It may also contain a small amount of salt. It is graded according to USDA standards for flavor, body, color, and salt content, although grading is not mandatory. Grades are AA, A, B, and C. Butter is marketed as sweet, unsalted, or lightly salted. Butter is firm when refrigerated and becomes soft at 85° to 90°F (29° to 32°C) and liquid at 98°F (37°C), reaching the smoking point at 260°F (127°C). Butter is preferred for cooking fat because of its flavor. It has no equal in sauce making and is often used as a sauce itself. Butter is more expensive, however, and some chefs use blends of clarified butter and oil. Following is a list of types of butter:

- Sweet butter is butter that is unsalted. It has a sweet, creamy taste and is often sold frozen because it is highly perishable.
- Lightly salted butter is butter that has had a small amount of salt added to flavor and preserve it. It also may contain annatto during parts of the year.
- Clarified butter is butter that has been heated, and the protein solids, salt, and whey have been removed, leaving just the butter (milk) fat. There are two common methods for making clarified butter:
  1. Place whole butter in a saucepan and bring to a boil. Skim to remove excess whey. Boil off all of the water. When the butter starts to get slightly golden, remove from heat. Let it sit for 15 minutes. Strain it through cheesecloth to remove any remaining whey.
  2. Place whole butter in a saucepan. Heat on medium low until the butter is completely melted. Heat for an additional 5 minutes after the butter is melted. Pour into a straight-sided, stainless steel container such as a bain-marie. Let the butter sit at room temperature for a half hour. The butterfat will separate from the water and whey. Place in the refrigerator or freezer overnight. The next day, remove the solid butter from the pot. Rinse under cold water to remove any whey. Pat dry and reheat the solid block of clarified butter for use. This method takes more planning, but there is no loss of butterfat.
- Whipped butter is butter that has been whipped and contains up to 50 percent more air than regular butter.

Butter Substitutes

Butter substitutes have been used for over 100 years.

- A French chemist invented margarine in the late 1800s upon a request from Napoleon III, who wanted a low-cost fat to feed his armies. Originally, it was produced from animal fat such as beef tallow. Today it is made from vegetable fats, mainly soy, canola, or corn oil; sometimes milk solids or whey; salt; emulsifiers; air; and water. It contains approximately 80 percent fat and 15 percent water like butter, and the remaining ingredients are used for flavor and color.
- Light butter usually contains 50 percent butter, and the remaining ingredients are water, emulsifying agents, flavoring agents, and coloring.
- Light, or nonfat, margarine usually contains small amounts of vegetable fats, water, emulsifying agents, flavorings, color, and a thickening agent such as gelatin, gums, or starch. This type of product can only be used as a spread—cooking with these products will leave a gummy, sticky substance on the pan. They have no lubrication properties.

>> Eggs

Eggs are the reproductive body produced by birds. They consist of egg white, or albumen, egg yolk, and a hard external shell composed of calcium. Albumen is the clear portion of the egg composing approximately two-thirds of the egg and is the chief source of nutrition for the developing chick. Egg albumen is primarily water with a protein matrix. This protein coagulates when heated and is used in fresh or dried form as a clarifying agent. The egg yolk contains all of the fat, vitamins, and minerals. It also contains lecithin, a fat-based substance used as an emulsifying agent in the preparation of other foods. The chalazae cord keeps the yolk in place. The fresher the egg, the larger and stronger the chalazae. In the cold kitchen, eggs are often used as a binding agent when added to ground poultry mixes or as a main component of a dish such as egg salad. They provide nutrition due to their high-quality protein, as well as flavor, structure, texture, and moisture. Egg yolks are used as a thickening agent in mayonnaise-based dressings.

There are three grades of eggs: AA, A, and B. Eggs are graded according to the size, spread, and thickness of the egg white, the lack of any defects or spots in the yolk, and the shape and cleanliness of the egg shell. Color has no bearing on grading or flavor. Brown eggs come from brown-feathered birds and there is no nutritional or flavor difference in the egg itself.

Most commercial egg products are chicken based; however, occasionally duck and quail eggs are used in the cold kitchen for sauces, pasta, and salads.

STORAGE OF EGGS

Eggs keep for 4 to 6 weeks if held at 36°F (2°C) but lose quality quickly at room temperature—they lose one full grade in one day if held at room temperature. Each day at room temperature equals one week at 36°F (2°C). Older (4 to 5 weeks) eggs have the same nutritional benefit as fresh eggs.

How important is it for eggs to be fresh when we use them? Fresh eggs have firm yolks and whites that stand up high and do not spread due to cellular breakdown. As eggs age, they lose moisture and become less dense. The white thins out and the yolk flattens out. An air pocket forms as the water evaporates through minute pores in the shell.

For a ready-to-serve egg such as a fried or shirred egg, use very fresh eggs.

It is better to use older eggs for hard-cooked eggs because they are easier to peel. Hold eggs for 2 weeks for peeling purposes. For baking, it is perfectly acceptable to use Grade B eggs, as appearance is not the main issue.

MARKET FORMS OF EGGS

When purchasing eggs, there are many market forms to choose from. Fresh or in shell eggs come in 15 dozen cases or individual dozen per carton. When using eggs for sauces that will not receive additional cooking, many state health codes require that frozen pasteurized egg products be used. They come packaged as whole eggs, yolks, whites, whole with extra yolks, and sugared yolks. Eggs also come in dry form sold as powdered whole eggs, egg whites, and dried egg yolks. For ease in banquet work, hard cooked, pre-sliced, and pre-diced are available. Eggs in a bag for banquet work come in plastic, boilable bags or raw egg product that are pasteurized.

EGG SUBSTITUTES

Egg substitutes are made with egg whites only and no yolk or albumen, from plant sources or soy, and a variety of protein-based chemicals. They are used for fat-restricted diets. They behave similarly to real eggs but have a slightly different flavor.

Figure 6-49 A variety of types of protein.

>> Seafood, Poultry, and Meat

Protein in the form of seafood, poultry, or meat is the most expensive raw material that a cold kitchen will process and utilize (Figure 6-49). The purchase of these tasty but perishable items, along with storing them in an optimal setting, are among the most important duties of the cold kitchen chef. As with produce, good chefs go to great lengths to secure the best proteins in their region. Items such as local, wild-caught, or sustainably raised seafood; free-range or organically raised poultry; and grass-fed, paddock-raised cattle and pigs are preferred but sometimes unavailable. Foodservice operations that establish a good rapport with farmers, growers, and fish purveyors benefit their guests by providing nutritious and tasty food. Chefs who order directly from the farm, coop, or other source also benefit the environment and become a part of the solution. Above all else, chefs know where their food comes from (Figure 6-50).

SEAFOOD

The rivers, seas, and oceans of the world provide us with quality protein sources of unlimited varieties and flavors. In this unit we will break down seafood into two main categories: (1) aquatic invertebrates known as crustaceans, mollusks, and cephalopods; and (2) vertebrates with cartilage, bones, muscle tissue, gills, fins, and scales known as finfish. Seafood is particularly rich in calcium, phosphorus, iron, copper, magnesium, and iodine. Although the amounts vary, they are rich in vitamins A, B, and D. Shellfish of all kinds are lean and low in salt. They are choices for low-calorie and low-sodium diets.

Inspection and Grading of Seafood

Inspection of seafood for wholesomeness is voluntary, unlike the mandatory inspections in the poultry and meat industries. That is why you must shop at a reputable seafood purveyor. How can you tell? Contact your local health department and talk to other chefs and restau-

Figure 6-50 Fresh seafood on display at Pike Place Market, Seattle, Washington.

rant owners. The reputation of a good or bad company is self-evident. Many purveyors and seafood companies pay for a fee-for-service inspection through the U.S. Department of Commerce (USDC). There are three types of seafood inspection services:

Type 1: Covers the plant itself, the products, and the processing practices from the fish that come off the boats to the final packaging and shipping. When a product is passed through this inspection process, it can receive the Packed Under Federal Inspection (PUFI) seal.

Type 2: Covers warehouses, cold storage facilities, and processing plants. An inspector visits the site and inspects random lots to ensure quality control and wholesomeness of stored products as well as compliance of size, package weight, and other conditions.

Type 3: Covers fishing vessels and plants that do processing. This is for sanitation standards only. If a boat or processing plant passes this inspection process, it is recognized as an officially approved establishment listed with the USDC.

Grading

Grading seafood, like inspection, is also voluntary. Only products listed under Type 1 inspection are eligible for grading. Fish and shellfish are graded A, B, or C based on configuration, flavor, lack of odor, and defects.

Shellfish

Simply put, shellfish are animals that have a shell. There are three varieties of shellfish: mollusks, crustaceans, and cephalopods.

Mollusks

Mollusks are shellfish that have soft unsegmented bodies inside a hard shell. There are two types of shelled mollusks: (1) the univalve, such as abalone and conch, and (2) bi-valves, such as clams, mussels, and oysters. They have many uses in the cold kitchen and are served raw or cooked, chilled or hot.

Figure 6-51 Oysters.

Oysters Easter oyster-*Crassostrea virginica;* European oyster-*Ostrea edulis;* Pacific oyster-*Crassostrea gigas;* Olympia oyster-*Ostrea lurida*

Oysters are bi-valve mollusks that attach themselves to piers, underwater structures, and, in the case of aquaculture oysters, on scallop shells that are strung up on steel wire (Figure 6-51). They live in brackish water near the mouth of rivers along the coasts in bays, inlets, and estuaries. Tough, irregular, and brittle shells characterize oysters. The flesh of the oyster is soft and delicate with a briny or sweetly metallic flavor profile, dependent upon where they are raised. Briny oysters come from coastal waters whereas oysters with a sweeter, more mineral finish tend to be from waters in bays and estuaries where there is more fresh water in the mix. Oysters are available year-round; however, oysters harvested in the cooler months usually have a better flavor and texture. Oysters are edible during the summer, but the flesh is softer due to spawning and warmer water conditions.

There are a few types of varieties of oysters grown in the United States, including the Pacific Northwest native, called Olympia. This native Pacific oyster is small, rarely reaching 2 inches. It is known for its coppery flavor and is a favorite of oyster aficionados. Other oysters available on the West Coast are the Pacific oysters originally from Japan and grown in dozens of aquaculture farms along the coast of California, Oregon, and Washington. They are all the same Pacific species but take on differing flavors based on the mineral content of the waters in which they live. Some of these are the Quilicene, Fanny Bay, and Hood Canal. The Kumamoto and Gigamoto are other successful Japanese varieties now grown in these West Coast locations. There have been recent successes with bringing the flat European oysters to the East and West coasts. Marennes and Belon oysters are just two of the European varieties now grown in the United States.

Oysters found along the shores of the Atlantic and Gulf coasts are the next category. These oysters go by the names of the areas in which they are found; the most common is the Bluepoint oyster. Some other Atlantic varieties are the Cape Cod, Chincoteague, Apalachicola, and, along the Texas and Louisiana coast, the Gulf oyster. The market forms for oysters are live in shell, shucked, either fresh or frozen, and canned.

Always purchase your shellfish from a reputable purveyor, and check oysters and other shellfish for freshness. The shell should feel heavy for its size, and it should be clamped tight. Oysters must be alive to be safely eaten. When shucked, they should have a very mild, sweet, almost cucumber-like smell or have a clean, briny smell. If they smell of ammonia, discard them, as they are dying or decomposing. Before opening oysters, brush and scrub the shells under running water to remove any mud or sand. Check to be sure that the shells are intact.

CHEF'S TIP
To open oysters that will be cooked, place them in an oven until they begin to open.

Opening an Oyster

1. Scrub oyster shells to remove any residue. Use a brush if necessary (Figure 6-52).

Figure 6-52 Scrubbing the oyster's shell.

2. To open the oyster, place the bowl side down with the flatter shell on the top. Place the oyster knife at a 45° angle at the point of the oyster. Pry open and slowly slide the oyster knife along the top shell to sever the muscle from the shell (Figures 6-53 and 6-54). Slide the knife under the oyster to dislodge from shell for raw bar service.

Figure 6-53 Oyster knife.

Figure 6-54 Use an oyster knife to pry the oyster open.

Oysters come from purveyors in net bags or in boxes. To store oysters before service, keep them in a drip pan in their original container. If they come in a plastic bag, remove the oysters from the bag and place them on a thin layer of ice with a damp towel over them to prevent them from drying out. Do not let them sit in a plastic bag—they will asphyxiate. When stored properly, fresh oysters can be kept for up to 1 week. Shucked oysters can be stored for up to 1 week in their original container at 30° to 34°F (−1° to +1°C). Frozen oysters should be kept at or below 0° (−18° C).

To cook oysters, heat just enough to cook through, keeping the oyster plump and juicy. Avoid overcooking. Other cooking methods for oysters include baking on the half-shell with a tasty stuffing, poaching, deep-frying, and adding them to soups and stews (Figure 6-55).

Clams Hard-shell or quahog-*Mercenaria mercenaria;* Soft-shell-*Mya arenaria;* Geoduck-*Panopea abrupta;* Surf-*Spisula solidissima*

Clams are bi-valves that live in sand and mud (Figure 6-56). They are found along coastal areas as well as in fresh water. There are two types of clams: hard-shell, or quahog as it is called in the New England states, and soft-shelled, or steamers. Hard-shelled clams are sold by age and size, the smallest being called the "littleneck," which is a 3- to 4-year-old hardshell clam. Cherrystones are 5-year-old clams, and clams older than 5 years are sold as

Figure 6-55 Oysters Rockefeller.

Figure 6-56 Clams.

chowder clams. Butter, Manilla, geoduck, horse clams, and pismos are found along the Pacific coast. Razor clams are found on both the Pacific and Atlantic coasts. Soft-shelled clams have a brittle, thin shell and tender, sweet flesh. To ensure that clams and other shellfish are sand free, the process of depuration is recommended.

Depuration

After shellfish are caught, they go through the process of **depuration.** In this process, they are placed in a treated water solution and allowed to purge sand, excrement, and other impurities. This treatment assures a higher standard of sanitation and a longer shelf-life in oysters, clams, and mussels. With the health concerns of contaminated seafood, this is a good way to ensure a safer product for dining customers.

Clams also come shucked fresh and frozen, canned whole, chopped or minced, and pre-breaded. When purchasing clams, check for freshness by looking for tight shells with little gaping. They should have little odor and, when opened, should smell sweet and briny.

Opening Clams

1. Scrub the shells thoroughly. If possible, keep the clams in a saltwater solution with cornmeal added to flush out any sand. Rinse after a few hours.
2. To open for clams on the half-shell, use a clam knife to pry open the shell (Figures 6-57 and 6-58).

Figure 6-57 Clam knife.

Figure 6-58 Opening clams.

Clams can be steamed, poached, deep fried, baked on the half-shell with a savory filling such as bacon and spinach, and, of course, added to flavorful soups and chowders. When baking clams, spread on sheet pans in the oven and cook just until the shells begin to open for easy removal of the clam meat. Razor clams should be stored in salt water until use and then steamed or plunged in boiling water for 30 seconds before shocking in an ice bath and being cleaned for use. Take care not to overcook them—clams can become excessively tough and chewy. When steaming, steam just enough to open the clams.

Once the shell is open, the knife tip can be used to release the clam from the shell.

Clams should be stored like oysters in their net bags or on a thin bed of ice in drip pans and covered with damp towels until use. Clams, as well as all shellfish, should be stored at 34° to 40°F (2° to 4°C).

Mussels Blue mussel-*Mytilus edulis;* Green-lipped-*Perna canaliculus*

Mussels have thin, shiny, black- or green-lipped shells with bright orange to yellow flesh (Figure 6-59). They have a stronger protein flavor than clams and are well suited to garlicky and spicy sauces. They are found on both the Pacific and Atlantic shorelines. The best mussels come from Prince Edward Island in Canada. The green-lip variety comes from the Southern Pacific, especially along the New Zealand coastline. Mussels come live, in shell, sold shucked, and packed in brine, vinaigrette, or pickled. They are also sold smoked as well as frozen. When buying fresh, live mussels, make sure the shells are clamped tight. Throw out any mussel that is gaping open and will not close when touched.

Cleaning Mussels

1. Scrub well under cold running water with a stiff-bristle brush (Figure 6-60).
2. Remove the hairy "beard" from between shells (Figure 6-61). This is a harmless protein substance that helps the mussels to attach themselves to piers and other underwater structures.
3. Soak mussels in salted water and cornmeal to remove any sand.
4. Refrigerate at 34° to 40°F (1° to 4°C) and keep covered with a damp towel to prevent them from drying out.

Figure 6-59 Mussels.

Figure 6-60 Clean the mussel with a brush under cold running water to remove sand and grit.

Figure 6-61 Use a paring knife to remove the beard from the mussels.

Mussels are rarely served raw. They do best when lightly steamed with white wine, garlic, and a touch of red pepper flakes. The broth may be served alongside the mussels. Mussels are delicious when served poached, then chilled with a tangy salsa or topped with a sesame, soy glaze and grilled.

Figure 6-62 Scallops.

Scallops Bay scallops-*Argopecten irradians;* Sea scallops-*Placopecten megallanicus*

Scallops are unique in that the edible portion of the scallop is the large muscle that enables the scallop to swim (Figure 6-62). Scallops are characterized by the creamy white, almost gelatinous flesh, which has a nutty, buttery, and sweet flavor. It is rare to purchase live scallops in the United States, as they are usually sold fresh shucked in a dry pack or wet brine pack. They are also available IQF frozen. There are two basic kinds of scallops sold in the United States: the small, delicate bay scallop and the larger, less tender sea or diver scallop. Diver scallops are hand-collected scallops from Maine. The process of dredging the ocean floor retrieves other large scallops. Large scallops from Alaska and the Calico scallop from the southern Atlantic coastal states, the Gulf of Mexico, and down to the coast of South America are also becoming more available. Scallops are available year-round. Because they are shucked, checking for freshness is key. Scallops should smell sweet and clean. Scallops have a small, tough side muscle that needs to be removed before cooking them. Scallops can be marinated in lemon juice and served ceviche style or sautéed, broiled, poached, baked, and grilled. They are also useful as an ingredient in seafood sausages and mousselines.

To store scallops, keep them covered with plastic wrap and refrigerated between 30° to 34°F (−1° to +1°C). Keep away from direct contact with ice and water, as they can absorb excess moisture, thus damaging the delicate proteins.

Other Mollusks

Univalves such as abalone, found along the Pacific Coast; periwinkles and whelks, found along the Atlantic coasts; conch *(Strombus gigas)* from the Florida coast; and escargot, a land-based univalve, are also popular shellfish items served from the cold kitchen. Abalone *(Haliotis rufescens)* is now available for foodservice. Periwinkles are small snails found in fresh water and salt water in Europe and off the Eastern coast of North America. They are handled like other mollusks and can be steamed and served with drawn butter.

Crustaceans

Crustaceans, which are distantly related to land spiders, are animals with a segmented shell and joined legs. Shrimp, crab, lobster, and crayfish are some of the more common examples.

Lobsters Northern or Maine-*Homarus americanus;* Spiny or Rock-*Panulirus argus;* Australian rock lobster-*Panulirus cygnus*

The edible meat of the lobster comes from the tail, claws, and legs (Figure 6-63). The red coral, or roe, and green tomalley, or liver, is considered a delicacy. Lobsters are classified by weight.

CATEGORIES OF LOBSTERS AND THEIR WEIGHTS

Name	Weight
Chicken	1 pound
Quarters	1 1/4 pound
Selects	1 1/2 pound up to 2 1/4 pound
Jumbos	2 1/4 pound

A 1-pound lobster will yield 4 ounces of cooked meat. Lobsters come live or cooked, either fresh or frozen in cryovac packages or canned. When purchasing lobsters live, the key word is "live." Live lobster must be alive when cooked. If alive, meat is firm and the tail is springy. Dying lobsters are called sleepers and should be cooked immediately to preserve the meat. Lobsters have an enzyme that causes the meat to turn to a sticky gel when the lobster is dead, making the meat unpalatable. When cooking lobster, the meat should smell fresh and sweet, and the texture should be tender.

There are two varieties of lobster available in the United States. From the East we have the Northern lobsters, which are found off the east coast from Maine to Massachusetts. These lobsters have large pincers as well as a robust, meaty tail. The other variety is called the spiny rock lobster, which has small pincers with large tails. They are found along the Southern Atlantic coast as well as the West Coast off of California.

Lobster can be cooked whole or cut up before cooking. When cleaning cooked lobster, the stomach sac should be discarded. The

Figure 6-63 Lobster.

tomalley can be eaten plain, mashed into butter for a nice compound sauce, or used in veloutè sauces. The coral, or roe, that is present only in females can be added to sauces as well.

Live lobster should be packed in moist seaweed; moist, heavy paper; or kept in a saltwater tank. Never place live lobster in fresh water—it will kill the lobsters instantly. Cooked lobster must be kept at 30° to 34°F (−1° to +1°C). To cook lobsters, simmer them in salted water or court bouillon. Be careful to avoid toughening lobster by cooking at too high a temperature or cooking too long. You can also sauté, bake, and broil lobsters. Lobster meat is used for salads, appetizers, and for many other uses.

Rock lobsters are used for their tail meat only. They come fresh but are now available IQF. They can be steamed, simmered, and broiled.

Crawfish or Crayfish *Procambarus clarkia, Procabarus zonangulus*

Crawfish are related to lobsters. They have similar body structures but live in fresh water and are much smaller in size (Figure 6-64). They are found in streams and creeks and have a sweet flavor. They are favored for their tail meat. In Louisiana, they are boiled fresh in large cauldrons.

Shrimp White-*Penaeus setilferus;* Bay shrimp-*Pandalus jordani and Pandalus borealis;* Large blue-*Macrobrachium rosenbergii*

Shrimp are one of the mainstays of the cold kitchen. From crisp, cold shrimp cocktails to bay shrimp appetizers and hors d' oeuvre, shrimp and prawns are one of the most versatile shellfish utilized in the cold kitchen (Figure 6-65). There are several species of shrimp available. Raw shrimp are sold and distinguished by their color. The common white shrimp from the Gulf of Mexico is actually a greenish gray

Figure 6-64 A crawfish lies next to a lobster.

color. Mexican or Brazilian browns have a reddish brown tint. Tiger shrimp from Southeast Asia are a blue-black striped variety with yellow spots. Other less common varieties are the Santa Barbara spot prawn, a super sweet and rare treat. (*Prawn* is a term commonly used to describe large shrimp. Technically true prawns have a thinner body and longer legs than

Figure 6-65 Shrimp.

shrimp.) The small, tender bay shrimp is the favorite for salads such as a shrimp Louie as well as for shrimp salad used in sandwich making. In Hawaii, there are large blue, freshwater prawns that are used not only for a flavorful menu addition but also for their dramatic looks. With their long antenna and thorny heads, they add a dash of excitement to any seafood display or dish.

All shrimp cook up into a pink to red color. Shrimp are found in most of the coastal waters of the United States, with the majority of wild caught shrimp coming from the Gulf Coast. Most aquaculture shrimp sold in the United States come from Mexico, India, and Southeast Asia.

Shrimp are sold by the count per pound. Generally speaking, only the tail is marketed and eaten. In other countries, the head is also served. The larger the shrimp, the higher the cost but the lower the labor in cleaning and deveining. One pound of shrimp will yield approximately 8 to 12 ounces (227 to 340 g) of flesh.

Shrimp are called "green" shrimp when raw in the shell. This type of shrimp is sold fresh, frozen, P/D (peeled and deveined), PDC (peeled, deveined, and cooked), and IQF, or individually quick-frozen. Frozen shrimp, whether in block form or IQF, are usually glazed in a saltwater solution and blast frozen. This glazing protects the shrimp from drying out in the freezing process.

To ensure a quality product, you should check for freshness. Frozen shrimp should not have any blanched or white spots. This would indicate freezer burn. Shrimp should smell sweet when defrosted, with no hint of ammonia or off smells. There should be no dark brown spots or sliminess. When received, the shrimp should be solidly frozen. Fresh shrimp should have a glossy shell, an almost translucent quality, and be true to their natural color. The meat should have little smell or a slightly sweet, briny smell. The flesh should be firm.

Bay shrimp should come packed in tubs, either fresh or frozen. The meat should smell sweet. Any shrimp with a strong ammonia or off smell should be rejected.

To properly store shrimp, freeze at 0°F (−18°C) or lower. It should be thawed overnight in the refrigerator and stored on crushed ice, wrapped with moisture-proof material. Fresh shrimp should be stored at between 32° and 34°F (0° and 1°C) due to its fragile nature.

Shrimp should be peeled and deveined before cooking to remove the sand vein. If possible, shrimp served chilled should be peeled after cooking to protect the flavor of the shrimp and chilled immediately. Shrimp can be steamed, simmered, boiled, broiled, coated and deep-fried, butterflied, stuffed, and baked. Cold shrimp is traditionally served with cocktail sauce and lemon wedges.

The term "scampi" is actually a distinct kind of crustacean found in the Mediterranean. In the United States, the term "scampi" generally refers to a dish made from large shrimp sautéed in garlic butter.

Crab Blue-*Callinectes sapidus, Portusnus pelagicus;* Dungeness-*Cancer magister;* Jonah-*Cancer borealis;* King-*Paralithodes camtschaticus;* Snow-*Chionoecetes opilio, C. bairdi, and C. tanneri;* Stone-*Meippe mercenaria and M. adina*

There are many types of crab products used in the cold kitchen (Figure 6-66). The king crab is the largest crab available in the United States and is also the most costly. The snow crab is a slightly smaller and less-expensive crab from the cold waters off of Alaska. The dungeness is the sweet and succulent variety that is found along the Pacific coast from Alaska to just south

Figure 6-66 Dungeness crab.

of San Francisco. The Jonah crab is located along both coasts, and the blue crab is found along the Atlantic and Gulf coasts.

Stone crabs and tanner crabs are not as well known. Stone crabs are used for their claws only. The crabs are caught, one claw is removed, and the crab is released. These crabs grow new claws to replace the missing claw. Soft-shell crabs are also popular. Soft-shell crabs are blue crabs that have molted or shed their outer carapace. This new shell takes approximately 24 hours to harden. When the crabs are in this fragile state, they are harvested. These types of crabs can be eaten shell and all. Crabs come as live, cooked fresh, or frozen. Crab meat comes cooked and frozen in cans or in small plastic carton packs in 6 ounce and 8 ounce (170 g and 227 g) sizes.

Dungeness crab comes whole frozen, or in 5 pound (2.27 kg) cooked and frozen or fresh pack cans. King and snow crab come in glazed and frozen leg and claw sections that are precooked.

For receiving and storage, live crabs should be kept alive until cooked. Like lobster, they should not be placed in fresh water. They should be covered with damp newspaper or seaweed until cooked. When purchasing live crab, the key word is "lively." They should be lively. Sleepers should be cooked immediately. When receiving frozen crab meat, it should be treated like any other frozen seafood product. Keep frozen crab at or below 0°F (−18°C). Crab and crab meat can be used in cold salads, hors d' oeuvre, appetizers, raw bars, and many other cold kitchen uses. Soft-shelled crabs are dredged in seasoned flour and sautéed or battered for deep frying. They may be used for many types of appetizers. Frozen meat should have excess moisture squeezed out and removed before use. Crab meat is used for many purposes such as stuffing, fillings, and cooked into patties. Frozen crab meat is already cooked and needs only to be heated through and sauced.

Cephalopods

Cephalopods have soft bodies; a thin, cartilage-like internal structure and a hard-shelled beak; and long, sucker-laden arms. They have the ability to swim rapidly through the water to great depths. Calamari, giant squid, and octopus are in this group. In the cold kitchen, these shellfish groups play an important part in banquets, catering, and restaurant meals.

Squid Loligo opalescens, L. pealei, Illex illecebrosus

Squid are also known by their Italian name of "calamari" (Figure 6-67). Squid come in various sizes; the smaller ones are used for deep frying and tempura—tentacles and all. The

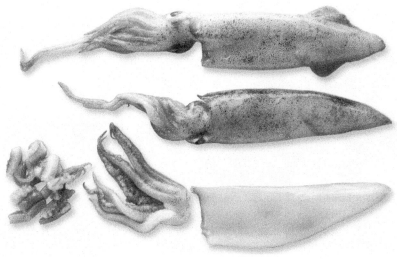

Figure 6-67 Squid.

Figure 6-68 Octopus.

medium ones are used for calamari rings or pounded out for mock abalone or "scallone," and the larger ones are used for stuffing. Small squid are brined or pickled and can be used for salads. They have tentacles and are similar to octopus, only smaller and more tender. Their ink sacs are used to color pasta and some sauces.

Octopus *Octopus* spp.

Octopus is firmer in texture in comparison to squid. They, too, have eyes and tentacles, but their tentacles are covered with suckers and, in most cases, must be blanched and peeled before use (Figure 6-68). Octopus should be slow simmered for a long period of time to tenderize. The flesh is sweet and, if handled correctly, can be tender.

Cuttlefish *Sepia* spp.

The cuttlefish is a 10-armed cephalopod closely related to the octopus and squid (Figure 6-69). It is larger and heavier than the squid and contains a valuable ink sac that is used to flavor sauces and color pastas. It is imported from Europe and Asia and can be used in place of squid in most recipes.

Figure 6-69 Cuttlefish.

LEARNING ACTIVITY 6-3

Visit a local fish market. Make a list of the types of seafood available. Note the varieties within each classification, such as the types of shrimp or mollusks available.

LEARNING ACTIVITY 6-4

Cooking Shrimp

In this exercise, you will learn the importance of timing when cooking shellfish.

In each of two separate stainless steel pots, place 2 quarts of water. Bring to a boil.

In the first pot, set the temperature to 160°F (71°C). In the second pot, set the temperature to 200°F (93°C). In each pot place five raw, peeled, and deveined shrimp. At 5 minutes, remove one shrimp from each pot. Repeat this action at 3-minute intervals, recording the differences and any changes noted.

Note the color, texture, flavor, and aroma of each sample and record your findings.

	Pot 1 160°F (71°C)	Pot 2 200°F (93°C)	Color	Texture	Aroma	Flavor
After 5 min.						
After 8 min.						
After 12 min.						
After 15 min.						

Fish

There are thousands of aquatic vertebrates, or fish, as we know them, with fins for swimming and gills for breathing. They are found in both salt and fresh water, and many varieties are edible. Finfish are classified into two categories by their bone structure as flatfish or round fish. There are also fish without true bones. One of the best sources for the list of available fish is through the FDA. They publish *The Seafood List: FDA Guide to Acceptable Market Names for Food Fish Sold in Interstate Commerce.* The list is published regularly and is handy for information regarding finfish and shellfish.

Flatfish

Flatfish have uneven, flattened bodies, both eyes on the top of their head, a light sandy to dark-camouflaged top skin to match the environment, and a snow white bottom side. They swim horizontally and are generally found in deep-ocean waters. The following is a short list of the common available flatfish.

Flounder and Sole Soleidae spp.

Sole are fish from the soleidae family, which is only found off the coast of Europe and Africa. Sole marketed in the United States are actually members of the flounder family. The FDA allows for flounder to be marketed as "sole" in the United States. Flounder are sold as fillets, both fresh and frozen (Figure 6-70).

Figure 6-70 Flounder.

Figure 6-71 Petrale sole.

Petrale Sole

Petrale sole is considered to be the finest of the smaller flatfish available in the market (Figure 6-71). Petrale "sole" is actually a flounder that is found off the coast of California, Oregon, and Washington. It has firm flesh and is usually sold in fillet form.

Lemon Sole

Lemon sole is from the East Coast and is the most common "sole." It is also known as the winter flounder. Lemon sole has a softer flesh than petrale. Whole fish average 2 pounds and are commonly sold in fillet form.

Pacific Flounder

Pacific flounder, also known as Domestic Dover, is a soft-fleshed fish sold usually in fillet form.

English Sole

English sole is another flounder caught off the West Coast of the United States. It is a mild-fleshed fish that is plentiful.

True Dover Sole *Solea vulgaris*

Dover sole is a lean fish found in the waters off the coasts of England. They are sold fresh but, more often, glazed and frozen whole. They need to be peeled before they are cooked.

Turbot *Scophthalmus maximus*

Turbot, another flatfish, has a distinctive diamond shape and has firm flesh and a delicate flavor (Figure 6-72). Turbot is found in European waters and off the Pacific coast.

Halibut *Hippoglossus stenolepsis*

Halibut is the largest of the flatfish—some of the larger fish come in at 200 to 300 pounds (Figure 6-73). There are two types of halibut: East Coast or the Atlantic halibut, and West Coast halibut, also known as the Pacific, Northern, Western, and Alaskan halibut. Large flounder caught off the West Coast are often called California halibut. Halibut are sold whole, drawn, and in sides, fletches, or fillets.

Figure 6-72 Turbot.

Figure 6-73 Halibut.

Figure 6-74 Catfish.

Round Fish

Symmetrical, round, or oval bodies characterize **round fish.** They have eyes on either side of their heads. They swim in an upright position and are found in all types of environments. Some round fish are hot blooded, such as those from the Tuna or Thon family. The following is a list of a variety of round fish used in the cold kitchen.

Catfish *Ictalurus punctatus, Ictalurus furcatus, Ameiurus catus*

Popular catfish varieties include channel, blue, and white. Catfish is a freshwater fish found in lakes and streams. It has no scales and is usually sold in fillets (Figure 6-74). It is considered to be one of the best-eating freshwater fish because of its firm, white flesh. It has a mild, sweet flavor as long as it has been harvested from clean water. It is a moderately fatty fish that can be fried, baked, or broiled.

Figure 6-75 Cod.

Cod *Gadus morhua*

In recent years, the Atlantic cod fisheries have collapsed, and what used to be one of the most popular fish in the United States has been over-fished to the point that they now face a danger of extinction. We have, however, many types of cod on both coasts still available for consumption. Cod has a delicate flavor and medium to firm white flesh that flakes when cooked (Figure 6-75). It is often served deep fried, pan fried, or baked. Small cod under 2 1/2 pounds are called "scrod" or "schrod."

West Coast cod, also known as grey cod, is available and has a mild flaky flesh. It is labeled true cod to distinguish it from other fish with similar names, such as rock cod. Cod is available in skinless fillets, steaks, or whole or drawn fish. It is often salted, dried, pickled, and smoked.

Haddock *Melanogrammus aeglefinus*

Haddock is a member of the cod family. It has a stronger flavor than true cod (Figure 6-76). The haddock has a black lateral line running along its white side and a distinctive dark mark similar to a thumbprint above the pectoral fin.

Figure 6-76 A haddock fillet ready for grilling, pan frying, or baking.

Figure 6-77 Herring.

Figure 6-78 Mackerel.

Herring *Clupea harengus*

Herring are small, oily fish resembling sardines (Figure 6-77). There are over 12 species of herring in North American waters. They are found in shallow temperate water, they move in large schools, and they attract many larger fish such as barracuda, tuna, and shark. They are salted, pickled, and smoked and can be grilled and served with a mayonnaise verte. Pilchards and sardines found in cans are commonly herring.

Mackerel *Scombridae* spp.

Mackerel is the name given to a number of different species of smaller, tuna-like fish in the large family, scrombrodae (Figure 6-78). They are found in tropical as well as temperate oceans and seas. Mackerel has a round, slim body and many fins. It is an oily fish with dark meat that is rich. Because they spoil easily, mackerel should be eaten within a day of catch. They are often cured with salt and smoked.

Monkfish *Lophius americanus*

The monkfish is an unusual fish that has a huge, inedible head and a small, edible tail (Figure 6-79). Its flesh has a similar taste and texture to lobster meat. It is known as anglerfish or mock lobster because of its unique design and flavor. The tail meat is the most marketable section, although whole fish are sometimes found in Asian seafood markets.

Orange Roughy *Hoplostethus atlanticus*

Orange roughy has been available to chefs for the past 30 years (Figure 6-80). It was first discovered in the early 1970s off the coasts of New Zealand and Australia. Orange roughy has firm, white flesh with an orange skin. It is marketed in sizes ranging from 12 to 16 inches long or as fillets.

Figure 6-79 Monkfish.

Figure 6-80 Orange roughy.

Figure 6-81 Pompano.

Pompano Trachinotus carolinus, Parastronmateus niger

The two common species of pompano include the Florida pompano and the black pomfret. Pompanos are thin, deep-bodied fish with a deeply forked caudal tail and dorsal fins. They have a silvery body, shading to metallic blue above and golden yellow ventrally (Figure 6-81). Pompanos are rich-tasting fish and are sold whole, drawn, or as fillets. They are often baked enpapillotte, pan seared, or sautéed.

Red Snapper Lutjanus campechanus

Red snapper is also known as pargo, snapper, American red snapper, Northern red snapper, Mixian snapper, and mutton snapper (Figure 6-82). This fish is known as a meaty, all-purpose fish that has many uses. It has white meat that is firm textured, mild and delicately flavored, and low in fat. It is sold as a whole fish or in fillets or steaks.

Figure 6-82 Red snapper.

 Rock cod.

Figure 6-84 Salmon.

Rock Cod/Rockfish *Sebastes auriculatus*

Rock cod is known by many different names, including ocean perch, Pacific red snapper, yellowtail, goldeneye, blue rockfish, bocaccio, chilipepper, and shortbelly. Rock cod is found in the waters off the northern Pacific Coast. It ranges in size from 5 to 15 pounds. The skin color comes in numerous hues ranging from deep red to brilliant orange, brown, and blue (Figure 6-83). Rock cod has a firm texture and white flesh with a sweet, mild taste. It is low in fat and is great broiled, baked, or sautéed.

Salmon

Salmon is one of the superstars of the cold kitchen (Figure 6-84). From a regal, poached whole salmon as a centerpiece to a magnificent buffet spread complete with mountains of cured, thinly sliced lox, salmon is a great-looking and tasting fish. With its oil-rich, scarlet flesh, it bursts with succulent flavor. Most species of salmon are high in omega-3s.

The following table takes a closer look at some of the popular species of salmon.

SALMON COMPARISONS

Name	Species	Characteristics	Size	Culinary Applications
Chinook/King	*Oncorhynchus tshawytscha*	Oil-rich, scarlet flesh, succulent flavor	18–20 lbs, 18 to 20 inches	Grilling, broiling, sautéing, baking, poaching, steaming, and smoking
Sockeye	*Oncorhynchus nerka*	Brilliant red, firm, rich flavor	6 lbs	Poaching, steaming, smoking, curing, grilling, baking, and sautéing
Silver/Coho	*Oncorhynchus kisutch*	Orange red flesh, firm flesh, moderately oil texture	12 lbs, 20 to 35 inches	Cured and smoked
Pink	*Oncorhynchus gorbuscha*	Lower in fat than most other species, high in protein; light rosy pink flesh, tender texture, delicate flavor	1–4 lbs	Canned, baked, and sautéed
Keta/chum/silverbright	*Oncorhynchus keta*	Orange pink color; firm texture, lower fat content, mild flavor	15–18 lbs	Curing, smoking, and grilling
Atlantic salmon	*Salmo salar*	Mild and oily flavor; flesh is softer due to the higher fat content; bright orange flesh	4–20 lbs	Fattier species good for grilling, broiling, and baking; if poaching, use a low temp 160°F (71°C)

Figure 6-85 Trout.

Figure 6-86 Tuna steaks.

Trout Oncorhynchus mykiss

Trout is the oldest aquaculture in North America, starting in the late 1800s. Most of today's farm-raised trout comes from Idaho. Rainbow trout is a mild-fleshed fish with a tender, flaky texture (Figure 6-85). It has a creamy white, orange, or light pink flesh, depending on its feed. Wild caught trout often have a reddish flesh. Steelheads are ocean going rainbow trout and are usually caught wild. Market size for rainbow trout is 8 to 16 ounces. It can be baked, broiled, grilled, poached, sautéed, cured in brine, or smoked for a tasty appetizer or hors d' oeuvre.

Tuna

Tuna are warm-blooded fish found in virtually all oceans of the world. Tuna are related to the mackerel and bonito and, as such, are subject to the same cautions. Tuna should be always kept as cold as possible to avoid the development of histamine, which can lead to scomboid poisoning. Top-grade tuna is preferred for use in sashimi. Fresh tuna steaks are grilled (Figure 6-86). Canned tuna has multiple applications.

The following table compares three popular species of tuna.

> **CHEF'S TIP**
> *If you are lucky enough to have access to live trout, try using the classic method of cooking called, "au bleu." The trout is kept alive until just before cooking. It is then immediately poached in a vinegar court bouillon. The skin becomes a deep blue in color, and the flesh is delicate and delicious.*

TUNA COMPARISONS

Name	Species	Characteristics	Culinary Applications
Albacore	*Thunnus alalunga*	White meat; fresh is fattier than most other species; high in omega-3s	Canned and used for salads, sandwiches, and other cooking applications; fresh grilled (rare), broiled, or sautéed
Ahi/yellowfin	*Thunnus albacares*	Bright yellow side markings; average size is 7 to 20 lbs; mild, meaty taste and a firm texture; bright red meat when raw (turns grayish tan when cooked)	Sashimi, grilled, broiled, sautéed, baked, and smoked
Bluefin	*Thunnus thynnus*	Largest commercially viable tuna (some weigh over a ton with a length of 12 ft); most are between 200 and 400 lbs; available in three grades based on fat content and color	Sashimi, grilling

Snapper/American Red Snapper/Red Snapper Lutjanus campechanus

The American red snapper is the only snapper in the United States that can be legally shipped interstate. Red snapper can grow to 35 pounds, although most commercial red

Figure 6-87 Red snapper.

Figure 6-88 Swordfish steaks in a lemon, dill marinade.

snapper is sold in the 4- to 6-pound size. Red snapper is sold whole, dressed, and in fillets (Figure 6-87). Snapper is a flavorful fish with a sweet, mild flavor and a medium firm texture. Red snapper can be cooked by just about every method, from steaming and poaching to baking, broiling, grilling, sautéing, and frying.

Swordfish *Xiphias gladius*

Swordfish is a nonschooling fish that is found worldwide. Most native-caught swordfish are harvested off the north banks of the North Atlantic off the eastern coast of Canada and the United States. Swordfish is a moist, flavorful fish with a firm texture similar to the texture of shark meat (Figure 6-88). The flesh is white to pink in color and burns beige after it is cooked. Swordfish is cooked in any manner that tuna is cooked—broiled, baked, grilled, smoked, and sautéed.

Whitefish/Shad *Coregonus clupeaformis*

Whitefish, also called shad or lake whitefish, is a pure white-fleshed member of the salmonidae family. It does not resemble trout or salmon, however. It is a freshwater and saltwater fish found in colder waters, giving it a high fat content (Figure 6-89). It is prized for its gold-colored roe. The market form of whitefish or shad is whole-dressed fish, fillets, and steaks. More often it is found smoked. Smoked whitefish lends itself to many tasty applications such as spreads, dips, and in chowders or fish stews.

Figure 6-89 Whitefish.

Nonbony-Type Fish

Symmetrical round or oval bodies characterize nonbony-type fish. These fish are some of the oldest types of animals living on the Earth. They have cartilage instead of bone structures and no scales. Sharks and rays fall into this category, as do sturgeon. Sturgeons have bony plates covering their bodies. Sturgeons and sharks are perhaps the most expensive and endangered fish today due to the value of their caviar, in the case of sturgeons, and sharks for their fins.

Shark *Isurus oxyrinchus*

The Mako shark is one of the most flavorful of the shark family. It is a tasty substitution for swordfish, with moister flesh. Shark steak is great for grilling. It has a firm flesh that holds together well when on the grill (Figure 6-90). It can also be baked, sautéed, or steamed and is especially delicious when steamed with ginger and garlic.

When using shark, remove the bloodline because it has a bitter flavor. Shark has urea in the blood; if not cleaned properly, it can have a strong ammonia smell. Reject any shark that has this odor.

Sturgeon *Acipenser transmontanus*

Since prehistory, the bony-plated sturgeon has been swimming in rivers and along the coasts of the world (Figure 6-91). It is the source of true caviar and, unfortunately, has been hunted almost to the brink of extinction. In the United States, there were originally seven different varieties of sturgeon; however, today only two are still harvested on the West Coast in small quantities.

Sturgeon is now farm-raised in California. The farm-raised white sturgeon is marketed in the 20-pound size. It is prized for its firm flesh and sweet, mild flavor resembling the gamed beluga sturgeon of Russia.

Sturgeon can be cured, smoked, grilled, marinated and boiled, poached, or sautéed.

Purchasing Fish

To purchase fish, you must always first look at the product and answer the following questions:

- Are the eyes clear and bright or cloudy?
- Are the gills bright red or dull brown?
- Does the fish smell clean and fresh like the ocean or like cucumber? Does it smell fishy?
- Is the flesh firm, and does it spring back to the touch?
- Are the scales bright, shiny, and tight?

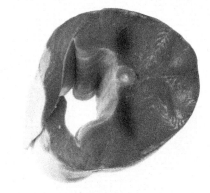
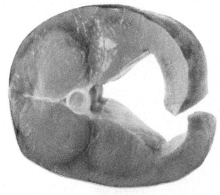

Figure 6-90 Shark steaks.

> **CHEF'S TIP**
> Never accept or purchase a fishy-smelling fish—the smell is an indication of old product.

> **CHEF'S TIP**
> Fish flesh should be shiny and bright, not dull or slimy. Old fish will show a separation of the flesh, especially near the belly cavity. This is called "belly burn." Refuse any fish that shows this age indicator.

Figure 6-91 Sturgeon.

Storing Fish

Fish should be kept at or below 34°F (1°C). It should be stored on crushed ice and lightly covered to keep moist. Ideally, fish should be stored in a lexan or a stainless steel drip pan to keep the flesh from sitting in its juices. Whole or drawn fish are not wrapped, but loosely covered and surrounded by crushed ice. Cut fish should be wrapped or left in its original wrapping and stored on crushed ice in a drip pan. It should not be stored beyond 2 days, and wrappings and pans should be changed daily.

Storing Frozen Fish

Frozen fish should be always stored at or below 0°F (−18°C). The majority of fish served in the United States is frozen. Frozen products should be frozen solid when received. There should be no appreciable odor and the packaging should show no signs of defrosting. Items should be well wrapped with no sign of freezer burn. The maximum storage time for frozen fatty fish is 2 months. Lean fish may be frozen for 6 months.

Thawing Frozen Raw Fish

Always thaw frozen raw fish in the refrigerator overnight with a drip pan under the package. Previously frozen fish should never be refrozen.

Cooking Fish for Use in the Cold Kitchen

There are many applications for fish in the cold kitchen. Poaching and simmering whole fish for displays and buffets is a popular method to prepare fish. Poaching with a court bouillon or a fish fumet is ideal for whole fish and thick cuts. Fish prepared with this method may be served hot or cold. Herbs, spices, mirepoix, or acids such as lemon juice or white wine are usually added to the liquid. The cooking temperature is 160° to 180°F (71° to 82°C) maximum to ensure a tender, flavorful, and juicy product.

Shellfish such as lobster, shrimp, and crab can be cooked in this same manner. Always start large fish in cold liquid. When finished and chilled, serve fish with an appropriate sauce or condiment.

POULTRY

Poultry is the term we use for meat that comes from commercially and domestically raised birds such as chicken, turkey, duck, quail, and geese. This list also includes pigeon or squab, guinea hen, and the nonflying birds known as **ratites,** such as ostrich, rhea, or emu.

Composition

Poultry flesh is similar to red meat in its composition. Generally speaking, many of the same cooking principles are applicable to both. Birds are usually much smaller and the cuts simpler, making them easier to fabricate in-house.

Poultry is composed of 70 to 73 percent water, 20 percent protein, 5 to 7 percent fat, and 1 percent other elements, including carbohydrates and minerals in small quantities.

This product ranks high as digestible meat, having shorter muscle fibers than beef, lamb, or pork.

Inspection and Grading

Inspection

Federal law requires that poultry be federally inspected to ensure that the product is wholesome and fit for human consumption. The U.S. Department of Agriculture (USDA) is responsible for the inspection of poultry processing plants and their products for cleanliness

Figure 6-92 Chicken breasts.

and sanitation processes. The stamp used to indicate wholesome and safe products is the round USDA inspection stamp (Figure 6-93).

Grading

Quality inspection, unlike inspections federally mandated for wholesomeness, is voluntary and not required by law. Quality is indicated by a shield stamp and a letter grade. U.S. grades are A, B, and C, and the grades are based on shape of carcass, amount of flesh, amount of fat, whether pinfeathers are present, skin tears, cuts, and broken bones. Most poultry used in foodservice is Grade A (Figure 6-94).

Grade Mark

Figure 6-93 A stamp of inspection for poultry from the U.S. Department of Agriculture.

Figure 6-94 The U.S. Department of Agriculture symbol denoting a specific type of meat to be at the high grade.

Purchasing

Most poultry in the United States is purchased dressed and drawn or in a ready-to-cook state. Always select birds that are odor free and very fresh with plump, well-rounded breasts. In immature birds, the tip of the breastbone should be flexible, which is a good sign of tenderness. Poultry for use in the cold kitchen can also be purchased canned, frozen, IQF in pieces, diced meat, pulled meat, or ground.

Poultry can have either yellow or white skin due to the type of feed given to the birds. This has little to no effect on quality and flavor. Age and classification of the bird indicate how tender it will be. Age and sex have a pronounced effect on the intended use of the poultry.

Chicken and turkey have both white and dark meat whereas Cornish game hens have all white meat, and ducks and geese have all dark meat. The white meat is usually drier because it has less fat; the darker meat is moister due to a higher fat content. Although dark meat has more fat, it is a better source of riboflavin and thiamin.

Storing

Poultry is very fragile and has a short shelf-life. It lasts no longer than 2 to 3 days under normal refrigeration temperatures of 32° to 40°F (0° to 4°C), so it is important to store it in cooler temperatures. Poultry that is frozen should always be stored at −0°F (−18°C) or colder. It can be held up to 6 months.

Thaw poultry under refrigeration in original wrappings unless the poultry is needed quickly. Run under cold water for a quicker thaw.

Never store poultry on a rack above other foods; instead, use the bottom rack with a pan under to catch liquid.

Never store raw product with cooked product. Keep all work surfaces clean and sanitized, use the correct cutting board, and never cross contaminate.

Chickens are classified as broilers, fryers, roasters, Cornish game hens, capons, and stewing chicken (Figure 6-95).

Figure 6-95 Three types of chicken: roaster, fryer, and broiler.

Figure 6-96 Tom turkey ready for roasting.

Broilers

Broilers are of either sex, are from 9 to 13 weeks old, and weigh from 1 to 1 1/2 pounds.

Fryers

Fryers are slightly older, from 9 to 16 weeks, and weigh from 2 1/2 to 3 1/2 pounds.

Roasters

Roasters are older, about 3 to 5 months, and weigh from 3 1/2 to 5 pounds.

Cornish Hen

Cornish hens are a breed of young chickens from 5 to 7 weeks old, weighing from 1 to 2 pounds.

CAPONS

Capons are male birds that have been castrated at about 8 weeks of age and slaughtered at 7 to 8 months, weighing from 5 to 8 pounds.

Stewing Chickens

Stewing chickens are older females over 10 months old that weigh from 3 to 6 pounds.

Turkeys

Turkeys are classified as fryers, roasters, young toms, and hens (Figure 6-96). Fryers and roasters are young birds up to 16 weeks old and weighing from 4 to 9 pounds. Young toms and hens are from 5 to 8 months old weighing 6 to 25 pounds, hens weighing less than toms.

Ducks

Ducks are marketed as broilers, fryers, or roasters (Figure 6-97). Duck broilers and fryers are under 8 weeks old and weigh 2 to 4 pounds. Roasters range from 8 to 16 weeks old, weighing from 4 to 6 pounds. **Magrets** are duck breasts taken from the ducks that produce the liver for foie gras.

Geese

Geese are classified as young or mature (Figure 6-98). A young goose is 6 months of age and under, and a mature goose is over 6 months. Weights of geese run from 4 to 20 pounds in the two classes.

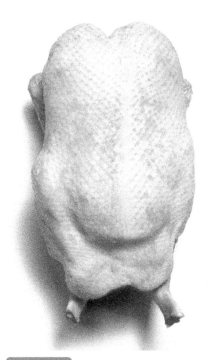

Figure 6-97 Duck with legs and wings removed.

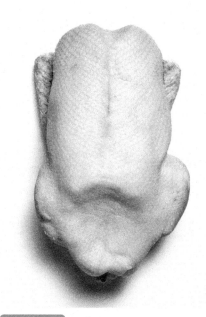

Figure 6-98 Plucked goose.

Additional Poultry

— Guinea hen, squab, and game birds such as pheasant, partridge and quail are also used in the cold kitchen. These birds have become more popular in recent years and can be a tasty addition to the menu.

Guinea Hen

These domesticated relatives of the pheasant average about 1 to 2 pounds in weight, and are similar to the taste of chicken with richer overtones.

Pheasant

These wild birds are popular game birds that are now available farm raised. They are 2 to 2 1/2 pounds dressed and have predominantly light meat that can dry out easily, so careful cooking is required.

Quail

These small game birds with dark rich meat weigh between 4 to 6 oz. dressed weight. They are available semi-boned and make an excellent first course choice.

Squab

Domesticated pigeons are small birds averaging just under 1 pound, dressed weight. They are mostly dark meat and very rich in flavor with slight gamey overtones.

LEARNING ACTIVITY 6-5

Determining Poultry Yield
This activity will help you to understand the relationship of bone to water.

1. Select two fryer or broiler chickens.
2. Weigh each bird separately and record the weight.
3. Place each bird in a roasting pan; label one bird A and the other B.
4. Place in a preheated 375°F (191°C) oven and bake for approximately 1 hour.
5. Remove both birds when they reach an internal temperature of 165°F (74°C).
6. Weigh each bird and record the weight.
7. Determine the percentage of weight loss from cooking and evaporation. (Subtract the weight you recorded in step 6 from the weight you recorded in step 2, and divide by the initial weight in step 2 (#2 − #6)/#2. This is the percentage of weight lost.)
8. Remove all usable meat from each bird and weigh the meat to determine edible portion. What remains is bone waste.
9. Determine the percentage of waste versus the actual edible portion. Record your findings in the chart below. Subtract #8 from #6 (waste = #6 − #8).

Divide waste by #6 (waste/#6) to determine the percentage of waste.
To determine percentage of edible portion, divide #8 by #6 (8/6).

Bird	Original Weight	Weight After Cooking	Weight of Edible Portion	Percentage of Waste
A				
B				

MEAT

The use of meat is unlimited in the cold kitchen, We use many kinds of meat in cold displays, in charcuterie, and in salads. In this next section, we will touch on the more common types and cuts of meat used for these purposes.

Meat is the flesh of furred animals (Figure 6-99). Domesticated meat such as beef, veal, lamb, and pork are the most common. Game meats—those of wild caught animals such as deer and elk venison, wild bore, antelope, and others—are also becoming popular again. In the United States, beef still reigns supreme and is the most popular. Pork shares the market with beef, with more than two-thirds of it is sold as cured products such as bacon and ham. Veal and lamb have a relatively small but important share as tasty alternatives to beef and pork. A beef roulade coupled with tasty mustard vinaigrette or a sophisticated pork loin stuffed with perhaps some tender foie gras mousseline and served with cherry chutney can bring in rave reviews for the cold kitchen.

Preparation

The correct cooking of a particular cut of meat requires the knowledge of where the piece was positioned on the carcass. This will influence whether moist or dry heat should be used. Meats that come from the harder-working muscles such as the leg, round, and shoulder area of the animal are tougher but have great flavor. Learning how to fabricate these particular meats is the goal of a good garde manger. Areas that have seen little or no use, such as the tenderloin, are tender and require a different type of cooking. The tissues are soft, with much intramuscular fat. The most important reason to cook meat is to make it tender by softening the collagen connective tissues. Excessive heat, however, can actually toughen tender cuts of meat because heat causes the muscle fibers in the lean portion of the muscle to shrink and lose water. Overcooking makes meat tough, rubbery, stringy, and dry.

Read through the following quick food science lesson, which describes how muscle tissues react to heat.

Figure 6-99 Meat (boneless strip loin).

When the steak hits the hot pan or grill, many reactions occur simultaneously:

1. The fat melts, rendering out and lubricating the meat. This occurs at a low temperature, as low as 90° to 95°F (32° to 35°C).
2. The protein in the meat, which is composed primarily of water, starts to immediately change into vapor. The vapor carries the glycogen or blood sugar to the surface. This sugar is composed of sucrose.
3. When the sucrose is heated, it slowly changes color, progressively deepening to a rich, dark brown color (Figure 6-100). This adds to the flavor of the meat, and the flavor takes on the richness based on at least 100 different reaction products, among them the sour organic acids, sweet and bitter derivatives, many fragrant volatile molecules, and brown-colored polymers.
4. At a higher temperature of 300° to 500°F (148° to 260°C), the Maillard Reaction occurs. The carbohydrate of the sucrose reacts with the amine-protein group, and a brown coloration and full, intense flavor results. (Proteins coagulate at 140° to 145°F or 60° to 63°C and cause the residual water to burst out of the cell walls; this is what can cause the meat to become tough during the cooking process.)

CHEF'S TIP
Think of cooking meat as a race against time and toughness. You want the surface to develop all of the wonderful flavors and carry through without losing the tenderness for palatability.

Figure 6-100 Steaks that have been properly cooked turn a rich color.

This activity will show you the importance of cooking meat to its correct temperature.

1. Place two, 2-pound eye of round roasts in separate roasting pans (use an adequate pan to fit each piece of meat).
2. Label each roast (A and B).
3. Place one roast in an oven set at 300°F (149°C).
4. Place the other roast in an oven set at 375°F (191°C).
5. Roast each piece of meat for an hour.
6. Remove each roast from the oven and let rest for 10 minutes.
7. Weigh each piece to determine the percentage of evaporative loss.
8. Slice each roast in the middle and visually note the difference in each piece.
9. Taste each roast and note the tenderness or toughness of each roast. Record your findings in the chart below:

Roast	Percentage of Evaporative Loss	Appearance	Taste
A			
B			

Muscle Composition

Why are some cuts butter-tender and some are as tough as leather?

Red meat flesh from furred animals consists of lean muscular tissue, connective tissues such as collagen that dissolve when cooked in a moist environment, and elastin, which is primarily protein-based but too tough to be edible, along with fat and bones.

The carcass is first cut into two halves, then divided up by the main location and protein groups into large, maneuverable pieces called **primal cuts.** Primal cuts are very rarely cooked whole—they are cut into smaller cuts called **subprimal cuts.** These cuts, in turn, are cut into even smaller, more manageable portions called **fabricated cuts.** These are represented by such cuts as rib steaks, flank steaks, pork chops, lamb stew meat, and so on.

According to the USDA, meat is composed of 75 percent water, 20 percent protein, and the remaining 5 percent fat, carbohydrates, and minerals.

Muscle Fiber and Fat Content

The size and thickness of the cell walls, the size of the cellular muscle bundles, and the collagen that holds them together form a type of matrix, or grain, of the meat. This grain determines the type of texture the meat will have. When the fiber bundles are small, the meat has an almost velvet-like, fine-grain texture. Grain also refers to the directionality of the muscle bundles. When animals are taken to the feedlot for 4 to 6 weeks for final fattening, some of the water in the meat and proteins are replaced with fat. This process is known as finishing, and intramuscular fat forms. The result is the marbling of the fat throughout the flesh.

Collagen and Elastin

Collagen is a protein-based substance that is water soluble. It is the soft connective tissue between muscles. It is tenderized by acids and renders down in the presence of low heat and moisture into gelatin and water. In preparing products such as aspic, headcheese, or other heavily aspic-based products, it is good to know which cuts work best for these processes.

Elastin is protein-based, golden-colored, ropey connective tissue that is not broken down by heat or moisture. Mechanical chopping of these fibers or total removal is the only way of tenderizing a food product.

Inspection and Grading

All meat sold in the United States is federally inspected and must be wholesome and fit for human consumption. Inspection is required by federal law and is done by the USDA (Figure 6-101). It is not an indicator of taste or quality. Quality inspection is voluntary, and is also done through the USDA.

At this point in time, the USDA is promoting a system that will identify every animal with a microchip so that it can be monitored throughout its life. If an animal is found with any disease that could possibly be transmitted after consumption, such as mad cow or avian flu, then a careful examination would be made of what other animals have been in contact with it. The animal would be killed before the disease could spread out of control. At this point in time, legislation is pending on this ID system.

There are several levels of quality grading with beef, veal, pork, and lamb:

Beef: USDA Prime (Figure 6-102), Choice, Select, Standard, Commercial, Utility, Cutter, and Canner
Veal: USDA Prime, Choice, Good, Standard, and Utility
Pork: USDA No. 1, No. 2, No. 3, and Utility
Lamb: USDA Prime, Choice, Good, and Utility

Figure 6-101 USDA meat inspection mark.

Beef

Beef is the meat from domesticated bovine animals. It has the largest amount of available flesh. Beef is the most popular red meat consumed in the United States. Due to the large amount of available flesh, it is also a popular menu item in the cold kitchen. It is important to understand how beef is processed and the optimum methods for cooking the various cuts of beef. Beef is sectioned into parts broken up into what are called "primals."

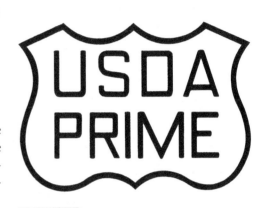

Figure 6-102 USDA prime stamp.

Processing

Cattle are brought to the processing plant, washed down, led to the kill floor, and dispatched. After the animals are killed, the carcasses are attached to a cable or chain, hoisted up, and bled. The heads and hides are removed and the visceral cavities emptied. The carcasses are inspected for sores, tumors, bruises, and other flaws. When the carcasses pass inspection, they are then broken down into halves, then quarters, and then to the primal cuts and fabricated cuts. These fabricated cuts include sides, quarters, foresaddles, and hindquarters or saddles.

It is rare to see whole sides and quarters of beef. In some high-end restaurants that specialize in prime beef, there is a trend toward dry aging and custom cutting. Generally speaking, however, most restaurants rely on primal cuts or boxed beef. The meat industry went through a revolution about 30 years ago. Because of the demand for meat by the fast food industry, the processing of beef changed. With a lack of trained meat cutters and higher labor costs, methods were designed to streamline and speed up the process. Cryovac technology enabled meat to be wet aged and boxed into sections more suitable for restaurants.

Most meat is broken down into primal cuts in the processing plants. Beef is cut into halves through the backbone. Sides are divided between the twelfth and thirteenth ribs into forequarter and hindquarter sections. The meat is then divided into the following cuts:

• Primal Cuts

Primal cuts are the wholesale cuts that are cut to industry standards. A system was devised by the meat industry to standardize all meats sold in the United States. The NAMPS or North American Meat Processors Association guidelines codified all meat primals, subprimals, and fabricated cuts so that a steak that is sold in Kansas City would have the same configuration and quality grading system in New York or in California. Primal cuts are the primary divisions of the quarter cuts. They are smaller and more manageable yet still large enough to allow a variety of cuts for different uses or needs. Primal cuts are easier to use in a restaurant than a full quarter or half cut.

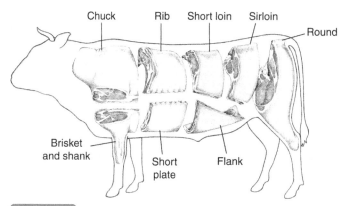

Figure 6-103 The eight primal sections of beef begin with chuck (or shoulders), ribs, short loin, sirloin, round, brisket/shank, short plate, and flank.

There are eight beef primal cuts according to the National Livestock and Meat Board (Figure 6-103), Starting from the front quarters, there is the chuck or shoulder of the beef. This section has very flavorful but tough meat due to the large amount of connective tissue, fat, and bone. The next section is the rib. This section is perfect for dry heat methods because this area is one of the least-used muscle groups. It has decent marbling and it is used for roasts and steaks. Next is the short loin, another tender section of meat. This section also contains the internal muscle mass we call the tenderloin of beef, a prize nugget of beef that is the most tender part of the beef. The round is just above the sirloin. The round is a heavily worked section of beef that benefits from long, slow cooking. Then there is the underside of the beef, or brisket/shank section. These areas are highly worked; consequently, the meat is also heavily grained and tough and benefits from long, slow, and moist cooking methods. The short plate and flank are often used as a corned product such as corned beef. Again, this section should be slow cooked or braised.

- **Subprimal Cuts**

Subprimal cuts are cut from a primal down to a more manageable size.

- **Fabricated Cuts**

Fabricated cuts such as roasts, steaks, chops, cutlets, stewing meats, ground meat, and so forth as set forth by the Institutional Meat Purchase Specifications IMPS/NAMPS specifications are even smaller cuts for foodservice.

Veal

Veal is the by-product of the dairy industry. Dairy cows must calve each year in order to produce milk, so the excess calves are used for veal production. The finest veal is milk fed or formula fed and slaughtered under the age of 16 weeks. Calf meat is from calves slaughtered after 5 months of age but less than 1 year. They have been fed solid food and have a more robust color and flavor.

Milk- and formula-fed veal is light pink in color with a mild flavor and low fat content. There are six primal cuts of veal: shoulder, rib, loin, sirloin, leg, breast/shank, and flank (Figure 6-104).

Lamb

Lamb is the meat of sheep. Most lamb sold in the United States is very young and very tender. Older lamb, or mutton as it is called, is tougher with a strong, waxy flavor that takes getting used to. We use lamb leg roasts, boned, stuffed, and tied, as well as lamb racks for many cold kitchen applications. Small chops can be used for one- or two-bite appetizers. Whole loins or racks can be used for stunning platter presentations.

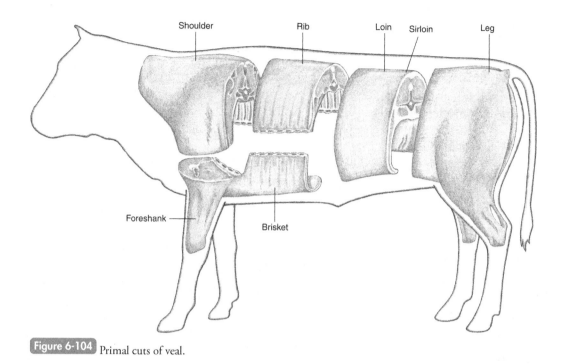

Figure 6-104 Primal cuts of veal.

The tougher cuts of lamb, such as lamb shoulder and neck meat, are useful for lamb sausages and forcemeats.

Primal and subprimal cuts of lamb include shoulder, rib, loin, sirloin, leg, flank, breast, shanks, and neck (Figure 6-105).

Pork

Pork is the meat of hogs. Hogs are usually butchered before the age of 1 year in the United States. After 1 year of age, pork meat becomes stringier and has a much stronger, gamy odor. Most pork is processed into cured products such as bacon and ham. Pork is the heart and soul of charcuterie (see Unit 17 on charcuterie). In the United States, pork is second only to beef in meat consumption. Pork is pale pink to light red in color, and, like all meats, its flavor can be enhanced by what type of feed the hog eats. Hogs used for proscuitto, as an example, are often fed acorns to improve the flavor profile of the finished product.

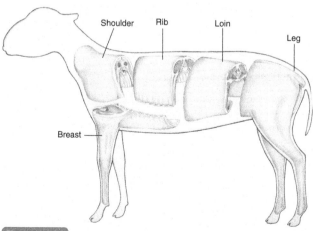

Figure 6-105 Primal cuts of lamb.

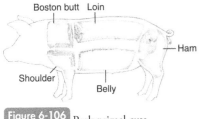

Figure 6-106 Pork primal cuts.

Primal (Figure 6-106) and subprimal cuts of pork include the following:

- **Shoulder**

The primal shoulder, known as the picnic ham, is the lower portions of the hog's front leg or foreleg. It accounts for 20 percent of the total percent of the carcass weight. Because it comes from a highly worked part of the body, it is somewhat tough.

Whole pork shoulders are preferred by many BBQ pitmasters. Shoulder meat is great for soups and stews.

- **Boston Butt**

This cut is located just above the primal pork shoulder. It accounts for 7 percent of the carcass. Boston butt has a large percentage of fat to lean meat, which makes it a good choice for roasting and a good choice for cutting into steaks or chops.

- **Belly**

Pork belly is a misnomer in that it also contains the spareribs as well as the underbelly of the pig. Spareribs are baked, cured and smoked, braised, and barbecued. Fresh pork belly is braised. Salt pork and pancetta is pork belly that is salted to cure it. Bacon is pork belly that is cured with salt, nitrates, and sugar. It may be smoked as well.

- **Loin**

The loin is a cut that comes from behind the shoulder section. It includes the rib section as well as the loin and a small section of the sirloin. This primal cut accounts for 20 percent of the carcass weight. The loin section of the pig is rarely cured in the United States. It is, however, cured in many parts of Eastern Europe. The loin is located on the back of the pig and does not receive much physical action, therefore making this a very tender type of muscle meat. The loin cut is great for dry heat cooking methods such as roasting and grilling. Smaller cuts are ideal for sauté. The tenderloin is also located in this primal cut.

- **Fresh Ham**

This is the pork equivalent to the round of beef. This cut contains the whole hind leg of the pork. The ham is the most commonly cured type of pork and is cured by pumping with a wet brine solution or by packing in salt and dry curing. It is a very meaty cut with few connective tissues. It is also a lean cut, which makes it a great cut for dieters. Ham can also be smoked. Unlike its beef counterpart, hams are somewhat tender and remain so in the cooking process. Fresh whole ham is baked; ham steaks are served fried, grilled, or broiled.

Buffet Meats

Large meat pieces, displayed properly carved on buffets, are popular. Following is a list of the most popular cuts and sizes.

Capon

A capon is a castrated male chicken. Practical sizes are 5 to 6 pounds (2.3 to 2.7 kg).

Turkey

The best size Tom turkey is 20 to 22 pounds (9.1 to 10 kg). For optimum roasting, make sure the pan fits the bird.

Ham, Bone In

MBG #501 is a short shank, precooked ham, whole including the aitch bone. The most practical sizes for buffets are 14 to 17 pounds (6.4 to 7.7 kg).

Lamb

Baby lamb in the weight range of 25 to 29 pounds (11.4 to 13.2 kg), with the pelt on, is manageable. There is little usable meat on the carcass, and the whole lamb will render only 25 to 35 servings on a buffet.

Roast Rib, Standing Rib

MBG #109 is an oven-ready rib, bone on. It is often sold netted. Good sizes are 17 to 19 pounds (7.7 to 8.6 kg). The meat can be handled without too much effort. If the meat is sliced on the action station, a smaller rib in the weight range of 14 to 16 pounds (6.4 kg to 7.3 kg) might be preferable because the slices are smaller. However, meat in that weight range is not available as top choice meat.

Suckling Pig

The best weight range is up to 25 pounds (11.4 kg). It will still fit in a standard-size convection oven. For pig galantine (filled boneless pig), the best size is about 10 pounds (4.6 kg).

>> Summary

Protein is the most expensive ingredient used in the cold kitchen. Its value as a nutritional powerhouse, coupled with its versatility, is unmatched by any other ingredient. Dairy, poultry, and meat are products from the farm brought to your table in many forms. Seafood comes to us through many sources from wild caught fish to aquaculture. The variety of shellfish and finfish is endless.

>> Review Questions

SHORT ANSWER

1. Explain why fresh cheese cannot be aged.
2. Describe kefir.
3. Explain the difference between butter and light butter.
4. Describe "fabricated cuts" in beef.
5. List the products that come from the belly primal cut of a hog.

MATCHING

Cheese

Match the type of cheese to its category. (You may use the category more than once.)

6. brie
7. Swiss
8. English stilton
9. asiago
10. provolone
11. Havarti
12. Italian gorgonzola
13. munster
14. gromage blanc
15. edam
16. brick
17. Monterey jack
18. mascarpone
19. boucheron

a. fresh cheese
b. soft-ripened cheese
c. washed-rind cheese
d. waxed-rind cheese
e. blue-veined cheese
f. pasta filata cheese
g. hard cheese
h. grana
i. goat cheese

Seafood

Match the type of seafood to its category. (You may use the category more than once.)

20. shrimp
21. clam
22. squid
23. mussel
24. octopus
25. lobster

a. mollusk
b. crustacean
c. cephalopod

Fish

Match the type of fish to its category. (You may use the category more than once.)

26. halibut
27. cod
28. flounder
29. turbot
30. trout
31. catfish
32. lemon sole

a. flatfish
b. round fish

Poultry

Match the type of poultry to its description.

33. capon
34. squab
35. young Toms
36. magrets
37. emu
38. guineas

a. ratite
b. domestic relative of the pheasant
c. weighs 6 to 25 pounds
d. breasts are taken from ducks that produce foie gras
e. young pigeons
f. male birds that have been castrated

Beef

Label the eight primal sections of a cow.

39. chuck
40. rib
41. short loin
42. sirloin
43. round
44. brisket/shank
45. short plate
46. flank

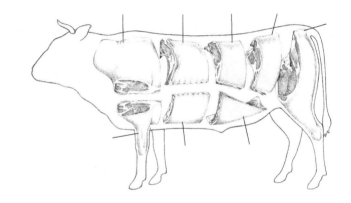

Starters

The dictionary defines appetizers as, "A food or drink served before a meal to stimulate the appetite" (Merriam Webster). The root of the word "appetizer" is derived from Latin and means "craving for food and drink," but also for power and other pleasures. The use of appetizers varies from country to country, reflecting different eating habits. Unit 7 covers hot and cold finger food served at receptions, often referred to as canapés.

Unit 8 discusses both plated cold and hot appetizers. They can be served at tables as a first course or at reception buffets.

>> Learning Objectives

After you have finished reading this unit, you should be able to:

- Discuss ways to create interesting and satisfying canapés.
- List the four components of a canapé.
- Explain the purpose of the spread.
- Describe typical garnishes used to top canapés.

>> Key Terms

agliata	base	focaccia	profiteroles
andalouse	bercy butter (*bair-SEE*)	(*foh-CAH-chee-ah*)	(*pro-FEHT-uh-rohl*)
(*ahn-dah-LOOZ*)	binding agent	glace de vinade (*glahs*	romescu
aspic	crissini	*duh vee-AHND*)	rouille (*roo-EE*)
barquette (*bahr-KEHT*)	croustade		tartelette

The French term "canapé" originally meant "a canopy or cover over a bed." Over time, the meaning of the term changed to "a type of day bed or couch." The term was adopted by chefs because canapés originally consisted of small slices of bread topped with flavorful foods such as cheese spreads, anchovies, ham, and other savory foods.

Frivolitiés was another French term for canapés and was coined in England by Auguste Escoffier, who was serving as the Savoy Hotel's first chef at the turn of the twentieth century. It means "of little or no weight, not serious or important," and is perhaps a good description for delicate canapés. The term is seldom used today in the United States.

>> Canapé Starters

Today's canapés are a caterer's bread and butter—no pun intended. These tasty, petite, cold, savory morsels consist of a base, a spread (binding agent), a topping, and a garnish, creating a true finger food. The **bases** can be traditional breads or updated versions consisting of pita wedges; rye or oat crackers; potato crisps; small, boiled creamer potatoes; vegetable chips such as beet chips; apple or pear crisps; corn and flour tortillas; chapattis; lavash; wonton; and rice paper.

Food placed on top of a base needs a binding agent or spread to prevent it from sliding off. The canapé spread, or **binding agent,** is usually flavored butter or a cheese mixture. The fat in these spreads keeps the bread from getting soggy from the toppings. Canapés using nonbread bases such as a fresh cucumber or zucchini slices are more difficult to keep together because most spreads will slide off the moist vegetables.

Canapés demonstrate the chef's creativeness and can showcase new taste ideas. They are also an outlet for creative and cost-effective usage of overproduction and trimmings. An example would be trimmings from smoked salmon combined with cream cheese to top a toasted rye bread round.

Canapés can be glazed with **aspic,** which is a clear, savory jelly made from meat, fish, or vegetable stock and gelatin. Aspic is very decorative and provides a beautiful shine that looks truly professional. It also helps to seal in the moisture in many of the ingredients and keep them fresh. Making aspic from scratch is labor-intensive and would be cost-prohibitive in many situations. Most operations use aspic powder, which requires only blending the powder with hot water. Chefs can apply a fine layer of aspic by spraying or brushing each canapé. The layer must be very thin and the aspic flavor compatible with the main ingredient. Customers may not appreciate a thick coating. Due to the limitless flavor combinations and types, canapés continue to be an excellent and popular type of hors d'oeuvre. Some types of canapés are smaller versions of open-faced sandwiches. (Many of the sandwich recipes presented in Unit 10 can be used for canapés.)

When designing canapés, remember that flavor, color, and texture contrasts will add interest. A soft filling could be combined with a crisp base or sprinkled with crunchy nuts.

Canapés Should Be
- Bite-sized—anything large is difficult to eat. People usually have a glass in one hand and the canapé in the other and must be able to eat the food in one bite.
- Dry—not wet or greasy. Guests are usually dressed up, and sticky fingers are not acceptable. Licking fingers in public is usually frowned upon.
- Made with strictly edible items. Don't use toothpicks, skewers, paper, sticks, unpitted olives, or anything that must be discarded.
- Free of surprises. Canapés should be seasoned well but not to the point that they are unexpectedly hot, garlicky, or salty.
- Interesting. Texture contrast adds interest to canapés. A soft filling could be combined with a crisp base or sprinkled with crisp nuts. However, the base should not crumble to the touch.

BASES

When creating canapés, great care must be taken to choose complementary bases or foundations. As was mentioned earlier, bases can be made of a variety of products. They should be sturdy enough to withstand the weight of the toppings and garnish and remain strong until the canapé is eaten. There's nothing worse than a canapé that falls apart between the hand and the mouth.

In France, the original canapé would have been made with a "pain de mie," or basic white pan bread. The close grain of this particular bread is good for keeping the canapé crisp. Pain de mie, called pan bread, can be baked into many shapes; however, the most common shape is rectangular loaf, also called Pullman loaf. It is available sliced lengthwise by specialty bakeries or can be sliced in-house. The best way is to freeze the bread and then slice it with an electric bread or meat slicer about 1/4-inch thick. By slicing the traditional Pullman loaf lengthwise and using cutters, many shapes such as hearts, rounds, squares, or triangles can be created (Figure 7-1). This practice is labor-intensive. Today, any type of bread can be adapted to canapé use.

Figure 7-1 Using star- and heart-shaped metal pastry cutters to create a variety of canapé bases.

The following list is just a small sampling of what can be used. Use this list as your starting point.

Rye. Light, medium, or dark, Pumpernickel, flavored ryes with nuts and dried fruits

White bread. Pullman, French baguettes, Italian, or Vienna

Other grains. Whole wheat, nine-grain, millet, barley or any mixed-grain bread

Flat breads. Focaccia, ciabatta, naan, chapatti, pita, corn or wheat tortillas, lavash

Nonbread bases. Egg roll or wonton skins, rice paper, shredded crisp potatoes, vegetable and fruit chips, rice cakes, fresh vegetable slices such as cucumber and zucchini rounds, hollowed-out cherry tomatoes, hollowed-out and cooked creamer or baby red, purple or yellow potatoes, cooked mushroom caps, melon round slices, apple rings, pear slices, lettuce and endive leaves

Pastry. Other flour bases including items made with short paste or pâte brisée, puff pastry, pâte à choux, and phyllo dough

Tartelettes and Barquettes

Round-shaped **tartelettes** and oval- or boat-shaped **barquettes** are small, baked dough shells. They are filled and topped with garnish.

Croustades and Bruschetta

Croustades is the French term for containers that can be filled with a variety of fillings. The most common are hollowed-out, thick bread slices, polenta or semolina slices, or deep-fried, little containers made with a special batter.

Bruschetta is garlic toast made with olive oil, garlic, and rosemary, often covered with peeled, diced tomatoes and Parmesan cheese. There are many regional variations. Bruschetta is one of the simplest canapés to make as well as one of the tastiest.

SPREADS

Spreads act as a sealer or coating to protect the base from getting soggy from a wet topping (Figure 7-2). Spreads add color, texture, and flavor to the finished canapé. They also act as an adhesive to keep the protein or topping from sliding off the canapé.

Here is a list of suggested spreads and coatings:

Butter

Simple butter, unsalted or salted, can be used in canapé assembly.

Compound Butter

The term "compound butter" refers to butter blended with a wide variety of ingredients to add flavor and texture. Typical flavor ingredients used on canapés include the following:

- Herbs, such as dill, cilantro, parsley, thyme, basil, lemon thyme, and many others
- Spices, such as paprika, curry, chili powder, and pepper
- Reductions of wine, juice, meat glace, and herb infusions
- Finely ground and chopped solid ingredients such as shrimp, lobster, and smoked meats

Some compound butters are used in the hot kitchen but are often made in the pantry.

For additional butter blends, try these:

- Butter mixed with chopped dill
- Butter mixed with toasted sesame seeds
- Roasted red bell pepper butter (purée canned, drained red pimentos can be used in a pinch)
- Lemon butter blended with grated lemon peel and lemon juice
- Mustard sage butter
- Citrus butter blended with grated orange and lime peel
- Tarragon butter blended with chopped tarragon

Figure 7-2 The spread is applied to the base and acts as a barrier between the toppings and the bread beneath them.

Figure 7-3 A compound butter is made by mixing butter and herbs.

Bercy butter is a French compound butter blended with white wine, parsley, lemon, shallots, salt, and pepper (Figure 7-3). It is served with grilled meat or fish. Other examples of compound butters might be chipotle and ancho chile butter used as a pork topping, red wine reduction with shallots and glace de viande butter for beef toppings, and cilantro lime butter for a grilled scallop canapé. (**Glace de vinade** is reduced brown stock that is similar to syrup in consistency.)

LEARNING ACTIVITY 7-1

To make compound butter, soften 1 pound of unsalted butter, add up to 4 ounces of desired flavorings, and mix well. Place butter on paper or plastic wrap, and shape into cylinder form. If using parchment paper, fold the paper over the butter and roll it up. Twist ends of paper, label, and store refrigerated (Figure 7-4). For canapés, the compound butter should be kept at spreadable temperatures.

Figure 7-4 The chef holds the ends of a tube or cylinder of butter wrapped in cling film or plastic wrap.

Mayonnaise and Oil-Based Emulsions

Mayonnaise and its many derivative sauces include pesto mayonnaise, **andalouse** (a French mayonnaise made with tomato purée and pimento), tartare, verte, aioli, **rouille** (paste made with hot chilies, garlic, olive oil, stock, and breadcrumbs), **romescu** (Spanish sauce made from sweet red peppers, tomatoes, olive oil, vinegar, almonds, or hazelnuts), and **agliata** (garlic and walnut sauce), to name a few. They add flavor but are controversial as a canapé spread because they tend to make the base soft, especially when the canapés are made ahead of time.

Cheese Spreads

Spreads based on soft cheeses are popular, easy to make, and practical. Some cheeses need to be blended with butter for spreadability. These are popular spread cheeses:

- Cream cheese or Neufchatel
- Mascarpone
- Bleu cheeses
- Chevre or brie
- Cheddar cheese blended with port wine

TOPPINGS

Toppings can be substantial items such as smoked or cured fish, seafood of all types, caviar, meat, poultry, eggs, preserved meats, raw or cooked vegetables, mushrooms, nuts, and cheese (Figure 7-5).

GARNISHES

Garnishes complement the overall flavors and add a "kiss of excitement" to each canapé. Everything from a simple sprig of dill to a brunoise of red pepper or a mini-wedge of lime can serve as an effective topper. The garnish must be edible. Some examples of typical garnishes follow:

- Finely diced red pepper
- Small lime or lemon slice
- Chopped herbs or small sprigs of herbs
- Gherkins, pickled onions, olive slices, capers, and other pickled vegetables
- Caviar
- Chopped eggs
- Chopped nuts or dried fruit

Figure 7-5 A variety of products can be used as canapé toppings. This photo shows canapés served with anchovy and prawn, cheese and spring onion, salami, and asparagus toppings.

The following canapé is especially good when made toward the end of the peach season in late summer when the peaches are at their juiciest. Choose a red or white variety for color contrast. This recipe uses canned foie gras mousse—an expensive product. It can be substituted with the Best Chicken Liver Pâté Mousse recipe found in Unit 17.

foie gras mousse with peach canapé
Yield: 40 pieces

Ingredients	Amounts U.S.	Metric	Procedure
Egg bread rounds, sliced	40 each	40 each	Cut 1 1/2-inch rounds to 1/4-inch thick.
Butter, melted	As needed	As needed	Brush melted butter on rounds and toast at 350°F (175°C) until golden brown.
Peach slices	40 slices	40 slices	Pan sear slices.
Honey	1 fl oz	30 ml	Add honey and wine to the peaches. Glaze and remove from pan. Reserve until assembly.
Madeira wine	1 fl oz	1 fl oz	
Foie gras mousse	1 lb	454 g	In a mixer or food processor, blend mousse until pipable consistency. Using a small French or star tip, fill a piping bag with foie gras mousse.
Almond, slices, toasted	40 each	40 each	Place a glazed peach slice on each buttered and toasted round. Pipe the foie gras mousse through the French tip and onto the peach. Top with a sliced toasted almond.

NUTRITIONAL INFORMATION PER SERVING: 73 Calories; 3 g Fat (40.0% calories from fat); 3 g Protein; 8 g Carbohydrate; trace Dietary Fiber; 51 mg Cholesterol; 65 mg Sodium. Exchanges: 1/2 Grain (Starch); 0 Lean Meat; 0 Vegetable; 1/2 fruit; 1 Fat.

Sometimes the most delicious and popular canapés are the simplest. This recipe is quick and delicious and will add variety to any canapé tray. You can use the Silky Chicken Liver Pâté Mousse recipe found in Unit 17 or any other chicken liver mousse.

chicken liver and apple canapés
Yield: 40 each ¾ oz (21 g) pieces

Ingredients	Amounts U.S.	Metric	Procedure
Chicken liver mousse	1 lb	454 g	Pipe or spread mousse on top of brioche slices. Top with apple chips.
Toasted brioche slices	40 each	40 each	
Dried apple chips, quarters	40 each	40 each	

NUTRITIONAL INFORMATION PER PIECE: 145 Calories; 3 g Fat (18.4% calories from fat); 4 g Protein; 27 g Carbohydrate; 3 g Dietary Fiber; 55 mg Cholesterol; 142 mg Sodium. Exchanges: 1/2 Grain (Starch); 0 Lean Meat; 1 Fruit; 1/2 Fat.

Stuffed celery is an old, tried-and-true standby that still satisfies. Stuffed celery adds crunch and color to any canapé collection.

stuffed celery   *Yield: 40 each*

Ingredients	Amounts U.S.	Metric	Procedure
Blue Cheese Spread			
Blue cheese	1 lb	454 g	Blend blue cheese, butter, and cream cheese in food processor.
Butter	4 oz	113 g	
Cream cheese	4 oz	113 g	
Celery stalks	As needed	As needed	Peel celery if necessary, wash well, and cut into 2 1/2-inch lengths. Center leaves can be left on for added flavor and eye appeal. Make sure the celery is dry before piping. Pipe filling into celery pieces.
Paprika	Sprinkle	Sprinkle	Sprinkle paprika on top of filling.

NUTRITIONAL INFORMATION PER PIECE: 74 Calories; 7 g Fat (79.2% calories from fat); 3 g Protein; 1 g Carbohydrate; trace Dietary Fiber; 18 mg Cholesterol; 208 mg Sodium. Exchanges: 0 Grain (Starch); 1/2 Lean Meat; 0 Vegetable; 1 Fat.

Use half of the blue cheese spread found in the stuffed celery recipe as the filling in the pea pods.

stuffed pea pods   *Yield: 40 each*

Ingredients	Amounts U.S.	Metric	Procedure
Blue cheese spread	1 lb	454 g	Soften spread to room temperature.
Sugar snap pea pods	40 large	40 large	Carefully split each pea pod, keeping ends together to form a small boat. Fill with cheese mixture.
Red pepper, fine dice	2 oz	57 g	Sprinkle red pepper on top of the cheese spread.

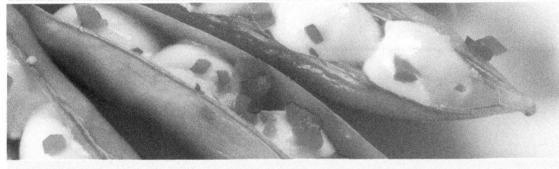

NUTRITIONAL INFORMATION PER PIECE: 76 Calories; 3 g Fat (40.4% calories from fat); 4 g Protein; 6 g Carbohydrate; 2 g Dietary Fiber; 9 mg Cholesterol; 163 mg Sodium. Exchanges: 1/2 Lean Meat; 0 Vegetable; 1/2 Fat.

This is perfect during fig season. For an added flavor enhancement, add some lemon or orange zest to the mascarpone cheese. Try using the bacon recipe from Unit 16.

fresh fig and mascarpone cheese canapés   *Yield: 40 each*

Ingredients	Amounts U.S.	Metric	Procedure
Fresh figs, ripe but not too soft	8 each	8 each	Slice figs into 40 equal slices, save ends for fruit salad if desired.
Mascarpone cheese	8 oz	227 g	Place dab of cheese on each biscuit or cracker, top with a fig slice, and sprinkle with crumbled bacon.
Water biscuit or cracker	40 each	40 each	
Bacon, cooked, crumbled	6 oz	170 g	

NUTRITIONAL INFORMATION PER PIECE: 81 Calories; 6 g Fat (64.2% calories from fat); 3 g Protein; 5 g Carbohydrate; 1 g Dietary Fiber; 13 mg Cholesterol; 118 mg Sodium. Exchanges: 0 Grain (Starch); 1/2 Lean Meat; 0 Fruit; 1 Fat.

The camembert in this recipe can be replaced with a gorgonzola or Roquefort cheese for a different twist. Pecans, hazelnuts, and other nuts can also be used in place of the toasted almonds for variety provided the name is changed.

camembert, grape, and almond canapés   *Yield: 40 pieces*

Ingredients	Amounts		Procedure
	U.S.	Metric	
Camembert cheese, ripe	8 oz	227 g	Process cheese, butter, and cream cheese in food processor.
Butter	4 oz	113 g	
Cream cheese	4 oz	113 g	
Cracker, toast or bread	40 pieces	40 pieces	Spread or pipe cheese spread on bread of choice.
Red or black grapes, seedless, cut into four wedges	10 whole	10 whole	Top with wedge of grape.
Almonds, toasted, chopped	4 oz	113 g	Dust with chopped almonds.

NUTRITIONAL INFORMATION PER PIECE: 78 Calories; 6 g Fat (73.2% calories from fat); 2 g Protein; 3 g Carbohydrate; trace Dietary Fiber; 13 mg Cholesterol; 119 mg Sodium. Exchanges: 0 Grain (Starch); 1/2 Lean Meat; 0 Fruit; 1 Fat.

This canapé has a touch of salty and sweet to excite the mouth. The chutney adds an intriguing flavor. Use a commercial product or use the Benchmark Mango Chutney recipe found in Unit 15 as well as the bacon recipe from Unit 16.

bacon, cream cheese, and mango chutney canapés
Yield: 40 pieces

Ingredients	Amounts		Procedure
	U.S.	Metric	
Mango chutney	8 fl oz	237 ml	Process chutney in a food processor until it is smooth and the chunks are gone.
Cream cheese	8 oz	227 g	Add cream cheese to mango chutney purée and blend.
Bacon sliced, cooked crisp, crumbled	8 each	8 each	Stir in bacon bits and season with cayenne pepper.
Cayenne pepper	To taste	To taste	
Crackers or bread of choice	40 each	40 each	Spread mixture on choice of bread.

NUTRITIONAL INFORMATION PER PIECE: 56 Calories; 3 g Fat (47.9% calories from fat); 1 g Protein; 6 g Carbohydrate; trace Dietary Fiber; 7 mg Cholesterol; 78 mg Sodium. Exchanges: 0 Grain (Starch); 0 Lean Meat; 1/2 Fruit; 1/2 Fat.

Whitefish is a high-fat, mild-flavored fish with a firm, white flesh. It is popular in the states bordering the Great Lakes. The dry cure recipe for salmon, sturgeon, or trout from Unit 16 will work with whitefish, if you prefer to smoke the fish in-house.

smoked whitefish canapés   *Yield: 40 pieces*

Ingredients	Amounts U.S.	Metric	Procedure
Smoked Whitefish Spread			
Cream cheese	8 oz	227 g	Mix cream cheese, fish, onion, dill, lemon juice, mayonnaise, and black pepper until well blended. Cover and chill until needed.
Smoked whitefish, skinned, boned, and flaked	1 lb	454 g	
Green onion, finely chopped	2 tbsp	28 g	
Fresh dill, chopped	1 tbsp	14 g	
Lemon juice	1 tsp	5 ml	
Mayonnaise	4 fl oz	118 ml	
Black pepper, freshly ground	To taste	To taste	
Cracker or toast points	40 each	40 each	Serve spread on top of crackers or toast points.
Lemon cut into tiny wedges, rind removed	40 wedges	40 wedges	Garnish with lemon wedge and a short sprig of fresh dill.
Fresh dill	40 short sprigs	40 short sprigs	

NUTRITIONAL INFORMATION PER PIECE: 67 Calories; 5 g Fat (62.3% calories from fat); 4 g Protein; 3 g Carbohydrate; trace Dietary Fiber; 11 mg Cholesterol; 188 mg Sodium. Exchanges: 0 Grain (Starch); 1/2 Lean Meat; 0 Vegetable; 0 Fruit; 1/2 Fat.

Zucchini slices for this recipe should be cut from small, very fresh zucchini no larger than 1 1/2-inch in diameter. Score the sides of the zucchini for visual contrast. Try using the Benchmark Recipe found in Unit 16 for the dry cure for salmon. Use the smoked salmon spread recipe that follows:

smoked salmon julienne on zucchini canapés
Yield: 40 each

Ingredients	Amounts U.S.	Metric	Procedure
Zucchini slices	40 each	40 each	Spread or pipe salmon spread on zucchini slices.
Smoked salmon or lox spread	1 lb	454 g	
Lox, cut short, julienne	8 oz	227 g	Arrange lox julienne on top.
Capers, drained	4 tbsp	56 g	Place 1–2 capers in the center.

NUTRITIONAL INFORMATION PER PIECE: 21 Calories; 1 g Fat (32.4% calories from fat); 3 g Protein; trace Carbohydrate; trace Dietary Fiber; 4 mg Cholesterol; 210 mg Sodium. Exchanges: 1/2 Lean Meat; 0 Vegetable; 0 Other Carbohydrates.

Lox is a type of smoked salmon that is brine cured and then cold smoked. Either type of smoked salmon works well with this recipe. If you prefer to smoke your salmon in-house, use the Dry Cure for Salmon, Sturgeon, or Trout recipe from Unit 16.

smoked salmon or lox and cream cheese spread
Yield: 1 lb 7 oz

Ingredients	Amounts U.S.	Metric	Procedure
Cream cheese	1 lb	454 g	Blend all ingredients in a food processor until smooth.
Smoked salmon or lox	6 oz	170 g	
Sour cream	1 fl oz	30 ml	
Lemon juice	1 tsp	5 ml	
Worcestershire sauce	1 tsp	5 ml	
Cayenne pepper	¼ tsp	2 g	

NUTRITIONAL INFORMATION PER RECIPE: 1,889 Calories; 176 g Fat (82.8% calories from fat); 68 g Protein; 14 g Carbohydrate; trace Dietary Fiber; 568 mg Cholesterol; 2,808 mg Sodium. Exchanges: 0 Grain (Starch); 9 1/2 Lean Meat; 0 Fruit; 31 Fat; 0 Other Carbohydrates.

This recipe works best if you use hydroponically grown seedless cucumbers. These cucumbers are grown suspended above a nutrient solution and are seedless and straight.

salmon roe on cucumber canapés *Yield: 40 each*

Ingredients	Amounts U.S.	Metric	Procedure
Cucumber slices, 1/4-inch thick	40 each	40 each	Lightly scoop without breaking through.
Sour cream, thick	4 fl oz	118 ml	Use a pastry bag and pipe a small dab of sour cream in the center of each cucumber slice. Make sure slices are very dry to prevent the sour cream from sliding off.
Salmon caviar	8 oz	227 g	Just prior to service, place a small spoonful of caviar in the center of the slice.

NUTRITIONAL INFORMATION PER PIECE: 23 Calories; 2 g Fat (58.6% calories from fat); 2 g Protein; 1 g Carbohydrate; trace Dietary Fiber; 35 mg Cholesterol; 87 mg Sodium. Exchanges: 0 Lean Meat; 0 Vegetable; 0 Nonfat Milk; 0 Fat.

This recipe combines the heat of the wasabi with the tangy, tart flavor of the pickled ginger. As a base, we use shrimp chips, which are sometimes called prawn chips. They are made with a shrimp and tapioca flour and are available from specialty distributors. The chips are inexpensive and puff up when fried.

shrimp and ginger canapés *Yield: 40 pieces*

Ingredients	Amounts U.S.	Metric	Procedure
Wasabi Cheese Spread			
Ginger, pickled, minced fine	1 tsp	5 g	Mix ginger, wasabi paste, soy sauce, and cream cheese until smooth.
Wasabi paste	3 tbsp	44 ml	
Soy sauce	3 tbsp	44 ml	
Cream cheese, softened	1 lb	454 g	
Shrimp chips, fried	40 pieces	40 pieces	Pipe wasabi cheese spread onto fried shrimp chips.
Wasabi paste	As needed	As needed	Top with a small dollop of wasabi paste, a shrimp, and a small piece of pickled ginger.
Bay or salad shrimp	40 each	40 each	
Ginger, pickled, chopped	2 tbsp	30 ml	

NUTRITIONAL INFORMATION PER PIECE: 63 Calories; 5 g Fat (67.4% calories from fat); 3 g Protein; 2 g Carbohydrate; trace Dietary Fiber; 31 mg Cholesterol; 144 mg Sodium. Exchanges: 0 Grain (Starch); 1/2 Lean Meat; 0 Vegetable; 1 Fat; 0 Other Carbohydrates.

This canapé comes from Central Mexico. Grilled shrimp may be substituted for the scallops. Use the Traditional Tomato Salsa Benchmark Recipe found in Unit 15. Make sure to drain the tomato salsa to remove excessive moisture.

grilled scallops with jicama, tomato, and lime
Yield: 40 each

Ingredients	Amounts		Procedure
	U.S.	Metric	
French bread (baguette), sliced into 1/4-inch thick rounds	40 each	40 each	Butter and toast the baguette on both sides.
Sea scallops	1 lb	454 g	Slice each scallop 1/4-inch thick; you should get 2–4 slices per scallop. Lightly oil scallops and grill each slice quickly. Make sure slices do not dry out. You should have at least 40 disks of grill-marked scallops. Cover and chill.
Jicama, fine dice	2 oz	57 g	Mix jicama with the salsa and place on toasted bread rounds. Top with scallop, mark side up. Place a small wedge of lime and a cilantro leaf on top.
Tomato salsa	8 fl oz	237 ml	
Cilantro leaves	40 each	40 each	
Lime wedges, without rind	40 each	40 each	

NUTRITIONAL INFORMATION PER PIECE: 53 Calories; 1 g Fat (9.9% calories from fat); 4 g Protein; 9 g Carbohydrate; 1 g Dietary Fiber; 5 mg Cholesterol; 129 mg Sodium. Exchanges: 1/2 Grain (Starch); 1/2 Lean Meat; 0 Vegetable; 0 Fruit; 0 Fat.

Lingonberries are popular in Scandinavia where the berries grow wild in the forests. The conserve is available through specialty suppliers. Fresh orange supremes may be too big, but they can be cut to fit. Canned mandarin orange wedges are just about the right size and can be substituted.

smoked duck, lingonberry, and orange canapés
Yield: 40 pieces

Ingredients	Amounts		Procedure
	U.S.	Metric	
Lingonberry conserves	8 fl oz	237 ml	Place lingonberries and cream cheese in a food processor and blend.
Cream cheese	8 oz	227 g	
French bread, buttered, toasted	40 each	40 each	Spread cheese mixture on bread. Place a small portion of the shredded smoked duck meat. Place a small orange wedge next to the duck meat as a garnish.
Smoked duck meat, boneless, shredded	8 oz	227 g	
Orange supreme wedges	40 pieces	40 pieces	

NUTRITIONAL INFORMATION PER PIECE: 162 Calories; 3 g Fat (15.3% calories from fat); 4 g Protein; 32 g Carbohydrate; 5 g Dietary Fiber; 11 mg Cholesterol; 98 mg Sodium. Exchanges: 1/2 Grain (Starch); 0 Lean Meat; 1 1/2 Fruit; 1/2 Fat.

Tartar steak is named for the ancient Mongolian horsemen, the Tartars, who invaded much of Eastern Europe in the twelfth and thirteenth centuries, and ate their beef raw, not taking time out from their pillaging to cook it. Tartar steak is a popular appetizer in Germany and is also used as canapé topping. It consists of ground lean, raw beef blended with spices and egg yolk, served raw with toast or pumpernickel bread. In many restaurants, tartar steak was blended tableside or the ground meat was surrounded with the garnishes for the customers to blend. The meat must be flavorful, without any fat or suet, and ground as close to serving time as possible in a chilled grinder. Although some recipes call for beef tenderloin, it is not the best meat to use because it is too mushy and relatively flavorless. The best cut is the chuck flatiron. You can familiarize yourself with this tender cut by locating it in the *Meat Buyer's Guide* PSO1 or 114D. The flatiron is considered the second-most tender cut after the tenderloin; because of its location in the chuck shoulder, it is very flavorful.

tartar steak *Yield: 1 lb (454 g) 2 each 8 oz (227 g) servings as main course*

Ingredients	Amounts		Procedure
	U.S.	Metric	
Egg yolk	1 each	1 each	Blend egg yolks with smashed anchovy fillets.
Anchovy fillets	2 each	2 each	
Extra virgin olive oil	1 fl oz	30 ml	Gradually add oil, like making mayonnaise.
Capers	1 tbsp	29 g	Blend in remaining ingredients.
Shallots, chopped very fine	1 tbsp	29 g	
Dijon mustard	1 tsp	5 ml	
Sea salt	To taste	To taste	
Pepper, freshly ground	To taste	To taste	
Chuck flatiron, ground fine	1 lb	454 g	
Toast points	As needed	As needed	Serve with toast points.

NUTRITIONAL INFORMATION PER SERVING (WITH FOUR TOAST POINTS): 704 Calories; 53 g Fat (68.6% calories from fat); 41 g Protein; 14 g Carbohydrate; 1 g Dietary Fiber; 241 mg Cholesterol; 604 mg Sodium. Exchanges: 1 Grain (Starch); 5 1/2 Lean Meat; 0 Vegetable; 7 Fat; 0 Other Carbohydrates.

This canapé is definitely luxurious. It looks spectacular and is still served at exquisite events. Use the Tartar Steak recipe above.

quail egg on tartar steak canapés   *Yield: 40 each*

Ingredients	Amounts		Procedure
	U.S.	Metric	
Tartar steak mix	16 oz	454 g	Just prior to service, place freshly made steak tartar on each toast round.
Toast rounds, 1 1/2-inch diameter	40 each	40 each	Make a slight indentation in the center. Break egg, separate yolk without breaking, and place in center. (Discard egg white or use for another recipe.) Decorate with parsley leaf.
Quail eggs, fresh, very small	40 each	40 each	
Italian parsley	40 leaves	40 leaves	

NUTRITIONAL INFORMATION PER PIECE: 67 Calories; 4 g Fat (53.9% calories from fat); 4 g Protein; 4 g Carbohydrate; trace Dietary Fiber; 88 mg Cholesterol; 67 mg Sodium. Exchanges: 1/2 Grain (Starch); 1/2 Lean Meat; 0 Vegetable; 1/2 Fat; 0 Other Carbohydrates.

Profiteroles are small balls made of pâte à choux paste (called puff paste in English) that can be filled with many exciting savory and sweet fillings. The next recipe uses a luxurious filling based on lobster. However, any type of shellfish salad, such as a shrimp salad, could be used instead. Pâte à choux freezes well, so the shells can be kept on hand for a quick canapé base.

Profiteroles are puff paste loaves or ovals, small enough to be eaten in one bite. Puff paste items are made in the pastry shop or purchased ready for filling. We have included the recipes for the puff paste used to make the profiteroles as well as the recipe for lobster salad filling.

pate choux profiteroles *Yield: 40 pieces*

Ingredients	Amounts U.S.	Metric	Procedure
Water	6 fl oz	177 ml	Bring the water, milk, and butter to a boil.
Milk	2 fl oz	59 ml	
Butter	4 oz	113 g	
All-purpose flour, sifted	4 1/2 oz	128 g	Dump the flour in all at once and stir with a wooden spoon. When the mixture comes off the sides of the pot and is shiny, place it into a mixing bowl.
Eggs, large AA	4 each	4 each	With the paddle attachment, work in the eggs, one at a time. Add the salt.
Salt	1 tsp	5 g	

With the paddle attachment, work in the eggs, one at a time. Add the salt. The mixture should be somewhat stiff but pliable to pipe out. On a parchment-covered sheet pan, pipe 40 1-inch balls.

Bake at 400°F (200°C) until golden brown.

NUTRITIONAL INFORMATION PER PIECE: 40 Calories; 3 g Fat (64.4% calories from fat); 1 g Protein; 3 g Carbohydrate; trace Dietary Fiber; 28 mg Cholesterol; 85 mg Sodium. Exchanges: 0 Grain (Starch); 0 Lean Meat; 0 Nonfat Milk; 1/2 Fat.

Lobster creates a sense of luxury and can command a high price.

lobster salad filling *Yield: 1 lb (454 g)*

Ingredients	Amounts U.S.	Metric	Procedure
Lobster meat, freshly cooked, diced small	1 lb	454 g	Gently fold the lobster, onion, celery, tarragon, and mayonnaise together. Chill.
Yellow onion, chopped	1 tbsp	15 g	
Celery stalk, finely diced	2 tbsp	30 g	
Tarragon leaves	1 tsp	5 g	
Mayonnaise	1/2 cup	118 ml	

NUTRITIONAL INFORMATION PER RECIPE: 1,244 Calories; 96 g Fat (67.8% calories from fat); 95 g Protein; 8 g Carbohydrate; 1 g Dietary Fiber; 365 mg Cholesterol; 2,365 mg Sodium. Exchanges: 0 Grain (Starch); 13 Lean Meat; 0 Vegetable; 8 Fat.

lobster profiteroles, assembly *Yield: 40 each*

Ingredients	Amounts U.S.	Metric	Procedure
Profiteroles	40 each	40 each	Split the profiteroles horizontally. The bottom of the profiterole should use 2/3 of the pastry, and the top or lid should use 1/3. Use a spoon to fill the bottom section of the profiterole with lobster. Replace the top. Put in small pastry cups for service.
Lobster salad filling	1 lb	454 g	
Paper pastry cups	40 each	40 each	

NUTRITIONAL INFORMATION PER PIECE: 70 Calories; 5 g Fat (67.1% calories from fat); 3 g Protein; 3 g Carbohydrate; trace Dietary Fiber; 39 mg Cholesterol; 134 mg Sodium. Exchanges: 0 Grain (Starch); 1/2 Lean Meat; 0 Vegetable; 0 Nonfat Milk; 1/2 Fat.

There are times when caviar is almost expected for elegant affairs. This is a simple and delicious recipe.

caviar canapés *Yield: 40 pieces*

Ingredients	Amounts U.S.	Metric	Procedure
Dark rye rounds, 1 1/2-inch, or squares 1 1/2-inch wide	40 each	40 each	Toast bread on each side only under broiler.
Butter, melted	2 fl oz	59 ml	When toast is cold, brush with melted butter.
Sour cream	4 fl oz	118 ml	Using a small French or star tip, pipe on a small dollop of sour cream and put caviar on top. Place a little red onion next to caviar for color.
Caviar (any kind)	8 oz	227 g	
Red onion, fine dice	4 oz	113 g	

NUTRITIONAL INFORMATION PER PIECE: 52 Calories; 3 g Fat (51.6% calories from fat); 2 g Protein; 4 g Carbohydrate; trace Dietary Fiber; 38 mg Cholesterol; 127 mg Sodium. Exchanges: 0 Grain (Starch); 0 Lean Meat; 0 Vegetable; 0 Nonfat Milk; 1/2 Fat.

Sometimes less is more. This simple recipe is another example that proves that canapés don't have to be elaborate productions. **Crissini** are thin Italian bread sticks. The crissini sticks can be broken in half if a smaller version is preferred.

crissini with prosciutto *Yield: 40 pieces*

Ingredients	Amounts		Procedure
	U.S.	Metric	
Crissini sticks, thin	40 each	40 each	Spread lightly with butter (about 2/3 of the length).
Butter, room temperature	As needed	As needed	
Prosciutto, thin slices	40 each	40 each	Wrap prosciutto around the butter and leave the unbuttered end exposed. Present in a basket with the unwrapped ends sticking out.

NUTRITIONAL INFORMATION PER PIECE: *57* Calories; 3 g Fat (42.8% calories from fat); 4 g Protein; 4 g Carbohydrate; 0 g Dietary Fiber; 11 mg Cholesterol; 357 mg Sodium. Exchanges: 1/2 Grain (Starch); 1/2 Lean Meat; 0 Fat.

Focaccia is an Italian soft, flat, pizza-like yeast bread. It is usually topped with onions, olives, herbs, and other ingredients. The word "focaccia" is derived from the Latin word "hearth-cake." The topping is usually kneaded in, unlike pizza, where the garnish is placed on top.

bruschetta with sun-dried tomato
Yield: 40 pieces

Ingredients	Amounts		Procedure
	U.S.	Metric	
Sun-dried tomatoes, packed in oil, drained, and cut in fine strips	8 oz	227 g	Place the drained sun-dried tomatoes and basil in a bowl and toss with the balsamic vinegar and extra virgin olive oil. Let this mixture rest for 30 minutes to meld the flavors.
Basil leaves, fresh, minced fine	10 each	10 each	
Balsamic vinegar	1 tbsp	15 ml	
Extra virgin olive oil	1 tbsp	15 ml	
Focaccia, sliced 1/4-inch thick	40 each	40 each	Slice focaccia and brush with olive oil. Lightly toast.
Olive oil	As needed	As needed	Place the sun-dried tomato mixture on top of the toasted focaccia.

NUTRITIONAL INFORMATION PER SERVING (EXCLUDING UNKNOWN ITEMS): 185 Calories; 5 g Fat (24.0% calories from fat); 4 g Protein; 30 g Carbohydrate; 2 g Dietary Fiber; 0 mg Cholesterol; 16 mg Sodium. Exchanges: 2 Grain (Starch); 0 Fruit; 1 Fat.

The flavors of this favorite mussel soup are combined into a tasty canapé. Saffron must be bloomed before it is used. This is accomplished by placing the wine in a saucepan. Top with the saffron strands and bring wine to a boil. Reduce heat and let the saffron steep for 10 minutes. Blooming releases the color of the saffron. The Leek Marmalade recipe will follow.

billi bi barquette   *Yield: 40 pieces*

Ingredients	Amounts		Procedure
	U.S.	Metric	
White wine	1 fl oz	30 ml	In a nonreactive pan, bloom the saffron in the white wine by warming the wine.
Saffron	5 strands	5 strands	
Cream cheese	8 oz	227 g	Add the cream cheese and leek marmalade to the saffron and white wine mixture. Mix until blended.
Leek marmalade	8 fl oz	240 ml	
Barquette shells, 2 inches, pre baked	40 each	40 each	Pipe cream cheese mixture from a pastry bag into the prebaked barquette pastry shells. Place a mussel on top.
Poached or smoked mussels	40 each	40 each	

NUTRITIONAL INFORMATION PER PIECE: 326 Calories; 21 g Fat (58.4% calories from fat); 6 g Protein; 28 g Carbohydrate; 1 g Dietary Fiber; 11 mg Cholesterol; 187 mg Sodium. Exchanges: 1 1/2 Grain (Starch); 1/2 Lean Meat; 1/2 Vegetable; 4 Fat; 0 Other Carbohydrates.

leek marmalade   *Yield: 8 fl oz (240 ml) 40 each 1/5 oz (6 g) servings*

Ingredients	Amounts		Procedure
	U.S.	Metric	
Leeks, 1 1/2 inch in diameter, julienne	8 each	8 each	In a nonreactive pot, sauté the leeks in the olive oil.
Olive oil	2 tbsp	30 ml	
Sauterne wine	8 fl oz	237 ml	Add the wine and sugar and cook down until the mixture is thick like jam.
Sugar	4 oz	113 g	

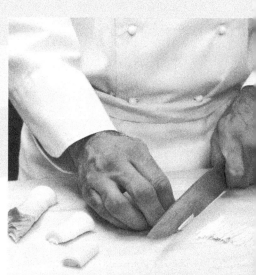

NUTRITIONAL INFORMATION PER SERVING: 32 Calories; 1 g Fat (22.4% calories from fat); trace Protein; 5 g Carbohydrate; trace Dietary Fiber; 0 mg Cholesterol; 4 mg Sodium. Exchanges: 1/2 Vegetable; 0 Fat; 0 Other Carbohydrates.

LEARNING ACTIVITY 7-2

Select a canapé recipe from this unit. Try the same recipe using three different bases. Suggestions might include vegetable, bread, puff pastry, pita, or tortillas. Note the differences in flavor, appearance, and texture. Which base did you prefer? Which base would be best for a formal event? Which base would lend itself to a catered pool-side party?

LARGE-SCALE CANAPÉ PRODUCTION

In most hotels and catering facilities, hundreds of canapé are produced daily. To make such a production simple and efficient, it is important to have a game plan for large-scale production. The catering departments of most hotels and catering facilities have specific lists of canapés that they make and use for any particular type of function. At a typical BEO (Banquet Event Order) meeting, the counts and amounts of specific canapé pieces are discussed. At this time, the chef, food and beverage manager, or catering manager takes the order sheets and batches the canapés for production.

The planning phase of production spells out how many of each item will be needed, and the executive chef gives the lists of assignments to the sous chef or garde manger to be further broken down into the tasks per each area in the kitchen or production department. For bread-based canapé, the baker will need to bake the necessary Pullman loaves or breads, or purchase the loaves to use in the canapé recipe. The bread products are then sent to the garde manger or cold kitchen. The garde manger department may be tasked to prepare the assorted butters, cheese spreads, and fillings for the necessary assortment of canapés.

Canapés are put together in an assembly-line fashion. One person cuts rounds; another coats them in clarified butter or other spread and toasts them off. Still another coats them with the toppings such as the meat, fish, or other main ingredient, and the next person garnishes the canapé. The final product is finished off so that each one looks identical to the next. In smaller operations, one or two individuals may have to build the canapés. The most important thing to remember is making sure that the entire mise en place is in effect:

1. The bases are cut from 1/8- to 1/4-inch thick and are either toasted bare or painted with clarified butter and toasted.
2. Toppings such as meat, seafood, and cheese are cut and ready. Fillings that will be piped should be placed in the appropriate bags with piping tips.
3. Garnishes are cut, trimmed, and further processed, if needed.
4. If aspic is to be used, it is prepared and ready to go.
5. Production of canapés takes up a lot of space. Make sure all counters and tables are cleaned and sanitized before use. Have all necessary sheet pans and speed racks ready for use.
6. Prepare parchment-covered sheet pans or trays. When mise en place is complete, the canapés are ready to be put together in an organized fashion as follows:
   - The toasted bases are laid out on parchment-covered sheet pans or trays (parchment keeps them neat).
   - The fat-based spread is applied to all of the bases with an even coating to seal out the moisture.
   - The main component of the body is artfully placed on the base, ensuring that all of the canapés are identical in placement.
   - Garnishment is then added with precision to ensure a uniform and consistent product.
   - The aspic is then applied, if required, or the canapés are covered with plastic wrap until service.
   - Canapés are placed on trays or mirrors for service.

>> Summary

Canapés are tasty, petite morsels that are served cold as a finger food. They consist of a base or foundation, which can be made out of all types of breads, chips, crackers, and even vegetables. They should be sturdy enough to withstand the weight of the toppings.

A spread of butter or cheese is needed to protect the base from getting soggy and to keep the topping from sliding off the canapé. Toppings can consist of a wide variety of delicious ingredients including smoked fish, seafood, caviar, poultry, eggs, meats, and vegetables.

Garnishes are placed above the topping and should complement the overall flavors of the canapé and add a visual punch. Aspic can be used to glaze the entire canapé and provide a glossy sheen and protection. Large-scale canapé production requires communication between the catering department and chefs and a good mise en place set up.

>> Review Questions

MATCHING

Match the term to its description.

1. _____ profiteroles
2. _____ focaccia
3. _____ rouille
4. _____ romescu
5. _____ crissini
6. _____ andalouse
7. _____ aspic
8. _____ barquette
9. _____ agliata

a. clear jelly
b. boat-shaped shell
c. type of French mayonnaise
d. garlic and walnut sauce
e. pâte à choux ball
f. spicy paste
g. Italian bread stick
h. pizza-like yeast bread
i. type of Spanish sauce

MULTIPLE CHOICE

10. Which is *not* characteristic of a canapé?
    a. made with only edible ingredients
    b. served warm
    c. bite-sized
    d. dry, not wet or greasy
11. Which of the following is *not* considered a flat bread?
    a. ciabatta
    b. pita
    c. millet
    d. lavash
12. Bercy is a type of
    a. bread.
    b. compound butter.
    c. topping.
    d. garnish.

13. It is advisable to make the base about _____ inch thick.
    a. 1/4- to 1/2-
    b. 1/4- to 3/4-
    c. 1/2- to 3/4-
    d. It doesn't matter as long as it is sturdy enough to hold the rest of the canapé ingredients.
14. Which component adds a "kiss of excitement" to the canapé?
    a. topping
    b. spread
    c. base
    d. garnish

SHORT ANSWER

Write the purpose of each of the main canapé components.

15. Base:

16. Spread (binding agent):

17. Topping:

18. Garnish:

Make a list of products that can be used as the

19. Base:

20. Spread (binding agent):

21. Topping:

22. Garnish:

Appetizers

>> Learning Objectives

After you have finished reading this unit, you should be able to:

- Define appetizers, amuse-bouche, and hors d'oeuvre.
- Compare and contrast appetizers and hors d'oeuvre.
- Prepare a variety of cold and hot appetizers.
- Classify a variety of caviars and explain their roles in the cold kitchen.

>> Key Terms

amuse-bouche
  (*ah-muz-boosh*)
antipasto
blini

bresaola (*brehsh-ay-
  OH-lah*)
chermoula (*chair-mulia*)
croquette (*kroh-keht*)

hummus
phyllo (Filo)
roe
tandoori

tapenade (*ta-pen-
  AHD*)
zampone (*dzahm-POH-
  nay*)

Appetizers should stimulate the desire to eat; therefore, portions should be small and flavorful (Figure 8-1). In many cases, the appetizer menu is where chefs try out their boldest, most creative, and most flavorful creations, knowing that diners feel more adventurous when they are only ordering a small bite. Quality appetizers give the guest a glimpse of good things to come.

Appetizers have gained in popularity because the portions are small and appealing to diet-conscious customers. "Savvy and flavor-intrepid diners have long ordered only from the left (appetizer) side of the menu. The idea has caught on, and appetizers now herald the trendiest way of dining—leisurely nibbling, drinking, and chatting one's way through an evening, sharing stimulating bites of this and that. Dining is today's entertainment and fun. We've become a nation of grazers, making meals of little plates of exotic fare," says Sandy Szwarc in an article printed in the *Austin Chronicle* ("The Appetizer Atlas: A World of Small Bites Review," April 11, 2003).

Figure 8-1 Appetizers should whet the appetite.

>> Amuse-Bouche

Amuse-bouche, or amuse-geule, is similar to an appetizer and has been described as "little bites of food to amuse the mouth, invigorate the palate, and whet the appetite." This somewhat old-fashioned French term has been resurrected by today's young chefs (Figure 8-2). Serving these little morsels, which are typically much smaller than an appetizer serving, is again a common practice in fine restaurants. Amuse-bouche is traditionally a little gift from the chef served to stimulate the guests' appetites and keep them happy until the first course is served.

In many operations, designated hot and cold appetizer and amuse-bouche stations are attached to the cold kitchen.

>> Appetizer or Hors d'Oeuvre?

Ask a number of chefs to explain the difference between an appetizer and hors d' oeuvre and you'll get a number of different answers. These terms are often used interchangeably. But for the sake of our discussion we will note a slightly different meaning between the two words. Hors d'oeuvre "means little snack foods, small items of food or light courses, served before or outside of ("hors") the main dish of a meal (the "oeuvres") that are intended to stimulate the appetite. Hors d'oeuvres are the small, savory bites, typically finger food, served before a meal whereas appetizers appear as the first course served at the table. The name "hors d'oeuvres" comes from French and is literally translated as "out of the work," but it's more logical

Figure 8-2 Rolled courgette ribbons stuffed with fresh mint leaves, chilies, and goat's cheese and presented to a table of guests as an amuse-bouche.

to think of it as meaning 'apart from (or before) the meal'" (*Linda's Culinary Dictionary, A Dictionary & History of Cooking, Food, and Beverage Terms* ©2004 by Linda Stradley). Hors d'oeuvre are served when a meal is not planned, such as at a stand-up function, reception, or cocktail party, and include those items that can be eaten with the fingers such as canapés and crudités or those requiring plates and forks such as hot hors d'oeuvre served with a sauce (Figure 8-3). In conclusion, the difference between appetizers and hors d'oeuvre has more to do with how and when they are served than the foods being served.

Figure 8-3 A lavish appetizer buffet.

>> Around the World

It seems as if every cuisine has its own favorite appetizers. In the United States, cold appetizers—also often called starters—could be shrimp cocktail, fruits, smoked salmon, and, in many cases, salads. Oysters and clams served on the half-shell are also popular appetizers. Cold soups are also served as appetizers, but their popularity is waning. Hot appetizers include a host of delicious options including hot crab dip, stuffed mushrooms, and much more.

In Germany, appetizers are called "Vorspeisen" and are generally more substantial than what is served in other countries. Popular cold appetizers consist of pickled fish, vegetable salads, sliced sausages, substantial salads and cold cuts, and even cold poultry dishes (Figure 8-4). Popular hot appetizers range from a patty shell filled with creamed wild mushrooms to grilled spicy sausages or fried oysters.

Antipasto is the Italian term given for "appetizers." (*Antipasti* is the plural form of the word "antipasto.") Most Americans are familiar with the antipasto platter, which consists of sliced Italian cold cuts, pickled vegetables, olives, and cheeses. In Italy, an antipasto could also consist of pasta dishes despite the name, fruits with melon and prosciutto (ham, usually dry-cured Italian ham), pickled vegetables, olives, canned sardines, or cheeses (Figure 8-5). In this unit, we will study a variety of antipasto platters and suitable components.

Figure 8-4 This vorspeisen comes with cheese, radish, smoked sausage pieces, cream cheese, and parsley.

On French menus, the heading "Hors d'oeuvre" could include a selection of cold and hot appetizers including a selection of many different salads, pickled fish, meats, soufflés, snails, croquettes, and seafood dishes (Figure 8-6). A large segment of French appetizers includes pâtés and related products. Some of them are rather expensive, especially when they are made with goose liver and truffles; others require complicated preparation.

Figure 8-5 Antipasto is a Roman starter that includes artichokes, olives, peppers, and seafood.

Figure 8-6 Escargots á la bourguignonne, served on a white plate with lemon garnish.

Empanadas and tapas come from Spain. The pastry turnovers, called empanadas, are traditionally filled with either savory or sweet ingredients (Figure 8-7). It is the savory, filled empanadas that find their way to appetizer plates. Spanish tapas consist of many small, individual dishes of food that can act as appetizers, or they can be eaten as an incredibly varied meal. Tapas are found in bars and restaurants in Spain and are often eaten with an aperitif such as sherry.

"In the middle of the nineteenth century, Western Europe gradually began to adopt the Russian style of serving a meal. The Russians served each course in turn and cleared the table in between. *Zakuski* was, and is, the appetizer course in a Russian meal (Figure 8-8). The word comes from the Russian for "piece" or "morsel"(from the *Zakuski Catalogue* introduction by

Figure 8-7 Empanadas with red sauce or salsa and sour cream.

Figure 8-8 Pickled mushrooms, beetroot, sour cream, rye bread, pickled cucumber, and herring fillets make up this zakuski plate.

curator Peter Ford, Off-Centre Gallery, Bristol, England). From caviar to pickled herring, Russian gourmands have long enjoyed their own version of the appetizer.

In Greece the appetizer course, or "meze," includes hummus, tarama, salata, and dolmas (Figure 8-9).

Mexican appetizers such as quesadillas, guacamole, and salsa with chips have become popular in the United States (Figure 8-10). Cachapas de Carabobo is a well-liked Venezuelan appetizer made of corn pancakes that are fried on a hot griddle or cast iron skillet and then served with cream or wrapped around a slice of cheese. Chipas is a corn and cheese bread that is very popular in Paraguay and Argentina. Some recipes call for freshly grated corn, others for tapioca flour or cornmeal. Brazilians love their salgadinhos (appetizers), and a favorite choice is Bolinhos de Bacalhau (salt cod fritters) of Portuguese origin.

The Chinese serve dim sum, which translated means "touching your heart" or "choose what your heart likes most." In China, dim sum is typically a mid-day meal, served with tea. In the United States we have taken components of the dim sum and used them as appetizers. There are steamed shrimp and pork dumplings, deep-fried egg rolls, taro-root dumplings, and green peppers with shrimp filling, to name a few favorites (Figure 8-11).

Figure 8-9 Filo pastries, dolmades, Middle Eastern meatballs, tomato and zucchini cups, apricot and almond tartlets, hummus in pepper cups with pita bread—all are delicious appetizers from Greece.

Figure 8-10 A bowl of guacamole amid an arrangement of nacho chips, hot sauce, and garnishes.

Figure 8-11 Plate of dim sum.

Figure 8-12   An ornate buffet spread of sushi.

Traditional Japanese appetizers include sushi, sashimi, and gyoza, which are deep- or pan-fried pot stickers (Figure 8-12).

It's easy to see that appetizers have found a prominent place on menus around the globe. With more awareness of world cuisines, these international appetizers are now finding their way onto menus right here in our own local bistros.

LEARNING ACTIVITY 8-1

When developing appetizer menus, chefs must understand the world's food customs and flavors. For this exercise, develop an appetizer menu based on a country or region of the world. Include indigenous foods and any special cultural influences.

>> Presentation

Appetizers should provide an inviting flavor and an attractive appearance. The choice of appetizers to preface a main course should correspond with the food to follow. Presentation is very important when serving appetizers because they set the tone for the whole meal. There are many new and interesting china and glass dishes available now to present appetizers. China spoons, glass timbales, and small cups inspire chefs to create interesting little dishes. Chefs are encouraged to create beautiful and stunning appetizers (Figure 8-13). Use the following tips when serving appetizers:

- Vary texture if possible—soft food pared with crisp food.
- Choose appetizers that complement rather than compete with your main dishes.
- Consider the aesthetics of the plate as a whole. Think about color and dimension. Don't overcrowd the plate.
- All cuts should be accurate and clean (Figure 8-14).

Figure 8-13   Appetizers give the chef an opportunity to create a visually appealing dish.

Figure 8-14 Artful array of crudites and dip with vegetables that have been carefully cut.

Figure 8-15 Beef skewers are garnished with an individual lettuce leaf and a sprinkle of colorful diced onions.

- Select appropriate garnishes (Figure 8-15). Vary the garnish choice with different appetizers. (Don't get in a rut using only parsley.)
- Serve cold appetizers "cold" and hot appetizers "hot." Match the plates to the type of appetizer by using cold plates for cold appetizers and hot or warm plates for hot items. Some appetizers are served lukewarm and created at the last moment, matching a hot garnish with a cold ingredient.
- Select plates that reflect the style of the food items (Figure 8-16).
- Make sure the plate is sparkling clean; check the edges once the food has been plated.
- If the food items are to be served on platters, butler style, make sure the plate is as presentable to the last guest as it was with the first. (Butler style is a type of service where the appetizers are place on hand-held trays and offered to guests by servers) (Figure 8-17).

A recent presentation trend has been to use spoons. Each spoon is attractively displayed (handles out) on a tray and filled with a variety of popular appetizer ingredients (Figure 8-18). A unique vase or container is usually included on the tray to hold the discarded spoons. Estimate three or four spoons per guest for a typical appetizer. Spoons are lighter because they don't require a base such as bread or tart shell to hold the ingredients—the spoon does that for you!

Figure 8-16 The right dish can complement the food, as in this quesadilla appetizer.

Figure 8-17 Platters should be kept clean and presentable throughout the service.

Figure 8-18 Decorative spoons filled with a variety of appetizers.

LEARNING ACTIVITY 8-2

Create an appetizer and plate it three different ways. Be creative and showcase the food. Show the three plates to your classmates and get their feedback on which presentation is most appealing and practical.

>> Cold Appetizers

In the United States, cold appetizers could be shrimp cocktail, fruits, smoked salmon, and, in many cases, salads. Oysters and clams served on the half-shell are also popular as appetizers. Cold soups are also served as appetizers and will be discussed in Unit 10. It is important to keep cold appetizers cold throughout the service period.

CLAMS ON THE HALF-SHELL

Clams or oysters are often served raw on the half-shell (Figure 8-19). That is why only the most tender clams are used for this application.

Preparation

Here are a few things to look for when selecting good-quality clams:

- Select clam shells that do not gape open.
- The shells should close quickly when tapped, which indicates that the clam is still alive.
- Discard any clams that have broken shells.
- Discard any dead clams.
- Once the shells are opened, look for meat that has a firm texture and is tan in color.
- Fresh clams have a fresh, mild smell; discard those clams that have a strong, fishy odor.
- Discard any clams that have meat that is dry or darker in color.
- Scrub the shells of the clams under cold, running water. Use a clam knife to pry open the clam and rinse out any remaining sand or grit. Gently separate the top and the bottom shells. Use the clam knife to loosen the clam in the shell, removing any further sand or grit that may have been hidden behind the clam meat. Leave the meat in the shell.
- If serving in a raw bar, set the clams on a bed of crushed ice to keep them steady.

OYSTERS ON A HALF-SHELL

Oysters served on the half-shell are usually placed on a bed of ice or seaweed and served with cocktail sauce, grated horseradish, and lemon wedges or halves (Figure 8-20). Preparations are the same as for clams on a half-shell. Serve with sauce Mignonnette from Unit 15.

Cooked mussels are served as cold appetizers on the half-shell with the following vinaigrette topping. This recipe also works well with a mussel salad. The following recipe is an adaptation to the Benchmark Recipe: Basic Vinaigrette Dressing, which is presented in Unit 14.

Dry, nonalcoholic wine can be used in schools if preferred.

Figure 8-19 Cherrystone clams on half-shells topped with pesto.

Figure 8-20 Six fresh oysters on a half-shell resting on a bed of ice and seaweed or kelp.

mussels vinaigrette *Yield: 6 servings of 4 mussels each*

Ingredients	Amounts U.S.	Metric	Procedure
Mussels, large, scrubbed	24 each	24 each	Combine mussels, shallots, and wine in a suitable pot. Cover and bring to a boil. Cook over high heat 2 minutes or until mussels have opened. Cool covered until the mussels have cooled enough to handle. Remove the mussels and save the stock. Remove the top shell and loosen the mussels from the bottom shell. Discard one of the shells and save the other. Refrigerate. Carefully strain the mussel stock in a smaller pot, making sure the sand collected at the bottom is left behind. Boil quickly to about 1/2 cup quantity. Chill.
Shallots, chopped	1 tbsp	15 g	
Wine, dry white	4 fl oz	118 ml	
Olive oil	1 oz	29 ml	Mix the olive oil, vinegar, capers, onions, red bell peppers, Kosher salt, lemon juice and parsley together. Add reduced mussel stock to the preceding mixture and toss with reserved mussels.
Champagne vinegar	1/2 oz	15 ml	
Capers	1 tbsp	15 g	Fill shell with mussel and sauce and serve chilled.
Onions, minced fine	1/2 oz	15 g	
Red bell peppers, minced	2 oz	58 g	
Parsley, minced	1 1/2 tbsp	22 g	
Lemon juice	1 tbsp	16 ml	
Kosher salt	to taste	to taste	
Reduced mussel stock	4 oz	118 ml	

NUTRITIONAL INFORMATION PER SERVING: 97 Calories; 4 g Fat (40.0% calories from fat); 8 g Protein; 5 g Carbohydrate; trace Dietary Fiber; 18 mg Cholesterol; 237 mg Sodium. Exchanges: 0 Grain (Starch); 1 Lean Meat; 0 Vegetable; 0 Fruit; 1/2 Fat.

The traditional salsa and chips won't do, try serving this Mexican delicacy. Poached mussels enseñada is a fun title that translates to "educated mussels."

poached mussels enseñada

Yield: 60 mussels, 6 each appetizer servings of 10 mussels each

Ingredients	Amounts		Procedure
	U.S.	Metric	
Red pepper, small dice	1 medium	1 medium	Toss together to make a fresh salsa.
Jalapeno pepper, small dice	1 small	1 small	
Anaheim chili, small dice	1 large	1 large	
Garlic, minced fine	2 cloves	2 cloves	
Lemon juice, fresh	3 medium	3 medium	
Olive oil	1 to 2 oz	30 to 60 ml	
Balsamic vinegar	1 tbsp	15 ml	
Cilantro, chopped	1 oz	28 g	
Kosher salt	To taste	To taste	
Cayenne	To taste	To taste	
Mussels	60	60	To steam mussels: First sauté the garlic and red pepper flakes in the olive oil. Add the wine and water and bring to a simmer. Place cleaned mussels in a steamer over the liquid and steam until the mussels open. Discard any closed ones. Chill. Remove the meat; save one shell. Replace the mussel; top with salsa and serve.
White wine	8 fl oz	237 ml	
Water	8 fl oz	237 ml	
Garlic, mashed	3 cloves	3 cloves	
Red pepper flakes	1 tsp	5 g	
Olive oil	1 fl oz	30 ml	

NUTRITIONAL INFORMATION PER SERVING: 306 Calories; 15 g Fat (48.7% calories from fat); 21 g Protein; 16 g Carbohydrate; 1 g Dietary Fiber; 45 mg Cholesterol; 513 mg Sodium. Exchanges: 0 Grain (Starch); 3 Lean Meat; 1/2 Vegetable; 0 Fruit; 2 1/2 Fat.

SHRIMP AND LOBSTER COCKTAIL

The term "cocktail," used traditionally for mixed short drinks, has been appropriated also for food when served in high-stemmed cocktail glasses. Crab and shrimp cocktail are found on many appetizer menus. The use of the stem glasses has gone out of fashion and returned again. Luxury hotels sometimes use silver stands, called supreme, filled with shaved ice, an insert with the crab or shrimp, and a ring to keep the insert in place.

There are many ways of serving seafood cocktails. Many operations put the seafood on a bed of shredded lettuce. Seafood cocktails are often garnished with shaved horseradish and a lemon wedge. Luxury operations add a half lemon, wrapped in gauze to prevent the pits of the lemon from falling into the food when squeezed.

The most expensive crab meat is lump crab meat, which is sold pasteurized in 16-ounce (450 g) cans. It should be handled as little as possible—it is highly perishable and will break easily. Any kind of crab meat can be used for crab meat cocktail. The Benchmark Recipe for Traditional Cocktail Sauce is in Unit 15.

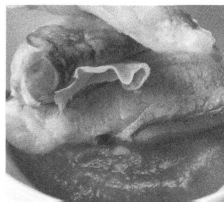

crab cocktail _Yield: 1 serving_

Ingredients	Amounts		Procedure
	U.S.	Metric	
Lump crab meat	5 oz	142 g	Serve as illustrated.
Cocktail sauce	1 fl oz	30 ml	
Shaved horseradish	1 oz	28 g	

NUTRITIONAL INFORMATION PER SERVING: 159 Calories; 2 g Fat (9.6% calories from fat); 26 g Protein; 9 g Carbohydrate; 1 g Dietary Fiber; 111 mg Cholesterol; 673 mg Sodium. Exchanges: 3 1/2 Lean Meat; 1/2 Other Carbohydrates.

Figure 8-21 Shrimp cocktail is served with sauce in a glass dish.

Shrimp cocktail is a popular appetizer (Figure 8-21). Some operations use very large shrimp, identified as U 10 count (fewer than 10 shrimp per pound, 454 g). Usually three shrimp are served.

Lobster cocktail is made with cooked, shelled lobster. The serving size is about 5 ounces (142 g), which is the approximate yield of a 1-pound (454 g) lobster. Often a section of the shell is added for a dramatic presentation.

CAVIAR

To give caviar is to honor the recipient.
To serve caviar is to honor the guest.

Author unknown

The name "caviar" has become synonymous with elegance and luxury. James Beard once pointed out that, "The **roe** or eggs of the Russian mother sturgeon has probably been present at more important international affairs than have all the Russian dignitaries of history combined. This seemingly simple article of diet has taken its place in the world along with pearls, sables, old silver, and Cellini cups." In many circles, caviar is considered an aphrodisiac. At this point in time, sturgeon roe from Russia is considered endangered and is only available in limited supply, even in Russia. Sturgeon roe is available in China, Iran, and the United States and most is farm raised. It is fitting that we include in our discussion of seafood appetizers this esteemed product.

Figure 8-22 A white caviar spoon with a sampling of black caviar from a large tin of caviar.

Figure 8-23 Caviar should be kept in a closed container, refrigerated, and used within 1 or 2 days after opening.

Caviar is fish roe (eggs) (Figure 8-22). In the United States, only sturgeon roe can be called "caviar." Roe from other species must be identified with the name of the fish preceding the word "caviar," such as salmon caviar or whitefish caviar.

Caviar Handling and Service

Sturgeon caviar is incredibly expensive and must be handled with extreme care. It is usually only purchased when there is a specific order, such as for a banquet. It should be received from a reputable purveyor and kept immediately under lock and key until issued to the kitchen as close to serving time as possible (Figure 8-23). Refrigerate upon opening. Do not freeze caviar—freezing and thawing will cause the eggs to burst.

Metal spoons can impart a metallic taste to caviar and should not be used. Special caviar spoons made of "mother of pearl," bone, or tortoise shells are ideal (Figure 8-24).

When caviar is sold in individual portions, which happens rarely in most restaurants, each portion should be weighed to avoid losses. The average serving is 1 ounce (28 g), about 1 heaping tablespoon. Years ago when caviar was more abundant—and therefore less expensive—caviar lovers were known to eat 8 ounces or more at a meal.

Caviar is always served chilled. It should be placed on ice when it is served, which will keep it at lower than room temperature for optimal taste. As soon as the chill wears off, both flavor and texture start to decline. Caviar is traditionally served in a caviar serving set or from a glass container that has been placed in a bowl of ice (Figure 8-25). When adding caviar to a hot dish, always add it at the last possible minute before service.

Figure 8-24 This caviar spoon is made of "mother of pearl."

Figure 8-25 Traditional caviar serving set.

Figure 8-26 Baby baked potatoes with sour cream are topped with caviar.

Because caviar is so costly, it is often served surrounded by garnishes or used sparingly as a topper on another ingredient (Figure 8-26).

Typical caviar garnishes include the following:

- Sieved egg yolk
- Chopped egg white
- Diced onion

Serve with:

- Toast points
- Melba toast
- Crackers
- Potato pancakes
- Blinis
- Endive leaf

Top with:

- Sour cream
- Cream cheese
- Crème fraîche

Caviar is often served with ice cold vodka or dry champagne.

Blinis

Blinis are a traditional accompaniment with caviar; they are small, buckwheat griddle cakes. Original Russian blinis are made with a yeast pancake batter. When there is not time to make yeast-leavened blinis, buckwheat pancake mix works well. In most operations, blinis are made in the breakfast pantry. Blinis are always made fresh, like any other pancake, and they should be served warm. For banquet service, blinis can be topped with a dollop of crème fraîche and a small spoonful of cold caviar. This could be messy because the crème fraîche will immediately melt on the warm blinis.

blinis _Yield: 40 pieces_

Ingredients	Amounts		Procedure
	U.S.	Metric	
Sugar	1 tsp	5 g	Blend the sugar with water and yeast to dissolve.
Water, lukewarm	6 fl oz	177 ml	
Yeast, dry	1 package	1 package	
Milk, warm	12 fl oz	355 ml	Combine the milk with salt and eggs.
Salt	1 tsp	5 g	
Eggs	6 oz	170 g	
Bread flour	5 oz	142 g	Sift flours together; add to milk and yeast. Whisk to make smooth batter. Add melted butter.
Buckwheat flour	10 oz	284 g	
Butter, melted	4 tsp	20 g	

Let batter proof in a warm place until bubbly. Make silver dollar-sized pancakes and drop into a hot skillet to fry.

Serve blinis with caviar and an assortment of garnishes.

NUTRITIONAL INFORMATION PER PIECE: 45 Calories; 1 g Fat (25.3% calories from fat); 2 g Protein; 7 g Carbohydrate; 1 g Dietary Fiber; 18 mg Cholesterol; 68 mg Sodium. Exchanges: 1/2 Grain (Starch); 0 Lean Meat; 0 Nonfat Milk; 0 Fat; 0 Other Carbohydrates.

SUSHI

Sushi is basic, traditional Japanese food. It consists of a special variety of rice, flavored with vinegar and combined while still warm with ice-cold ingredients, usually raw fish. Often, but not necessarily so, the rice combination is rolled in seaweed sheets called nori. Sushi is made to order in restaurants by specially trained chefs.

Making sushi is considered an art in Japan. It takes sushi chefs years to learn the exact way to cut fish and combine it with other cold ingredients. Aesthetical presentation, often including carved vegetables, is very important.

Sashimi is sushi without rice. Both are usually served with wasabi paste, the pungent green horseradish.

Sushi has become popular in the United States to the extent that it is often available in the refrigerated compartments in supermarkets or made to order in supermarkets. Obviously, the rice is no longer warm because the emphasis is on keeping the main ingredients cold. Using the proper rice variety is essential to making sushi. Japanese short grain rice called kome is the best option. Most restaurants and households in Japan use automatic electric rice cookers, which make perfect rice every time.

sushi rice *Yield: 6 cups*

Ingredients	Amounts U.S.	Metric	Procedure
Japanese short grain rice (kome)	21 oz	595 g	Thoroughly rinse rice in cool water, drain well. Repeat process. Cook the rice in a pan (cover and simmer with water and sake for 20 minutes or until water is absorbed). Do not lift lid during cooking. Remove pan from heat and let stand for 10 minutes or use rice cooker.
Water	3 pints	1.42 l	
Saki	2 fl oz	60 ml	
Rice wine vinegar	2 1/2 fl oz	74 ml	Prepare sushi vinegar (sushizu) by mixing rice vinegar, sugar, and salt in a small pan. Put the pan on low heat and cook until the sugar dissolves. Cool the vinegar mixture. Spread the cooked hot rice onto a plastic-lined half-sheet pan by spatula. Sprinkle the vinegar mixture over the rice and fold the rice very quickly. Be careful not to smash the rice. To cool and remove the moisture of the rice well, use a fan as you mix sushi rice. This will give sushi rice a shiny look. Make sushi immediately with this rice, as cooled rice is very hard to work with.
Sugar	1 oz	28 g	
Salt	1/4 oz	6 1/2 g	

NUTRITIONAL INFORMATION PER RECIPE: 2,333 Calories; 4 g Fat (1.6% calories from fat); 42 g Protein; 509 g Carbohydrate; 8 g Dietary Fiber; 0 mg Cholesterol; 4,340 mg Sodium. Exchanges: 31 Grain (Starch); 2 Other Carbohydrates.

Another popular type of sushi is an inside-out roll. The nori is in the middle of the roll and sesame seeds and rice are on the outside. Follow these instructions to create an inside-out roll:

1. Make sure the bamboo sushi mat is wrapped with plastic wrap; this will prevent the roll from sticking to the mat.
2. Cut a nori into thirds as three wide rectangles. Orient the sushi mat so that it will roll away from you, not left to right or the opposite.
3. Place one of the nori rectangles wide on the mat, then gently spread the rice over the entire area of the nori, making sure the rice is spread evenly along the edges. You should press down on the rice a bit more than when you're making regular sushi, because any loose rice will fall off when this type of roll is sliced. This will help in shaping the roll into a uniform cylinder.
4. Garnish the roll by sprinkling a spoonful of tobiko (a type of roe used in sushi) with your finger evenly across the rice covering the nori. This will ultimately be on the outside of the roll and will be decorated with the sprinkles of tobiko.
5. Carefully flip over the riced nori on the mat so that the rice is on the bottom next to the mat. Try to reposition the nori so that the bottom or wide edge, which is closer to you, is aligned with the bottom of the sushi mat.
6. Gently lay the fillings across the middle of the nori.
7. Lift the bamboo mat with the nori and the filling from underneath. Carefully roll over the bottom of the nori (wide edge closer to you) onto the top of the nori (the wide edge away from you), making sure the edges of the nori meet closely but without too much overlapping.
8. Position both hands over the sushi mat. Give a few gentle pushes to fuse the nori together on both ends and form a log.
9. Once the roll is complete, the inside of the nori should contain the filling. The outside is wrapped around with the sushi rice.
10. Carefully slice the roll. If too much rice is leaving the roll, tightly wrap the roll while using the minimum amount of plastic wrap. Slice the wrapped roll. Carefully remove the plastic strips around each sliced roll after slicing (Figure 8-27).

This popular New England dish is a lobster salad served in a soft, elongated roll. Note that in many states the health department recommends dipping diced celery into boiling water to sanitize.

> **CHEF'S TIP**
> *Inside-out rolls need more filling so that when the nori is rolled into its final shape, the filling will occupy the entire inner circle.*

Figure 8-27 Inside-out roll.

California rolls opened up the world of sushi to those who didn't want to eat raw fish. These rolls were invented by a chef in California and feature cooked crab, avocado, carrots, onion, and cucumber. Today there are many variations that do not include raw fish.

California sushi roll *Yield: 8 full rolls, for approx. 80 pieces*

Ingredients	Amounts		Procedure
	U.S.	Metric	
Avocado	1 medium	1 medium	Peel avocado. Sprinkle with lemon juice to keep from browning. Cut into thin strips.
Dungeness or Blue Fin crab meat, cleaned, cooked	1 lb	454 g	Put crab meat in a bowl and mix with soy sauce, grated ginger, and sesame oil.
Soy sauce	1 tsp	5 ml	
Fresh ginger, grated	1 tsp	5 g	
Sesame oil	2 tsp	10 ml	

Nori seaweed sheets	8 sheets	8 sheets	
Sushi rice, cooked	36 oz	1.020 kg	
Sesame seeds	2 tsp	10 g	
Wasabi paste	1 tsp	5 g	

Cover a bamboo mat with plastic wrap.

Put a sheet of dried seaweed on top of the mat.

Spread sushi rice on top of the seaweed and press firmly.

Carrots, peeled and julienned	2 medium	2 medium
Green onions, cut into 8 long strips	2 each	2 each
English-style cucumber, julienned	1 medium	1 medium

Place avocado, julienned carrots, cucumbers, green onions, and crab meat lengthwise on the seaweed.

Roll the bamboo mat forward while holding the ingredients with your fingers. Use your thumbs to roll the mat. Stretch the mat as you roll. One hand is on top of the mat while the other is on the roll.

Press the bamboo mat firmly with your hands.

Remove the rolled sushi. Cut the sushi roll into bite-sized pieces.

Wipe the knife with a wet cloth before slicing the sushi.

NUTRITIONAL INFORMATION PER PIECE: 59 Calories; 1 g Fat (10.7% calories from fat); 2 g Protein; 11 g Carbohydrate; trace Dietary Fiber; 3 mg Cholesterol; 25 mg Sodium. Exchanges: 1/2 Grain (Starch); 0 Lean Meat; 0 Vegetable; 0 Fruit; 0 Fat.

mini lobster roll *Yield: 6 rolls, each containing 4 oz (113 g) per roll*

Ingredients	Amounts U.S.	Metric	Procedure
Lobster meat, diced	1 lb	454 g	Mix diced lobster with the following ingredients.
Celery, finely diced	3 oz	85 g	
Sherry vinegar	1 tsp	5 ml	
Mayonnaise	4 fl oz	118 ml	
Cayenne pepper	1/4 tsp	2 g	
Tarragon, fresh, minced	1 tsp	5 g	
Worcestershire sauce	1/4 tsp	2 g	
Soft rolls, miniature, split	6 each	6 each	Divide the mixture to fill the soft rolls. Serve cold.

NUTRITIONAL INFORMATION PER SERVING: 288 Calories; 18 g Fat (56.2% calories from fat); 17 g Protein; 15 g Carbohydrate; 1 g Dietary Fiber; 79 mg Cholesterol; 486 mg Sodium. Exchanges: 1 Grain (Starch); 2 Lean Meat; 0 Vegetable; 1 1/2 Fat; 0 Other Carbohydrates.

The salmon must be absolutely fresh and should not be oily. Belly salmon is more oily than back fillet. The salmon must be ice cold and chopped by hand to order. Toast points are usually served with this dish. Only fresh, high-quality salmon should be used in this recipe. Make sure that all bones have been removed. If not, remove them with pliers.

The same dish can be made with high-quality tuna fish.

salmon tartar *Yield: 1 serving*

Ingredients	Amounts U.S.	Metric	Procedure
Salmon, skinless, boneless	6 oz	170 g	Cut the salmon into even 1/4-inch pieces.
Capers	1 tsp	5 g	Chop the capers and the shallots.
Shallots	1 tsp	5 g	
Sesame oil, mild	1/2 tsp	2.5 ml	Blend the salmon, capers, shallots, oils, lemon peel, vinegar, and salt and pepper. Shape into an attractive patty.
Grated lemon peel	1/2 tsp	2 g	
Olive oil	1 tbsp	15 ml	
Balsamic vinegar	1/2 tsp	2.5 ml	
Pepper	To taste	To taste	
Sea salt	To taste	To taste	
Lettuce leaves	3 each	3 each	Place the patty on the lettuce and top with caviar.
Salmon roe	1 tsp	5 g	

NUTRITIONAL INFORMATION PER SERVING: 350 Calories; 22 g Fat (57.7% calories from fat); 35 g Protein; 2 g Carbohydrate; trace Dietary Fiber; 104 mg Cholesterol; 449 mg Sodium. Exchanges: 0 Grain (Starch); 5 Lean Meat; 0 Vegetable; 0 Fruit; 3 Fat; 0 Other Carbohydrates.

RAW BARS

Raw bars have become a popular appetizer (Figure 8-28). They usually consist of clams, oysters, cooked shrimp, lobsters, and crab meat garnished with seaweed and supplemented with different sauces and dips.

This recipe calls for sashimi quality tuna, the best belly cut from large fish. Togarashi is a Japanese-style chili powder. It is readily available in most Asian markets. Just a touch of it goes a long way.

Figure 8-28 This raw bar features fresh crab legs and is adorned with an ice carving.

tuna tataki *Yield: Tuna 1 lb Sauce 5 1/2 fl oz, 4 each 4 oz (113 g) tuna portions*

Ingredients	Amounts U.S.	Metric	Procedure
Tuna, sashimi quality	1 lb	454 g	Roll tuna in cracked black pepper.
Black pepper, freshly cracked coarse	1 tsp	5 g	Sear it in a very hot cast iron pan without oil; cool.
Peanut oil	2 fl oz	60 ml	Blend peanut oil, sesame oil, soy sauce, lemon juice, garlic, ginger, and spice powder to create a sauce. Slice tuna very thin; serve with sauce and garnish with pickled ginger.
Sesame oil	1 fl oz	30 ml	
Soy sauce	2 fl oz	60 ml	
Lemon juice	1 tsp	5 ml	
Garlic, minced fine	1/2 oz	14 g	
Ginger, minced fine	1/2 oz	14 g	
Togarashi	To taste	To taste	

NUTRITIONAL INFORMATION PER SERVING: 361 Calories; 26 g Fat (65.1% calories from fat); 28 g Protein; 4 g Carbohydrate; trace Dietary Fiber; 43 mg Cholesterol; 1,141 mg Sodium. Exchanges: 0 Grain (Starch); 3 1/2 Lean Meat; 1/2 Vegetable; 0 Fruit; 4 Fat.

Carpaccio originated at the restaurant Cipriani in Venice. It consists of ice-cold, thinly sliced beef tenderloin sprinkled with crushed pepper, and dribbled with virgin olive oil, herbs, and, when in season, shaved fresh truffles.

The following carpaccio uses tuna. Serve it with the Zesty Wasabi aioli and Tangy Ponzu Sauces found in Unit 16.

tuna carpaccio   *Yield: 6 each 2 1/2 oz (70 g) servings*

Ingredients	Amounts U.S.	Metric	Procedure
Sushi-grade tuna	1 lb	454 g	Place into freezer until semi-frozen. Slice with electric meat slicer about 18 slices. Separate slices with plastic wrap and put on an oiled sheet pan. Keep frozen until use. The tuna will defrost by the time it is served. Take three tuna slices and arrange them on a 10-inch plate, alternating so that the tuna slices look like the petals of a flower.
Extra virgin olive oil	1 fl oz	30 ml	Brush olive oil onto the tuna and drizzle with Wasabi Aioli Sauce and Ponzu Sauce (see sauce recipes in Unit 16).
Black sesame seeds	2 tsp	10 g	Sprinkle with black sesame seeds and nori seaweed, fine julienned. A small daub of wasabi and a tiny lemon slice may also be used to garnish this dish.
Nori (dried seaweed), fine julienne	1 tsp	5 g	

NUTRITIONAL INFORMATION PER SERVING: 152 Calories; 8 g Fat (51.5% calories from fat); 18 g Protein; trace Carbohydrate; trace Dietary Fiber; 29 mg Cholesterol; 30 mg Sodium. Exchanges: 0 Grain (Starch); 2 1/2 Lean Meat; 0 Vegetable; 1 Fat.

SMOKED CURED FISH SERVICE

Smoked fish tastes best when served still warm or at least at room temperature. Smoked fish is perishable, so this is not an easy task because it must be kept refrigerated; however, at least the fish can be plated on room-temperature plates.

Smoked Salmon

Smoked salmon is probably the most popular type of smoked fish. It is used sliced as an appetizer and as a component in appetizers. See Unit 16 for the Benchmark Recipe for Dry Cure for Salmon, Sturgeon, or Trout, if you prefer to smoke the salmon in-house. Slicing smoked salmon requires much skill and practice. It is no wonder that many operations purchase ready-to-serve, machine-sliced salmon. New York delicatessen restaurants famous for smoked salmon use only highly skilled employees to hand-slice salmon to order. Refer to the caviar section for instructions on how to prepare the onions.

Slicing Smoked Salmon

1. Remove all bones with needle pliers.
2. Begin slicing, starting at the tail end.
3. Plate (Figure 8-29).

Figure 8-29 A silver tray of smoked salmon.

Slicing Smoked Salmon on Electric Meat Slicer

1. Remove all bones with needle pliers.
2. Cut the smoked salmon into 2-inch-wide chunks.
3. Remove the skin.
4. Chill to almost frozen.
5. Slice on a meat slicer.
6. Set on wax paper until service.

Smoked Trout Plate

Many individuals consider smoked trout to be a very special treat. See the Benchmark Recipe in Unit 16 for Dry Cure for Salmon, Sturgeon, or Trout for smoking trout. To serve, remove the skin and bones (Figure 8-30). Many operations serve smoked trout with horseradish cream sauce (see the recipe for Horseradish Cream Sauce in Unit 15). If you are planning on using purchased horseradish preserved in vinegar, drain it first.

Smoked Sturgeon

Sturgeon is prized for its dense, boneless flesh, as well as its caviar (Figure 8-31). To smoke sturgeon in-house, see the Benchmark Recipe in Unit 16 for Dry Cure for Salmon, Sturgeon, or Trout. Sturgeon is easier to slice than most other smoked fish. Because the fish has no bones, it is often sliced on the electric slicer. Serve and garnish smoked sturgeon like a smoked salmon plate.

Salt Cod

Salt cod is also known as baccalá, bacalao, bacalhau, or morue. In Italy, it is a popular, basic ingredient on antipasti platters. Before soaking, salt cod smells and looks like a dried-up fish. It takes on a magical transformation once it has been soaked in numerous water changes. It will swell up succulently and taste good.

The salad can be dressed up with olives, capers, or diced pimentos.

Figure 8-30 Skinning a smoked trout.

Figure 8-31 Fillet of smoked sturgeon.

salt cod salad   *Yield: 10 servings 4 oz (120 g) portions*

Ingredients	Amounts		Procedure
	U.S.	Metric	
Salt cod	2 lbs	907 g	Soak the salt cod overnight.
			Change the water and soak again for 12 hours. Cover the fish with fresh water; bring to a simmer and cook for 15 minutes. Cool in the stock. Remove the fish and carefully pick out its bones.
			Flake the deboned fish.
Garlic, chopped	3 tbsp	44 g	Mix together the garlic, lemon juice, and olive oil. Stir in the flaked fish. Serve on a bed of crisp lettuce and sliced tomatoes.
Lemon juice	2 fl oz	60 ml	
Olive oil	6 fl oz	177 ml	

NUTRITIONAL INFORMATION PER SERVING: 555 Calories; 35 g Fat (57.0% calories from fat); 57 g Protein; 1 g Carbohydrate; trace Dietary Fiber; 138 mg Cholesterol; 6,381 mg Sodium. Exchanges: 8 Lean Meat; 0 Vegetable; 0 Fruit; 6 1/2 Fat.

ANTIPASTI

In Italy, the term "antipasti" is used for both hot and cold appetizers. Most customers in the United States expect antipasto to be served cold. There are so many variations of cold antipasti that only a few typical samples can be detailed in this unit. The list of antipasto ingredients could be almost endless and is only limited by the imagination of the chef. Following are typical examples:

- Sliced meats such as prosciutto, salami, **bresaola** (dried, salted beef fillet), **zampone** (sausage made of pork, seasoned with nutmeg, cloves, and pepper), smoked birds, and ready-to-eat sausages served with fruits and/or marinated vegetables
- Marinated seafood such as shrimp, mussels, squid, and scallops
- Smoked fish, fresh sardines grilled and served cold, anchovies, and salt cod
- Marinated prepared vegetables
- Marinated wild and cultivated mushrooms
- Raw vegetable salads made with fennel, celeriac, or peppers
- Olives
- Assorted cheeses
- Raw vegetables with dips

Antipasti Platters

Antipasti platters can come in a wide assortment of products. Some are seafood-based, others showcase the cured meats, and others the pickled vegetables (Figures 8-32, 8-33, and 8-34).

Figure 8-32 Antipasto of carved meats and hams including mortadella, Parma ham, proscuitto cotto, and wild boar salami.

Figure 8-33 Antipasto di Frutti di Mare, Italian starter of a fish and seafood platter with scallops, squid, bream, crab, prawns, and mussel.

Figure 8-34 Antipasto plate of sliced char-grilled courgettes, aubergines, marinated artichokes, and roasted red peppers.

The following ingredients could be used on antipasti platters or served alone.

sweet and sour roasted peppers
Yield: 6 lbs/ 24 – 4 oz. (113 g) servings

Ingredients	Amounts		Procedure
	U.S.	Metric	
Bell peppers, green, red, and yellow	6 lbs	2.722 kg	Drizzle oil over the peppers and roast in a hot oven or over an open flame until the skin is black and blisters.
Oil	1 fl oz	30 ml	Place in a bowl and cover with plastic wrap. The steam will facilitate removing the skin. Wait until the peppers cool and remove the skin under warm water. Remove the seeds and cut in attractive squares.

Water	1 pint	473 ml	Combine all the remaining ingredients; bring to a boil; reduce the temperature and simmer for 10 minutes. Cool and pour over the peppers. Store refrigerated until used.
Salt	1 tbsp	15 g	
Balsamic vinegar	8 fl oz	236 ml	
Lemon peel, grated	1 tbsp	15 g	
Sugar	1 tbsp	15 g	
Bay leaves	2 each	2 each	
Olive oil	8 fl oz	237 ml	
Garlic, crushed	1 tbsp	15 g	

NUTRITIONAL INFORMATION PER SERVING: 97 Calories; 10 g Fat (85.6% calories from fat); trace Protein; 3 g Carbohydrate; 1 g Dietary Fiber; 0 mg Cholesterol; 268 mg Sodium. Exchanges: 1/2 Vegetable; 0 Fruit; 2 Fat; 0 Other Carbohydrates.

Tuscans, in particular, have a love affair with artichokes. They serve them raw with a little lemon juice, olive oil, and fresh parmesan; stewed with tomatoes and garlic; and dipped in batter, fried, marinated, and served on an antipasto plate as in the following recipe.

baby artichokes in oil and lemon juice
Yield: 8 servings of 6 split pieces

Ingredients	Amounts U.S.	Metric	Procedure
Baby artichokes	24 each	24 each	Trim artichokes, but leave stem on. Split in half.
Olive oil	8 fl oz	237 ml	Put the remaining ingredients in a large pot. Simmer for 10 minutes. Add artichokes and simmer until fork tender. Cool and let marinate in the broth refrigerated for at least 24 hours before service.
Onions, diced	4 oz	113 g	
Garlic, crushed	1 tbsp	15 g	
Pepper, coarsely crushed	1 tbsp	15 g	
Bay leaf	1 each	1 each	
Oregano, fresh, chopped	1 tsp	5 g	
Salt	1 tsp	5 g	
Lemon juice	4 fl oz	118 ml	
Water	1 pint	473 ml	

NUTRITIONAL INFORMATION PER SERVING: 386 Calories; 27 g Fat (58.9% calories from fat); 10 g Protein; 33 g Carbohydrate; 16 g Dietary Fiber; 0 mg Cholesterol; 540 mg Sodium. Exchanges: 0 Grain (Starch); 6 Vegetable; 0 Fruit; 5 1/2 Fat.

This appetizer is popular in Southern France. It calls for the white part of the leeks. Use the stem ends and leave a small part of the stem to keep the leaves together.

marinated leeks *Yield: 10 servings*

Ingredients	Amounts		Procedure
	U.S.	**Metric**	
Leeks, white part only	30 pieces (3 in long)	30 pieces (75 mm long)	Split leeks in half but leave the stem end on the halves to keep the leek leaves together. Carefully wash under flowing water between each leaf layer to remove all sand. Arrange leeks tightly together in a cooking pan. 
Olive oil	8 fl oz	237 ml	Put the remaining ingredients in a pot. Simmer for 10 minutes.
Onions, diced	4 oz	113 g	Pour hot marinade over the leeks.
Garlic, crushed	1 tbsp	15 g	Cover with foil and place a suitable pan on top to keep the leeks submerged.
Black pepper, coarsely crushed	1 tbsp	15 g	
Bay leaf	1 each	1 each	Simmer slowly about 1/2 hour until the leeks are tender. Cool in marinade and serve chilled after 24 hours.
Oregano, fresh, chopped	1 tsp	5 g	
Lemon juice	4 fl oz	118 ml	
Water	1 pint	473 ml	

NUTRITIONAL INFORMATION PER SERVING: 363 Calories; 22 g Fat (53.1% calories from fat); 4 g Protein; 40 g Carbohydrate; 5 g Dietary Fiber; 0 mg Cholesterol; 56 mg Sodium. Exchanges: 0 Grain (Starch); 7 1/2 Vegetable; 0 Fruit; 4 1/2 Fat.

Mozzarella is one of the most popular Italian cheeses. It is a cow's milk—or buffalo milk—cheese and is available fresh as little balls preserved in brine. As the cheese matures it is sold as solid blocks and is the topping on pizza. Smoked mozzarella is a popular sandwich cheese.

marinated mozzarella   *Yield: 10 servings*

Ingredients	Amounts		Procedure
	U.S.	Metric	
Mozzarella balls, small (bocconcini)	40 each	40 each	Drain the mozzarella balls and set aside in a noncorrosive bowl.
Water	2 fl oz	60 ml	Combine water, sun-dried tomatoes, onions, olive oil, lemon juice, salt, and capers.
Sun-dried tomatoes, chopped	1 oz	28 g	
Onions	2 oz	57 g	Bring to a boil; reduce the temperature and simmer for ten minutes. Pour over mozzarella balls and refrigerate overnight.
Olive oil	4 fl oz	118 ml	
Lemon juice	1 tbsp	15 ml	
Salt	1 tsp	5 g	
Capers	1 tbsp	15 g	
Basil, fresh, chopped	1 tbsp	15 g	Top with fresh herbs just prior to service.
Oregano, fresh, chopped	1/2 tbsp	7 g	
Parsley, chopped	1 tbsp	15 g	

NUTRITIONAL INFORMATION PER SERVING: 462 Calories; 39 g Fat (75.2% calories from fat); 25 g Protein; 4 g Carbohydrate; trace Dietary Fiber; 101 mg Cholesterol; 705 mg Sodium. Exchanges: 0 Grain (Starch); 3 1/2 Lean Meat; 0 Vegetable; 0 Fruit; 6 Fat; 0 Other Carbohydrates.

This famous dish was described earlier with the Tuna Carpaccio recipe.

traditional beef carpaccio   *Yield: 8 servings 2 oz (56 g) each*

Ingredients	Amounts		Procedure
	U.S.	Metric	
Beef tenderloin, center cut, completely trimmed including the silver skin	1 lb	454 g	Place tenderloin in freezer until semi-frozen. Slice as thin as possible with a chef's knife or on meat slicer. Arrange fan-like on a large plate.
Parmesan cheese	4 oz	113 g	Sprinkle with cheese.
Black pepper, freshly ground	To taste	To taste	Add pepper and capers and drizzle oil over the meat.
Capers	1 oz	28 g	Serve at once while meat is still ice cold.
Olive oil, extra virgin	4 fl oz	118 ml	

NUTRITIONAL INFORMATION PER SERVING: 324 Calories; 31 g Fat (85.8% calories from fat); 11 g Protein; trace Carbohydrate; trace Dietary Fiber; 43 mg Cholesterol; 86 mg Sodium. Exchanges: 0 Grain (Starch); 1 1/2 Lean Meat; 5 Fat; 0 Other Carbohydrates.

Beef is always a popular choice. In this recipe, the beef tenderloin is marinated and roasted and then chilled and served on a roll or baguette slice with a mustard or plum sauce.

Asian-style tenderloin bites   *Yield: 48 each 1 oz (28 g) servings*

Ingredients	Amounts		Procedure
	U.S.	Metric	
Hoisin sauce	4 fl oz	118 ml	Mix all the ingredients (except the tenderloin) in a bowl to make the marinade.
Plum sauce	2 fl oz	60 ml	
Oyster sauce	2 fl oz	60 ml	
Rice wine vinegar	1 fl oz	30 ml	
Sesame oil	1 fl oz	30 ml	
Brown sugar	3 oz	85 g	
Chili oil	1 tbsp	15 ml	
Fresh ginger, grated	1 oz	28 g	
Garlic, finely minced	5 cloves	5 cloves	
Beef tenderloin	3 lbs	1,360 kg	Rub the marinade over the tenderloin, reserving some for basting. Make some slits lengthwise about 1/2-inch deep to allow the marinade to penetrate.

Refrigerate the tenderloin and let it marinate for two hours or overnight. Roast the tenderloin at 475°F (240°C), brushing occasionally with the reserved marinade.

Cook until the internal temperature reaches 120°F (50°C), about 20 minutes. Let cool; then refrigerate until chilled, about 3 hours. Slice the meat across the grain into very thin slices. The tenderloin can be prepared, covered with plastic wrap, and refrigerated up to 24 hours before serving. Serve chilled or at room temperature with baguette slices or rolls.

It can be served with mustard or Asian plum sauce.

NUTRITIONAL INFORMATION PER SERVING: 103 Calories; 7 g Fat (65.8% calories from fat); 5 g Protein; 4 g Carbohydrate; trace Dietary Fiber; 20 mg Cholesterol; 72 mg Sodium. Exchanges: 0 Grain (Starch); 1/2 Lean Meat; 0 Vegetable; 0 Fruit; 1 Fat; 0 Other Carbohydrates.

Tapenade is a traditional French-Italian dish made with olives and anchovies and then seasoned with spices and lemon juice. It provides the perfect dip for bread or vegetables. Use any French or Italian olives. Kalamata olives can be substituted, although they are from Greece.

tapenade *Yield: 24 oz, 24 each 1 oz (28 g) servings*

Ingredients	Amounts U.S.	Metric	Procedure
Garlic, chopped	2 cloves	2 cloves	Combine garlic, olives, anchovies, capers, thyme, parsley. and lemon juice in a food processor.
Olives, pitted	1 lb	454 g	
Anchovy fillets, rinsed	1 (2 oz) can	56 g	
Capers	2 oz	56 g	
Fresh thyme, chopped	1 tsp	5 g	
Fresh Italian parsley, chopped	1 tsp	5 g	
Lemon juice, fresh squeezed	3 tbsp	44 ml	
Olive oil	3 fl oz	89 ml	Slowly drip the olive oil into the food processor while you are blending the ingredients together. Transfer the tapenade into a bowl and store until service. Blend until a paste is formed. Serve with bread or pita triangles, or as a dip for vegetables.

NUTRITIONAL INFORMATION PER SERVING: 58 Calories; 6 g Fat (84.6% calories from fat); 1 g Protein; 1 g Carbohydrate; 1 g Dietary Fiber; 2 mg Cholesterol; 302 mg Sodium. Exchanges: 0 Grain (Starch); 0 Lean Meat; 0 Vegetable; 0 Fruit; 1 Fat; 0 Other Carbohydrates.

Hummus has become synonymous with Middle Eastern and Mediterranean cuisine. This dip is an exotic blend of ground chickpeas, lemon, tahini, and spices. The important ingredient is oily tahini—or tahini paste, consisting of ground sesame seeds. It is available canned. Sumac is a sour spice powder popular in Middle Eastern cooking.

hummus *Yield: 26 fl oz (780 ml), 26 each 1 oz (30 ml) serving*

Ingredients	Amounts		Procedure
	U.S.	Metric	
Chickpeas, or Great Northern beans, drained	1 (15 oz) can	425 g	Place the beans, oil, lemon juice, cumin, sumac, tahini, garlic, and hot water in a food processor.
Extra virgin olive oil	1 oz	30 ml	Pulse till the mixture is smooth. If too thick, add a small amount of water.
Lemon juice, fresh squeezed	2 oz	60 ml	
Cumin, ground	1 tsp	5 g	
Sumac, ground	1/2 tsp	2 g	
Tahini	5 oz	142 g	
Garlic, mashed	6 to 8 cloves	6 to 8 cloves	
Hot water	1 fl oz	30 ml	
Kosher salt	2 tsp	10 g	Add salt and continue blending. Add cilantro or parsley and pulse into the mixture if desired.
Cilantro or parsley, chopped (optional)	1 oz	28 g	Garnish with cilantro leaves, sumac, and cumin dust, and wedges of tomatoes and lemons.
			Serve with lavash pita bread, crackers, or fresh cut vegetables. It is also a delicious sandwich spread.

NUTRITIONAL INFORMATION PER SERVING: 67 Calories; 4 g Fat (54.7% calories from fat); 2 g Protein; 6 g Carbohydrate; 1 g Dietary Fiber; 0 mg Cholesterol; 202 mg Sodium. Exchanges: 1/2 Grain (Starch); 0 Lean Meat; 0 Vegetable; 0 Fruit; 1 Fat.

For the roasted pears recipe that follows, use ripe, but not too soft, Bartlett pears.

roasted pears with blue cheese and nuts *Yield: 10 servings*

Ingredients	Amounts U.S.	Metric	Procedure
Bartlett pears, medium	10 each	10 each	Peel pears, leave stem intact. From the bottom, carefully remove the core with a melon baller or other suitable tool.
Blue cheese, crumbled	10 oz	284 g	Blend the cheese, nuts, and egg white. Fill the pears.
Pecan nuts, chopped	4 oz	113 g	
Egg white	1 each	1 each	
Oil	1 tbsp	15 ml	Rub with oil and lemon juice.
Lemon juice	1 tbsp	15 ml	Place the pears upright on a small roasting pan. Wrap each stem with aluminum foil. Roast in a very hot oven until the pears are light brown and cooked. Do not overcook.
Lettuce leaves	10 each	10 each	Remove foil and serve at room temperature upright on a lettuce leaf.

NUTRITIONAL INFORMATION PER SERVING: 289 Calories; 18 g Fat (52.6% calories from fat); 8 g Protein; 28 g Carbohydrate; 5 g Dietary Fiber; 21 mg Cholesterol; 402 mg Sodium. Exchanges: 0 Grain (Starch); 1 Lean Meat; 0 Vegetable; 1 1/2 Fruit; 3 Fat.

This simple appetizer is popular in catering halls. No dressing is needed because the grapefruit sections are acidic.

grapefruit sections and avocado *Yield: 6 servings*

Ingredients	Amounts U.S.	Metric	Procedure
Grapefruit sections	3 lbs	1.360 kg	Arrange grapefruit and avocado sections on top of the lettuce leaves.
Avocado, slices, ripe	18 pieces	18 pieces	
Boston Bibb lettuce leaves	As needed	As needed	
Pecan nuts, toasted and chopped	3 oz	85 g	Lightly toast the pecans. Sprinkle the grapefruit and avocado sections with the toasted nuts and a couple of grinds of fresh cracked pepper.
Pepper, fresh cracked	As needed	As needed	

NUTRITIONAL INFORMATION PER SERVING: 178 Calories; 14 g Fat (66.0% calories from fat); 2 g Protein; 14 g Carbohydrate; 3 g Dietary Fiber; 0 mg Cholesterol; 9 mg Sodium. Exchanges: 0 Grain (Starch); 0 Lean Meat; 0 Vegetable; 1/2 Fruit; 3 Fat.

>> Hot Appetizers

The major concern when serving hot appetizers is to keep them hot throughout the service period. Another consideration is to make sure they are not too hot as to burn someone's mouth.

Steamed clams and casino clams are two popular hot clam appetizers. The first step in preparing clams is to make sure that they are alive and properly cleaned before cooking. Tap the shells to see if the clams are alive. They should close up immediately. If they are gaping, throw them out.

steamed clams   *Yield: 8 to 10 appetizer or buffet servings (1/2 lb per guest)*

Ingredients	Amounts U.S.	Metric	Procedure
Live small clams	4 to 6 lbs	2 to 3 kg	One hour before serving, scrub clams with brush in cold water, and rinse with water until free of sand. (Adding a little coarse kosher salt to the water will help to remove the sand from the clams.)
Olive oil	3 tbsp	45 ml	In a steamer pot or large kettle, add the olive oil and heat.
White onion, coarsely chopped	1 small	1 small	Sauté the onion and garlic until soft.
Garlic, chopped	6 cloves	6 cloves	
Dry white wine	34 fl oz	1 lt	Add the wine, pepper flakes, and the optional dill or fennel seeds and bring to a slow simmer. Add the clams and cover the pot with a tight-fitting lid. Steam the clams over low heat just until the clams open, about 5 to 10 minutes. Do not overcook, as the clams will become tough and rubbery. (Discard any clams that do not open.) Use tongs or a slotted spoon to transfer the clams to large individual soup bowls. Pour broth through a cheesecloth-lined strainer to remove any sand. The broth can either be used as a dunking liquid for French bread or placed in mugs to drink. Serve the clams with individual cups of melted butter.
Red pepper flakes	1 tsp	5 g	
Dill or fennel seeds (optional)	1 tsp	5 g	

NUTRITIONAL INFORMATION PER SERVING: 236 Calories; 7 g Fat (27.4% calories from fat); 33 g Protein; 8 g Carbohydrate; trace Dietary Fiber; 85 mg Cholesterol; 142 mg Sodium. Exchanges: 0 Grain (Starch); 5 Lean Meat; 1/2 Vegetable; 1 Fat.

For convenience sake, make the casino butter ahead of time and refrigerate until needed.

casino butter   *Yield: 16 oz (448 oz) servings, 32 each 1/2 oz*

Ingredients	Amounts U.S.	Metric	Procedure
Butter, unsalted, softened	8 oz	227 g	Blend all of the ingredients together to make a compound butter.
Green bell pepper, minced fine	2 oz	57 g	
Red bell pepper, minced fine	2 oz	57 g	
Garlic, minced fine	2 cloves	2 cloves	
Shallots, minced fine	1 oz	28 g	
Parsley, minced	2 oz	57 g	
Tabasco sauce	1/4 tsp	1 ml	
Salt	1 tsp	5 g	
Black pepper, freshly ground	1/2 tsp	3 g	
Lemon juice, freshly squeezed	1/2 fl oz	15 ml	

Use a half tablespoon of the casino butter per clam if small, or a full tablespoon if clam is large.

clams casino *Yield: 32 clams*
Serving: 1 clam with 1/2 oz topping and 1/2 ounce butter

Ingredients	Amounts U.S.	Metric	Procedure
Little neck or other clams approx. 2 inches across	32 each	32 each	Shuck the clams, reserving the bottom shell. Place the clam meat back on the bottom shell and place in a baking pan that has been layered with rock salt. This keeps the shells from tipping over and steadies them on the baking plaque.
Green bell pepper, minced	3 oz	85 g	To make the casino butter:
Onion, minced	3 oz	85 g	Mix together the green pepper, onion, bacon, and garlic. Season with salt and pepper. Place a tablespoon of this mixture on top of each clam.
Bacon, precooked, minced	4 each	4 each	
Garlic, minced	2 cloves	2 cloves	
Salt	To taste	To taste	
Pepper	To taste	To taste	
Breadcrumbs	4 oz	113 g	Sprinkle breadcrumbs over all and then sprinkle with lemon juice. Bake uncovered 10 to 15 minutes or until the edges of the clams begin to curl. Remove from the oven and serve immediately.
Lemon juice, freshly squeezed	3 tbsp	45 ml	

NUTRITIONAL INFORMATION PER SERVING: 31 Calories; 1 g Fat (21.2% calories from fat); 3 g Protein; 3 g Carbohydrate; trace Dietary Fiber; 6 mg Cholesterol; 60 mg Sodium. Exchanges: 0 Grain (Starch); 1/2 Lean Meat; 0 Vegetable; 0 Fruit; 0 Fat.

Pernod is a French aperitif with a distinctive anise flavor. You can serve Oysters Stuffed with Spinach and Pernod on a bed of rock salt as an attractive hot appetizer. When the spinach is blended with cooked watercress and the cheese is omitted, the dish is called Oysters Rockefeller.

The following recipe makes 12 oysters, which can work for a buffet line or can be plated for two appetizer plates of six each.

oysters stuffed with spinach and pernod   *Yield: 12 oysters*

Ingredients	Amounts U.S.	Metric	Procedure
Garlic, minced fine	1 each	1 each	Sauté the garlic and shallots until soft.
Shallots, minced fine	1 large	1 large	
Spinach, chopped	2 bunches	2 bunches	Combine the spinach, Pernod, salt, and pepper. Sauté until the spinach is tender.
Pernod	1 to 2 fl oz	30 to 60 ml	
Salt	To taste	To taste	
Pepper	To taste	To taste	
Goat cheese, mild (Montrachet)	12 oz	340 g	Add the goat cheese and breadcrumbs. Mix thoroughly.
Breadcrumbs	6 oz	170 g	
Oysters	12 each	12 each	Shuck the oysters, loosen the oysters, and reserve the bottom shell. Place each oyster on the bottom shell in a baking pan that has been liberally sprinkled with rock salt. Top the oyster with a generous amount of the above mixture.
Limes, juice and zest	2 each	2 each	Top with juice and zest. Bake at 350°F (175°C) until mixture is bubbly.

NUTRITIONAL INFORMATION PER SERVING: 220 Calories; 11 g Fat (41.9% calories from fat); 11 g Protein; 23 g Carbohydrate; 1 g Dietary Fiber; 34 mg Cholesterol; 224 mg Sodium. Exchanges: 1/2 Grain (Starch); 1 1/2 Lean Meat; 0 Vegetable; 1 Fruit; 1 1/2 Fat; 0 Other Carbohydrates.

These BBQ oysters are the perfect appetizer for an outdoor catered event and are a good use for the extra large Pacific oysters.

teriyaki BBQ oysters
Yield: Sauce 18 fl oz (522 ml)

24 servings with 3/4 oz sauce

Ingredients	Amounts U.S.	Metric	Procedure
Soy sauce	8 fl oz	237 ml	Combine the ingredients and heat until the sugar is dissolved. Reserve as baste.
Brown sugar	4 oz	113 g	
Pineapple juice	4 fl oz	118 ml	
Sesame oil	1 fl oz	30 ml	
Garlic, minced fine	1 large clove	1 large clove	
Ginger, fresh, grated	1 tbsp	15 g	
Oysters (large Pacific oysters)	24 each	24 each	Shuck the oysters. Loosen the oyster and place on its bottom shell. Baste with teriyaki sauce. Set the oyster shells on a BBQ grate and grill for a maximum of 3 minutes.

NUTRITIONAL INFORMATION PER SERVING: 78 Calories; 2 g Fat (26.6% calories from fat); 5 g Protein; 9 g Carbohydrate; trace Dietary Fiber; 25 mg Cholesterol; 741 mg Sodium. Exchanges: 1/2 Lean Meat; 1/2 Vegetable; 0 Fruit; 0 Fat; 1/2 Other Carbohydrates.

The most common forms of anchovies are salted and canned in oil and sold as flat or rolled fillets. Anchovies are often the secret "punch" found in recipes. This anchovy dip is served warm with raw vegetables. It is from Valle d'Aosta in Northern Italy and translates as "hot bath" in the local Piedmont dialect.

bagna caôda
Yield: 4 servings of the sauce

Ingredients	Amounts U.S.	Metric	Procedure
Anchovy fillets, canned	4 oz	113 g	Chop anchovy fillets and save the oil from the can.
Olive oil	4 fl oz	118 ml	Combine all ingredients except butter in small saucepan and cook over very low heat for approximately 10 minutes.
Garlic, chopped	1 tbsp	15 g	
Butter	3 oz	85 g	Add butter to melt, stir and serve warm as a dip with raw vegetables.

NUTRITIONAL INFORMATION PER SERVING: 454 Calories; 47 g Fat (92.0% calories from fat); 8 g Protein; 1 g Carbohydrate; trace Dietary Fiber; 71 mg Cholesterol; 1,216 mg Sodium. Exchanges: 1 Lean Meat; 0 Vegetable; 9 Fat.

Croquettes are cooked ingredients such as meats or vegetables thickened with sauce, shaped when cold, breaded, and fried. A close cousin is cromesquis, which are batter dipped and fried. This croquette recipe is a popular Spanish tapa. Be sure to serve the croquettes as soon as possible after frying, while they are crisp—the breading will quickly absorb moisture from the air.

mussels croquettes *Yield: 5 lbs (2.28 kg), 40 each 2 oz servings*

Ingredients	U.S.	Metric	Procedure
Fresh live mussels	5 lbs	2.269 kg	Place mussels in a skillet with 2 cups water, sliced lemons, and bay leaves. Bring water to a boil and remove mussels as they open.
Water	8 fl oz	237 ml	
Lemons, sliced into 1/2 inch thick round	3 each	3 each	Reserve 1 to 2 cups of the cooking liquid. Boil down to half the amount. Discard the mussel shells and chop the meat finely. Set aside until later.
Bay leaves	2 each	2 each	
Butter	6 oz	170 g	Heat butter and olive oil in a pan. Add the flour and make a roux, cooking for 3 to 5 minutes.
Extra virgin olive oil	2 fl oz	60 ml	
Bread flour	8 oz	227 g	
Milk	1 pt + 2 fl oz	532 ml	Pour in the milk to make a thick béchamel.
Serrano or proscuitto ham, minced	8 oz	227 g	Add the ham and mussel meat and continue cooking till thickened.
Salt	To taste	To taste	Add salt and pepper to taste. Carefully fold in cooked mussels. Spread mixture on an oiled cookie sheet, cover with plastic wrap, and chill.
Black pepper	To taste	To taste	
Eggs	6 each	6 each	Blend eggs with water to make an egg wash.
Water, cold	3 fl oz	89 ml	
Flour	8 oz	227 g	Put some flour in a flat container, and the bowl of egg wash in the center flanked by a flat container with breadcrumbs. With wet hands, take enough mixture—the size of a large walnut—and shape it into an oval ball. Coat first with flour, then egg wash, and roll in the breadcrumbs. Continue until all the mixture is rolled.
Breadcrumbs	10 oz	284 g	
Oil	For frying	For frying	Fry at 375°F (190°C) until golden brown and crunchy. Serve immediately.

NUTRITIONAL INFORMATION PER SERVING: 212 Calories; 11 g Fat (45.1% calories from fat); 12 g Protein; 17 g Carbohydrate; trace Dietary Fiber; 63 mg Cholesterol; 436 mg Sodium. Exchanges: 1 Grain (Starch); 1 1/2 Lean Meat; 0 Fruit; 0 Nonfat Milk; 1 1/2 Fat.

Pancetta is Italian rolled bacon. It is not easily obtainable—regular sliced bacon can be substituted.

pancetta wrapped scallops   *Yield: 8 portions*
32 to 40 scallops 3.5 lbs (1.6 kg)

Ingredients	Amounts U.S.	Metric	Procedure
Garlic, peeled, mashed	2 cloves	2 cloves	Blend garlic, soy sauce, brown sugar, olive oil, and vinegar.
Soy sauce	1 tbsp	15 ml	
Brown sugar	1/2 oz	14 g	
Olive oil, extra virgin	4 fl oz	118 ml	
Balsamic vinegar	1/2 fl oz	15 ml	
Scallops	2 lbs	907 g	Clean the scallops and place in a shallow, nonreactive bowl. Blend the scallops with the above marinade and marinate for 1 hour. Remove from marinade and pat dry.
Pancetta, thinly sliced into strips, precooked	1 1/2 lbs	680 g	Wrap each scallop with a slice of pancetta. Secure with toothpicks. Place on oiled sizzle pan and cook under broiler for 2 minutes on each side until pancetta is cooked crisp. Serve immediately with or without a sauce.

NUTRITIONAL INFORMATION PER SERVING: 394 Calories; 21 g Fat (50.1% calories from fat); 43 g Protein; 5 g Carbohydrate; trace Dietary Fiber; 97 mg Cholesterol; 2,606 mg Sodium. Exchanges: 6 Lean Meat; 0 Vegetable; 0 Fruit; 2 1/2 Fat; 0 Other Carbohydrates.

Bourguignonne in the following recipe refers to the Burgundy region of France, where world-famous wines are made. Snails are tolerated in the vineyards because they feed on superfluous foliage, allowing more sun to reach the grapes. Before harvest, the snails are collected and eaten.

escargot à la bourguignonne   *Yield: 4 servings (24 snails)*

Ingredients	Amounts U.S.	Metric	Procedure
Parsley, finely minced	1 oz	30 g	Combine the parsley, shallot, and garlic.
Shallot, finely minced	1 oz	30 g	
Garlic, finely minced	1 oz	30 g	
Salt	1 tsp	5 g	Add the salt, pepper, wine, cognac, and nutmeg.
Black pepper, freshly ground	1/2 tsp	2.5 g	
White wine	1 fl oz	30 ml	
Cognac	2 tsp	10 ml	
Nutmeg	Dash	dash	
Butter, unsalted, softened	8 oz	227 g	Blend all the ingredients with butter. This seasoned butter can be made ahead and stored.
Snails, canned	24 extra large	24 extra large	Remove snails from the can, drain, and rinse.
Brandy	As needed	As needed	Sprinkle the snails with brandy. Take a teaspoon of the seasoned butter and put that in the snail shell or in individual escargot pots. Add the snail and then top with another teaspoon of the butter sauce.
Breadcrumbs	2 oz	57 g	Sprinkle with breadcrumbs. Preheat oven to 425°F (220°C). Bake for 10 minutes or until snails are warm.

NUTRITIONAL INFORMATION PER SERVING: 74 Calories; 1 g Fat (11.9% calories from fat); 5 g Protein; 4 g Carbohydrate; trace Dietary Fiber; 15 mg Cholesterol; 585 mg Sodium. Exchanges: 0 Grain (Starch); 1/2 Lean Meat; 0 Vegetable; 0 Fat.

Shrimp are versatile and can be cooked a wide variety of ways for appetizer menus. Serve the coconut shrimp with the Orange Mango Chutney (see the recipe in Unit 8).

coconut shrimp   *Yield: 8 portions of 4 shrimp each*

Ingredients	Amounts U.S.	Metric	Procedure
Shrimp, gulf or tiger	2 lbs (16/20)	907 g (16/20)	Peel and devein shrimp. Rinse with cold water.
Coating			
Flour	3 oz	85 g	Toss shrimp in flour to coat. Chill for 5 minutes.
Batter			
Flour	8 oz	227 g	Combine the dry ingredients.
Cornstarch	3 oz	85 g	
Garlic powder	1 tsp	5 g	
Ginger powder	1 tsp	5 g	
Beer, one can	12 fl oz	355 g	Mix all the wet ingredients and add to the dry mixture, incorporating thoroughly. Let rest, covered, at room temperature for half an hour.
Egg white, beaten to foam	4 each	4 each	
Soy sauce	1 tsp	5 ml	
Coconut Coating			
Coconut, angel flake shredded, not sweet	24 oz	670 g	Mix the coconut with the panko crumbs. Place the cornstarch-coated shrimp into the beer batter, taking care not to overcoat at this stage. Roll the batter-dipped shrimp into the coconut and crumb mix, coating thoroughly. Chill or freeze until cooking time. To cook: Place the coated shrimp in hot oil at 355°F (180°C) and fry for 3 to 5 minutes until the shrimp are cooked and the coating is golden brown. Serve with orange mango chutney.
Panko Japanese-style breadcrumbs	6 oz	170 g	

NUTRITIONAL INFORMATION PER SERVING: 818 Calories; 31 g Fat (34.3% calories from fat); 34 g Protein; 98 g Carbohydrate; 6 g Dietary Fiber; 173 mg Cholesterol; 643 mg Sodium. Exchanges: 3 1/2 Grain (Starch); 3 1/2 Lean Meat; 0 Vegetable; 2 1/2 Fruit; 5 1/2 Fat.

Tandoori is a waist-high clay oven heated by charcoal. It is used for India's version of barbecue and for baking whole wheat yeast bread, called tandoori roti or tandoori chapatti. The bread is baked clinging to the rough sides of the oven. Most tandoori dishes are accompanied by freshly cut onions and lime wedges. Indian marinades usually are yogurt-based and require marinating.

Tandoori barbecues are lowered into the pit on long skewers. In lieu of a tandoori oven, we can put the shrimp on short skewers and cook them in the broiler. This recipe can also be used with chicken.

shrimp tandoori *Yield: 4 pieces per skewer, about 8 to 9 skewers*

Ingredients	Amounts U.S.	Metric	Procedure
Yogurt, plain	8 fl oz	237 ml	Mix the ingredients.
Coconut milk, unsweetened	4 fl oz	118 ml	
Lime juice and zest	1 1/2 fl oz	45 ml	
Cayenne pepper	1/2 tsp	2.5 g	
Turmeric	1/4 tsp	1 g	
Paprika	2 tsp	10 g	
Garlic, finely minced	2 cloves	2 cloves	
Ginger, fresh, grated	1 tbsp	15 g	
Coriander leaves (cilantro), chopped	1 1/2 oz	43 g	
Shrimp, raw, shell on	2 lbs of 16–20 size	907 g	Peel and devein shrimp. Marinate for 4 to 6 hours. Put four shrimp each on metal skewers. Grill 2 to 3 minutes per side.

NUTRITIONAL INFORMATION PER SERVING: 119 Calories; 5 g Fat (34.7% calories from fat); 16 g Protein; 3 g Carbohydrate; 1 g Dietary Fiber; 139 mg Cholesterol; 171 mg Sodium. Exchanges: 0 Grain (Starch); 2 Lean Meat; 0 Vegetable; 0 Fruit; 0 Nonfat Milk; 1 Fat; 0 Other Carbohydrates.

Szechwan food is famous in Chinese history and is legendary for spicy dishes and extraordinary variety and richness. Chili oil used in the following recipe adds a powerful punch to this popular hot appetizer. It is interesting to note that chili peppers originated in South America and entered Asia via Portuguese traders.

Szechwan-style spicy shrimp stuffed wontons

Yield: 50 pieces

Ingredients	Amounts		Procedure
	U.S.	Metric	
Shrimp, raw, peeled, and deveined	2 lbs	907 g	Prepare the shrimp. Set aside.
Sesame oil, mild	2 fl oz	60 ml	Heat the sesame oil and add onion, garlic, and ginger. Brown over low heat.
Onion, finely minced	4 oz	113 g	
Ginger, shredded	1 tbsp	15 g	
Garlic, minced	3 cloves	3 cloves	
Dried shiitake mushrooms, soaked for 2 hours, dried off, and minced	2 oz	57 g	Add the mushrooms to the above mixture and cook until hot. Let cool.
Chili oil	1 tsp	5 ml	Mince the shrimp and add to the cooked ingredients. Add the chili oil, soy sauce, scallions, sherry, brown sugar, and egg to the cooked mixture.
Soy sauce	1 fl oz	30 ml	
Scallions, minced (white parts with some green)	1 bunch	1 bunch	
Sherry	1 1/2 fl oz	44 ml	
Brown sugar	1 tbsp	15 g	
Egg	1 each	1 each	
Wonton skins	1 package-50 ct	1 package-50 ct	Use the above mixture to fill the wonton skins. Place 1 1/2 tsp of the filling in the center of each wonton wrapper. With a finger dipped in water, moisten the edges of the wrapper. Then bring one corner up over the filling to the opposite corner; do the same with the other two corners, creating a purse.
Egg for wash	1 each	1 each	

Pinch together the ends. Cover filled wontons with a dry cloth until fried. If wontons have to wait for 30 minutes or longer, cover with plastic wrap and refrigerate. Whip an egg and brush on each wonton.

Ingredients	Amounts		Procedure
Oil for frying	As needed	As needed	Deep fry wontons in oil at 375°F (190°C) for 2 minutes or until they are golden brown.

NUTRITIONAL INFORMATION PER PIECE: 114 Calories; 7 g Fat (55.7% calories from fat); 6 g Protein; 7 g Carbohydrate; trace Dietary Fiber; 59 mg Cholesterol; 157 mg Sodium. Exchanges: 1/2 Grain (Starch); 1/2 Lean Meat; 0 Vegetable; 1 1/2 Fat; 0 Other Carbohydrates.

Chermoula is a Moroccan marinade made with a variety of herbs and spices. It is usually used to flavor fish, but it can be used with vegetables or other meats. This recipe uses very large shrimp, fewer than 15 per pound.

prawns chermoula   *Yield: 7 servings, 2 shrimp each*

Ingredients	Amounts U.S.	Metric	Procedure
Cilantro	1 bunch	1 bunch	Blend the ingredients (not shrimp) in a food processor.
Garlic	4 cloves	4 cloves	
Spanish paprika, smoked	1/2 tsp	2 1/2 g	
Cumin, ground	1/2 tsp	2 1/2 g	
Coriander seeds, ground	1 tsp	5 g	
Cayenne	1/4 tsp	1 g	
Lemon juice	2 fl oz	59 ml	
Olive oil	3 fl oz	89 ml	
Shrimp, skewered	2 lbs (U-15's)	907 g	Clean the shrimp; devein. Skewer, if desired. Marinate in the above mixture for 4 to 6 hours. Grill skewers for 2 to 3 minutes on each side.

NUTRITIONAL INFORMATION PER SERVING: 257 Calories; 15 g Fat (51.7% calories from fat); 27 g Protein; 4 g Carbohydrate; trace Dietary Fiber; 197 mg Cholesterol; 197 mg Sodium. Exchanges: 0 Grain (Starch); 3 1/2 Lean Meat; 0 Vegetable; 0 Fruit; 2 1/2 Fat.

This crab artichoke bake is similar to a small casserole. It should be served bubbly hot after the cheese has turned a golden brown.

crab artichoke bake   *Yield: 8 each 5 oz (143 g) servings*

Ingredients	Amounts U.S.	Metric	Procedure
Artichoke hearts, canned, packed in water	14 oz	397 g	Drain artichoke hearts and chop.
Garlic, chopped	4 cloves	4 cloves	Add the garlic, mayonnaise, cream cheese, cheese (reserve a little asiago to use as topping), Worcestershire sauce, and cooked crab meat. Mix. Put in four baking dishes.
Mayonnaise	4 fl oz	118 ml	
Cream cheese	2 oz	57 g	
Asiago, grated	2 oz	57 g	
Worcestershire sauce	1 tbsp	15 ml	
Crab meat, any kind, defrosted	1 lb	454 g	
Green onions, chopped	2 oz	57 g	Top with green onions and reserved cheese. Bake at 350°F (175°C) until hot and bubbly. Serve with crackers or toast.

NUTRITIONAL INFORMATION PER SERVING: 229 Calories; 17 g Fat (63.4% calories from fat); 15 g Protein; 7 g Carbohydrate; 3 g Dietary Fiber; 63 mg Cholesterol; 419 mg Sodium. Exchanges: 1 1/2 Lean Meat; 1 Vegetable; 1 1/2 Fat; 0 Other Carbohydrates.

BENCHMARK RECIPE

While crab cakes are most often associated with Maryland and the Chesapeake Bay area, this recipe comes from the other side of the country. The addition of red bell peppers gives it a unique and delicious flavor.

San Francisco style crab cakes   *Yield: approx 8 pieces*

Ingredients	Amounts U.S.	Metric	Procedure
Dungeness or lump crab	1 lb	454 g	Mix all the ingredients, except the crab meat, in a bowl to blend thoroughly. Carefully fold in the crab meat to prevent breaking.
Breadcrumbs, dry	6 oz	170 g	
Eggs, beaten	2 each	2 each	
Mayonnaise	4 fl oz	118 ml	
Dijon mustard	1 tbsp	15 ml	
Worcestershire	1 tsp	5 ml	
Green onions, minced	1 stalk	1 stalk	Shape by hand or use a cylinder cutter to create small rounds, approx. 1 1/2 inch in diameter, and 3/4 inch thick.
Red bell pepper, fine dice	2 oz	56 g	
Cayenne pepper	1/4 tsp	1 g	
Salt	1/2 tsp	2.5 g	
Parsley, minced fine	1 1/2 oz	43 g	
Vegetable oil or clarified butter	As needed	As needed	

For Coating

Ingredients	Amounts U.S.	Metric	Procedure
Eggs, beaten	3 each	3 each	Egg wash and coat with crumbs.
			Chill for 1 hour. Heat oil in a pan to medium heat and cook until golden, turning on each side or deep fry in 350°F (175°C) oil.
			Serve with remoulade or sweet pepper aioli sauce and lemon wedges, or go traditional with tartar sauce.
Toasted or panko breadcrumbs	10 oz	284 g	

NUTRITIONAL INFORMATION PER SERVING: *579* Calories; 31 g Fat (47.9% calories from fat); 27 g Protein; 49 g Carbohydrate; 2 g Dietary Fiber; 228 mg Cholesterol; 1,160 mg Sodium. Exchanges: 3 Grain (Starch); 2 1/2 Lean Meat; 0 Vegetable; 3 1/2 Fat; 0 Other Carbohydrates.

The catfish of today doesn't even resemble the catfish of yesterday. Most of the catfish available to restaurants have been farmed under carefully controlled conditions in fresh water from underground sources. Catfish is versatile and can be fried, poached, grilled, sautéed, blackened, or oven baked. It's lean and has a delicate, slightly sweet taste. This recipe for fried catfish is delicious when served with the Creole Mustard Sauce found in Unit 16.

cornmeal fried catfish   *Yield: 12 4 oz (113 g) portions*

Ingredients	Amounts U.S.	Metric	Procedure
Catfish fillets	3 lbs	1.35 kg	Cut into 2-inch cubes or strips. Set aside.
Cornmeal	2 oz	57 g	Pour the cornmeal, flour, onion powder, cayenne, garlic powder, curry, salt, and pepper through a sieve to blend and remove any lumps. Set aside.
Flour	2 oz	57 g	
Onion powder	1 tsp	5 g	
Cayenne	1/2 tsp	2 1/2 g	
Garlic powder	1 tsp	5 g	
Curry	1/4 tsp	1 g	
Salt	To taste	To taste	
Black pepper	To taste	To taste	
Eggs, beaten	2 large	2 large	In a separate bowl, beat the egg, then add beer and minced onions. Mix well.
Beer	12 fl oz (can)	355 ml	
Onion, minced	2 oz	57 g	
Vegetable oil	As needed	As needed	Heat the vegetable oil. Roll the catfish in the flour mixture, then dip into the egg-beer solution, then back into the flour. Place dipped catfish pieces into the hot oil. Cook until golden brown. Serve with Creole Mustard Sauce (Unit 16).

NUTRITIONAL INFORMATION PER SERVING: 215 Calories; 11 g Fat (48.3% calories from fat); 20 g Protein; 6 g Carbohydrate; trace Dietary Fiber; 101 mg Cholesterol; 85 mg Sodium. Exchanges: 1/2 Grain (Starch); 2 1/2 Lean Meat; 0 Vegetable; 1 1/2 Fat.

Quiche Lorraine is a custard and cheese dish flavored with bacon or ham. It originated in Alsace Lorraine, a French province bordering Germany. There are many variations deviating from the original recipe based on different flavor fillings, such as broccoli, mushrooms, seafood, and many others. Quiche can be served as an entrée, for lunch and breakfast, or as shown below in mini forms for a tasty appetizer. To smoke the salmon in-house, use the Benchmark Recipe found in Unit 16 for Dry Cure for Salmon, Sturgeon, or Trout.

mini-smoked salmon quiche *Yield: 32, mini quiches*

Ingredients	Amounts U.S.	Metric	Procedure
Smoked salmon, crumbled	6 oz	170 g	Prepare the ingredients as directed.
Chives, chopped	1 oz	28 g	
Chevre goat cheese, crumbled	4 oz	113 g	
Gruyere cheese, shredded	4 oz	113 g	

Ingredients Custard

Heavy cream	4 fl oz	118 ml	Mix the cream, milk, and eggs, blending well. Add seasonings. Set aside.
Milk	12 fl oz	355 ml	
Eggs	6 eggs	6 eggs	
Nutmeg	1/4 tsp	1 g	
Salt	To taste	To taste	
Pepper	To taste	To taste	
Thyme, fresh, minced	1/4 tsp	1 g	

Mini Tart Shells

Flour, all-purpose	16 oz	907 g	Mound the flour on the bench and sprinkle the salt over it. Make a well in the center. Cut the butter into small pieces and put them in the well with the egg. Mix with your fingers, moving from the well outwards. Do not knead. When it ceases to stick to your fingers, roll it into a ball and put it in a plastic bag. Refrigerate for 15 minutes. Roll out the dough. Butter the mini-tart shell pans and line with the dough. Sprinkle the crumbled salmon, onions, and cheese over the tart shell. Cover with custard. Bake at 325°F (160°C) until firm.
Unsalted butter	10 oz	284 g	
Cold water	2 fl oz	59 ml	
Egg yolk	3 fl oz	89 ml	
Salt	2 tsp	10 g	

NUTRITIONAL INFORMATION PER SERVING: 132 Calories; 11 g Fat (76.2% calories from fat); 4 g Protein; 4 g Carbohydrate; trace Dietary Fiber; 76 mg Cholesterol; 291 mg Sodium. Exchanges: 0 Grain (Starch); 1/2 Lean Meat; 0 Vegetable; 0 Nonfat Milk; 2 Fat.

Bruschetta is the generic Italian term for toasted garlic bread, usually served warm when it comes out of the oven. Bruschetta can be topped with many different ingredients such as diced tomatoes, cheese, olives and many others.

Bresaola used in this recipe is rather salty, very dry, and must be sliced as thin as possible on the electric slicer. Use ciabatta bread if available; if not, a French baguette will work.

bresaola bruschetta with herbed goat cheese
Yield: 32 pieces

Ingredients	Amounts U.S.	Metric	Procedure
Cream cheese	1 lb	454 g	Purée cheese and blend with herbs, salt, and pepper.
Goat cheese	1 lb	454 g	
Thyme, fresh, crushed	1 tbsp	15 g	
Parsley, minced fine	1 tbsp	15 g	
Kosher salt	1 tsp	5 g	
Black pepper, fresh cracked	1 tsp	5 g	
Roasted garlic, mashed	3 oz	85 g	Combine the garlic with oil.
Olive oil	8 fl oz	237 ml	
Ciabatta	2 loaves- 1 lb	2 loaves- 454 g	Slice the bread diagonally into 1/4 in-thick pieces. Paint with garlic oil. Toast lightly on the oiled side. Spread the cheese mixture onto the toasted bread.
Dried beef, shaved or Bresaola (büundnerfleisch), shaved	1 lb	454 g	Top toasts with 1/2 oz bresaola. (Bresaola is known for its bright red color and intense flavor.)

NUTRITIONAL INFORMATION PER PIECE: 308 Calories; 21 g Fat (60.6% calories from fat); 10 g Protein; 20 g Carbohydrate; 1 g Dietary Fiber; 40 mg Cholesterol; 302 mg Sodium. Exchanges: 1 Grain (Starch); 1 Lean Meat; 0 Vegetable; 3 1/2 Fat.

Leeks have been an important flavoring ingredient in European recipes for hundreds of years. This recipe elevates the humble leek to a new high and becomes the star of this delicious appetizer.

candied leeks and goat cheese bruschetta
Yield: 50 oz (1.418 kg); use 1 oz (28 g) per slice, 25 1/4-inch slices per loaf

Ingredients	Amounts U.S.	Metric	Procedure
Candied Leeks			
Leeks, white part only, julienned	12 each	12 each	Split the leeks and wash thoroughly. There is often sand between the layers. Trim the root end off of each leek.
Olive oil	2 fl oz	59 ml	
Optional:			Cut into fine strips about 2 in (5 cm) long.
Water	1 fl oz	30 ml	Put the leeks and oil in a heavy sauce pan and cook slowly until the leeks become soft and start to color. A small amount of water may be added.
Sauterne wine	8 fl oz	237 ml	Once the leeks are caramelized, add the Sauterne wine and sugar and allow to cook down into marmalade-like consistency. Set aside.
Sugar	3 oz	85 g	
Cheese Spread			
Goat cheese	2 lbs	907 g	Mix the cheese with garlic, thyme, pepper, parsley, and salt; taste and adjust for seasoning. Set aside.
Garlic, roasted and mashed	3 oz	85 g	
Fresh thyme, crushed	1 tbsp	15 g	
Black pepper, freshly cracked	1 tsp	5 g	
Parsley, minced	1 tbsp	15 g	
Kosher salt	2 tsp	10 g	
Olive oil	3 fl oz	89 ml	Mix the crushed garlic and the olive oil.
Garlic, crushed	1 clove	1 clove	
Walnut bread	2 each-1 lb	2 each-454 g	Brush slices of bread with the garlic-flavored olive oil. Cut into 1/4-inch croustates. Toast at 375°F (190°C). Remove, cool, and top each toast piece with 1/2 to 1 oz of cheese mixture and 1 tbsp of candied leeks. Warm in oven until heated through. Serve immediately.

NUTRITIONAL INFORMATION PER SERVING: 352 Calories; 20 g Fat (50.7% calories from fat); 15 g Protein; 28 g Carbohydrate; 3 g Dietary Fiber; 38 mg Cholesterol; 477 mg Sodium. Exchanges: 1 Grain (Starch); 1 1/2 Lean Meat; 1 1/2 Vegetable; 3 Fat; 0 Other Carbohydrates.

This is a quick and delicious appetizer. The apple ring serves as the base. Use the Ham Mousse recipe found in Unit 17.

ham mousse on apple rings   *Yield: 1 serving*

Ingredients	Amounts U.S.	Metric	Procedure
Ham mousse	4 oz	112 g	Peel, core, and slice apple rings.
Apple rings	2 each	2 each	Sprinkle the rings with lemon juice and sugar. Place under the broiler until light brown.
Lemon juice	1 tsp	5 ml	
Sugar	1 tsp	5 g	Garnish according to your taste.

NUTRITIONAL INFORMATION PER SERVING: 277 Calories; 19 g Fat (65.0% calories from fat); 12 g Protein; 11 g Carbohydrate; trace Dietary Fiber; 84 mg Cholesterol; 1,034 mg Sodium. Exchanges: 0 Grain (Starch); 1 1/2 Lean Meat; 0 Fruit; 0 Nonfat Milk; 3 Fat; 1/2 Other Carbohydrates.

Grilled Portobellos have a meaty taste and texture and are used in place of meat in many vegetarian recipes. Portobellos get a meatier taste the longer they are grilled. Cook them at least 5 minutes per side.

grilled portobello mushrooms   *Yield: 8 servings*

Ingredients	Amounts U.S.	Metric	Procedure
Portobello mushroom caps, large	8 each	8 each	Wash and remove sand from the mushroom caps.
Olive oil	2 fl oz	59 ml	Sprinkle with oil, salt, and pepper. Grill on both sides until done. Cut each cap in half and plate.
Salt	To taste	To taste	
Black pepper, coarsely ground	To taste	To taste	
Oregano, fresh, chopped	1 tsp	5 g	Sprinkle with herbs and vinegar. Serve at room temperature.
Parsley, chopped	2 tsp	10 g	
Balsamic vinegar, high quality	2 fl oz	59 ml	

NUTRITIONAL INFORMATION PER SERVING: 101 Calories; 7 g Fat (59.9% calories from fat); 3 g Protein; 8 g Carbohydrate; 2 g Dietary Fiber; 0 mg Cholesterol; 40 mg Sodium. Exchanges: 0 Grain (Starch); 1 1/2 Vegetable; 0 Fruit; 1 1/2 Fat.

This pan-seared foie gras is a luxury appetizer commanding a high price. If the pears are not light brown, place under a broiler. We recommend that you serve this recipe with the Blackberry Gastrique recipe from Unit 16.

pan-seared foie gras with pears and port *Yield: 8 servings*

Ingredients	Amounts U.S.	Metric	Procedure
Pear Sauce			
Bosc pears, sliced, thin	2 medium	2 medium	Sauté the pears, shallots, and garlic in butter. Season with salt and pepper. Cook until slightly caramelized.
Shallots, minced fine	1 large clove	1 large clove	
Garlic, minced fine	1 clove	1 clove	
Butter, unsalted	1/2 oz	15 g	
Salt	To taste	To taste	
Pepper	To taste	To taste	
Port	5 fl oz	148 ml	Add port wine and flame off. Strain the pear sauce through cheesecloth and reserve the pears. Reduce the liquid by half, almost to a syrup stage.
Whole Grade A goose or duck foie gras lobe	1 lb	454 g	Clean each lobe piece carefully, striping out and removing the vein.
Milk	12 fl oz	355 ml	Soak the liver in milk for 2 hours, refrigerated. Rinse and pat dry. Slice into eight 1/2-in slices.
Kosher salt	1 1/2 tsp	8 g	Sprinkle with kosher salt. Preheat a sauté pan. Carefully place each slice into the medium hot pan; make sure to cook two slices at a time. Sear for 1 minute on each side; remove and keep warm.
Brioche crouton, toasted lightly	2 in diameter, 1/2 in thick	51 mm	Place each slice of liver on a toasted brioche crouton and top with sautéed pears. Drizzle reduced with Blackberry Gastrique (Unit 16) or a similar sauce around the crouton.

NUTRITIONAL INFORMATION PER SERVING: 356 Calories; 27 g Fat (73.1% calories from fat); 7 g Protein; 15 g Carbohydrate; 1 g Dietary Fiber; 89 mg Cholesterol; 859 mg Sodium. Exchanges: 0 Grain (Starch); 1 Lean Meat; 0 Vegetable; 1/2 Fruit; 4 1/2 Fat; 0 Other.

orange thyme smoked chicken ravioli *Yield: 40 to 50 pieces,*
10 servings of 4 to 5 pieces each

Ingredients	Amounts U.S.	Metric	Procedure
Pasta			
All purpose flour	8 oz	227 g	Place the flour, semolina, orange zest, and thyme in the bowl of a food processor with a blade attachment.
Semolina flour	8 oz	227 g	
Orange zest	1/2 oz	15 g	
Fresh thyme leaves, chopped	1/4 oz	7 g	
Whole eggs	4 each	4 each	In a bowl, blend the eggs, oil, and orange juice together and, while the machine is running, slowly add liquid through the feed tube. Pulse/blend until a ball forms.
Olive oil	1 fl oz	30 ml	
Orange juice	1 fl oz	30 ml	
			Remove from the bowl and knead until smooth. Cover the dough ball with plastic and let rest for 30 minutes at room temperature.
			Roll out pasta into 3-in-wide strips. A standard pasta machine can be used to cut the strips.
Filling			
Garlic, minced fine	1 clove	1 clove	Sauté the garlic, shallots, and thyme in olive oil.
Shallots, minced fine	1 large clove	1 large clove	
Fresh thyme, chopped	1 tsp	5 g	
Olive oil	1 tbsp	15 ml	
Chicken liver, cleaned and trimmed	2 oz	57 g	Add the chicken liver and sauté until the livers are fully cooked.
Madeira wine	1 fl oz	30 ml	Flame with wine.
Smoked chicken, dark meat, shredded	1 lb	454 g	Toss the chicken and seasonings with the flamed ingredients and heat until warm. Remove from heat and cool for 10 minutes.
Nutmeg	1 pinch	1 pinch	
Salt	To taste	To taste	
Black pepper	To taste	To taste	

Breadcrumbs	3 oz	85 g
Cream cheese	4 oz	113 g
Egg	1 large	1 large
Water, cold	1 fl oz	30 ml

Add the breadcrumbs, cream cheese, and egg to bind the above ingredients. Adjust the seasonings and cool.

To Assemble

Lay out sheets of pasta. Place 1/2 oz dollop of smoked chicken/cheese mixture, 2 in apart, across the sheet. Use the heel of your hand to press the sheets together between each dollop.

Egg wash the sheet and place another sheet of pasta over the first, covering the fillings. With the back side of a circle cutter or a ravioli press, seal the mixture in. Cut the raviolis and place in refrigerator uncovered on parchment or semolina-dusted sheet pans.

To Cook

Bring salted water to a boil and add the pasta. Cook for 2 to 3 minutes or until the pasta floats. Al dente.

Pasta can be served with a mushroom cream sauce or deep fried.

NUTRITIONAL INFORMATION PER SERVING: 385 Calories; 17 g Fat (40.1% calories from fat); 17 g Protein; 40 g Carbohydrate; 2 g Dietary Fiber; 173 mg Cholesterol; 171 mg Sodium. Exchanges: 2 1/2 Grain (Starch); 1 1/2 Lean Meat; 0 Vegetable; 0 Fruit; 2 1/2 Fat.

Polenta is corn mush and hails from Northern Italy, where it is used more often than pasta. In this recipe the polenta cakes serve as a first course. "Confit" comes from the French word meaning "preserved." It was described earlier in this unit.

herb polenta cake with duck confit   *Yield: 24 portions*

Ingredients	Amounts U.S.	Metric	Procedure
Polenta Cake			
Garlic, minced fine	2 cloves	2 cloves	Sauté the minced garlic and shallots in olive oil until golden brown.
Shallot, minced fine	1 each	1 each	
Olive oil	1 tbsp	15 ml	
Chicken stock	2 1/2 pints	1.183 l	Add the stock, salt, and pepper and bring the mixture to a boil. Add the polenta and stir with a wire whisk. The mixture will splatter. Cover with a lid and simmer over low heat.
Salt	To taste	To taste	
Pepper	To taste	To taste	
Polenta meal	10 oz	284 g	
Butter	4 oz	112 g	Add the butter, thyme, and orange zest. Spread hot polenta onto a plastic-covered half-sheet pan.
Thyme, fresh	1/4 oz	7 g	
Orange zest	1/2 oz	15 g	Chill for 1 hour until the polenta is firm. When firm, cut 24 pieces with 1 1/2-in round biscuit or cookie cutter or cut off disks to eliminate waste.
Oil	As needed	As needed	Heat oil in pan and sear each round until golden brown on both sides.
Duck Confit			
Moulard duck, average size, 5 lb	1 whole	1 whole	Cut the duck into six pieces: two legs, two thighs, and two breasts. (Reserve any duck fat found in the cavity.)
Duck fat, rendered (schmaltz)	4 lbs	1.814 kg	
Kosher salt	To taste	To taste	Season the duck with the salt and pepper. Place the duck into a roasting pan to just fit the duck. Melt the reserved duck fat and pour over the duck, placing a bay leaf on top of the duck. Braise in duck fat in 200°F (90°C) oven for 4 hours. When the duck is tender, remove the pieces and drain from the fat. Reserve the fat for other uses. Pull the meat from the bones and mash. Use this mashed or pulled duck meat as a topper for crispy herb polenta cakes. This makes approx. 1 1/2 lbs of pulled meat.
Black pepper, cracked	To taste	To taste	
Bay leaf	1 each	1 each	

To Serve: Place 1 tbsp of duck on top of a round of toasted herb polenta, and garnish with a kiss of mandarin cherry relish or something fruity.

NUTRITIONAL INFORMATION PER SERVING: 690 Calories; 56 g Fat (74.8% calories from fat); 14 g Protein; 29 g Carbohydrate; 3 g Dietary Fiber; 106 mg Cholesterol; 2,085 mg Sodium. Exchanges: 2 Grain (Starch); 1 1/2 Lean Meat; 0 Vegetable; 0 Fruit; 10 1/2 Fat.

Ravioli has long been a favorite Italian main dish. It is now a popular appetizer, whether breaded and deep-fried or boiled and served with a complementary sauce. See the Poultry Brine recipe in Unit 16 to smoke the chicken in house.

Tapas can be eaten at lunch or dinner if the quantity or variety of tapas is enough to satisfy the appetite. In general, tapas make the perfect appetizer. Our Spanish Chicken and Roasted Red Pepper Skewers are a tapa-style appetizer.

Spanish chicken and roasted red pepper skewers
Yield: 24 skewers

Ingredients	Amounts		Procedure
	U.S.	Metric	
Bamboo skewers, soaked in water	24	24	Soak skewers in water for 30 minutes.
Boneless, skinless chicken breasts	2 lbs	907 g	Cut the chicken and peppers into 1/2-in strips. Thread alternating chicken and pepper strips on the skewers.
Peppers, fire roasted, seeded	1 lb	454 g	Place in a shallow baking pan.
Mayonnaise	8 fl oz	237 ml	Combine the remaining ingredients until well blended. Pour over skewers and marinate in refrigerator for a minimum of 2 hours, but preferably 2 to 4 hours. Remove skewers from marinade; discard leftovers and place skewers on the rack of the broiler. Broil 4 to 6 in from the heat for 10 minutes or bake in a 375°F (190°C) oven until chicken is cooked through.
Garlic, minced	2 cloves	2 cloves	
Smoked Spanish paprika	1/2 oz	15 g	
Red pepper flakes	1 tsp	7 g	
Sherry vinegar	1/2 fl oz	15 ml	

NUTRITIONAL INFORMATION PER PIECE: 114 Calories; 8 g Fat (64.2% calories from fat); 9 g Protein; 1 g Carbohydrate; trace Dietary Fiber; 25 mg Cholesterol; 77 mg Sodium. Exchanges: 0 Grain (Starch); 1 Lean Meat; 0 Vegetable; 1/2 Fat; 0 Other Carbohydrates.

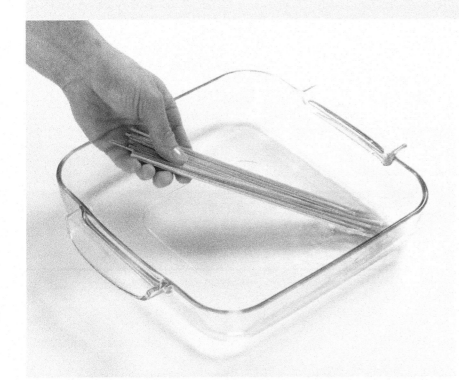

In years past, lamb was only available in the spring during the lambing season. Today, fresh lamb is available year-round. Lamb pairs well with a broad range of seasonings.

Sates consist of small, marinated cubes of meat, fish, or poultry. They are threaded on skewers and grilled or broiled. In the following recipe, the lamb is marinated in an Asian marinade requiring two new, unfamiliar ingredients: lemon grass and fish sauce. Lemon grasses are long stalks available fresh. The brown outer leaves must be removed, and the stalks split and squashed. They are not eaten. Fish sauce is made with fermented fish and has a pungent, unusual taste. It should be used with caution. Sates are traditionally served with a spicy peanut sauce (see Unit 16).

Thai sate of lamb (pork, beef, or chicken can be used, too) *Yield: 10 to 12 skewers 4 oz (113 g) servings*

Ingredients	Amounts U.S.	Metric	Procedure
Lamb, loin or leg meat, completely trimmed and lean	2 1/2 lbs	1.134 kg	Cut the meat into even 1/2 in cubes.

Marinade

Ingredients	U.S.	Metric	Procedure
Red onion, chopped	1 medium	1 medium	Combine the ingredients. Mix thoroughly in a blender and use it to coat the meat cubes.
Garlic, minced	2 cloves	2 cloves	
Lemon grass	4 stalks	4 stalks	Marinate for 2 hours. Place 4 to 5 pieces of meat on soaked wooden skewers.
Cumin powder	2 tsp	10 g	
Turmeric powder	1 tsp	5 g	Grill over a charcoal fire, turning and basting frequently with additional marinade.
Tamarind paste	1 fl oz	30 ml	Grill until meat is medium rare, approximately 8 minutes.
Brown sugar	2 oz	57 g	
Shrimp paste	1 tsp	5 g	Serve with spicy sate peanut sauce recipe found in Unit 16.
Salt	1 tsp	5 g	
Soy sauce	1 pint	473 ml	
Pinch red pepper	Dash	Dash	
Peanut oil	8 fl oz	237 ml	

NUTRITIONAL INFORMATION PER SERVING: (Lamb): 426 Calories; 34 g Fat (70.8% calories from fat); 18 g Protein; 13 g Carbohydrate; 1 g Dietary Fiber; 56 mg Cholesterol; 3,244 mg Sodium. Exchanges: 0 Grain (Starch); 2 Lean Meat; 1 1/2 Vegetable; 0 Fruit; 5 1/2 Fat; 0 Other Carbohydrates.

Kufte is the generic term used for meatballs throughout the Middle East. Lamb meat is usually used.

kufte (Middle Eastern lamb meatballs) *Yield: 40 meatballs*
1 oz (28 g); serves 10, 4 meatballs

Ingredients	Amounts U.S.	Metric	Procedure
Cracked wheat	6 oz	168 g	Cover cracked wheat with hot water and let sit 1 hour. Drain off water; squeeze dry and cool.
Lamb, ground, not too fat	1 lb	454 g	Add the remaining ingredients. Shape into meatballs. Bake the meatballs and serve with chopped mint and lemon juice.
Onions, ground	2 oz	56 g	
Garlic, chopped	1 tbsp	15 g	
Pine nuts	2 oz	56 g	
Rosemary, dried, chopped	1/2 tsp	2 g	
Thyme, dried	1/2 tsp	2 g	
Lemon peel, grated	1 tsp	5 g	
Salt	To taste	To taste	
Black pepper	To taste	To taste	

NUTRITIONAL INFORMATION PER SERVING: 177 Calories; 10 g Fat (50.1% calories from fat); 10 g Protein; 13 g Carbohydrate; 2 g Dietary Fiber; 25 mg Cholesterol; 48 mg Sodium. Exchanges: 1 Grain (Starch); 1 Lean Meat; 0 Vegetable; 0 Fruit; 1 1/2 Fat.

Squash blossoms have been a long-time favorite in Mexican and Italian cuisines and have now found favor in fine restaurants around the world. The recipe works well served with the Roasted Red Pepper Aioli Dip; the recipe is found in Unit 16.

squash blossom fritters   *Yield: 6 servings (4 blossoms each)*

Ingredients	Amounts		Procedure
	U.S.	Metric	
Squash blossoms, stamen removed	24 each	24 each	Clean the squash blossoms; remove any bugs or dirt. Remove the stamen as these are bitter.
Garlic, minced, sautéed until golden	2 cloves	2 cloves	In a sauté pan, fry 2 cloves of garlic, minced, in 2 tbsp olive oil. Reserve.
Olive oil	1 fl oz	30 ml	
Corn, fire roasted, kernels removed	2 medium ears	2 medium ears	Fire roast 2 ears of corn and 2 red bell peppers. When the peppers are blistered, place in a bowl and cover with plastic. When the peppers are cool, peel them and seed them. Chop them into medium dice and add to the garlic mixture. Cut the roasted kernels off the corn cob and place with the pepper mixture.
Red bell peppers, fire roasted and diced	2 each	2 each	
Goat cheese, crumbled	1 lb	454 g	Add the goat cheese, pine nuts, breadcrumbs, salt, pepper, and chiffonade of sage. Mix until combined. Open each blossom and stuff with 2 tbsp filling.
Pine nuts	2 oz	56 g	
Soft breadcrumbs	3 oz	85 g	
Salt	To taste	To taste	Twist the end gently to seal in.
Black pepper	To taste	To taste	
Sage leaves, fresh, chiffonade	1 tsp	5 g	
Flour	4 1/2 oz	126 g	Roll stuffed blossoms in flour and dip in batter.
Batter (tempura or beer batter—see other recipes)	As needed	As needed	Deep fry in wire basket to keep intact at 365°F (185°C) until batter is golden brown. Serve with Roasted Red Pepper Aioli Dip (see Unit 16 for recipe).
Oil for frying	As needed	As needed	

NUTRITIONAL INFORMATION PER SERVING: 645 Calories; 42 g Fat (57.8% calories from fat); 31 g Protein; 38 g Carbohydrate; 3 g Dietary Fiber; 115 mg Cholesterol; 446 mg Sodium. Exchanges: 2 Grain (Starch); 3 1/2 Lean Meat; 1/2 Vegetable; 6 Fat.

Phyllo, or filo, is a paper-thin dough of Middle Eastern origin. It is available in 16 oz (450 g) packages. The defrosted dough is ready to use. It will dry rapidly and must be kept covered at all times. It is best worked on moist (not wet) kitchen towels.

wild mushroom phyllo rolls *Yield: 72 servings with 1 oz (28) filling*

Ingredients	Amounts		Procedure
	U.S.	Metric	
Filling			
Butter	2 oz	56 g	Sauté the shallots, garlic, re-hydrated mushrooms, crimini mushrooms, and thyme in butter until semi-dry (Duxelle).
Shallots, chopped	1 tbsp	15 g	
Garlic, chopped	1 tbsp	15 g	
Dried wild mushrooms, hydrated	4 oz	112 g	
Crimini mushrooms, chopped	2 lbs	906 g	
Thyme, fresh, minced	1 tbsp	15 g	
Flour	2 oz	56 g	Add flour and make a roux.
Heavy cream	1 pt	448 ml	Whisk in cream. Cook 2 minutes until thick.
Goat cheese, crumbled	4 oz	112 g	Remove from heat and add goat cheese and cream cheese.
Cream cheese	4 oz	112 g	
Breadcrumbs	4 oz	112 g	Add breadcrumbs, salt, and pepper to taste. Mix thoroughly. Cool and save for filling.
Salt	To taste	To taste	
Pepper	To taste	To taste	
Phyllo			
Phyllo sheets	1 package	1 package	Spread out a single phyllo sheet. Brush on a thin layer of clarified butter. Top with a second sheet of phyllo.
Clarified butter	1 lb	454 g	

Repeat the butter stage. Top with a third sheet of phyllo. Place 1/2-in-thick ribbon of mushroom mix on the long side of the triangle. Roll the buttered phyllo around the filling. Cut roll into 1 oz pieces. This recipe will make approx. 72 pieces. Chill until needed.

Bake at 375°F (190°C) until rolls are golden brown and filling is hot.

NUTRITIONAL INFORMATION PER SERVING: 159 Calories; 13 g Fat (79.7% calories from fat); 3 g Protein; 5 g Carbohydrate; 1 g Dietary Fiber; 62 mg Cholesterol; 81 mg Sodium. Exchanges: 1/2 Grain (Starch); 0 Lean Meat; 1/2 Vegetable; 0 Nonfat Milk; 2 1/2 Fat.

Brie is considered one of the greatest dessert cheeses and is probably the most famous of any French cheese. Here it is coupled with apricots to create a delicious savory appetizer.

apricot and brie tartlets *Yield: 16 3-in individual tartlets*

Ingredients	Amounts U.S.	Metric	Procedure
Pâté brisée pastry, prepared or homemade	1 lb	454 g	Roll the pastry and stamp out 3-in circles to fit in a tartlet or muffin tin and then chill for 30 minutes. Bake the pastry shells blind (use pie weights or beans) for 10 minutes at 350°F (175°C). Remove from oven.
Dried apricots, soaked and diced	8 oz	227 g	Put 1/2 oz of apricots and two to three small cubes of brie in each pastry case.
Brie cheese, cut into 1/2-inch cubes	1 lb	454 g	
Heavy cream	4 fl oz	112 ml	Whisk together the cream, milk, egg yolks, eggs, salt, and pepper.
Milk	4 fl oz	112 ml	
Egg yolks	4 each	4 each	Fill each tartlet evenly with custard. Top with a few slices of almonds. Bake for approximately 10 to 15 minutes at 350°F (175°C) until raised and golden brown.
Eggs	6 each	6 each	
Almonds, blanched, sliced	4 oz	112 g	
Salt	To taste	To taste	
Black pepper	To taste	To taste	

NUTRITIONAL INFORMATION PER SERVING: 275 Calories; 18 g Fat (57.6% calories from fat); 7 g Protein; 22 g Carbohydrate; 2 g Dietary Fiber; 162 mg Cholesterol; 109 mg Sodium. Exchanges: 1 Grain (Starch); 1/2 Lean Meat; 1/2 Fruit; 0 Nonfat Milk; 3 Fat.

The following recipe is a traditional snack from South America. It can add diversity of flavor to any appetizer plate.

cachapas de carabobo *Yield: 12 servings*

Ingredients	Amounts U.S.	Metric	Procedure
Yellow corn	10 each	10 each	Remove the kernels and purée in food processor.
Heavy cream	2 fl oz	60 ml	Mix the cream, eggs, flour, sugar, and salt into the corn purée. Cover and rest in the refrigerator for 20 minutes.
Eggs	2 fl oz	57 g	
Bread flour	2 oz	57 g	Heat the griddle or cast iron pan and place a small amount of oil or clarified butter in the pan. With a small ladle or spoon, put 2 oz of batter on the pan. Fry each pancake, turning once until lightly browned and firm on both sides. Remove from the hot pan and wrap around the cheese sticks. Serve warm.
Sugar	1 oz	28.35 g	
Salt	1/4 tsp	2 g	
Gouda or Jack cheese	12 oz	340 g	Cut cheese into 1 oz (28 g) sticks.

NUTRITIONAL INFORMATION PER SERVING: 236 Calories; 11 g Fat (41.2% calories from fat); 12 g Protein; 25 g Carbohydrate; 3 g Dietary Fiber; 64 mg Cholesterol; 301 mg Sodium. Exchanges: 1 1/2 Grain (Starch); 1 Lean Meat; 0 Nonfat Milk; 1 1/2 Fat; 0 Other Carbohydrates.

>> Summary

Appetizers are meant to whet the appetite. Appetizers are sometimes also called *hors d'oeuvre* and "amuse-bouche." We have defined appetizers as the first course served at the table. Hors d'oeuvre are small items of food, typically finger foods served apart from the meal, as in a reception held before the meal is served. Amuse-bouche is a tiny bite often presented as a gift of the chef to welcome guests and stimulate appetites.

Appetizers are an important component in most any cuisines. Many of our favorite appetizers have origins from foreign sources.

It is important to serve cold appetizers "cold" and hot appetizers "hot." Because appetizers give diners a glimpse of what's to come, they should be carefully prepared and beautifully served.

>> Review Questions

SHORT ANSWER

1. Explain the differences between appetizers and hors d'oeuvre, according to this text.
2. Appetizers should be attractive and have an inviting flavor. List at least three serving tips.
3. Describe a method used to determine if a mollusk is still alive.

MATCHING

Match the country with the appetizer.

4. cold cuts, pickled vegetables, olives, cheese
5. pickled herring
6. soufflé
7. salt cod fritter
8. tarama
9. grilled spicy sausages
10. taro root dumplings
11. gyoza
12. empanada
13. corn and cheese bread

a. Spain
b. Greece
c. Germany
d. Brazil
e. Japan
f. France
g. Argentina
h. Russia
i. Italy
j. China

Match the appetizer to its description.

14. anchovy dip
15. fattened goose or duck liver
16. Indian-style barbecue
17. Kalamata olives and anchovies, lemon juice, and spices
18. Moroccan marinade made with herbs and spices
19. ground chickpeas, lemon, tahini, and spices
20. fried cooked meats or vegetable mixtures
21. raw sliced beef tenderloin

a. hummus
b. carpaccio
c. chermoula
d. croquettes
e. bagna caôda
f. foie gras
g. tandoori
h. tapenade

MULTIPLE CHOICE

22. Blinis are often served with
    a. artichoke crab dip.
    b. fresh cut vegetables.
    c. caviar.
    d. dim sum.
23. Raw clam meat should have a firm texture and be _____ in color.
    a. gray
    b. tan
    c. pink
    d. orange
24. Which of the following ingredients is *not* found on a typical antipasto plate?
    a. bresaola
    b. marinated vegetables
    c. truffles
    d. olives
25. Sate is grilled or
    a. pan fried.
    b. baked.
    c. stir-fried.
    d. broiled.

Sandwiches and Cold Soups

>> Unit 9

Sandwiches

>> Unit 10

Cold Soups

The chef in the cold kitchen has many responsibilities, and those vary depending on the type of facility and the menu. Sandwiches are a mainstay on many lunch and dinner menus and have recently filtered down to breakfast menus as well. The task of preparing sandwiches usually falls on the shoulders of the cold kitchen staff. Unit 9 discusses the elements of sandwich preparation and includes a number of traditional and contemporary sandwiches.

Cold soups are both refreshing and healthy, particularly on hot days. With a slice of bread, a cold soup can be a satisfying meal in itself. Cold soups have also found their way to the dessert menu. Unit 10 focuses on cold soups and includes a host of both savory and sweet recipes.

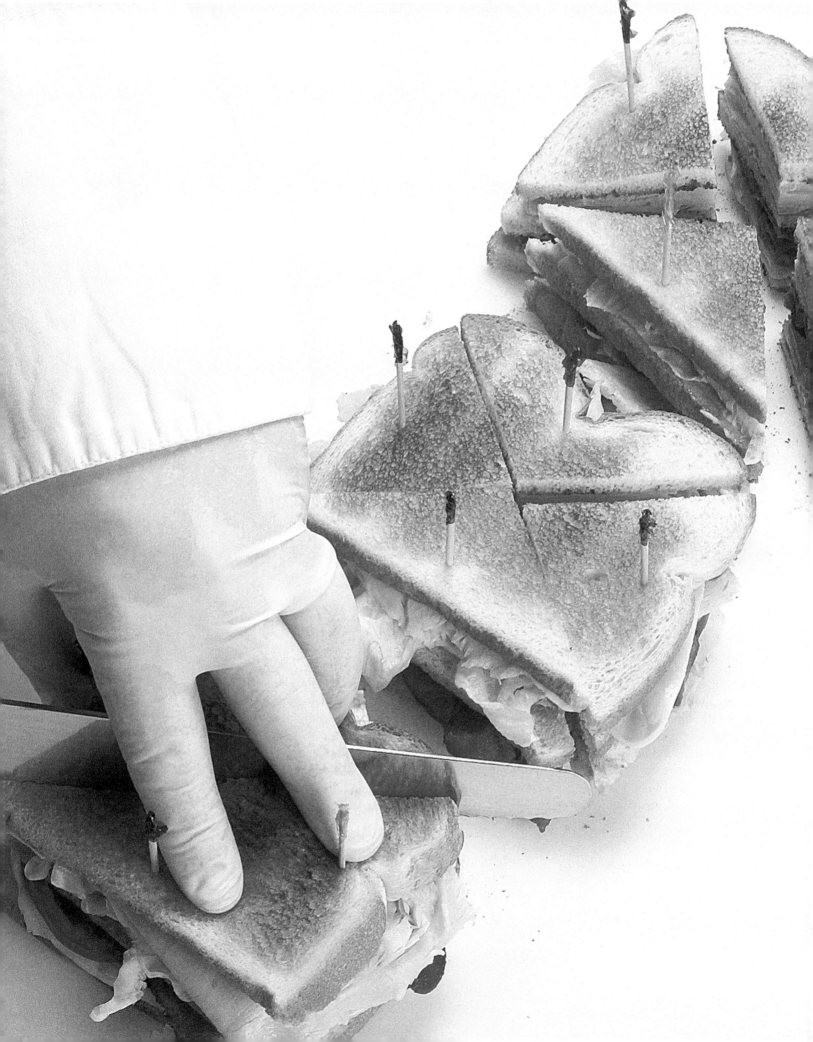

9

Sandwiches

>> Learning Objectives

After you have finished reading this unit, you should be able to:

- Distinguish among a wide variety of breads.
- Prepare an assortment of sandwich fillings.
- Set up the sandwich station.
- Make individual hot and cold sandwiches.
- Understand the principles of storing sandwiches.
- Recognize sandwich terminology.

>> Key Terms

à la minute	mise en place (*meez*	panini	surimi
gyro (*YEE-roh*)	*ahn plahs*)	roquette	

In this unit, you will be learning about the sandwich and the important role it plays in any successful foodservice operation. Sandwich prep is one of the mainstays of the cold kitchen. Meats are sliced, and fillings, spreads, and garnishes are prepped. The mise en place for the sandwich station is key to the success of any sandwich production. You will learn about the parts of the sandwich, from the bread to the spread, and you will learn how to set up a typical sandwich station. One of the first jobs for most chefs and cooks just starting out in a professional kitchen is the sandwich station. Many sandwiches are filled with a salad-type filling similar to those used in main course salads. Usually sandwiches are served with side orders or garnishes such as pickles, small salads, relishes, cold sauces, or just lettuce and tomato slices. Learning to practice "mise en place" is excellent training for more advanced cooking skills.

The hamburger is the most popular sandwich in the world, so we often associate sandwiches with fast-food operations, cafeterias, coffee shops, and diners. Fast-food establishments, diners, and coffee shops have even created their own language to speed up service. In this unit, some of these terms will be used to give you the flavor of this fast-paced work. The diner is a popular type of restaurant that uses large, all-day menus and is sometimes open around the clock. The diner-style of restaurant originated in New England where food was once sold from horse-drawn wagons. Eventually diners adopted the architectural style of railroad dining cars.

325

Depending on the facility where you work, you might have to prepare sandwiches to order. In restaurants, the waitstaff usually types in the order electronically on a POS (point of sale) terminal, or writes down the orders, called "dupes" or duplicate order tickets, and brings them to the kitchen. They are usually printed out directly at the station.

The pantry cook must read the orders and make the sandwiches as quickly as possible. The process is called "to order." Another term for "to order" is **à la minute,** a French term that is sometimes used in upscale restaurants and refers to on-the-spot preparation.

>> History of the Sandwich

While we think of sandwiches as a typically American food, the history of the sandwich is as old as recorded history. In the first century BC, the famous Rabbi Hillel talks of the Passover custom of sandwiching a mixture of nuts, fruits, spices, and wine between two matzohs to eat with the bitter herbs. All served as a reminder of the suffering of the Jews before their deliverance from the Egyptians. During the Medieval era, between the sixth and sixteenth century, thick blocks of bread called "trenchers" were used as a type of plate. Meat and other foods were stacked on these trenchers and, as the diner would eat his or her fill, the remains were given to the lower classes or the dogs. The term "sandwich" was first published in 1762 in the journal of Edward Gibbons. He recorded what he had seen at a gentleman's club in London. Around the same time, John Montague (1718–1792), the Fourth Earl of Sandwich, is credited with inventing the sandwich while partaking of a poker game at one of these clubs. He had a reputation as a hardened gambler, sometimes refusing to get up from the game table even for a meal. The legend has it that he ordered his servant to bring him some beef tucked between two pieces of bread. Others picked up on this novel idea and started ordering their meal, "the same as Sandwich."

>> Classification of Sandwiches

The concept of a sandwich has changed since the time of the Earl of Sandwich. Many cultures feature sandwiches in unique forms, such as Mexican burritos, Chinese egg rolls, Indian samosas, Italian pizzas, and the New Orleans Muffalata. Even these different types of sandwiches have a few things in common with the burger and the hero—they have a base that is usually made of wheat or some other grain, a filling, and some dressing or garnish.

There are many types of sandwiches, including the following:

- Canapés—tea sandwiches, finger sandwiches, appetizers, and zakuski sandwiches; served hot or cold
- Cold sandwiches
- Hot sandwiches
- International sandwiches—made with wheat or grain-based wrappers, dough, or bread with fillings; served hot or cold

>> Components of the Sandwich

Sandwiches are composed of the bread, the spread, the filling, and garnishes:

- Bread is the base of the sandwich and can be yeast breads and rolls, focaccia, pizza dough, wrappers such as tortillas, naan, rice paper, egg roll wrappers, and a hundred other bread types. The bread or wrap is what holds the fillings together in a sandwich (Figure 9-1).

Figure 9-1 Bread is the most common base for sandwiches; a host of varieties are used.

- Spreads give flavor and moisture to a sandwich (Figure 9-2). They can be butter based, cheese, dressings and mayonnaise based, nut butters, mustard, cheese based such as cream cheese, puréed beans, and guacamole. The spread is sometimes referred to as the glue that holds a sandwich together. Some spreads are fat based and are used to keep wet fillings from making the bread or wrapper too soggy.
- Fillings are the stars of the sandwich and can be sliced, shredded, or ground meats, cheese, seafood, pork, both fresh and cured products, sausages, bound salads, fruits, and vegetables (Figure 9-3). Fillings give substance to the sandwich. A good standard proportion for a sandwich is 1/4 cup to 1/2 cup of salad-type filling, or 2 to 4 ounces of meat, cheese, or vegetarian-type of filling.
- Garnishes add eye appeal and another flavor profile to any sandwich. Garnishes are those extra ingredients that complement the filling such as lettuce, sliced avocado, sprouts, pickles, sliced onion, or tomato (Figure 9-4). In many operations the executive chef will post photographs of garnished sandwiches to make sure the staff maintains consistency, and that all types of sandwiches are served the same way.

>> Sandwich Presentation

Sandwiches are relatively simple and easy to prepare. To increase eye appeal and customer satisfaction, presentation is important. The size, shape, and pattern of china plates and platters used for serving help to turn simple sandwiches into exciting dishes.

COLD SANDWICH PRODUCTION

Most restaurants and hotels have a sandwich station. A typical scenario might be that sandwiches are prepared on refrigerated deli counters. These counters usually have a number of refrigerated wells to keep all ingredients handy. Over the counter are two shelves for plates, for extra supplies, and for the dupe printer. There is usually a rack to keep the dupes posted in the sequence they are received. When the sandwich is finished, the dupe is placed next to the order. When the order is picked up, all dupes are stored on a spindle.

Figure 9-2 Mayonnaise is just one type of sandwich spread that adds flavor and moisture to the sandwich.

Figure 9-3 All kinds of meats, cheeses, salads, and vegetables can be used to create delicious fillings for sandwiches.

Figure 9-4 Garnishes add interest to the sandwich. Sandwich toppers include cucumbers, tomatoes, and hard-boiled eggs.

The equipment needed is the sandwich spreader and a sharp French knife. On the table behind the counter is the toaster, meat slicer, and other equipment as needed. Depending on the volume of orders, meat is presliced or sliced to order.

In order to prepare sandwiches rapidly, all ingredients needed must be ready on hand. The French term **mise en place** surely applies to sandwich production; this term is frequently used in professional kitchens and refers to having ready and at hand all ingredients and equipment needed for a recipe or for executing an order.

>> Breads

Hundreds of varieties of breads, in many different sizes and shapes, are used in sandwich making. A sampling of the many types of breads includes bagels, baguettes, byali, brioche, ciabatta, focaccia, hero rolls, Kaiser rolls, lavosh, Parker House rolls, pita bread, pumpernickel bread, rye bread, and tortilla wraps, just to name a few. Breads are an important component of a restaurant's signature sandwich.

It is important to know the terminology and yield of basic sandwich loaves. Commercial sandwich loaves are classified by the dimension of the slice. The following chart shows the number of slices available from a 2-pound (900 g) loaf, depending on the thickness of each slice.

Type of Slice	Size of Slices		Yield
Average	1/2 inch	12 1/2 mm	32 slices
Thin	1/3 inch	7 1/2 mm	34 slices
Extra thin	1/4 inch	6 1/4 mm	40 slices

>> Spreads

Sandwich spreads are usually flavored butter, mayonnaise, mustard, or a cheese mixture. The fat in these spreads keeps the bread from getting soggy from the fillings. Spreads also add extra flavor to the sandwich. A variety of spread ideas are found in Unit 7. Sandwiches filled with salads, such as tuna salad, normally do not require a spread because the salad already contains a binding agent like mayonnaise.

>> Fillings

The most popular filling is a type of meat or cheese, but vegetables can also be used. The filling is usually the part of the sandwich that is spotlighted. The bread and spread should complement the filling. Sandwich fillings should not be wet. All ingredients should be as dry as possible when blended. Many ingredients shed liquid during storage and, in many cases, the sandwich fillings must be drained. Sandwich fillings are so easy to make rapidly that they should be made in small quantities just before service.

The amount of filling needed per sandwich varies greatly depending on price point and other factors such as the size of the sandwich. Generally, 3 to 4 ounces (85 to 112 g) are calculated for each sandwich.

A Boston lettuce leaf or shredded iceberg lettuce is frequently put on all sandwiches. The leaf provides crispness and flavor. As mentioned, sandwiches can be made with toasted or nontoasted bread, and the bread varieties are enormous. In busy operations, the meat is presliced, weighed, and the portions put on wax paper. These are called sandwich set-ups. This method helps to control the meat quantity.

Common sandwich filling ingredients include chicken, turkey, bologna, liverwurst, salami, capacole, corned beef brisket, lamb or beef (gyro), ham, liver, lobster (fresh, frozen, or canned), pastrami, cooked roast beef, shrimp (frozen or canned), surimi products, tongue, tuna fish (canned), and turkey products.

CHEESE

In sandwich making, any cheese that can be sliced or spread works well. Some favorites are Muenster, blue, gouda, provolone, and brie. Popular sandwich cheeses include processed cheese, Swiss cheese, cheddar cheese, Monterey Jack cheese, Muenster, blue, gouda, provolone, and brie.

FILLING RECIPES

Mixed fillings such as tuna and chicken salads have become popular in sandwiches. Unit 11 covers traditional, bound, salad-style fillings that can be used in salads or as sandwich fillings. The following filling recipes are for contemporary sandwiches. They can spark a menu and add excitement to any sandwich line-up.

Salmon is one of the richest sources of omega-3, which is a known aid in the prevention of heart problems and inflammatory problems such as arthritis. Many consumers are trying to find ways to include salmon in their regular diet. This recipe for salmon salad will make a great lunch on its own, a first course for dinner, or a great sandwich filling.

Pacific northwest salmon sandwich filling
Yield: 24 oz (680 g)

Ingredients	Amounts U.S.	Metric	Procedure
Soy sauce	2 fl oz	58 ml	Place soy sauce, sesame oil, and finely grated ginger into a small stainless steel bowl. Mix into a marinade.
Sesame oil	1 tbsp	15 ml	
Ginger, fresh, finely grated	1/2 oz	15 g	
Salmon	1 lb	454 g	Paint the salmon with the above marinade. Grill or pan sear the salmon. Cool and remove all bones and crumble into bite-sized pieces.
Celery	4 oz	114 g	Finely dice the celery and apple.
Apple, peeled and cored	4 oz	114 g	
Mayonnaise	4 fl oz	118 ml	Combine all the ingredients and chill. Store refrigerated.
Chives, chopped	1 tbsp	15 g	

NUTRITIONAL INFORMATION PER SERVING: 195 Calories; 15 g Fat (69.0% calories from fat); 12 g Protein; 3 g Carbohydrate; 1 g Dietary Fiber; 34 mg Cholesterol; 642 mg Sodium. Exchanges: 1 1/2 Lean Meat; 1/2 Vegetable; 0 Fruit; 1 1/2 Fat. Bound Sandwich.

Surimi is a Japanese imitation shellfish product that is made from fish protein with carbohydrate binders, soy extenders, and sometimes egg white or albumen, as well as the namesake material such as crab or lobster. It is processed, flavored, shaped, and colored to resemble crab, lobster, or scallop meat. The product is not as tasty as the real shellfish but it has a place in modern foodservice. It is economical and is often used in salad fillings. It is unfortunate that surimi is called crab or lobster in some establishments—this is not ethical, and it is wrong to call the resulting product "crabmeat salad." More consumers are accepting surimi as a delicious and low-cost alternative to higher-priced seafood.

surimi salad filling *Yield: 16 oz (454 g)*

Ingredients	Amounts U.S.	Metrics	Procedure
Surimi, frozen	8 oz	227 g	Defrost surimi and drain. Chop into small pieces.

Ingredients	Amounts U.S.	Metrics	Procedure
Celery	4 oz	113 g	Dice the celery.
Mayonnaise	4 fl oz	118 ml	Combine all the ingredients and chill. Store refrigerated.
Paprika	1 tsp	5 g	

NUTRITIONAL INFORMATION PER SERVING: 129 Calories; 12 g Fat (79.6% calories from fat); 5 g Protein; 2 g Carbohydrate; trace Dietary Fiber; 13 mg Cholesterol; 125 mg Sodium. Exchanges: 0 Grain (Starch); 1/2 Lean Meat; 0 Vegetable; 1 Fat; 0 Other Carbohydrates.

Any of the salad filling recipes given in Unit 11 can be used as the key ingredient in a bound salad type of sandwich. Notice that spread is usually not added when using a salad filling. In this sandwich, 4 ounces (113 g) of any bound salad filling is used with two slices of your choice of bread.

bound salad sandwich   *Yield: 1 sandwich*

| Ingredients | Amounts | | Procedure |
	U.S.	Metric	
Bread	2 slices	2 slices	Top one slice of bread with bound salad and the lettuce leaf. Cover with the second slice of bread.
Bound salad	4 oz	113 g	
Lettuce leaf	1 each	1 each	

Nutritional analysis depends on the type of bound salad and bread that are used for this recipe.

Ham and cheese sandwiches are a standard in the United States and are made by putting cheese and sliced ham between two pieces of bread. A variety of breads are used including rye, whole wheat, and white. The bread is sometimes toasted. American, cheddar, and Swiss are the types of firm cheese that are typically used in this type of sandwich. Common garnishes include lettuce and/or tomato. Spreads range from mayonnaise, butter, and mustard. Always use a good-quality ham. Check out the recipe for ham in Unit 16.

ham and cheese sandwich *Yield: 1 serving*

Ingredients	Amounts		Procedure
	U.S.	**Metric**	
Bread	2 slices	2 slices	Spread both slices of bread with butter or mayonnaise.
Butter, mayonnaise, or spread	1/2 fl oz	15 ml	

Lettuce leaf	1 each	1 each	Place lettuce leaf on top of one slice of bread, add ham and cheese, put second slice on top (spread down), secure with two toothpicks, if desired, and cut across diagonally.
Ham	2 oz	55 g	
American, cheddar, or Swiss cheese	2 oz	55 g	

NUTRITIONAL INFORMATION PER SERVING (MADE WITH WHOLE WHEAT, MAYONNAISE, AND CHEDDAR CHEESE): 598 Calories; 39 g Fat (58.0% calories from fat); 29 g Protein; 34 g Carbohydrate; 2 g Dietary Fiber; 97 mg Cholesterol; 1,514 mg Sodium. Exchanges: 2 Grain (Starch); 3 1/2 Lean Meat; 0 Vegetable; 4 1/2 Fat.

Roast beef sandwiches are frequently ordered on rye bread. Applying a suitable, fat-based spread is important to prevent any juice from the cooked beef from seeping into the bread and making it soggy. The meat must be completely trimmed of all fat and gristle and sliced thin.

roast beef sandwich *Yield: 1 sandwich*

Ingredients	Amounts		Procedure
	U.S.	**Metric**	
Bread	2 slices	2 slices	Slice roast beef on a meat slicer or by hand.
Spread of choice	1/2 fl oz	15 ml	Apply spread to both slices of bread. Take one slice of bread and top with the roast beef and lettuce leaf. Add the second slice of bread, spread side down.
Roast beef, cut thin	4 oz	113 g	
Lettuce leaf	1 each	1 each	

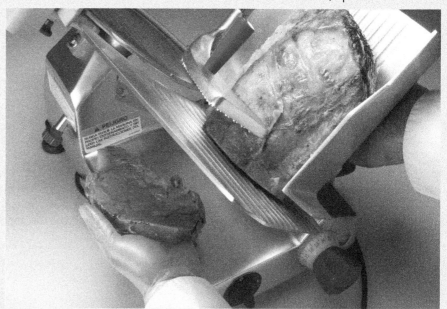

NUTRITIONAL INFORMATION PER SERVING: 488 Calories; 26 g Fat (49.2% calories from fat); 24 g Protein; 37 g Carbohydrate; 2 g Dietary Fiber; 69 mg Cholesterol; 501 mg Sodium. Exchanges: 2 1/2 Grain (Starch); 2 1/2 Lean Meat; 0 Vegetable; 3 Fat.

Turkey sandwiches can be ordered on a variety of breads such as raisin bread, whole wheat bread, or sunflower seed bread. In diner and coffee shop lingo, "high and dry" means the customer wants a plain sandwich without any spreads. With modern POS systems, this quaint and charming language has all but disappeared in the kitchen.

The club sandwich is a staple in most restaurants. A club is typically a sandwich made with three slices of bread. Double decker sandwiches are sometimes ordered by customers wanting to eat just two slices of bread.

Clubs are filled with turkey, crisp bacon, lettuce, and tomato. They are usually served on toast and the quality of bread used is important; cheap bread will dry out rapidly or will get soggy. Potato chips and cole slaw are often served with a club sandwich.

turkey breast club sandwich *Yield: 1 sandwich*

Ingredients	Amounts U.S.	Metric	Procedure
Bread, toasted	3 slices	3 slices	Spread mayonnaise on one side of all three slices of bread.
Mayonnaise	1 fl oz	30 ml	
Lettuce	1 leaf	1 leaf	Place lettuce on one slice of bread. Top with tomatoes and bacon. Put the second slice of toast on top, mayonnaise side down. Add a little mayonnaise to the top side of the second piece of toast and top with the turkey. Put the third slice of toast, mayonnaise side down, on top of the turkey. Plunge four toothpicks into the sandwich and cut into four wedges.
Tomatoes, sliced	3 slices	3 slices	
Bacon, crisp	3 slices	3 slices	
Turkey, sliced	3 oz	85 g	

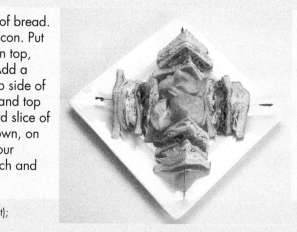

NUTRITIONAL INFORMATION PER SERVING: 764 Calories; 42 g Fat (48.9% calories from fat); 31 g Protein; 69 g Carbohydrate; 7 g Dietary Fiber; 98 mg Cholesterol; 2,080 mg Sodium. Exchanges: 3 1/2 Grain (Starch); 2 1/2 Lean Meat; 3 1/2 Vegetable; 5 Fat.

Vegetarian sandwiches are in demand. These simple sandwiches are made on toasted whole-wheat, low-fat bread. They are served open faced and consist of two slices of bread laid next to each other on a platter. A mustard spread can be substituted for the cream cheese.

sliced cucumber sandwich *Yield: 1 sandwich*

Ingredients	Amounts U.S.	Metric	Procedure
Whole-wheat, low-fat bread, toasted	2 slices	2 slices	Spread cream cheese on one slice of bread.
Cream cheese	1 oz	30 g	
Cucumbers, seedless	5 oz	142 g	Peel cucumber and slice thin. Place cucumber slices on top of cream cheese in an attractive pattern.
Paprika	Sprinkle	Sprinkle	Sprinkle lightly with paprika and a little salt. Top with the second slice of bread.
Salt	To taste	To taste	

NUTRITIONAL INFORMATION PER SERVING: 290 Calories; 13 g Fat (38.4% calories from fat); 10 g Protein; 37 g Carbohydrate; 6 g Dietary Fiber; 31 mg Cholesterol; 722 mg Sodium. Exchanges: 2 Grain (Starch); 1/2 Lean Meat; 1 Vegetable; 2 1/2 Fat.

This sandwich is an attractive, low-calorie luncheon sandwich. The peppery flavor of the arugula, which is sometimes called **roquette,** is a nice match to the sweet flavor of the ripe tomatoes.

arugula tomato sandwich   *Yield: 1 sandwich*

Ingredients	Amounts U.S.	Metric	Procedure
Crusty Italian loaf	1 large or 2 small slices	1 large or 2 small slices	Toast the bread and place on a platter. Sprinkle with oil, and put arugula on the bread with tomatoes on top. Sprinkle with pepper and vinegar.
Olive oil	As needed	As needed	
Arugula, coarse cut	8 fl oz	237 ml	
Tomatoes, thick slices	3 each	3 each	
Pepper	To taste	To taste	
Balsamic vinegar	As needed	As needed	

NUTRITIONAL INFORMATION PER SERVING: 367 Calories; 17 g Fat (39.7% calories from fat); 9 g Protein; 49 g Carbohydrate; 6 g Dietary Fiber; 0 mg Cholesterol; 389 mg Sodium. Exchanges: 2 Grain (Starch); 3 1/2 Vegetable; 0 Fruit; 3 Fat.

This all-American favorite is a standard in many operations. With the option of adding a few slices of avocado, this is sure to please. In kitchen slang, the bacon, lettuce, and tomato sandwich is called the "BLT." You can use the bacon recipe from Unit 16. Try adding 3 1/4-inch slices of peeled avocado.

bacon, lettuce, and tomato sandwich   *Yield: 1 sandwich*

Ingredients	Amounts U.S.	Metric	Procedure
Bread slices	2 each	2 each	Toast the bread and spread with mayonnaise. Put lettuce, then tomatoes, and, finally, the bacon on top of one slice of bread. Close the sandwich with the second slice of bread, mayonnaise side down. Insert toothpicks to hold the sandwich together. Cut diagonally in half.
Mayonnaise	1/2 fl oz	15 ml	
Boston lettuce	2 leaves	2 leaves	
Tomato slices	3 each	3 each	
Bacon slices, crisp	4 each	4 each	

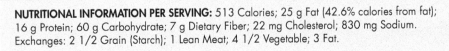

NUTRITIONAL INFORMATION PER SERVING: 513 Calories; 25 g Fat (42.6% calories from fat); 16 g Protein; 60 g Carbohydrate; 7 g Dietary Fiber; 22 mg Cholesterol; 830 mg Sodium. Exchanges: 2 1/2 Grain (Starch); 1 Lean Meat; 4 1/2 Vegetable; 3 Fat.

SUBS, HOAGIES, AND GRINDERS

The following sandwich is made in a long loaf of white Italian bread and is known under many names such as grinder, hoagie, and submarine. The term "hoagie" became popular during World War II when shipbuilders working on Hog Island would order these sandwiches to go. The deli workers called the sandwiches "hoagies" after the submarine and shipbuilders who ordered them. The ham and pastrami recipes are located in Unit 16.

submarine or hoagie sandwich   *Yield: 3 servings*

Ingredients	Amounts U.S.	Metric	Procedure
Italian or French bread, crusty	One 18-inch loaf	457 mm	Split the loaf of bread in half lengthwise.
Mayonnaise	2 fl oz	59 ml	Mix mayonnaise and Italian dressing together. Spread onto both sides of the loaf.
Italian vinaigrette dressing	2 fl oz	59 ml	
Tomato, thinly sliced	2 small	2 small	Layer the bottom half of the bread with tomato, meats, and cheeses.
Ham, thinly sliced	4 oz	113 g	
Salami, thinly sliced	4 oz	113 g	
Pastrami, thinly sliced	4 oz	113 g	
Cheddar cheese, thinly sliced	4 oz	113 g	
Provolone cheese, thinly sliced	4 oz	113 g	
Red onion, thinly sliced	1 small	1 small	Top with onions and lettuce. Cover with the top half of the bread. Cut into three servings.
Iceberg lettuce, shredded	1/4 head	1/4 head	

NUTRITIONAL INFORMATION PER SERVING:
618 Calories; 38 g Fat (55.2% calories from fat);
26 g Protein; 43 g Carbohydrate; 3 g Dietary Fiber;
77 mg Cholesterol; 1,481 mg Sodium. Exchanges:
2 1/2 Grain (Starch); 2 1/2 Lean Meat; 1/2 Vegetable;
5 Fat; 0 Other Carbohydrates.

>> Hot and Grilled Sandwiches

Many favorite sandwiches are served cold, but there are many that are best served hot. They can be baked, grilled, or pan-fried to perfection. Food flavors intensify when heated. There is something very comforting about melted cheese oozing out the sides of the sandwich.

A good grilled cheese sandwich is deceptively hard to produce correctly. It's a test of the cook's skill—the bread should be toasted golden brown, the cheese melting through and through. Most types of cheese will work, although American cheese melts more uniformly. This sandwich could be made open-faced or closed. Customers often order the sandwich with tomatoes or with bacon. In coffee shop or diner shorthand, the server might write AC, noting that the sandwich is to be made with American cheese. When written "full house" it means a grilled cheese, bacon, and tomato sandwich.

When making an open-faced grilled cheese sandwich with tomatoes, the sandwich should first be put under the salamander or top broiler without the tomato slices; otherwise, the cheese will not melt under the tomato. When the cheese is melted, the tomato slices are put on top and the sandwich finished in the oven.

grilled cheese sandwich   *Yield: 1 sandwich*

Ingredients	Amounts U.S.	Metric	Procedure
White bread	2 slices	2 slices	Place cheese on one slice of bread. Brush the outsides of both slices of bread with butter and cook on a griddle. The cheese should melt in the center. Add tomato slices cooked separately or cooked bacon, if desired.
Butter	As needed	As needed	
Cheese, sliced	4 oz	113 g	

NUTRITIONAL INFORMATION PER SERVING: 728 Calories; 50 g Fat (61.4% calories from fat); 31 g Protein; 39 g Carbohydrate; 2 g Dietary Fiber; 139 mg Cholesterol; 2,142 mg Sodium. Exchanges: 2 1/2 Grain (Starch); 3 1/2 Lean Meat; 7 1/2 Fat.

Bruschetta is a well-known Italian sandwich and is made in many versions. Basically it is bread topped with fresh, diced tomatoes. When good quality tomatoes are unavailable, sun-dried tomatoes will make an acceptable substitution.

bruschetta *Yield: 1 sandwich*

Ingredients	Amounts		Procedure
	U.S.	Metric	
Crusty Italian bread	2 slices	2 slices	Toast the bread on one side.
Tomatoes, peeled and seeded	4 oz	113 g	Put the toasted side down and add all the ingredients on top. Place in a hot oven for a few minutes to heat the sandwich.
Sun-dried tomatoes in oil	2 oz	57 g	
Parmesan cheese, grated	1 oz	28 g	
Thyme, fresh	1 sprig	1 sprig	
Olive oil	Drizzle	Drizzle	

NUTRITIONAL INFORMATION PER SERVING: 248 Calories; 9 g Fat (32.6% calories from fat); 10 g Protein; 34 g Carbohydrate; 5 g Dietary Fiber; 8 mg Cholesterol; 503 mg Sodium. Exchanges: 2 Grain (Starch); 1/2 Lean Meat; 1 Vegetable; 1 1/2 Fat.

This sandwich was once a luncheon favorite at country clubs and white-glove luncheon clubs. It is making a retro food comeback today. A similar sandwich is called the Croque Madame, which is the same as the Croque Monsieur except that sliced turkey is used in place of the ham. Many restaurants also omit the cheese, although the turkey with cheese tastes much better. For an in-house ham, check out the recipe in Unit 16.

croque monsieur *Yield: 1 sandwich*

Ingredients	Amounts		Procedure
	U.S.	**Metric**	
White bread	2 slices	2 slices	Spread mustard on both slices of bread. Place ham and cheese on one slice of bread. Cover with the second slice. Press down.
Mustard	1/2 fl oz	15 ml	
Ham, large slice	2 oz	57 g	
Swiss cheese, large slice	2 oz	57 g	
Egg, large	1 each	1 each	Combine the egg with cream. Dredge the sandwich through the egg and cream mixture.
Heavy cream	1 fl oz	30 ml	

Butter	As needed	As needed	Griddle fry with butter until both sides of the sandwich are brown and the cheese is melted.

NUTRITIONAL INFORMATION PER SERVING: 682 Calories; 52 g Fat (68.8% calories from fat); 25 g Protein; 28 g Carbohydrate; 1 g Dietary Fiber; 361 mg Cholesterol; 1,110 mg Sodium. Exchanges: 1 1/2 Grain (Starch); 2 1/2 Lean Meat; 0 Nonfat Milk; 8 1/2 Fat; 0 Other Carbohydrates.

This sandwich changes names when it crosses state lines; it is called grinder in some places and hoagie in others. The filling changes along with the name—in some places, it is tomato sauce and grilled Italian sausages, topped with mozzarella cheese; in other places, a breaded veal cutlet, tomato sauce, and Parmesan cheese; and in still other places, a breaded eggplant slice with tomato sauce. All of these sandwiches could be made in the hot kitchen, but in other places they are produced in the pantry. As was previously mentioned, the recipe for preparing ham in-house is located in Unit 16.

Italian grinder   *Yield: Serves 4*

Ingredients	Amounts U.S.	Metric	Procedure
Green bell pepper, seeded and sliced into thin rings	1 each	1 each	Sauté pepper, onions, and garlic in olive oil until tender.
Onions, diced	2 oz	57 g	
Garlic, minced	1 clove	1 clove	
Olive oil	1 fl oz	30 ml	
French bread	12-inch loaf	304 1/2 mm loaf	Cut bread in half lengthwise.
Ham, thinly sliced	6 oz	170 g	Layer the ham, green pepper mixture, fresh basil, and cheese on the bottom half of the bread. Drizzle olive oil on top of the ingredients. Cover with the top half of the bread and wrap the entire loaf in aluminum foil. Bake in a 350°F (177°C) oven for 10 to 15 minutes until the cheese is melted. Remove foil and slice into four servings.
Basil, fresh	4 leaves	4 leaves	
Mozzarella cheese	4 oz	113 g	
Olive oil	As needed	As needed	

NUTRITIONAL INFORMATION PER SERVING: 558 Calories; 22 g Fat (35.5% calories from fat); 24 g Protein; 65 g Carbohydrate; 5 g Dietary Fiber; 50 mg Cholesterol; 1,370 mg Sodium. Exchanges: 4 Grain (Starch); 2 Lean Meat; 1/2 Vegetable; 3 Fat.

This New Orleans specialty is popular with tourists and locals. It is said to be the New Orleans version of the hoagie, submarine, grinder, or hero sandwich. Benny and Clovis Martin first served it in the late 1920s. Fried oysters, roast beef, and shrimp are the three common types of filling for a Po' Boy, but actually any meat or seafood can be used. In New Orleans, Po' Boys are often served with gravy and garnished with lettuce, tomato, and pickles.

Po' Boy *Yield: 1 sandwich*

Ingredients	Amounts U.S.	Metric	Procedure
French bread	6-inch loaf	152 mm loaf	Split the French bread and scoop out the center to create a small "boat." Fill with lettuce and top with oysters. Spread tartar sauce on the bread. Close the sandwich.
Iceberg lettuce, shredded	2 oz	59 g	
Oysters, breaded and fried	6 each	6 each	
Tartar sauce	2 fl oz	59 ml	

NUTRITIONAL INFORMATION PER SERVING: 716 Calories; 46 g Fat (57.2% calories from fat); 10 g Protein; 67 g Carbohydrate; 3 Dietary Fiber; 46 mg Cholesterol; 1,176 mg Sodium. Exchanges: 4 Grain (Starch); 1/2 Vegetable; 1/2 Fruit; 9 Fat.

This is an example of a typical, old-fashioned sandwich. Homestyle sandwiches have made a comeback and are called "comfort food." The key is to start with a high-quality meat loaf.

meat loaf on kaiser roll   *Yield: 1 sandwich*

Ingredients	Amounts U.S.	Metric	Procedure
Kaiser roll, large	1 each	1 each	Split the Kaiser roll and toast. Top with hot meat loaf. Serve the sandwich open faced with lettuce, tomato, and cole slaw on the side.
Meat loaf, heated and sliced	6 oz	170 g	
Lettuce leaf	1 each	1 each	
Tomato slices	2 each	2 each	
Cole slaw	4 oz	113 g	

NUTRITIONAL INFORMATION PER SERVING: 733 Calories; 22 g Fat (26.3% calories from fat); 27 g Protein; 112 g Carbohydrate; 7 g Dietary Fiber; 49 mg Cholesterol; 1,393 mg Sodium. Exchanges: 5 1/2 Grain (Starch); 1 Lean Meat; 2 1/2 Vegetable; 3 1/2 Fat; 1 Other Carbohydrates.

Grilled vegetables are usually prepared just ahead of service at the broiler station. The most suitable vegetables are zucchini, yellow squash, mushrooms, eggplant, tomato slices, and cooked asparagus spears. This sandwich is frequently presented as open face.

grilled vegetable sandwich *Yield: 1 sandwich*

Ingredients	Amounts U.S.	Metric	Procedure
Crusty Italian loaf	2 slices	2 slices	Toast the bread and place on a plate.
Grilled vegetable assortment	6 oz	170 g	Arrange picturesque vegetables on top.

Olive oil	1/2 fl oz	15 ml	Sprinkle with oil and vinegar.
Balsamic vinegar	1/2 fl oz	15 ml	

NUTRITIONAL INFORMATION PER SERVING: 230 Calories; 15 g Fat (57.8% calories from fat); 4 g Protein; 21 g Carbohydrate; 1 g Dietary Fiber; 0 mg Cholesterol; 234 mg Sodium. Exchanges: 1 1/2 Grain (Starch); 0 Fruit; 3 Fat.

This old-fashioned sandwich probably originated in Colorado where it is called the Denver omelet sandwich. In some operations, the pantry prepares the whole sandwich; in others, the hot kitchen makes the omelet. Unit 16 features a recipe for ham that would be a delicious addition to the following sandwich.

western omelet sandwich *Yield: 1 sandwich*

Ingredients	Amounts		Procedure
	U.S.	Metric	
Butter or oil	As needed	As needed	Sauté the scallions, peppers, and ham in the butter or oil.
Scallions, chopped	1/2 oz	15 g	
Green peppers, diced	1/2 oz	15 g	
Ham, small dice	1 oz	30 g	
Egg	1 each	1 each	Break the egg in a bowl and whisk. Pour the egg mixture over the vegetables and ham. Cook over low heat to set, flip over, and cook on the other side.
White bread	2 slices	2 slices	Toast the bread and put the omelet on top of one slice. Put the second slice on top and cut across diagonally.

NUTRITIONAL INFORMATION PER SERVING: 347 Calories; 21 g Fat (55.3% calories from fat); 12 g Protein; 26 g Carbohydrate; 1 g Dietary Fiber; 217 mg Cholesterol; 451 mg Sodium. Exchanges: 1 1/2 Grain (Starch); 1 Lean Meat; 0 Vegetable; 3 1/2 Fat.

Panini is the Italian term for "sandwiches." The term is based on the Latin word for bread and has become trendy during the last years. Paninis can be filled with any filling, but sliced meats and cheese are the most popular. Panini sandwiches are grilled on a panini grill, which has grooves. When the sandwich is placed in the grill, the grooves press down on the sandwich, leaving the grill marks.

mozzarella, napoli salami, and sun-dried tomato panini *Yield: 1 sandwich*

Ingredients	Amounts U.S.	Metric	Procedure
Hero loaf	1 each	1 each	Split the loaf in half. Sprinkle the bottom half of the loaf with olive oil. Place the salami, tomatoes, and oregano evenly on the loaf. Put cheese on top and make sure it is not hanging over the bread. Cover with the second half of the loaf. Place on the panini grill and toast until the cheese is melted. Cut in half and place on a plate.
Olive oil	Sprinkle	Sprinkle	
Napoli salami, sliced	3 oz	85 g	
Sun-dried tomatoes in oil, chopped	1 oz	30 g	
Oregano leaves, dried	1/4 tsp	7 g	
Mozzarella, sliced	2 oz	57 g	

NUTRITIONAL INFORMATION PER SERVING: 819 Calories; 38 g Fat (41.6% calories from fat); 37 g Protein; 82 g Carbohydrate; 5 g Dietary Fiber; 106 mg Cholesterol; 1,939 mg Sodium. Exchanges: 5 Grain (Starch); 3 1/2 Lean Meat; 5 1/2 Fat.

Here's another panini recipe. The fresh basil truly complements the flavor of the smoked provolone cheese and makes a memorable sandwich favorite. Use the Fresh Pesto Sauce recipe found in Unit 16. In some operations one boneless, skinless chicken breast, 5 to 6 ounces (140 to 170 g) is used. Normally the broiler cook grills a number of chicken breasts just before service time. They will be used in the pantry when ordered. They are normally sliced on a bias into three or four slices.

chicken pesto ciabatta panini   *Yield: 6 sandwiches*

Ingredients	Amounts U.S.	Metric	Procedure
Chicken breasts, boneless	6 each	6 each	Marinate the chicken breasts in the olive oil, basil, and lemon juice for 1 hour.
Olive oil	2 fl oz	59 ml	
Basil, fresh, minced fine	1 tbsp	15 g	
Lemon juice	2 tsp	20 ml	
Salt	To taste	To taste	Drain and season with the salt and pepper. Grill the chicken skin side down to mark. Turn over and grill until the chicken is done with an internal temperature of 165°F (74°C).
Pepper	To taste	To taste	
Smoked provolone cheese	6, 1-oz slices	6, 30 g slices	Place a slice of cheese on top of each chicken breast.
Ciabatta rolls, split	6 each	6 each	Split and toast the ciabatta.
Fresh basil pesto sauce	2 oz	57 g	Dress the ciabatta with the pesto and mayonnaise. Place the grilled chicken breast and cheese on top of the ciabatta.
Mayonnaise	2 fl oz	59 ml	
Tomato, sliced	6 slices	6 slices	Garnish the sandwich with a tomato slice and lettuce. Cover with the top of the ciabatta. Place in a hot panini grill and cook until the cheese melts, about 2 to 3 minutes.
Romaine lettuce leaves, chiffonade	6 each	6 each	

NUTRITIONAL INFORMATION PER SERVING: 784 Calories; 46 g Fat (52.3% calories from fat); 66 g Protein; 27 g Carbohydrate; 3 g Dietary Fiber; 173 mg Cholesterol; 839 mg Sodium. Exchanges: 1 1/2 Grain (Starch); 8 1/2 Lean Meat; 1 Vegetable; 0 Fruit; 5 Fat; 0 Other Carbohydrates.

This sandwich is basically street food in Greek neighborhoods. The term **gyro** refers to meat that has been cooked on a vertical spit. In Greek, *gyro* means to "turn." The meat is typically either lamb or beef. It is listed here as an interesting example of a completely different type of sandwich.

pita pockets with gyro *Yield: 1 sandwich*

Ingredients	Amounts		Procedure
	U.S.	Metric	
Pita bread	1 each	1 each	Open the pita bread pocket and place the meat in the bottom. Top with onions, tomatoes, and lettuce. Sprinkle oil, vinegar, hot sauce. and oregano on top.
Gyro meat, thinly sliced	4 oz	113 g	
Onions, diced	1 oz	30 g	
Tomatoes, diced	1 oz	30 g	
Lettuce, shredded	1 oz	30 g	
Olive oil	Sprinkle	Sprinkle	
Vinegar	Sprinkle	Sprinkle	
Hot sauce	Dash	Dash	
Oregano	Sprinkle	Sprinkle	

NUTRITIONAL INFORMATION PER SERVING: 413 Calories; 20 g Fat (43.9% calories from fat); 22 g Protein; 36 g Carbohydrate; 2 g Dietary Fiber; 66 mg Cholesterol; 403 mg Sodium. Exchanges: 2 Grain (Starch); 2 Lean Meat; 1/2 Vegetable; 2 1/2 Fat; 0 Other Carbohydrates.

Deli is the abbreviation for delicatessen sandwich stores/restaurants, which are popular in New York City. This European concept was brought over by German and Jewish immigrants from Central and Eastern Europe.

New York delis are famous and tradition reigns. The menu rarely changes and, in some delis, deviations are not permitted. Staples are corned beef and pastrami sandwiches served on freshly sliced rye bread and accompanied with a fresh pickle and mustard. Anything else is superfluous and considered with scorn. There is a story that has been circulating for some time about a tourist who walked into a delicatessen and ordered a corned beef sandwich on white toast with mayonnaise. The counterman fainted and had to be revived with a bottle of "two cents plain," which is old-fashioned New York City slang for soda water or seltzer. A hot corned beef sandwich is prepared in the same manner, just substitute well-trimmed, steaming hot, paper-thin corned beef for the pastrami. To prepare pastrami in-house, use the recipe found in Unit 16.

hot pastrami sandwich *Yield: 1 sandwich*

Ingredients	Amounts		Procedure
	U.S.	**Metric**	
Rye bread, soft, freshly sliced	2 slices	2 slices	To build the sandwich, place one slice of bread on a plate. Slice hot pastrami paper thin and heap on the center of the bread.
			Close the sandwich and insert a toothpick. Cut once in half.
Hot pastrami, sliced paper thin (Pastrami is usually kept hot in the steam table until needed. It is then sliced paper thin and piled high on the sandwich.)	5 oz	141 g	

NUTRITIONAL INFORMATION PER SERVING: 660 Calories; 43 g Fat (60.0% calories from fat); 30 g Protein; 35 g Carbohydrate; 4 g Dietary Fiber; 132 mg Cholesterol; 2,162 mg Sodium. Exchanges: 2 Grain (Starch); 3 1/2 Lean Meat; 6 1/2 Fat; 1/2 Other Carbohydrates.

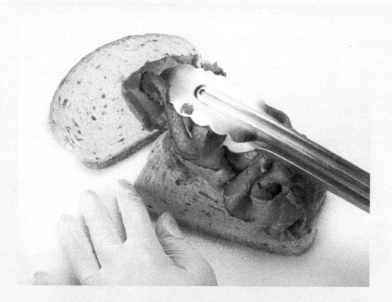 

There are several stories floating around about the origin of the Reuben. The most widely accepted story talks about a group of gentlemen in the 1920s who liked to play poker late into the evenings at the Blackstone Hotel in Omaha, Nebraska. One of the regulars was Reuben Kulakofsky. When the men got hungry, they would request fixings and make their own sandwiches. Everyone's favorite was the sandwich that Reuben created. The owner of the Blackstone Hotel liked Reuben's sandwich so much that he added it to his menu and named it after his customer. There are, however, many Reuben diehards from New York who would dispute this story and place the origin of the Reuben sandwich squarely in the realm of the old Jewish delicatessens from the late 1800s. In any event, this sandwich is a favorite of anyone who likes a large, hearty, hot sandwich.

Traditionally, a Reuben sandwich consists of sour dough pumpernickel bread, sauerkraut, Swiss cheese, and thinly sliced, kosher-style corned beef. It is topped with Russian dressing and the bread is buttered and grilled. Make sure the cheese is melted—it might be necessary to put the sandwich under the salamander or, as a last resort, in the microwave oven. To make corned beef, refer to the recipe in Unit 16.

grilled reuben sandwich *Yield: 1 sandwich*

Ingredients	Amounts		Procedure
	U.S.	Metric	
Rye bread or soft pumpernickel	2 slices	2 slices	Build the sandwich by spreading dressing on both pieces of bread. Place sauerkraut, cheese, and corned beef on one slice. Put the second slice of bread on top, dressing side down. Grill on the griddle until brown. Make sure the cheese is melted.
Russian dressing	1 fl oz	30 ml	
Sauerkraut, slightly chopped	2 oz	57 g	
Swiss cheese	2 oz	57 g	
Corned beef, sliced	4 oz	113 g	
Butter or oil	As needed	As needed	

NUTRITIONAL INFORMATION PER SERVING: 624 Calories; 38 g Fat (54.6% calories from fat); 31 g Protein; 40 g Carbohydrate; 5 g Dietary Fiber; 90 mg Cholesterol; 1,247 mg Sodium. Exchanges: 2 Grain (Starch); 3 Lean Meat; 1/2 Vegetable; 1/2 Fruit; 5 1/2 Fat.

Chopped liver is a staple in Jewish delicatessens and is also served as a spread on buffets. Chicken, beef, or veal liver can be used. If it is truly kosher, it must come from an animal slaughtered under rabbinical supervision.

chopped liver sandwich *Yield: 12 sandwiches 3 lbs (1.361 kg)*

Ingredients	Amounts U.S.	Metric	Procedure
Liver	2 lbs	907 g	Wash the liver in hot water, and trim off any skin and nerves. Cut the liver in pieces and place in a deep roasting pan.
Chicken fat, rendered	8 fl oz	237 ml	Add all the other ingredients, except the bagel or bun. Slow roast at least 1 hour until well done and the onions are soft. Coarsely chop the mixture, as it should be grainy.
Onions, peeled	8 oz	227 g	
Eggs, hard-boiled	4 each	4 each	
Salt	To taste	To taste	
Pepper	To taste	To taste	
Marjoram, dry	1/2 tsp	5 g	
Bagel or bun, toasted	12 each	12 each	Serve the chopped liver mixture on a toasted bagel or bun.

NUTRITIONAL INFORMATION PER SERVING: 522 Calories; 30 g Fat (51.4% calories from fat); 13 g Protein; 50 g Carbohydrate; 3 g Dietary Fiber; 128 mg Cholesterol; 528 mg Sodium. Exchanges: 3 Grain (Starch); 1/2 Lean Meat; 1/2 Vegetable; 5 1/2 Fat.

A beef on weck is a tasty roast beef sandwich that is served on a coarse salt-topped Kaiser roll called a kummelweck. This sandwich originated in Buffalo, New York, and is served with lots of horseradish sauce and beef au jus. The Horseradish Cream Sauce given in Unit 15 works well with this sandwich.

beef on weck *Yield: 1 sandwich*

Ingredients	Amounts U.S.	Metric	Procedure
Kummelweck or Kaiser roll	1 each	1 each	Slice the roll and spread with horseradish sauce and mayonnaise. Top with sliced roast beef. Serve with plenty of au jus on the side. This sandwich is traditionally served with kosher pickle slices.
Horseradish sauce	1 tbsp	15 ml	
Mayonnaise	1 tbsp	15 ml	
Roast beef, sliced paper thin	4 oz	113 g	
Kosher pickle slice, on side	2 each	2 each	
Beef au jus, on side	2 fl oz	59 ml	

NUTRITIONAL INFORMATION PER SERVING: 390 Calories; 19 g Fat (44.2% calories from fat); 22 g Protein; 33 g Carbohydrate; 3 g Dietary Fiber; 51 mg Cholesterol; 1,710 mg Sodium. Exchanges: 2 Grain (Starch); 2 1/2 Lean Meat; 1/2 Vegetable; 2 Fat; 0 Other Carbohydrates.

Salmon is one of the most versatile fish on the market. It can be served hot or cold, as the center of the plate, baked in pastry, and even made into mousse. This delicious sandwich features a salmon fillet. Other fish such as red snapper, escolar, or halibut may be used in place of the salmon, if desired. See Unit 16 for the recipe for the Lime Chipotle Aioli.

grilled salmon with lime chipotle aioli sandwich
Yield: 1 sandwich

Ingredients	Amounts U.S.	Metric	Procedure
Salmon fillet	5 oz	142 g	Marinate the salmon in olive oil, lime juice, zest, chili powder, garlic, and salt and pepper for at least 30 minutes. Drain and cook on a hot grill or under a salamander. Grill to medium rare.
Olive oil	1 tbsp	15 ml	
Lime juice	1 tsp	5 ml	
Lime zest	1 tsp	5 g	
Chili powder	1 tbsp	15 ml	
Garlic, minced	1 clove	1 clove	
Salt	To taste	To taste	
Pepper	To taste	To taste	
Baguette, cut into 6-in lengths	1 each	1 each	Split and toast the baguette, and spread with lime chipotle aioli. Place the cooked salmon on the baguette and serve open-faced with lettuce and tomato slices.
Lime chipotle aioli	1 tbsp	15 ml	
Butter lettuce	1 leaf	1 leaf	
Tomatoes, sliced	2 slices	2 slices	

NUTRITIONAL INFORMATION PER SERVING: 672 Calories; 34 g Fat (44.9% calories from fat); 38 g Protein; 57 g Carbohydrate; 8 g Dietary Fiber; 79 mg Cholesterol; 996 mg Sodium. Exchanges: 3 Grain (Starch); 4 Lean Meat; 2 1/2 Vegetable; 0 Fruit; 4 1/2 Fat.

The muffaletta is said to have originated in the late 1800s in New Orleans at the Central Grocery store. Locals now call the sandwich the "muff." It is made with a tasty olive and caper spread. The muffaletta bun is a round Italian-style loaf similar to focaccia and is a suitable substitute if round Italian loaves are unavailable.

This is a large, round sandwich that can serve up to six people when cut into wedges. The spread recipe may also be added to 1 pound of cream cheese for a dip or spread. The ham recipe found in Unit 16 can work for a muffaletta sandwich.

muffaletta sandwich *Yield: 6 portions per 10-inch sandwich*

Ingredients	Amounts U.S.	Metric	Procedure
Olive Spread			
Black olives, coarsely chopped	4 oz	113 g	Mix the olives, capers, onion, celery, garlic, and spices.
Pimiento stuffed green olives, coarsely chopped	4 oz	113 g	
Capers, drained and chopped	1 oz	28 g	
Yellow onion, grated	1 oz	28 g	
Celery, fine diced	1 oz	28 g	
Garlic, mashed and finely chopped	2 cloves	2 cloves	
Celery seed	1/2 tsp	5 g	
Oregano, dried leaf	2 tsp	20 g	
Parsley, fresh, chopped fine	2 tsp	20 g	
Pepper, freshly cracked fine	1 tsp	10 g	
Olive oil	4 fl oz	118 ml	Add the oil, vinegar, and pepper sauce. Stir and let sit covered in the refrigerator to meld the flavors for at least 1 hour. Use as the spread for muffalata sandwiches.
Red wine vinegar	1 fl oz	30 ml	
Tabasco or Louisiana-style chili sauce	1/2 tsp	5 g	
For the Sandwich			
Muffaletta bun, Italian bread, or focaccia	1, 10-in round	1, 25-cm round	Split the bread in half horizontally and remove the top half.
Extra virgin olive oil	1 fl oz	30 ml	Drizzle olive oil over both the top and bottom slices of the bread.
Genoa salami, sliced thin	4 oz	113 g	Place meats and cheeses on the bottom half of the bread. Top with the olive spread (recipe above). Replace the top half of the bread, then cut the sandwich into six equal pieces.
Smoked ham, sliced thin	4 oz	113 g	
Mortadella, sliced thin	4 oz	113 g	
Mozzarella cheese, sliced thin	2 oz	57 g	
Provolone cheese, sliced thin	2 oz	57 g	

NUTRITIONAL INFORMATION PER SERVING: 641 Calories; 39 g Fat (55.2% calories from fat); 18 g Protein; 54 g Carbohydrate; 4 g Dietary Fiber; 38 mg Cholesterol; 774 mg Sodium. Exchanges: 3 1/2 Grain (Starch); 1 1/2 Lean Meat; 1/2 Vegetable; 0 Fruit; 7 Fat; 0 Other Carbohydrates.

A hot meatball sandwich with tangy red sauce and a blend of melted Italian cheeses is the epitome of a hearty sandwich that's a meal in itself.

hot meatball sandwich   Yield: 4 sandwiches

Ingredients	U.S.	Metric	Procedure
Meatballs			
Ground beef, lean	1 lb	450 g	Mix the ingredients together. Shape the mixture into 16 meatballs. Bake at 350°F (177°C) for 25–30 minutes until cooked through.
Italian breadcrumbs	4 oz	113 g	
Eggs	2 each	2 each	
Onion, chopped	1 medium	1 medium	
Garlic, minced	1 clove	1 clove	
Parmesan cheese, grated	2 oz	57 g	
Salt	1 tsp	5 g	
Parsley, chopped	1 oz	30 g	
Oregano, crushed	1 tsp	5 g	
Pepper	Dash	Dash	
Sauce			
Onion, chopped	2 oz	57 g	Sauté onion and garlic in the olive oil and cook until tender.
Garlic, minced	1 clove	1 clove	
Olive oil	1 tbsp	15 ml	
Whole tomatoes, crushed	16 fl oz	473 ml	Stir in the remaining ingredients and bring to a boil. Reduce to a simmer and let it cook for 1 hour.
Tomato sauce	16 fl oz	473 ml	
Tomato paste	4 fl oz	118 ml	
Salt	To taste	To taste	
Pepper	To taste	To taste	
Basil, dried	To taste	To taste	
Marjoram	To taste	To taste	
Oregano	To taste	To taste	
To Assemble Sandwich			
Italian sandwich rolls	4, 6-in rolls	4, 15-cm rolls	Split the rolls and put four meatballs in each roll. Spoon an ample amount of sauce over the meatballs. (Beware of adding too much sauce—the sandwiches will become too soggy.)
Italian meatballs from above recipe	16 each	16 each	
Italian cheese blend, shredded	4 oz	113 g	Top with cheese. Wrap the rolls in aluminum foil and bake at 350°F (175°C) until the cheese melts.

NUTRITIONAL INFORMATION PER SERVING: 687 Calories; 37 g Fat (47.8% calories from fat); 41 g Protein; 49 g Carbohydrate; 7 g Dietary Fiber; 214 mg Cholesterol; 2,476 mg Sodium. Exchanges: 1 1/2 Grain (Starch); 4 1/2 Lean Meat; 4 Vegetable; 4 1/2 Fat.

>> Summary

Sandwiches are popular and are very important in most cold kitchen and pantry operations. In this unit, students were exposed to many different hot and cold sandwiches, including traditional New York deli sandwiches and trendy panini.

Sandwich station set-up and operations were also discussed. This type of work is invaluable because knowledgeable sandwich makers will always be in demand.

>> Review Questions

TRUE/FALSE

1. À la minute means preparing food to order.
2. John Montague was a gambler.
3. Dupes are usually printed out directly at the station.
4. The panini press has grooves.
5. Sauerkraut is an important ingredient in a Reuben sandwich.
6. The term "sandwich" originated in Colorado.
7. Pita bread has a pocket.
8. Gyro is a Greek sausage.
9. Muffalata buns are always round.
10. A kummelweck is a type of olive spread.

MULTIPLE CHOICE

11. Deli is the abbreviation for
    a. delicatessen store/restaurant.
    b. delicious food.
    c. delicate food.
    d. fluffy chocolate pastry.
12. _____ is considered to be the "star" of any sandwich.
    a. Bread
    b. Spread
    c. Filling
    d. Garnish
13. Surimi is
    a. a spread made with Japanese horseradish.
    b. usually served with chutney.
    c. an Indian specialty sandwich.
    d. Japanese imitation crab.
14. The New Orleans version of a hoagie sandwich is called a
    a. grinder.
    b. Po' Boy.
    c. submarine.
    d. hero.

FILL IN THE ANSWERS

15. Delicatessen restaurants are of _____ origin.
16. The term "sandwich" is defined as _____.
17. Dupes are _____.
18. Triple-decker sandwiches are (provide a description) _____.
19. A gyro sandwich is (provide a description)_____.
20. Panini is what type of sandwich?_____.

>> Learning Objectives

After you have finished reading this unit, you should be able to:

- Describe a number of classic cold soup recipes.
- Make cold consommé and other clear soups.
- Make basic cold vegetable soups to include a purée.
- Prepare basic cold fruit soups.
- Make basic cold dairy soups.
- Make an assortment of garnishes for cold soups.
- Fold napkins into artichoke shape for cold soup service.

>> Key Terms

aesthetic garnishes	chiffonade	consommé	kaltschale
agar agar	(*chef-fon-nahd*)	(*kwang-soh-may*)	(*KAHLT-shaaler*)
alginates	component garnishes	gazpacho	raft
borscht (*BOHR-sh*)	concassé	(*gahz-PAH-choh*)	vichyssoise
	(*kon-kaas-SAY*)		(*VEE-shee-swahz*)

The soup is served. Before you sits a bowl of glistening, jewel-like liquid, the color of ruby gemstones, shiny and dark, cool and refreshing—the perfect addition to a summer luncheon menu. Cold soups have a special place in the cold kitchen. They are made from the freshest of fruits and vegetables and the clearest of stocks. The flavors must be intense as these soups are served chilled and, in some cases, nearly frozen. A gelled consommé is the true test of a cold kitchen chef. This delicacy must have true color and flavor, be firm and yet tender, instantly melting the second it hits the warmth of the tongue. In this unit, we will be covering a variety of cold soups, from crystal clear consommés to frosty fruit-based soups.

We find cold soups in many cultures. They are refreshing, nourishing, and in many cases, low in calories. Cold soups, in general, have low material cost, keep refrigerated for a few days, and are easy to make. Cold soups can be used on the menu as a tantalizing appetizer, a palate refresher, a glistening first course, a cooling summer or tangy winter entrée, or as a dessert soup.

Cold soups may consist of a base ingredient that can be prepared ahead of time. With the addition of new flavors, many varieties can be created. Vichysoisse is a classic example. With the addition of avocado, a creamy version of avocado soup is possible. Add curry powder to the same soup, and you have a curried version.

Cold soups are becoming more common with the availability of new techniques and thickening agents such as agar agar and starch gels. **Agar agar** comes from red algae and is used as a thickener in Asian foods and many types of processed foods including baked goods, jellies, custards and soups.

Most cold soups are easy to make, and can be garnished and presented in new and exciting ways. As with all cold foods, cold soups should be well flavored because of the blunting power of cold on the tongue. In other words, our taste buds don't pick up flavors that are cold as easily as they do warm flavors. Some compensation must be made for that phenomenon. Care must be taken, however, to avoid overpowering the palate. A cold soup portion size is usually 6 fluid ounces (180 ml) or less.

Soups served cold or chilled can be classified into the following groups:

- **Clear Soups**

Clear soups are those based on a clarified stock or clear fruit juice. These types of soups can be jelled naturally due to the high gelatin content of the base meat and bones. Powdered or sheet gelatin is also used to gel this type of soup. For a vegetarian- or fruit-based soup, agar agar and other seaweed-based gels are used. **Alginates** are also becoming more popular for various gel-type soups and soup garnishes; these agents are derived from carageenan and other seaweeds. They are flavorless and useful for many other types of gel applications. With the addition of citric acid and other ingredients, fruit "caviars" can be made and used as intriguing garnishes. For more on this procedure, see Unit 20, decorating in the cold kitchen.

- **Dairy or Cream Soups**

These soups are made with dairy products such as milk, cream, sour cream, or yogurt. They can be made with a roux base such as a velouté or béchamel, or thickened with a starch slurry or cultured dairy product. Served chilled and garnished, these soups are a rich addition to the menu.

- **Vegetable Soups**

These are some of the most popular cold soups. They may be cooked or served raw. The vegetables and legumes can be puréed or chopped.

- **Fruit Soups**

Fruit soups are made with raw or cooked fruits that are chopped, juiced, puréed, and gelled. Fruit soups are especially refreshing in hot weather.

One of the major selling points to cold soups is their presentation. Because many include raw ingredients, the colors and textures are bright and crisp. Cold soups that are garnished nicely and presented in a beautiful way look stunning when brought to the table. Garnishing plays an important part in our soup presentations.

We distinguish two types of garnishes:

1. **Component, or internal, garnishes** consist of finely cut major ingredients or related ingredients for color contrast and mouth feel. Note that any component garnish must be completely edible. Some examples are mango caviar for a fruit soup made using Chef Ferran Adria's unique technique, miniature melon balls or avocado balls for a fruit soup or gazpacho, or fine-diced beets for a borscht.

2. **Aesthetic, or external, garnishes** are placed on the soup, on the side of the cup or bowl, or next to the soup bowl to increase eye appeal. They could consist of crunchy bacon bits or a potato crisp served on a chilled potato soup, a sprig of herb compatible with the soup, an attractive sliver of the main ingredient, or a leaf or suitable flower with low scent.

Chilled soup can be served in any type of suitable bowl or container, bedded in shaved ice, or placed in cups or bowls on top of salad plates. A folded napkin in the shape of an artichoke can be placed on the plate to steady the cup or bowl to keep it from sliding and to add eye appeal to the plate. Soup cups or bowls should be chilled.

LEARNING ACTIVITY 10-1

Folding napkins in the traditional shape of an artichoke, rose, or water lily (all three names have been used to describe this type of fold) is easy and illustrated below with step-by-step instructions.

NOTE: *The napkins should be lightly starched and, if possible, made of linen. Napkins made of synthetic material do not hold up very well. The napkins should measure 12 inches × 12 inches or 16 inches × 16 inches.*

Step 1
Spread the napkin out on a flat surface. Fold each of the four corners to the center, creating a square (Figure 10-1).

Figure 10-1 Take each corner and fold it to the center of the square.

Step 2
Fold the new points to the center again, creating an even smaller square (Figure 10-2).

Figure 10-2 Take each new corner and fold it to the center.

Step 3

Hold the center points in place with one hand and carefully flip the napkin over so that the fold side is down (Figure 10-3).

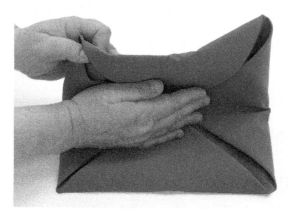

Figure 10-3 Flip the napkin over so that the folds are underneath.

Step 4

Use your hand to anchor the center, or place a cup or glass in the center of the napkin. Reach underneath the napkin and pull out one of the loose corners. Continue until you have brought over all four corners (Figure 10-4).

Figure 10-4 Slip your hand underneath and pull out each of the folded corners.

Step 5

Give each of those corners a tug to make it stand up and look like the petals of the artichoke (Figures 10-5 and 10-6).

Figure 10-5 Shape each of the four petals.   **Figure 10-6** The completed artichoke fold.

>> Clear Soups

For a stock-based consommé or other stock-based clear soup, the hallmark of a quality, finished cold soup is intense, true-to-the-base material flavor and clarity. (**Consommé** is the French generic term for a clarified stock.)

There are as many ways to make a soup as there are chefs. There has been, and continues to be, great debate over the techniques used for soup-making. There are those who advocate simmering the bones first before adding the mirepoix, and others who prefer adding all the ingredients at one time. Some treat one type of meat stock differently from others. We have included a basic recipe for making quality stock. Once you have tried it, you may want to try simmering the bones first and adding the other ingredients later to determine which method you prefer.

Steps for Making a Quality Stock

1. Start with clean bones; fresh, clean mirepoix; and fresh herbs and spices. The old habit of using a stock as a dumping ground for trimmings is outdated and unsuitable for quality consommé.
2. Cover the ingredients with cold water, and simmer, in most cases, several hours to draw out all the flavors and protein.
3. Skim to remove the protein and fat scum that initially forms. This refining process will ensure a clear stock full of bright flavor.
4. Strain the finished soup and refrigerate.

To Make a Consommé

After the stock has been strained and chilled, a finishing step is required for what we call consommé.

1. We use a "clearmeat" to clarify and refine the soup even further. This consists of albuminous material such as chopped or ground, fat-free beef when making beef consommé, or poultry when making a poultry-based consommé, or lean fish for a fish consommé, mirepoix, and egg whites. This clearmeat is mixed with the cold stock, brought to a slight boil, and then reduced to a simmer.
2. In the process, the stock is reduced to concentrate the flavor, and any stray bits of material are trapped in the "raft" (Figure 10-7).

The **raft** is a congealed protein mass that forms on the top of the stock. As the liquid heats up, convection occurs, bringing any tiny bits of protein and refuse to the top of the stock. This matter sticks to the albumen and forms a lid or raft on the top of the stock. This raft is the filter that the stock bubbles through. In a few hours, the results are a clear liquid, with intense flavor, that (when refrigerated), usually gels from the resultant gelatin released from the bones and connective tissue.

Figure 10-7 The raft is formed on top of the consommé.

The classic consommé served cold is Consommé Madrilène. It is flavored with tomatoes and celery. The acidity of the tomatoes gives the soup a tangy, refreshing flavor. The name refers to Madrid, the capital of Spain (Spain is a large producer of tomatoes). The soup should be light reddish brown.

The basic consommé can be served hot or cold. Consommé served cold should be slightly jellied, tender but not too firm. The soup will jell when cold if calf's feet or veal knuckles are used in the preparation of the basic stock. Gelatin may be added to get the desired consistency. While the soup is cooling it should not be stirred to avoid formation of air bubbles.

Optional garnishes include diced, seeded tomatoes and chopped celery greens.

consommé Madrilène *Yield: 1 qt (960 ml)*   *About 5 servings*

Ingredients	Amounts	
	U.S.	Metric
Beef stock	3 pints	1.420 l
Carrots, diced	4 oz	113 g
Celery, diced	4 oz	113 g
Celery greens	4 oz	113 g
Leeks	4 oz	113 g
Onions, diced	4 oz	113 g
Tomatoes, crushed, ripe, seeds	8 oz	226 g
Garlic, chopped	1/4 tsp	1 1/2 g
Egg whites	2 each	2 each
Peppercorns, crushed	5 each	5 each
Salt	To taste	To taste
Gelatin, powdered, optional	1 tsp	5 g

Procedure

Warm the stock slightly and blend all the ingredients thoroughly.

Heat to around 140°F (60°C), stirring occasionally. Stop stirring and simmer at 180°F (80°C) until the stock is clear, approximately 45 minutes to 1 1/2 hours. Season, strain through cheesecloth, and cool until set. Serve in a coupe or soup bowl.

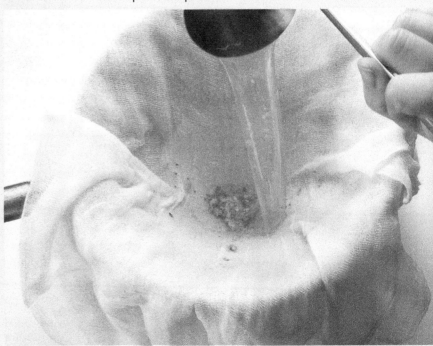

NUTRITIONAL INFORMATION PER SERVING: *57* Calories; trace Fat (8.0% calories from fat); 3 g Protein; 7 g Carbohydrate; 2 g Dietary Fiber; 0 mg Cholesterol; 2,223 mg Sodium. Exchanges: 0 Grain (Starch); 0 Lean Meat; 1 Vegetable; 0 Fat; 0 Other Carbohydrates.

The French king, *Henri* de Bourbon, commonly known as Henry IV supposedly declared that every French person should have a chicken in his or her pot. French chefs named this hearty soup made with beef and chicken stock and served with diced beef, chicken, and soup vegetables after Henry IV. It may be served hot or chilled. A "marmite" is the French term for a large metal or ceramic soup kettle and the flavorful, hearty clear soup made in it.

A standard marmite is served as a complete meal with all meats and soup vegetables. This more refined version uses meat and vegetables as component garnishes. Optional garnishes might include diced, boiled meat and chicken; small carrot and celery bâtonnets, boiled in meat stock; and chopped chives. When using bâtonnets as soup garnish, they should not be much longer than the soup spoon, or approximately 1/2-inch long.

jellied marmite Henry IV Yield: 1 qt (960 ml)   About 5 servings

Ingredients	Amounts U.S.	Metric	Procedure
Beef stock	2 pints	946 ml	Warm the stock slightly and blend all the ingredients thoroughly. Heat to 140°F (60°C), stirring occasionally. Do not stir any longer; bring to a slow simmer for about 40 minutes. Strain and cool.
Chicken stock	1 pint	473 ml	
Carrots, diced	4 oz	113 g	
Celery, diced	4 oz	113 g	
Leeks	4 oz	113 g	
Onions, diced	4 oz	113 g	
Tomatoes, crushed, seeds and all	4 oz	113 g	
Egg whites	2 each	2 each	
Peppercorns, crushed	5 each	5 each	
Thyme, fresh	Small sprig	Small sprig	
Bay leaf, small	1/2 each	1/2 each	
Salt	To taste	To taste	
Gelatin, powdered	1 tsp	5 g	

NUTRITIONAL INFORMATION PER SERVING: 58 Calories; trace Fat (7.7% calories from fat); 3 g Protein; 8 g Carbohydrate; 2 g Dietary Fiber; 0 mg Cholesterol; 2,230 mg Sodium. Exchanges: 0 Grain (Starch); 0 Lean Meat; 1 Vegetable; 0 Fat; 0 Other Carbohydrates.

Borscht is a traditional Eastern European or Russian soup that has hundreds, if not thousands, of variations. Borscht is traditionally made with either beef or pork; root vegetables such as carrots, rutabaga. and turnips; vegetables such as cabbage and potatoes; and, always, beets. Borscht is popular with Jews of Ashkenazi ancestry and is made with beef or lamb. (Ashkenazi Jews are of Central or Eastern European ancestry and are distinguished from the Western Sephardim branch by different religious customs. Many Jews living in New York City are Ashkenazi descendants.)

The following version is typical of the borscht prepared in many Jewish households. Diced small beets may be used as an optional garnish along with sour cream on the side.

jellied borscht   *Yield: 80 fl oz (2.4 l)*   *10 servings*

Ingredients	Amounts U.S.	Metric	Procedure
Beef stock	3 pints	1.420 l	Warm the stock slightly and blend all the ingredients thoroughly. Heat to around 180°F (80°C), stirring occasionally. Do not stir any longer; bring to a slow simmer for 40 minutes. Strain, season, and cool.
Carrots, diced	4 oz	113 g	
Celery, diced	4 oz	113 g	
Leeks	4 oz	113 g	
Onions, diced	4 oz	113 g	
Parsnips	4 oz	113 g	
Tomatoes, crushed, seeds and all	4 oz	113 g	
Beets, fresh, peeled, coarsely chopped	8 oz	226	
Egg whites	2 each	2 each	
Peppercorns, crushed	5 each	5 each	
Salt	To taste	To taste	
Vinegar	1 tbsp	15 ml	
Gelatin, powdered	1 tsp	5 g	

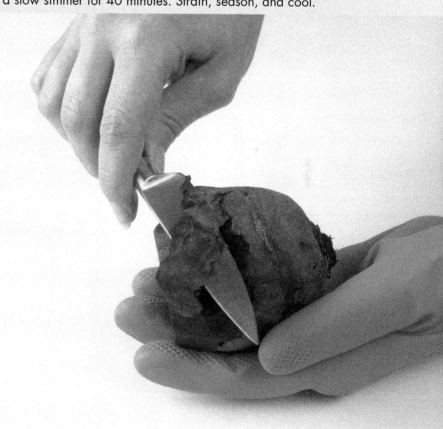

NUTRITIONAL INFORMATION PER SERVING: 46 Calories; trace Fat (5.9% calories from fat); 2 g Protein; 7 g Carbohydrate; 2 g Dietary Fiber; 0 mg Cholesterol; 1,339 mg Sodium. Exchanges: 0 Grain (Starch); 0 Lean Meat; 1 Vegetable; 0 Fat; 0 Other Carbohydrates.

This meatless version of borscht, served with sour cream, is available in many Jewish dairy restaurants. It contains no beef stock but uses a vegetable stock instead. Chopped boiled beets, small dill sprigs, and sour cream can be served on the side.

vegetarian borscht *Yield: 84 oz (2,520 ml)* *8 servings*

Ingredients	Amounts		Procedure
	U.S.	Metric	
Porcini mushrooms, dried	4 oz	113 g	Soak the mushrooms in water.
Water	8 fl oz	237 ml	Lift the mushrooms out of the water and chop coarsely. Save the mushroom water, but make sure there is no sand at the bottom.
Oil	1 fl oz	30 ml	Sauté all vegetables in oil.
Onion, chopped	4 oz	113 g	
Beets, peeled and ground	8 oz	226 g	
Carrots, fine dice	4 oz	110 g	
Celery, fine dice	4 oz	110 g	
Cabbage, chopped	1 lb	453 g	
Garlic, chopped	2 tsp	10 g	
Tomato juice	8 fl oz	237 ml	Add the tomato juice, stock, and mushroom water. Bring to a boil; reduce the temperature and simmer for 40 minutes.
Vegetable stock	1 qt	946 ml	
Apple cider vinegar	1 tbsp	15 ml	Add vinegar and chill soup.

NUTRITIONAL INFORMATION PER SERVING: 194 Calories; 6 g Fat (24.6% calories from fat); 6 g Protein; 33 g Carbohydrate; 6 g Dietary Fiber; 1 mg Cholesterol; 967 mg Sodium. Exchanges: 1 Grain (Starch); 4 Vegetable; 0 Fruit; 1 Fat.

"Sopa de Lima" is a chicken and lime soup of South American origin. Chopped cilantro and thin slices of lime provide the perfect garnish.

sopa de Lima—chicken soup with lime
Yield: 2 qt (1,920 ml)   *About 10 servings*

Ingredients	Amounts U.S.	Metric	Procedure
Chicken stock	2 pints	946 ml	Warm the chicken stock.
Oil	1 tbsp	15 ml	Sauté the vegetables in oil and add to the chicken stock. Add the hot pepper, salt, and lime zest. Bring to a boil; reduce the temperature and simmer for 30 minutes. Purée and chill.
Carrots, small dice	4 oz	113 g	
Onions, small dice	8 oz	226 g	
Tomatoes, peeled, seeded	8 oz	226 g	
Lima beans, small, frozen	1 lb	454 g	
Hot pepper	1/4 tsp	1 g	
Salt	To taste	To taste	
Lime zest	1 tbsp	15 g	
Lime juice	3 tbsp	44 ml	Add lime juice just prior to serving.

NUTRITIONAL INFORMATION PER SERVING: 192 Calories; 2 g Fat (8.7% calories from fat); 11 g Protein; 33 g Carbohydrate; 10 g Dietary Fiber; 0 mg Cholesterol; 900 mg Sodium. Exchanges: 2 Grain (Starch); 1/2 Lean Meat; 1/2 Vegetable; 0 Fruit; 1/2 Fat.

The secret to this recipe is in the roasted tomatoes, which give it a powerful flavor. It can be garnished with a tomato **concassé** (peeled, seeded, and diced tomatoes) and fresh basil **chiffonade** (finely chopped). Fresh basil can be used but it will turn grey due to the acidity level in this recipe.

roasted tomato soup *Yield: 1 1/2 qt (1,440 ml)   9 servings*

Ingredients	Amounts U.S.	Metric	Procedure
Roma tomatoes	2 lbs	907 g	Wash and split the tomatoes. Blend with the oil and roast in a hot oven.
Olive oil	2 fl oz	59 ml	(Be careful not to burn the tomatoes.) Purée and save the pulp and juice.

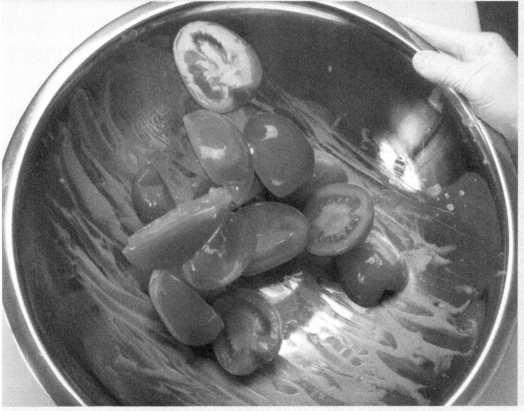

Stock	1 pint	473 ml	Add the stock, bring to a boil.
Cornstarch	1 tbsp	15 g	Dissolve the cornstarch in a little cold water. Add the mixture to the boiling soup.
Water	1 fl oz	30 ml	
Basil, dried	1 tsp	5 g	Add the basil, sugar, salt, and pepper. Chill.
Sugar	1 tsp	5 g	
Salt	To taste	To taste	
Pepper	To taste	To taste	

NUTRITIONAL INFORMATION PER SERVING: 78 Calories; 6 g Fat (68.7% calories from fat); 1 g Protein; 6 g Carbohydrate; 1 g Dietary Fiber; 0 mg Cholesterol; 38 mg Sodium. Exchanges: 0 Grain (Starch); 1 Vegetable; 1 Fat; 0 Other Carbohydrates.

The best-known cold, cream soup is **vichyssoise,** a cold potato and leek soup, created by the French Chef Louis Diat at the Ritz hotel on Madison Avenue in New York City. He called the soup "vichyssoise" because he grew up near Vichy in France, and his mother made this soup. The soup was introduced to New York at the beginning of the twentieth century when the tunnels leading to the Grand Central station were constructed. The nearby Ritz Hotel had a roof garden and the dust and noise of construction made the distinguished clientele unhappy. Chef Diat created the soup to mollify complaints and to add a new dish to his menu. During World War II, French chefs in New York City tried to change the name to Crème Gaulloise because they hated the Nazi-associated Vichy government. The name change never took hold.

Although vichyssoise is not seen much on today's menu, it is still considered to be a classic cold soup and, therefore, is included in this unit. The base for the soup is chicken stock flavored with onions and white parts of leeks, which is thickened with Russet potatoes. The rather thick purée, when chilled, is blended with cream, seasoned, and stored in small quantities ready for serving. The potato base can be used to make many variations by blending with other vegetable purées and spices.

Some chefs prefer to use heavy cream instead of the light cream suggested in this recipe. Chopped chives can be used as an optional garnish.

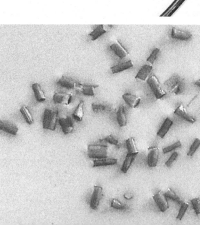

vichyssoise *Yield: 2 qt. (1.9 l)*   *Approximately 6 servings*

Ingredients	Amounts U.S.	Metric	Procedure
Chicken stock	1 qt	946 ml	Combine the stock, leeks, onions, and potatoes. Add salt and pepper. Bring the mixture to a boil; reduce the temperature and simmer until potatoes are very soft and fall apart.
Leek, whites only, well washed and diced	8 oz	227 g	
Onions, white, diced	8 oz	227 g	
Russet potatoes, peeled and coarse dice	1 lb	454 g	
Salt	To taste	To taste	
Pepper	To taste	To taste	
Cornstarch	1 tbsp	15 g	Make a slurry and add to the boiling soup. Bring it back to a boil. Purée the soup and chill.
Cold stock or water	1 fl oz	30 ml	
Light cream	8 fl oz	237 ml	Blend the soup with cream, then adjust the consistency and seasoning.
Chilled stock	As needed	As needed	
Worcestershire sauce	To taste	To taste	

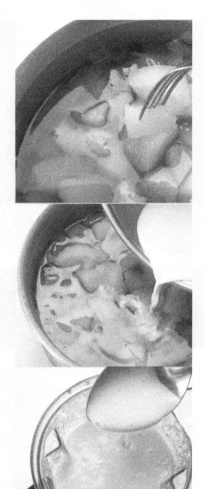

NUTRITIONAL INFORMATION PER SERVING: 169 Calories; 8 g Fat (44.2% calories from fat); 4 g Protein; 19 g Carbohydrate; 2 g Dietary Fiber; 26 mg Cholesterol; 1,731 mg Sodium. Exchanges: 1 Grain (Starch); 1 Vegetable; 1 1/2 Fat; 0 Other Carbohydrates.

VICHYSSOISE VARIATIONS

Any flavorful, cooked vegetable purée added to vichyssoise can make many new creations.

Some suggestions include puréed carrots, tomatoes (both puréed and paste), sweet potatoes, broccoli, and avocado.

This avocado vichyssoise includes a touch of cayenne pepper, which gives it a little kick. Avocados will oxidize, so the purée should be made at the last moment and added right away to the soup. Light cream could be substituted with sour cream. Top with diced avocados, if desired.

avocado vichyssoise *Yield: 3 pints (1.42 liter)*   *Approximately 7 servings*

Ingredients	Amounts		Procedure
	U.S.	Metric	
Vichyssoise base soup	2 pints	947 ml	Combine the ingredients and season to taste.
Avocado purée	8 fl oz	237 ml	
Light cream	8 fl oz	237 ml	
Cayenne pepper	To taste	To taste	
Salt	To taste	To taste	

NUTRITIONAL INFORMATION PER SERVING: 251 Calories; 23 g Fat (81.5% calories from fat); 3 g Protein; 9 g Carbohydrate; 1 g Dietary Fiber; 70 mg Cholesterol; 276 mg Sodium. Exchanges: 0 Grain (Starch); 0 Fruit; 0 Nonfat Milk; 4 1/2 Fat; 0 Other Carbohydrates.

Chervil is a member of the parsley family and has a taste similar to parsley with a touch of anise. Chervil's flavor is lost when cooked or dried. That is why it should be sprinkled on food in its fresh, raw state. Use additional chopped chervil sprinkled on top of each serving as a possible garnish.

chervil cream vichyssoise
Yield: 42 fl oz (1,260 ml)   Approximately 7 servings

Ingredients	Amounts U.S.	Metric	Procedure
Vichyssoise base soup	1 qt	946 ml	Combine the base with pepper.
White pepper, ground	To taste	To taste	
Salt	To taste	To taste	Add all the other ingredients just prior to service. Adjust to taste.
Light cream	8 fl oz	227 ml	
Chervil, chopped	1 oz	30 g	
Parsley, chopped	1 oz	30 g	

NUTRITIONAL INFORMATION PER SERVING: 156 Calories; 10 g Fat (58.0% calories from fat); 4 g Protein; 13 g Carbohydrate; 1 g Dietary Fiber; 34 mg Cholesterol; 681 mg Sodium. Exchanges: 1/2 Grain (Starch); 1 Vegetable; 2 Fat; 0 Other Carbohydrates.

This vichyssoise variation uses fresh peas. A possible garnish would be snow peas, cut in fine strips and sprinkled on top of each serving, or a swirl of cream or sour cream.

green pea vichyssoise   *Yield: 6 cups (1.3 liter)   Approximately 8 servings*

Ingredients	Amounts U.S.	Metric	Procedure
Green peas, fresh (If unavailable, use frozen peas)	1 lb	454 g	Boil or steam the peas until tender. Plunge them into cold water to arrest the cooking process. Drain immediately and purée.
Vichyssoise soup base	1 1/2 pts	710 ml	Blend the pea purée with all the ingredients. Adjust seasoning to taste.
White pepper, ground	To taste	To taste	
Salt	To taste	To taste	
Light cream	8 fl oz	237 ml	

NUTRITIONAL INFORMATION PER SERVING: 220 Calories; 18 g Fat (71.5% calories from fat); 4 g Protein; 12 g Carbohydrate; 2 g Dietary Fiber; 62 mg Cholesterol; 242 mg Sodium. Exchanges: 1/2 Grain (Starch); 0 Nonfat Milk; 3 1/2 Fat; 0 Other Carbohydrates.

ADDITIONAL COLD FAVORITES

Sorrel has a sweet and spicy flavor. Some say it reminds them of kiwi fruit.

chilled cream of sorrel
Yield: 96 fl oz (2.84 l)   Approximately 12 servings

Ingredients	Amounts U.S.	Metric	Procedure
Sorrel, fresh	1 1/2 lbs	680 g	Clean and stem the sorrel. Chop.
Chicken stock	1 1/2 qt	1.42 l	Use a nonreactive pot and simmer the sorrel in the chicken stock for 10 minutes, until tender. Strain out half of the sorrel and place in a blender or food processor to purée. Add the puréed sorrel back into the soup and chill.
Heavy cream	8 fl oz	237 ml	When the soup is cold, add the heavy cream and sour cream and whisk until blended.
Sour cream	8 fl oz	237 ml	
Salt	2 tsp	10 g	Add the salt, nutmeg, pepper, and Worcestershire sauce.
Nutmeg	1/2 tsp	2 g	
White pepper, ground	1/2 tsp	2 g	
Worcestershire sauce	1 tsp	5 ml	
Eggs, hard boiled	2 each	2 each	Garnish with sieved hard boiled egg and a small sorrel leaf.
Sorrel leaves, for garnish	8 each	8 each	

NUTRITIONAL INFORMATION PER SERVING: 134 Calories; 12 g Fat (85.8% calories from fat); 3 g Protein; 2 g Carbohydrate; trace Dietary Fiber; 71 mg Cholesterol; 1,461 mg Sodium. Exchanges: 0 Grain (Starch); 0 Lean Meat; 0 Nonfat Milk; 2 1/2 Fat; 0 Other Carbohydrates.

Dairy-based dessert soups are popular in Scandinavian countries. The next soup is a Danish soup based on buttermilk. It is tangy from both the buttermilk and the lemon, but very refreshing. The dusting of the gingersnap cookie crumbs adds a special sweet and spicy note.

Denmark is famous for dairy products and is a large exporter of cheese and butter. Pasteurized eggs should be used in this recipe.

Danish buttermilk soup   *Yield: 1 qt (946 ml)   6 servings*

Ingredients	Amounts U.S.	Metric	Procedure
Eggs, whole (pasteurized)	3 each	3 each	Combine all the ingredients (except for the buttermilk) in a mixer. Whip until well blended.
Lemon zest, grated	1 tsp	5 g	
Lemon juice	1 fl oz	30 ml	
Sugar	3 oz	85 g	
Vanilla extract	1 tsp	5 ml	
Buttermilk	1 qt	946 ml	Add the buttermilk and continue whipping at medium speed. Chill and serve ice cold. Garnish with crushed gingersnaps.

NUTRITIONAL INFORMATION PER SERVING: 155 Calories; 4 g Fat (22.8% calories from fat); 9 g Protein; 21 g Carbohydrate; trace Dietary Fiber; 112 mg Cholesterol; 207 mg Sodium. Exchanges: 1/2 Lean Meat; 0 Fruit; 1/2 Nonfat Milk; 1/2 Fat; 1 Other Carbohydrates.

Here's another soup with a buttermilk base. This refreshing and hearty soup is perfect for a summer reception dinner or light supper.

chlodnik or cold cucumber and buttermilk soup with shrimp   *Yield: 2 qt   Approximately 8 servings*

Ingredients	Amounts U.S.	Metric	Procedure
Buttermilk	2 pints	946 ml	Blend the buttermilk and sour cream together until smooth.
Sour cream	12 fl oz	354 ml	
English cucumbers, large	2 each	2 each	Peel, seed, and dice fine. Add to the buttermilk mixture.
Yellow onion, finely grated	3 oz	85 g	Add the remaining ingredients (not the eggs) to the liquid and blend. Adjust the seasonings if needed.
Chives, sliced thin	1 oz	30 g	
Dill weed, fresh, chopped	2 tsp	10 g	
Fennel seeds, toasted and ground fresh	2 tsp	10 g	
Garlic, fine mince	1 clove	1 clove	
Bay shrimp, cooked	8 oz	227 g	
Salt	To taste	To taste	
Pepper	To taste	To taste	
Eggs, hard boiled	2 each	2 each	Serve in iced cold soup bowls or cups. Garnish with chopped egg on top of each serving.

NUTRITIONAL INFORMATION PER SERVING: 207 Calories; 12 g Fat (51.6% calories from fat); 14 g Protein; 11 g Carbohydrate; 1 g Dietary Fiber; 120 mg Cholesterol; 243 mg Sodium. Exchanges: 0 Grain (Starch); 1 Lean Meat; 0 Vegetable; 1/2 Nonfat Milk; 2 Fat.

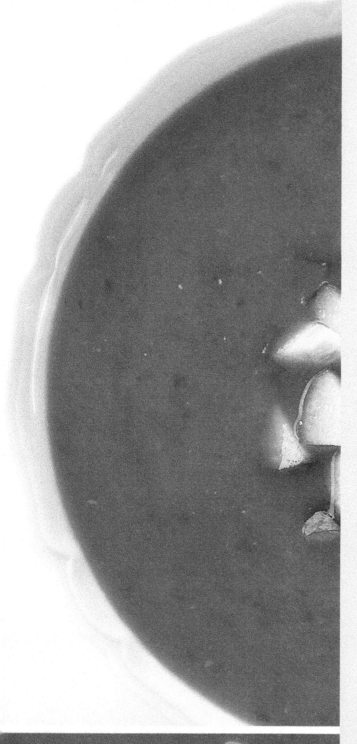

One of the most popular cold, puréed soups made with raw vegetables is the well-known signature soup of Spain, **gazpacho.** Its texture can be compared to a cold vegetable drink and minced salad combined. The dish may have originated with the Romans who liked to eat bread soaked with vinegar and olive oil, and the word "gazpacho" may have come from the old Roman word "caspa" for residue or fragment. It allegedly travelled with the Moors (Arabs) to present-day Spain, who conquered and occupied the Iberian Peninsula from 800 AD to about 1400 AD. The term "gazpacho" probably was adapted to the Arabic word for soaked bread.

Serving cold soups based on chopped vegetables made a lot of sense in hot climates because they eliminated the need to make fire and made use of local products. In the United States, gazpacho is customarily a soup made with chopped or ground cucumbers, tomatoes, tomato juice, vinegar, olive oil, green peppers, and spices.

Both tomatoes and peppers came from the Americas and were unheard of when the Arabs made gazpacho. Tomatoes originated in Central America, were transported to Europe by the Portuguese and Spanish explorers, and were initially shunned as a food plant due to the plant's familial relationship with the deadly "nightshade" plant family. It was treated as a botanical curiosity, and it took years before tomatoes were considered safe for raw eating.

Many variations of gazpacho exist in different regions of Spain and not all contain tomatoes. Many soups use bread or ground almonds as a thickening agent. American restaurants serve gazpacho with a garnish of chopped onions, green peppers, diced tomatoes, and toasted croutons. In Spain, gazpacho is often served with cubed white bread, not toasted, and most restaurants shun the garnishes served traditionally in American restaurants. In some parts of Spain, the gazpacho is blended with a little heavy cream at the moment of service.

It is important to wait and blend the cream into the soup at the moment of service and not beforehand. The acidity level in the soup could curdle the cream if it is allowed to sit.

Andalusia is a hot region of Spain, famous for sherry wine, Seville oranges, and for growing luscious tomatoes. This type of gazpacho is the best-known version served in American restaurants. Optional garnishes may include peeled and seeded cucumbers finely diced on top.

andalusia gazpacho *Yield: 2 qts (1.89 l) Approximately 8 servings*

Ingredients	Amounts U.S.	Metric
Tomatoes, peeled and seeded	2 lbs	907 g
Green bell pepper, coarse dice	8 oz	227 g
Onion, coarse dice	8 oz	227 g
Cucumber, peeled, seeded, coarse dice	8 oz	227 g
Sherry or red wine vinegar	2 fl oz	59 ml
Olive oil	1 fl oz	30 ml
White bread, crust removed	2 slices	2 slices
Sugar	1 tsp	5 g
Tarragon, fresh, chopped	1 tsp	5 g
Cayenne pepper	1/4 tsp	1 g
Salt	To taste	To taste
Tomato juice	4 oz	113 ml
Ice cubes	4 each	4 each

Procedure

Combine the tomatoes, bell pepper, onion, cucumber, vinegar, olive oil, bread, sugar, tarragon, salt, and pepper in a food processor and process to medium fine consistency.

Chill and let the soup marinate at least overnight in the refrigerator.

Thin with tomato juice or cold stock if necessary. Blend in ice cubes for added coolness and moisture just prior to service.

NUTRITIONAL INFORMATION PER SERVING: 94 Calories; 4 g Fat (36.1% calories from fat); 2 g Protein; 14 g Carbohydrate; 3 g Dietary Fiber; trace Cholesterol; 129 mg Sodium. Exchanges: 0 Grain (Starch); 0 Lean Meat; 2 Vegetable; 1/2 Fat; 0 Other Carbohydrates.

This is a pure-white gazpacho made with almonds, garlic, and olive oil and not a trace of tomato. As the name implies, it is popular in the city of Malaga. The soup can be garnished with sliced or whole grapes stirred into the soup.

white malagan-style gazpacho
Yield: 1 qt (946 ml)   *Approximately 5 servings*

Ingredients	Amounts		Procedure
	U.S.	Metric	
Almonds, peeled, slivered	8 oz	227 g	Combine all the ingredients (except for the grapes) in a food processor and process until well blended. Chill and let marinate refrigerated overnight. Adjust the thickness/consistency with added water, if needed.
Garlic, chopped	1 tbsp	15 g	
Bread, white, crust removed	6 slices	6 slices	
Olive oil	2 fl oz	59 ml	
White sherry vinegar	2 fl oz	59 ml	
Ice water	1 1/2 pints	710 ml	
Salt	To taste	To taste	
White grapes, seedless, split	30 each	30 each	Arrange the sliced grapes onto the soup, just prior to service.

NUTRITIONAL INFORMATION PER SERVING: 355 Calories; 27 g Fat (65.0% calories from fat); 8 g Protein; 24 g Carbohydrate; 4 g Dietary Fiber; trace Cholesterol; 223 mg Sodium. Exchanges: 1 1/2 Grain (Starch); 1/2 Lean Meat; 0 Vegetable; 0 Fruit; 5 Fat; 0 Other Carbohydrates.

Brazil is the largest country in South America. As in the United States, a number of different ethnic groups settled the country. To describe Brazilian cuisine in a sentence or two is virtually impossible. Each region varies but beans are commonly served throughout most of the country. They find their way onto most Brazilian tables at least once a day. Black beans are common in Brazilian dishes, and are called "feijoadas" in Portuguese, the country's national language. This chilled black bean soup combines coconut milk, shrimp, cream, lime, and hot pepper sauce for a zesty and tangy flavor.

chilled Brazilian black bean soup

Yield: 3 1/2 pints (1.66 liter)   *Approximately 8 servings*

Ingredients	Amounts U.S.	Metric	Procedure
Cooked black or turtle beans	24 fl oz	710 ml	Rinse the beans. Purée the beans in a food processor with 8 fl oz of the chicken stock until smooth.
Chicken stock	24 fl oz	710 ml	Add the remaining stock and coconut milk. Stir until completely blended.
Coconut milk, fresh or canned, unsweetened	4 fl oz	113 ml	
Shrimp, 30/35 ct	24 each	24 each	Mince the shrimp and add to the bean mixture. (Save out 6 whole shrimp to use as a garnish.)
Hot pepper sauce	1 tsp	5 g	Add the hot sauce, salt, pepper, cream, lime juice, and cilantro.
Salt	To taste	To taste	
Pepper	To taste	To taste	
Heavy cream	2 fl oz	59 ml	
Lime juice, fresh squeezed	1 fl oz	30 ml	
Cilantro, fine mince	1 tbsp	15 g	
Lime, sliced into 8 rounds	1 each	1 each	Serve chilled and garnish with one whole shrimp per bowl and a lime round.

NUTRITIONAL INFORMATION PER SERVING: 177 Calories; 7 g Fat (34.8% calories from fat); 10 g Protein; 19 g Carbohydrate; 6 g Dietary Fiber; 43 mg Cholesterol; 897 mg Sodium. Exchanges: 1 Grain (Starch); 1 Lean Meat; 0 Fruit; 0 Nonfat Milk; 1 1/2 Fat; 0 Other Carbohydrates.

>> Fruit Soups

Fruit soups are used chiefly for desserts or palate refreshers in large, multi-course meals. In Northern and Central Europe, you find many of these fruit soups made with berries and stone fruits such as cherries, lingon berries, and currants. In hot climates, such as in the Mediterranean, South America, Mexico, and the Caribbean, cool soups act as a refreshing repast on hot days, with citrus, melons, and tropical fruits playing the starring role. Cold fruit soups are sometimes thickened with tapioca or rice flour.

Kaltschale is the German term for cold soup and is also used to describe soups made with uncooked fruits and berries and chopped or diced fruits marinated with liqueur or wine.

This recipe calls for the use of a sachet bag. Wrap the spices in a small cheesecloth square and tie off the end with string. Red wine should be semi-dry. Nonalcoholic wine can be used in schools. An optional garnish is grated gingerbread sprinkled on top of the soup.

German sour cherry kaltschale
Yield: 3 pints (1.42 l)   Approximately 8 servings

Ingredients	Amounts U.S.	Metric	Procedure
Sour cherries, frozen with juice	2 pints	946 ml	Combine the cherries, water, wine, sugar, and lemon juice in a noncorrosive pot.
Water	8 fl oz	237 ml	
Red wine	8 fl oz	237 ml	
Sugar	2 oz	57 g	
Lemon juice	1/2 tbsp	8 ml	
Cinnamon stick	1/2 each	1/2 each	Make a sachet bag with the spices. Add to the cherry mixture and bring to a boil. Reduce the temperature and simmer for 20 minutes. Remove the sachet bag and discard. Put the mixture into a blender or food processor and purée.
Cloves, whole	2 each	2 each	
Vanilla bean, split	1 small	1 small	
Cornstarch	1 tbsp	15 g	Make a slurry with cornstarch and water. Add to the cherry mixture and bring it to a boil once more.
Water	2 tbsp	30 ml	
Lemon zest	1 tsp	5 g	Chill the soup. Add zest to each serving. Garnish with fresh cherries, if desired.

NUTRITIONAL INFORMATION PER SERVING: 104 Calories; trace Fat (4.6% calories from fat); 1 g Protein; 21 g Carbohydrate; 2 g Dietary Fiber; 0 mg Cholesterol; 33 mg Sodium. Exchanges: 0 Grain (Starch); 1/2 Fruit; 0 Fat; 1/2 Other Carbohydrates.

Use the preceding recipe as a base for this gooseberry soup.

Hungarian gooseberry soup

Yield: 48 fl oz (1,440 ml) Approximately 8 servings

Ingredients	Amounts U.S.	Metric	Procedure
Gooseberries, fresh or frozen	1 lb	454 g	In a nonreactive pot, boil the gooseberries with sugar until soft, about 15 minutes.
Water	1 pint	473 ml	
Sugar	4 oz	113 g	

Ingredients	Amounts U.S.	Metric	Procedure
Cornstarch	1 oz	30 g	Make a slurry with the cornstarch and water. Add it to the boiling soup, bring the mixture back up to a boil, and remove it from the stove. Cool for a few minutes, process briefly in the food processor, but leave the gooseberries in chunks.
Water	2 fl oz	60 ml	
Lemon juice	1/2 fl oz	15 ml	Stir in the remaining ingredients. Chill, stirring occasionally to prevent skin from forming on top.
Sour cream	8 fl oz	237 ml	
Lemon zest	1 tbsp	15 g	

NUTRITIONAL INFORMATION PER SERVING: 200 Calories; 8 g Fat (36.7% calories from fat); 2 g Protein; 31 g Carbohydrate; 3 g Dietary Fiber; 17 mg Cholesterol; 24 mg Sodium. Exchanges: 0 Grain (Starch); 1/2 Fruit; 0 Nonfat Milk; 1 1/2 Fat; 1 1/2 Other Carbohydrates.

These soups are commonly made with dairy products such as yogurt, sour cream, ricotta cheese, or low-fat cottage cheese. They can be considered breakfast dishes, desserts, or even main courses for slimming diets.

Cold, uncooked fruit soups typically are made as close to service time as possible. The fruits are peeled and diced, the berries washed and then slightly squashed and mixed with sugar (if used) to macerate before the dairy product is added.

Depending on the type of fruit used, the flavor is adjusted with a little lemon juice or sugar. Soups made with a thicker dairy substance, such as cottage cheese or ricotta, should be puréed in the food processor to smooth out the soup and enhance the look. They can be garnished with some fresh fruit pieces.

These soups are very perishable and tend to separate (curdle) easily because of the interaction of the acid from the fruits and the dairy products, so they should be served immediately.

Top this soup with fresh blueberries or an edible flower.

blueberry yogurt soup
Yield: 1 qt (32 fl oz) or 946 ml   Approximately 8 4 oz servings

Ingredients	Amounts	
	U.S.	Metric
Blueberries, fresh	1 pt	473 ml
Yogurt	1 pt	473 ml
Sugar	2 oz	57 g
Lemon zest	1 tbsp	15 g
Grape juice	1 fl oz	30 ml

Procedure

Combine the ingredients in a food processor and blend until smooth.

Make the soup as close to service time as possible and serve very cold.

NUTRITIONAL INFORMATION PER SERVING: 117 Calories; 3 g Fat (25.2% calories from fat); 4 g Protein; 19 g Carbohydrate; 2 g Dietary Fiber; 12 mg Cholesterol; 49 mg Sodium. Exchanges: 1/2 Fruit; 1/2 Nonfat Milk; 1/2 Fat; 1/2 Other Carbohydrates.

SOUPS MADE WITH UNCOOKED FRUITS

To make a good melon soup, the melon must be very ripe and sweet. Suitable choices are cantaloupe or Crenshaw melons. Try topping the soup with toasted almond slivers or an edible flower.

cream of melon soup   *Yield: 1 qt (32 fl oz) or 946 ml*
Approximately 8 4 oz servings

Ingredients	Amounts U.S.	Metric	Procedure
Melon, seeded, coarse dice	1 1/2 lbs	680 g	Put all the ingredients in a food processor and process to a smooth consistency. Chill. Prepare the soup as close to the service time as possible.
Lime juice	1 fl oz	30 ml	
Black pepper, ground	1 tsp	5 g	
Ricotta cheese	8 oz	227 g	
Mascarpone cheese	4 oz	113 g	

NUTRITIONAL INFORMATION PER SERVING: 175 Calories; 12 g Fat (58.5% calories from fat); 7 g Protein; 12 g Carbohydrate; 1 g Dietary Fiber; 40 mg Cholesterol; 59 mg Sodium. Exchanges: 0 Grain (Starch); 1 Lean Meat; 1/2 Fruit; 2 Fat.

This soup has a touch of balsamic vinegar to balance the flavors. It is perfect on a hot summer day. You can top each serving with a small basil leaf, diced strawberry, drizzle of balsamic vinegar, and a small swirl of crème fraîche.

strawberry basil soup   *Yield: 40 fl oz (1.2 l)*   *Approximately 8 servings*

Ingredients	Amounts U.S.	Metric	Procedure
Strawberries, fresh, sliced	2 pints	946 ml	Put all the ingredients in a food processor and process to smooth consistency. Chill. Prepare the soup as close to service time as possible.
Basil leaves, minced	1 oz	30 g	
Apple juice	8 fl oz	237 ml	
Balsamic vinegar	1 fl oz	30 ml	

NUTRITIONAL INFORMATION PER SERVING: 46 Calories; trace Fat (7.1% calories from fat); 1 g Protein; 11 g Carbohydrate; 3 g Dietary Fiber; 0 mg Cholesterol; 3 mg Sodium. Exchanges: 0 Grain (Starch); 1/2 Fruit; 0 Fat.

Garnish this delicious Thai-inspired soup with diced honeydew melon.

Thai melon soup *Yield: 2 qt (1.89 l)*   *Approximately 8 servings*

Ingredients	Amounts		Procedure
	U.S.	Metric	
Honeydew melon, rind removed, seeded and cut into cubes	2 lbs	907 g	Blend all the ingredients in a blender or food processor.
Watermelon, rind removed, seeded and cut into cubes	1 lb	454 g	Put into serving bowls or cups and garnish with watermelon balls.
Yogurt	4 fl oz	118 ml	
Banana, peeled and sliced	6 oz	170 g	
Honey	3 oz	85 g	
Crushed ice	3 oz	85 g	

NUTRITIONAL INFORMATION PER SERVING: 82 Calories; 1 g Fat (7.4% calories from fat); 1 g Protein; 20 g Carbohydrate; 1 g Dietary Fiber; 2 mg Cholesterol; 14 mg Sodium. Exchanges: 1/2 Fruit; 0 Nonfat Milk; 0 Fat; 1/2 Other Carbohydrates.

The combination of guava, pineapple, and lime juices with honeydew melon makes this an especially unique and refreshing soup.

tropical fruit soup *Yield: 2.5 qts (2.37 l)*   *Approximately 10 8 oz servings*

Ingredients	Amounts		Procedure
	U.S.	Metric	
Guava juice	32 fl oz	946 ml	Blend all the ingredients in a food processor or blender.
Honeydew melon, rind removed, seeded and cut into cubes	16 oz	454 g	
Pineapple juice	16 fl oz	473 ml	
Lime juice	4 fl oz	118 ml	
Honey	4 oz	113 g	
Crushed Ice	8 oz	226 g	Add crushed ice and blend to make a frosty soup. Pour into serving cups or bowls and serve immediately.

NUTRITIONAL INFORMATION PER SERVING: 124 Calories; trace Fat (1.4% calories from fat); 1 g Protein; 33 g Carbohydrate; 4 g Dietary Fiber; 0 mg Cholesterol; 8 mg Sodium. Exchanges: 1 Fruit; 1 Other Carbohydrates.

Garnish the Bali Dream soup with a pineapple wedge or carrot curls. A lime wedge would work as a garnish as well. Canned (unsweetened) coconut milk is used in the recipe. Canned pineapple can be used if fresh pineapple is not available.

Bali dream (a taste of the island's beauty)

Yield: 3.25 qt (3.08 l)   Approximately 16 servings

| Ingredients | Amounts | | Procedure |
	U.S.	Metric	
Carrot juice, fresh or canned	1 pt	473 ml	Blend all the ingredients. Add crushed ice and blend until thick and frothy. Pour into serving bowls and cups.
Pineapple, fresh, puréed	1 qt	946 ml	
Papaya pulp	1 qt	946 ml	
Yogurt	8 oz	227 g	
Coconut milk	8 fl oz	237 ml	
Honey or palm sugar	4 oz	113 g	
Crushed ice	8 oz	226 g	

NUTRITIONAL INFORMATION PER SERVING: 150 Calories; 4 g Fat (23.8% calories from fat); 2 g Protein; 29 g Carbohydrate; 1 g Dietary Fiber; 2 mg Cholesterol; 22 mg Sodium. Exchanges: 1/2 Vegetable; 1 1/2 Fruit; 0 Nonfat Milk; 1 Fat; 1/2 Other Carbohydrates.

Use fresh strawberries, small dice, as a garnish for this melon berry soup. The cayenne pepper will give it a touch of kick.

melon berry delight *Yield: 1.15 qt (1.09 l)*   *Approximately 4 servings*

Ingredients	Amounts		Procedure
	U.S.	Metric	
Cantaloupe, rind removed, seeded, cut into 1–in cubes	1 pt	450 ml	Purée the melon with honey, salt, and water.
Honey	1 tbsp	15 g	
Salt	1/2 tsp	2 g	
Ice water	4 fl oz	118 ml	
Strawberries, fresh, sliced	1 pint	473 ml	Purée the strawberries with cayenne pepper and vinegar. Strain, then pour into a bowl and refrigerate. At serving time, pour both purées into the bowl. Avoid mixing. Add ice water if consistency is too thick.
Cayenne pepper	1/2 tsp	2 g	
Balsamic vinegar	1 tsp	5 ml	

NUTRITIONAL INFORMATION PER SERVING: 67 Calories; 1 g Fat (6.1% calories from fat); 1 g Protein; 16 g Carbohydrate; 2 g Dietary Fiber; 0 mg Cholesterol; 0 mg Sodium. Exchanges: 0 Grain (Starch); 1 Fruit; 0 Fat; 1/2 Other Carbohydrates.

>> Summary

Cold soups can be made with clarified meat stock, with meat stock not clarified, as vegetarian soup, with cooked vegetable purée, and with raw vegetables. These soups originated in various parts of the world, usually in areas with a warm climate.

Completely different types of cold soups are made with fruits, either cooked and puréed or just with fresh chopped fruits.

A Danish soup is even based on buttermilk, slightly sweetened and flavored with vanilla. Cold soups are delicious and also practical to serve on banquets because the soup bowls can be filled in the kitchen and brought with appropriate garnishes to the table just before the guests come to the banquet room.

>> Review Questions

TRUE/FALSE

1. Consommé is the French term for a clarified stock.
2. Vichyssoise is a cold, cream soup made with potatoes and leeks.
3. Andalusia is famous for Seville oranges and tomatoes.
4. Component garnishes are not eaten.
5. A flower could be considered an aesthetic garnish.

MULTIPLE CHOICE

6. Kaltschale is the German term for
   a. refrigerator.
   b. beer soup.
   c. cold fruit soup.
   d. cocktail made with Schnapps.
7. Why blend cream into the tomato gazpacho at the last moment before service?
   a. to save time
   b. to adjust the color
   c. to prevent curdling
   d. all of the above
8. A raft
   a. is a congealed protein mass.
   b. acts as a filter.
   c. forms on top of the stock.
   d. all of the above
9. Marmite is the French term for
   a. navy bean.
   b. a metal or ceramic soup kettle and the soup made in it.
   c. white vinegar.
   d. b and c
10. Andalusia is a region of
    a. Italy.
    b. Portugal.
    c. Spain.
    d. California.
11. A veloutè is a
    a. roux base.
    b. garnish.
    c. cold soup.
    d. alginate.
12. Gelatin can be used to gel this type of soup.
    a. cream soup
    b. vegetable soup
    c. clear soup
    d. all of the above

FILL IN THE ANSWERS

13. Why place a napkin under a soup cup?
14. Why should cold consommé not be stirred vigorously while it is cooling?
15. Describe a sachet bag and explain its use in soup making.

Salads

>> **Unit 11**

Salad Basics

>> **Unit 12**

Side Salads

>> **Unit 13**

Main-Course Salads

The salad course is usually one of the first courses ordered. It is, therefore, one of the first items to either impress or disappoint. The significance of serving only fresh, clean produce is paramount—many salads are raw and sanitation is the most important factor in quality salad production. Quality ingredients, carefully cleaned and prepared, are served in many creative ways. Greens are one of the most popular types of salad. Many other salads are also prepared in the salad or pantry station. This section will cover the preparation of vegetable and fruit salads, including a focus on greens (Unit 11), side salads (Unit 12), and main-course salads (Unit 13). Section 6 will cover dressings and sauces used for salads.

Salad Basics

>> Learning Objectives

After you have finished reading this unit, you should be able to:

- Discuss the history of the salad.
- Demonstrate how to clean, prepare, and store common salad components.
- List a variety of salad toppings and garnishes.
- Demonstrate an ability to prepare popular garnishes.
- Explain how to prepare a variety of fruits for fruit salads and breakfast service.
- Discuss the steps to plating salads.
- Understand the challenges related to serving banquet salads.

>> Key Terms

al dente (*al DEN-tay*)	concassé (*kon-kaas-SAY*)	crouton hydroponically	lardon panzanella

The earliest humans collected the tender shoots that came up in spring: ramps, sorrel, fiddlehead fern shoots, poke salad, and wild lettuce. These greens were welcomed after the long winters when fresh vegetables were only memories from the past. Greens have always been associated with health and lightness, and in this unit, our focus is on green salads, toppings, and presentation.

In this unit we will learn how to purchase, store, wash, and make ready for service a large variety of salad greens. Special attention is paid to washing salad greens. Lettuces and other salad greens grow in sandy soil, so most varieties have large amounts of dirt and sand trapped between the leaves. Serving customers gritty greens is a physical contaminant and is totally undesirable; thus, having the highest sanitation standards when cleaning greens is imperative.

Delicious salads have great components and garnishes. A variety of salad toppings and garnishes will be discussed. We will also learn how to cut lemons in wedges and wrap lemon halves as well as how to peel, seed, and chop tomatoes into concassé. Additionally, we will focus on basic pantry work such as peeling fruits, preparing grapefruits for breakfast service, making grapefruit sections, peeling peaches, and handling pineapples. We will also learn how to make a basic selection of fruit and vegetable decorations and garnishes.

Figure 11-1 A salad with apple slices served around a bed of curly endive and topped with walnuts and a gorgonzola cheese not only tastes good, but it looks good.

Salads, like all foods, should be "eaten with the eyes" first, so the final task in this unit is learning plating techniques to bring out the best look of side salads, such as basic mixed green salad, cole slaw, sliced tomato salad, and more exotic salads (Figure 11-1). Illustrations will also show how to prepare salads for large banquets.

>> History of the Salad

Salads have a long history dating back to the Egyptians, Romans, and Greeks. Hieroglyphics from Egyptian tombs depict Egyptians eating mixed greens as early as 2500 B.C. The Romans served greens such as lettuce with a sprinkling of salt. This was called "herba salta," meaning salted herb. The word "salad" comes from this term. The Romans also made a sauce with lemon, egg yolks, and olive oil, somewhat similar to our modern mayonnaise.

The Greeks used olive oil, vinegar, and herbs to dress greens, and Hippocrates believed raw vegetables were easily digested and "did not create obstructions"; therefore, these were often served at the beginning of a meal.

After the fall of the Roman Empire, salads were eaten less, and the emphasis was more on the medicinal quality of greens, herbs, and vegetables rather than on the enjoyment of eating them. Salads were a feature of Byzantine cookery and were popular in Spain and in Italy during the Renaissance. During this period salads were commonly vegetables that were pickled in vinegar or salt. Without refrigeration, storage of vegetables relied on these methods.

In Asia, the use of night soil or animal fertilizer discouraged consumption of raw vegetables and greens in the form of salads. Highly acidic or salted vegetables were the norm. In the 1400s, mixed herbs and greens were popular in England. The "salmagundi" was a term from the seventeenth century describing a salad composed of herbs, eggs, cold roast capon, other meats or fish, onions, and a dressing of oil and condiments.

In the 1800s, greens were popular with the French. It is said that King Louis XIV liked his greens served with violets and other edible flowers (Figure 11-2).

Salads were popular in early American history. Native Americans used wild onions, garlic, sorrel, and leeks along with herbs as medicinal treatment. Thomas Jefferson was fond of salads made of wild lettuce, watercress, and sorrel. The Scottish and Irish immigrants who settled in the Appalachian Mountains relied on the spring greens and sour grasses to be a tonic after a long winter of stale food and salted beef. These greens were loaded with vitamins and minerals and were used to "cleanse the blood."

At the end of the nineteenth century, the homemaker became the domestic engineer, and salads of greens gave way to orderly and balanced structures, oftentimes composed of chopped or shredded vegetables and gelatin. Scientific salad making became the norm, with molded, protein-based salads or salads composed of grains, cheese, shellfish and fin fish, and fruit. During the mid-twentieth century, eating green salads actually fell out of favor in most parts of America; the

Figure 11-2 King Louis XIV appreciated salads made with edible flowers.

Figure 11-3 Green salads feature a wide variety of lettuce.

Figure 11-4 This carrot salad with raisins is made with citrus vinaigrette and topped with sunflower seeds. It is just one example of a vegetable-based salad.

exception being on the West Coast, especially California. There, lettuce was still a very popular item. After refrigerated freight cars were perfected in the early 1920s, lettuce again began to show up on mid-American tables. After World War II, greens were not as popular; in fact, they were deemed old-fashioned. Canned and frozen vegetables replaced fresh greens. It wasn't until the advent of salad bars in the 1960s that fresh greens became fashionable again. Since then, salads composed of assorted greens have become popular worldwide. Romaine, Napa cabbage, Radicchio, and Lola Rossa are just a few of the hundreds of varieties found on dining tables today.

>> Types of Salads

Before we get further into our discussion of salads, it's important to discuss the basic types of salads. Obviously, there are thousands of varieties, but most will fall under one of the following categories:

- *Green salads* are those made primarily with a selection of green or red lettuce. They are traditionally dressed with vinaigrette, a creamy mayonnaise-based dressing, or a fruit dressing. Green salads are considered a palate refresher (Figure 11-3).
- *Vegetable salads* can be raw or cooked and dressed with either mayonnaise-based creamy dressings, vinaigrettes, or low-calorie dressings. The vegetables can be raw, roasted, grilled, toasted, or charred. Vegetable salads can be served with the protein entrée as a side dish or served as a stand-alone, main dish salad (Figure 11-4).
- *Potato salads* are made from potatoes that have been cooked to fork tender. Waxy potatoes hold their shape better than other starchy potatoes, making them a better choice for salad making. Potato salads are generally dressed with either a vinegar-based or a mayonnaise dressing (Figure 11-5).

Figure 11-5 Potato salad is one of the most popular salads.

Figure 11-6 Pasta salads can include most any type of pasta such as this salad made with farfalle pasta, tomatoes, broccoli, zucchini, and other vegetables.

Figure 11-7 Lentil and other types of legumes provide a hearty and delicious base to salads.

Figure 11-8 Grapes are being added to this chicken salad, a type of bound salad.

- *Pasta and grain salads* are composed of cooked grains or pasta. These grains or pastas are cooked until tender to the bite, or **al dente.** Care should be taken to avoid overcooking—once the pasta is mixed with the dressing it can become mushy. Because cooked grains and pasta absorb moisture, the seasonings may need to be adjusted after the product has had a chance to sit (Figure 11-6).
- *Legume salads* are made from beans, peas, or lentils. Some legumes such as dried beans should be soaked and cooked before use. Cook until tender and then season. Vinegar-based dressings work well with cooked legume salads. Care should be taken to avoid soaking the legumes in acidic dressings for long periods of time because the acid will cause the legumes to harden or toughen over an extended length of time (Figure 11-7).
- *Bound salads* are composed of protein products such as cooked chicken or turkey, seafood, or beef as the main component of the salad. These ingredients are diced or shredded and bound together with a mayonnaise-based dressing. The dressing holds the meat and accompanying seasonings such as celery and onions together so that this style of salad can be scooped for salad samplers, luncheon plates, and sandwich fillings (Figure 11-8).
- *Fruit salads* need special consideration because many fruits need acidulation to keep them from oxidizing. Crisp fruits such as apples, pears, or firm bananas can be acidulated with fresh lemon juice. Fruit salads are usually dressed with a creamy, mayonnaise-based sauce or honey-based dressings. Fruit salads can used as a side salad or as desserts and palate cleansers (Figure 11-9).

Figure 11-9 Apple slices, orange slices, blueberries, raspberries, and grapes combine to make a refreshing fruit salad.

Figure 11-10 Tuna nicoise salad, a type of composed salad, is made with green beans, romaine lettuce, boiled egg, sliced tomatoes, potato slices, black olives, and anchovies.

- *Composed salads* are made by carefully arranging items on a plate rather than randomly tossing them together. Usually a main protein item is the central player in a composed salad. These salads have a base or bed, the body or main ingredient, dressing, and garnish. These salads have contrasting textures and flavors and are composed neatly versus just tossing and plating. A classic example of a composed salad is a Tuna Nicoise (Figure 11-10).
- *Entrée salads* are made from proteins, dairy products, grains, and vegetables. They are served as a complete entrée (Figure 11-11).
- *Side salads* can be virtually any type of salad and are served to enhance the entrée (Figure 11-12).

Figure 11-11 Entrée salads serve as the main dish of the meal and usually include greens, vegetables, and meat.

Figure 11-12 Side salads should complement the main dish.

>> Basic Knife Skills Used in the Salad Station

In Unit 3, you were introduced to the tools and equipment used in the cold kitchen. Most chefs would agree that the single most important tool in the kitchen is the knife. The correct usage of knives makes for efficiency in the kitchen. Each knife has a specific use. The following section will demonstrate the proper methods for handling both the chef's and paring knives.

Always remember these knife-handling safety pointers:

- Knives must be kept sharp. Dull knives are dangerous.
- Keep knives clean and sanitized. When cleaning knives, never leave them in the sink unguarded. Wash, rinse, and sanitize knives after use. Allow knives to dry before putting them into a knife holder. Never put knives unguarded into a drawer.
- When cutting, know where your fingers are in relationship to the edge of the blade.
- Always walk with a knife pointed down next to your leg. Never run with knives.
- Never engage in knife horseplay in a kitchen. Serious injuries will always be the result of a knife handled carelessly.
- Do not try to catch a falling knife.

CHEF'S KNIFE

A chef's knife is the basic cutting tool used by professional chefs (Figure 11-13). This all-purpose knife is used for chopping, slicing, dicing, and mincing, and for trimming vegetables and meat. The side of the blade can be used for crushing garlic and whole spices.

The knife's efficiency will increase when it is held properly (Figure 11-14):

1. Place the thumb and index finger on opposite sides of the blade just above the bolster.
2. Wrap the remaining three fingers around the handle.

It is also important to properly hold the item that is being cut (Figure 11-15). Curl the fingertips under the item. Hold the item you are cutting with your small finger and thumb.

The slightly curved, rigid blade works well with a rocking motion that promotes even chopping and lessens hand fatigue (Figure 11-16).

PARING KNIFE

A paring knife looks similar to a small version of the chef's knife (Figure 11-17). Like the chef's knife, it is also considered an all-purpose utility knife. Paring knives are used for

Figure 11-13 Chef's knives measure between 6 and 10 inches long. The blade is triangular in shape and is made of rigid steel.

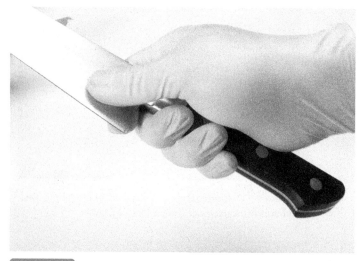

Figure 11-14 When held properly, the knife becomes an extension of the chef's hand, giving control and eliminating fatigue.

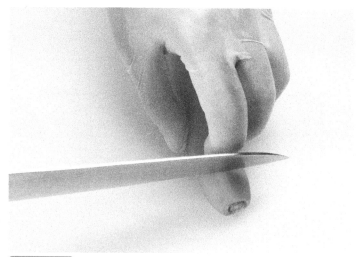

Figure 11-15 Keep fingers out of the knife's blade line.

Figure 11-16 The tip of the knife remains on the cutting board as the handle of the knife is repeatedly lifted up and down in a rocking motion.

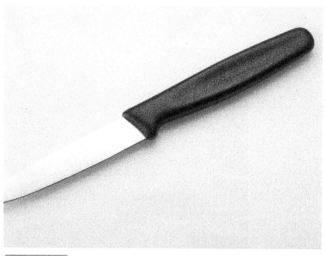

Figure 11-17 Paring knives are used for small jobs.

peeling, slicing, trimming, and hand-held jobs such as shaping mushrooms. Paring knives usually measure between 2 1/2 and 4 inches in length. Hold the knife between the thumb and the index finger.

Tomato Concassé

Basically, a **concassé** is roughly chopped tomatoes that have been peeled and seeded prior to chopping. Tomato concassé is commonly served over pasta, and used in many types of salads or in salsas. High-quality, firm tomatoes make the best concassé. Follow these steps to make a tomato concassé:

1. Use a paring knife to remove the stem by carving a V-shaped piece out of the top of the tomato.
2. Score an "X" in the bottom of the tomato. Each cut should be approximately 1 inch long (Figure 11-18).
3. Place the tomatoes in a pot of boiling water and boil for about 20 seconds. (The length of time required is variable depending on the ripeness of the tomato. Don't cook too long—the tomatoes will become mushy.)
4. Use a strainer to remove the tomatoes and place them in ice water or under cold running water (Figure 11-19).

Figure 11-18 Score tomatoes and make incision.

Figure 11-19 Remove tomatoes from boiling water.

Figure 11-20 Remove the seeds.

Figure 11-21 Cut or dice seedless tomato.

5. Let the tomatoes cool, slide the paring knife under the loose skin made from the "X" at the bottom of the tomato, and pull the skin away to peel. Continue until the tomato is skinned.
6. Cut the tomatoes in half. Use a teaspoon to remove the seeds. Some chefs prefer to squeeze out the seeds (Figure 11-20).
7. Use a rough chop cut to complete the concassé (Figure 11-21).

>> Salad Greens

In Unit 5, you were introduced to the many forms of greens available for use in salads. The purchase and storage of these greens is important to the overall quality of the finished salad. Try to purchase from nearby sources if possible and keep seasonality in mind. By using local sources when possible, you provide a unique and more healthful experience for your diner's pleasure. By purchasing from area markets, you not only encourage the local farming community but also help protect the environment. Using locally grown winter greens such as bok choy, nappa cabbage, tat soi, frisee, and endive in a salad that you serve in January will make the salad fresher and more interesting than using the cardboard tomato and watery iceberg that comes from thousands of miles away.

LEARNING ACTIVITY 11-1

Place all available salad greens on the bench or table. Start a food journal.

Write their names and descriptions in your notebook. Use this list to:

- Describe their shape and color—round, elongated, pointed, green, yellow, bronzed?
- Sample them and taste their flavors—peppery or mild; bitter, sweet, or nutty; pleasant and smooth to the tongue; tangy, lemony, or herb-like?
- Describe their texture—soft, crisp, curly, flat, crunchy?

Keep the journal and add other food categories. Go back and consult the list when you are developing menus and recipes.

>> Fresh Herbs

Fresh herbs have become widely available over recent years, and many ambitious chefs have embraced their use. Fresh herbs such as basil, borage, sage, and others are used in herb-laced salads. By placing them with other young greens, they add a fresh note to the salad. Other hardier, fresh herbs such as rosemary and thyme are used in vinegars, oils, vinaigrettes, and other liquid seasoning mediums. The soil and climate where the herbs are grown, and the care they received in harvesting and handling, make a difference in the quality of fresh herbs, as in all agricultural products. Fresh herbs are sold in small bunches, by the ounce, or by the pound. Fresh herbs have a short shelf-life, so they should be used within a day or two of purchase for the best flavor. For a complete list of herbs used in salad making, refer to Unit 4.

LEARNING ACTIVITY 11-2

Using the flavor journal that you used with vegetables in the preceding learning activity, lay out on the bench or table a nice selection of fresh herbs and dried herbs (preferably whole-leaf—ground dried herbs lose most of their flavor and become stale very quickly).

Write their names and descriptions in your notebook. Use this list to:

- Describe their shape and color—round, elongated, pointed, green, yellow, bronzed?
- Sample them and notice their tastes—peppery or mild; bitter, sweet, or nutty; pleasant and smooth to the tongue; tangy, lemony, or herb-like?
- Describe their texture—soft, crisp, curly, flat, crunchy?
- Compare each of the fresh herbs with its corresponding dried herb and check for taste and aroma.

Following is a listing of greens and salad herbs arranged by their cultivation season. Obviously, there are some climates with longer growing seasons. This list provides a general time frame for most greens and herbs.

Spring	Summer	Autumn	Winter
Sorrel	Iceberg lettuce	Bok choy	Escarole
Watercress	Bronze leaf lettuce	Swiss chard	Kale
Beet greens	Basil	Beet greens	Cabbage
Chard	Thyme	Fennel	Savoy cabbage
Chervil	Borage	Garlic	Celery root
Dandelion greens	Sage blossoms		Chicories
Frisee	Garlic		Endive
Arugula			Collard
Mustard greens			Mache (lamb's lettuce)
Nettles			
Lettuces			Radicchio
Fiddlehead ferns			Mizuna
Garlic scapes			Shiso leaves

Figure 11-22 Spinach is grown in a hydroponics greenhouse.

>> Organics

Organically grown produce is reaching food markets in increasing quantities. The definition of "organically grown" has undergone many changes. Current guidelines, developed by the U.S. Department of Agriculture (USDA) and the Organic Trade Association (OTA), in a nutshell, state that organic farmers feed the soil and not the plants and are prohibited from using pesticides and chemical fertilizers. The trend of returning to the soil as much vegetable matter as possible has been around for a long time. With rising shipping costs, just about all produce is trimmed in the field and the waste plowed under or composted and returned to the soil. As production costs get less expensive, the cost of organic produce will go down. Whether the organically grown produce is better for your health and for the environment is a judgment call.

Some greens are grown **hydroponically;** "hydro" is the Greek word for "water." Hydroponics are grown without soil in a special growing medium and fed a controlled amount of nutrients in a wet environment (Figure 11-22). With this system, lettuces and other vegetables such as tomatoes become a year-round product with consistent flavor and texture. The flavor of hydroponically grown vegetables and salad greens is a higher quality than the flavor of produce that may be shipped thousands of miles under sometimes questionable conditions. In countries with short growing seasons and cold climates, this form of farming affords residents quality produce. Because these types of plants are grown without soil, there is little contamination from sand and dirt. The end product is a clean product with a nice taste.

Be an informed chef so that you can help educate your staff, as well as the dining public, on the benefits of healthy and clean greens and vegetables. Perception plays a big part in what our customers want to eat; by providing them with a cleaner, safer product, everyone wins.

>> Salad Prep

In the cold kitchen, lettuce is cleaned, cored, and cut; and for a crisp dry salad, greens can be tumble dried in a salad spinner. This device consists of a perforated drum mounted vertically on a pivot inside a larger container. The salad is placed in the drum, the drum is turned rapidly by hand or electrically and the water clinging to the salad leaves is spun out by centrifugal force, leaving the lettuce dry (Figure 11-23). Cleaned greens should be stored in lexan tubs if possible, with damp towels and lids to keep in the freshness.

Salad greens and raw vegetables should be refrigerated in their original packaging as soon as received. Some bigger varieties of lettuce and vegetables come in large boxes or lugs. It is necessary at times to trim or reduce the size of the packaging for storage.

Salad greens such as lettuce, spinach, and other fragile-leafed products should be checked for cleanliness and freshness when received and should be purchased as frequently as needed. Lettuce and other greens do not improve with age! Remember that these products are generally eaten raw, so every caution must be taken to avoid cross-contamination during storage. Salad ingredients should be stored away from certain vegetables such as mushrooms, as these cause the fragile leaves to mold and break down. Never store vegetables near meat or other raw protein products due to the close proximity of raw juices.

Figure 11-23 Washed greens are placed in the basket of a salad spinner and spun for approximately 30 seconds.

CLEANING, PREPARING, AND STORING SALAD COMPONENTS

Depending on the quantities required, a salad ingredient is received in the pantry either in the original cases or crates, as loose heads, in bunches, or as pre-cleaned, bagged salads. Modern packaging for bagged salads removes the need to open the bag until use. For most products, cleaning is a necessity. It is obviously a messy procedure and must be well organized.

Washing salad greens is easy, providing the basic principles are well understood and the proper sinks are available. Stones and sand are heavier than salad greens and will sink to the bottom if given a chance. Some pieces of debris can float but are easily identified and picked out. Some operations add antioxidants, such as an ascorbic acid-based product, to the rinse water to keep salads looking fresh.

Figure 11-24 Move the greens from one sink to another filled with fresh water.

1. Fill clean, sanitized double sinks with cold water.
2. Place all the ingredients except the salad greens out of the way to avoid contamination with the unwashed greens. Clear the station of everything except the cutting board. In some operations, the pantry is busy with breakfast service in the morning, and salad preparation would interfere with service. In that case, the salads must be cleaned in another part of the kitchen or at some other time.
3. Cleaning salad greens generates waste, so it is essential to have the proper-sized, plastic-lined garbage can next to the sink, exactly where you need it. Some salad greens are dirtier than others; some varieties are needed in larger amounts than others. It is advisable to process every variety separately even when all are used in the same salad blends.
4. Remove any bruised, badly wilted, or rotten parts and discard.
5. Remove wholesome outer leaves from such items as escarole or chicory. They may be set aside for cooking.
6. Trim root ends that often contain embedded soil or sand and discard.
7. Immerse a reasonable amount of salad greens in one sink. There should be enough water to allow the leaves to move around freely and enough so that the water reaches all parts of the product.
8. Agitate the greens to loosen soil, insects, and other debris.
9. Lift, so debris settles into the water and not back onto the product. Put greens in the adjacent sink. You can use a colander or wire strainer to lift the salads out of the water, speeding the process.
10. Clean the first sink and remove all the sand and dirt that settled on the bottom. Rinse out the sink. Run your hand over the bottom to make sure the sand is totally gone. Fill with water.
11. Repeat the process; lift the salad greens from one sink and put them into the fresh water (Figure 11-24). Swish or agitate the greens until no debris or grit remains.
12. Depending on the type and quality of the salad greens, repeat the process until you are completely satisfied that the greens are clean. Customers do not want to bite into sand or stones when eating salad.
13. Lift the greens gently and put them into a colander to drain (Figure 11-25). The counter surrounding the sinks should have a marine edge, or small lip, if possible, which prevents water from dripping on the floor. If the counter does not have this type of lip, then the colander can be placed in one of the sinks.
14. When the salad has drained, it can be dried additionally with a salad spinner.

Figure 11-25 Allow the clean greens to drain in a colander.

Figure 11-26 Lift out the core and discard.

PRE-WASHED SALAD COMPONENTS

Many operations purchase washed and ready-to-use salad blends. They are more costly than salad components purchased in bulk, but when the cost of receiving, storing, and preparing is considered, the pre-cut material can be cost effective because of saved labor in the kitchen. The salads are ready for use, so there is little or no waste to discard—an expensive issue in many cities. Chefs can just take them out of the box and use them with no work needed. When ready-cut salads were developed, a porous plastic material had to be manufactured to allow the components to "breathe."

Preparation

Almost all salad ingredients must be cut or torn into bite-size pieces. According to type and end use, either separate into leaves or sections or cut and tear to the desired size. Salads cut into small pieces spoil faster than those with larger pieces; and some varieties oxidize (get brown at the cut), diminishing eye appeal. Yet, salads should be bite size—they are eaten with a fork, and customers should be able to eat the salad without having to use a knife. The chef or management should decide and demonstrate how to cut the salad greens.

Each variety requires special treatment:

- The core from the iceberg lettuce must be removed, but the head is usually kept whole until ready to use. Loosen the core by gripping the head and smacking the core on the cutting board. Do not use too much force or you might bruise the lettuce (Figure 11-26).
- The core or bottom rib from romaine should be removed as well, but the inner core should be kept intact.
- Boston lettuce and other soft lettuce varieties should be carefully rinsed but seldom cut and the head is usually kept intact.
- Stems from spinach should be torn off and discarded.

Never store salad greens in water. Many vitamins are water soluble and will leech out. Salads should be dry when served.

LEARNING ACTIVITY 11-3

Look for sand and stones in unwashed salad greens such as curly leaf spinach.

- Fill a sink with water.
- Put unwashed, curly leaf spinach in the sink.
- Swish around.
- Put your hand on the sink bottom. Feel the sand and tiny stones.
- Drain the sink without lifting the spinach out.
- Taste some leaves and notice the sand and grits.
- Wash the spinach properly as previously described.
- Taste the spinach now. Notice the lack of sand.

Storing

Keep salad ingredients cool and dry until service. A plastic container that is perforated with holes is ideal for salad storage. The product can be covered with damp paper towels and plastic wrap.

SALAD TOPPINGS AND GARNISHES

Green salads made with the traditional iceberg or green leaf lettuce would be boring if served without contrasting colors and textures. Toppings and garnishes add interest, flavor, color, and a pleasant texture to salads. The array of topping ingredients is almost unlimited and includes raw shredded vegetables, slivers of cheese, cooked proteins, bits of fresh or dried fruits, nuts, or a shower of sieved egg.

Use restraint when selecting toppings and garnishes. A few well-chosen items will enhance a salad—too many might create a confusing jumble. One item that adds crispness and texture is usually enough if the right item is selected. However, some salads gain interest with several crisp toppings. The items should harmonize with each other and the dressing. Toppings can be a salad component or blended into the dressing. Some garnishes, such as diced celery or peppers in a bound tuna or chicken salad, are internal—that is, they are mixed in with the salad itself. Toppings can also be added to the salad after the dressing has been added, so that it is the final component of the salad.

Garnishes add a touch of class or interest to a prepared dish. They should in no way detract from the dish, but should enhance it instead. Most garnishes are served raw, so it is important to remember to use foodservice prep gloves (if required) or to thoroughly wash your hands to ensure proper food-handling procedures.

Some of the salad ingredients that are featured here have been discussed in previous units or will be covered more extensively in the following units. However, because they are used in this lecture, a short overview is appropriate.

Bacon/Lardons or Lardoon

Crisp bacon pieces or bits are popular toppings (Figure 11-27). They can be purchased ready for use and also as vegetarian product. In some foodservice operations, bacon that was not used in breakfast service is often turned over to the pantry. It requires careful heating and draining off of all fat. Bacon used in salads should be so crisp that it will crumble when cold. Bacon is purchased sliced by weight, usually in 1-pound (450 g) layers. Unit 16 gives a recipe for making bacon. The usual number of slices per pound are 16 to 18 or 18 to 20 slices. The flavor of bacon is influenced by the type of wood used for smoking; for example, hickory or apple wood-smoked bacon.

Layout bacon is sliced bacon placed on a sheet of pan-size parchment paper and can be cooked as is. Pre-cooked bacon is partially cooked and is less dangerous to use because a smaller amount of fat is rendered out during the cooking process. Burns and fires are hazards from hot bacon fat.

Pancetta is the Italian version of bacon. It is made of rolled, cured pork belly and can be cut in pieces and fried until crisp.

Lardon is the French term for slab bacon. It is cut into small rectangular pieces, boiled about 20 minutes to reduce the salt content, and then baked or rendered until crisp. Thrifty chefs save the flavorful fat and use it in other preparation.

Ideally, bacon preparations should be prepared as close to service time as possible. If the cooked product must be held under refrigeration, re-warm before service, because cold, congealed fat is unpleasant to the palate.

Bacon flakes or bacon-flavored soy bits are canned products frequently used on salad bars. The product is available as vegetarian made with non-meat ingredients.

Croutons

There are many bread varieties on the market. The croutons explained in this lesson can be made with herb bread, focaccia, olive bread, sourdough, rye, pumpernickel, and firm cornbread. **Croutons** are small pieces of bread that are

Figure 11-27 This salad features red cabbage on greens that are topped with bacon bits and blue cheese. The bacon adds flavor and texture to the salad.

Figure 11-28 Croutons are easy to make and can turn an ordinary salad into a signature dish.

either toasted or sautéed in butter until crisp and pleasantly crunchy to the bite. While some operations purchase flavored croutons ready for use, from a flavor standpoint, making in-house croutons is a good way to enhance the flavor of your signature salad (Figure 11-28).

Generally, white bread has always been used; however, croutons made with flavored breads such as a vanilla brioche, two-color breads, rye, focaccia, sourdough, pumpernickel, and herb breads, even a firm cornbread, can add a great flavor dimension to a specialty salad. Follow these steps to make delicious croutons.

1. Cube bread to bite size (about 1 inch).
2. To add flavor to croutons, toss bread cubes in a bowl with selected herbs or spices and butter or oil. Cooking croutons in a pan with drawn butter infuses a real buttery flavor and is a more traditional way of cooking them.
3. Toast the bread cubes at 350°F (175°C), turning the croutons every 2 to 3 minutes until all of them are gently browned.

Cheese Toppings

Toppings made with cheese are always popular. Cheese cubes made with firm or semi-firm cheese are easy to make. The famous Greek salad is made with cubed feta cheese. Cheese shards and shavings are often made with Parmigiano Reggiano, the original cheese from Parma, Italy, although less-expensive cheese can also be used (Figure 11-29). Suitable cheeses are aged gouda, domestic parmesan, cheddar, goat cheese, or pecorino, a sheep's milk cheese. The cheese should be hard but not so aged as to be brittle. Cut the cheese with a vegetable peeler or grater into shreds or strips. The shreds can be baked on Silpats®, which is a flexible, nonstick baking mat, or greased sheet pans into tasty cheese tuiles or crisps. Fresh parmesan is often used to make crisps that are called parmesan tuiles. The following is a simple recipe for these crunchy tidbits.

Figure 11-29 This Caesar salad was made with romaine lettuce and topped with dressing, croutons, and tangy shavings of parmesan cheese.

Crisp garnishment has always been popular with cool crisp salads. Using a drier grating or "grana" cheese works well for this purpose.

cheese crisps, also called tuiles _Yield: 8 oz (227 g) Approximately 24 crisps_

Ingredients	Amounts		Procedure
	U.S.	Metric	
Cheese, grated	8 oz	227 g	Arrange the grated cheese into small heaps on a Silpat® or Teflon®-coated baking mat.

Bake in a 350°F (175°C) oven until the cheese is melted. Remove the crisps while warm and allow them to set up into crispy disks when they cool. To create a shaped crisp, place the hot disk over a rolling pin or glass to form a curved form.

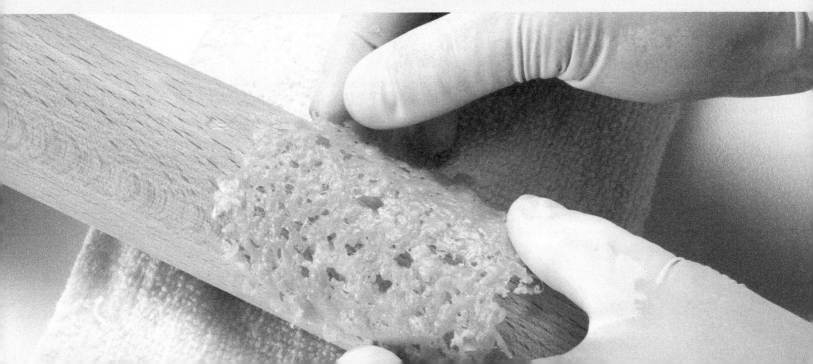

This crostini recipe can be used as a side garnish to a salad or chopped into bite-sized pieces and used as a topping.

goat cheese crostini Yield: 1 1/2 oz (43 g) 8 garnishes

Ingredients	Amounts		Procedure
	U.S.	Metric	
French bread, cut on a bias	8 slices	8 slices	Brush the bread slices with oil and toast in the oven until golden brown.
Walnut or pecan oil	As needed	As needed	

Goat cheese	8 oz	227 g	Combine the cheese, cream, and sugar to make a smooth paste. Spread on the toasted bread slices. Sprinkle with nuts. Bake in a 350°F (175°C) oven until the cheese spread is brown, about 3–4 minutes.
Heavy cream	1.5 fl oz	44 ml	
Brown sugar	1 tbsp	15 g	
Pecans or walnuts, chopped	3 oz	85 g	

NUTRITIONAL INFORMATION PER SERVING: 258 Calories; 17 g Fat (58.7% calories from fat); 11 g Protein; 15 g Carbohydrate; 1 g Dietary Fiber; 37 mg Cholesterol; 253 mg Sodium. Exchanges: 1 Grain (Starch); 1 Lean Meat; 0 Nonfat Milk; 2 1/2 Fat; 0 Other Carbohydrates.

CHEF'S TIP

Some dried fruits need to be plumped up slightly before use. Very dry fruits can be soaked in water, fruit juice, or wine an hour before service to plump them up. Apples, pears, and, occasionally, lemon slices are used. Baked fruit chips make a unique and attractive garnish on fruit platters and desserts. They should be stored in an airtight container between layers of parchment paper to keep out moisture.

Duck or Turkey Skins

Duck or turkey skin can be slow-roasted in the oven until the fat is rendered and the skin is crisp. When crumbled, the skin resembles the flavor and texture of bacon crisps. By making these cracklings with duck or turkey, they can be used when dietary restrictions prohibit the use of pork products.

Crisp Pork Skins

The product called "chicharon" is popular in South America as a snack. The pork skin should be boiled and then deep fried until crisp and glossy. Crumbled up, it makes a nice salad topping. The product is usually purchased.

Dried Fruits

Currents, cranberries, cherries, and raisins are purchased by weight. They add sweet flavor to counterbalance salty ingredients, and add texture dimension to salads. They should be tossed in when adding the dressing to the salad or sprinkled on top.

A play on the crisp potato chip by using a slice of apple or pear works well in this garnishing procedure. Slice the fruit paper thin for a crisp chip.

dried fruit chips *Yield: 30 chips*

Ingredients	Amounts		Procedure
	U.S.	Metric	
Fruit (apples or pears), sliced	30 slices	30 slices	Slice the fruit very thin on a slicing machine.

Place the slices on a Silpat®-lined baking tray. Bake in a 225°F (105°C) oven for 1–2 hours, depending upon their water content. The chips should be firm and crisp like a potato chip. Turn off the oven and let them continue to dry in the warm environment of the oven for up to 12 hours. Store in an air-tight container.

NUTRITIONAL INFORMATION PER SERVING: 8 Calories; trace Fat (4.9% calories from fat); trace Protein; 2 g Carbohydrate; trace Dietary Fiber; 0 mg Cholesterol; 0 mg Sodium. Exchanges: 0 Fruit.

Other fruits such as pineapple and citrus fruits can be dried but should be frozen first, tempered in the refrigerator for half an hour, sliced paper thin, placed on a Silpat® tray, and then dusted with 10X powdered sugar before going into the oven.

Sugar syrups help to preserve the color of some fruits by keeping them from oxidizing. In addition, the syrup can help to speed up the drying process.

sugar-coated dried fruit chips *Yield: 30 chips*

Ingredients	Amounts		Procedure
	U.S.	Metric	
Water	8 fl oz	237 ml	Combine the water, sugar, and lemon juice and let it simmer for 5 minutes to evaporate some of the water.
Sugar	14 oz	397 g	
Lemon juice	1/2 fl oz	15 ml	

Apples or pears, sliced thin	30 slices	30 slices	Immerse the sliced fruit into the solution and let it soak for 1 minute. Remove the fruit, dry it off carefully, and place it on Silpat®-lined baking trays. Top with a dusting of 10X confectioner's sugar and bake in a 225°F (105°C) oven for 1 hour to crisp. Store with parchment paper between the layers in an air-tight container.

NUTRITIONAL INFORMATION PER SERVING: 59 Calories; trace Fat (0.7% calories from fat); trace Protein; 15 g Carbohydrate; trace Dietary Fiber; 0 mg Cholesterol; trace Sodium. Exchanges: 0 Fruit; 1 Other Carbohydrates.

Fresh Vegetables

Using raw vegetables is probably the least-expensive option for adding a little extra excitement to salads. The best known are carrot curls.

How to Make Carrot Curls

1. Cut thin slices on the slicing machine.
2. Roll the slices into a curl and secure with a toothpick (Figure 11-30).
3. Store in ice-cold water in the refrigerator.
4. Let curls remain in the refrigerator for 2 to 3 hours.
5. Remove toothpicks and serve.

Shredded red cabbage, sliced radishes, shredded cucumbers, and sliced mushrooms are frequently used. Thrifty chefs save broccoli and cauliflower stems; when peeled, sliced, and briefly cooked, they make crunchy salad ingredients. Vegetable toppings can be tossed quickly in light vinaigrette prior to topping or sprayed with flavored oils to enhance flavor and shine.

Fried Asian-Style Noodles

To make these tasty garnishes, fry Asian-style yaki soba noodles or any other wheat-based, dried noodles in a fryer. You can slice wonton skins into chiffonade and deep fry at 350°F (175°C).

Dried rice noodles and Thai-style shrimp chips, when deep fried, are great Asian salad garnishes.

Fried Onions, Vegetables, and Herbs

Lightly flour-dusted and deep-fried onion slices are wonderful and inexpensive salad enhancers. Other vegetables such as beet or garlic chips work well. You may also fry herbs such as basil and sage for the added dimension of texture and flavor to your salads.

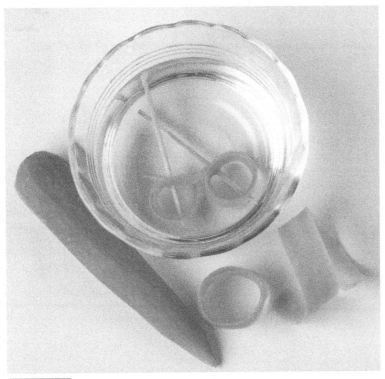

Figure 11-30 Carrot curls will retain their shape when the toothpicks are removed.

The dough can be rolled out through a pasta machine or by hand when very cold and then cut into strips or small shapes and deep-fat-fried or baked.

savory dough for frying or baking *Yield: 3 1/2 lbs (675 g)*

Ingredients	Amounts U.S.	Metric
Cream cheese	1 lb	457 g
Butter	1 lb	457 g
All-purpose flour	20 oz	567 g
Parmesan cheese, grated	4 oz	113 g
Egg yolks	2 each	2 each
Pepper, ground	1 tsp	5 g
Nutmeg	1/2 tsp	2 g
Salt	1 tsp	5 g

Procedure

Make sure all the ingredients are cold. Cut the butter and cream cheese into the dry mixture. Add the egg yolks and make the dough. Knead on a pastry bench or table. Chill the dough before use.

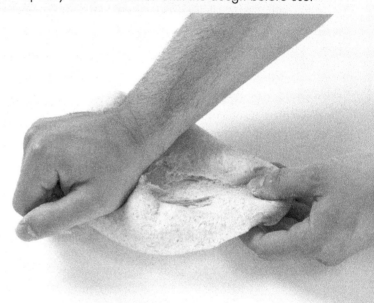

NUTRITIONAL INFORMATION PER RECIPE: 7,399 Calories; 567 g Fat (68.5% calories from fat); 136 g Protein; 450 g Carbohydrate; 16 g Dietary Fiber; 1,980 mg Cholesterol; 8,739 mg Sodium. Exchanges: 28 1/2 Grain (Starch); 10 Lean Meat; 106 Fat.

Fried Savory Dough

This dough can be rolled out with a rolling pin and cut into any desired cracker shape. Alternatively, the dough can be rolled out with a pasta machine and cut in strips and deep-fat-fried or baked in a 400°F (204° C) oven for 7 minutes.

paprika herb water biscuits

Yield: 2 lbs dough (907 g) Approximately 64 small biscuits

Ingredients	Amounts U.S.	Metric	Procedure
All-purpose flour	22 oz	624 g	Sift the flour, sugar, baking soda, salt, and paprika together.
Sugar	1 3/4 oz	50 g	
Baking soda	1 1/2 tbsp	22 g	
Salt	2 1/3 tbsp	34 g	
Paprika	1 tbsp	15 g	
Butter	4 oz	113 g	Cut the butter into the dry ingredients. Add the thyme and sour cream. Mix until smooth. Refrigerate for 30 minutes.
Thyme, fresh, chopped	2 fl oz	59 g	
Low-fat sour cream	7 fl oz	207 ml	

NUTRITIONAL INFORMATION PER PIECE: 55 Calories; 2 g Fat (27.1% calories from fat); 1 g Protein; 9 g Carbohydrate; 1 g Dietary Fiber; 4 mg Cholesterol; 338 mg Sodium. Exchanges: 1/2 Grain (Starch); 0 Lean Meat; 1/2 Fat; 0 Other Carbohydrates.

Crackers

Small commercial crackers could make economical salad toppings. They should be toasted to improve crispness.

Herbs

Fresh herbs add flavor to salads. They should be used with a light touch because some herbs are more potent than others and can overshadow the other flavors of the salad.

Nuts

Almonds, hazelnuts, peanuts, pecans, macadamia, pine nuts (called pignoli nuts), pistachios, and walnuts are often used. Nuts used as salad toppings can be purchased whole, whole blanched, coarsely chopped, sliced, or slivered. There is a big price difference between whole nuts or halves and chopped nuts. Nuts are perishable and should be stored tightly covered in the freezer once the can, box, or bag is opened. They should be toasted lightly before use. Toasting nuts brings out the flavor and aroma trapped in aromatic oils. Pecans, walnuts, hazelnuts, and many others are suitable for toasting.

Toasting Nuts

1. Place nuts or seeds on a sheet pan and place in a 350°F (175°C) moderate oven.
2. Shake the pan or stir the nuts with a spoon occasionally to ensure even toasting (Figure 11-31).
3. Use caution when toasting nuts or seeds—they can burn easily! Use your nose as well as your eyes. When the fragrance is obvious, remove the pan from the oven immediately and toss nuts or seeds on a dry pan or container to stop the cooking process. Burnt nuts are bitter and unusable.

Figure 11-31 Chef stirs the almonds during the toasting process.

High in nutrition, taste and versatility, toasted nuts are a crunchy addition to salads of all kinds. Nuts such as pecans, walnuts, almonds and hazelnuts can be flavored with a variety of herbs, spices and salts.

spicy pecans *Yield: 1 lb (450 g)*

Ingredients	Amounts		Procedure
	U.S.	Metric	
Egg whites	2 each	2 each	Combine the egg whites with water.
Water	1 fl oz	30 ml	
Pecan halves	1 lb	454 g	Blend the pecans with the remaining ingredients and then coat them evenly with the egg white/water mixture. Spread evenly on a baking sheet and place in a 300°F (150°C) oven to dry thoroughly. When dry, raise the temperature to 450°F (230°C) and toast the pecans until golden brown.
Salt	1 tbsp	15 g	
Cayenne pepper	1 tsp	5 g	
Sugar	1 tbsp	15 g	
Oil	1 fl oz	30 ml	

NUTRITIONAL INFORMATION PER RECIPE: 1,933 Calories; 190 g Fat (83.6% calories from fat); 26 g Protein; 58 g Carbohydrate; 19 g Dietary Fiber; 0 mg Cholesterol; 6,509 mg Sodium. Exchanges: 3 Grain (Starch); 2 Lean Meat; 36 1/2 Fat; 1 Other Carbohydrates.

Figure 11-32 Start at one end of the apple and peel spirally, working toward the other end.

Seeds

Many seeds such as poppy, pumpkin, sesame, and sunflower can be added to salads. Seeds become rancid quickly, so purchase only enough for a week or two and store in the freezer. Pumpkin seeds should not be served raw but must be toasted for digestibility and flavor. Toast seeds using the same method described earlier for nuts.

ADDITIONAL FRUIT PREP PANTRY WORK

The task of preparing fruit usually lands in the cold kitchen. It is suggested that you wash all fruit thoroughly before slicing to remove any potential bacteria. This applies to all fruit, even if you will be removing the rind or skin. Fruit prepared in the pantry is used as a garnish, as a breakfast item, or as ingredients in salsas or fruit salads. The following section will focus on basic fruit preparation.

Peeling Apples

1. Use a potato or apple peeler or paring knife and remove the peel (Figure 11-32).
2. Most apples oxidize rapidly. Keep the peeled fruit in grapefruit or lemon juice. Fruits will get mushy if kept in the juice too long. Some operations do not peel red delicious apples because the color of the skin is attractive.

Dicing Apples

1. Put the peeled apple on a cutting board; with a chef's knife, remove the ends to get level surfaces.
2. Cut down just beyond the core.
3. Dice the apple.

Apple Bird of Paradise

This is a popular and easy-to-make garnish for fruit salads or fruit banquet displays.

1. Hold an apple upright with the stem facing upward. Cut a vertical slice measuring one-fourth to one-third of the apple (Figure 11-33). This will create a smooth surface so that the bird will lie flat on a plate.
2. Take the piece of apple that the was just removed. Use a paring knife to carve out the bird's head and neck (Figure 11-34). Sprinkle it with lemon juice and set it aside.

Figure 11-33 Cut off a bottom section of the apple to create a smooth surface.

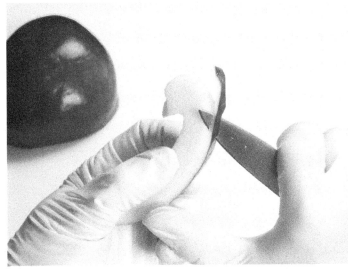

Figure 11-34 Carve the bird's neck and head out of the slice of apple.

Figure 11-35 Make a "V-shaped" wedge cut to the left of the middle intact strip of apple.

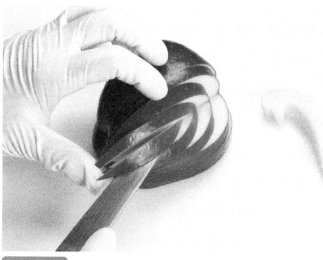

Figure 11-36 Tan out slices for wings.

3. Tip the apple so that the stem is horizontal or parallel to the cutting board (remove the stem).
4. Divide the apple into thirds, leaving a strip down the middle of the apple. To do this, use a paring knife to make a "V-shaped" wedge cut to the left of the strip of apple (Figure 11-35). Make three to five additional wedges out of the initial wedge. They should be about 1/8-inch inside the last wedge cut. You will end up with a series of wings (Figure 11-36).
5. Repeat on the opposite side.
6. Sprinkle lemon juice on all cuts, and lay the wings next to the center ridge. Spread out the V-cuts so that they look like feathers (Figure 11-37). Repeat on the other side.
7. Push the neck and head piece into the dip where the stem grew. Secure it with a straight pin (Figure 11-38 and Figure 11-39).

Figure 11-37 Spread out the V-cuts to look like feathers.

Figure 11-38 Attach the neck and head to complete the garnish.

Figure 11-39 Completed Bird of Paradise.

Peeling Figs

Some people eat the peeling of figs. Others prefer to remove the outside and enjoy the sweet flesh.

1. Place the fig on a cutting board, bottom end up.
2. Use a sharp knife to cut the fig in fourths from the apex (Figure 11-40).
3. Lift the flesh from the skin with the blade of the knife.

Preparing Grapefruits for Breakfast

One of the first jobs in hotel pantries consists of cutting grapefruits into halves and loosening the sections. Cut grapefruits will dry out during storage and must be covered with parchment paper. Before service, a few drops of grapefruit juice should be added to restore juiciness. Most operations put a strawberry or other fruit in the center for decoration. Some add a few sections for a stunning presentation.

1. Place a grapefruit on the cutting board and cut it in half.
2. Remove the pithy center with a curved grapefruit knife.
3. Insert the grapefruit knife and cut the membrane that lies between the grapefruit's sections (Figure 11-41). Score each section.
4. Run the knife around the back of each section between the rind (Figure 11-42).
5. Remove all seeds.
6. Place the grapefruits on a plastic refrigerator tray and hold until service.

Figure 11-40 Cut the fig in half and then cut the half in half until the fig is quartered.

Figure 11-41 Each section will easily lift up if scored properly before service.

Figure 11-42 Cutting between the flesh and the inner pith.

Grapefruit sections provide a beautiful, tangy, and refreshing addition to any salad.

Preparing Grapefruit Sections

Grapefruit sections, or supremes, are often used for a breakfast or brunch citrus fruit salad.

1. To peel, slice off the stem end of the fruit. Score the peel with a knife into quarters so that it looks like the lines on a basketball. Use your fingers to pull the peel off the grapefruit. Remove as much of the flesh and white membranes as possible.
2. Hold the grapefruit firmly on a cutting board and use a paring knife to cut between the membranes of each grapefruit section (Figure 11-43).

Cutting Lemon Wedges

1. Cut both of the ends off the lemon.
2. Cut the lemon into six wedges.

Wrapping Lemon Halves

Luxurious operations serve lemon halves wrapped in cheesecloth, primarily as an accompaniment for fish and seafood entrées. Precut pieces of gauze and ribbons are commercially available and used in many operations. Much money can be saved by using kitchen cheesecloth cut into squares.

1. Cut cheesecloth into squares.
2. Wrap the lemon halves; moisten the corners of the cheesecloth, twist and tie with a color-fast ribbon, add a sprig of parsley if desired (Figure 11-44).

Figure 11-44 A lemon half wrapped in cheesecloth topped with parsley.

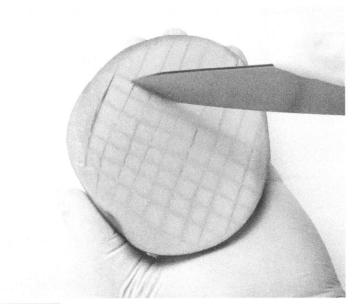

Figure 11-45 Score the mango one direction before turning it and scoring the other direction.

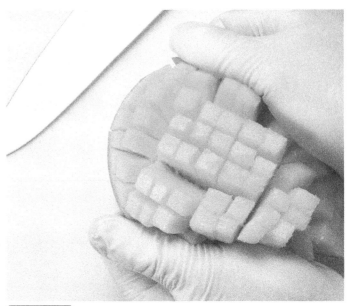

Figure 11-46 Apply pressure on the back of the scored mango half and pop out the rind so that the cubes can be easily cut off.

Cutting Mangos

Mangos are an intensely flavored, succulent tropical fruit with a slightly acidic, sweet taste. The fruit is elongated with a thin skin that is green when unripe and yellowish red when ripe. It has one large pit that is difficult to remove because the flesh clings to it. The key to cutting off the flesh is to work around the pit. Cutting mangos for breakfast service requires practice.

1. Place the mango on its side on a cutting board. Use a chef's knife and slice it in half (slightly off center to avoid hitting the seed). Cut from the top of the fruit to the bottom of it.
2. Turn the mango around and slice off the other side.
3. First score the cubes. Take each half and score the flesh without cutting through the skin. Start at the top of one half and score to the other end of the fruit. Move over 1/2 to 3/4 inch and make another line. (The size of the cubes depends on what you will be doing with the mango. If making salsa, you may want to go with a smaller cube.) Then turn the mango 90° and score it again in the other direction, moving from one side to the other (Figure 11-45). You will end up with a bunch of squares that are still attached to the rind.
4. Pick up the scored half with both hands and push the skin from underneath to pop out the scored flesh. Some people say it looks like a porcupine (Figure 11-46).
5. Hold the scored half over a bowl and slice the cubes off the rind and into a bowl.
6. There will still be mango clinging to the seed. Use a paring knife and insert it as close to the rind as possible and next to the flesh. Score around the rind. Make an incision and remove the rind. Cube as much of the remaining flesh as possible and discard the pit.

Making Cantaloupe Halves

Cantaloupe melons are sometimes served in halves. The pantry person is responsible for removing the seeds. Cut melons will dry out in storage and should be kept refrigerated and covered with parchment paper or plastic.

Figure 11-47 Once the cantaloupe is cut in half, the seeds can be easily removed.

1. Use a cutting board and chef's knife. Lay the melon on the board and cut it in half (Figure 11-47).
2. Remove the seeds and any fibrous membranes with a spoon.

Figure 11-48 Melon balls can easily be scooped from the flesh by bending and twisting a melon baller.

Making Melon Balls

Cantaloupe, honeydew, and watermelons are often scooped into balls and served in salads or fruit cups.

1. There is no need to peel the melons. Use a cutting board and chef's knife. Cut the melon in half. Use a spoon to remove the seeds and any fibrous membranes that are found in the center of the melon.
2. Use a melon baller or Parisian scoop to twist out the melon into balls or oblong-shapes (Figure 11-48). Slight imperfections are permissible.
3. Store the melon balls in the refrigerator until needed.

Serving Melon Wedges

Melon wedges are often served with the breakfast menu but they also provide color and an added treat when served on a luncheon plate alongside a sandwich, quiche, or other entrée. Most restaurants keep the rind on the melon if serving a wedge.

1. Use a cutting board and chef's knife. Cut the melon in half and scoop out the seeds and membranes that are found in the center of the melon.
2. Continue to cut the melon into quarters or even eighths, depending on the size of slice you want (Figure 11-49).

Figure 11-49 Melon wedges are easy to create; simply cut the melon melon in half, remove the seeds, and cut the size of slice needed.

Peeling Peaches

1. Place the peaches in a wire basket. Put the basket in boiling water for a few seconds, depending on their ripeness.
2. Put the peaches immediately in ice-cold water to reduce the heat.
3. Slip off the skin with your fingers or lift up a piece with a paring knife and pull off the loose skin (Figure 11-50).

Peeling Pineapples

Fresh pineapple is a fantastic addition to any fruit salad, particularly those featuring other tropical fruits. A slice of fresh pineapple is a simple and appreciated garnish and can be served with a host of menus.

1. Use a cutting board and a chef's knife. Place the pineapple on its side and cut off the top or crown of the pineapple.
2. Cut off the bottom or base.
3. Set the pineapple upright on the cutting board (Figure 11-51). Using a chef's knife, cut down to remove the peel.
4. Remove the "eyes" with a paring knife.
5. Cut in quarters and remove the core.
6. Cut in slices or small wedges.

Pineapple Basket/Boat

Pineapple baskets, boats, or shells can be filled with fruits or seafood salads and served as an appetizer or as a light main course dish.

1. Trim away any brown or ugly leaves. Keep the green, healthy-looking leaves.
2. Use a cutting board and a chef's knife. Lay the pineapple on its side and split it in half vertically, from the top (at the crown or leaves) to the bottom.
3. If the pineapple won't set flat on the cutting board, cut a slice off the backside to create a smooth surface.

> **CHEF'S TIP**
> *There is a pineapple peeling and coring device on the market, often used in supermarkets. The device is easy to use. Pineapples can be cut by hand using a variety of methods.*

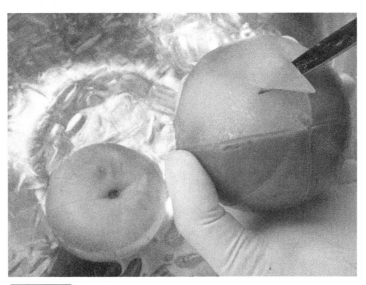

Figure 11-50 The skin on the blanched peach will buckle. Use your fingers or the point of a paring knife to lift and remove.

Figure 11-51 Cut pineapple exposing the core.

Figure 11-52 A hollowed pineapple basket filled with tropical fruit pieces becomes a festive presentation.
Tomas del Amo/PacificStock.com

4. Remove the core and take out the fruit flesh.
5. Discard the core and dice pineapple.
6. Use the pineapple basket in place of a serving bowl (Figure 11-52). Fill with fruit or seafood salad.

>> Plating Salads

The simple green, or house, salad is a preparation of one or more lettuces or leafy greens. It should look attractive and can reach the elevated status of a signature salad with the addition of various shades of color from a variety of greens such as radicchio leaves with irregular stripes of deep red and white or ruby red lolla rossa lettuce or deep green tat soi. The deeply wrinkled veins of savoy cabbage leaves can work as a stunning "bowl" to hold the other ingredients. The mixed colors of mesclun are decorative in themselves. A combination of iceberg, romaine, and chicory has varied shades of greens. The simple salad should be made from no more than three to four basic components that are married together with a dressing of choice, garnished appropriately with tasty toppings sprinkled over the salad.

Portion control is important in making house salads. Standardized recipes are important to determine the sizes of each item in the salad for a consistent product each time. Food costs can be maintained when tools such as portion scales are used to measure the size of salad items.

Salad dressings are normally added by the service staff. The proper size ladles for each dressing variety must be provided. The standard service size for vinaigrette dressings is 1 fluid ounce (30 ml). The service size for emulsified and cream dressings is 2 fluid ounces (45 ml) because the dressing is thick and does not spread easily.

Portion sizes depend, to a large extent, on the size of plates and bowls. Tiny bowls filled to the rim with greens and topped with a dollop of dressings are messy to eat. A good size for a house salad is an 8-inch plate. Larger plates can be used to good effect. The rim of the plate should be immaculately clean—this gives definition to the dish, with positive space somewhat like the frame to a painting.

CHEF'S TIP
Always serve cold salads on a chilled plate.

The following recipe is for a typical house salad. Cherry tomatoes, tomato wedges, sliced cucumber, slivered red onions, or black olives can be added or used instead of the radishes.

typical house salad garnished with croutons *Yield: 8 servings*

Ingredients	Amounts		Procedure
	U.S.	Metric	
Lettuce leaves	24 each	24 each	Place three salad leaves on each plate.

Ingredients	Amounts		Procedure
Dressing of your choice	As needed	As needed	Place the dressing in a stainless steel bowl and add the salad greens. Toss gently and place in a mound on the center of a plate. Sprinkle with radish shreds and croutons. Garnish as desired.
Assorted salad greens, packed loosely	2 qt	1.89 l	
Red radish, shredded	4 oz	113 g	
Croutons of your choice	4 oz	113 g	

NUTRITIONAL INFORMATION PER SERVING (WITHOUT DRESSING): 22 Calories; trace Fat (12.8% calories from fat); 1 g Protein; 4 g Carbohydrate; 2 g Dietary Fiber; 0 mg Cholesterol; 22 mg Sodium. Exchanges: 0 Grain (Starch); 1/2 Vegetable; 0 Fat.

Wilted salads are made when a warm dressing is poured over cold, crisp greens. A wilted salad can be considered a comfort food of the salad world. Canned chicken stock can be used in the following recipe. The mixed greens can be replaced with spinach leaves. Unit 16 features a bacon recipe that can be used with this salad.

salad with warm bacon dressing and crispy fried onions *Yield: 6 servings*

Ingredients	Amounts U.S.	Metric	Procedure
Bacon strips	6 each	6 each	Coarsely dice the raw bacon. Fry the bacon until crisp. Set aside.
Onions, chopped	1 oz	28 g	Discard the bacon fat. Add the onions; sauté until brown.
White wine vinegar	2 fl oz	59 ml	Add the vinegar, sugar, and 1/2 cup of the chicken stock to the onions. Bring to a boil. Reduce to a simmer.
Sugar	1 tsp	5 g	
Chicken stock	8 fl oz	237 ml	
Arrowroot	1 tbsp	15 g	Blend the arrowroot with the remaining cold stock. Add to the simmering stock. Stir and bring to a boil.
Oil	1 1/2 fl oz	45 ml	Add the oil, salt, and pepper to the above mixture.
Salt	To taste	To taste	
Pepper	To taste	To taste	
Onions, sliced paper thin	6 oz	170 g	Toss the sliced onions in flour and deep-fry until crisp.
Flour	1 tbsp	15 g	
Salad greens	2 qt	1.9	Toss the salad with the above mixture (dressing). Arrange on six plates. Top with fried onions and diced bacon.

NUTRITIONAL INFORMATION PER SERVING: 134 Calories; 10 g Fat (67.6% calories from fat); 3 g Protein; 8 g Carbohydrate; 2 g Dietary Fiber; 5 mg Cholesterol; 511 mg Sodium. Exchanges: 0 Grain (Starch); 1/2 Lean Meat; 1/2 Vegetable; 2 Fat; 0 Other Carbohydrates.

The following sliced tomatoes and mozzarella side salad recipe is sometimes called a Caprese salad or Insalata Caprese, which means it is a salad that was inspired by the Isle of Capri. It is generally served in the summer months and showcases garden-fresh, vine-ripened tomatoes. Only fresh mozzarella should be used as well as fresh basil leaves. The Balsamic Vinaigrette Dressing recipe found in Unit 15 can serve as dressing.

sliced tomatoes with mozzarella side salad *Yield: 1 serving*

Ingredients	Amounts		Procedure
	U.S.	Metric	
Tomato, ripe	1 large	1 large	Slice the tomato and place on a lettuce leaf. Arrange the cheese on top. Sprinkle with dressing and garnish with a basil leaf.
Boston lettuce leaf	1 each	1 each	
Mozzarella Ciliegini (small balls)	3 each	3 each	
Balsamic vinaigrette dressing	1 fl oz	30 ml	
Basil leaf, fresh	1 each	1 each	

NUTRITIONAL INFORMATION PER SERVING: 438 Calories; 37 g Fat (74.7% calories from fat); 20 g Protein; 9 g Carbohydrate; 1 g Dietary Fiber; 76 mg Cholesterol; 365 mg Sodium. Exchanges: 2 1/2 Lean Meat; 1 Vegetable; 6 Fat.

Wedge salads are quick and easy to prepare and give the diner a feeling of abundance. Use the Favorite Ranch Dressing recipe found in Unit 15 as the dressing.

Boston lettuce with egg wedges and ranch dressing
Yield: 1 serving

Ingredients	Amounts		Procedure
	U.S.	Metric	
Boston lettuce heart	1 each	1 each	Cut the lettuce heart in half and place one half on a plate.
Hard-boiled egg	1 each	1 each	Quarter the egg and arrange it on the plate.
Ranch dressing	1 1/2 fl oz	44 ml	Cover with the dressing and sprinkle with radish julienne.
Radish, julienne	1 tbsp	15 g	

NUTRITIONAL INFORMATION PER SERVING: 318 Calories; 29 g Fat (81.8% calories from fat); 9 g Protein; 6 g Carbohydrate; 1 g Dietary Fiber; 220 mg Cholesterol; 569 mg Sodium. Exchanges: 1 Lean Meat; 1/2 Vegetable; 5 1/2 Fat; 0 Other Carbohydrates.

This salad, which comes from Russia, features cooked potatoes and an unusual array of other fresh ingredients that are tossed with mayonnaise. A light version can be dressed with low-fat sour cream.

chicken olivia   *Yield: 45 oz (1.276 kg) 6 servings side order*

Ingredients	Amounts		Procedure
	U.S.	Metric	
Chicken breast, cooked, julienned	16 oz	454 g	Gently toss all the ingredients.
Apples, peeled, julienned	4 oz	113 g	
Cucumbers, julienned	4 oz	113 g	
Potatoes, cooked, julienned	5 oz	141 g	
Carrots, blanched, julienned	4 oz	113 g	
Green peas, frozen	4 oz	113 g	
Mayonnaise	4 oz	113 g	
Parsley, chopped	1 tbsp	15 g	
Hard-boiled egg, diced	4 oz	113 g	

NUTRITIONAL INFORMATION PER SERVING: 319 Calories; 24 g Fat (64.8% calories from fat); 17 g Protein; 12 g Carbohydrate; 2 g Dietary Fiber; 116 mg Cholesterol; 175 mg Sodium. Exchanges: 1/2 Grain (Starch); 2 Lean Meat; 1/2 Vegetable; 0 Fruit; 1 1/2 Fat

This simple salad is light and refreshing. Don't scrimp on the cheese. Use a flavorful cheese such as parmigiano reggiano, pecorino romano, an aged goat cheese, dry jack, or aged gouda. Allow for the full marinating time so that the cucumbers have a chance to absorb some of the flavor from the dressing.

cherry tomatoes and cucumber salad
Yield: 20 oz (472 g) 2 servings

Ingredients	Amounts		Procedure
	U.S.	Metric	
Cherry tomatoes, halved	4 oz	113 g	Combine the cucumbers and tomatoes with dressing. Marinate for 20 minutes.
Cucumbers, seeded and diced	4 oz	113 g	
Balsamic dressing	1 fl oz	30 ml	
Herb croutons	1 tbsp	15 g	Plate and sprinkle with croutons and cheese shards.
Cheese shards	1 tbsp	15 g	

NUTRITIONAL INFORMATION PER SERVING (EXCLUDING UNKNOWN ITEMS): 40 Calories; 2 g Fat (32.7% calories from fat); 2 g Protein; 6 g Carbohydrate; 1 g Dietary Fiber; 4 mg Cholesterol; 43 mg Sodium. Exchanges: 0 Grain (Starch); 0 Lean Meat; 1 Vegetable; 0 Fruit; 0 Fat.

Panzanella is a refreshing, Tuscan, stale-bread salad with onions, tomatoes, basil, olive oil, vinegar, and seasonings. Use focaccia or crusty Italian bread. Use high-quality olive oil and red wine vinegar as well as ripe, flavorful tomatoes. The ingredients are approximate and must be adjusted according to the bread type.

panzanella *Yield: 8 servings side order*

Ingredients	Amounts	
	U.S.	**Metric**
Stale bread, diced	1 qt	946 ml
Red onions, diced	6 oz	170 g
Tomatoes, seeded and diced	8 oz	227 g
Basil leaves, chopped	1 oz	28 g
Black olives, chopped	4 oz	113 g
Olive oil	6 fl oz	177 ml
Red wine vinegar	2 fl oz	59 ml
Pepper, coarsely ground	1 tbsp	15 g

Procedure

The bread must be stale and, if necessary, oven dried.

Combine all the ingredients and let rest for 1 hour. The bread should not be soaking wet but should remain somewhat dry in the center.

NUTRITIONAL INFORMATION PER SERVING: 423 Calories; 24 g Fat (51.0% calories from fat); 8 g Protein; 45 g Carbohydrate; 3 g Dietary Fiber; 0 mg Cholesterol; 543 mg Sodium. Exchanges: 2 1/2 Grain (Starch); 1/2 Vegetable; 0 Fruit; 5 Fat; 0 Other Carbohydrates.

This recipe for Hungarian Cucumber Salad features Hungarian paprika. Paprika powder is made from a type of ground red peppers. These peppers are sweeter and milder than chili peppers, but paprika can range from mild to hot. Hungarian paprika is considered to provide the strongest and richest flavor of all the types of paprika. Not only does paprika add flavor to a dish but it also adds a beautiful color.

Hungarian cucumber salad *Yield: 6 servings side order*

Ingredients	Amounts U.S.	Metric	Procedure
Cucumbers, seeded and sliced	3 pints	1.42 l	Combine the cucumbers and salt. Let rest for 1 hour. Drain off any liquid and use the back of a spoon to squeeze out the extra juices.
Salt	2 tsp	10 g	
Sugar	2 tsp	10 g	Combine the remaining ingredients. Pour over the cucumbers.
Hungarian paprika	1 tbsp	15 g	
Oil	2 fl oz	59 ml	
White vinegar	2 fl oz	59 ml	
Dill, fresh	1/2 oz	14 g	

NUTRITIONAL INFORMATION PER SERVING: 104 Calories; 9 g Fat (76.8% calories from fat); 1 g Protein; 5 g Carbohydrate; 1 g Dietary Fiber; 0 mg Cholesterol; 713 mg Sodium. Exchanges: 0 Grain (Starch); 0 Lean Meat; 1/2 Vegetable; 2 Fat; 0 Other Carbohydrates.

According to the *Oxford Encyclopedia of Food and Drink in America,* written by Andrew F. Smith (Oxford University Press, New York, 2004, Volume 1, p. 147), "The earliest European settlers on North America's eastern shores brought cabbage seeds with them, and cabbage was a general favorite throughout the colonies. The Dutch who founded New Netherland (New York State) . . . grew cabbage extensively along the Hudson River. They served it in their old-country ways, often as koolsla (shredded cabbage salad). This dish became popular throughout the colonies and survives as cole slaw."

Cole slaw will shed liquid in storage, and at the same time the cabbage will get soft. If crisp slaw is desired, it should be served right away; soft slaw can be stored overnight. The yield will be smaller if the salad is stored.

cole slaw and raisin salad *Yield: 6 servings side order*

Ingredients	Amounts U.S.	Metric	Procedure
Raisins	3 oz	85 g	Cover the raisins with water and bring to a boil. Let stand for 10 minutes and drain. Save the liquid.
Cabbage, shredded	24 oz	680 g	Combine all the ingredients and store refrigerated for 4 hours. Taste; if sweetness is needed, add some of the raisin liquid.
Vinegar, white	2 fl oz	59 ml	
Mayonnaise	4 fl oz	118 ml	
Oil	2 fl oz	59 ml	
Salt	To taste	To taste	
Pepper	To taste	To taste	

NUTRITIONAL INFORMATION PER SERVING: 268 Calories; 25 g Fat (77.9% calories from fat); 2 g Protein; 14 g Carbohydrate; 2 g Dietary Fiber; 6 mg Cholesterol; 164 mg Sodium. Exchanges: 0 Grain (Starch); 1/2 Vegetable; 1/2 Fruit; 3 Fat; 0 Other Carbohydrates.

Inventive cooks took cole slaw recipes and added other favorite ingredients. This recipe includes apple and celery stalks. It's creamy and refreshing, the perfect accompaniment to a sandwich or pork dish.

apple slaw *Yield: Approximately 6–8 servings*

Ingredients	Amounts U.S.	Metric	Procedure
Mayonnaise	4 fl oz	118 ml	Combine the mayonnaise, vinegar, sugar, celery salt, and pepper in a large bowl. Whisk until the sugar is dissolved.
Cider vinegar	1 1/2 fl oz	44 ml	
Sugar	1 1/2 oz	43 g	
Celery salt	1 tsp	5 g	
Black pepper	1 tsp	5 g	
Green cabbage	1 small head	1 small head	Finely chop the cabbage, onion, apple, and celery in a food processor, running the machine in short bursts and working in several
Onion, quartered	1 small	1 small	
Red Delicious apple, quartered	1 medium	1 medium	
Celery stalks	2 each	2 each	

batches so as not to overcrowd the processor bowl. Pour into a bowl. Combine with dressing; adjust the seasonings if necessary.

NUTRITIONAL INFORMATION PER SERVING: 156 Calories; 14 g Fat (72.7% calories from fat); 1 g Protein; 11 g Carbohydrate; 1 g Dietary Fiber; 6 mg Cholesterol; 329 mg Sodium. Exchanges: 0 Grain (Starch); 1/2 Vegetable; 0 Fruit; 1 Fat; 1/2 Other Carbohydrates.

Grated carrot salads were popular in the 1950s. This one is updated with the addition of cumin and honey.

carrot nut salad *Yield: 6 servings side order*

Ingredients	Amounts		Procedure
	U.S.	Metric	
Carrots, grated	1 lb	454 g	Combine all the ingredients except the nuts. Marinate the carrots for 2 hours.
Honey	1 tbsp	15 g	
Cumin	1 tsp	5 g	
Lemon juice	2 fl oz	59 ml	
Oil	1/2 fl oz	15 ml	
Pepper, coarsely ground	2 tsp	10 g	
Salt	To taste	To taste	

Cashews or peanuts, toasted	2 oz	57 g	Plate and sprinkle with nuts.

NUTRITIONAL INFORMATION PER SERVING: 104 Calories; 5 g Fat (41.1% calories from fat); 2 g Protein; 15 g Carbohydrate; 3 g Dietary Fiber; 0 mg Cholesterol; 76 mg Sodium. Exchanges: 0 Grain (Starch); 0 Lean Meat; 1 1/2 Vegetable; 0 Fruit; 1 Fat; 0 Other Carbohydrates.

This salad includes curry and amchoor powder, giving it a wonderful taste twist. Raw zucchini is a great alternative to other fresh salad ingredients. Make sure that only fresh, firm zucchini is used. Amchoor powder is an acidic powder made from green mangos. It is available in Indian stores or specialty distributors.

zucchini and nut salad *Yield: 6 servings side order*

Ingredients	Amounts U.S.	Metric	Procedure
Zucchini, firm, small, diced	1 lb	454 g	Combine all the ingredients except the nuts. Marinate the zucchini for 2 hours. Plate and sprinkle with nuts.
Curry powder	1 tbsp	15 g	
Oil	2 fl oz	59 ml	
Amchoor powder	1 tsp	5 g	
Lemon juice	1 fl oz	30 ml	
Brown sugar	1 tsp	5 g	
Cayenne pepper	1/4 tsp	1 g	
Salt	To taste	To taste	
Cashews, toasted, chopped	2 oz	57 g	

NUTRITIONAL INFORMATION PER SERVING: 152 Calories; 14 g Fat (77.9% calories from fat); 3 g Protein; 6 g Carbohydrate; 2 g Dietary Fiber; 0 mg Cholesterol; 404 mg Sodium. Exchanges: 0 Grain (Starch); 0 Lean Meat; 1/2 Vegetable; 0 Fruit; 2 1/2 Fat; 0 Other Carbohydrates.

Cactus leaf salad is usually served on lettuce leaves, garnished with chili peppers, and topped with a Mexican white cheese called *queso blanco*.

Mexican cactus leaf salad   *Yield: 10 servings side order*

Ingredients	Amounts U.S.	Metric	Procedure
Nopales leaves, raw, diced	2 lbs	907 g	With gloved hands, carefully cut out the spines of the nopales cactus pads. Dice and let drain for 1 hour.
Tomatoes, peeled, seeded, chopped	6 oz	170 g	Combine the remaining ingredients. Pour over the diced nopales and let marinate for at least 2 hours.
Olive oil	2 fl oz	59 ml	
Red wine vinegar	2 fl oz	59 ml	
Onions, chopped	4 oz	113 g	
Oregano, fresh, chopped	1 tbsp	15 g	
Serrano chili, chopped	1 tbsp	15 g	
Cilantro, chopped	1 tbsp	15 g	
Salt	To taste	To taste	

NUTRITIONAL INFORMATION PER SERVING: 65 Calories; 6 g Fat (73.0% calories from fat); 1 g Protein; 4 g Carbohydrate; 1 g Dietary Fiber; 0 mg Cholesterol; 35 mg Sodium. Exchanges: 0 Grain (Starch); 0 Lean Meat; 1/2 Vegetable; 1 Fat; 0 Other Carbohydrates.

 CHEF'S TIP
If using tuna packed in oil, make sure to lightly rinse the tuna in cold water to remove the excess oil. Always drain the tuna thoroughly before using it.

>> Bound Salads

Bound salads are very popular for lunch entrée items. They can be served strictly as a salad course—garnished and plated; usually on a large, clean, unblemished outer leaf of Boston bibb lettuce or Iceberg lettuce. This underlayer acts as a bed for the salad, giving it eye appeal and a fresh look. These bound salads are also used as sandwich fillings. Tuna, chicken, salmon, and egg are the most common of the protein-based bound salads. By changing flavors and garnishes, these fillings can go from boring to bold.

Tuna salad is tops when it comes to bound salads. Many other proteins can be used as a replacement for the tuna in the next recipe. Grilled or poached chicken is popular. A bound salad is a good way to use excess turkey or other cooked meats such as roast beef or pork loin. These salads not only can serve a hungry lunch crowd, but are a smart way to strengthen the bottom line. Crisp fruit such as apples and pears can be added for flavorful and colorful variations. Crunchy foods such as toasted almonds and pecans also add texture as well as flavor. Unique spices and herbs can turn a standard salad recipe into the chef's signature dish.

Our Benchmark Recipe for Tuna Salad Filling is simple and uncomplicated. Chefs can use the basic recipe, expand it, and customize it to a particular usage. Diced red or green bell peppers, capers, finely grated lemon zest, minced flat leaf parsley, dill weed, and finely diced hard-cooked eggs combine well with the taste of tuna. Avoid using too much of your garnish ingredients—they are used for color and flavor, not for filler.

Bound salads such as the ever popular tuna salad is found on many types of menus. Salmon, cooked chicken or turkey and other proteins can be substituted for the tuna.

tuna salad filling *Yield: 16 oz (454 g) 4 each, 4 oz (110 g) servings*

Ingredients	Amounts U.S.	Metric	Procedure
Tuna fish, canned or vacuum packed	8 oz	227 g	Drain the tuna and flake it with a fork.
Celery	4 oz	110 g	Dice the celery.
Onion	1 tbsp	15 g	Grate the onion.
Mayonnaise	4 fl oz	118 ml	Combine the tuna, celery, and onion with the mayonnaise. Do not purée. Store refrigerated.

NUTRITIONAL INFORMATION PER SERVING: 268 Calories; 24 g Fat (76.9% calories from fat); 15 g Protein; 1 g Carbohydrate; trace Dietary Fiber; 27 mg Cholesterol; 370 mg Sodium. Exchanges: 2 Lean Meat; 0 Vegetable; 2 Fat.

Cooked fish such as canned mackerel or sockeye tuna work well in place of tuna. Try turning the basic tuna salad filling recipe into roast beef salad by pairing roast beef with blue cheese or grated sharp cheddar and the addition of horseradish or mustard in the spread. Roast pork salad can be made by substituting pork for the tuna and adding fire-roasted red sweet or hot peppers; a touch of jalapeno jelly; or canned, chopped, and drained pineapple to the mayonnaise. Adding other ingredients such as crumbled bacon pieces, chopped nuts, chutney, and diced apples, grapes, and dates can expand chicken salad fillings. Try adding different spices and herbs to further alter the basic recipe. Different cooking methods also alter the flavor of the chicken salad. Grilled or baked chicken provides a rich flavor. Steamed or poached chicken has a subtle flavor.

basic chicken salad filling
Yield: 16 oz (454 g) 4 each, 4 oz (110 g) servings

Ingredients	Amounts U.S.	Metric	Procedure
Chicken, cooked	8 oz	227 g	Dice the cooked chicken. Cool.
Celery	4 oz	113 g	Dice the celery.
Mayonnaise	4 fl oz	118 g	Combine all the ingredients and chill. Store refrigerated.

NUTRITIONAL INFORMATION PER SERVING: 289 Calories; 30 g Fat (88.7% calories from fat); 8 g Protein; 1 g Carbohydrate; trace Dietary Fiber; 47 mg Cholesterol; 207 mg Sodium. Exchanges: 1 Lean Meat; 0 Vegetable; 2 1/2 Fat.

To make a chicken curry salad, add sliced grapes, diced apples, toasted almonds, or macadamia nuts, add a touch of curry powder to the mayonnaise (depending on the desired taste), and add a few tablespoons of mango chutney to the dressing. Toss the chicken with the ingredients and chill.

In our next standard classic, we start with egg salad. With several interesting additions, we can create a unique and flavorful luncheon salad or sandwich filling. Most egg salad recipes include pickle relish. Any type of pickle relish can be used including dill or sweet pickles, depending on your preference.

egg salad filling   *Yield: 24 oz (680 g) 6 each, 4 oz (110 g) servings*

Ingredients	Amounts U.S.	Metric	Procedure
Eggs, hard boiled	8 each	8 each	Chop the eggs.
Celery	4 oz	113 g	Dice the celery.
Red bell pepper	1 oz	28 g	Mince the pepper.
Mayonnaise	4 fl oz	118 ml	Blend the eggs, celery, and red pepper with mayonnaise and any of the optional ingredients listed (Dijon mustard, jalapeno pepper, capers, pickle relish). Top with paprika. Store refrigerated.
Dijon mustard, coarse ground, optional	1 tbsp	15 g	
Jalapeno pepper, diced fine, optional	1 oz	28 g	
Capers, optional	1 tbsp	15 g	
Pickle relish, optional	1 tbsp	15 g	
Smoked paprika	1 tsp	5 g	

NUTRITIONAL INFORMATION PER SERVING: 246 Calories; 23 g Fat (80.9% calories from fat); 9 g Protein; 3 g Carbohydrate; 1 g Dietary Fiber; 289 mg Cholesterol; 267 mg Sodium. Exchanges: 0 Grain (Starch); 1 Lean Meat; 0 Vegetable; 2 Fat; 0 Other Carbohydrates.

Shrimp creates an image of opulence in most people's minds. Serve this salad at any up-scale event. Use a crisp lacy Nappa or Savoy cabbage leaf on the liner between the chilled plate and salad. Lobster or crab can be substituted for the shrimp.

Asian-style shrimp salad filling
Yield: 24 oz (680 g) 6 each, 4 oz (110 g) servings

Ingredients	Amounts U.S.	Metric	Procedure
Shrimp (salad or bay), fresh or frozen, cooked	16 oz	454 g	Thaw the shrimp, if frozen.
Celery	2 oz	56 g	Finely mince the celery.
Water chestnuts	2 oz	56 g	Finely mince the water chestnuts.
Ginger root	1/2 tbsp	8 g	Grate the ginger root.
Mayonnaise	3 fl oz	89 ml	Combine the shrimp, celery, water chestnuts, ginger root, mayonnaise, sesame oil, and paprika. Store refrigerated.
Sesame oil	1 fl oz	29 ml	
Paprika	1/2 tbsp	8 g	
Sesame seeds, toasted	1 tsp	5 g	Just prior to service, garnish with toasted sesame seeds.

NUTRITIONAL INFORMATION PER SERVING: 234 Calories; 18 g Fat (67.3% calories from fat); 16 g Protein; 4 g Carbohydrate; 1 g Dietary Fiber; 120 mg Cholesterol; 199 mg Sodium. Exchanges: 0 Grain (Starch); 2 Lean Meat; 0 Vegetable; 2 Fat.

>> Banquet Salads

Banquet salad service poses its own set of challenges. Whether the salad is preset before the banquet or served during the course of the event, space is always the challenge on a banquet table set for eight or ten guests. Banquet salads generally are served on the charger plate, or this plate is removed before service of the salad. Banquet salads are made in the same manner as any other salad, with an emphasis on servability (Figure 11-53). If a banquet salad is stacked too high, the server may have difficulty in getting many plates served to a table at the same time. Freshness is also a key, so many banquet salads are served undressed with the dressing passed or served tableside.

At very formal dinners, the salad is served after the main course as accompaniment to a small serving of exquisite cold meat. Usually, burgundy wines are served at that stage, and the salad must be dressed very lightly with olive oil, lemon juice, salt, and pepper.

Figure 11-53 A chef delicately moves pre-made salads from a large tray to individual plates before serving them at a banquet.

>> Summary

In this unit we discussed how to prepare salad ingredients and how to store them properly. We learned that green salads can be cultivated without soil in a nutritious solution, and this process is called hydroponic gardening. These salads are usually more expensive but contain no sand and give a better yield. Salad greens should never be left soaking in water because water-soluble vitamins will get washed out.

We practiced working with knives and learned important safety pointers for handling them. Salad toppings were discussed, including many diverse ingredients that can be added to a salad to give it texture and additional flavor. A variety of basic garnishment techniques were also introduced.

>> Review Questions

TRUE/FALSE

1. Knives should be placed in the sink to get washed by the pot washer.

2. Plants can be grown without soil.
3. Organic farmers feed the soil and not the plants.

MULTIPLE CHOICE

4. Chiffonade is
   a. pie with a meringue topping.
   b. fancy fabric used by women.
   c. shredded greens or herbs.
   d. ribbons on gift boxes.
5. OTA stands for
   a. Organization of Technical Assistance.
   b. Over the Counter Transactions.
   c. Orders Taken by Assistant servers.
   d. Organic Trade Association.
6. Hydro is a(n)
   a. fancy name for a fire plug.
   b. island in the Pacific.
   c. Greek word for water.
   d. technical term for hoist.
7. Hippocrates believed raw vegetables
   a. were poisonous.
   b. were hard on the bowels and should be eaten sparingly.
   c. were easily digested and did not create obstructions.
   d. were medicinal and should be eaten when sick.
8. King Louis XIV liked his greens served with
   a. cheese.
   b. capers.
   c. game meats.
   d. edible flowers.

9. The term "al dente" refers to cooking grains or pastas
   a. tender to the bite.
   b. thoroughly cooked through.
   c. in boiling water.
   d. using a parboiled method.
10. A tuiles is a
    a. French gadget used in creating salad garnishes.
    b. Spanish edible flower.
    c. cheese crisp.
    d. bacon crisp.
11. Always serve cold salads on
    a. a lettuce leaf.
    b. a chilled plate.
    c. a salad bowl.
    d. a rimless bowl or plate.
12. Most egg salad is made with _____ pickle relish.
    a. dill
    b. sweet
    c. bread and butter
    d. any type of
13. Bound salads are bound together with
    a. a mayonnaise-based dressing.
    b. a vinaigrette.
    c. eggs.
    d. oil.

FILL IN THE ANSWERS

14. Centrifugal force is _____.
15. Why shouldn't salads greens be stored in water? _____
16. Describe a composed salad. _____
17. The main purpose of a side salad is to _____.

18. Silpat® is a trade name for _____.
19. Croutons are _____.
20. Describe amchoor powder. _____
21. What is panzella? _____

Side Salads

>> Learning Objectives

After you have finished reading this unit, you should be able to:

- Identify at least five starch-based side salads.
- Demonstrate how to make the Benchmark Recipes for potato salad and macaroni salad.
- Discuss ways to create ethnically inspired side salads based on basic recipes.
- Demonstrate how to trim and prepare small artichokes for use in side salads.
- Identify some of the concerns associated with stocking a salad bar.

>> Key Terms

celeriac	mimosa	quinoa (*KEEN-wah*)	succotash
cereal grains	pulses	sneeze guard	teff

I n previous units, you learned to identify and select salad ingredients for quality. You also learned preparation techniques for those ingredients and prepared a variety of both green and composed main-course salads. In this unit, we will be working with versatile side salads.

Side salads have a long history in modern foodservice. A cookbook written in 1893 by the chef de cuisine of Delmonico's restaurant in New York City, Charles Ranhofer, lists 33 vegetable- or starch-based salads. Many of these same salads are still very popular today and are served as side salads to accompany an entrée or sandwich plate. What is a picnic without potato salad? Or a crusty, hot po'boy sandwich without a side of cole slaw or three-bean salad? Many side salads are composed of cooked starch items such as potatoes, beans, pasta, rice, and other grain-based products. The best-known starch salads include the potato salad and the ubiquitous macaroni salad. Some side salads are composed of raw or cooked vegetables such as tomatoes, beets, broccoli, and cabbage. Other sides feature fruits. Just about any ingredient can find its way into a side salad.

Side salads can be served as appetizer courses or as accompaniments to many main-course meals and sandwiches. They can also make a perfect addition to buffet tables and salad bars. Side-salad serving sizes vary. For a first course or light meal, a portion size might run 4 to 6 ounces and, in some cases, up to 8 ounces by volume. At other times, a small size such as 2 to 4 ounces would be appropriate. In this unit, we will also focus on salad bars and their ingredients and set-up procedures. Salad bars continue to be very popular and cost-effective in many restaurants.

>> Starch-Based Salads

Starch-based salads are the foundation of any hotel or institutional foodservice operation. Caterers use starches, legumes, potatoes, and cereal grains in many creative ways. **Cereal grains** are those plants that yield an edible grain such as wheat, rye, oats, rice, or corn. With today's focus on health issues, whole grains and beans are becoming popular menu items. They add flavor and healthy salads to any menu. Many grains new to the United States are ancient and commonplace in their native homeland. These new grains, such as quinoa, amaranth, and **teff,** along with the legumes, or **pulses,** such as beans, peas, and lentils, are adding a new dimension to many side-salad menus (Figure 12-1).

Figure 12-1 Grains and legumes, along with potatoes, provide the key ingredients in starch-based salads.

If there was one side salad that is considered an all-American side, it would be the potato salad. Potato-salad-type recipes were actually introduced to America by European settlers who adapted local ingredients to their traditional recipes. This accounts for regional potato salad variations found throughout the United States. Cold potato salads came from British and French recipes. Warm potato salads followed the German preference for hot vinegar and bacon dressings served over vegetables. This is a basic cold potato salad recipe. The potato peels can be left on to give added color and fiber, if desired.

potato salad   *Yield: 8–10 servings side order*

Ingredients	Amounts U.S.	Metric	Procedure
Red potatoes (1 1/2–2 in diameter), peeled and cut into quarters	2.25 lbs	1.02 kg	Put the potatoes in a pot and cover with cold, salted water. Bring the potatoes to a simmer and cool until they can be easily pierced with a fork. Drain, let dry, and cool. Dice into medium dice.
Water	2 qt	1.9 l	
Salt	1 oz	30 g	
Eggs, hard-boiled	4 each	4 each	Mix the mustard, mayonnaise, and Worcestershire sauce. Gently toss over the eggs, green onions, and chilled potatoes.
Green onions, diced	4 oz	113 g	
Mustard	1 fl oz	59 ml	
Mayonnaise	1 pt	473 g	
Worcestershire sauce	1/2 tsp	2 g	
Salt	To taste	To taste	Season to taste. Chill.
Pepper	To taste	To taste	

NUTRITIONAL INFORMATION PER SERVING: 477 Calories; 44 g Fat (78.5% calories from fat); 6 g Protein; 21 g Carbohydrate; 2 g Dietary Fiber; 111 mg Cholesterol; 1,818 mg Sodium. Exchanges: 1 Grain (Starch); 1/2 Lean Meat; 0 Vegetable; 3 1/2 Fat; 0 Other Carbohydrates.

There's a division between those who like mustard in their potato salad and those who do not. This is a creamy potato salad without mustard.

creamy potato salad *Yield: 8–10 servings side salads*

Ingredients	Amounts U.S.	Metric	Procedure
Red potatoes (1 1/2–2 in diameter), peeled and cut into quarters	2 lbs	907 g	Put the potatoes in a pot and cover with cold, salted water. Bring the potatoes to a simmer and cool until they can be easily pierced with a fork. Drain, let dry, and cool. Dice into medium dice.
Water	2 qt	1.9 l	
Eggs, hard-cooked, peeled, diced	4 each	4 each	Blend the eggs, celery, onion, chilled potatoes, mayonnaise, sour cream, and garlic powder. Season to taste.
Celery, diced	4 oz	113 g	
Green onion, diced	1 oz	28 g	
Yellow onion, grated	1 oz	28 g	
Mayonnaise	8 fl oz	237 g	
Sour cream	4 fl oz	118 ml	
Garlic powder	1 tbsp	15 g	
Salt	To taste	To taste	
Pepper	To taste	To taste	
Paprika	Dust	Dust	Dust the top with paprika. Optional garnishes could include sliced radishes, green onions, and celery.

NUTRITIONAL INFORMATION PER SERVING: 319 Calories; 26 g Fat (69.8% calories from fat); 6 g Protein; 20 g Carbohydrate; 2 g Dietary Fiber; 108 mg Cholesterol; 215 mg Sodium. Exchanges: 1 Grain (Starch); 1/2 Lean Meat; 0 Vegetable; 0 Nonfat Milk; 2 1/2 Fat.

This is a very popular salad similar to German-style potato salads made with hot or warm bacon dressing. Red bliss potatoes are waxy and perfect for this recipe. Use the Hot Dressing for Potato Salad recipe found in Unit 15 for this recipe.

red bliss potato salad *Yield: 6 servings side order*

Ingredients	Amounts		Procedure
	U.S.	Metric	
Red bliss potatoes (1 1/2–2 in diameter)	2 lbs	907 g	Scrub the potatoes and cut the large potatoes in half. Peel once around to expose some white, but leave some peel on. Steam the potatoes.

Vidalia onions, chopped	2 oz	57 g	When potatoes have cooled, add the onions and dressing. Marinate about 2 hours at room temperature.
Hot bacon dressing	8 fl oz	236 ml	
Chives, chopped	1 oz	28 g	Chill and serve sprinkled with chives.

NUTRITIONAL INFORMATION PER SERVING: 391 Calories; 30 g Fat (67.1% calories from fat); 3 g Protein; 29 g Carbohydrate; 3 g Dietary Fiber; 9 mg Cholesterol; 57 mg Sodium. Exchanges: 1 1/2 Grain (Starch); 0 Vegetable; 6 Fat.

Along with potato salad, pasta and macaroni are some of the most popular types of starchy salads. How many recipes are there for macaroni salad? How many chefs are there?

macaroni salad *Yield: 4–6 servings side order*

Ingredients

Ingredients	U.S.	Metric
Elbow macaroni, cooked, cooled	1 pt	473 ml
Celery, diced	4 oz	113 g
Green peppers, diced	4 oz	113 g
Red bell peppers, diced	4 oz	113 g
Peas, cooked	4 oz	113 g
Mayonnaise	6 fl oz	177 ml
White vinegar	2 fl oz	59 ml
Salt	To taste	To taste
Pepper	To taste	To taste

Procedure

Blend all the ingredients. Let the salad marinate overnight. If desired, peas can be added just before service to preserve the color.

NUTRITIONAL INFORMATION PER SERVING: 344 Calories; 29 g Fat (70.8% calories from fat); 4 g Protein; 22 g Carbohydrate; 2 g Dietary Fiber; 12 mg Cholesterol; 270 mg Sodium. Exchanges: 1 Grain (Starch); 1/2 Vegetable; 2 1/2 Fat; 0 Other Carbohydrates.

Here's another version of macaroni salad. You may want to try both versions and then experiment with your favorite ingredients and come up with your own signature recipe.

basic pasta salad *Yield: 6–8 servings side order*

Ingredients	Amounts U.S.	Metric	Procedure
Shell pasta, cooked, cooled	2 pt	946 ml	Combine all the ingredients with just enough mayonnaise to bind them together. Season to taste with salt and pepper.
Onions, diced	4 oz	113 g	
Green pepper, diced	4 oz	113 g	
Olives, sliced	4 oz	113 g	
Garlic, mashed	2 cloves	2 cloves	
Mayonnaise, as needed	12 fl oz	355 ml	
Salt	To taste	To taste	
Pepper	To taste	To taste	

NUTRITIONAL INFORMATION PER SERVING: 734 Calories; 38 g Fat (45.4% calories from fat); 15 g Protein; 87 g Carbohydrate; 3 g Dietary Fiber; 14 mg Cholesterol; 350 mg Sodium. Exchanges: 5 1/2 Grain (Starch); 1/2 Vegetable; 0 Fruit; 3 Fat.

Any shape of pasta can be used for any of these pasta salads. This one calls for bow tie pasta, but any pasta will work. However, pasta shapes with holes or ridges are more suited to pasta salads. This recipe includes favorite Mexican ingredients. Kidney beans can be used in place of the black beans, if desired.

Mexicana pasta salad   *Yield: 6–8 servings side order*

Ingredients	Amounts		Procedure
	U.S.	Metric	
Bow tie pasta, cooked, cooled	2 lbs	907 g	Combine all the ingredients with just enough mayonnaise to bind together. Season to taste with salt and pepper.
Corn, fresh (if available) or frozen, cooked	4 oz	113 g	
Red bell peppers, diced	4 oz	113 g	
Olives, sliced	4 oz	113 g	
Black beans, cooked	8 fl oz	237 ml	
Mayonnaise	As needed	As needed	
Lime, add the zest and juice of 1 medium lime	1 each	1 each	
Cilantro, chopped	1/2 oz	15 g	
Salt	To taste	To taste	
Pepper	To taste	To taste	

NUTRITIONAL INFORMATION PER SERVING: 724 Calories; 27 g Fat (32.5% calories from fat); 21 g Protein; 103 g Carbohydrate; 7 g Dietary Fiber; 10 mg Cholesterol; 275 mg Sodium. Exchanges: 7 Grain (Starch); 1/2 Lean Meat; 0 Vegetable; 0 Fruit; 2 Fat.

LEARNING ACTIVITY 12-1

The preceding salad is an example of an ethnically inspired salad. It is based on the traditional pasta salad with added ingredients. In this learning activity, you are to create two different ethnically inspired pasta salads. Use our basic pasta salad recipe as a basis for your new recipes. Decide which type of cuisine you want to feature and then add two or three ingredients representing that type of cuisine. You might want to consider doing a salad inspired by Asian, Moroccan, Tuscan, Thai, Hawaiian, North African, or Greek cuisine. Use the Internet or any other resources to determine the cuisine and to select the ingredients that represent it and will work in a pasta salad recipe.

Record the recipes that you made in the space below.

Recipe #1

Recipe #2

Tamarind paste has a sweet/sour taste and is available in many Asian and Hispanic markets. If unavailable, substitute with puréed prunes and lemon juice. Fenugreek seeds, both whole and ground, can be found in Indian and Middle Eastern markets.

Curry leaves, which are the small, green leaves of the Kari plant, have a scent resembling citrus fruits. They can be found in many Asian markets.

Indian rice salad   *Yield: 6–8 servings side order*

Ingredients	Amounts U.S.	Metric	Procedure
Peanut oil	4 fl oz	110 ml	Heat the oil, add curry powder, and sauté over low heat.
Curry powder	1/2 oz	15 g	
Tamarind paste	2 tsp	10 g	Dissolve the tamarind paste in the rice vinegar.
Rice vinegar	8 fl oz	237 ml	
Fenugreek seeds, ground	1 tsp	1 tsp	Combine the sautéed curry powder, dissolved tamarind paste with the rice, and raisins. Salt to taste.
Rice, boiled and rinsed	2 lbs	907 g	
Raisins, plumped	4 oz	113 g	
Salt	To taste	To taste	
Curry leaves	As needed	As needed	Plate and garnish with curry leaves.

NUTRITIONAL INFORMATION PER SERVING: 567 Calories; 16 g Fat (26.1% calories from fat); 8 g Protein; 97 g Carbohydrate; 3 g Dietary Fiber; 0 mg Cholesterol; 46 mg Sodium. Exchanges: 5 1/2 Grain (Starch); 0 Lean Meat; 1/2 Fruit; 3 Fat; 0 Other Carbohydrates.

Quinoa is considered the mother grain of the Andean plateau cultures of the Incas. They called it "chisaya mama," or the mother of all grains. It is not a true grain, as it is not a grass plant. It is, however, a sustaining seed used as a grain. It is a complete protein and is gluten free. Quinoa has a pleasing, nutty flavor and an attractive shape, making it a natural for cold salads.

quinoa salad *Yield: 6–8 servings side order*

Ingredients	Amounts U.S.	Metric	Procedure
Quinoa	1 lb	450 g	Wash the quinoa in cold water and rinse well. In a large saucepot bring salted water to a boil, add the quinoa, stir, and reduce the temperature to a simmer until the kernels are tender. Drain, saving some water.
Water	1 qt	946 ml	

Tomatoes, peeled and diced	8 oz	226 g	Blend the cooked quinoa with all the remaining ingredients. If the salad is too dry, add some reserved quinoa stock.
Chili peppers, mild, chopped	1 oz	30 g	
Chili sauce	4 fl oz	118 ml	
Basic vinaigrette (see Unit 14 for recipe)	8 fl oz	236 ml	
Chives, diced	2 oz	57 g	
Salt	To taste	To taste	

NUTRITIONAL INFORMATION PER SERVING: 413 Calories; 22 g Fat (46.3% calories from fat); 9 g Protein; 48 g Carbohydrate; 5 g Dietary Fiber; 0 mg Cholesterol; 61 mg Sodium. Exchanges: 3 Grain (Starch); 1/2 Vegetable; 4 1/2 Fat; 0 Other Carbohydrates.

This salad exists in many variations throughout the Middle East. It is used as part of a mezze, which is the term used in Greek and Turkish cuisines for the first course. The predominant flavors are lemon, mint, and parsley. Bulgur is fully cooked, dried wheat.

tabbouleh—bulgur and vegetable salad
Yield: 8 servings side order

Ingredients	Amounts		Procedure
	U.S.	Metric	
Bulgur	1 lb	454 g	Cover the bulgur with boiling water and let sit 1 hour. Stir occasionally because some kernels might float and not stay submerged. 
Olive oil	8 fl oz	237 ml	Drain the water off the bulgur and combine it with the remaining ingredients except for the mint leaves. Marinate overnight.
Lemon juice	2 fl oz	55 ml	
Lemon rind, grated	1 tsp	1 tsp	
Black olives, pitted, packed in oil	4 oz	113 g	
Parsley, chopped	1 oz	28 g	
Tomatoes, diced	8 oz	227 g	
Mint leaves, fresh chopped	1 oz	28 g	
Paprika	1 tsp	1 tsp	
Sesame oil	1 tbsp	15 ml	
Salt	To taste	To taste	
Pepper	To taste	To taste	
Mint leaves	As needed	As needed	Plate the salad and garnish with mint leaves.

NUTRITIONAL INFORMATION PER SERVING: 470 Calories; 30 g Fat (56.0% calories from fat); 8 g Protein; 46 g Carbohydrate; 12 g Dietary Fiber; 0 mg Cholesterol; 123 mg Sodium. Exchanges: 3 Grain (Starch); 0 Lean Meat; 1/2 Vegetable; 0 Fruit; 6 Fat.

Lentils range in color from bright orange to jet black. The taste does not vary much regardless of the color. Lentil salads make a colorful addition to many dishes or as a salad bar component. Lentils need no soaking and cook rather fast compared with other dried legumes.

lentil salad *Yield: 5–6 servings side order*

Ingredients	Amounts		Procedure
	U.S.	**Metric**	
Leeks, cooked	8 fl oz	237 ml	Combine all the ingredients and marinate overnight.
Carrots, diced, cooked	8 fl oz	237 ml	
Lentils, cooked	1 pt	473 ml	
Cilantro	1 tbsp	15 g	
Cumin	1 tbsp	15 g	
Apple cider vinegar	4 fl oz	118 ml	
Salt	To taste	To taste	
Pepper	To taste	To taste	

NUTRITIONAL INFORMATION PER SERVING: 249 Calories; 1 g Fat (3.3% calories from fat); 19 g Protein; 44 g Carbohydrate; 21 g Dietary Fiber; 0 mg Cholesterol; 64 mg Sodium. Exchanges: 2 1/2 Grain (Starch); 1 1/2 Lean Meat; 1 Vegetable; 0 Fruit; 0 Fat.

>> Vegetable and Fruit Side Salads

Vegetables and fruits are the basis of many popular side salads (Figure 12-2). Take your pick—almost any vegetable or fruit can be included in a fresh salad. Produce makes every bite memorable and also adds great color as well as a variety of textures to side salads.

Figure 12-2 Fruit and vegetable sides are healthy and tasty.

This salad is useful for buffets and banquets. It is quick, easy to make, and maintains its bright colors even with an acidic-style dressing. Red onion can be used in place of the red peppers, if desired. The recipe for the Pistachio Vinaigrette is found in Unit 14.

wax bean salad *Yield: 10 servings side order*

Ingredients	Amounts		Procedure
	U.S.	Metric	
Wax beans, frozen, cut	2 1/2 lbs	1.1 kg	Boil the wax beans until tender but still firm. Cool.

Ingredients	Amounts		Procedure
Red peppers, diced	4 oz	113 g	Mix the ingredients. Add the dressing and chill. Marinate in the refrigerator for at least 6 hours.
Pistachios, toasted, chopped	2 oz	56 g	
Pistachio vinaigrette	4 fl oz	118 ml	

NUTRITIONAL INFORMATION PER SERVING: 116 Calories; 9 g Fat (62.6% calories from fat); 3 g Protein; 9 g Carbohydrate; 4 g Dietary Fiber; 0 mg Cholesterol; 6 mg Sodium. Exchanges: 0 Grain (Starch); 0 Lean Meat; 1 1/2 Vegetable; 1 1/2 Fat.

Three-bean salad is a standard catering and banquet salad that never goes out of fashion. We have added some fresh herbs and a touch of diced red pepper for added color and spark. Use the Basic Vinaigrette Dressing recipe found in Unit 14.

three-bean salad *Yield: 6 servings side order*

Ingredients	Amounts		Procedure
	U.S.	Metric	
Kidney beans, canned, drained	8 fl oz	237 ml	Combine all the ingredients and marinate refrigerated.
Navy beans, canned, drained	8 fl oz	237 ml	
Chick peas, canned, drained	8 fl oz	237 ml	
Onion, diced	2 oz	57 g	
Red pepper, diced or pimiento	2 oz	57 g	
Basil, fine chop	1 tbsp	15 g	
Parsley, minced	2 tsp	10 g	
Basic vinaigrette dressing	8 fl oz	237 ml	

NUTRITIONAL INFORMATION PER SERVING: 326 Calories; 22 g Fat (58.4% calories from fat); 8 g Protein; 27 g Carbohydrate; 6 g Dietary Fiber; 0 mg Cholesterol; 464 mg Sodium. Exchanges: 1 1/2 Grain (Starch); 1/2 Lean Meat; 0 Vegetable; 4 1/2 Fat.

This salad is often served as an appetizer salad. It should be made with fresh asparagus. The term **mimosa** refers to the garnish of chopped eggs resembling mimosa tree blossoms.

asparagus salad mimosa *Yield: 4 servings*

Ingredients	Amounts U.S.	Metric	Procedure
Asparagus stalks, thick, cooked firm, chilled	16 each	16 each	Place two lettuce leaves on a side plate and top with four asparagus stalks.
Leaf lettuce	8 leaves	8 leaves	
Pimiento strips	8 each	8 each	Garnish with pimiento strips.
Dressing, your choice	6 fl oz	177 ml	Drizzle with dressing and top with chopped, hard-boiled egg.
Eggs, hard-boiled, chopped	2 each	2 each	

NUTRITIONAL INFORMATION PER SERVING (WITHOUT DRESSING): 56 Calories; 3 g Fat (43.1% calories from fat); 5 g Protein; 4 g Carbohydrate; 2 g Dietary Fiber; 106 mg Cholesterol; 34 mg Sodium. Exchanges: 1/2 Lean Meat; 1/2 Vegetable; 1/2 Fat.

This salad is best made with small sugar-pie-style pumpkins. It is a refreshing fall salad that will surely become a favorite. You can substitute diced apples for the cucumbers for a variation.

marinated pumpkin and cucumber salad
Yield: Approximately 12 each, 4 oz (120 g) servings

Ingredients	Amounts U.S.	Metric	Procedure
Pumpkin, fresh	1 lb	454 g	Dice the pumpkin. Cover the pumpkin with water and simmer until tender. Drain and cool.
Seedless cucumbers, whole	2 lbs	907 g	Peel the cucumbers, split, remove the seeds, and slice.
Extra virgin olive oil	1 fl oz	30 ml	Combine the remaining ingredients and combine them with cucumbers and pumpkin. Marinate for 2 hours before serving.
Honey	1 fl oz	30 ml	
Mint, fresh, chopped	1 tbsp	15 g	
Salt	To taste	To taste	

NUTRITIONAL INFORMATION PER SERVING: 422 Calories; 28 g Fat (56.1% calories from fat); 8 g Protein; 42 g Carbohydrate; 8 g Dietary Fiber; 0 mg Cholesterol; 288 mg Sodium. Exchanges: 1/2 Grain (Starch); 5 1/2 Vegetable; 5 1/2 Fat; 1/2 Other Carbohydrates.

In Lancaster County, Pennsylvania, you will find this roast beet salad on many restaurant tables, representing an example of the seven sweets and seven sours typically found in Amish or Mennonite communities.

roast beet salad *Yield: 6–8 servings side order*

Ingredients	Amounts U.S.	Metric	Procedure
Small beets, greens removed	2 lbs	907 g	Scrub and wash the beets, then blend with 2 tbsp oil. Place in a roasting pan and roast at 325°F (160°C) until tender. Trim and peel the beets. Cut in wedges.
Oil	1 fl oz	30 ml	
Vinegar	4 fl oz	118 ml	Bring the vinegar and caraway seeds to a boil and pour hot over the beets.
Sugar	2 oz	57 g	
Caraway seeds	1 tsp	5 g	
Mint, fresh, chopped	1/2 oz	30 g	Add the mint leaves, additional oil, and seasonings. Chill. Serve cold.
Oil	4 fl oz	118 ml	
Salt	To taste	To taste	
Pepper	To taste	To taste	

NUTRITIONAL INFORMATION PER SERVING: 241 Calories; 20 g Fat (70.9% calories from fat); 1 g Protein; 17 g Carbohydrate; 3 g Dietary Fiber; 0 mg Cholesterol; 106 mg Sodium. Exchanges: 0 Grain (Starch); 1 1/2 Vegetable; 4 Fat; 1/2 Other Carbohydrates.

This is a nice variation on the basic beet salad. The balsamic dressing highlights the sweetness of the beets. Use the Balsamic Dressing recipe found in Unit 14.

sliced beet salad *Yield: 6 servings side order*

Ingredients	Amounts U.S.	Metric	Procedure
Red beets, greens removed	2 lbs	907 g	Scrub the beets and boil until tender. Slip off the skins while the beets are still warm. Slice on a mandolin. Cool.
Red onion, thinly sliced	4 oz	113 g	Add the remaining ingredients, including the dressing, and marinate refrigerated for at least 6 hours.
Parsley, minced	1 tbsp	15 g	
Balsamic dressing	8 fl oz	237 ml	

NUTRITIONAL INFORMATION PER SERVING: 238 Calories; 21 g Fat (76.9% calories from fat); 2 g Protein; 12 g Carbohydrate; 3 g Dietary Fiber; 0 mg Cholesterol; 80 mg Sodium. Exchanges: 2 Vegetable; 4 Fat.

This salad, consisting of boiled, cooked vegetables dressed with mayonnaise, is well known in many countries. The origin of the name is not documented.

Russian salad *Yield: 6 servings side order*

Ingredients	Amounts		Procedure
	U.S.	Metric	
Carrots, diced, cooked	4 oz	113 g	Chill all the cooked vegetables. Blend all the ingredients with mayonnaise and season to taste. Chill again before serving.
Potatoes, diced, cooked	4 oz	113 g	
Peas, cooked	4 oz	113 g	
Corn kernels, cooked	4 oz	113 g	
Sweet pickles, diced	2 oz	57 g	
Mayonnaise	4 oz	113 g	
Apple cider vinegar	1 tbsp	15 ml	
Salt	To taste	To taste	
Pepper	To taste	To taste	

NUTRITIONAL INFORMATION PER SERVING: 190 Calories; 16 g Fat (71.9% calories from fat); 2 g Protein; 12 g Carbohydrate; 2 g Dietary Fiber; 7 mg Cholesterol; 250 mg Sodium. Exchanges: 1/2 Grain (Starch); 1/2 Vegetable; 0 Fruit; 1 1/2 Fat; 0 Other Carbohydrates.

Ratatouille is a fragrant vegetable side dish originally from Provence, France. It is "mixed up," which is how the dish got its name—from the French word "touiller," meaning "to stir." This salad includes the ingredients found in most ratatouille and combines diced eggplant, tomatoes, onions, bell peppers, zucchini, garlic, and herbs simmered in olive oil. It is served cold.

ratatouille salad *Yield: 6 servings side order*

Ingredients	Amounts		Procedure
	U.S.	Metric	
Olive oil	4 fl oz	118 ml	Sauté the garlic in olive oil without getting color.
Garlic, mashed	1 tbsp	15 g	
Green peppers, coarse dice	8 oz	227 g	Add all the ingredients, stir, cover, and simmer about 15 minutes. Stir occasionally and check for moisture; usually the vegetables have enough liquid for braising. Chill and let marinate at least 1 day before serving.
Onions, coarse dice	8 oz	227 g	
Zucchini, coarse dice	8 oz	227 g	
Eggplant, coarse dice	8 oz	227 g	
Tomatoes, peeled, seeded	8 oz	227 g	
Thyme, fresh	1 sprig	1 sprig	
Pepper, coarse	1 tsp	5 g	
Salt	To taste	To taste	

NUTRITIONAL INFORMATION PER SERVING: 194 Calories; 18 g Fat (81.7% calories from fat); 1 g Protein; 8 g Carbohydrate; 2 g Dietary Fiber; 0 mg Cholesterol; 50 mg Sodium. Exchanges: 0 Grain (Starch); 1 1/2 Vegetable; 3 1/2 Fat.

Caponata is a Sicilian salad or relish. It is made from eggplants, onions, tomatoes, fennel, olives, pine nuts, red peppers, capers, and vinegar, simmered together in fragrant olive oil. It is best served at room temperature, which brings out its rich flavors.

caponata   *Yield: 4 cups approximately 8 servings side order*

Ingredients	Amounts U.S.	Metric	Procedure
Eggplant, peeled and cut in thick strips	1 lb	453 g	Combine the eggplant with salt. Rest for 1 hour. Squeeze out the excess juices.
Salt	1 tsp	1 tsp	
Virgin olive oil	4 fl oz	118 ml	Sauté the garlic in oil.
Garlic, mashed	1 tbsp	15 g	
Red onions, sliced	4 oz	113 g	Combine the eggplant, garlic, red onions, peppers, zucchini, tomatoes, fennel, capers, chili peppers, green olives, and pine nuts. Cook on the stovetop for 15 minutes until the vegetables are cooked but crisp.
Red peppers, sliced	6 oz	170 g	
Zucchini, sliced	6 oz	170 g	
Tomatoes, diced	2 oz	57 g	
Fennel, sliced	4 oz	113 g	
Capers, chopped	1 oz	30 g	
Chili peppers, chopped	1/2 oz	15 g	
Green olives, pitted, chopped	1 oz	30 g	
Pine nuts	2 oz	57 g	
Basil, fresh, chopped	2 tsp	10 g	Add the remaining ingredients and refrigerate.
Oregano, fresh	2 tsp	10 g	
Parsley, chopped	2 tsp	10 g	
Lemon peel, grated	1 tsp	5 g	
Red wine vinegar	1 fl oz	30 ml	
Salt	To taste	To taste	

NUTRITIONAL INFORMATION PER SERVING: 173 Calories; 16 g Fat (79.1% calories from fat); 2 g Protein; 7 g Carbohydrate; 3 g Dietary Fiber; 0 mg Cholesterol; 326 mg Sodium. Exchanges: 0 Grain (Starch); 0 Lean Meat; 1 Vegetable; 0 Fruit; 3 Fat; 0 Other Carbohydrates.

This simple stewed vegetable dish can be eaten hot or cold as an appetizer or as a main course. The original recipe uses lard, but we have substituted the more heart-friendly vegetable oil. Covering the pan traps steam and adds moisture to the salad.

Hungarian lecó *Yield: 8 servings appetizer*

Ingredients	Amounts		Procedure
	U.S.	Metric	
Vegetable oil	2 fl oz	59 ml	Sauté the onions in oil until light brown.
Onions, diced	4 oz	113 ml	
Bell peppers, red and green	2 lbs	907 g	Split the peppers and remove the seeds; cut into slivers.
Tomatoes, skinned, seeds removed, and diced	1 lb	454 g	Add all the other ingredients, stir, and cook over low heat about 10 minutes.
Sugar	1 tbsp	15 g	
Salt	1 tbsp	15 g	
Pepper	1 tsp	1 tsp	
Hungarian paprika	1 tbsp	30 g	

NUTRITIONAL INFORMATION PER SERVING: 112 Calories; 7 g Fat (54.7% calories from fat); 2 g Protein; 12 g Carbohydrate; 3 g Dietary Fiber; 0 mg Cholesterol; 806 mg Sodium. Exchanges: 0 Grain (Starch); 0 Lean Meat; 1 1/2 Vegetable; 1 1/2 Fat; 0 Other Carbohydrates.

LEARNING ACTIVITY 12-2

It's important that you know how to trim fresh, small artichokes for use in salads. In this learning activity you will have the opportunity to trim a small artichoke and prepare an artichoke bottom. Follow these instructions:

Trimming a Small Artichoke

1. Wash the artichoke thoroughly, rinsing between the leaves without pulling on them. Turn the artichoke upside down and shake out any excess water. Dry with a clean towel (Figure 12-3).
2. Pull off any of the tough outer, dark green leaves.
3. Trim the top by slicing off the top inch of the leaves.
4. Split the artichoke in half (vertically) and clean out the hairy fibers (Figure 12-4).

Figure 12-3 Thoroughly clean and dry the artichoke.

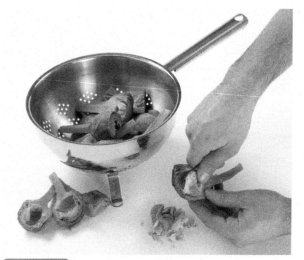

Figure 12-4 Scoop out the soft flesh and hairy fibers.

5. Simmer the artichoke in water that has lemon juice added, as oxidation will take place once the artichoke is exposed to air and will start to turn a darker color. The acidulated water will prevent the oxidation from taking place. (Use 1/2 ounce lemon juice per quart of water.)
6. Chill. Just prior to service, cut the artichokes into sizes needed for the recipe.

artichoke and pimiento salad *Yield: 6 servings side order*

Ingredients	Amounts U.S.	Metric	Procedure
Baby artichokes	6 each	6 each	Split and clean the artichokes as explained in the previous text (steps 1–4). Boil until tender, yet still firm. Chill in stock. Remove the artichokes, cool, and cut into bite-sized pieces.
Acidulate water (add 1/2 oz of lemon juice per quart of water)	3 qt	2.8 l	

Ingredients	Amounts U.S.	Metric	Procedure
Lemon juice	1 tbsp	15 ml	In a nonreactive saucepan, combine the lemon juice, wine, peppercorns, and coriander seeds. Simmer for 10 minutes, then remove from heat.
White wine, dry	8 fl oz	237 ml	
Peppercorns, crushed	1 tsp	5 g	
Coriander seeds	1/2 tsp	2 g	
Capers	1 tbsp	15 g	Add the capers, olive oil, and pimientos. Add the artichokes; they should be covered with liquid. Add a small amount of water if necessary to cover the ingredients. Refrigerate for at least 1 hour to marinate the artichokes.
Olive oil	2 fl oz	59 ml	
Pimientos, large dice	4 oz	113 g	
Salt	To taste	To taste	

NUTRITIONAL INFORMATION PER SERVING: 153 Calories; 9 g Fat (59.4% calories from fat); 3 g Protein; 11 g Carbohydrate; 5 g Dietary Fiber; 0 mg Cholesterol; 154 mg Sodium. Exchanges: 0 Grain (Starch); 1 1/2 Vegetable; 0 Fruit; 2 Fat; 0 Other Carbohydrates.

The name **succotash** is derived from the Narraganset, Rhode Island, Indians and is a dish that traditionally includes lima beans and corn. This salad can be served either cold or hot.

succotash salad *Yield: 6 servings side order*

Ingredients	Amounts U.S.	Metric	Procedure
Green peppers, diced	4 oz	113 g	Cook the green peppers in boiling water until tender but firm. Drain thoroughly. Chill.
Water	1 qt	946 ml	
Corn, canned, drained	8 fl oz	237 ml	Combine with all the other ingredients. Marinate and refrigerate overnight.
Red pimientos, diced	4 fl oz	118 ml	
Baby lima beans, cooked	8 fl oz	237 ml	
Red onions, diced	2 oz	57 g	
Olive oil	2 fl oz	59 ml	
Nutmeg	Dash	Dash	
Red wine vinegar	2 fl oz	59 ml	
Salt	To taste	To taste	
Pepper	To taste	To taste	

NUTRITIONAL INFORMATION PER SERVING: 152 Calories; 9 g Fat (53.2% calories from fat); 3 g Protein; 16 g Carbohydrate; 2 g Dietary Fiber; 0 mg Cholesterol; 155 mg Sodium. Exchanges: 1 Grain (Starch); 0 Lean Meat; 1/2 Vegetable; 2 Fat; 0 Other Carbohydrates.

Root vegetables are perfect for autumn and winter salads. **Celeriac,** or knob celery, is a specially adapted variety of celery, grown for its large root. The celeriac is the size of a small potato and is used cooked as well as fresh.

celeriac salad *Yield: 6 servings side order*

Ingredients	Amounts U.S.	Metric	Procedure
Celeriac, raw, no leaves	1 1/2 lbs	680 g	Peel the celery. The knob is hard and is best peeled with a paring knife. Cut in half if the knob is very large and heavy.
Lemon juice	1 fl oz	30 ml	Boil the peeled celeriac in lemon-flavored water until done but still firm. Chill in stock. Remove and cut with a serrated knife into attractive slices.
Water	4 qt	3.78 l	
Oil	2 fl oz	59 ml	Combine the remaining ingredients and pour over the slices to marinate.
Balsamic vinegar	2 fl oz	59 ml	
Sage, chopped	1 tsp	5 g	
Salt	To taste	To taste	
Pepper	To taste	To taste	

NUTRITIONAL INFORMATION PER SERVING: 131 Calories; 9 g Fat (61.4% calories from fat); 2 g Protein; 12 g Carbohydrate; 2 g Dietary Fiber; 0 mg Cholesterol; 177 mg Sodium. Exchanges: 0 Grain (Starch); 2 Vegetable; 0 Fruit; 2 Fat.

This typical French salad is often served as a first course or appetizer salad. Its tangy taste comes from the capers and cornichons. It makes a great side salad served with any type of beef or cured meat sandwich.

celeriac remoulade *Yield: 6 servings side order*

Ingredients	Amounts U.S.	Metric	Procedure
Celeriac, no leaves	1 1/2 lbs	680 g	Peel the celeriac. The knob is hard and is best peeled with a paring knife. Cut in half if the knob is very large and heavy. Use a mandolin or chef's knife to cut into fine julienne.

Remoulade Sauce

Ingredients	Amounts U.S.	Metric	Procedure
Lemon juice	1 fl oz	30 ml	Blend the other ingredients into a sauce. Combine the celeriac with the remoulade sauce and marinate refrigerated overnight.
Capers, chopped	1 tbsp	15 g	
Cornichons, chopped	1 tbsp	15 g	
Dijon mustard	1 tsp	5 g	
Tarragon vinegar	2 fl oz	59 ml	
Tarragon leaves, chopped	1 tsp	5 g	
Tabasco sauce	Dash	Dash	
Chives, chopped	1 tbsp	15 g	
Mayonnaise	6 fl oz	148 g	
Salt	To taste	To taste	

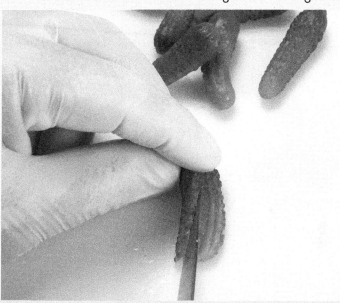

NUTRITIONAL INFORMATION PER SERVING: 253 Calories; 24 g Fat (78.5% calories from fat); 2 g Protein; 12 g Carbohydrate; 2 g Dietary Fiber; 10 mg Cholesterol; 407 mg Sodium. Exchanges: 0 Grain (Starch); 0 Lean Meat; 2 Vegetable; 0 Fruit; 2 Fat; 0 Other Carbohydrates.

The original Waldorf salad was created around 1893 at The Waldorf-Astoria Hotel in Manhattan, located at the site where the Empire State Building stands today. Today, this salad is served as a side salad for sandwiches and lunch entrées and is included on many holiday menus.

Waldorf salad   *Yield: 4 servings side order*

Ingredients	Amounts U.S.	Metric	Procedure
Celery, peeled, diced	8 oz	227 g	Blend the celery with apples, lemon juice, and mayonnaise. Serve on lettuce leaves and sprinkle with walnuts.
Red Delicious apples, diced with peel on	8 oz	227 g	
Lemon juice	1 tbsp	15 ml	
Mayonnaise	6 fl oz	177 ml	
Walnuts, chopped	1 oz	30 g	
Boston lettuce leaves	8 each	8 each	

NUTRITIONAL INFORMATION PER SERVING: 343 Calories; 37 g Fat (91.0% calories from fat); 2 g Protein; 6 g Carbohydrate; 2 g Dietary Fiber; 14 mg Cholesterol; 261 mg Sodium. Exchanges: 0 Grain (Starch); 0 Lean Meat; 0 Vegetable; 1/2 Fruit; 3 1/2 Fat.

The first historical reference to balsamic vinegar dates back to 1046, when a bottle of balsamic vinegar was reportedly given to Emperor Enrico III of Franconia as a gift. In the Middle Ages, it was used as a disinfectant. It also had a reputation as a miracle cure—good for everything from sore throats to labor pains. Today there are a lot of grades of balsamic vinegar available. For this recipe, use a high-quality balsamic. The sugar in this recipe can be adjusted, depending on the natural sweetness of the fresh fruit.

peach and strawberry balsamico *Yield: 6–8 servings side order*

Ingredients	Amounts U.S.	Metric	Procedure
Peaches (approx. 3 to 4 in diameter), fresh, peeled, pitted, and sliced	6 each	6 each	Combine the sliced fruits in a large serving bowl and toss gently.
Strawberries, fresh, hulled, and sliced	1 lb	454 g	
Sugar	1 oz	28 g	Sprinkle the fruit with sugar.
Balsamic vinegar, good quality	1 oz	30 ml	Whisk together the vinegar and the walnut oil. Pour over the fruit and toss gently to combine. Serve chilled.
Walnut oil	1/2 tbsp	8 ml	

NUTRITIONAL INFORMATION PER SERVING: 75 Calories; 1 g Fat (10.2% calories from fat); 1 g Protein; 17 g Carbohydrate; 3 g Dietary Fiber; 0 mg Cholesterol; 1 mg Sodium. Exchanges: 1 Fruit; 0 Fat; 0 Other Carbohydrates.

With over 500 farmers' markets in the country, there's bound to be a market near you offering a wide range of quality, local, and ethically retailed, reared, or produced foods. Many chefs are finding that their local farmers' market provides a gold-mine of high-quality produce and meats.

farmers' market melon and papaya salad

Yield: 4–6 servings side salad

Ingredients	Amounts		Procedure
	U.S.	Metric	
Watermelon, seedless, peeled, and cut into 1-in balls	4 oz	113 g	Combine melons and papaya and set aside.
Honeydew melon, peeled, seeded, and cut into 1-in balls	4 oz	113 g	
Cantalope, peeled, seeded, and cut into 1-in balls	4 oz	113 g	
Charentais or Juane Canary melon, peeled, seeded, and cut into 1-in balls	4 oz	113 g	
Papaya, peeled, seeded, and cut into 1-in balls	4 oz	113 g	
Honey	1 1/2 oz	45 g	In a small nonreactive bowl, combine the honey, lime juice, zest, cayenne pepper, and mint. Gently toss the melon and papaya balls with this mixture. Serve chilled.
Lime juice, fresh	1/2 fl oz	15 ml	
Lime zest	3/4 tsp	3 g	
Cayenne pepper	1/4 tsp	1 g	
Mint, fresh, minced fine	1/2 tbsp	8 g	

NUTRITIONAL INFORMATION PER SERVING: 65 Calories; trace Fat (2.3% calories from fat); 1 g Protein; 17 g Carbohydrate; 1 g Dietary Fiber; 0 mg Cholesterol; 11 mg Sodium. Exchanges: 0 Grain (Starch); 0 Vegetable; 1/2 Fruit; 0 Fat; 1/2 Other Carbohydrates.

>> The Salad Bar

Many lower- to middle-priced restaurants and even some fast-food operations have a salad bar in the dining room (Figure 12-5). Many health-oriented and vegetarian restaurants, as well as some ethnic restaurants, also include salad bars. They are a convenient and quick way to serve guests. Sanitation is the key issue with salad bars. Modern salad bars are required to have **sneeze guards,** which are transparent panels or canopies mounted above a salad bar or food counter. They provide a sanitary barrier between the customer and the food. Sneeze guards must be continually monitored for cleanliness and sanitation. Because the guest has free reign, the responsibilities of maintaining the salad bar rests with the dining room management to ensure that all health regulations are followed to the letter. The cold kitchen staff should also monitor the salad bar to ensure a well-stocked station. One person in the dining room should be in charge of the salad bar and made fully responsible for the operation.

Stationary or built-in salad bars need to maintain a temperature of no more than 40°F (4°C) (Figure 12-6). The refrigeration compressor should be remote to avoid noise and heat in the dining room. Well-designed stations have plate-chilling cabinets to keep plates cold. Some salad bars consist of an ice bin to keep the food cold. These bins must be filled with crushed ice, maintained, and frequently checked throughout service time, then drained and cleaned at the end of service. Special attention should be paid to the cleanliness of the sneeze guards. They should be inspected periodically and wiped with a sanitizer. Glass cleaners and similar chemicals must not be used when food is on display.

Foodservice operations should be aware of the following issues and problems that often occur with having a salad bar:

- Some customers take too much.
- Some customers take only the expensive items.
- Some customers waste food.
- Dining room personnel keep the salad bar containers overfilled.
- Dining room personnel do not provide a sufficient number of service utensils.

Figure 12-5 Salad bars are an easy and quick way to serve guests.

Strategies to keep the cost of salad bars under control include the following:

- Have smaller plates available.
- Have containers in various sizes. When business slows, smaller containers can be used.
- Control the choices on the salad bar and switch when seasonal items become too expensive.
- Practice careful purchasing, taking advantage of purveyor specials.
- Dressing ladles should not be bigger than 1 fluid ounce (30 ml).
- Serving utensils should be convenient to use for customers and should not be too big.

Salad bars, like buffets, must always look neat, clean, and sumptuous (Figure 12-7). Half-empty containers should be either refilled immediately or the contents transferred to smaller containers. This should be done in the back of the house.

Figure 12-6 Temperatures must be checked on a regular basis to ensure that the proper temperatures are maintained.

Figure 12-7 Regular checks must be made to keep the salad bar sparkly clean and tidy.

SIMPLE SALAD BAR INGREDIENTS

Salad bars are often priced by the ounce or pound in many modern foodservice operations, as well as grocery stores. Salads such as potato salad and heavier salads have become an asset instead of a liability when it comes to cost. By offering a large selection of salad bar ingredients, guest satisfaction rises.

The following is just a sampling of items for simple salad bars.

Vegetables
Artichoke hearts
Bamboo shoots
Bell peppers (raw or roasted)
Broccoli
Cabbage (shredded)
Carrots (shredded or sliced)
Cauliflower
Celery (sliced)
Corn (kernels)
Cucumber (sliced or chopped)
Green beans
Hearts of Palm
Lettuce (a variety of options)
Mushrooms (sliced or marinated)
Olives (green or black, pitted)
Onions (green or red, diced)
Peppers (green, red, or yellow, diced)
Radishes
Spinach
Sprouts (bean or alfalfa)
Tomatoes, sliced, cherry or grape
Turnip (sliced)
Water chestnuts (sliced)
Yellow squash
Zucchini (sliced or chopped)

Other Ingredients
Beans (garbanzo, pinto, red, black, or
    kidney)
Corn relish
Cottage cheese
Pickles (dill and sweet)

Fruits (sliced or diced)
Apples
Avocado

Cantaloupe
Grapefruit
Grapes
Honeydew melon
Mango
Oranges
Pears
Watermelon

Toppings
Bacon bits
Capers
Chow mein noodles
Croutons
Deli meats (ham, chicken, or turkey)
Dressings (three or more flavors)
Grated cheese
Hard-cooked eggs
French-fried onions
Fresh herbs
Fried tortilla chips
Nuts (sliced almonds, pine, pecans,
    pistachios, cashews)
Seafood such as shrimp, crab, salmon,
    or tuna
Seeds (pumpkin or sunflower)
Tofu

Popular Side Salads
Cole slaw
Cottage cheese
Fresh fruit salad
Macaroni salad
Pasta salad
Potato salad
Three-bean salad

>> Summary

Side salads add interest and value to a meal. By mastering the skills needed to make side salads, you will be able to transfer these skills to the more elaborate main-course salads, sandwiches, and appetizers. The meal components you have learned to produce are used in many other preparations and food applications. Cooking is a step-by-step process, and just about all dishes served in restaurants consist of many parts prepared in the cold kitchen.

In this unit, you learned about side salads featuring vegetable and starch ingredients. Some of the vegetables need cooking and others can be used raw. You also learned about salads that can be made with grains such as rice, bulgur, quinoa, and legumes or pulses such as lentils and beans. Try experimenting with ingredients to create new salad combinations with different flavors.

Side salads add variety and interest to a buffet or salad bar. It is important for you to understand the operation of salad bars, including the safety issues involved.

>> Review Questions

TRUE/FALSE

1. Cereal grains are those plants that yield an edible grain such as wheat, rye, oats, rice, or corn.
2. Pulses is another term used for legumes such as beans, peas, and lentils.
3. German-style potato salad is made with hot or warm bacon dressing.
4. Tamarind paste has a sweet/sour taste.
5. Bulgur is considered the mother grain of the Andean plateau cultures of the Incas.
6. Lentils can be white.
7. Mimosa is a type of dressing made with egg whites.
8. Cut artichokes will turn colors due to oxidation.
9. Succotash traditionally contains lima beans and green beans.
10. Waldorf salad usually contains celery, red apples, and walnuts.

MULTIPLE CHOICE

11. Celeriac is also known as
    a. pascal celery.
    b. celery juice.
    c. knob celery.
    d. turnip.
12. Amaranth is a
    a. legume.
    b. grain.
    c. liquer.
    d. oil.
13. Curry leaves
    a. don't exist; curry is a blend of spices.
    b. come from a small citrus tree.
    c. are the small green leaves of the Kari plant.
    d. taste like puréed prunes.
14. Quinoa is
    a. a complete protein.
    b. a seed, used as a grain.
    c. gluten-free.
    d. all of the above.
15. Bulgur is
    a. fully cooked, dried wheat.
    b. a pulse.
    c. a seed, used as a grain.
    d. a type of rice.
16. Lentils
    a. should be soaked overnight.
    b. should be soaked for an hour.
    c. need no soaking.
    d. none of the above.
17. Salad bars must maintain a temperature of no more than
    a. 40°F (4°C).
    b. 42°F (5°C).
    c. 38°F (3°C).
    d. 36°F (2°C).
18. Red Bliss potatoes are
    a. waxy.
    b. mealy.
    c. both.
    d. interchangeable with Russet potatoes.

FILL IN THE ANSWERS

19. List three cereal grains. _____
20. List three pulses. _____
21. List three concerns when using a salad bar. _____
22. List three strategies for keeping the cost of the salad bar under control. _____

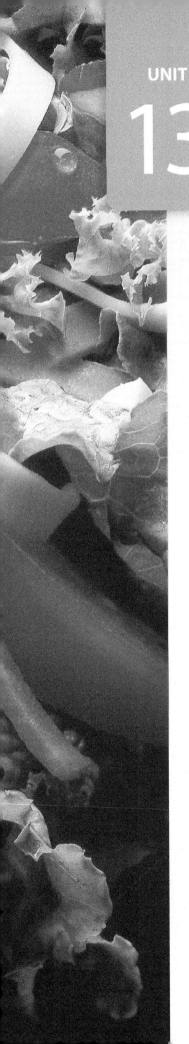

Main-Course Salads

>> Learning Objectives

After you have finished reading this unit, you should be able to:

- Discuss ways to create interesting and satisfying main-course salads.
- Identify the four components generally found in main-course salads.
- Share the history of the Cobb salad.
- Recognize classical main-course salads.
- List a number of foods that fall in each flavor category: sweet, sour, bitter, spicy, salt, and umami.

>> Key Terms

albacore   galangal root   orange supreme   ravigote (*rah-vee-GOT*)

Main-course salads are served as a complete meal. They can be served hot, room temperature, or cold, depending on the central protein or starch component. Main-course salads can be an inexpensive menu addition, or they can be expensive if ingredients such as tenderloin or beef, shellfish, or poultry such as Moulard duck breasts are used.

When developing a main-course salad, the same rules apply as are used for any other menu item. Balance in flavors, the use of contrasting colors and textures, and fresh ingredients are important considerations. When foods are served cold, bright bold flavors are necessary as cold can deaden the taste sensations.

This unit is divided into two sections: Classic Main-Course Salads and Contemporary Main-Course Salads.

Main-course salads are not a new idea; however, their popularity is increasing with our active and health-conscious lifestyles. Old cookbooks list entrée or main-course salads as part of elaborate multiple course meals. While large and elaborate menus are no longer fashionable, many customers order just a salad for lunch and occasionally only a main-course salad for dinner.

Fast-food restaurants have recognized this and are serving a hot protein, such as a chicken breast, on a bed of lettuce as a meal itself (Figure 13-1). Salads can be a profitable addition to the menu and impact the bottom line in a positive way.

>> Main-Course Salad-Making Tips

To create interesting and satisfying main-course salads, attention should be paid to the following:

- Freshness, seasonality, and quality of ingredients (Figure 13-2)
- Proper cooking procedures for all cooked ingredients
- Texture contrast
- Attractive presentations that are easy to access and eat (bite-sized pieces of lettuce, as an example)

Figure 13-1 Fast-food franchises discovered that there was a need for a healthier option than burgers and began introducing main-course salads to fill the need.

COMMON COMPONENTS

In general, there are four components found in most main-course salads:

1. The featured, center-of-the-plate protein or heavy carbohydrate item; for example, baked goat cheese, grilled duck or chicken breast, poached fish, lobster meat, grilled tofu or tempeh, bean cake, or smoked fish.
2. Some type of greens such as lettuce, endive, escarole, Chinese cabbage, or other leafy-type vegetable.
3. Garnishes of vegetables, starches, fruits, or other signature items. Examples might be duck cracklings, wasabi croutons, diced fruit, or edible blossoms.
4. Dressing, which should enhance the salad, bringing together the flavors harmoniously.

Figure 13-2 Only the freshest ingredients should be used in salads.

There are always exceptions to these four components, as the typical seafood salad has no starch component, relying instead on the seafood and perhaps a chopped hard-boiled egg, vegetables such as tomatoes or celery, a bed of greens, and dressing.

FLAVOR

When composing new salad combinations, it is important to understand how flavors work. To create harmonious flavor combinations, chefs must think about flavors, train their palates, and taste the combinations they create. For that reason, we will review the essence of flavor, which was discussed in depth in Unit 4.

Sweet = Ripe fresh fruits, sweet balsamic, honey. Sweets balance acids and harmonize with salt.

Sour = Lemon, vinegars, capers, and sour greens such as sorrel. Sours intensify the sensation of taste and add a sharp tinge to foods.

Bitter = Almond, coffee, bitters, artichokes. Bitter foods produce a dry, acrid sensation in the mouth. Bitter compounds in food lend a hand to enhancement of sweets or sours in small quantities.

Spicy = Peppers, curry, horseradish. Spicy flavors are generally combined with sweet or salty flavors in most applications and add surprise to the taste of food.

Salty = Sea salt or table salt, anchovies, parmesan cheese. Salt wakes up flavors by enhancing the conductivity of saliva. When coupled with sweet flavors, salty foods will balance out the flavors.

Umami = Aged meat and cheeses, seaweed, oily fish, mushrooms, soy sauce. Umami is called the fifth flavor (sweet, sour, salty, bitter, and umami) and lends a savory note to food.

LEARNING ACTIVITY 13-1

You have been hired by a large, casual-dining restaurant chain to revamp its main-course salad menu. They want you to include two classical main-course salads and three contemporary salads. Use any sources to determine the menu. Provide the recipe and write a description for each salad as it will appear on the menu.

>> Classic Main-Course Salads

CHEF'S TIP
Grill or broil the chicken breast; season lightly; do not overseason. Make sure the bacon is crisp.

The general public has come to appreciate a number of classic salads and knows what to expect when ordering them. It is, therefore, not recommended that you stray very far from these classic recipes unless the names are changed. Chefs may want to include a number of classic salads on their menus along with a few contemporary choices where their creative ideas can be expressed. Foodservice operations with a captive audience such as private clubs, conference centers, and residential feeding services should feature some classic salads the customers know and are comfortable with such as chef salad, Cobb salad, and other favorites. There are also a number of classic salads made popular in fashionable hotel dining rooms such as crab and shrimp Louis, Caesar salad, crab ravigote, cold poached salmon, and many others.

The original "Cobb salad" was invented at the Brown Derby restaurant in Los Angeles, California, in 1937. It was a favorite of the early Hollywood legends such as Sid Grauman and Clark Gable. Robert Cobb, the Brown Derby's owner and manager, missed his dinner one evening, so he went to the refrigerator and pulled out what he could find: a Haas avocado, celery, tomato, and bacon—and a classic was born. Later he added chopped breast of chicken, chives, watercress, and some hard-boiled eggs. Traditionally, Cobb salad is served with Roquefort cheese crumbles. The original lettuce used was leaf green lettuce. However, a mixture of greens such as romaine, butter, or limestone lettuce is sometimes used. Some modern versions use a blue cheese dressing or vinaigrette dressing on the side. The bacon recipe found in Unit 16 works well with this Cobb salad recipe.

This classic composed salad is an example of the best of utilization. It was a salad that came to life based on left overs in a restaurant kitchen, turned into an all American favorite.

This is an excellent example of a composed salad served as an entree at lunch or early dinner. Cooked turkey breast may be substituted for chicken if preferred.

traditional cobb salad *Yield: 1 serving*

Ingredients	Amounts U.S.	Metric	Procedure
Romaine lettuce	3 oz	85 g	Chop or tear the lettuce into bite-sized pieces and distribute into an individual salad bowl.
Tomatoes, ripe, seeded, and diced	1 each medium	1 each medium	Layer the tomatoes in diagonal lines across the lettuce. Next add the avocado, eggs, cheese, chicken, bacon, and celery. Top with a sprinkling of chives and serve the dressing on the side.
Avocado, diced	3 oz	85 g	
Eggs, hard-boiled, diced	1/2 large	1/2 large	
Roquefort cheese, crumbled	1 oz	28 g	
Chicken breast, cooked, diced	2 oz	57 g	
Bacon, cooked, diced	1 oz	28 g	
Celery, diced	1 oz	28 g	
Chives, snipped	1 tsp	5 g	
Blue cheese or favorite vinaigrette dressing	1 fl oz	30 ml	

NUTRITIONAL INFORMATION PER SERVING: 558 Calories; 40 g Fat (64.2% calories from fat); 38 g Protein; 13 g Carbohydrate; 4 g Dietary Fiber; 203 mg Cholesterol; 1,465 mg Sodium. Exchanges: 5 Lean Meat; 1 1/2 Vegetable; 0 Fruit; 5 1/2 Fat.

Always recognizable, the chef salad is the traditional main-course salad appearing on menus across the nation. It has many protein variations including turkey, chicken, ham, and assorted cheeses. The original salad was made with boiled, smoked ox tongue. Try using the ham recipe from Unit 16. The chef salad is very colorful, and many people consider it a type of salad comfort food.

> **CHEF'S TIP**
> *Remember that lettuce, coarsely chopped, should be bite-sized so that diners can easily eat it.*

chef salad *Yield: 1 serving*

Ingredients	Amounts U.S.	Metric	Procedure
Lettuce, coarsely chopped or torn into bite-sized pieces	2 oz	57 g	Place lettuce in a bowl and arrange meats and cheeses in four bundles on top.
Ham, julienne	1 oz	28 g	
Swiss cheese, julienne	1 oz	28 g	
Cheddar cheese, julienne	1 oz	28 g	
Turkey breast, julienne	1 oz	28 g	

Tomatoes, cut in wedges	1 medium	1 medium	Put tomatoes in the center.
Egg, hard-boiled, cut in wedges	1 large	1 large	Garnish with the egg, olives, and sprinkle green onions on top.
Black olives, sliced	1 oz	28 g	
Green onions	1 tbsp	15 g	

Salad dressing of choice	2 fl oz	59 ml	Serve dressing on the side.

NUTRITIONAL INFORMATION PER SERVING: (WITHOUT DRESSING) 467 Calories; 31 g Fat (60.0% calories from fat); 34 g Protein; 13 g Carbohydrate; 4 g Dietary Fiber; 300 mg Cholesterol; 1,012 mg Sodium. Exchanges: 4 1/2 Lean Meat; 1 1/2 Vegetable; 0 Fruit; 3 1/2 Fat.

This recipe is a California classic. It is still served at many of the restaurants up and down the coast. Legend has it that it originated at the St. Francis Hotel in San Francisco.

shrimp or crab louie   *Yield: 1 serving*

Ingredients	Amounts U.S.	Metric	Procedure
Capers	1 tsp	5 g	To make the sauce: mix the capers, mayonnaise, chili sauce, cocktail sauce, whipped cream, and lemon juice and set aside.
Mayonnaise	2 tbsp	30 ml	
Chili sauce	1 tbsp	15 ml	
Cocktail sauce	1 tbsp	15 ml	
Heavy cream, whipped	1 tbsp	15 ml	
Lemon juice	1 tsp	5 ml	
Iceberg lettuce, shredded	2 oz	57 g	Place lettuce on the individual salad plate. Top with crab or shrimp and cover with the sauce.
Bay shrimp or Dungeness crab	7 oz	198 g	
Egg, hard-boiled, chopped	1 large	1 large	Garnish salad with the remaining ingredients.
Tomato, cut in wedges	1 small	1 small	
Black olives, sliced	2 tsp	10 g	
Green onions, sliced	2 tsp	10 g	

NUTRITIONAL INFORMATION PER SERVING: 520 Calories; 36 g Fat (61.7% calories from fat); 41 g Protein; 10 g Carbohydrate; 2 g Dietary Fiber; 548 mg Cholesterol; 760 mg Sodium. Exchanges: 5 1/2 Lean Meat; 1 Vegetable; 0 Fruit; 0 Nonfat Milk; 3 1/2 Fat; 1/2 Other Carbohydrates.

Ravigote comes from the French *ravigoter*, which means to add a new figure. In culinary arts, a ravigote is cold, French vinegar-based sauce that contains capers, onions, and herbs. Here the sauce is used as a dressing for the salad. This classic preparation is still modern. Once it is plated, it should be served immediately.

crab ravigote *Yield: 1 serving*

Ingredients	Amounts U.S.	Metric	Procedure
Olive oil	1 fl oz	30 ml	Combine the olive oil, chives, capers, onions, tarragon, parsley, vinegar, mustard, and salt and pepper to make a dressing.
Chives, chopped	1 tbsp	15 g	
Capers	1 tbsp	15 g	
Onions, chopped	1 tbsp	15 g	
Tarragon, fresh, chopped	1 tsp	5 g	
Parsley, chopped	1 tsp	5 g	
Vinegar, mild	1 tsp	5 ml	
Dijon mustard, prepared	1 tsp	5 g	
Salt	To taste	To taste	
Pepper	To taste	To taste	
Lettuce	As needed	As needed	Place lettuce leaves on the center of a salad plate.
Crab meat	7 oz	198 g	Center the crab meat on top of the lettuce, and cover evenly with the dressing.

NUTRITIONAL INFORMATION PER SERVING: 457 Calories; 30 g Fat (59.5% calories from fat); 42 g Protein; 4 g Carbohydrate; 1 g Dietary Fiber; 177 mg Cholesterol; 1,074 mg Sodium. Exchanges: 0 Grain (Starch); 5 1/2 Lean Meat; 1/2 Vegetable; 5 1/2 Fat; 0 Other Carbohydrates.

Salad Niçoise is named after the city Nice on the French Riviera. The original recipe calls for the best-quality canned tuna caught in the Mediterranean. Modern chefs replace canned tuna with fresh-seared tuna, which was completely unknown when the salad was created. If canned tuna is used, it should be **albacore** tuna, which is a species of tuna known for its white meat that has a dry texture and a taste that resembles the taste of chicken meat. Cherry tomatoes can be used in place of larger varieties.

salad Niçoise *Yield: 1 serving*

Ingredients	Amounts U.S.	Metric	Procedure
Green beans, cooked	1 oz	28 g	Cut beans into 1-in pieces.
New red potatoes, cooked, diced	2 oz	57 g	Gently blend the green beans, potatoes, tomatoes, tuna (including the oil from the tuna), olives, tarragon, vinegar, salt, and pepper.
Tomatoes, coarse diced	2 oz	57 g	
Albacore tuna canned in oil or fresh seared tuna	6 oz	170 g	
Ripe olives in oil	1 tbsp	15 g	
Tarragon, chopped	To taste	To taste	
White wine vinegar	1 tbsp	15 ml	
Salt	To taste	To taste	
Pepper	To taste	To taste	
Lettuce leaves	As needed	As needed	Arrange the lettuce leaves on a salad plate. Top with the salad mixture.
Anchovy fillets	2 each	2 each	Garnish with the anchovy fillets and capers.
Capers	1 tsp	5 g	

NUTRITIONAL INFORMATION PER SERVING: 317 Calories; 6 g Fat (17.8% calories from fat); 50 g Protein; 13 g Carbohydrate; 3 g Dietary Fiber; 77 mg Cholesterol; 1,339 mg Sodium. Exchanges: 1/2 Grain (Starch); 7 Lean Meat; 1 Vegetable; 0 Fruit; 0 Fat; 0 Other Carbohydrates.

This traditional salad can be made with turkey instead of chicken; however, if substituted, the menu should reflect the proper name of the ingredient and be listed as turkey salad. Variety can be added by including nuts, citrus fruits, grapes, or raisins. Try using smoked chicken. Choose an avocado that is ripe enough to eat but not so ripe that it's mushy. The amount to use will depend on the operation. Remember that avocado oxidizes quickly and should be added just prior to service.

chicken salad with avocado *Yield: 1 serving*

Ingredient	Amounts U.S.	Metric	Procedure
Chicken, boiled or roasted and diced	6 oz	170 g	Blend the chicken and celery with mayonnaise and vinegar.
Celery, diced	2 oz	57 g	
Mayonnaise	1 fl oz	30 ml	
Tarragon vinegar	1 fl oz	30 ml	

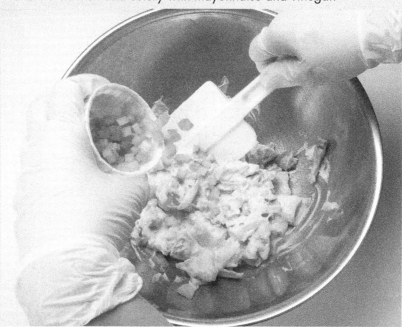

Ingredient	Amounts U.S.	Metric	Procedure
Avocado, diced to blend and slices reserved to top the salad	As needed	As needed	Carefully blend the diced avocado into the chicken mixture.
Lettuce, shredded	2 oz	57 g	Arrange the lettuce on a salad plate. Top with the chicken salad. Garnish with avocado slices and pimento strips.
Red pimento strips	6 each	6 each	

NUTRITIONAL INFORMATION PER SERVING: 1,161 Calories; 109 g Fat (79.6% calories from fat); 46 g Protein; 17 g Carbohydrate; 4 g Dietary Fiber; 137 mg Cholesterol; 796 mg Sodium. Exchanges: 1/2 Grain (Starch); 5 1/2 Lean Meat; 1 1/2 Vegetable; 1/2 Fruit; 10 Fat.

The following Beef Tenderloin Salad recipe is an excellent way to utilize the smaller end or head end of a beef tenderloin. The Mustard Chive Dressing recipe can be found in Unit 14.

beef tenderloin salad *Yield: 1 serving*

Ingredients	Amounts U.S.	Metric	Procedure
Beef tenderloin steak, well trimmed	6 oz	170 g	Marinate the steaks overnight. Drain. Cook the steaks when ordered and cool while preparing the salad. Cut into 1/2-in strips. Season with pepper.
Pepper, coarsely ground	1 tsp	5 g	
Red wine, dry	1 fl oz	30 ml	

Ingredients	Amounts U.S.	Metric	Procedure
Romaine lettuce, coarse cut	1 oz	28 g	Dress the lettuce with the vinaigrette and place on the center of the plate. Top with the strips of beef.
Mustard chive dressing	2 fl oz	59 ml	
Tomato, diced	1 tbsp	15 g	Arrange diced tomatoes and four onion slices on top of the salad. Sprinkle croutons over the top of the salad.
Red onion, slices	4 each	4 each	
Croutons	1 tbsp	15 g	

NUTRITIONAL INFORMATION PER SERVING: 845 Calories; 72 g Fat (78.0% calories from fat); 33 g Protein; 13 g Carbohydrate; 3 g Dietary Fiber; 121 mg Cholesterol; 496 mg Sodium. Exchanges: 0 Grain (Starch); 4 1/2 Lean Meat; 1 Vegetable; 11 1/2 Fat; 0 Other Carbohydrates.

This traditional Greek salad is a staple item on many menus. Originating on Cos, one of the Greek Islands, this salad should be made with romaine lettuce.

classic Greek salad   *Yield: 1 serving*

Ingredients	Amounts U.S.	Metric	Procedure
Romaine lettuce, cut in bite-sized pieces	2 oz	57 g	Place the lettuce in an individual salad serving bowl or on a plate. Add the tomatoes, cucumbers, and beans; sprinkle with oregano.
Tomatoes, diced or sliced	4 oz	113 g	
Cucumbers, seeded, diced, or sliced	4 oz	113 g	
Garbanzo beans	4 oz	113 g	
Oregano leaves, dried	Sprinkle	Sprinkle	
Kalamata olives in oil, drained	1 oz	30 g	Remove the pits from the olives and sprinkle the olives over the salad.
Feta cheese, diced or sliced	4 oz	113 g	Add the cheese.
Red wine vinegar	1 fl oz	30 ml	To order, combine the vinegar and oil and pour the mixture over the salad.
Olive oil	1 1/2 fl oz	45 ml	
Pita bread	1 each	1 each	Cut the bread in quarters and place them around the bowl or plate. Garnish with banana peppers, if desired.

NUTRITIONAL INFORMATION PER SERVING: 1,303 Calories; 80 g Fat (54.1% calories from fat); 43 g Protein; 109 g Carbohydrate; 21 g Dietary Fiber; 101 mg Cholesterol; 2,096 mg Sodium. Exchanges: 6 Grain (Starch); 3 1/2 Lean Meat; 1 1/2 Vegetable; 0 Fruit; 14 Fat; 0 Other Carbohydrates.

This is a nice salad for fall, especially when made with Granny Smith or Gravenstein apples. It is also an effective way to utilize leftover ham or use ham prepared in-house with the recipe found in Unit 16. The recipe for Spicy Pecans can be found in Appendix I.

diced apples and ham salad *Yield: 1 serving*

Ingredients	Amounts U.S.	Metric	Procedure
Ham, diced	4 oz	113 g	Combine the salad ingredients and marinate refrigerated for 2 hours.
Granny Smith apples, diced	4 oz	113 g	
Dijon mustard, prepared	1 tsp	5 g	
Horseradish, grated, preserved	1 tsp	5 g	
Cucumbers, seeded, diced	2 oz	57 g	
Mayonnaise	1 fl oz	30 ml	
Cayenne pepper	Dash	Dash	
Lettuce leaves	3 each	3 each	Plate the salad on lettuce leaves, garnish with apple chips, and sprinkle with spicy pecans.
Dried apple chips	2 each	2 each	
Spicy pecans	1 tbsp	30 g	

NUTRITIONAL INFORMATION PER SERVING: 509 Calories; 38 g Fat (65.6% calories from fat); 21 g Protein; 24 g Carbohydrate; 3 g Dietary Fiber; 74 mg Cholesterol; 1,756 mg Sodium. Exchanges: 0 Grain (Starch); 3 Lean Meat; 0 Vegetable; 1 Fruit; 2 1/2 Fat; 0 Other Carbohydrates.

This beef salad is a great use for leftover prime rib, steamship rounds, or any large cuts of roasted beef. The Chive Mustard Dressing recipe is located in Unit 14.

traditional beef salad *Yield: 1 serving*

Ingredients	Amounts U.S.	Metric	Procedure
Grilled or roasted leftover prime rib	6 oz	170 g	Trim the leftover beef of all visible fat and connective tissue. Slice into thin (1/2-in) strips. Blend with the dressing.
Chive mustard dressing	1 fl oz	30 ml	
Red onion, sliced thin	2 oz	57 g	Combine all the remaining ingredients except for the cucumber. Marinate the vegetables for 2 hours.
Green peppers, julienne	2 oz	57 g	
Red peppers, julienne	2 oz	57 g	
Dill pickle, julienne	2 oz	57 g	
Mustard, prepared	1 tsp	5 ml	
Olive oil	1 fl oz	30 ml	
Red wine vinegar	1 fl oz	30 ml	
Salt	To taste	To taste	
Pepper	To taste	To taste	
Cucumbers, sliced thin lengthwise	6 slices	6 slices	Line an individual serving bowl with cucumber slices. Arrange the salad in the center. Top with the beef strips. Garnish as desired.

NUTRITIONAL INFORMATION PER SERVING: 816 Calories; 71 g Fat (78.3% calories from fat); 32 g Protein; 13 g Carbohydrate; 3 g Dietary Fiber; 119 mg Cholesterol; 1,294 mg Sodium. Exchanges: 0 Grain (Starch); 4 1/2 Lean Meat; 1 1/2 Vegetable; 1 1/2 Fat; 1/2 Other Carbohydrates.

>> Contemporary Main-Course Salads

In recent years, chefs have created distinctive and contemporary salad combinations. The dictionary defines "contemporary" as "of the present time or modern." We define it as food that is "now." Contemporary cuisine is often inspired by classical dishes, substituting cutting-edge ingredients, technique, and dietary knowledge. Contemporary salads use fresh ingredients and allow individual creativity, stressing natural flavors and unique combinations.

LEARNING ACTIVITY 13-2

Create a signature, contemporary main-course salad that combines sweet, sour, and salty flavors. Create a second recipe combining hot and bitter flavors. You may need to refer back to the discussion on flavors found early on in this unit.

ANOTHER CONSIDERATION

Cost is a major consideration when developing salads to dress up a menu. Using items because they are expensive-sounding or trendy without understanding how to use them is unprofessional and costly. The challenge is creating interesting combinations within the established cost structure.

Smart chefs look at the profitable synergy between main-course salads and by-products from other menu items; for example, by using the following:

- Smaller chicken breasts—about 5 ounces (125 g) grilled on salad
- Salmon tail pieces, skin on and sliced on a bias, quickly cooked on a griddle until crisp
- Cold roast beef made into an interesting salad
- Cold baked ham end cuts with diced apples as ham salad

Opposite temperature combinations such as a warm meat or fish served on cold salad greens are gaining in popularity. Examples would be grilled salmon salad on a bed of arugula or grilled chicken with seasonal berries and fresh greens. We have collected a few of our recent favorites for you to try.

Pesto is a favorite in Northern Italy. It is typically made by blending fresh basil leaves, pine nuts, garlic, parmesan cheese, and olive oil. Prepared pesto can be purchased.

pesto chicken and pine nut salad *Yield: 1 serving*

Ingredients	Amounts U.S.	Metric	Procedure
Chicken	5 oz	140 g	Cook and dice the chicken. Chill.
Pesto, prepared	1 fl oz	30 ml	Combine the chicken, pesto, mayonnaise, olive oil, and balsamic vinegar.
Mayonnaise, prepared	1 tbsp	15 ml	
Olive oil	1 tbsp	15 ml	
Balsamic vinegar	1/2 tbsp	8 ml	
Toasted pine nuts	1 tsp	5 g	Top with pine nuts.

NUTRITIONAL INFORMATION PER SERVING: 512 Calories; 42 g Fat (73.0% calories from fat); 32 g Protein; 3 g Carbohydrate; 1 g Dietary Fiber; 79 mg Cholesterol; 358 mg Sodium. Exchanges: 0 Grain (Starch); 4 1/2 Lean Meat; 0 Fruit; 6 1/2 Fat; 0 Other Carbohydrates.

Highlighting the flavors of Thailand, this next salad combines peanuts, lime, and coconut in a tasty combination that travels well for catered events or can be properly chilled in box lunches. This recipe calls for ginger root, or **galangal root,** which is a plant native to Southeast Asia that has a peppery, ginger-like flavor and texture.

> **CHEF'S TIP**
> *Many of the salad recipes in this unit have been geared to one individual serving. But there are some recipes that are especially geared for buffet and banquet service. Those recipes will have an increased yield, as in the Thai Pork Salad recipe.*

Thai pork salad *Yield: 6 main course portions*

Ingredients	U.S.	Metric	Procedure
Pork loin, boneless	36 oz	1.02 kg	Cut into 1/2-in stir-fry strips.
Rice noodles	8 oz	227 g	Cook the noodles according to the package directions, drain, and set aside.
Dressing			
Sesame oil	2 fl oz	60 ml	Combine the oil, vinegar, juice, zest, peanut butter, soy sauce, coconut milk, brown sugar, ginger root, and red pepper flakes. Blend until smooth.
Rice wine vinegar	1 fl oz	30 ml	
Lime juice	1 fl oz	30 ml	
Lime zest	2 tsp	20 g	
Peanut butter	3 oz	85 g	
Soy sauce	2 fl oz	59 ml	
Coconut milk	2 fl oz	59 ml	
Brown sugar	2 oz	57 g	
Ginger root or galangal root	2 tsp	10 g	
Red pepper flakes, crushed	1/2 tsp	2 g	
Vegetable oil	4 tsp	20 ml	Heat the vegetable and sesame oil in a large skillet over medium-high heat. Add the bell pepper and onion and stir-fry for 1–2 minutes or until onions are crisp and tender. Remove the vegetables from the skillet. Add the pork strips to the hot skillet. Cook and stir for 2–3 minutes or until cooked through; return the vegetables to the skillet and add the cooked noodles. Cook and stir about 1 minute more or until heated through. Remove from the heat. Pour the dressing over the mixture in the skillet. Toss lightly to coat.
Sesame oil	4 tsp	20 ml	
Red bell pepper, diced	2 medium	2 medium	
Green onions, chopped	2 oz	57 g	
Chinese cabbage, shredded	18 oz	510 g	Divide the pork mixture and place on the shredded Chinese cabbage.
Cashews or peanuts	2 oz	57 g	Top with cashews or peanuts.

NUTRITIONAL INFORMATION PER SERVING (WITH CASHEWS): 565 Calories; 32 g Fat (49.6% calories from fat); 27 g Protein; 45 g Carbohydrate; 3 g Dietary Fiber; 53 mg Cholesterol; 811 mg Sodium. Exchanges: 2 1/2 Grain (Starch); 3 1/2 Lean Meat; 1 Vegetable; 0 Fruit; 5 Fat; 0 Other Carbohydrates.

This salad is a spin-off of the traditional grilled chicken breast salad. The spicy flavor comes from the mustard greens and sprouts. Top it with the Asian-Style Dressing from Unit 14.*

Asian-style grilled chicken salad *Yield: 12 main-course servings*

Ingredients	Amounts U.S.	Metric	Procedure
Bean sprouts	1 lb	454 g	Mix together the sprouts, cabbage, greens, pepper, carrots, water chestnuts, and green onion.
Cabbage or broccoli sprouts	1/2 lb	227 g	
Asian mustard greens (red or green) chopped fine	1 lb	454 g	
Chinese cabbage, chopped	1 1/2 lbs	680 g	
Red bell pepper, julienne	8 oz	227 g	
Carrots, finely shredded	8 oz	227 g	
Water chestnuts, sliced	8 oz	227 g	
Green onions, sliced bias cut	4 oz	113 g	
Chicken breast, skinless	2 lbs	907 g	Grill the chicken and slice it into thin 1/4-in × 1/4-in strips, about 2 in long. Chill.

*Asian dressing	20 fl oz	592 ml	Blend the vegetables, chicken, and dressing.
Mandarin or Navel orange sections	1 1/2 lbs	680 g	Plate and sprinkle with the orange sections and nuts.
Cashews, roasted, chopped	4 oz	113 g	

NUTRITIONAL INFORMATION PER SERVING: 444 Calories; 32 g Fat (62.0% calories from fat); 20 g Protein; 24 g Carbohydrate; 6 g Dietary Fiber; 35 mg Cholesterol; 77 mg Sodium. Exchanges: 1/2 Grain (Starch); 2 Lean Meat; 2 Vegetable; 1/2 Fruit; 6 Fat.

*Asian Dressing is found in Unit 14, Dressings on page 559.

Lobster salad may be the perfect menu choice when a high-end salad is needed to round out a salad menu. One pound of lobster (454 g) will yield about 5 ounces (142 g) when cooked and shelled. Some chefs reserve the claw meat as a garnish.

lobster salad with grapes and fennel *Yield: 1 serving*

Ingredients	Amounts		Procedure
	U.S.	Metric	
Lobster, cooked, shelled	5 oz	142 g	Cut the lobster in coarse pieces; save the claws.
Thompson grapes, fresh	2 oz	57 g	Combine all the ingredients except for the lettuce and dill sprigs.
Fennel, diced	2 oz	57 g	
Sour cream	1 fl oz	30 ml	
Horseradish, grated	1 tsp	5 g	
Dill, fresh, chopped	1 tsp	5 g	
Salt	To taste	To taste	
Pepper	To taste	To taste	
Lettuce leaves	3 each	3 each	Place the lettuce leaves on a salad plate. Top with the lobster salad and garnish with the claws and dill sprig.
Dill sprig	1 each	1 each	

NUTRITIONAL INFORMATION PER SERVING: 235 Calories; 8 g Fat (28.7% calories from fat); 29 g Protein; 13 g Carbohydrate; 3 g Dietary Fiber; 147 mg Cholesterol; 743 mg Sodium. Exchanges: 0 Grain (Starch); 3 1/2 Lean Meat; 0 Vegetable; 1/2 Fruit; 0 Nonfat Milk; 1 Fat; 0 Other Carbohydrates.

The grilled salmon slices for the following salad should be cut on a bias, skin on, and should be about 1/2 inch thick. They can be cut ahead of time, marinated at will, and kept in oil until service. Use the Basic Vinaigrette Dressing recipe found in Unit 14.

grilled salmon slices on arugula *Yield: 1 serving*

Ingredients	Amounts U.S.	Metric	Procedure
Celeriac	2 oz	57 g	Julienne the celeriac.
Tomatoes	2 oz	57 g	Dice the tomatoes.
Arugula	2 oz	57 g	Shred the arugula and toss it with the tomatoes and celeriac.
Basic vinaigrette dressing	1 1/2 oz	45 ml	Combine the dressing and lemon juice. Plate the vegetables and top with the dressing mixture.
Lemon juice	1 tsp	5 ml	
Salmon slices	6 to 7 oz	170 to 200 g	Make sure the grill or broiler is smoking hot. Salt and pepper the salmon slices. Place salmon slices on the grill and cook over high heat. Turn over when brown, grill one moment longer, and serve on top of the salad. The slices and skin should be crisp.
Salt	To taste	To taste	
Pepper	To taste	To taste	

NUTRITIONAL INFORMATION PER SERVING: 471 Calories; 31 g Fat (58.6% calories from fat); 41 g Protein; 8 g Carbohydrate; 1 g Dietary Fiber; 103 mg Cholesterol; 446 mg Sodium. Exchanges: 0 Grain (Starch); 5 1/2 Lean Meat; 1 Vegetable; 0 Fruit; 4 1/2 Fat.

The Roasted Asparagus and Smoked Salmon Salad is garnished with chopped egg whites and sieved egg yolks. Use the Basic Vinaigrette Dressing recipe found in Unit 14. To smoke the salmon in-house, use the Benchmark Recipe for Dry Cure for Salmon, Sturgeon, or Trout found in Unit 16.

roasted asparagus and smoked salmon salad
Yield: 1 serving

Ingredients	Amounts U.S.	Metric	Procedure
Asparagus, fresh	4 to 8 spears	4 to 8 spears	Steam the asparagus until cooked yet firm. Brush the steamed asparagus with oil and put it on a hot surface of the stove. Turn when brown or almost charred. Plate.
Oil	1 tsp	5 ml	

Smoked salmon	5 oz	142 g	Slice the salmon. Drape the salmon slices over the asparagus.
Onions	1/2 oz	14 g	Fine mince the onions and sprinkle on the above.
Hard-boiled egg white	1/2 tsp	2 g	Chop the egg whites. Chop the egg yolks. Arrange in two strips on top of the above mixture with one strip of egg whites and one strip of yolks.
Hard-boiled egg yolk	1/2 oz	14 g	
Basic vinaigrette dressing	1 tbsp	15 ml	Drizzle vinaigrette over the above mixture.
Parsley	1 tsp	5 g	Chop the parsley and sprinkle it over the salad.

NUTRITIONAL INFORMATION PER SERVING: 419 Calories; 24 g Fat (51.2% calories from fat); 38 g Protein; 14 g Carbohydrate; 6 g Dietary Fiber; 245 mg Cholesterol; 1,180 mg Sodium. Exchanges: 4 1/2 Lean Meat; 2 1/2 Vegetable; 3 Fat.

If possible, use white balsamic vinegar for the following recipe. If white balsamic vinegar isn't available, you may substitute it with regular balsamic vinegar. To obtain the **orange supreme** from the orange, use a paring knife to completely remove the skin and the pith. Carefully cut the orange into segments, or supremes, by cutting next to the segment layer, removing the meat between each membrane, being careful to remove all skin and seeds.

seared scallops with white truffle vinaigrette
Yield: 4 servings

Ingredients	Amounts U.S.	Metric	Procedure
Large sea scallops	16 oz	454 g	Clean the scallops by removing the small, tough muscle attachment.
Soy sauce	1 tbsp	15 ml	Combine the soy sauce, orange juice, and zest to make a marinade. Toss the scallops in the marinade and let sit for 30 minutes.
Orange juice	1 fl oz	30 ml	
Orange zest	1/2 tsp	2 g	
White truffle oil	2 fl oz	55 ml	Make the white truffle vinaigrette with the truffle oil, white balsamic vinegar, Dijon mustard, and salt and pepper.
White balsamic vinegar	1 fl oz	30 ml	
Dijon mustard	1 tsp	5 ml	
Salt	To taste	To taste	
Pepper	To taste	To taste	
Assorted mesclun greens	12 oz	340 g	Toss the greens with the vinaigrette and place on individual salad plates. Heat a sauté pan to a hot temperature. The pan must be very hot to sear and caramelize quickly. Pan-sear the scallops, caramelizing both sides for 2 minutes. You can also broil the scallops. This gives them nice crosshatch marks. Do not overcook the scallops.
Orange supremes, segments	4 oz	113 g	Serve the scallops on the bed of greens, alternating with the orange supremes.

NUTRITIONAL INFORMATION PER SERVING: 265 Calories; 16 g Fat (51.2% calories from fat); 23 g Protein; 11 g Carbohydrate; 4 g Dietary Fiber; 46 mg Cholesterol; 586 mg Sodium. Exchanges: 0 Grain (Starch); 3 Lean Meat; 1 Vegetable; 1/2 Fruit; 3 Fat; 0 Other Carbohydrates.

Turmeric is a component in most curry powders, but it can also be used alone. This Indian-inspired duck salad calls for a touch of turmeric, cilantro, and mango.

mango ginger duck salad with turmeric curry infused oil *Yield: 4 servings*

Ingredients	Amounts U.S.	Metric	Procedure
Grape seed oil	1 1/2 fl oz	44 ml	To make a marinade, combine the grape seed oil, first mango pureé, vinegar, ginger, and garlic.
Mango pureé	2 fl oz	59 ml	
Cider vinegar	1 fl oz	30 ml	
Fresh ginger, grated fine	1 tbsp	15 g	
Garlic, mashed	2 cloves	2 cloves	
Moulard duck breast	4 - 4 oz breasts	4 -113 g breasts	Score each duck breast. Pour marinade over each duck breast and marinate for 1 hour.
Turmeric powder	1 tsp	5 g	Heat the turmeric and curry in a small sauté pan for 20 seconds to toast lightly and bring out the flavors. Add the oil and simmer over low heat for 5 minutes to infuse the oil. Remove from heat and let cool. Strain through cheesecloth into a squeeze bottle. Reserve for the salad assembly.
Curry powder	1/2 oz	15 g	
Grape seed oil	4 fl oz	118 ml	
Cilantro, chopped	1/2 oz	15 g	To make the dressing: Mix the cilantro, mango, green onions, celery, mango pureé, and mayonnaise together.
Mango, seeded and diced small	1 each	1 each	
Green onion, diced	1 stalk	1 stalk	
Celery rib, diced fine	1 stalk	1 stalk	
Mango pureé	1 tbsp	15 ml	
Mayonnaise	1 1/2 fl oz	44 ml	
Assorted baby greens	8 oz	227 g	To assemble the salad: Remove the duck breasts from the marinade. Let dry. Grill until the duck is rare. Dice the duck into medium squares and toss with the dressing. Place the mixed greens on a salad plate and top with the duck salad. Garnish with the toasted almonds and drizzle the plate with the spiced oil.
Toasted almond slices	4 oz	113 g	

NUTRITIONAL INFORMATION PER SERVING: 970 Calories; 94 g Fat (83.6% calories from fat); 16 g Protein; 26 g Carbohydrate; 7 g Dietary Fiber; 33 mg Cholesterol; 121 mg Sodium. Exchanges: 1/2 Grain (Starch); 1 1/2 Lean Meat; 1 Vegetable; 1 Fruit; 17 Fat; 0 Other Carbohydrates.

You will find this salad on many menus in California and Oregon. When possible, use fresh crab meat. Blue crab meat is an acceptable substitution when dungeness is unavailable.

dungeness crab stuffed avocado salad   *Yield: 4 servings*

Ingredients	Amounts U.S.	Metric	Procedure
Haas avocados, split, pitted, and skin removed	2 large	2 large	Split the first two avocados, removing the pit. With a large metal spoon, carefully remove the flesh intact.

Ingredients	Amounts U.S.	Metric	Procedure
Mixed greens	8 oz	227 g	Place the greens on individual salad plates. Place one-half avocado on each salad.
Red onion, diced fine	2 oz	57 g	In a separate bowl, mix the onions, mayonnaise, lime juice, cilantro, chili sauce, spices, and seasonings.
Mayonnaise	2 fl oz	59 ml	
Lime juice	1 fl oz	30 ml	
Cilantro, minced fine	1 tsp	5 ml	
Chili sauce	1/2 fl oz	15 ml	
Cayenne pepper	To taste	To taste	
Cumin	1/2 tsp	2 g	
Salt	To taste	To taste	
Pepper	To taste	To taste	
Dungeness crab meat, leg and body pieces	16 oz	454 g	Toss in the crab meat, making sure to pick through to remove any remaining shells.
Haas avocado, split, pitted, skinned, diced	1 large	1 large	Gently toss in the diced avocado. Fill each avocado half with 4 oz of the crab and avocado salad.
Lime, sliced	1 medium	1 medium	Garnish with a twist of lime.

NUTRITIONAL INFORMATION PER SERVING: 541 Calories; 48 g Fat (73.6% calories from fat); 20 g Protein; 18 g Carbohydrate; 6 g Dietary Fiber; 60 mg Cholesterol; 506 mg Sodium. Exchanges: 0 Grain (Starch); 2 Lean Meat; 1/2 Vegetable; 1 Fruit; 6 1/2 Fat; 0 Other Carbohydrates.

Some chefs boil octopus with wine bottle corks to tenderize. There is no scientific reason for this but it is something you might want to try sometime.

octopus salad *Yield: 4 servings*

Ingredients	Amounts		Procedure
	U.S.	Metric	
Water	1 gallon	3.79 l	Bring the water to a boil, and then reduce the temperature and simmer the octopus until tender or about 1 hour. Cool in the stock.
Salt	1 tbsp	15 g	
Baby octopus	8 each	8 each	
Dressing			
Garlic cloves, crushed	4 each	4 each	Combine the ingredients to make the dressing.
Olive oil	2 fl oz	59 ml	
Lemon juice	1 fl oz	30 ml	
Grated lemon peel	1 tsp	5 g	
Oregano leaves, fresh	1 tsp	5 g	
Pepper, coarse	To taste	To taste	
Salt	To taste	To taste	
Tomatoes	8 oz	227 g	Dice the tomatoes.
Greek olives, pitted	2 oz	58 g	Remove the octopus from the stock, drain, and cut into bite-sized pieces. Blend with the dressing. Serve on lettuce leaves and top with diced tomatoes and olives.
Lettuce leaves	As needed	As needed	

NUTRITIONAL INFORMATION PER SERVING: 243 Calories; 17 g Fat (61.7% calories from fat); 17 g Protein; 7 g Carbohydrate; 1 g Dietary Fiber; 51 mg Cholesterol; 1,991 mg Sodium. Exchanges: 0 Grain (Starch); 2 Lean Meat; 1/2 Vegetable; 0 Fruit; 3 Fat.

This North African-inspired salad features couscous. Bulgur wheat can be substituted for the couscous. The lamb roast should be lean cut and trimmed of all visible fat, because cold lamb fat has a strong tallow taste.

grilled lamb and fig salad *Yield: 1 serving*

Ingredients	Amounts U.S.	Metric	Procedure
Lamb roast, cooked	6 oz	170 g	Slice lamb into thin slices and then into 1-in squares.
Pitted dried dates	2 oz	57 g	Julienne the dates.
Couscous, cooked	4 oz	113 g	Combine all the ingredients except for the mint leaves and figs. Marinate refrigerated for 1 hour.
Lemon juice	1 tbsp	15 ml	
Grated lemon peel	1/2 tsp	2 g	
Cinnamon, ground	Dash	Dash	
Olive oil	1 tbsp	15 ml	
Hot pepper	To taste	To taste	
Salt	To taste	To taste	
Mint leaves, fresh	As needed	As needed	Plate the above mixture. Sprinkle with mint leaves and garnish with a quartered fig.
Fig, ripe	1 each	1 each	

NUTRITIONAL INFORMATION PER SERVING: 907 Calories; 30 g Fat (29.5% calories from fat); 49 g Protein; 111 g Carbohydrate; 10 g Dietary Fiber; 122 mg Cholesterol; 368 mg Sodium. Exchanges: 4 1/2 Grain (Starch); 5 Lean Meat; 0 Vegetable; 3 Fruit; 2 1/2 Fat.

A trip to the local farmer's market not only ensures a fresh and original salad, but it supports sustainability. Any seasonal vegetable or herb can be used as a substitution in this salad. This recipe uses golden beets, which can be blended with other ingredients without the bleeding that you would find with regular red beets.

farmer's market penne pasta *Yield: 10 servings*

Ingredients	Amounts U.S.	Metric	Procedure
Marinade and Dressing			
Red wine vinegar	4 fl oz	118 ml	In a small mixing bowl, combine the mustard, garlic, salt, and pepper. Add the vinegar and stir to blend thoroughly. Slowly drizzle in the olive oil, blending. Split the mixture into two portions. Use one of the portions to marinate the chicken breast. Marinate the chicken for no less than 1 hour and no more than 4 hours.
Extra virgin olive oil	12 fl oz	355 ml	
Course ground mustard	1 fl oz	30 ml	
Garlic, crushed, mashed fine	4 cloves	4 cloves	
Kosher salt	To taste	To taste	
Pepper, freshly cracked	To taste	To taste	
Boneless, skinless chicken breasts	10 each/ 6 oz	10 each/ 170 g	Marinate the breasts in half of the above mixture. Grill until an internal temperature of 165°F (75°C) is reached. Let cool and cut into 1/2-in strips.
Penne pasta	1 lb dry	454 g	Boil the penne pasta in salted water. When tender, drain and place in a large bowl.
Salt	2 to 3 tbsp	30 to 45 g	
Water	6 qt	5.68 l	
Asparagus	1 lb	454 g	Steam or boil the asparagus until just tender, approximately 2 to 3 minutes in rapidly boiling water. Drain, and cut into 2-in diagonal cuts. Add to the pasta in a large bowl. Do not toss at this time.
Golden beets, leaves removed	1 lb	454 g	Steam or boil the golden beets, let cool to touch, peel and cut into 1/4-in squares, and add to the bowl.
Roma tomatoes	1 lb	454 g	Remove the stem spot on the tomatoes and slice the Roma tomatoes into 1/4-in slices. Add to the bowl.
Green onions	1 bunch	1 bunch	Remove the root end of the green onions and slice into diagonal slices. Add the onions to the bowl.
Basil leaves, fresh	1 bunch	1 bunch	Remove the stems off the basil leaves, reserving five of the nicest larger leaves for garnish. Cut the remaining leaves into fine julienne strips. Add to the bowl.
Yellow or orange cherry tomatoes	4 oz	113 g	Pour the remaining dressing over the pasta, cooked chicken, and vegetables. Toss all of the ingredients together to coat and mix well. Garnish with large basil leaves and a few whole yellow or orange cherry tomatoes.

NUTRITIONAL INFORMATION PER SERVING: 691 Calories; 38 g Fat (49.5% calories from fat); 45 g Protein; 42 g Carbohydrate; 3 g Dietary Fiber; 104 mg Cholesterol; 1,799 mg Sodium. Exchanges: 2 Grain (Starch); 5 1/2 Lean Meat; 1 1/2 Vegetable; 6 1/2 Fat; 0 Other Carbohydrates.

This salad brings a taste of the Middle East to your menu. Saffron comes from the crocus plant and is one of the most exotic and costly spices available to chefs. With the green peas, red peppers, and yellow orange saffron, this is a visually beautiful salad to serve at banquets and buffets. This recipe uses the larger couscous, known as Israeli couscous.

chicken and saffron Israeli couscous with peas

Yield: 4 main-course servings

Ingredients	Amounts U.S.	Metric	Procedure
Chicken breasts, boneless, skinless	4 each- 6 oz	4 each- 170 g	Grill the breasts, cool, and slice into 1/2–in strips.
Chicken broth or water	1 pint	473 ml	Bring the broth or water to a boil. Add the salt and couscous. Simmer for 6 minutes. Drain and set the couscous aside.
Israeli couscous	8 oz	227 g	
Salt	1/2 tsp	2 g	
Olive oil	1 fl oz	30 ml	Heat the olive oil in a sauté pan and add the white wine. Soak strands of saffron in the hot oil and wine mixture until the saffron threads color the liquid.
White wine	2 fl oz	59 ml	
Saffron threads	A pinch	A pinch	
Red pepper, chopped	6 oz	170 g	Add the peppers, green onions, tarragon, and peas. Add the couscous and toss together.
Green onions, chopped	3 whole	3 whole	
Tarragon leaves, fresh, minced	1/2 oz	15 g	
Green peas, fresh or frozen	12 oz	340 g	
Salt	To taste	To taste	Salt and pepper to taste.
Pepper	To taste	To taste	

NUTRITIONAL INFORMATION PER SERVING: 511 Calories; 13 g Fat (23.0% calories from fat); 50 g Protein; 45 g Carbohydrate; 6 g Dietary Fiber; 104 mg Cholesterol; 874 mg Sodium. Exchanges: 3 Grain (Starch); 5 1/2 Lean Meat; 1/2 Vegetable; 1 1/2 Fat.

>> Summary

A well-balanced and attractive salad selection on the menu serves two purposes. First, customers like attractive main-course salads, especially for lunch and increasingly for dinner, especially in warm weather. Second, main-course salads are a way to add excitement and interest to a menu and to introduce new flavors to the guest. Plated main-course salads served for lunch or banquets can also balance the workload because they can be prepared ahead of time, providing that suitable refrigeration is available. In the kitchen, it helps to balance the workload between the hot kitchen and the cold kitchen.

While many people enjoy eating meals that are attractive and cool (temperature wise), they also appreciate the cost effectiveness of main-course salads. An attractive salad section on the menu can offer interesting, well-priced choices for the customer. It also gives the kitchen an opportunity to utilize many ingredients, as many main-course salads use by-products from other preparations, making the menu item very profitable.

Care must be taken to ensure good sanitation standards because many salads are prepared and served without additional cooking.

Classic salads are recognized by customers and it is advisable not to alter the classic recipe unless the name is changed. Contemporary salads are those that allow the chef more freedom and let his or her imagination run wild.

>> Review Questions

MATCHING

Go back and review the recipes for the following main-course salads. Match the salad with one of its unique ingredients.

1. _____ Salad Niçoise
2. _____ Classic Greek Salad
3. _____ Cobb Salad
4. _____ Traditional Beef Salad
5. _____ Chef Salad
6. _____ Crab Louie

a. turkey breast, julienne
b. cocktail sauce
c. Roquefort cheese
d. tuna
e. dill pickles
f. Kalamata olives

MULTIPLE CHOICE

7. To create successful salads, attention must be paid to
   a. the freshness and quality of ingredients.
   b. the proper cooking procedures of all cooked ingredients.
   c. guest-centered presentations that are easy to access and eat.
   d. all of the above.
8. Which of the following is *not* a common component of a main-course salad?
   a. protein or heavy carbohydrate
   b. dressing
   c. greens
   d. base
9. A ravigote is a(n)
   a. French crab.
   b. Italian olive.
   c. spiral pasta.
   d. cold, French vinegar-based sauce.

10. Refer back to the text regarding flavor at the beginning of this unit and answer the following question: What flavor adds surprise to food?
    a. sweet
    b. sour
    c. spicy
    d. umami
11. What ingredient is not typically found in pesto?
    a. capers
    b. basil
    c. pine nuts
    d. olive oil
12. Mimosa garnish refers to
    a. sieved egg yolks.
    b. the city Mimosa Park, Louisiana.
    c. champagne and orange juice drink.
    d. minimal use of garnish.

SHORT ANSWER

13. What's the difference between a classic main-course salad and contemporary salads?

14. List three tips for making satisfying main-course salads.

15. What meats and cheese are used to make a traditional chef salad?

16. What protein is generally used in Louie salads?

17. Cobb salad originated in what famous Los Angeles restaurant?

18. Which country did the salad Nicoise originate in?

Dressings, Dips, and Cold Sauces

>> **Unit 14**

Dressings

>> **Unit 15**

Cold Sauces, Dips, Aioli, Salsas, Relishes, and Chutneys

In many cases it is the dressing, dip, or sauce that brings the dish to life. While there are a wide variety of prepared products on the market, most chefs know how to make them from scratch. In many settings, signature, made-from-scratch products are used to set that business apart from the competition. It is important for budding chefs to understand the types of dressings, such as vinaigrettes, emulsified, cream, cooked, and low-fat preparations, discussed in Unit 14.

Unit 15 focuses on cold sauces, dips, aiolis, salsas, relishes, and chutneys, all of which complement other foods. They add flavor, texture, and color and are generally prepared in the cold kitchen.

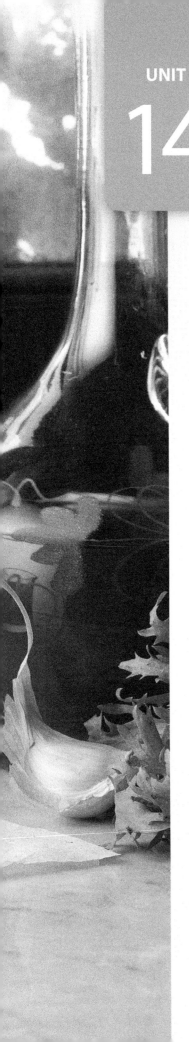

Dressings

>> Learning Objectives

After you have finished reading this unit, you should be able to:

- Describe the differences between the basic types of salad dressings.
- Demonstrate how to prepare a vinaigrette dressing.
- Explain the emulsification process.
- Create a cream dressing.
- Demonstrate how to prepare a basic cooked dressing.
- Define what makes a dressing "low-fat."

>> Key Terms

cooked dressings	emulsifiers	vinaigrette
cream dressings	emulsions	*(vihn-uh-GREHT)*
emulsified dressings	low-fat dressings	wilted salads

This unit discusses the basic categories of salad dressings. While many restaurants and home cooks purchase ready-made dressings and vinaigrettes, preparing dressings from scratch is inexpensive and easy. As students progress through this unit, they should compare the quality and cost-effectiveness of purchased dressings with the dressings made in class.

Salad dressings have been used for centuries to "dress" up blander ingredients such as lettuce and vegetables that are typically used in salads. Their purpose is to enhance the flavors of the ingredients of the salad, not to mask or overtake them. It's important not to use too much dressing and to choose a dressing that complements the ingredients in the salad.

>> Dressing Classifications

Salad dressings can be classified in a number of categories:

- **Vinaigrettes** are simple dressings that consist of oil or other acidic ingredients, herbs, and spices.
- **Emulsified dressings** consist of mayonnaise, egg yolks or other thickening agents, herbs, spices, and flavorful ingredients.
- **Cream dressings** contain dairy products.
- **Cooked dressings** are made with a variety of ingredients that are cooked before being served. The dressing can be used hot or cold, depending on the recipe.

- **Low-fat dressings** made with low-fat dairy products or oils and seasoning reduce fat content as well as calories.

You can alter the flavor of most salad dressing recipes by using any or all of the following variations:

- Fresh, chopped herbs
- Flavored vinegars or oils (the color of the vinegar may change the color of the dressing)
- A variety of spices or spice combinations
- Mustards, Worcestershire sauce, Tabasco sauce, soy sauce, catsup, and other prepared condiments to alter the flavor.

>> Vinaigrettes

The simplest dressing consists of oil, an acid, and spices (Figure 14-1). This basic dressing is called *vinaigrette* because about one-third of the blend consists of vinegar.

There is a French jingle that says it takes four people to make the vinaigrette dressing for the perfect salad:

> *The stingy person to add salt*
> *The miser to add vinegar*
> *The generous person to add oil*
> *A fool who will vigorously toss all together.*

CHEF'S TIP
Vinaigrettes must be stirred before every use.

The basic vinaigrette dressing is made with oil, vinegar, salt, and pepper. Using fresh ingredients and high-quality oils and vinegars will enhance the salad. Some chefs prefer using extra virgin olive oil for salad dressings. That is clearly a matter of taste and budget—extra virgin olive oil is more expensive than many other types of oil. Salt will dissolve in vinegar but not in oil and should, therefore, be added before the oil. Oils in liquids do not remain suspended; even after vigorous blending, the liquids will settle to the bottom and the oils will stay on top (Figure 14-2). Vinaigrettes are used mostly on salads but are finding their way into other dishes including hot pasta, broiled meats and fish, and even cold meat, poultry, and fish dishes.

Figure 14-1 Vinaigrette set-up.

Figure 14-2 The oil floats on top of the vinegar and must be mixed just prior to serving.

This type of simple dressing is basically made by blending liquid ingredients with spices and oil. These dressings are popular but have the disadvantage of not clinging to salad greens, especially when the greens are wet. As you know, water and oil do not mix and putting oil-based dressings on wet leaves causes the dressing to run off. To remedy this challenge, chefs created slightly thickened, simple vinaigrette dressings.

Several of the dressings listed next contain small amounts of thickening ingredients but are still classified as *vinaigrette dressings*.

basic vinaigrette dressing   *Yield: 1 quart (960 ml) Approximately 30 each 1 fl oz (30 ml) servings*

Ingredients	Amounts		Procedure
	U.S.	Metric	
White wine vinegar, mild	8 fl oz	237 ml	Combine the vinegar with salt and pepper. Stir until the salt is dissolved.
Salt	1 tbsp	15 g	
Pepper, coarse ground	1 tbsp	15 g	

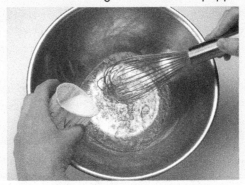

Oil, neutral or light olive oil	24 fl oz	710 ml	Add the oil and stir. The dressing can be stored without refrigeration.

NUTRITIONAL INFORMATION PER SERVING: 194 Calories; 22 g Fat (98.7% calories from fat); trace Protein; 1 g Carbohydrate; trace Dietary Fiber; 0 mg Cholesterol; 213 mg Sodium. Exchanges: 0 Grain (Starch); 4 1/2 Fat; 0 Other Carbohydrates.

This vinaigrette is made with balsamic vinegar, which has an intense flavor, color, and texture. Its richness comes from the aging process, which uses a series of different wood casks that concentrate the flavors and natural sugars.

balsamic dressing
Yield: 28 oz (840 ml) Approximately 28 each 1 fl oz (30 ml) servings

Ingredients	Amounts		Procedure
	U.S.	Metric	
Balsamic vinegar	8 fl oz	237 ml	Mix the vinegar, honey, shallots, and mustard in a food processor.
Honey	2 fl oz	59 g	
Shallots, chopped	1 1/2 oz	43 g	
Dijon mustard	1 fl oz	30 ml	
Olive oil	1 pint	473 ml	While the processor is running, drizzle in the oil so that it emulsifies.
Salt	To taste	To taste	Season with salt and pepper.
Pepper	To taste	To taste	

NUTRITIONAL INFORMATION PER SERVING: 148 Calories; 15 g Fat (91.3% calories from fat); trace Protein; 3 g Carbohydrate; trace Dietary Fiber; 0 mg Cholesterol; 23 mg Sodium. Exchanges: 0 Grain (Starch); 0 Lean Meat; 0 Vegetable; 0 Fruit; 3 Fat; 0 Other Carbohydrates.

To bring out the flavor, lightly toast the pistachio nuts just prior to serving. To toast, spread the nuts in a baking sheet and bake at 400°F (205°C) for 7 to 10 minutes until they start to turn golden.

Crème fraîche is a slightly acidic, thick cream and a basic ingredient used in many French dishes. If it is not available, you can make a batch by combining 2 tablespoons sour cream with 2 cups heavy cream. Cover the container and allow it to ferment overnight at room temperature.

pistachio vinaigrette
Yield: 1 qt (960 ml) Approximately 30 each 1 fl oz (30 ml) servings

Ingredients	Amounts		Procedure
	U.S.	Metric	
White wine vinegar	8 fl oz	237 ml	Use a powerful blender to emulsify all the ingredients to create a smooth dressing.
Canola oil	12 fl oz	354 ml	
Pistachio oil	12 fl oz	354 ml	
Pistachio nuts, shelled	6 oz	170 g	
Crème fraîche	2 fl oz	59 ml	
Salt	To taste	To taste	
Pepper	To taste	To taste	
Sugar	To taste	To taste	

NUTRITIONAL INFORMATION PER SERVING: 216 Calories; 24 g Fat (96.6% calories from fat); 1 g Protein; 1 g Carbohydrate; trace Dietary Fiber; 2 mg Cholesterol; 10 mg Sodium. Exchanges: 0 Grain (Starch); 0 Lean Meat; 0 Nonfat Milk; 4 1/2 Fat; 0 Other Carbohydrates.

Red Wine Vinaigrette is a standard recipe and is used in many restaurants. The dry mustard creates more assertive vinaigrette, which is good with stronger greens such as romaine or escarole.

red wine vinaigrette
Yield: 1 qt (960 ml) Approximately 32 each 1 fl oz (30 ml) servings

Ingredients	Amounts		Procedure
	U.S.	Metric	
Red wine vinegar	8 fl oz	225 ml	Blend the vinegar, mustard, and seasonings.
Dijon mustard	1 fl oz	30 ml	
Dry mustard	1 tsp	5 g	
Sugar	1 tbsp	15 g	
Garlic, crushed	2 cloves	2 cloves	
Salt	To taste	To taste	Add salt and pepper, to taste.
Black cracked pepper	To taste	To taste	
Canola oil	12 fl oz	355 ml	Slowly add the oils to emulsify.
Extra virgin olive oil	12 fl oz	355 ml	

NUTRITIONAL INFORMATION PER SERVING: 192 Calories; 21 g Fat (97.9% calories from fat); trace Protein; 1 g Carbohydrate; trace Dietary Fiber; 0 mg Cholesterol; 20 mg Sodium. Exchanges: 0 Grain (Starch); 0 Lean Meat; 0 Vegetable; 4 1/2 Fat; 0 Other Carbohydrates.

This vinaigrette is excellent with main course salads made with grilled pork or chicken. Consider using a blender to mix this recipe. A stronger and creamier dressing will result.

port wine sesame vinaigrette

Yield: 48 fl oz (1.42 l) Approximately 48 each 1 fl oz (30 ml) servings

Ingredients	Amounts		Procedure
	U.S.	Metric	
Shallots, minced	2 fl oz	59 ml	Sauté the shallots in the butter. Add the port wine and reduce the mixture to 1 ounce. Be careful not to burn the mixture. Once reduced, place the mixture in a blender.
Butter	1 oz	30 g	
Port wine	12 fl oz	354 ml	

Ingredients	Amounts		Procedure
Egg yolk, liquid pasteurized	4 fl oz	118 ml	Add the egg yolk, vinegar, and lime juice. Blend with the above mixture.
Rice wine vinegar	4 fl oz	118 ml	
Lime juice	2 fl oz	59 ml	
Safflower oil	16 fl oz	473 ml	Slowly add the oil. If the mixture is too thick, adjust it with the consommé.
Consommé	6 fl oz	177 ml	
Salt	To taste	To taste	Adjust the seasoning with salt and pepper, and add sesame oil to taste.
White pepper	To taste	To taste	
Sesame oil	1 fl oz	30 ml	

NUTRITIONAL INFORMATION PER SERVING: 179 Calories; 17 g Fat (92.8% calories from fat); 1 g Protein; 2 g Carbohydrate; trace Dietary Fiber; 52 mg Cholesterol; 35 mg Sodium. Exchanges: 0 Grain (Starch); 0 Lean Meat; 0 Vegetable; 0 Fruit; 3 1/2 Fat; 0 Other Carbohydrates.

A variety of citrus juice and segments can be substituted in this recipe for a flavorful twist.

lemon vinaigrette

Yield: 1 qt (960 ml) Approximately 30 each 1 fl oz (30 ml) servings

Ingredients	Amounts U.S.	Metric	Procedure
Lemon segments	2 1/2 oz	71 g	Finely chop the lemon segments, tarragon, and mint.
Tarragon, fresh	1 oz	28 g	
Mint, fresh	1 oz	28 g	
Lemon juice, freshly squeezed	6 fl oz	178 ml	In a blender mix the lemon juice, vinegar, and oils for 2 to 3 minutes.
Apple cider vinegar	4 fl oz	118 ml	
Olive oil	12 fl oz	355 ml	
Grapeseed oil	8 fl oz	237 ml	
Salt	To taste	To taste	Whisk in by hand the lemon segments, tarragon, mint, and remaining ingredients.
Pepper	To taste	To taste	
Honey	1 oz	30 g	
Candied lemon peel	1 oz	30 g	

NUTRITIONAL INFORMATION PER SERVING: 171 Calories; 18 g Fat (92.5% calories from fat); trace Protein; 3 g Carbohydrate; trace Dietary Fiber; 0 mg Cholesterol; 10 mg Sodium. Exchanges: 0 Grain (Starch); 0 Lean Meat; 0 Vegetable; 0 Fruit; 3 1/2 Fat; 0 Other Carbohydrates.

Mirin is a rice wine made from sweet rice. It adds a slightly sweet, memorable taste to the typical Thai ingredients found in this dressing. Thai basil has purple leaves and concentrated flavor. You might want to increase the amount of basil the recipe calls for if Thai basil is not available. The peanuts are optional and will give an added crunch to the recipe.

Thai basil dressing *Yield: 32 oz (946 ml) Approximately 32 1 fl oz servings*

Ingredients	Amounts U.S.	Metric	Procedure
Brown sugar	8 oz	227 g	Blend the sugar, lime juice, mirin, Thai fish sauce, and garlic together.
Lime juice	2 fl oz	59 ml	
Mirin	3 fl oz	85 ml	
Thai fish sauce	1/2 fl oz	15 ml	
Garlic, minced	1 tbsp	15 g	
Sesame oil	3 fl oz	85 ml	Whisk in the oils to blend.
Salad oil	12 fl oz	354 ml	
Fresh Thai basil	1 oz	30 g	Chop the basil. Grate the lime zest. Add the basil and zest to the above mixture.
Lime zest	2 tsp	10 g	
Roasted peanuts	2 oz	57 g	Chop the peanuts and add them to the dressing.

NUTRITIONAL INFORMATION PER SERVING: 189 Calories; 17 g Fat (80.9% calories from fat); 1 g Protein; 8 g Carbohydrate; 1 g Dietary Fiber; trace Cholesterol; 4 mg Sodium. Exchanges: 0 Grain (Starch); 0 Lean Meat; 0 Vegetable; 0 Fruit; 3 1/2 Fat; 1/2 Other Carbohydrates.

Here's another Asian favorite. This goes well with the Asian-Style Grilled Chicken Salad recipe found in Unit 13.

Asian-style dressing
Yield: 28 fl oz (840 ml) Approximately 28 each 1 fl oz (30 ml) servings

Ingredients	Amounts U.S.	Metric	Procedure
Mirin or sweet rice wine vinegar	6 fl oz	177 ml	Combine all the ingredients. This may be used for marinades as well as dressing.
Soy sauce	2 fl oz	59 ml	
Peanut oil	14 fl oz	414 ml	
Sesame oil	4 fl oz	118 ml	
Lemon juice	1/2 fl oz	15 ml	
Brown sugar	2 oz	58 g	
Fresh ginger root, grated	1/2 oz	15 g	
Fresh garlic, mashed	2 cloves	2 cloves	
Green onions, minced	1 tbsp	15 g	

NUTRITIONAL INFORMATION PER SERVING: 164 Calories; 17 g Fat (93.4% calories from fat); trace Protein; 3 g Carbohydrate; trace Dietary Fiber; 0 mg Cholesterol; 148 mg Sodium. Exchanges: 0 Vegetable; 0 Fruit; 3 1/2 Fat; 0 Other Carbohydrates.

For a more intense tomato taste, 4 oz (113 g) dry weight minced reconstituted sun-dried tomatoes can be substituted for fresh tomatoes.

tomato vinaigrette dressing
Yield: 1 qt (946 ml) Approximately 32 each 1 fl oz (30 ml) servings

Ingredients	Amounts		Procedure
	U.S.	Metric	
Red wine vinegar	4 fl oz	118 ml	Blend the vinegar, mustard, cheese, chopped herbs, and sugar in a food processor.
Dijon mustard	1 fl oz	30 ml	
Parmesan cheese, freshly grated	1 oz	28 g	
Fresh basil, chopped	1 tbsp	15 g	
Fresh oregano, chopped	1 tbsp	15 g	
Sugar	1 tbsp	15 g	
Salt	To taste	To taste	Add salt and pepper to taste. Blend.
Pepper, freshly cracked	To taste	To taste	
Salad oil	8 fl oz	237 ml	When thoroughly blended, stream in the salad oil to emulsify.
Extra virgin olive oil	8 fl oz	237 ml	Add the olive oil, whisking in to blend.
Tomatoes, peeled, seeded, and chopped	8 oz	227 g	Add concasse and tomato paste and whisk to blend.
Tomato paste	1 fl oz	30 ml	

NUTRITIONAL INFORMATION PER SERVING: 138 Calories; 15 g Fat (94.3% calories from fat); 1 g Protein; 1 g Carbohydrate; trace Dietary Fiber; 1 mg Cholesterol; 48 mg Sodium. Exchanges: 0 Grain (Starch); 0 Lean Meat; 0 Vegetable; 3 Fat; 0 Other Carbohydrates.

Greek Kalamata olives are plump and juicy with a powerful salty and acidic flavor. Try this recipe with any assortment of leafy greens.

Kalamata olive vinaigrette
Yield: 1 qt (946 ml) Approximately 32 each 1 fl oz (30 ml) servings

Ingredients	Amounts U.S.	Metric	Procedure
Red wine vinegar	8 fl oz	237 ml	Blend the vinegar, cheese, chopped herbs, and capers in a food processor.
Greek Kaseri cheese, freshly grated	2 oz	57 g	
Parsley, fresh, chopped	1 tbsp	15 g	
Oregano, fresh, chopped	1 tbsp	15 g	
Capers	1 tbsp	15 g	
Salt	To taste	To taste	Add salt and pepper to taste. Blend.
Pepper, freshly cracked	To taste	To taste	
Salad oil or olive oil blend	16 fl oz	450 ml	When thoroughly blended, stream in the oil and whisk to blend.
Kalamata olives, pitted, chopped	12 oz	340 g	Add the chopped olives to the mixture and blend.

NUTRITIONAL INFORMATION PER SERVING: 168 Calories; 18 g Fat (95.6% calories from fat); trace Protein; 1 g Carbohydrate; trace Dietary Fiber; 2 mg Cholesterol; 210 mg Sodium. Exchanges: 0 Grain (Starch); 0 Lean Meat; 0 Vegetable; 0 Fruit; 3 1/2 Fat; 0 Other Carbohydrate.

Lentils are the surprise ingredient in this recipe. They are puréed, so guests may not be able to recognize them and will wonder what gives this vinaigrette its earthy, wholesome flavor. Boil the lentils for 30 to 40 minutes until tender. Cool before using in this salad.

lentil vinaigrette
Yield: 1 qt (946 ml) Approximately 32 each 1 fl oz (30 ml) servings

Ingredients	Amounts U.S.	Metric	Procedure
Lentils, cooked	8 oz	227 g	Place the cooked lentils and other ingredients in a blender. Pulse to purée. If too thick, thin with a small amount of cold water.
Extra virgin olive oil	8 fl oz	237 ml	
Champagne vinegar	8 fl oz	237 ml	
Pimento, canned, diced	2 oz	57 g	
Parsley, fresh, minced	1 tbsp	15 g	
Lemon juice, freshly squeezed	1 tbsp	15 ml	
Lemon zest	1 tbsp	15 g	
Kosher salt	To taste	To taste	
Pepper, freshly cracked	To taste	To taste	

NUTRITIONAL INFORMATION PER SERVING: 74 Calories; 7 g Fat (84.9% calories from fat); 1 g Protein; 2 g Carbohydrate; 1 g Dietary Fiber; 0 mg Cholesterol; 9 mg Sodium. Exchanges: 0 Grain (Starch); 0 Lean Meat; 0 Vegetable; 0 Fruit; 1 1/2 Fat; 0 Other Carbohydrates.

Fruit-flavored dressings can be used on green salads and on very ripe and sweet fruits such as cubed melon pieces. The dried cranberries provide a tangy and colorful addition to the vinaigrette.

cranberry vinaigrette

Yield: 1 qt (946 ml) Approximately 32 each 1 fl oz (30 ml) servings

Ingredients	Amounts U.S.	Metric	Procedure
Shallots	1/2 oz	15 g	Chop the shallots.
Cranberries, dried	6 oz	170 g	Bring the cranberries, shallots, sugar, vinegar, and water to a boil. Reduce the temperature and simmer for 5 minutes and purée in a blender.
Sugar	3 oz	85 g	
Berry vinegar	6 fl oz	178 ml	
Water	10 fl oz	295 ml	

Peanut oil	16 fl oz	473 ml	While the blender is running, slowly add the peanut oil.

NUTRITIONAL INFORMATION PER SERVING: 147 Calories; 14 g Fat (80.3% calories from fat); trace Protein; 7 g Carbohydrate; trace Dietary Fiber; 0 mg Cholesterol; 1mg Sodium. Exchanges: 0 Vegetable; 1/2 Fruit; 2 1/2 Fat; 0 Other Carbohydrates.

Papaya has a sweet, astringent flavor. The combination of fresh mint and papaya creates an exceptional dressing.

papaya vinaigrette
Yield: 1 qt (946 ml) Approximately 32 each 1 fl oz (30 ml) servings

Ingredients	Amounts U.S.	Metric	Procedure
Papaya, fresh puréed	8 fl oz	237 ml	Combine the papaya purée with the salt and pepper.
Salt	1 tsp	5 g	
Pepper, coarse ground	2 tsp	10 g	

Ingredients	Amounts U.S.	Metric	Procedure
Grapeseed oil	12 fl oz	355 ml	Mix the purée with the grapeseed oil and rice vinegar.
Rice vinegar, sweet	8 fl oz	237 ml	
Mint, fresh	1/4 oz	7 g	Chop the mint, fresh papaya, and dried papaya into very small pieces. Add the chopped items to the above mixture.
Papaya, fresh, small dice	2 oz	57 g	
Papaya, dried	2 oz	57 g	

NUTRITIONAL INFORMATION PER SERVING: 97 Calories; 10 g Fat (92.7% calories from fat); trace Protein; 2 g Carbohydrate; trace Dietary Fiber; 0 mg Cholesterol; 67 mg Sodium. Exchanges: 0 Grain (Starch); 0 Vegetable; 0 Fruit; 2 Fat; 0 Other Carbohydrates.

Choose a flavorful apple such as a Rome Beauty, Winesap, or McIntosh for the following recipe.

apple vinaigrette dressing

Yield: 40 fl oz (1.18 l) Approximately 40 each 1 fl oz (30 ml) servings

Ingredients	Amounts		Procedure
	U.S.	Metric	
Shallots	2 oz	57 g	Sauté the shallots in the olive oil until soft.
Olive oil	1 fl oz	30 ml	
Apple	12 oz	340 g	Peel, core, and shred the apple. There will be about 1 cup of grated apple.

Ginger, fresh, chopped	1/2 tbsp	7 g	Finely chop the ginger.
Pepper, ground white	1 tbsp	15 g	Purée all the ingredients in the food processor.
Apple cider	8 fl oz	237 ml	
Champagne vinegar	8 fl oz	237 ml	
Salt	1 tbsp	15 g	
Walnut oil	8 fl oz	237 ml	

NUTRITIONAL INFORMATION PER SERVING: 85 Calories; 8 g Fat (83.9% calories from fat); trace Protein; 3 g Carbohydrate; trace Dietary Fiber; 0 mg Cholesterol; 214 mg Sodium. Exchanges: 0 Grain (Starch); 0 Vegetable; 0 Fruit; 1 1/2 Fat; 0 Other Carbohydrates.

Balsamic vinegar is made in Modena, Italy, and is aged in barrels made from different types of wood. During this aging process, the vinegar becomes thick and syrupy, and develops an intense flavor. The finest balsamic is well-aged 20 years and longer and can be very expensive. Commercial varieties are less expensive but are still very flavorful compared to standard red wine vinegar. Use high-quality commercial vinegar for the following recipe. The combination of anise honey, with its hint of licorice, along with cherry syrup and vinegar makes this a truly distinguished salad topping. Cherry syrup can be purchased bottled.

cherry balsamic dressing
Yield: 1 qt (946 ml) Approximately 32 each 1 fl oz (30 ml) servings

Ingredients	Amounts		Procedure
	U.S.	Metric	
Mint, fresh	1/4 oz	7 g	Chop the mint and basil.
Basil, fresh	1/4 oz	7 g	
Cherry syrup	2 fl oz	59 ml	Combine all the items including the chopped ingredients in a blender. Blend for 1 to 2 minutes.
Extra virgin olive oil	8 fl oz	237 ml	
Grapeseed oil	12 fl oz	354 ml	
Balsamic vinegar	8 fl oz	237 ml	
Anise honey	1 1/2 fl oz	44 ml	
Salt	To taste	To taste	
Pepper	To taste	To taste	

NUTRITIONAL INFORMATION PER SERVING: 175 Calories; 18 g Fat (92.9% calories from fat); trace Protein; 3 g Carbohydrate; trace Dietary Fiber; 0 mg Cholesterol; trace Sodium. Exchanges: 0 Grain (Starch); 0 Vegetable; 0 Fruit; 3 1/2 Fat; 0 Other Carbohydrates.

Use the cherry syrup as a key ingredient in the previous Cherry Balsamic Dressing recipe.

cherry syrup *Yield: 2 fl oz (60 ml) servings*

Ingredients	Amounts U.S.	Metric	Procedure
Cherry juice, fresh, frozen, canned, or bottled	1 1/2 fl oz	45 ml	Mix the juice with the sugar in a nonreactive sauce pot. Bring to a boil and skim off any foam. When the sugar is completely dissolved, remove the mixture from the stove and let it cool to room temperature.
Sugar	1 1/2 oz	43 g	

NUTRITIONAL INFORMATION PER SERVING: 186 Calories; trace Fat (0.2% calories from fat); trace Protein; 48 g Carbohydrate; trace Dietary Fiber; 0 mg Cholesterol; 2 mg Sodium. Exchanges: 1/2 Fruit; 3 Other Carbohydrates.

The citrus vinaigrette works well with any of the following herbs: rosemary, sage, basil, or mint. A combination of the herbs is also nice. Note that the green color of fresh herbs is affected by acidity. The herbs should be added when needed.

citrus vinaigrette
Yield: 1 qt (946 ml) Approximately 32 each 1 fl oz (30 ml) servings

Ingredients	Amounts U.S.	Metric	Procedure
Sugar	1 oz	30 g	Combine the sugar with water. Boil for 5 minutes and chill.
Water	2 fl oz	59 ml	
Lime juice, fresh	4 fl oz	118 ml	Combine the sugar and syrup with the remaining ingredients.
Lemon juice, fresh	2 fl oz	59 ml	
Orange juice, fresh	8 fl oz	237 ml	
Grapefruit juice, fresh	2 fl oz	59 ml	
Grapeseed oil	8 fl oz	237 ml	
Champagne or pear vinegar	8 fl oz	237 ml	
Salt	To taste	To taste	
Pepper	To taste	To taste	
Herbs, fresh chopped (see suggestions above)	1 oz	30 g	Add the herbs before service.

NUTRITIONAL INFORMATION PER SERVING: 77 Calories; 7 g Fat (82.2% calories from fat); trace Protein; 3 g Carbohydrate; trace Dietary Fiber; 0 mg Cholesterol; 1 mg Sodium. Exchanges: 0 Grain (Starch); 0 Fruit; 1 1/2 Fat; 0 Other Carbohydrates.

The combination of grape juice, tarragon, and anise honey in this dressing is pleasant.

anise honey grape dressing
Yield: 1 qt (946 ml) Approximately 32 each 1 fl oz (30 ml) servings

Ingredients	Amount U.S.	Metric	Procedure
Tarragon, fresh, minced	1/2 oz	15 g	Combine all the ingredients in a blender and blend until smooth.
Champagne vinegar	8 fl oz	237 ml	
Grapeseed oil	12 fl oz	355 ml	
Grape juice, white	8 fl oz	237 ml	
Anise honey	6 fl oz	177 ml	
Salt	1 tsp	5 g	
Pepper, ground	1 tsp	5 g	

NUTRITIONAL INFORMATION PER SERVING: 129 Calories; 11 g Fat (73.2% calories from fat); trace Protein; 9 g Carbohydrate; trace Dietary Fiber; 0 mg Cholesterol; 1 mg Sodium. Exchanges: 0 Grain (Starch); 0 Lean Meat; 0 Fruit; 2 Fat; 1/2 Other Carbohydrates.

The dark red interior flesh of the blood orange provides the beautiful color of this dressing. Blood oranges are slightly less acidic than regular table oranges. Other orange juice can be used but the taste and appearance will change.

blood orange juice vinaigrette

Yield: 1 qt (946 ml) Approximately 32 each 1 fl oz (30 ml) servings

Ingredients	Amounts		Procedure
	U.S.	Metric	
Sage, fresh, minced	2 tbsp	30 g	Combine all the ingredients in a food processor or blend with a whisk. Mix thoroughly.
Blood orange juice	8 fl oz	237 ml	
Grapeseed oil	8 fl oz	237 ml	
Olive oil	8 fl oz	237 ml	
Lime juice, fresh	4 fl oz	118 ml	
Champagne vinegar	2 fl oz	59 ml	
Honey	2 fl oz	59 ml	
Salt	To taste	To taste	
Pepper	To taste	To taste	

NUTRITIONAL INFORMATION PER SERVING: 142 Calories; 15 g Fat (89.4% calories from fat); trace Protein; 4 g Carbohydrate; trace Dietary Fiber; 0 mg Cholesterol; trace Sodium. Exchanges: 0 Grain (Starch); 0 Fruit; 3 Fat; 0 Other Carbohydrates.

This dressing is suitable for green salads. The best tarragon to use for this recipe is the kind that is preserved in vinegar. To enhance the presentation, sprinkle some fresh raspberries on top of the plated salad.

raspberry honey dressing
Yield: 1 qt (946 ml) Approximately 32 each 1 fl oz (30 ml) servings

Ingredients	Amounts		Procedure
	U.S.	Metric	
Tarragon, preserved in vinegar	1 1/2 tbsp	22 g	Chop the tarragon.
Raspberry vinegar	8 fl oz	237 ml	Combine all the ingredients in a food processor or blender until thoroughly blended.
Grapeseed oil	16 fl oz	450 ml	
Olive oil	8 fl oz	237 ml	
Honey	4 fl oz	118 g	
Raspberry purée, frozen or fresh, strained to remove seeds, unsweetened	4 fl oz	118 g	
Salt	To taste	To taste	
Pepper	To taste	To taste	

NUTRITIONAL INFORMATION PER SERVING: 212 Calories; 22 g Fat (90.0% calories from fat); trace Protein; 5 g Carbohydrate; trace Dietary Fiber; 0 mg Cholesterol; trace Sodium. Exchanges: 0 Fruit; 4 1/2 Fat; 1/2 Other Carbohydrates.

The combination of strawberry and fresh basil creates an extraordinary salad dressing.

strawberry basil vinaigrette
Yield: 1 qt (946 ml) Approximately 32 each 1 fl oz (30 ml) servings

Ingredients	Amounts		Procedure
	U.S.	Metric	
Fresh strawberries, wash and stem	6 oz	170 g	In a blender or food processor, combine the vinegars, strawberries, and basil. Pulse to purée.
Cider vinegar	4 fl oz	118 ml	
Balsamic vinegar	6 fl oz	177 ml	
Fresh basil, chopped	1 oz	30 g	

Ingredients	Amounts		Procedure
Light olive oil	8 fl oz	237 ml	Slowly add the oils to blend.
Canola oil	8 fl oz	237 ml	
Salt	To taste	To taste	Adjust the seasonings and use with field greens, butter head, Boston lettuce, or any other soft lettuce.
Pepper	To taste	To taste	

NUTRITIONAL INFORMATION PER SERVING: 132 Calories; 15 g Fat (95.7% calories from fat); trace Protein; 1 g Carbohydrate; trace Dietary Fiber; 0 mg Cholesterol; trace Sodium. Exchanges: 0 Grain (Starch); 0 Fruit; 3 Fat; 0 Other Carbohydrates.

>> Emulsified Dressings

Emulsified and creamy dressings go one step further than vinaigrettes—they cling to salad leaves and other ingredients better than thinner vinaigrette dressings. In the cold kitchen, the term *emulsified dressing* is used for dressings that no longer separate into separate ingredients. High-speed blenders or blending sticks can mechanically emulsify dressings without adding thickening agents and provide a very thick product, which will remain suspended for a while, but not as long as when an emulsifier is used.

The following dressings are classified as emulsions because the oil and water-based ingredients are bound in a suspension that doesn't readily separate. **Emulsions** are colloidal dispersions of water and oil. Vinegar, which is composed mostly of water, and oil do not dissolve into each other. However, they can disperse in each other with the aid of an emulsifier. Typical **emulsifiers** are egg yolks, mayonnaise, reduced stocks, mustard, vegetable gums, arrow root, and cornstarch (Figure 14-3).

Figure 14-3 Oil and vinegar are being mixed with mustard, serving as the recipe's emulsifier.

In years past, chefs used raw eggs in many of their emulsified dressing recipes. That practice is no longer acceptable with current health standards. Instead, pasteurized eggs are used. They are readily available in the shelled bulk form and now in flash pasteurized shell form. These pasteurized shell eggs have recently hit the market and enable the chef to make dressings without fear of salmonella. One large whole egg equals 2 fluid ounces of egg. We have listed all eggs in fluid ounces.

French dressing was created in the United States. It is sometimes called Catalina. The basic dressing is made with vinegar, sugar, and catsup or another tomato product. Do not confuse this with the traditional French vinaigrette.

basic French dressing Yield: 1 qt (946 ml) Approximately 32 each 1 fl oz (30 ml) servings

Ingredients	Amount		Procedure
	U.S.	Metric	
Egg yolk, pasteurized	6 fl oz	177 ml	Combine the egg yolk, salt, garlic, mustard, paprika, lemon juice, Worcestershire sauce, and catsup.
Salt	1 tsp	5 g	
Garlic, mashed to a paste	1 tsp	5 g	
Dry mustard	2 tsp	10 g	
Paprika	2 tsp	10 g	
Lemon juice	6 fl oz	177 ml	
Worcestershire sauce	2 tsp	10 ml	
Tomato catsup	4 fl oz	118 ml	

Oil	16 fl oz	473 ml	Slowly add the oil, continually whisking.

NUTRITIONAL INFORMATION PER SERVING: 156 Calories; 16 g Fat (92.4% calories from fat); 1 g Protein; 2 g Carbohydrate; trace Dietary Fiber; 75 mg Cholesterol; 53 mg Sodium. Exchanges: 0 Grain (Starch); 0 Lean Meat; 0 Vegetable; 0 Fruit; 3 Fat; 0 Other Carbohydrates.

Caesar dressing has an interesting past. It was invented in 1924 by Caesar Cardini in Tijuana, Mexico, when he found himself with a last minute rush of Hollywood movie stars and only a few ingredients in the kitchen. Caesar salad is always made with Romaine lettuce, which should be broken into chunks and not cut. The salad is traditionally sprinkled with bread croutons. In some restaurants, the dressing is made tableside. Coddled eggs are made by dipping eggs for 1 minute in boiling water.

Caesar dressing *Yield: 1 qt (946 ml) Approximately 20 each 1 1/2 fl oz (45 ml) servings*

Ingredients	Amounts U.S.	Metric	Procedure
Garlic cloves, mashed	6 each	6 each	Combine the garlic, eggs, cheese, lemon juice, anchovies, salt, and pepper in the bowl of a food processor and process until smooth, approximately 1 minute.
Egg yolks (from coddled eggs)	4 each	4 each	
Parmigiano-Reggiano, grated	6 oz	170 g	
Lemon juice, freshly squeezed	3 fl oz	88 ml	
Anchovy fillets, rinsed and mashed to a paste	4 oz	113 g	
Salt	2 tsp	10 g	
Pepper, freshly cracked	1 tsp	5 g	

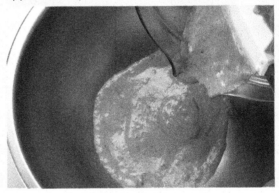

Virgin olive oil	16 fl oz	473 ml	Add the oil and process until smooth.

NUTRITIONAL INFORMATION PER SERVING: 255 Calories; 26 g Fat (89.9% calories from fat); 5 g Protein; 1 g Carbohydrate; trace Dietary Fiber; 49 mg Cholesterol; 160 mg Sodium. Exchanges: 1/2 Lean Meat; 0 Vegetable; 0 Fruit; 4 1/2 Fat.

Mayonnaise acts as an emulsifier in many salad dressings. Eggs, which contain the emulsifier lecithin, help to bind the ingredients together and prevent separation. Mayonnaise is made by combining lemon juice or vinegar with egg yolks, salt, and spices. Then, oil is added drop by drop as the mixture is rapidly whisked. Adding oil too quickly (or by insufficient whisking) will keep the two liquids from combining (emulsifying). The key element is combining eggs and the acids with the oil at room temperature. Once the mixture begins to thicken, and emulsify, the oil can be added more rapidly. Homemade mayonnaise can be stored for 3 or 4 days if properly refrigerated. Most operations purchase mayonnaise ready made. It is lighter than the homemade product and is consistent in quality. Commercial mayonnaise can be stored at ambient temperature until opened.

mayonnaise *Yield: 1 qt (946 ml) Approximately 32 each 1 fl oz (30 ml) servings*

Ingredients	Amounts U.S.	Metric	Procedure
Egg yolks, pasteurized	8 fl oz	237 ml	Place the egg yolks in a mixing machine kettle. Add the salt, pepper, and mustard. Use a whisk and stir at medium speed to combine.
Salt	1/2 tsp	2 g	
White pepper	2 tsp	10 g	
Dijon mustard	2 tsp	10 ml	
Vinegar or lemon juice	1 oz	30 ml	Add the vinegar or juice to the egg mixture.
Oil	24 fl oz	710 ml	Add the oil slowly while mixing at medium speed. If the sauce gets too thick, dilute with 1 tbsp hot water.

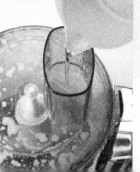

Reprinted with permission of the Thousand Island Inn

NUTRITIONAL INFORMATION PER SERVING: 222 Calories; 24 g Fat (97.1% calories from fat); 1 g Protein; trace Carbohydrate; trace Dietary Fiber; 100 mg Cholesterol; 43 mg Sodium. Exchanges: 0 Grain (Starch); 0 Lean Meat; 4 1/2 Fat; 0 Other Carbohydrates.

For decades, salad lovers around the world have enjoyed the appealing flavor of Thousand Island dressing. Although national sales figures rank it as one of the most popular dressings with consumers, many people do not associate it with the popular upstate New York resort area, while many others don't even associate it with any actual geographic locale. In reality, it is the only salad dressing named for any region of the United States.

The history of the dressing dates back to the early days of the century and centers in the small resort village of Clayton, New York. In those days, George LaLonde, Jr., a popular fishing guide, led visiting anglers as they fished for black bass and northern pike through the scenic, fish-filled waters of the 1,000 Islands.

George Jr. would serve a different and unusual salad dressing to his fishing parties as part of their shore dinners. On one particular occasion, George was guiding a very prominent New York City stage actress of the period, May Irwin, and her husband. Miss Irwin, a renowned cook and cookbook authoress in her own right, was particularly impressed with the dressing and asked George for the recipe. The dressing was actually created and made by George's wife Sophia, who was flattered by the request and willingly gave the recipe to Miss Irwin. At the same time, George's wife gave the recipe to Mrs. Ella Bertrand, whose family owned the Herald Hotel, one of the most popular hotels in the area and where Miss Irwin and her husband stayed during their early vacations in the islands. Mrs. Bertrand prepared the dressing for Miss Irwin and her husband and also added it to the other choices of salad dressing offered to her dining room customers.

It was Miss Irwin who gave the dressing the name *"Thousand Island"* and it was Mrs. Bertrand, at the Herald Hotel, who first served it to the dining public. Upon her return to New York City, Miss Irwin gave the recipe to fellow 1,000 Islands summer visitor George C. Boldt, owner of the Waldorf Astoria Hotel in New York, the Bellevue Stratford in Philadelphia, and also the builder of Boldt Castle on nearby Heart Island. Equally impressed with its flavor, Mr. Boldt directed his world-famous maitre d', Oscar Tschirky, to put this dressing from the 1,000 Islands on the hotel's menu at once. In doing so, Oscar earned credit for introducing the dressing to the "world."

Thousand Island dressing can be served with chilled seafood such as crab meat, shrimp, or lobster. It is good on sandwiches as well as salads. The dressing recipe on the facing page includes raw onions. If the dressing is made ahead and stored, the onions should be omitted because they ferment easily.

Thousand Island dressing

Yield: 1 qt (946 ml) Approximately 32 each 1 fl oz (30 ml) servings

Ingredients	Amounts U.S.	Metric	Procedure
Green stuffed olives, chopped	2 oz	60 g	Combine all the ingredients and mix well.
Dill pickle relish	2 oz	60 g	
Celery, fine diced	4 oz	110 g	
Green bell pepper, fine diced	2 oz	55 g	
Yellow onion, fine diced	4 oz	110 g	
Hard-boiled egg, fine diced	1 each	1 each	
Mayonnaise	16 fl oz	473 ml	
Chili sauce	6 fl oz	177 ml	
Prepared horseradish	1/2 tbsp	7 ml	
Worcestershire sauce	1 tbsp	15 ml	
Lemon juice, fresh squeezed	2 tbsp	30 ml	
Salt	To taste	To taste	
Pepper, fresh cracked	To taste	To taste	

NUTRITIONAL INFORMATION PER SERVING: 112 Calories; 13 g Fat (95.1% calories from fat); trace Protein; 1 g Carbohydrate; trace Dietary Fiber; 12 mg Cholesterol; 116 mg Sodium. Exchanges: 0 Grain (Starch); 0 Lean Meat; 0 Vegetable; 0 Fruit; 1 Fat; 0 Other Carbohydrates.

Traditional Italian dressing is a simple vinaigrette. By adding the egg yolk and creating an emulsion, this dressing bursts with flavor and creamy texture while preserving the great blend of Italian herbs.

creamy Italian dressing
Yield: 1 qt (946 ml) Approximately 20 each 1 1/2 fl oz (45 ml) servings

Ingredients	Amounts		Procedure
	U.S.	Metric	
Egg yolk, pasteurized	2 fl oz	59 ml	Combine the egg yolk, salt, garlic, herbs, red wine vinegar, and Worcestershire sauce in a food processor or blender and mix well.
Salt	1/2 tsp	2 g	
Garlic, mashed to a paste	1/2 tsp	2 g	
Basil, fresh, chopped	2 tsp	10 g	
Oregano, fresh, chopped	2 tsp	10 g	
Thyme, fresh, chopped	1 tsp	5 g	
Parsley, fresh, chopped	1 tbsp	15 g	
Red wine vinegar	8 fl oz	237 ml	
Worcestershire sauce	1 tsp	5 ml	
Oil	24 fl oz	710 ml	Slowly add the oil, whisking constantly.

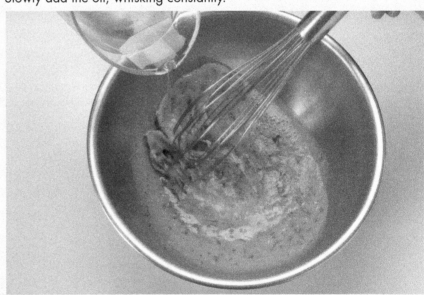

NUTRITIONAL INFORMATION PER SERVING: 302 Calories; 34 g Fat (98.5% calories from fat); 1 g Protein; 1 g Carbohydrate; trace Dietary Fiber; 38 mg Cholesterol; 57 mg Sodium. Exchanges: 0 Grain (Starch); 0 Lean Meat; 0 Vegetable; 6 1/2 Fat; 0 Other Carbohydrates.

LEARNING ACTIVITY 14-1

Take 1 quart (946 ml) of dry salad greens, cut in bite-size pieces, and blend with 4 fluid ounces (118 ml) of vinaigrette dressing. Take 1 quart (946 ml) of dry salad greens, cut in bite-size pieces, and blend with 6 fluid ounces (177 ml) of Creamy Italian dressing from the recipe on the facing page. Toss well.

Which dressing coats the salad greens evenly? Which do you prefer?

Dijon mustard was created in Dijon, France. Originally it was made with verjuice, which is the sour juice of unripe grapes, instead of vinegar. Today, Dijon mustard is always made from either brown or black mustard seeds, coupled with vinegar, wine, or green grape juice. The blend of the Dijon and grainy Pomeray mustard with the fresh herbs in this recipe creates a tantalizing and refreshing salad topper.

mustard herb salad dressing
Yield: 1 qt (946 ml) Approximately 20 each 1 1/2 fl oz (45 ml) servings

Ingredients	Amounts U.S.	Metric	Procedure
Dijon mustard	2 fl oz	59 ml	Whisk the mustards, shallot, and vinegar together in a small bowl.
Pomeray mustard	2 fl oz	59 ml	
Shallot, minced	1 tbsp	15 g	
White wine vinegar	4 fl oz	118 ml	
Salad oil	24 fl oz	710 ml	Slowly add the oil to the vinegar mixture. The quality of the emulsion depends on how well and how slowly you incorporate the oil and the vinegar.
Salt	2 tsp	10 g	Add the salt, pepper, and sugar. Adjust the acid taste with the sugar. Add more if needed.
Pepper	2 tsp	10 g	
Sugar	1 tbsp	15 g	
Thyme, fresh, chopped	1 tbsp	15 g	Add all the herbs. If the dressing is not used right away, add the herbs just prior to service.
Basil, fresh, chopped	1 tbsp	15 g	
Chives, fresh, chopped	1 tbsp	15 g	
Chervil, fresh, chopped	1 tbsp	15 g	

NUTRITIONAL INFORMATION PER SERVING: 299 Calories; 33 g Fat (97.2% calories from fat); trace Protein; 2 g Carbohydrate; trace Dietary Fiber; 0 mg Cholesterol; 289 mg Sodium. Exchanges: 0 Grain (Starch); 0 Lean Meat; 0 Vegetable; 6 1/2 Fat; 0 Other Carbohydrates.

Like French dressing, Russian salad dressing is the creation of an American chef. It was a specialty at The Plaza Hotel in Manhattan.

Russian dressing

Yield: 1 qt (946 ml) Approximately 20 each 1 1/2 fl oz (45 ml) servings

Ingredients	Amounts		Procedure
	U.S.	Metric	
Mayonnaise	20 fl oz	592 g	Combine the ingredients and season to taste.
Worcestershire sauce	1 tbsp	15 ml	
Horseradish, grated	1 1/2 oz	43 g	
Chili sauce	8 fl oz	237 g	
Chopped sweet pickle	4 oz	113 g	
Salt	To taste	To taste	
Pepper	To taste	To taste	

Eggs, hard-boiled, chopped	4 each	4 each	Sprinkle the chopped eggs on the dressing at the moment of service.

NUTRITIONAL INFORMATION PER SERVING: 222 Calories; 24 g Fat (93.0% calories from fat); 2 g Protein; 2 g Carbohydrate; trace Dietary Fiber; 52 mg Cholesterol; 234 mg Sodium. Exchanges: 0 Grain (Starch); 0 Lean Meat; 2 Fat; 0 Other Carbohydrates.

The shredded apple adds texture to this luscious dressing.

apple cider and walnut dressing
Yield: 1 qt (946 ml) Approximately 20 each 1 1/2 fl oz (45 ml) servings

Ingredients	Amounts		Procedure
	U.S.	Metric	
Apple cider vinegar	6 fl oz	177 ml	In a stainless steel bowl, using a balloon whisk, blend the vinegar, shallots, honey, and mustard together.
Shallots, finely minced	1 bulb	1 bulb	
Blossom honey	1 fl oz	30 ml	
Dijon mustard	1 tbsp	15 ml	
Walnut oil	6 fl oz	177 ml	Slowly whisk in the oils to emulsify.
Salad oil	12 fl oz	355 ml	
Granny Smith apple, shredded	4 oz	57 g	Add the apple and seasonings.
Salt	To taste	To taste	
Pepper	To taste	To taste	

NUTRITIONAL INFORMATION PER SERVING: 234 Calories; 26 g Fat (96.2% calories from fat); trace Protein; 2 g Carbohydrate; trace Dietary Fiber; 0 mg Cholesterol; 23 mg Sodium. Exchanges: 0 Grain (Starch); 0 Lean Meat; 0 Vegetable; 0 Fruit; 5 Fat; 0 Other Carbohydrates.

Using a variety of salts can change the flavor profile of any salad dressing. The following Mustard Chive Dressing recipe calls for kosher salt, which generally has no additives and a distinctive flavor. Try altering your choice of salts from table, sea salt, to kosher to determine your preference.

mustard chive dressing

Yield: 1 qt (946 ml) Approximately 20 each 1 1/2 fl oz (45 ml) servings

Ingredients	Amounts		Procedure
	U.S.	Metric	
Shallot bulb, minced fine	1 bulb (2 oz)	55 g	Add shallots to a little of the oil in a blender and purée.

Ingredients	Amounts		Procedure
Dijon mustard	8 fl oz	237 ml	Add the remaining ingredients and continue to purée.
Honey	3 fl oz	88 g	
Chives	2 tbsp	30 g	
White wine vinegar	3 fl oz	88 ml	
Olive oil	16 fl oz	473 ml	
Kosher salt	1/2 oz	15 g	
Black pepper, cracked	1/4 oz	7 g	

NUTRITIONAL INFORMATION PER SERVING: 148 Calories; 15 g Fat (87.1% calories from fat); trace Protein; 4 g Carbohydrate; trace Dietary Fiber; 0 mg Cholesterol; 278 mg Sodium. Exchanges: 0 Grain (Starch); 0 Lean Meat; 0 Vegetable; 3 Fat; 1/2 Other Carbohydrates.

Tahini is ground sesame paste available in cans and jars. The oily paste must be stirred to incorporate any oil that separated during storage. Tahini can be used as a dressing ingredient or as a dip for pita bread or vegetables.

tahini parsley dip
Yield: 1 qt (946 ml) Approximately 20 each 1 1/2 fl oz (45 ml) servings

Ingredients	Amounts		Procedure
	U.S.	Metric	
Tahini paste	12 fl oz	355 ml	Place the tahini, yogurt, garlic, salt, lemon juice with zest, and hot water in a food processor. Pulse until smooth, adding more water if
Yogurt, plain	12 fl oz	355 ml	
Garlic, mashed	2 cloves	2 cloves	
Salt	1 tsp	5 g	
Lemon juice with zest, freshly squeezed	2 fl oz	59 ml	
Hot water	6 fl oz	177 ml	

Parsley, flat leaf, chopped	1 tbsp	15 g	Fold in the parsley by hand into above mixture until incorporated. Store in the refrigerator for up to 1 week.

NUTRITIONAL INFORMATION PER SERVING: 20 Calories; 10 g Fat (72.5% calories from fat); 4 g Protein; 5 g Carbohydrate; 2 g Dietary Fiber; 2 mg Cholesterol; 136 mg Sodium. Exchanges: 1/2 Grain (Starch); 1/2 Lean Meat; 0 Vegetable; 0 Fruit; 0 Nonfat Milk; 2 Fat; 0 Other Carbohydrates.

Use the basic Tahini Parsley Dip recipe on the previous page as an ingredient in this dressing.

carrot tahini dressing
Yield: 1 qt (946 ml) Approximately 20 each 1 1/2 fl oz (45 ml) servings

Ingredients	Amounts		Procedure
	U.S.	Metric	
Carrots, shredded	8 fl oz	237 ml	Purée the carrots, onion, and garlic in a food processor.
Onion, diced	1 oz	30 g	
Garlic	2 cloves	2 cloves	

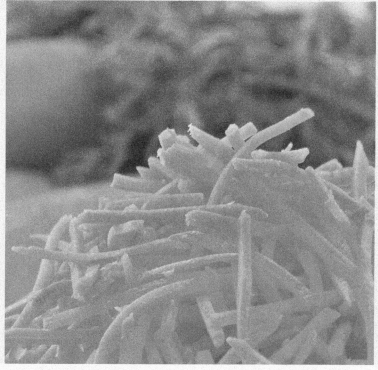

Ginger, fresh, chopped	2 tsp	10 g	Add the ginger and Tahini Parsley Dip to the food processor and process.
Tahini Parsley Dip	24 fl oz	709 ml	

NUTRITIONAL INFORMATION PER SERVING: 218 Calories; 19 g Fat (74.8% calories from fat); 6 g Protein; 8 g Carbohydrate; 4 g Dietary Fiber; 0 mg Cholesterol; 44 mg Sodium. Exchanges: 1/2 Grain (Starch); 1/2 Lean Meat; 0 Vegetable; 3 1/2 Fat.

This dressing is perfect with Tex-Mex or Southwest-inspired salads. The tabasco adds a touch of heat.

zesty lime herb dressing
Yield: 1 qt (946 ml) Approximately 20 each 1 1/2 fl oz (45 ml) servings

Ingredients	Amounts U.S.	Metric	Procedure
Lime juice, fresh squeezed	8 fl oz	237 ml	In a stainless steel bowl, using a balloon whisk, blend the juice, onion, garlic, herbs, and seasonings together. Adjust the seasonings to taste.
Yellow onion, diced fine	2 oz	60 g	
Garlic cloves, minced fine	2 each	2 each	
Cilantro, chopped	1 oz	28 g	
Oregano, dried	1 tbsp	15 g	
Cumin, ground	1 tsp	5 g	
Salt	2 tsp	10 g	
Sugar	2 tsp	10 g	
Black pepper	2 tsp	10 g	
Tabasco sauce	2 tsp	10 ml	
Olive oil	8 fl oz	237 ml	Slowly whisk in the oils.
Salad oil	12 fl oz	355 ml	
Lime zest	1 oz	30 g	Add the lime zest and adjust the seasonings to taste.

NUTRITIONAL INFORMATION PER SERVING: 248 Calories; 27 g Fat (96.2% calories from fat); trace Protein; 2 g Carbohydrate; trace Dietary Fiber; 0 mg Cholesterol; 217 mg Sodium. Exchanges: 0 Grain (Starch); 0 Lean Meat; 0 Vegetable; 0 Fruit; 5 1/2 Fat; 0 Other Carbohydrates.

Chef Edward G. Leonard, CMC, AAC, is a past president of the American Culinary Federation and executive chef at the famed Westchester Country Club in Rye, New York. Chef Leonard has spent the last 25 years working in the cooking profession and is one of less than 70 Certified Master Chefs in the United States.

chef Ed Leonard's gorgonzola dressing
Yield: 1 qt (946 ml) Approximately 20 each 1 1/2 fl oz (45 ml) servings

Ingredients	Amounts		Procedure
	U.S.	Metric	
Olive oil	2 fl oz	59 ml	Sauté the onion and garlic until very soft and light brown. Deglaze the pan with pear vinegar and reserve.
Garlic, minced	1 tbsp	15 g	
Sweet onion, small dice	2 tbsp	30 g	
Pear vinegar	2 fl oz	59 ml	
Dry mustard	1 tsp	5 g	Dissolve the mustard in red wine vinegar.
Red wine vinegar	1 tbsp	15 ml	
Mayonnaise	12 fl oz	354 ml	Combine the onions, mustard, and wine mixture with the mayonnaise, pear vinegar, paprika, honey, Worcestershire sauce, pepper, and salt in a blender and blend well.
Pear vinegar	4 fl oz	118 ml	
Hungarian paprika	1 tsp	5 g	
Anise honey	1 tbsp	15 ml	
Worcestershire sauce	1 tsp	5 ml	
White pepper	1 tsp	5 g	
Kosher salt	1 tbsp	15 g	
Olive oil	8 fl oz	236 ml	
Gorgonzola cheese, crumbled	10 oz	284 g	Add 6 oz of the cheese to the dressing and blend with a blender stick. Stir in the remaining cheese chunks by hand.

NUTRITIONAL INFORMATION PER SERVING: 295 Calories; 32 g Fat (92.7% calories from fat); 3 g Protein; 2 g Carbohydrate; trace Dietary Fiber; 18 mg Cholesterol; 686 mg Sodium. Exchanges: 0 Grain (Starch); 1/2 Lean Meat; 0 Vegetable; 4 1/2 Fat; 0 Other Carbohydrates.

>> Cream Dressings

Cream dressings are emulsified dressings that contain cream or other dairy products such as sour cream, Mascarpone cheese, buttermilk, or yogurt as a major ingredient. Typical examples of cream dressings are Blue Cheese Dressing, Green Goddess, and Ranch-style dressings (Figure 14-4).

Figure 14-4 Quartered iceberg lettuce with a variety of cream dressings.

LEARNING ACTIVITY 14-2

Take 1 pint (474 ml) vinaigrette dressing and place it on the counter. Take 1 pint (474 ml) blue cheese dressing (one-half the recipe on the next page) and place it on the counter. Check both dressings 15 minutes later. How do they look? What has happened to the vinaigrette? Is the blue cheese still emulsified?

Blue cheese is considered a standard dressing in this category of salad dressings. You'd be hard-pressed to find a restaurant that doesn't serve it. This is a delicious version of the old standard. Please note that Roquefort cheese is a registered trademark and must be used as an ingredient if the dressing is called Roquefort Dressing.

blue cheese dressing *Yield: 1 qt (946 ml) Approximately 20 each 1 1/2 fl oz (45 ml) servings*

Ingredients	Amounts		Procedure
	U.S.	Metric	
Sour cream	8 fl oz	237 ml	Blend in a food processor or immersion blender all the ingredients except the second blue cheese.
Mayonnaise	8 fl oz	237 ml	
Lemon juice	1 tbsp	15 ml	
Buttermilk	8 fl oz	237 ml	
Worcestershire sauce	1 tsp	5 ml	
Tabasco sauce	To taste	To taste	
White pepper	To taste	To taste	
Blue cheese, crumbled	8 oz	227 g	

Blue cheese, crumbled	4 oz	113 g	Fold the remaining cheese chunks into the dressing. Refrigerate.

NUTRITIONAL INFORMATION PER SERVING: 169 Calories; 17 g Fat (86.0% calories from fat); 5 g Protein; 2 g Carbohydrate; trace Dietary Fiber; 22 mg Cholesterol; 321 mg Sodium. Exchanges: 0 Grain (Starch); 1/2 Lean Meat; 0 Vegetable; 0 Fruit; 0 Nonfat Milk; 2 Fat; 0 Other Carbohydrate.

Green Goddess dressing originated at the famous Palace Hotel in San Francisco. The chef created it in honor of George Arliss, a stage and screen actor from the 1920s, who was starring at the time in a play titled "The Green Goddess."

green Goddess dressing
Yield: 1 qt (946 ml) Approximately 20 each 1 1/2 fl oz (45 ml) servings

Ingredients	Amounts		Procedure
	U.S.	Metric	
Parsley, stems removed	1 bunch	1 bunch	In a food processor, purée the parsley, fresh spinach, chopped defrosted spinach, chives, and anchovy fillets with oil and chopped garlic. Set aside.
Spinach, fresh, washed	4 oz loose leaf	113 g	
Spinach, frozen, chopped, defrosted, drained	10 oz	284 g	
Chives, chopped	1 oz	28 g	
Anchovy fillets with oil	5 oz	140 g	
Garlic, minced	1 tbsp	15 g	

Mayonnaise	16 fl oz	473 ml	In a separate bowl, blend the mayonnaise, sour cream, lemon juice, tarragon, and tarragon vinegar. Blend with the flavoring purée.
Sour cream	8 fl oz	237 ml	
Lemon juice	1/2 fl oz	15 ml	
Tarragon, fresh chopped	1 tbsp	15 g	
Tarragon vinegar	1/2 fl oz	15 ml	

NUTRITIONAL INFORMATION PER SERVING: 203 Calories; 22 g Fat (91.0% calories from fat); 3 g Protein; 2 g Carbohydrate; 1 g Dietary Fiber; 19 mg Cholesterol; 405 mg Sodium. Exchanges: 0 Grain (Starch); 1/2 Lean Meat; 0 Vegetable; 0 Fruit; 0 Nonfat Milk; 2 Fat; 0 Other Carbohydrates.

Ranch dressing has fast become one of the most popular types of dressings. It was created in Alaska but gained fame when it was served at Hidden Valley Guest Ranch near Santa Barbara, California. Guests begged to purchase bottles to take home. Soon seasoning packets were available that could be mixed with buttermilk and mayonnaise.

favorite ranch dressing
Yield: 1 qt (946 ml) Approximately 20 each 1 1/2 fl oz (45 ml) servings

Ingredients	Amounts U.S.	Metric
Parsley, fresh, chopped	2 tbsp	30 g
Buttermilk	8 fl oz	237 ml
Mayonnaise	8 fl oz	237 ml
Sour cream	8 fl oz	237 ml
Garlic, minced	1 tbsp	30 g
Anchovy fillets, mashed	1 oz	30 g
Chives, chopped	1 oz	30 g
Onion, grated	4 oz	113 g
Tarragon, fresh, chopped	1 tbsp	15 g
Lemon juice, fresh squeezed	1 fl oz	30 ml
Red wine vinegar	1 fl oz	30 ml
Worcestershire sauce	1 tsp	5 ml
Salt	To taste	To taste
Pepper	To taste	To taste

Procedure

Combine all the ingredients. Mix well. Season to taste.

NUTRITIONAL INFORMATION PER SERVING: 203 Calories; 22 g Fat (91.0% calories from fat); 3 g Protein; 2 g Carbohydrate; 1 g Dietary Fiber; 19 mg Cholesterol; 405 mg Sodium. Exchanges: 0 Grain (Starch); 1/2 Lean Meat; 0 Vegetable; 0 Fruit; 0 Nonfat Milk; 2 Fat; 0 Other Carbohydrates.

We associate eggnog with the holiday season. Serve this delicious, creamy dressing to add a festive touch to any meal. It works well on mild salads such as iceberg, butter head, or on a fruit salad.

eggnog dressing
Yield: 1 qt (946 ml) Approximately 20 each 1 1/2 fl oz (45 ml) servings

Ingredients	Amounts U.S.	Metric	Procedure
Eggnog	16 fl oz	473 ml	Whisk all the ingredients together and adjust the seasoning.
Mayonnaise	4 fl oz	118 ml	
Olive oil	4 fl oz	118 ml	
Sea or kosher salt	1 1/2 tbsp	22 g	
Champagne or pear wine vinegar	8 fl oz	237 ml	
White pepper	To taste	To taste	

NUTRITIONAL INFORMATION PER SERVING: 123 Calories; 12 g Fat (83.9% calories from fat); 1 g Protein; 4 g Carbohydrate; trace Dietary Fiber; 17 mg Cholesterol; 470 mg Sodium. Exchanges: 0 Grain (Starch); 2 Fat; 1/2 Other Carbohydrates.

The dressing is very pretty because of the black poppy seeds. It can be used in a green salad but is particularly nice on a fruit salad. Be sure that you continually whisk the mixture over the simmering water to prevent the egg yolks from scrambling.

creamy citrus dressing for fruit salad
Yield: 1 qt (946 ml) Approximately 20 each 1 1/2 fl oz (45 ml) servings

Ingredients	Amounts U.S.	Metric	Procedure
Orange juice	8 fl oz	237 ml	Combine all the ingredients, except for the cream, in a stainless steel bowl. Place the bowl over slightly simmering water and whip vigorously until thick and creamy. Remove the bowl and stir the dressing until cool. Place in the refrigerator.
Grapefruit juice	8 fl oz	237 ml	
Sugar	2 oz	57 g	
Egg yolk, pasteurized	2 oz	57 g	
Pepper, coarsely ground	2 tsp	10 g	
Poppy seeds	1 tbsp	15 g	
Heavy cream, 36%	8 fl oz	237 ml	Whip the cream. Just prior to serving, fold the whipped cream into the completely chilled dressing.

NUTRITIONAL INFORMATION PER SERVING: 69 Calories; 5 g Fat (62.3% calories from fat); 1 g Protein; 6 g Carbohydrate; trace Dietary Fiber; 27 mg Cholesterol; 8 mg Sodium. Exchanges: 0 Grain (Starch); 0 Lean Meat; 0 Fruit; 0 Nonfat Milk; 1 Fat; 0 Other Carbohydrates.

Curry is a blend of spices generally associated with Indian cuisine. Coupled with apple, this apple curry dressing is positively delightful.

apple curry dressing

Yield: 1 qt (946 ml) Approximately 20 each 1 1/2 fl oz (45 ml) servings

Ingredients	Amounts		Procedure
	U.S.	Metric	
Apple cider vinegar	6 fl oz	177 ml	Place the vinegar, juice, apple, green onions, grated ginger, soy sauce, spices, and honey in a blender or food processor.
Frozen apple juice, concentrate	4 fl oz	118 ml	
Tart green apple, peeled and shredded	8 oz	227 g	
Green onions, sliced	1 tbsp	15 g	
Ginger, fresh, grated	1 tbsp	15 g	
Soy sauce	1 tbsp	15 ml	
Turmeric, powder	1 tsp	5 g	
Ginger, ground	1 tsp	5 g	
Cayenne, powder	1/4 tsp	1 g	
Cumin, ground	1 tsp	5 g	
Curry	1/2 tsp	2 g	
Honey	1 tbsp	15 g	

Peanut oil	8 fl oz	237 ml	Slowly blend in the oils.
Sesame oil	2 fl oz	59 ml	
Salt	To taste	To taste	Taste and adjust the seasonings.
Pepper	To taste	To taste	

NUTRITIONAL INFORMATION PER SERVING: 134 Calories; 14 g Fat (89.6% calories from fat); trace Protein; 3 g Carbohydrate; trace Dietary Fiber; trace Cholesterol; 69 mg Sodium. Exchanges: 0 Grain (Starch); 0 Lean Meat; 0 Vegetable; 0 Fruit; 2 1/2 Fat; 0 Other Carbohydrates.

The secret ingredient to this amazing dressing is the grilled onions. Once grilled, they are puréed and combined with mayonnaise, vinegars, and cream.

charred onion dressing
Yield: 1 qt (946 ml) Approximately 20 each 1 1/2 fl oz (45 ml) servings

Ingredients	Amounts		Procedure
	U.S.	Metric	
Onion, sliced	2 lbs	907 g	Brush the onions with olive oil, salt, and sugar. Grill both sides of the sliced onion until sweet and tender.
Olive oil	2 fl oz	59 ml	
Salt	1 tbsp	15 g	Purée the cooled onions in food processor.
Sugar	1 tbsp	15 g	

Mayonnaise	8 fl oz	237 ml	Blend the remaining ingredients into the puréed onion mixture. Thin with water or stock if too thick. Adjust the seasonings.
Olive oil	8 fl oz	237 ml	
Balsamic vinegar	4 fl oz	118 ml	
Dry mustard	1 tbsp	15 g	
Heavy cream	3 fl oz	89 ml	

NUTRITIONAL INFORMATION PER SERVING: 233 Calories; 25 g Fat (91.0% calories from fat); 1 g Protein; 5 g Carbohydrate; 1 g Dietary Fiber; 10 mg Cholesterol; 385 mg Sodium. Exchanges: 0 Grain (Starch); 0 Lean Meat; 1/2 Vegetable; 0 Fruit; 0 Nonfat Milk; 4 Fat; 0 Other Carbohydrates.

>> Cooked Dressings

Cooked dressings are simply salad dressings that are cooked prior to service. They are used in a variety of ways. In some cases, the dressings are heated to combine the flavor ingredients and are poured hot over cooked salad ingredients. Some are cooked and cooled before use. Others are heated to order, called *à la minute* in French, and poured over green salads called **wilted salads** (Figure 14-5). Cooked dressings can also be made with fat-free chicken stock, thickened with cornstarch, and seasoned for a lower-fat product.

Figure 14-5   Spinach salad is topped with hot bacon dressing.

This cole slaw dressing keeps well refrigerated. It can be enhanced with chopped herbs at the moment of service.

cole slaw dressing   Yield: 1 qt (946 ml) Approximately 20 each 1 1/2 fl oz (45 ml) servings
(Sufficient for about 4 lbs [1,810 g] shredded cabbage)

Ingredients	Amounts		Procedure
	U.S.	Metric	
Apple cider vinegar	18 fl oz	532 ml	Bring the apple cider vinegar to a boil in a stainless steel 2 qt saucepan.

Water	12 fl oz	355 ml
Cornstarch	2 tbsp	30 g
Cumin, ground	1 tsp	5 g
Sugar	1 tbsp	15 g
Egg yolks	2 each	2 each
Dry mustard	1 tbsp	15 g
Cayenne pepper	1/4 tsp	1 g
Salt	To taste	To taste
Pepper	To taste	To taste

Combine all the remaining ingredients and add to the boiling vinegar. Stir well, then bring to a boil.

Salad oil	4 fl oz	118 ml

Add the oil. Pour while still hot over the shredded cabbage.

NUTRITIONAL INFORMATION PER SERVING: 65 Calories; 6 g Fat (79.8% calories from fat); trace Protein; 3 g Carbohydrate; trace Dietary Fiber; 21 mg Cholesterol; 15 mg Sodium. Exchanges: 0 Grain (Starch); 0 Lean Meat; 0 Fruit; 1 Fat; 0 Other Carbohydrates.

Some restaurants serve this dressing over warm potatoes for a warm salad. Others cool it and then use it on cold potatoes. It's delicious served either way.

hot bacon dressing for potato salad
Yield: 1 qt (946 ml) Approximately 20 each 1 1/2 fl oz (45 ml) servings

Ingredients	Amounts		Procedure
	U.S.	Metric	
Bacon, small dice	8 oz	227 g	Cook the bacon in a heavy sauce pot over medium heat until crisp. Add the shallots and cook briefly.
Shallot, chopped	2 tbsp	30 g	
White vinegar	12 fl oz	355 ml	Add the vinegar, sugar, and water. Bring to a boil.
Sugar	2 oz	57 g	
Water	6 fl oz	177 ml	
Oil	12 fl oz	355 ml	Add the remaining ingredients. Cool to lukewarm and pour over the prepared potato salad. Blend and refrigerate immediately or serve warm, if desired.
Tarragon, fresh, chopped	2 tbsp	30 g	
Chives, snipped	2 tbsp	30 g	
Salt	To taste	To taste	
Pepper	To taste	To taste	

NUTRITIONAL INFORMATION PER SERVING: 210 Calories; 19 g Fat (78.3% calories from fat); 5 g Protein; 7 g Carbohydrate; 1 g Dietary Fiber; 0 mg Cholesterol; 327 mg Sodium. Exchanges: 0 Grain (Starch); 1/2 Lean Meat; 0 Vegetable; 3 1/2 Fat; 1/2 Other Carbohydrates.

This dressing is served warm over cold spinach or greens. The hot dressing will wilt the salad, so it should be served immediately.

hot bacon dressing for spinach salad

Yield: 1 qt (946 ml) Approximately 20 each 1 1/2 fl oz (45 ml) servings

Ingredients	Amounts U.S.	Metric	Procedure
Bacon, diced	1 lb	454 g	Cook the bacon in a heavy sauce pot over medium heat until crisp. Remove the bacon with a slotted spoon and set aside.
Yellow onion, chopped	4 oz	113 g	Sauté the onion in the bacon fat and cook for 5 minutes until the onion is soft.
Salad oil	6 fl oz	177 ml	Add the oil.
Apple cider vinegar	8 fl oz	237 ml	Add the remaining ingredients except the cornstarch and cold water. Bring to a boil.
Water	6 fl oz	177 ml	
Brown sugar	2 oz	57 g	
Salt	To taste	To taste	
Pepper	To taste	To taste	
Cornstarch	2 tsp	10 g	Make a slurry with the cornstarch and cold water. Add it to the boiling dressing. Remove from the heat and keep hot. Add the cooked bacon. Use hot over the salad.
Cold water	2 tsp	10 ml	

NUTRITIONAL INFORMATION PER SERVING: 188 Calories; 14 g Fat (61.9% calories from fat); 9 g Protein; 10 g Carbohydrate; 2 g Dietary Fiber; 0 mg Cholesterol; 641 mg Sodium. Exchanges: 1/2 Grain (Starch); 1 Lean Meat; 0 Vegetable; 0 Fruit; 2 Fat; 0 Other Carbohydrates.

>> Low-Fat Dressings

Consumers are looking for healthier food options. Salads are considered a healthy choice, but dressings can sabotage even the best intentions. Low-fat dressings contain less fat than do traditional dressings (Figure 14-6). Many restaurants are including low-fat and lower-calorie dressings, and the simple answer is to serve commercially prepared dressings that are often thickened with gum paste.

It isn't difficult to prepare delicious, low-fat dressings from scratch. In general, this is done by using less oil and substituting it with stock or juice that has been thickened with arrowroot or cornstarch.

This spa-style vinaigrette is a low-calorie dressing that packs a flavor punch. Serve grilled chicken or fish on greens with this dressing for a complete meal. It is also good for grain-based salads such as wild rice or quinoa.

Figure 14-6   This yogurt and mint dressing is just one example of a low-fat dressing.

spa-style vinaigrette

Yield: 1 qt (946 ml) Approximately 20 each 1 1/2 fl oz (45 ml) servings

Ingredients	Amounts U.S.	Metric	Procedure
Chicken stock	8 fl oz	237 ml	Bring the chicken stock to a boil.
Cornstarch	1 tbsp	15 g	Make a slurry with the cornstarch and water. Add to the chicken stock. Cool the chicken stock, stirring frequently to prevent a skin from forming.
Cold water	1 tbsp	15 ml	
Cold-pressed safflower, olive or walnut oil	8 fl oz	237 ml	Combine with all the ingredients and whisk until blended. Store in the refrigerator.
Rice wine vinegar	8 fl oz	225 ml	
Orange juice, freshly squeezed	4 fl oz	110 ml	
Stone ground mustard	2 tbsp	30 g	
Shallots, finely minced	1 oz	28 g	
Chives, fresh, chopped	3 tbsp	90 g	
Pepper, freshly ground	To taste	To taste	

NUTRITIONAL INFORMATION PER SERVING: 107 Calories; 11 g Fat (91.8% calories from fat); trace Protein; 2 g Carbohydrate; trace Dietary Fiber; 0 mg Cholesterol; 129 mg Sodium. Exchanges: 0 Grain (Starch); 0 Vegetable; 0 Fruit; 2 Fat; 0 Other Carbohydrates.

LEARNING ACTIVITY 14-3

The flavor and, in some instances, the color of a salad dressing can be altered by changing the type of vinegar and oil used. For this learning activity, select one dressing recipe in this unit that contains both vinegar and oil. Make it as stated in the recipe. Then make it again using a different type of vinegar and a different type of oil. Taste both dressings and note the changes in flavor and appearance. It should become apparent that infinite possibilities can be created by taking a recipe and replacing some of the basic ingredients. To gain added experience, make another batch. This time, substitute the vinegar for another acidic liquid such as lime juice, orange juice, or lemon juice. See and taste the difference.

This light yogurt dressing is the perfect alternative to high-calorie cream dressings. The basic flavor of the dressing is dependent on the selected herbs. Use any combination of herbs, according to taste preference and season.

light yogurt dressing
Yield: 1 qt (946 ml) Approximately 20 each 1 1/2 fl oz (45 ml) servings

Ingredients	Amounts		Procedure
	U.S.	Metric	
Low-fat yogurt	20 fl oz	592 ml	Combine all the ingredients except for the herbs.
Low-fat sour cream	8 fl oz	237 ml	
Lemon juice	2 fl oz	59 ml	
Salt	To taste	To taste	
Pepper	To taste	To taste	
Water	4 fl oz	118 ml	

Herbs, your choice, chopped	2 oz	60 g	Add the herbs just before service.

NUTRITIONAL INFORMATION PER SERVING 38 Calories; 1 g Fat (25.1% calories from fat); 2 g Protein; 5 g Carbohydrate; 1 g Dietary Fiber; 4 mg Cholesterol; 48 mg Sodium. Exchanges: 0 Grain (Starch); 0 Fruit; 0 Nonfat Milk; 0 Fat; 0 Other Carbohydrates.

One way to cut the fat in salad dressings is to use a low-fat mayonnaise in place of traditional mayonnaise. This recipe uses arrowroot and egg yolks as the primary emulsifiers.

low-fat mayonnaise
Yield: 1 qt (946 ml) Approximately 20 each 1 1/2 fl oz (45 ml) servings

Ingredients	Amounts		Procedure
	U.S.	Metric	
Chicken stock	16 fl oz	473 ml	Bring the chicken stock to a boil. Make a slurry with the arrowroot and cold water and add the slurry to the boiling water. Remove and cool.
Arrowroot	3 tbsp	45 g	
Cold water	3 tbsp	44 ml	
Egg yolks, pasteurized	2 fl oz	59 ml	Put the thickened stock, egg yolks, vinegar, salt, pepper, mustard, and sugar in a food processor and blend.
Vinegar	4 fl oz	118 ml	
Salt	1 tsp	5 g	
Pepper	1/2 tsp	2 g	
Mustard	1 fl oz	30 ml	
Sugar	1 tsp	5 g	
Vegetable oil	8 fl oz	237 ml	Slowly add the oil, while processing.

NUTRITIONAL INFORMATION PER SERVING: 116 Calories; 12 g Fat (91.3% calories from fat); 1 g Protein; 2 g Carbohydrate; trace Dietary Fiber; 38 mg Cholesterol; 342 mg Sodium. Exchanges: 0 Grain (Starch); 0 Lean Meat; 2 1/2 Fat; 0 Other Carbohydrates.

Many consumers are trying to add soy bean products to their diets. This simple mayonnaise is made with tofu.

low-fat tofu mayonnaise

Yield: 1 qt (946 ml) Approximately 20 each 1 1/2 fl oz (45 ml) servings

Ingredients	Amounts		Procedure
	U.S.	Metric	
Silken low-fat tofu	30 oz	850 g	Place all the ingredients in a food processor or blender and blend until smooth.
Lemon, fresh, juice	2 fl oz	59 ml	
Champagne vinegar	2 fl oz	59 ml	
Egg yolk, pasteurized	1 fl oz	30 ml	
Kosher salt	2 tsp	10 g	

NUTRITIONAL INFORMATION PER SERVING: 48 Calories; 1 g Fat (22.7% calories from fat); 2 g Protein; 7 g Carbohydrate; trace Dietary Fiber; 18 mg Cholesterol; 110 mg Sodium. Exchanges: 0 Lean Meat; 0 Fruit; 0 Fat; 1/2 Other Carbohydrates.

Use tarragon leaves that have been preserved in vinegar. If not available, use fresh leaves that have been dipped in hot water to remove the raw flavor.

light tarragon vinegar and sour cream dressing

Yield: 1 qt (946 ml) Approximately 20 each 1 1/2 fl oz (45 ml) servings

Ingredients	Amounts U.S.	Metric	Procedure
Low-fat sour cream	16 fl oz	473 ml	Combine all the ingredients and refrigerate overnight before use.
Low-fat ricotta cheese	12 fl oz	354 ml	
Tarragon vinegar, mild	4 fl oz	118 ml	
Paprika, mild	2 tbsp	30 g	
Tarragon, chopped	2 tbsp	30 g	
Salt	To taste	To taste	
Pepper	To taste	To taste	

NUTRITIONAL INFORMATION PER SERVING: 48 Calories; 1 g Fat (22.7% calories from fat); 2 g Protein; 7 g Carbohydrate; trace Dietary Fiber; 18 mg Cholesterol; 110 mg Sodium. Exchanges: 0 Lean Meat; 0 Fruit; 0 Fat; 1/2 Other Carbohydrates.

Many pasta salads are made with a modified mayonnaise dressing. Canned chicken broth can be used if desired.

light mayonnaise dressing   Yield: 16 oz (473 ml) 16 each 1 oz (30 ml) servings

Ingredients	Amounts		Procedure
	U.S.	Metric	
Mayonnaise	4 fl oz	118 ml	Combine all the ingredients with a blender stick.
Chicken broth	8 fl oz	237 ml	
Oil	4 fl oz	118 ml	
Mustard, prepared	1 tbsp	15 ml	
Salt	To taste	To taste	
Pepper	To taste	To taste	

NUTRITIONAL INFORMATION PER SERVING: 113 Calories; 13 g Fat (98.1% calories from fat); trace Protein; trace Carbohydrate; trace Dietary Fiber; 2 mg Cholesterol; 115 mg Sodium. Exchanges: 0 Grain (Starch); 0 Lean Meat; 2 Fat; 0 Other Carbohydrates.

This Asian dressing features a number of traditional Asian sauces including soy (light version), mushroom, and oyster sauce, along with sesame oil, rice vinegar, and garlic chili paste to give it a complex taste profile.

light Asian dressing *Yield: 12 fl oz (355 ml) 1 fl oz (29 ml) servings*

Ingredients	Amounts U.S.	Metric	Procedure
Chicken broth	8 fl oz	237 ml	Bring the chicken broth to a boil. Make a slurry with arrowroot and a little water, and add it to the boiling broth to thicken. Chill.
Arrowroot	1/2 tbsp	8 g	
Water, cold	2 fl oz	59 ml	

Light soy sauce	4 fl oz	118 ml	Combine all the other ingredients except for the scallions. Sprinkle the salad with scallions at the moment of service.
Mushroom soy sauce	1 fl oz	30 ml	
Oyster sauce	1 fl oz	30 ml	
Sesame oil, mild	1 fl oz	30 ml	
Rice vinegar	1 fl oz	30 ml	
Sugar	1/2 oz	14 g	
Garlic chili paste	1/2 tbsp	8 g	
Scallions, sliced	As needed	As needed	

NUTRITIONAL INFORMATION PER SERVING: 225 Calories; 1 g Fat (6.1% calories from fat); 15 g Protein; 35 g Carbohydrate; 1 g Dietary Fiber; 0 mg Cholesterol; 7,884 mg Sodium. Exchanges: 1/2 Grain (Starch); 1 Lean Meat; 2 1/2 Vegetable; 1 Other Carbohydrates.

Canned chicken broth can be used for the following Soy Dressing recipe, if desired.

soy dressing *Yield: 12 fl oz (355 ml)*

Ingredients	Amounts U.S.	Metric	Procedure
Chicken broth	8 fl oz	237 ml	Bring the chicken broth to a boil, make a slurry with the arrowroot and a little water, and add it to the boiling broth to thicken. Chill.
Arrowroot	1/2 tbsp	7 g	

Light soy sauce	4 fl oz	118 ml	Combine the thickened broth with the soy sauces, oyster sauce, sesame oil, rice vinegar, sugar, and garlic chili paste.
Mushroom soy sauce	1 fl oz	30 ml	
Oyster sauce	1 fl oz	30 ml	
Sesame oil, mild	1 fl oz	30 ml	
Rice wine vinegar	1 fl oz	30 ml	
Sugar	1/2 oz	15 g	
Garlic chili paste	1/2 tbsp	7 ml	
Scallions, sliced	As needed	As needed	Sprinkle the salad with scallions at the time of service.

NUTRITIONAL INFORMATION PER SERVING: 37 Calories; 2 g Fat (58.2% calories from fat); 1 g Protein; 3 g Carbohydrate; trace Dietary Fiber; 0 mg Cholesterol; 776 mg Sodium. Exchanges: 0 Grain (Starch); 0 Lean Meat; 0 Vegetable; 1/2 Fat; 0 Other Carbohydrates.

>> Summary

Salad dressings made from scratch are cost-effective and easy to make. In most cases they provide a superior product when compared to ready-made dressings. Dressings fall into a number of categories. Vinaigrettes are made with oil, an acid ingredient, and spices. They separate quickly and must be mixed prior to each use. Emulsified dressings contain emulsifiers that act as a bridge between the oil and liquid and hold the blend. Creamy dressings are a type of emulsified dressing and contain a dairy product as a key ingredient. Cooked dressings are cooked and then chilled or served hot, depending on the recipe.

Salads have long been associated with healthy eating. In reality, the dressings can substantially raise the caloric content of a salad. Many consumers are looking for low-fat alternatives.

>> Review Questions

TRUE/FALSE

1. Salt will not dissolve in vinegar.
2. Mirin is vinegar that is made with rice.
3. Blood oranges are slightly less acidic than regular table oranges.
4. Emulsified dressings cling to salad ingredients better than vinaigrette dressings.
5. Caesar dressing contains anchovy fillets that are mashed to a paste.
6. Caesar dressing was named after a famous movie star.
7. Mayonnaise acts as an emulsifier.
8. Dijon mustard is made with either brown or black mustard seeds.
9. Russian dressing comes from Russia.
10. Any blue cheese dressing can be called Roquefort dressing.
11. Green Goddess isn't really green.
12. *À la minute* is a French term that means preparing food at the last minute, or to order.

MULTIPLE CHOICE

13. Crème fraîche is a
    a. French sour cream.
    b. slightly acidic, thick cream.
    c. sweetened cream.
    d. whipped cream.
14. In vinaigrettes, salt should be added before the
    a. vinegar.
    b. pepper.
    c. oil.
    d. fresh herbs.
15. Which of the following is *not* considered an emulsifier?
    a. egg yolks
    b. mayonnaise
    c. mustard
    d. vinegar
16. What type of eggs should be used in salad dressings?
    a. homogenized
    b. pasteurized
    c. whole
    d. brown
17. Another name for French dressing is
    a. Russian.
    b. Thousand Island.
    c. Catalina.
    d. Green Goddess.
18. _____ dressing was invented in Tijuana, Mexico.
    a. Russian
    b. Green Goddess
    c. Caesar
    d. Ranch
19. Which of the following is *not* considered a cream dressing?
    a. Blue cheese
    b. Ranch
    c. Green Goddess
    d. cole slaw dressing
20. Green Goddess was invented in what city?
    a. Los Angeles
    b. Miami
    c. San Francisco
    d. Las Vegas

SHORT ANSWER

21. What are the four basic ingredients of a vinaigrette?
22. Give a brief description of the emulsification process.
23. What happens to fresh herbs when they come in contact with acidity?
24. Describe cream dressings.
25. What is used in place of some of the oil in low-fat dressings?

Cold Sauces, Dips, Aioli, Salsas, Relishes, and Chutneys

After you have finished reading this unit, you should be able to:

- Describe the differences between the basic types of cold sauces.
- Share the history of cocktail sauce.
- Identify the main ingredient in sauce dijonnaise, sauce verte, sauce Andalouse, and sauce Chantilly.
- List the traditional bases used for making dips.
- Describe a typical Mexican salsa.
- Define the terms *chutney* and *relish*.

>> **Key Terms**

aioli (*ay-OH-lee*)	cold sauces	relish	sauce verte (*vehrt*)
chow chow	dip	salsa	tartar sauce
chutney	piccalilli	sauce Andalouse	

This unit covers a host of cold accompaniments, such as sauces, salsas, chutneys, and relishes, that can be served with sandwiches, appetizers, and main-course salads and entrées. Accompaniments, which are sometimes called condiments, add flavor, color, and sometimes interesting textures to the dish. In many cases they are strongly flavored and added sparingly.

The most basic cold sauce is mayonnaise, which was mentioned already in Unit 14. Many sauces are based on mayonnaise, but there are others thickened with a wide range of products. Aioli is a garlic mayonnaise from France that is used as a sauce and a condiment.

Chutneys and many cold sauces came to England from India and Southeast Asia. England was a seafaring nation; as its ships sailed the world, British sailors encountered foreign cuisines that they then adapted to their own tastes.

Dips and salsas are very important and play an increasing role in restaurants. People love to eat finger food or items they can dip in flavorful concoctions. Dips have become a favorite party food. There is seldom a reception or a gathering of people that does not include a dip. When it comes to making dips, there is no limit to the imagination. You will find many interesting dips in this unit.

In some countries, there is little difference between salads and dips. In hot countries, green salads are seldom eaten because they do not grow well and wilt rapidly unless refrigerated. In these countries, dips are served as salads.

Salsa is just one of the many contributions Mexico has made to the culinary arts. Translated, *salsa* is the Spanish word for sauce. Salsa has gained tremendous popularity throughout the United States.

>> Cold Sauces

Cold sauces are simply thickened liquids that are used to flavor or enhance other foods. Sauces can be based on mayonnaise as well as on vegetable and fruit purées (Figure 15-1). For example, a popular cold sauce served with beef in Vienna is applesauce blended with a generous amount of horseradish. Other cold sauces are based on tomatoes like the Cocktail Sauce listed later in this unit. Well-known is the French mayonnaise-based **sauce verte** (literally translated "green sauce") made with puréed herbs and served with cold fish. In French cooking, there are many cold mayonnaise-based sauces, and there is no limit to a chef's imagination for creating even more. Famous also is sauce Dijonnaise, which, as the name indicates, is flavored with mustard. Dijon is the capital of Burgundy, a province of France, and is famous for mustards.

Sauce Andalouse is named after the Spanish province and is, logically, flavored with tomato paste and puréed pimentos (red peppers). The minimum serving size is at least 2 fluid ounces (59 ml), although some customers like more than that.

Figure 15-1 Sauces add flavors and piquancy to foods.

The key ingredients in most cocktail sauce recipes are ketchup and horseradish. Cocktail sauces started appearing on menus in the early 1900s. Typically, they are served as a condiment with oysters, shrimp, and other chilled, cooked seafood. During the 1920s, at the height of prohibition, restaurateurs begin calling it *cocktail sauce*. They served it in cocktail glasses that had been used to serve cocktails prior to prohibition. This was a way to create an interest in the dish and to find a use for the glasses.

In Europe, whipped cream and brandy are sometimes added to the recipe. Many foodservice establishments use prepared cocktail sauce, but the current trend is to prepare sauces in-house. Some chefs add variations to traditional sauces to create signature recipes unique to their restaurant.

traditional cocktail sauce *Yield: 44 fl oz (1.3 l) About 20 each 2 oz (60 ml) servings*

Ingredients	Amounts		Procedure
	U.S.	Metric	
Tomato purée, coarse if desired	8 fl oz	237 ml	Blend all the ingredients. Refrigerate until use. This sauce gets better after storing it overnight.
Chili sauce	16 fl oz	473 ml	
Ketchup	16 fl oz	473 ml	
Horseradish, grated	4 fl oz	118 ml	
Lemon juice	1 fl oz	30 ml	
Salt	To taste	To taste	
Tabasco sauce	1 tbsp	15 ml	
Sugar	1 tbsp	15 g	

NUTRITIONAL INFORMATION PER SERVING: 40 Calories; trace Fat (2.5% calories from fat); 1 g Protein; 10 g Carbohydrate; 1 g Dietary Fiber; 0 mg Cholesterol; 364 mg Sodium. Exchanges: 0 Vegetable; 0 Fruit; 1/2 Other Carbohydrates.

Tartar sauce is a staple served with fried fish and consists of mayonnaise blended with chopped, flavorful ingredients. Generally the base is made ahead of time and stored in the refrigerator. When needed, it is blended with mayonnaise at a ratio of one part base with three parts mayonnaise.

> **CHEF'S TIP**
> The basic tartar sauce mix will stay preserved in the walk-in cooler because the vinegar in the pickles and capers acts as a preservative. Once it is blended with mayonnaise, it will become perishable. It must be refrigerated and should be used within 3 days of blending.

tartar sauce base
Yield: About 1 1/2 qt (1.42 l) without the mayonnaise. The base mix below is for 1 gallon (3.8 l) mayonnaise.

Ingredients	U.S.	Metric
Onion, coarsely chopped	1 lb	454 g
Dill pickle, chopped	2 lbs	907 g
Parsley, chopped, no stems	1 bunch	1 bunch
Watercress, chopped, no stems	1 bunch	1 bunch
Capers, not drained	4 oz	113 g
Garlic cloves, chopped	3 each	3 each
Chives	1 bunch	1 bunch

Procedure

Grind the ingredients in a food processor. Store in the refrigerator in a glass, plastic, or stainless steel container. (Don't use an aluminum container.) Blend with 1 gallon (3.8 l) mayonnaise when needed.

NUTRITIONAL INFORMATION PER SERVING: 365 Calories; 3 g Fat (6.4% calories from fat); 13 g Protein; 80 g Carbohydrate; 21 g Dietary Fiber; 0 mg Cholesterol; 12,322 mg Sodium. Exchanges: 15 Vegetable; 1/2 Other Carbohydrates.

The following recipe for mignonnette sauce comes from France. Sauce mignonnette can be served with clams or oysters.

sauce mignonnette   *Yield: 8 fl oz (240 ml) 1 oz (30 ml) of sauce served with 6 oysters on the half shell servings*

Ingredients	Amounts		Procedure
	U.S.	Metric	
White peppercorns	1 tbsp	15 g	Coarsely crush the peppercorns.

Ingredients	Amounts		Procedure
White vinegar, mild	8 fl oz	237 ml	Combine the peppercorns with vinegar and water.
Water	2 fl oz	59 ml	

Shallots, chopped	1 tbsp	15 g	Add shallots to the above mixture. Bring to a boil and chill. Serve chilled.

NUTRITIONAL INFORMATION PER SERVING: 365 Calories; 3 g Fat (6.4% calories from fat); 13 g Protein; 80 g Carbohydrate; 21 g Dietary Fiber; 0 mg Cholesterol; 12,322 mg Sodium. Exchanges: 15 Vegetable; 1/2 Other Carbohydrates.

This simple sauce was originally served in Europe with boiled beef. The Jewish population in New York brought the custom to the city and still serves it with boiled short ribs or brisket. Try it on ham. Most operations use grated horseradish preserved in vinegar. If that is the case, it should be drained. Fresh horseradish can be used. It will oxidize rapidly and turns dark. If fresh is used, prepare just prior to serving.

Viennese apple horseradish *Yield: 1 qt (946 ml)*
32 each 1 oz (30 ml) servings

Ingredients	Amounts		Procedure
	U.S.	Metric	
Applesauce, unsweetened	28 fl oz	828 ml	Stir together the ingredients and serve cold as a side order with boiled beef.
Horseradish, grated	4 oz	113 g	
Pepper, freshly ground	To taste	To taste	
Lemon rind, grated	1/2 tsp	2 g	

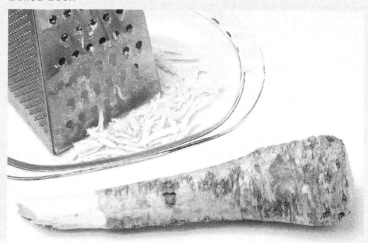

NUTRITIONAL INFORMATION PER SERVING: 28 Calories; trace Fat (1.3% calories from fat); trace Protein; 7 g Carbohydrate; 1 g Dietary Fiber; 0 mg Cholesterol; 10 mg Sodium. Exchanges: 0 Grain (Starch); 1/2 Fruit; 0 Fat; 0 Other Carbohydrates.

Vienna, Austria, is the home to some of our most beloved recipes, including wiener schnitzel, cheese Danish, and apple strudel, as well as many delicious sauce recipes. The following chive sauce is thickened with white bread and hard-boiled egg yolks.

Viennese chive sauce   *Yield: 1 qt (946 ml) 32 each 1 oz (30 ml) servings*

Ingredients	Amounts U.S.	Metric	Procedure
Bread, soft white	16 slices	16 slices	Remove the crust from the bread and discard or save for bread crumbs. 
Milk, cold	4 fl oz	118 ml	Combine all the ingredients except the chives and mix in a food processor. Adjust the consistency. If too runny, add more bread. If too thick, add more beef broth.
Egg yolks, hard-boiled	8 each	8 each	
Beef broth, cold	4 fl oz	118 ml	
Mayonnaise	8 fl oz	237 ml	
Sour cream	8 fl oz	237 ml	
Vinegar, white	2 fl oz	59 ml	
Salt	To taste	To taste	
Pepper	To taste	To taste	
Chives, chopped	3 oz	85 g	Add the chives.

NUTRITIONAL INFORMATION PER SERVING: 28 Calories; trace Fat (1.3% calories from fat); trace Protein; 7 g Carbohydrate; 1 g Dietary Fiber; 0 mg Cholesterol; 10 mg Sodium. Exchanges: 0 Grain (Starch); 1/2 Fruit; 0 Fat; 0 Other Carbohydrates.

Sauce Dijonnaise features the prepared mustard made in the Dijon region of France with black or brown mustard seeds. It is excellent with cold smoked meat.

sauce Dijonnaise *Yield: 1 qt (946 ml) 32 each 1 oz (30 ml) servings*

Ingredients	Amounts U.S.	Metric	Procedure
Dijon mustard	8 fl oz	237 ml	Combine the ingredients except the chives with a stick blender (a blender will also work).
Mayonnaise	6 fl oz	177 ml	
Lemon juice	2 tsp	10 ml	
Sour cream	16 fl oz	473 ml	
Pepper	To taste	To taste	
Sugar	To taste	To taste	
Chives, chopped	1 tbsp	28 g	Fold in the chives.

NUTRITIONAL INFORMATION PER SERVING: 157 Calories; 16 g Fat (89.7% calories from fat); 2 g Protein; 2 g Carbohydrate; trace Dietary Fiber; 17 mg Cholesterol; 297 mg Sodium. Exchanges: 0 Grain (Starch); 0 Lean Meat; 0 Vegetable; 0 Fruit; 0 Nonfat Milk; 2 Fat; 0 Other Carbohydrates.

This spicy mustard sauce works well with fish dishes or appetizers such as the Cornmeal Fried Catfish recipe found in Unit 8.

creole mustard sauce *Yield: 20 oz (0.6 l) 1 oz (30 ml) per servings*

Ingredients	Amounts U.S.	Metric	Procedure
Mayonnaise	16 fl oz	473 ml	Blend all the ingredients and chill.
Creole-style mustard	4 fl oz	118 ml	
Horseradish, prepared	1/2 fl oz	15 ml	
Worcestershire sauce	1/4 tsp	1 ml	
Sherry wine vinegar	1 tsp	5 ml	
Louisiana hot sauce	1 tsp	5 ml	
Salt	1/2 tsp	3 g	
Curry powder	1/4 tsp	1 g	
Tarragon leaves, minced fine	1/4 tsp	1 g	
Green onions, sliced thin	1 stalk	1 stalk	
Garlic cloves, mashed into purée	2 each	2 each	
Green bell pepper, finely minced	1 oz	28 g	
Red bell pepper, finely minced	1 oz	28 g	
Celery, finely minced	1 oz	28 g	
White onion, finely minced	1 oz	28 g	

(Before the tarragon can be minced, the leaves should be removed from the stalk and the stalk discarded.)

NUTRITIONAL INFORMATION PER RECIPE: 3,411 Calories; 394 g Fat (96.7% calories from fat); 12 g Protein; 18 g Carbohydrate; 5 g Dietary Fiber; 165 mg Cholesterol; 5,270 mg Sodium. Exchanges: 0 Grain (Starch); 1/2 Lean Meat; 1 1/2 Vegetable; 33 1/2 Fat; 1/2 Other Carbohydrates.

Sauce verte is a popular sauce in French cuisine and is served with cold fish. *Vert(e)* in French means "green." This sauce is green due to the spinach and herbs. The amount of herb purée added to the mayonnaise depends on the flavor desired.

sauce verte (green sauce)   *Yield: About 1 cup purée (0.24 l)*

Ingredients	Amounts U.S.	Metric	Procedure
Spinach, chopped, no stems	6 oz	170 g	Wash the herbs carefully. Toss the herbs into boiling water. As soon as the water returns to a boil, drain and chill immediately in cold water. Drain and squeeze out any excess water. When almost dry, purée in a food processor to a paste consistency.
Italian parsley, no stems	1 bunch	1 bunch	
Chervil, no stems	1 bunch	1 bunch	
Tarragon, no stems	3 oz	85 g	
Mayonnaise (optional)	16 fl oz	473 ml	Add mayonnaise as needed for a creamy consistency. For a creamier version, you can add 4 oz. (118 ml) to 8 oz. (236 ml.) mayonnaise to the green sauce.

NUTRITIONAL INFORMATION PER RECIPE: 47 Calories; 1 g Fat (18% calories from fat); 4 g Protein; 8 g Carbohydrate; 2 g Dietary Fiber; 0 mg Cholesterol; 28 mg Sodium. Exchanges: 1/2 Grain (Starch); 0 Lean Meat; 1/2 Vegetable; 0 Fat; 0 Other Carbohydrates.

The pimento, ketchup, cayenne pepper, and tomato paste give this sauce a beautiful, bright red color. This sauce can be chilled up to 1 day; however, bring it to room temperature before serving.

sauce Andalouse *Yield: 1 qt (946 ml) 32 each 1 oz (30 ml) servings*

Ingredients	Amounts U.S.	Metric	Procedure
Pimentos, canned, drained, diced	8 oz	227 g	Combine all the ingredients in a food processor until thoroughly blended.
Ketchup	4 fl oz	118 ml	
Anchovy fillets, chopped	4 each	4 each	
Cayenne pepper	1/2 tsp	2 g	
Tomato paste	2 fl oz	59 ml	
Mayonnaise	16 fl oz	473 ml	

NUTRITIONAL INFORMATION PER RECIPE: 225 Calories; 25 g Fat (93.1% calories from fat); 1 g Protein; 3 g Carbohydrate; trace Dietary Fiber; 11 mg Cholesterol; 336 mg Sodium. Exchanges: 0 Grain (Starch); 0 Lean Meat; 0 Vegetable; 2 Fat; 0 Other Carbohydrates.

This Italian specialty sauce is served over cold, roasted veal, but can be served independently as a dip. In that case, it is called Tonnato Dip.

vitello tonnato *Yield: 1 qt (946 ml) 32 each 1 oz (30 ml) servings*

Ingredients	Amounts U.S.	Metric	Procedure
Tuna fish packed in oil, not drained	2 each 8 oz (227 g) cans	454 g	Combine all the ingredients except the capers in a food processor. Stir in the capers. You might want to save some capers for garnish.
Anchovy fillets	10 each	10 each	
Lemon juice	1 fl oz	30 ml	
Lemon rind, grated	2 tsp	10 g	
Mayonnaise	12 fl oz	354 ml	
Garlic, chopped very fine	1 tsp	5 g	
Capers, small, drained	2 oz	57 g	

NUTRITIONAL INFORMATION PER SERVING: 224 Calories; 21 g Fat (82.7% calories from fat); 10 g Protein; trace Carbohydrate; trace Dietary Fiber; 15 mg Cholesterol; 351 mg Sodium. Exchanges: 1 1/2 Lean Meat; 0 Vegetable; 0 Fruit; 1 1/2 Fat; 0 Other Carbohydrates.

Chantilly, a village in northern France, is a region known for its fine porcelain and delicate lace. Chantilly cream is a popular dessert topper made with whipped cream, sweetener, and vanilla or some other flavoring agent. The name *Chantilly* is generally associated with a dish that contains whipped cream. This cold sauce is served with cold poached fish and, true to its name, contains whipped cream. This sauce cannot be stored and must be mixed just prior to service. It is delicious when served with grilled or smoked fish or pork.

sauce Chantilly *Yield: 1 qt (946 ml) 32 each 1 oz (30 ml) servings*

Ingredients	Amounts U.S.	Metric	Procedure
Mayonnaise	16 fl oz	473 ml	Fold the whipped cream and pepper into the mayonnaise.
Whipping cream, whipped	16 fl oz	473 ml	
Cayenne pepper	1 pinch	1 pinch	

NUTRITIONAL INFORMATION PER SERVING: 320 Calories; 37 g Fat (97.8% calories from fat); 1 g Protein; 1 g Carbohydrate; trace Dietary Fiber; 54 mg Cholesterol; 179 mg Sodium. Exchanges: 0 Grain (Starch); 0 Nonfat Milk; 4 1/2 Fat.

Many operations serve mint jelly with roasted lamb. In England, a mint sauce is often served instead of mint jelly. This sauce is easy to make and it provides a nice change from the traditional mint jelly.

mint sauce *Yield: 1 1/2 pint (709 ml) Approximately 24 each 1 fl oz (30 ml) servings*

Ingredients	Amounts U.S.	Metric	Procedure
Apple cider vinegar	16 fl oz	473 ml	Bring the vinegar and sugar to a boil.
Sugar	8 oz	227 g	
Mint leaves, chopped	4 oz	113 g	Pour the hot liquid over mint leaves. Refrigerate before use.

NUTRITIONAL INFORMATION PER SERVING: 113 Calories; 0 g Fat (0.0% calories from fat); trace Protein; 29 g Carbohydrate; 1 g Dietary Fiber; 0 mg Cholesterol; 4 mg Sodium. Exchanges: 0 Vegetable; 0 Fruit; 2 Other Carbohydrates.

This traditional English sauce is easy to make. It keeps well and works nicely with cold ham and cold game.

cumberland sauce *Yield: 1 qt (946 ml) 32 each 1 oz (30 ml) servings*

Ingredients	Amounts U.S.	Metric	Procedure
Red currant jelly	16 fl oz	473 ml	Combine the ingredients, except the horseradish, and bring to a boil. Chill.
Orange juice	8 fl oz	237 ml	
Shallots, chopped	2 tbsp	30 g	
Orange zest	2 tbsp	30 g	
Ginger, fresh, chopped	2 tsp	10 g	
Cayenne pepper	1 tsp	5 g	
Mustard	1 tbsp	15 g	
Horseradish, grated, prepared	4 oz	113 g	Add the horseradish. Store for 24 hours before use.

NUTRITIONAL INFORMATION PER RECIPE: 141 Calories; 2 g Fat (12.7% calories from fat); 1 g Protein; 32 g Carbohydrate; 1 g Dietary Fiber; 4 mg Cholesterol; 56 mg Sodium. Exchanges: 0 Grain (Starch); 0 Lean Meat; 0 Vegetable; 0 Fruit; 1/2 Fat; 2 Other Carbohydrates.

Ponzu is a citrus-flavored soy sauce. This recipe goes well with the Tuna Carpaccio recipe found in Unit 8.

ponzu sauce *Yield: 12 fl oz (360 ml)*

Ingredients	Amounts U.S.	Metric	Procedure
Soy sauce	8 fl oz	237 ml	Put the soy sauce in a saucepan. Bring it to a boil. Remove from heat.
Dried bonito flakes	2 oz	57 g	Add the bonito flakes to the pan of soy sauce and cool.

Lemon juice, fresh squeezed	4 fl oz	118 ml	Mix the soy sauce, lemon juice, vinegar, and sake.
Rice wine vinegar	2 fl oz	59 ml	
Sweet sake	2 fl oz	59 ml	

NUTRITIONAL INFORMATION PER RECIPE: 357 Calories; 8 g Fat (22.6% calories from fat); 13 g Protein; 49 g Carbohydrate; 2 g Dietary Fiber; 8 mg Cholesterol; 12,966 mg Sodium. Exchanges: 4 1/2 Vegetable; 1/2 Fruit; 1 1/2 Fat; 1 Other Carbohydrates.

This zesty sauce goes perfectly with sate such as the Thai Sate of Lamb recipe found in Unit 8.

spicy Thai peanut sauce *Yield: Approximately 3 qt (2.84 l) 48 each 2 fl oz (58 ml) servings*

Ingredients	Amounts		Procedure
	U.S.	Metric	
Chunky peanut butter	4 lbs	1.814 kg	Place all the ingredients into a stainless steel saucepan and mix together until the sugar is dissolved. Thin with a little hot water, if needed.
Canned coconut milk	15 1/2 fl oz	458 ml	
Brown sugar	8 oz	227 g	
Honey	8 fl oz	237 ml	
Hot chili paste	2 tbsp	30 ml	
Lime juice	2 fl oz	59 ml	
Lime zest	1 tbsp	30 ml	
Curry powder	2 tsp	10 g	
Soy sauce	2 fl oz	59 ml	
Hot water to thin	2 fl oz	59 ml	

NUTRITIONAL INFORMATION PER SERVING: 270 Calories; 19 g Fat (59.9% calories from fat); 10 g Protein; 19 g Carbohydrate; 3 g Dietary Fiber; 1 mg Cholesterol; 281 mg Sodium. Exchanges: 1/2 Grain (Starch); 1 Lean Meat; 0 Vegetable; 0 Fruit; 0 Nonfat Milk; 3 Fat; 1/2 Other Carbohydrates.

This Turkish cucumber walnut sauce is thickened with nuts rather than flour, which is typical for sauces from Eastern Mediterranean countries.

Turkish cucumber sauce *Yield: 1 qt (946 ml)*
32 each 1 oz (30 ml) servings

Ingredients	Amounts U.S.	Metric	Procedure
Cucumbers, fresh	3 lbs	1.36 kg	Peel the cucumbers, split lengthwise, remove the seeds with a tablespoon. Grate or chop fine.
Salt	1 tbsp	15 g	Add salt and refrigerate. Drain off all the cucumber juice and discard.
Lemon juice	1 tbsp	15 ml	Add all the other ingredients and blend by hand.
Garlic, chopped	1 tsp	5 g	
Green peppers, seeded and chopped	8 oz	227 g	
Walnuts, chopped fine	8 oz	227 g	
Pepper	1 tsp	5 g	
Mint, fresh, chopped	2 tbsp	30 g	

NUTRITIONAL INFORMATION PER SERVING: 161 Calories; 13 g Fat (67.0% calories from fat); 7 g Protein; 8 g Carbohydrate; 3 g Dietary Fiber; 0 mg Cholesterol; 643 mg Sodium. Exchanges: 0 Grain (Starch); 1/2 Lean Meat; 1 Vegetable; 0 Fruit; 2 Fat.

Cranberry sauce is a standard for holiday buffets that feature roasted turkey. From scratch, this sauce is a real treat.

cranberry sauce   *Yield: 1 qt (946 ml) 32 each 1 oz (30 ml) servings*

Ingredients	Amounts		Procedure
	U.S.	Metric	
Cranberries, fresh	12 oz	340 g	Combine all the ingredients and bring to a boil. Simmer for 10 minutes. Skim and cool.
Sugar	12 oz	340 g	
Water	8 fl oz	237 ml	
Cinnamon stick	1 each	1 each	

NUTRITIONAL INFORMATION PER SERVING: 99 Calories; trace Fat (0.6% calories from fat); trace Protein; 26 g Carbohydrate; 1 g Dietary Fiber; 0 mg Cholesterol; 1 mg Sodium. Exchanges: 0 Grain (Starch); 0 Fruit; 0 Fat; 1 1/2 Other Carbohydrates.

Oranges provide a unique twist to traditional cranberry sauce.

cold orange cranberry sauce   *Yield: 1 qt (946 ml) Approximately*
20 each 1 1/2 fl oz (0.045 ml) servings

Ingredients	Amounts		Procedure
	U.S.	Metric	
Oranges, whole	2 lbs	907 g	Peel the oranges. Cut them in half and remove as many seeds as possible.
Cranberries, fresh	1 lb	454 g	Wash and drain the cranberries. Grind the oranges and cranberries through a medium-fine plate of a meat grinder.
Lemon rind, grated	1 tbsp	15 g	Mix in the lemon peel, spices, and sugar. Store in the refrigerator for a minimum of 1 week prior to service, to marry the ingredients. More sugar might be needed according to taste preference.
Allspice, ground	1 tsp	5 g	
Sugar	12 oz	340 g	

NUTRITIONAL INFORMATION PER SERVING: 93 Calories; trace Fat (0.8% calories from fat); trace Protein; 24 g Carbohydrate; 2 g Dietary Fiber; 0 mg Cholesterol; trace Sodium. Exchanges: 0 Grain (Starch); 1/2 Fruit; 0 Fat; 1 Other Carbohydrates.

>> Gastriques

Gastriques come from France. They are composed mainly of brown or granulated sugar and an acidic, water-based liquid such as wine or fruit juice. Gastriques are cooked down to a syrup and are used for garnishing plates and as secondary sauces. They complement and contrast with both color and flavors and can liven up an unexciting plate of food. Unlike many other French sauces, gastriques do not contain fat. They are thickened just by the reduction of liquid.

Gastriques typically work well when paired with most types of rich or fatty meats. Their acidic nature helps to cut the richness of the dish and balance out the flavors, and they add a nice contrast to the taste. Use this blackberry version with foie gras such as the Pan-Seared Foie Gras with Pears and Port recipe found in Unit 8.

blackberry gastrique *Yield: 1 qt (946 ml) 32 each 1 oz (30 ml) servings*

Ingredients	Amounts U.S.	Metric	Procedure
Red wine	8 fl oz	237 ml	Mix all the ingredients in a saucepan and bring to a boil.
Blackberries, fresh, mashed to liquid	16 fl oz	473 ml	
Balsamic vinegar	4 fl oz	118 ml	
Sugar	4 oz	113 g	

Cook 5 minutes on low heat. Crush the berries. Strain the mixture through chinoise (strainer). Return to the pan and reduce to a syrup consistency.

NUTRITIONAL INFORMATION PER SERVING: 24 Calories; trace Fat (1.5% calories from fat); trace Protein; 5 g Carbohydrate; trace Dietary Fiber; 0 mg Cholesterol; 5 mg Sodium. Exchanges: 0 Fruit; 0 Other Carbohydrates.

Citrus fruits also make nice gastriques. Here is a recipe for a lemon version to be used as a garnish for a smoked salmon salad, or any application where a little touch of flavor is needed.

lemon gastrique *Yield: 22 fl oz (638 ml) 22 each 1 oz (30 ml) servings*

Ingredients	Amounts		Procedure
	U.S.	Metric	
Lemon juice	4 fl oz	116 ml	Squeeze lemon.
Champagne vinegar	8 fl oz	232 ml	
Sugar	8 oz	224 g	

In a nonreactive stainless steel pot, place the lemon juice, vinegar, and sugar. Cook over low heat to melt the sugar, then raise the heat to medium and reduce it to a syrup. This will take approximately 10 to 15 minutes. The gastrique is ready when it coats the back of a spoon.

Lemon zest	2 tsp	10 g	Add the lemon zest.

NUTRITIONAL INFORMATION PER SERVING: 43 Calories; trace Fat (0.0% calories from fat); trace Protein; 11 g Carbohydrate; trace Dietary Fiber; 0 mg Cholesterol; trace Sodium. Exchanges: 0 Fruit; 1/2 Other Carbohydrates.

This sauce is easy to make and is suitable for serving with batter-fried shrimp. This sauce was created by the late Albert Stöckli, the corporate chef for Restaurant Associates in New York City.

dipping sauce for fried shrimp   *Yield: 1 qt (946 ml) Approximately*
10 each 3 fl oz (0.09 l) servings

Ingredients	Amounts		Procedure
	U.S.	Metric	
Orange marmalade	14 fl oz	414 ml	Grind all the ingredients through the coarse blade of a meat grinder. Dilute with warm water, if necessary, to adjust the consistency.
Mango chutney	14 fl oz	414 ml	
Horseradish, grated, preserved	6 fl oz	177 ml	
Ginger, powder	1 tsp	5 g	
Tabasco® sauce	1 tsp	5 ml	

NUTRITIONAL INFORMATION PER SERVING: 256 Calories; trace Fat (0.7% calories from fat); trace Protein; 67 g Carbohydrate; 4 g Dietary Fiber; 0 mg Cholesterol; 65 mg Sodium. Exchanges: 0 Grain (Starch); 0 Vegetable; 2 Fruit; 0 Fat; 2 1/2 Other Carbohydrates.

Try serving this creamy horseradish sauce with smoked trout as discussed in Unit 8.

horseradish cream sauce   *Yield: 16 fl oz (480 ml) Approximately*
8 each 2 oz servings

Ingredients	Amounts		Procedure
	U.S.	Metric	
Heavy cream, 36%	8 fl oz	237 ml	Whip the cream until stiff.
Apple, Granny Smith, grated	4 fl oz	118 ml	Add all the other ingredients to the whipped cream and whisk. Note: This sauce will not keep well and should be made in small quantities.
Horseradish, grated	4 fl oz	118 ml	
Lemon juice and zest	1 medium	1 medium	
White pepper, ground	1 tsp	5 g	
Sugar	Dash	Dash	

NUTRITIONAL INFORMATION PER SERVING: 117 Calories; 11 g Fat (81.4% calories from fat); 1 g Protein; 5 g Carbohydrate; 1 g Dietary Fiber; 41 mg Cholesterol; 29 mg Sodium. Exchanges: 0 Grain (Starch); 0 Fruit; 0 Nonfat Milk; 2 Fat; 0 Other Carbohydrates.

>> Dips

Dips are thick condiments created to enhance raw vegetables, crackers, chips, and appetizers (Figure 15-2). Traditionally, dips are made with a sour cream, mayonnaise, or cream cheese base that is coupled with herbs and spices. In most professional kitchens, dips are prepared and served from the pantry.

Figure 15-2 Dips are used to accompany vegetables, fruits, crackers, and snack foods.

Guacamole comes from the Aztec Indian word *ahuacatl*, from which the word *avocado* is derived. More avocados are sold in the United States around Super Bowl Sunday than at any other time of the year. Most of those avocados make their way into the popular dip called *guacamole*. Guacamole is made to order in fine Mexican restaurants. Using perfectly ripe avocados is essential to producing a high-quality guacamole dip. The heat level depends on the amount of peppers that are used.

This recipe uses fresh chili peppers, which can cause discomfort to the skin. Wear gloves when handling peppers and avoid contact with your eyes until the gloves are removed. Any pepper residue can cause burning. To enhance the flavor of the tomatoes and chilies, fire-roast them under the broiler until the skin blackens. Once cooled, the skin of the tomatoes and peppers can be easily removed.

guacamole   *Yield: 1 qt (946 ml) Approximately 10 each 3 fl oz (0.09 l) servings*

Ingredients	Amounts		Procedure
	U.S.	Metric	
Avocados	3 each, approx. 1 1/2 lbs	3 each, approx. 680 g	Halve the avocados, scoop out the flesh, and dispose of the seed and skin. Immediately add the lemon juice to avoid discoloration.
Lemon juice	1 1/2 tbsp	22 ml	
Onions, chopped	1 1/2 oz	45 g	Add all the ingredients and blend by hand. Guacamole should be chunky. Serve at once.
Tomatoes, peeled, seeded	6 oz	170 g	
Serrano chili peppers, chopped	To taste	To taste	
Cilantro, fresh, chopped	2 tbsp	30 g	
Salt	To taste	To taste	

NUTRITIONAL INFORMATION PER SERVING: 102 Calories; 9 g Fat (74.9% calories from fat); 1 g Protein; 6 g Carbohydrate; 2 g Dietary Fiber; 0 mg Cholesterol; 35 mg Sodium. Exchanges: 0 Grain (Starch); 0 Lean Meat; 0 Vegetable; 1/2 Fruit; 2 Fat.

Cheese dip has many uses. It's great with crackers or chips as well as a delicious topping on baked potatoes. Some restaurants use a dollop on hamburgers or as a topper for raw or cooked vegetables.

cheese dip
Yield: 1 qt (946 ml) Approximately 10 each 3 fl oz (0.09 l) servings

Ingredients	Amounts		Procedure
	U.S.	Metric	
Cheddar cheese, aged, grated	1 lb	454 g	Combine all the ingredients except the chives in a blender until smooth.
Roquefort or other blue cheese	4 oz	113 g	
Cream cheese	4 oz	113 g	
Cottage cheese	10 oz	284 g	
Butter	3 oz	85 g	
Tabasco sauce	1 tbsp	15 ml	
Salt	To taste	To taste	
Pepper	To taste	To taste	
Chives, chopped	2 oz	57 g	Stir in the chives.

NUTRITIONAL INFORMATION PER SERVING: 350 Calories; 30 g Fat (76.2% calories from fat); 19 g Protein; 2 g Carbohydrate; trace Dietary Fiber; 90 mg Cholesterol; 692 mg Sodium. Exchanges: 0 Grain (Starch); 2 1/2 Lean Meat; 0 Vegetable; 4 1/2 Fat.

The next popular dip can be thickened with boiled potatoes or white bread. Bread is preferred. Do not add salt because the roe is salty. The amounts indicated are approximate because the moisture content of the Tarama (roe) varies. If the dip is too salty or too loose, add some white bread, briefly soaked in water and squeezed.

taramasalata (Greek carp roe dip) *Yield: 1 qt (946 ml)*
Approximately 10 each 3 fl oz (0.09 l) servings

Ingredients	Amounts		Procedure
	U.S.	Metric	
Tarama (roe)	10 oz	284 g	Combine the Tarama, bread, and water in a blender until smooth.
White bread	16 slices	16 slices	
Water, cold	6 fl oz	177 ml	

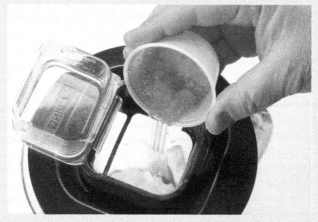

Onions, chopped	2 tbsp	30 g	Add the onions, garlic, and lemon juice to the above mixture and blend.
Garlic, chopped	2 tsp	10 g	
Lemon juice	2 fl oz	59 ml	
Olive oil	16 fl oz	473 ml	Add the oil in a steady stream until incorporated.

NUTRITIONAL INFORMATION PER RECIPE: 531 Calories; 46 g Fat (77.3% calories from fat); 10 g Protein; 21 g Carbohydrate; 1 g Dietary Fiber; 106 mg Cholesterol; 242 mg Sodium. Exchanges: 1 1/2 Grain (Starch); 1 Lean Meat; 0 Vegetable; 0 Fruit; 9 Fat.

Cooking vegetables in olive oil is basic in Turkish cooking. The original recipe for Imambayildi calls for scorching the eggplant skin over an open fire to remove and to embed a smoky flavor. Removing the seeds is optional—if desired, remove the seeds with a spoon after the eggplant is split in half. Some recipes call for chopped tomatoes. This recipe is similar to the popular Baba Ganoosh.

Imambayildi—the delight of Imam (Turkish eggplant dip)
Yield: 1 qt (0.94 l) Approximately 10 each 3 fl oz (0.09 l) servings

Ingredients	Amounts U.S.	Metric	Procedure
Eggplants, medium sized	About 4 lbs	1.8 kg	Use a fork to puncture the eggplants and rub them with oil.
Olive oil	8 fl oz	237 ml	

Put each eggplant in a roasting pan and set the oven to broil. Place each eggplant directly underneath. Cook until the skins start to blister. Turn each eggplant over slightly until the skin is charred evenly. Carefully remove them from the oven and put each eggplant in a large bowl with cold water. When cooled, remove them from the water and take off as much of the charred skin as possible. Be careful, as the eggplant might still be steaming hot inside. Put each eggplant on a cutting board, split it horizontally, and remove the seeds. |
Onions, chopped	4 oz	113 g	Sauté the onions and garlic in oil. Add the and the tahini and lemon juice to the cooked and peeled eggplant pulp and mash together.
Garlic, chopped	2 tbsp	30 g	
Tahini (sesame paste)	8 fl oz	237 ml	
Lemon juice	2 fl oz	59 ml	
Salt	To taste	To taste	Season to taste.
Pepper	To taste	To taste	
Black olives, pitted, sliced	4 oz	227 g	Sprinkle the olives on top for garnish

NUTRITIONAL INFORMATION PER SERVING: 395 Calories; 36 g Fat (78.3% calories from fat); 6 g Protein; 17 g Carbohydrate; 7 g Dietary Fiber; 0 mg Cholesterol; 177 mg Sodium. Exchanges: 1/2 Grain (Starch); 1/2 Lean Meat; 2 Vegetable; 0 Fruit; 7 Fat.

This is another popular dip made with eggplant pulp; the eggplants should be peeled by fire because the smoky taste is expected. When no open flame is available, the eggplants can be put under the broiler until the skin is black or just peeled and baked, although the smoky flavor won't be as pronounced as in those cooked over an open flame.

batinjaan imfasak (Turkish eggplant yogurt dip)
Yield: 1 qt (946 ml) 32 each 1 oz (30 ml) servings

Ingredients	Amounts		Procedure
	U.S.	Metric	
Eggplant, small	2 lbs	907 g	Spear the eggplants on a kitchen fork and hold them over a flame, turning until the skin is black. Plunge the eggplants into cold water. Slice in two and scoop out the flesh. Eggplants should be soft and mushy at this point. If not soft, bake the peeled eggplant in a 350°F (175°C) oven until mushy. Tiny black specks are acceptable.

Yogurt	8 fl oz	237 ml	Combine the eggplant with all the other ingredients and blend in a blender.
Olive oil	8 fl oz	237 ml	
Lemon juice	2 tbsp	30 ml	
Tomatoes, peeled and seeded	6 oz	170 g	
Onions, chopped	2 tbsp	30 g	
Pepper	1 tsp	5 g	
Salt	To taste	To taste	

NUTRITIONAL INFORMATION PER SERVING: 231 Calories; 23 g Fat (85.2% calories from fat); 2 g Protein; 7 g Carbohydrate; 2 g Dietary Fiber; 3 mg Cholesterol; 42 mg Sodium. Exchanges: 0 Grain (Starch); 1 Vegetable; 0 Fruit; 0 Nonfat Milk; 4 1/2 Fat; 0 Other Carbohydrates.

This dip is popular throughout the Mediterranean countries and is fast becoming an American favorite as well. Serve this dip with pita, crackers, or chips. It can be garnished with black marinated olives, if desired.

hummus (chickpea dip) *Yield: 1 qt (946 ml) Approximately 10 each 3 fl oz (89 ml) servings*

Ingredients	Amounts		Procedure
	U.S.	Metric	
Chickpeas, cooked (canned and drained will do)	1 1/2 lbs	680 g	Combine all the ingredients and blend in a blender until smooth.
Tahini paste	6 fl oz	177 ml	
Garlic, chopped	1 1/2 tsp	7 g	
Lemon juice	1 fl oz	30 ml	
Lemon peel, zest	1 tsp	5 g	
Cayenne pepper	1/2 tsp	2 g	
Salt	To taste	To taste	
Parsley, chopped	2 tbsp	30 g	Sprinkle parsley over the mixture.

NUTRITIONAL INFORMATION PER SERVING: 255 Calories; 9 g Fat (32.1% calories from fat); 12 g Protein; 33 g Carbohydrate; 10 g Dietary Fiber; 0 mg Cholesterol; 53 mg Sodium. Exchanges: 2 Grain (Starch); 1/2 Lean Meat; 0 Vegetable; 0 Fruit; 1 1/2 Fat.

This dip is very easy to make. It can be served as is, or baked until bubbly and served warm with crackers or chips for a delicious appetizer. Bake at 350°F (175°C) for 10 minutes.

artichoke dip   *Yield: 1 qt (946 ml) Approximately 10 each 3 fl oz (90 ml) servings*

Ingredients	Amounts		Procedure
	U.S.	Metric	
Artichokes, small, whole, canned	24 oz	680 g	Drain the artichokes and combine them with all the other ingredients. Blend in a blender until smooth.
Mayonnaise	12 fl oz	355 ml	
Pepper, freshly ground	1 tsp	5 g	
Salt	To taste	To taste	
Lemon juice	1 tbsp	15 ml	
Parmesan, Romano, Asiago cheese or a blend	8 oz	227 g	
Green onions, minced	2 oz	57 g	

NUTRITIONAL INFORMATION PER SERVING: 354 Calories; 35 g Fat (84.1% calories from fat); 11 g Protein; 4 g Carbohydrate; 2 g Dietary Fiber; 29 mg Cholesterol; 662 mg Sodium. Exchanges: 0 Grain (Starch); 1 1/2 Lean Meat; 1/2 Vegetable; 0 Fruit; 3 Fat.

This dip features Tahini paste, an oily substance resembling peanut butter but made with lightly toasted sesame seeds. This dip is best when served with pita bread.

Egyptian mazza *Yield: 1 qt (946 ml) 32 each 1 oz (30 ml) servings*

Ingredients	Amounts		Procedure
	U.S.	Metric	
Tahini paste	20 fl oz	592 ml	Combine all the ingredients and blend in a blender until smooth.
Garlic, chopped	2 oz	57 g	
Lemon juice	1 fl oz	30 ml	
Olive oil	4 fl oz	118 ml	
Water, warm	8 fl oz	237 ml	
Cumin, ground	2 tsp	10 g	
Salt	To taste	To taste	

NUTRITIONAL INFORMATION PER SERVING: 460 Calories; 43 g Fat (79.7% calories from fat); 10 g Protein; 14 g Carbohydrate; 6 g Dietary Fiber; 0 mg Cholesterol; 98 mg Sodium. Exchanges: 1 Grain (Starch); 1 Lean Meat; 0 Vegetable; 0 Fruit; 8 Fat.

This cheese dip was originally made with sheep's milk cheese. Fine curd cottage cheese can be substituted. It is a well-known dip or spread in beer gardens in Austria and Hungary. Don't compromise by using just any paprika—it is important to use only genuine Hungarian paprika.

Hungarian liptó cheese dip (liptauer)   *Yield: 1 qt (946 ml)*
32 each 1 oz (30 ml) servings

Ingredients	Amounts U.S.	Metric	Procedure
Soft sheep's milk cheese or cottage cheese, fine curd	1 1/2 lbs	680 g	Combine all the ingredients and blend in a blender until smooth. Chill and store refrigerated.
Butter, salted	8 oz	227 g	
Hungarian paprika, sharp	1 tbsp	15 g	
Mustard, prepared	2 tsp	10 g	
Onions, chopped	2 oz	57 g	
Caraway seeds, chopped	1 tsp	5 g	
Chives, cut	1 oz	28 g	

NUTRITIONAL INFORMATION PER SERVING: 477 Calories; 43 g Fat (80.0% calories from fat); 21 g Protein; 3 g Carbohydrate; trace Dietary Fiber; 121 mg Cholesterol; 436 mg Sodium. Exchanges: 0 Grain (Starch); 3 Lean Meat; 0 Vegetable; 7 Fat; 0 Other Carbohydrates.

Chilled clam dip is delicious with chips, crackers, or as a vegetable dipper. This clam dip is made with a panada of white bread as a thickener.

clam dip *Yield: 16 fl oz (473 ml) 16 each 1 oz (30 ml) servings*

Ingredients	Amounts		Procedure
	U.S.	Metric	
Clams, canned, chopped, not drained	12 oz	340 g	Combine all the ingredients in a food processor. Process until smooth. Add more bread if it's too runny.
White bread, crust removed	8 slices	8 slices	
Olive oil	1 tbsp	15 ml	
Mayonnaise	2 fl oz	59 ml	
Oregano, fresh, chopped	2 tsp	10 g	
Lemon peel, grated	1 tsp	5 g	
Salt	To taste	To taste	
Pepper	To taste	To taste	

NUTRITIONAL INFORMATION PER SERVING: 98 Calories; 5 g Fat (42.9% calories from fat); 7 g Protein; 7 g Carbohydrate; trace Dietary Fiber; 16 mg Cholesterol; 127 mg Sodium. Exchanges: 1/2 Grain (Starch); 1 Lean Meat; 0 Fruit; 1/2 Fat; 0 Other Carbohydrates.

Tapenade comes from southern France and can be considered a condiment, a relish, or a spread on toasted bread as an appetizer. It is also used on grilled fish. The blend will resemble a thick, black mayonnaise and will be pungent.

tapenade   *Yield: 16 fl oz (473 ml) 16 each 1 oz (30 ml) servings*

Ingredients	Amounts		Procedure
	U.S.	Metric	
Black Niçoise olives	4 oz	113 g	Remove the pits from the olives. You will end up with about 3/4 cup.
Anchovy fillets, drained	10 each	10 each	Purée all the ingredients in a food processor. Store covered with a thin layer of olive oil to seal out the air. Refrigerate.
Capers	1 oz	30 g	
Tuna fish, canned, drained	4 oz	113 g	
Olive oil	4 fl oz	118 ml	
Lemon juice	1 fl oz	30 ml	
Mustard	1 fl oz	30 ml	

NUTRITIONAL INFORMATION PER SERVING: 174 Calories; 16 g Fat (82.6% calories from fat); 6 g Protein; 2 g Carbohydrate; 1 g Dietary Fiber; 9 mg Cholesterol; 563 mg Sodium. Exchanges: 1/2 Lean Meat; 0 Fruit; 3 Fat; 0 Other Carbohydrates.

This very aromatic spread is flavored with berbere, a spice mixture from North Africa. The spice is hot and should be used with caution. The spread is often served in North African restaurants as an appetizer and with bread.

lentil dip   *Yield: 1 qt (946 ml) Approximately 10 each 3 fl oz (90 ml) servings*

Ingredients	Amounts		Procedure
	U.S.	Metric	
Lentils, green or yellow	1 lb	454 g	Cover the lentils with about the same volume of water. Add the onions and garlic. Simmer until the lentils are very soft. Check the liquid periodically, as the lentils should be just covered.
Onions, peeled, quartered	8 oz	227 g	
Garlic, chopped	1 tbsp	15 g	
Tomato paste	1 fl oz	30 ml	Add the remaining ingredients and process to a purée. Store refrigerated and serve at room temperature.
Pimento, canned, drained	4 oz	227 g	
Berbere seasoning (see next recipe)	1 tsp or to taste	1 tsp or to taste	
Sun-dried tomatoes in oil	2 oz	57 g	
Paprika	1 tsp	5 g	
Salt	To taste	To taste	
Olive oil	2 fl oz	59 ml	

NUTRITIONAL INFORMATION PER SERVING: 121 Calories; 6 g Fat (43.2% calories from fat); 5 g Protein; 13 g Carbohydrate; 4 g Dietary Fiber; 0 mg Cholesterol; 89 mg Sodium. Exchanges: 1/2 Grain (Starch); 1/2 Lean Meat; 1/2 Vegetable; 1 Fat.

Berbere is a hot pepper seasoning mix that was originally created in Ethiopia where it is used, first and foremost, to flavor stews.

basic berbere seasoning mix *Yield: Approximately 5 oz (141 g)*

Ingredients	Amounts		Procedure
	U.S.	Metric	
Cloves	1/4 tsp	1 g	Toast the whole cloves, cardamom, coriander, allspice, fenugreek, cinnamon, and nutmeg in a saucepan over low heat for 2–4 minutes. Shake the pan to prevent the spices from burning.
Cardamom	1/4 tsp	1 g	
Coriander	1/2 tsp	2 g	
Allspice	1/4 tsp	1 g	
Fenugreek	1/2 tsp	2 g	
Cinnamon	1/2 tsp	2 g	
Nutmeg	1/2 tsp	2 g	
Paprika	2 oz	57 g	Add the remaining ingredients and continue to toast for 2 more minutes. The blend should be cooled and ground and then put in a tight container and stored.
Cayenne pepper	1 oz	28 g	
Salt	1 oz	28 g	
Pepper, freshly ground	1 tsp	5 g	

NUTRITIONAL INFORMATION PER SERVING: 252 Calories; 12 g Fat (30.6% calories from fat); 11 g Protein; 48 g Carbohydrate; 20 g Dietary Fiber; 0 mg Cholesterol; 2820 mg Sodium. Exchanges: 3 Grain (Starch); 1/2 Lean Meat; 0 Vegetable; 2 Fat.

>> Aioli

Aioli is a garlic mayonnaise that is used as a condiment or sauce. Traditionally, it was made in a mortar and pestle and consisted of raw garlic, cooked waxy potatoes, a touch of Dijon mustard, and extra virgin olive oil. It was used primarily with boiled vegetables. Aioli originated in Provence, a subtropical area in southern France between the Rhône River and Italy. It was traditionally served with boiled fish.

Today's young chefs have discovered aioli and given it a place on American menus for a number of different uses. Today, it is made mostly with mashed garlic, egg yolk, and oil. It is used as a cold sauce for vegetables, fish or seafood, rotisserie chicken, or as a condiment or dip for fresh vegetables (Figure 15-3).

Figure 15-3 Roast red pepper aioli, roast garlic aioli, and chili lime aioli prove that aioli has come a long way from the basic garlic condiment.

This basic aioli recipe is loaded with garlic.

basic aioli *Yield: 1 pint (473 ml) 32 each 1 tbsp servings*

Ingredients	Amounts		Procedure
	U.S.	Metric	
Garlic cloves, peeled	8 each	8 each	Purée the garlic with salt in a food processor until it becomes a very fine paste.
Salt	2 tsp	10 g	
Egg yolks, pasteurized	4 fl oz	118 ml	Add the egg yolks and pulse briefly.
Olive oil, good quality	12 fl oz	355 ml	Add the oil slowly and allow the mixture to thicken to the consistency of mayonnaise. If the mixture gets too thick, add a few drops of warm water. Store refrigerated in a covered container.

NUTRITIONAL INFORMATION PER SERVING: 36 Calories; 3 g Fat (84.8% calories from fat); 1 g Protein; trace Carbohydrate; trace Dietary Fiber; 1 mg Cholesterol; 176 mg Sodium. Exchanges: 0 Lean Meat; 0 Vegetable; 0 Fruit; 1/2 Fat; 0 Other Carbohydrates.

Many chefs will flavor aioli with extra touches of fresh herbs, such as basil or cilantro, or use fire-roasted bell pepper purée. The next aioli recipe features wasabi, the Japanese name for horseradish. The plant is difficult to grow and expensive. Most restaurants use wasabi powder, which is actually a blend of horseradish, a touch of true wasabi, and green food coloring. The powder is blended with cold water to make a pungent green paste. Wasabi paste is a basic component of Japanese sushi and sashimi plates. Serve this sauce with the Tuna Carpaccio recipe found in Unit 8.

wasabi aioli sauce   *Yield: 9 fl oz (270 ml) 16 servings (heaping tablespoon)*

Ingredients	Amounts		Procedure
	U.S.	Metric	
Wasabi powder	1 tbsp	15 g	Blend the wasabi powder with the cold water to make a smooth paste.
Water, cold	1 fl oz	30 ml	

Ingredients	Amounts		Procedure
Egg yolks	2 each	2 each	Put the egg, garlic, and wasabi paste in a small food processor or blender and process until well blended.
Garlic, minced	1/2 clove	1/2 clove	
Salad oil	8 fl oz	237 ml	Slowly drizzle in the salad oil until the mixture thickens.
Salt	To taste	To taste	Season with salt and pepper.
Black pepper	To taste	To taste	

NUTRITIONAL INFORMATION PER SERVING: 128 Calories; 14 g Fat (98.5% calories from fat); trace Protein; trace Carbohydrate; trace Dietary Fiber; 27 mg Cholesterol; 18 mg Sodium. Exchanges: 0 Grain (Starch); 0 Lean Meat; 0 Vegetable; 3 Fat.

The following Lime Chipotle Aioli recipe is a key ingredient in the Grilled Salmon with Lime Chipotle Aioli Sandwich recipe found in Unit 9.

lime chipotle aioli *Yield: 9 fl oz (270 ml) 16 servings (heaping tablespoon)*

Ingredients	Amounts		Procedure
	U.S.	Metric	
Mayonnaise	8 fl oz	236 ml	Mix all the ingredients together to meld the flavors.
Lime zest	1 tsp	5 g	
Chipotle chili, minced fine	1 small	1 small	
Cilantro leaves	1 tbsp	15 g	
Lime juice	1 fl oz	30 ml	
Yellow onion, grated	1 oz	28 g	

NUTRITIONAL INFORMATION PER SERVING: 103 Calories; 12 g Fat (98.0% calories from fat); trace Protein; trace Carbohydrate; trace Dietary Fiber; 5 mg Cholesterol; 81 mg Sodium. Exchanges: 0 Vegetable; 0 Fruit; 1 Fat.

The fire-roasted peppers add a smoky and zesty component to this versatile dip.

roasted red pepper aioli dip   *Yield: 1 qt (946 ml) 32 each*
1 oz (30 ml) servings

Ingredients	Amounts		Procedure
	U.S.	Metric	
Garlic, mashed to purée	6 cloves	6 cloves	Mash the garlic and sauté in olive oil until soft and slightly colored. Remove from heat.
Olive oil	1 fl oz	30 ml	
Egg yolks	3 each	3 each	In a food processor, add the sautéed garlic, egg yolks, sherry vinegar, and salt.
Sherry vinegar	1 fl oz	30 ml	
Kosher salt	2 tsp	10 g	Start to blend. While the food processor is running, slowly add the canola oil in a steady stream.
Canola oil	12 fl oz	355 ml	
Extra virgin olive oil	6 fl oz	177 ml	When the mixture is emulsified, remove from the processor and place in a steel bowl.
Red bell peppers, fire roasted	2 each	2 each	Fire roast the peppers; cover and steam. When cooled, peel and seed. Mince fine. Whisk in the remaining olive oil. Add the peppers to the mixture above. Adjust the seasonings. Serve with Squash Blossom Fritters or as a dip with crudite.
Cayenne pepper	1/2 tsp	2 g	

NUTRITIONAL INFORMATION PER SERVING: 157 Calories; 17 g Fat (97.2% calories from fat); trace Protein; 1 g Carbohydrate; trace Dietary Fiber; 20 mg Cholesterol; 118 mg Sodium. Exchanges: 0 Grain (Starch); 0 Lean Meat; 0 Vegetable; 3 1/2 Fat; 0 Other Carbohydrates.

>> Salsa

Salsa is the Spanish term for "sauce"; technically, any sauce is a salsa. The methods of making sauces and soups with uncooked vegetables came from the Arabs to Spain and eventually to the New World. The term *salsa* is generally used to describe the Mexican-type cold sauce, made of tomatoes, chilies, and spices (Figure 15-4). However, it can be used for vegetable or fruit dips that are made without a binding agent and produce a loose and chunky product. Salsa also is a Latin American dance.

Figure 15-4 Typical Mexican salsa made with fresh tomatoes, chilies, and spices.

This salsa is a daily staple in most Mexican households. The amounts change according to taste. Use gloves when handling the chili peppers. Salsas tend to thicken when stored overnight. If that happens, simply dilute with a little cold water.

traditional tomato salsa   *Yield: 1 qt (946 ml) 16 each 2 oz (59 ml) servings*

Ingredients	Amounts		Procedure
	U.S.	Metric	
Red ripe tomatoes, coarsely chopped	2 lbs	907 g	Combine all the ingredients.
Yellow onion, chopped	4 oz	113 g	
Serrano chilies, seeds removed, chopped (or a blend of Serrano, Poblano, or Jalapeno chilies)	6 each, medium	6 each, medium	
Cilantro, fresh, chopped	2 tbsp	30 g	
Red wine vinegar	4 fl oz	118 ml	
Olive oil	2 fl oz	59 ml	
Salt	To taste	To taste	

NUTRITIONAL INFORMATION PER SERVING: 75 Calories; 6 g Fat (63.6% calories from fat); 1 g Protein; 6 g Carbohydrate; 1 g Dietary Fiber; 0 mg Cholesterol; 36 mg Sodium. Exchanges: 0 Grain (Starch); 0 Lean Meat; 1 Vegetable; 1 Fat; 0 Other Carbohydrates.

This salsa provides a colorful and flavorful condiment. It can be used as a refreshing side salad or to top a variety of grilled fish or meats such as halibut or chicken.

salsa de naranja *Yield: 1 qt (946 ml) 32 each 1 oz (30 ml) servings*

Ingredients	Amounts U.S.	Metric	Procedure
Orange sections, chopped	12 fl oz	354 ml	Coarsely chop the orange sections.
Red ripe tomatoes, chopped	6 oz	170 g	Mix with chopped tomatoes.
Red onions, chopped	6 oz	170 g	Combine with all the other ingredients.
Red wine vinegar	2 fl oz	55 ml	
Orange juice	4 fl oz	110 ml	
Orange zest	1 tbsp	15 g	
Jalapeno chilies, chopped	3 tsp	15 g	
Salt	To taste	To taste	
Pepper	To taste	To taste	

NUTRITIONAL INFORMATION PER SERVING: 27 Calories; trace Fat (3.7% calories from fat); 1 g Protein; 7 g Carbohydrate; 1 g Dietary Fiber; 0 mg Cholesterol; 28 mg Sodium. Exchanges: 0 Grain (Starch); 1/2 Vegetable; 1/2 Fruit; 0 Fat; 0 Other Carbohydrates.

This green salsa is bright and fresh and works well with most Mexican dishes or as a topper for scrambled eggs. As we've mentioned before, always wear gloves when chopping fresh chilies. To add a smoky flavor, put the tomatillos and chilies under a broiler to blister before chopping.

salsa verde or salsa cruda   *Yield: 1 qt (946 ml) 32 each*
1 oz (30 ml) servings

Ingredients	Amounts		Procedure
	U.S.	Metric	
Green tomatillos	2 lbs	907 g	Remove the papery husk and wash the tomatillos. Blister either by direct burner heat or under a salamander. Cut into halves and place in a blender. Pulse in the blender; don't purée. It should be coarse.
Serrano or Poblano chilies, chopped	4 each	4 each	Combine with all the other ingredients.
Onions, chopped	8 oz	227 g	
Garlic cloves, chopped	4 each	4 each	
Cilantro, fresh, chopped	2 tbsp	30 g	
Lime juice	4 fl oz	118 ml	
Sugar	1 tsp	5 g	
Salt	To taste	To taste	
Water, cold	4 fl oz	118 ml	

NUTRITIONAL INFORMATION PER SERVING: 14 Calories; trace Fat (17.1% calories from fat); trace Protein; 3 g Carbohydrate; 1 g Dietary Fiber; 0 mg Cholesterol; 9 mg Sodium. Exchanges: 0 Grain (Starch); 0 Lean Meat; 1/2 Vegetable; 0 Fruit; 0 Fat; 0 Other Carbohydrates.

This salsa is very hot (spicy) and should be served with caution. Wear gloves when handling the habaneras. You may want to try using Seville orange juice in place of the lime juice.

salsa picante de yucatan
Yield: 16 fl oz (473 ml) Approximately 20 each 3/4 fl oz servings

Ingredients	Amounts U.S.	Metric	Procedure
Habanero chilies	6 oz	170 g	Split the chilies in half and remove the seeds. Coarsely chop in a blender.
Lime juice	8 fl oz	237 ml	Mix in the juice and salt.
Salt	To taste	To taste	

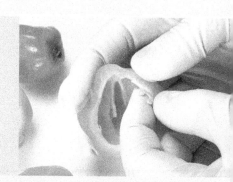

NUTRITIONAL INFORMATION PER SERVING: 6 Calories; trace Fat (2.4% calories from fat); trace Protein; 2 g Carbohydrate; trace Dietary Fiber; 0 mg Cholesterol; 14 mg Sodium. Exchanges: 0 Vegetable; 0 Fruit.

This Mexican condiment sauce or dip is known under a number of names such as Salsa Fría or Salsa Fresca. Be careful when handling the chilies.

pico de gallo
Yield: 1 qt (946 ml) 32 each 1 oz (30 ml) servings

Ingredients	Amounts U.S.	Metric	Procedure
Jalapeno chiles	4 each	6 each	Combine all the ingredients and marinate overnight in the refrigerator.
Onions, chopped fine	8 oz	227 g	
Tomatoes, seeded and chopped	16 oz	454 g	
Garlic, chopped	3 tbsp	45 g	
Cilantro, chopped	2 oz	57 g	
Olive oil	2 fl oz	59 ml	
Sherry vinegar	1 fl oz	30 ml	

NUTRITIONAL INFORMATION PER SERVING: 71 Calories; 6 g Fat (68.3% calories from fat); 1 g Protein; 5 g Carbohydrate; 1 g Dietary Fiber; 0 mg Cholesterol; 6 mg Sodium. Exchanges: 0 Grain (Starch); 0 Lean Meat; 1 Vegetable; 1 Fat; 0 Other Carbohydrates.

The chilies, sweet smoked paprika, and chipotle powder give this avocado salsa its unique, smoky flavor. The avocados are diced, not mashed, making it a salsa rather than a guacamole.

smoky avocado salsa *Yield: 1 qt (946 ml) 32 each 1 oz (30 ml) servings*

Ingredients	Amounts U.S.	Metric	Procedure
Haas avocados, peeled, pitted, and 1/4-in dice	3 medium	3 medium	In a medium nonreactive bowl, combine all the ingredients. Toss gently to maintain its chunky consistency.
Lime, juice and zest	1 large	1 large	
Tomatoes, 1/4-in dice	2 large	2 large	
Yellow onion, finely chopped	3 oz	89 g	
Garlic, minced	2 cloves	2 cloves	
Anaheim chili, seeded, 1/4-inch dice	1 each	1 each	
Cilantro, fresh, chopped	1/2 oz	15 g	
Cumin, ground	1/2 tsp	2 g	
Sweet smoked paprika	1 tsp	5 g	
Chipotle powder, dried, ground	1/4 tsp	1 g	
Salt	To taste	To taste	

NUTRITIONAL INFORMATION PER SERVING: 35 Calories; 3 g Fat (68.0% calories from fat); 1 g Protein; 3 g Carbohydrate; 1 g Dietary Fiber; 0 mg Cholesterol; 103 mg Sodium. Exchanges: 0 Grain (Starch); 0 Lean Meat; 0 Vegetable; 0 Fruit; 1/2 Fat.

COLD SAUCES, DIPS, AIOLI, SALSAS, RELISHES, AND CHUTNEYS

>> Chutney and Relish

The terms *relish* and *chutney* are almost interchangeable (Figure 15-5). Relishes have a long history going back to colonial times. Typically, **relish** is a cooked or pickled sauce of vinegar and sugar made of vegetables or fruits. Housewives historically prepared relishes to stretch their fruits and vegetables to last through the winter. The pickled vegetables became important side dishes when fresh produce was no longer available.

The best-known chutney, available in many variations in most supermarkets, is Mango Chutney. The basic recipe follows on the next page.

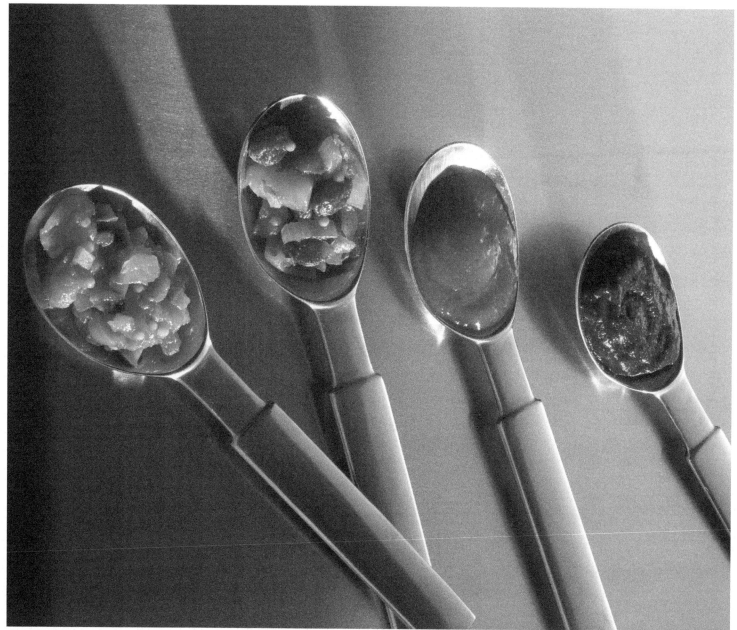

Figure 15-5 Chutney and relishes are flavorful and colorful condiments.

The cold kitchen is often responsible for the preparation and service of chutneys. The word *chutney* comes from the Sanskrit word *chatni*, meaning "to lick." In India today, the word simply means "mixture." **Chutney** can be fresh or cooked but is generally made from fruit, vinegar, sugar, and spices. It can range in texture from smooth to chunky and varies from mild to hot, depending on the recipe. Mango is often associated with chutney, but many other fruit and vegetable combinations exist. Chutney is normally a combination of sweet, sour, and pungent flavors. It entered the English language through the British when they governed India and learned to appreciate acidic and sweet accompaniments.

mango chutney *Yield: 1 qt (946 ml), 32 each 1 oz (30 ml) servings*

Ingredients	Amounts U.S.	Metric
Mangos, ripe, peeled, chopped	1 lb	454 g
Water	8 fl oz	237 ml
Brown sugar	1 lb	454 g
Vinegar	8 fl oz	237 ml
Salt	1 tsp	5 g
Cardamom, ground	1 tsp	5 g
Cayenne pepper	1/4 tsp	1 g
Cloves, ground	1/4 tsp	1 g
Cinnamon, ground	1/4 tsp	1 g
Black cumin seeds	1/4 tsp	1 g
Nutmeg, ground	1/4 tsp	1 g
Lime juice	1 tbsp	15 ml
Raisins	4 oz	113 g
Ginger, ground	1/4 tsp	1 g

Procedure

Combine all the ingredients in a noncorrosive pan such as a glass or stainless steel pan and simmer slowly together until the mixture is mushy, thick, and reduced to 1 quart. Store refrigerated.

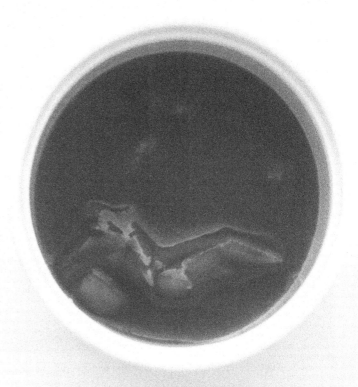

NUTRITIONAL INFORMATION PER SERVING: 110 Calories; trace Fat (0.7% calories from fat); trace Protein; 29 g Carbohydrate; 1 g Dietary Fiber; 0 mg Cholesterol; 117 mg Sodium. Exchanges: 0 Grain (Starch); 0 Lean Meat; 1/2 Fruit; 0 Fat; 1 1/2 Other Carbohydrates.

This recipe calls for grated fresh ginger. Use a ceramic grater found in Asian markets or a microplane, which is a very fine grater. The Coconut Shrimp recipe in Unit 8 goes well with this Orange Mango Chutney recipe.

orange mango chutney · Yield: 1 qt (946 ml) 32 each
1 oz (30 ml) servings

Ingredients	Amounts U.S.	Metric	Procedure
Yellow onion, chopped fine	1 medium	1 medium	Combine all the ingredients in a stainless steel pot. Simmer for 20 minutes. Serve hot or cold with coconut shrimp.
Orange, peeled and chopped, seeds removed	1 medium	1 medium	
Orange zest	1 tbsp	15 g	
Mangos, peeled and cut into bite-sized chunks	2 medium	2 medium	
Sultanas	4 oz	113 g	
Zante currants	2 oz	57 g	
Nutmeg	1/2 tsp	2 g	
Cinnamon	1 tsp	5 g	
Allspice	1/2 tsp	2 g	
Ginger, fresh, grated	1 tsp	5 g	
Curry powder	1/2 tsp	2 g	
Brown sugar	6 oz	170 g	
Orange juice	6 fl oz	177 ml	

NUTRITIONAL INFORMATION PER SERVING: 48 Calories; trace Fat (1.8% calories from fat); trace Protein; 12 g Carbohydrate; 1 g Dietary Fiber; 0 mg Cholesterol; 3 mg Sodium. Exchanges: 0 Grain (Starch); 0 Vegetable; 1/2 Fruit; 0 Fat; 1/2 Other Carbohydrates.

This chutney is a recipe from The Waldorf-Astoria Hotel in New York City. It is made with Italian plums, when in season. It freezes well.

plum chutney *Yield: 1 qt (946 ml) 32 each 1 oz (30 ml) servings*

Ingredients	Amounts		Procedure
	U.S.	Metric	
Italian plums	2 lbs	907 g	Wash the plumbs, split, and remove the pits. Set aside.
Brown sugar	6 oz	170 g	Combine the remaining ingredients in a noncorrosive bowl such as a glass or stainless steel bowl and bring to a boil. Add the pitted plums. Simmer until the plumbs are soft and the mixture is fairly thick. Stir frequently.
Cider vinegar	8 fl oz	237 ml	
Garlic, minced	1 tsp	5 g	
Ginger, fresh, grated	1 tsp	5 g	If the mixture is too thick, add a small amount of water during the cooking process. Store refrigerated.
Cayenne pepper	1/4 tsp	1 g	
Salt	1 tsp	5 g	
Pepper, coarsely ground	1/2 tsp	2 g	
Raisins	4 oz	113 g	
Lemon peel, grated	1 tsp	5 g	

NUTRITIONAL INFORMATION PER SERVING: 64 Calories; trace Fat (3.7% calories from fat); trace Protein; 16 g Carbohydrate; 1 g Dietary Fiber; 0 mg Cholesterol; 110 mg Sodium. Exchanges: 0 Grain (Starch); 0 Vegetable; 1/2 Fruit; 0 Fat; 1/2 Other Carbohydrates.

Sour cherries, sometimes called pie cherries, provide a tangy taste and colorful appearance to this simple chutney. The cherries should be marinated overnight before grinding. The vinegar will toughen the cellulose, which will help the cherries to retain their texture after grinding.

sour cherry chutney   *Yield: 1 qt (946 ml) 32 each 1 oz (30 ml) servings*

Ingredients	Amounts		Procedure
	U.S.	Metric	
Sour cherries, frozen, pitted	2 lbs	907 g	Defrost the cherries, and save the juice.
Brown sugar	8 oz	227 g	Combine the cherry juice, brown sugar, vinegar, peppercorns, water, and spices, except for the mustard. Bring the mixture to a boil. Pour the boiling hot mixture over the cherries.
Cider vinegar	8 fl oz	237 ml	
Peppercorns	1 tbsp	15 g	
Water	8 fl oz	237 ml	
Ginger, powder	1 tsp	2 g	
Allspice, whole	5 to 6 each	5 to 6 each	
Mustard, prepared	1 tbsp	15 g	Stir in the mustard. Refrigerate at least 24 hours. Stir occasionally. Grind the mixture in a food processor.

NUTRITIONAL INFORMATION PER SERVING: 69 Calories; trace Fat (3.2% calories from fat); 1 g Protein; 18 g Carbohydrate; 1 g Dietary Fiber; 0 mg Cholesterol; 19 mg Sodium. Exchanges: 0 Grain (Starch); 0 Lean Meat; 1/2 Fruit; 0 Fat; 1 Other Carbohydrates.

The Amish belong to the religious Mennonite group that came to the United States from Germany and Switzerland in the 1730s and 1740s. There are Amish settlements in 22 states and in Ontario, Canada. Some Amish settled in Lancaster County, Pennsylvania where they are called Pennsylvania Dutch because they spoke German (deutsch) originally. The Amish stress family values, community service, and forgiveness. Many Amish continue to live a simple life and use horses and buggies instead of cars; they don't use electricity and they send their children to private, one-room schoolhouses. The Amish are known for serving delicious, home-style food. This relish is a perfect example of their cuisine.

Amish red beet relish *Yield: 1 qt (946 ml) 32 each 1 oz (30 ml) servings*

Ingredients	Amounts		Procedure
	U.S.	Metric	
Beets, raw, peeled	2 lbs	907 g	Grind the beets through the medium plate of the meat grinder. Set aside.
Cider vinegar	8 fl oz	237 ml	Bring the remaining ingredients to a boil and pour the hot mixture over the ground beets. Store refrigerated in a noncorrosive pot or bowl, such as a glass or stainless steel container, for at least 24 hours. Stir occasionally.
Water	4 fl oz	118 ml	
Sugar	4 oz	113 g	
Caraway seeds	1 tsp	5 g	
Salt	2 tsp	10 g	
Garlic, chopped	1 tsp	5 g	

NUTRITIONAL INFORMATION PER SERVING: 23 Calories; trace Fat (1.5% calories from fat); trace Protein; 6 g Carbohydrate; 1 g Dietary Fiber; 0 mg Cholesterol; 148 mg Sodium. Exchanges: 1/2 Vegetable; 0 Fat; 1/2 Other Carbohydrates.

This relish is excellent with ham steaks. The tang of the rhubarb combined with the sugar and vinegar gives it a memorable flavor.

rhubarb relish   *Yield: 1 qt (946 ml) 32 each 1 oz (30 ml) servings*

Ingredients	Amounts		Procedure
	U.S.	Metric	
Rhubarb stalks	1 1/2 lbs	680 g	Peel the rhubarb and cut into 1-in pieces.
Sugar	1 lb 4 oz	567 g	Combine the remaining ingredients. Add the rhubarb and simmer in a noncorrosive pot until the rhubarb is tender and starts to fall apart. Refrigerate until service.
Vinegar, white	4 fl oz	118 ml	
Cinnamon stick	1 each	1 each	
Water	4 fl oz	118 ml	

NUTRITIONAL INFORMATION PER SERVING: 118 Calories; trace Fat (0.5% calories from fat); trace Protein; 30 g Carbohydrate; 1 g Dietary Fiber; 0 mg Cholesterol; 2 mg Sodium. Exchanges: 0 Grain (Starch); 0 Fruit; 0 Fat; 2 Other Carbohydrates.

This tomato and celery relish is a traditional recipe.

tomato and celery relish   *Yield: 1 qt (946 ml) 32 each 1 oz (30 ml) servings*

Ingredients	Amounts		Procedure
	U.S.	Metric	
Celery, diced	1 lb	454 g	Combine all the ingredients and bring to a boil. Reduce the temperature and simmer for 25 minutes. Chill and store refrigerated.
Tomatoes, seeded, diced	1 lb	454 g	
Red peppers, diced	8 oz	227 g	
Brown sugar	4 oz	113 g	
Vinegar, white	4 fl oz	118 ml	
Water	4 fl oz	118 ml	
Allspice, whole	3–4 each	3–4 each	
Cloves, ground	1/2 tsp	2 g	
Mustard, prepared	1 tbsp	15 g	

NUTRITIONAL INFORMATION PER SERVING: 23 Calories; trace Fat (4.9% calories from fat); trace Protein; 6 g Carbohydrate; 1 g Dietary Fiber; 0 mg Cholesterol; 23 mg Sodium. Exchanges: 0 Grain (Starch); 0 Lean Meat; 1/2 Vegetable; 0 Fat; 1/2 Other Carbohydrates.

This is an old-fashioned chutney recipe made popular in the American South. Its very concept can evoke curiosity and will brighten any entrée.

watermelon rind chutney   *Yield: 1 qt (946 ml) 32 each*
1 oz (30 ml) servings

Ingredients	Amounts U.S.	Metric	Procedure
Watermelon rind, cut in 1-in squares (Leave on some white flesh.)	2 lbs	907 g	Boil the melon rind with the salt in a generous amount of water for 1 hour.
Salt	2 tbsp	30 g	Drain and discard the water. Set the rind aside.

Sugar	1 lb	454 g	Combine the sugar, lemon juice, spices, and water; bring to a boil to make syrup. Once it thickens, add the melon rinds and bring to a boil. Reduce the temperature and simmer until the rinds are tender. Refrigerate until service.
Lemon juice	2 tbsp	30 g	
Cinnamon stick	1 each	1 each	
Cloves, ground	1 tsp	5 g	
Nutmeg	1 tsp	5 g	
Water	16 fl oz	473 ml	

NUTRITIONAL INFORMATION PER SERVING: 101 Calories; trace Fat (1.9% calories from fat); trace Protein; 26 g Carbohydrate; 1 g Dietary Fiber; 0 mg Cholesterol; 642 mg Sodium. Exchanges: 0 Grain (Starch); 0 Fruit; 0 Fat; 1 1/2 Other Carbohydrates.

Chow chow is a relish made with green tomatoes, onions, and other typical garden vegetables. It comes from the Southern United States and is still a popular chunky condiment with beans or cooked greens.

chow chow   *Yield: Approximately 1.25 qt (1.2 l) 40 each 1 oz (30 ml) servings*

Ingredients	Amounts U.S.	Metric	Procedure
Green tomatoes, diced	8 oz	227 g	Combine the vegetables and sprinkle with salt. Let sit overnight and drain off any liquid.
Cucumbers, peeled, seeded, diced	8 oz	227 g	
Red peppers, diced	6 oz	170 g	
Cauliflower rosettes, small	8 oz	227 g	
Celery stalks, diced	4 oz	113 g	
Pearl onions, peeled	4 oz	113 g	
String beans, cut in 1-in pieces	8 oz	227 g	
Salt	2 tbsp	30 g	
Vinegar	16 fl oz	473 ml	Combine the vinegar with the spices, then bring to a boil. Add the vegetables, cover, and simmer for 15 minutes, stirring occasionally. Cool and store refrigerated.
Mustard seeds	1 tbsp	15 g	
Turmeric, powder	1 tsp	5 g	
Allspice, whole	4–5 each	4–5 each	
Peppercorns, crushed	1 tsp	5 g	
Cloves, whole	3–4 each	3–4 each	

NUTRITIONAL INFORMATION PER SERVING: 15 Calories; trace Fat (15.7% calories from fat); 1 g Protein; 4 g Carbohydrate; 1 g Dietary Fiber; 0 mg Cholesterol; 334 mg Sodium. Exchanges: 0 Grain (Starch); 0 Lean Meat; 1/2 Vegetable; 0 Fat; 0 Other Carbohydrates.

The first recorded recipes for piccalilli appeared in the 1800s. **Piccalilli** traditionally consists of vegetables, including green tomatoes that are finely diced. The sauce is made of vinegar, spices, and mustard. In this case, the mustard flavor comes from the mustard seeds.

piccalilli *Yield: 1 qt (946 ml) 32 each 1 oz (30 ml) servings*

Ingredients	Amounts U.S.	Metric	Procedure
Green tomatoes, chopped	1 lb	454 g	Grind the vegetables through the coarse plate of a meat grinder.
Green peppers, chopped	1 lb	454 g	
Onions, diced	1 lb	454 g	
Cabbage, green	1 lb	454 g	
Salt	2 tbsp	30 g	Blend the ground vegetables with salt and let sit overnight. The next day, drain off the liquid.
Mustard seeds	1 tbsp	15 g	Use a piece of cheesecloth to make a bundle for the spices. Combine the marinated vegetables with the spice bundle in a pot.
Cinnamon sticks	2 each	2 each	
Whole allspice seed	3 each	3 each	
Brown sugar	8 oz	227 g	Add the brown sugar, mustard, and vinegar to the pot and bring to a boil. Simmer for 20 minutes. Store refrigerated and remove the spice bundle after 24 hours.
Mustard, prepared	1 tbsp	15 g	
Vinegar	16 fl oz	473 ml	

NUTRITIONAL INFORMATION PER SERVING: 75 Calories; trace Fat (5.0% calories from fat); 1 g Protein; 19 g Carbohydrate; 2 g Dietary Fiber; 0 mg Cholesterol; 662 mg Sodium. Exchanges: 0 Grain (Starch); 0 Lean Meat; 1 Vegetable; 0 Fat; 1 Other Carbohydrates.

>> Summary

Cold sauces, aiolis, dips, salsas, chutneys, and relishes are used to add flavor and interest to many dishes. These types of dishes are part of all cuisines in myriad combinations and made with many ingredients.

Most sauces are simply thickened liquids that are used to accompany, flavor, or enhance other foods. The most basic cold sauce is the egg-based mayonnaise; many other ingredients, including tomatoes, mustard, and whipped cream, are used to change flavor and consistency.

Dips are thick condiments that are usually made with a sour cream, mayonnaise, or cream cheese base and puréed vegetables. Dips are served with crudities, crackers, chips, and appetizers.

Aioli was originally a heavily garlic-flavored cold sauce from France, often thickened with cold potatoes. Aioli today is lighter and often resembles mayonnaise. It is used as a cold sauce with vegetables, fish, seafood, or chicken. Daring chefs are adding unusual ingredients, and you'll find many unique varieties on menus today.

The term *salsa* is most associated with the Mexican type of cold sauce, made with chunky tomatoes, chilies, and spices. Chutneys are usually made from fruits, vinegar, sugar, and spices boiled together. They range in a variety of textures and hotness, depending on the recipe. Mango is the most common fruit used for chutneys. Relishes are very similar to chutneys. They are typically made with vegetables or fruits combined with vinegar and sugar.

>> Review Questions

TRUE/FALSE

1. The key ingredients in most cocktail sauce recipes are mayonnaise, horseradish, and ketchup.
2. Once a tartar sauce base is blended with mayonnaise, it becomes perishable.
3. Chantilly is associated with dishes that contain whipped cream.
4. The key ingredient in Imambayildi is hummus.
5. Tahini paste is made with chickpeas.
6. Panada is generally made of boiled potatoes.
7. Tapenade comes from southern France and resembles a thick, black mayonnaise.
8. Basic aioli features mashed garlic.
9. *Salsa* is the Spanish term for "fire."
10. Mango is associated with chutney.

MATCHING

Match the sauce with its primary use.

11. tonnato sauce
12. sauce Dijonnaise
13. mint sauce
14. cranberry sauce
15. sauce Chantilly
16. cumberland sauce

a. cold poached fish
b. roasted lamb
c. cold ham or game
d. cold smoked meat
e. roasted turkey
f. cold roasted veal

MULTIPLE CHOICE

17. Sauce verte is
    a. an Italian specialty sauce.
    b. a French mayonnaise-based sauce.
    c. thickened with white bread and hard-boiled eggs.
    d. made with ketchup and horseradish.
18. Guacamole features
    a. tomatoes.
    b. a variety of chili peppers.
    c. avocados.
    d. Mexican cheese.
19. Hummus originated in Mediterranean countries and is made with
    a. chickpeas.
    b. lentils.
    c. roasted eggplant.
    d. sheep's milk cheese.
20. Berbere comes from North Africa and is a
    a. hot pepper seasoning mix.
    b. peanut paste.
    c. type of chutney.
    d. fig relish.

21. Aioli was traditionally made with garlic, olive oil, and
    a. egg yolks.
    b. fresh herbs.
    c. waxy potatoes.
    d. mayonnaise.
22. Green salsa gets its color from
    a. green tomatoes.
    b. spinach.
    c. green onions.
    d. tomatillos.
23. Chutney comes from the Sanskrit word *chatni* meaning
    a. delicious.
    b. pungent.
    c. mango.
    d. to lick.
24. The terms *chutney* and ___ are almost interchangeable.
    a. preserved
    b. relish
    c. pungent
    d. pickled

Fabrication

>> **Unit 16**

Curing, Smoking, Marinating, Drying, and Pickling

>> **Unit 17**

Basic Charcuterie

From the handmade duck sausage served in a tiny restaurant in Napa Valley to the cured Atlantic salmon in a fashionable New York bistro, trend-setting chefs from Los Angeles to London are practicing the ancient art of Charcuterie. In today's kitchens, some of the finest signature dishes contain house-made sausages, pâtés, terrines, and smoked, dried, and cured products. These items trace their path back to the humble beginnings of history. Salting, smoking, and other forms of curing meat started as a means of preserving the hunt and progressed to the production of the ground and cured protein products that we call "Charcuterie."

Unit 16 covers the art of curing, smoking, marinating, drying, and pickling. Unit 17 includes discussions of sausage making, pâtés, terrines, mousse, and foie gras.

>> Learning Objectives

After you have finished reading this unit, you should be able to:

- Explain the differences between dry curing and wet curing.
- Describe basic smoking terms and principles.
- List the functions of marinades.
- Explain the drying process and the use of rubs.
- Define the term *pickling*.

>> Key Terms

à la greque *(ah-lah-GREHK)*

brining

cold smoking

curing

gravlax *(GRAHV-lahks)*

hot smoking

jerk

marinades

pickling

TCM

Curing, smoking, drying, and pickling were the first methods of preserving food employed by prehistoric humans. The hunter who brought home wild game or fish soon discovered that meat hung close to the smoky fire or hearth to safeguard against marauding predators would last longer (Figure 16-1), By sheer observation, these early humans discovered that smoking was a way to extend the usefulness of the hunt or catch. People who lived near sources of salt also took note that the bodies of animals that died close to salt water or salt sources did not rot like other dead carrion.

Salting became one of the most vital methods of preserving foods. In areas of high heat and low humidity, it was also noted that animal flesh would dry out. This early form of dried meat or jerky was mixed with water to become a palatable source of food. Native Americans would add berries or dried fruits to this desiccated (dried) meat, then add melted fat and pound it into a paste. This "pemmican" would serve as food for the long winter months when fresh food was scarce.

Throughout the ages, as tools improved from those made of stones and sticks to those of iron and bronze, the hunt was preserved in the methods that were known at the time. Here are a few facts to consider:

- Today, refrigeration is still the exception in three-quarters of the world.
- Curing, smoking, marinating, drying, and pickling continue as the standard methods for food preservation.
- In areas that have modern refrigeration, these procedures are used not only for the preservation of food, but for the flavors that they impart.
- Drying concentrates and intensifies flavor.
- Curing increases the taste of meat or poultry, and it enhances the color and texture.
- Many of today's trend-setting chefs take pride in their ability to use these techniques to produce unique signature items.
- Smoking ingredients is popular, and it brings out the caramelization of the sugars in the various woods such as apple wood, cherry wood, alder, and hickory to give meat, poultry, and fish extraordinary flavor.

Modern machinery and equipment have made curing and smoking foods possible in restaurant kitchens. The art of smoking food is gaining interest among food professionals as methods change and improve. Most smoked food sold today is lightly smoked with aromatic woods to enhance the flavor (Figure 16-2). Ancient smoking was done to the point of blackening the product for safekeeping, and one must imagine that these meats tasted of resins and tar. Today, liquid-based smoke flavors are used as well as smoked salts to impart a fragrant, smoky flavor. This unit will introduce you to the methods for basic curing, smoking,

Figure 16-1 Strips of beef hang on a line over a fire as they are smoked and preserved.

Figure 16-2 This Manhattan Italian deli displays a variety of smoked meats.

drying, and pickling of foods for flavor as well as for preservation. A collection of marinade recipes used in the pre-cooking process of smoking foods will also be presented in this unit.

>> Curing

What does the term **curing** mean? Curing is a method of processing foods to stop them from spoiling. In order to preserve foods, specifically meat, poultry, and seafood proteins, a preserving chemical or curing agent must be used. Salt (nitrate or nitrite), sugar, and other chemical compounds are used to preserve the flesh, as well as enhance or protect the color and flavor. Salting is a type of curing that uses only salt. This method, thought to be of Celtic origin, is often called *corning* after the large salt "corns" or course crystals that are the size of corn kernels.

Salt pork or beef was a standard provision on board sailing ships during the 1500s and into the 1900s (Figure 16-3). This salted meat was the provision that made long voyages possible when sailing ships ventured beyond the coastlines and landed in other continents.

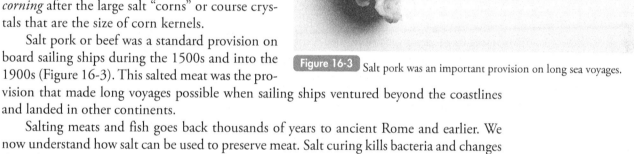

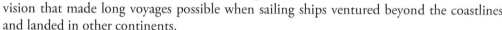
Figure 16-3 Salt pork was an important provision on long sea voyages.

Salting meats and fish goes back thousands of years to ancient Rome and earlier. We now understand how salt can be used to preserve meat. Salt curing kills bacteria and changes the soft, squishy texture of raw meat into the buttery and satiny texture that we now enjoy in prosciutto, bresaola, or bunderfleisch.

Curing is done either dry or wet. Ingredients such as salt/sugar mixtures are used as a dry cure.

DRY CURE

Dry curing or salting is perhaps the oldest method of curing. Early humans did not understand the reasons why burying the meat in salt worked to protect the hunt. As was previously mentioned, salt inhibits the growth of microbes by *plasmolysis*. In this process, water is pulled out of the microbe by osmosis due to the high concentration of salt outside the cell wall. The water is leached out of the microbe, thus rendering it harmless. The percentage of salt can vary, but 3 percent salt is known to kill *Salmonella*. Most bacteria and microbes are destroyed at low rates of salt cure. Other bacteria, such as *Listeria monocytogenes* and *Staphylococcus*, can survive higher levels of salt curing—from 12 percent on up to 20 percent. For this reason, many types of brine contain nitrites. These additional chemicals render many bacteria harmless (USDA, FSIS 1997A).

While there is still controversy as to whether N-nitrosamines are considered carcinogenic in humans, nitrates and nitrites in curing mixtures are still used as preventatives of serious bacteria such as *Clostridium botulinum*. The use of these chemicals inhibits the growth of this deadly and fatal bacteria and may inhibit other equally dangerous bacteria such as *Campylobacter*, *Salmonella*, and *E. coli* as well, if used in large enough quantities. Nitrate use has been prohibited in bacon, and the concentration of nitrites in other products has been reduced to a safer concentration. When foods that contain nitrites or nitrates are heated to an excessive temperature, potential carcinogenic materials in the form of nitrosamines form. The use of sodium acorbate or vitamin C is believed to help defuse these potential carcinogenic properties.

There are many products available commercially for preparing cures and brines. Following is a list of the more common ones found in commercial foodservice.

CURING AGENTS

A number of curing agents are available for the professional as well as the home cook. These blends usually combine sugar, spices, nitrate or nitrite compounds, and a large quantity of salt. Some have additional ingredients such as sodium erythorbate and sodium ascorbate to set color and accelerate the curing process. As with all manufactured products, please read and follow the manufacturers' directions.

TCM

Tinted Curing Mixture (**TCM**) is a product made of 94 percent salt, 6 percent sodium nitrite, and some red food coloring, which adds a pink tinge. The salt and nitrite mixture in the form of TCM or pink salt is mixed and rubbed onto the surface of the meat or mixed into wet cures. Only use this premix in recipes that specifically name it as an ingredient. Always carefully measure the amount of premix that you use, never exceeding the recommended amounts. This mixture has a slight amount of red dye commonly added to avoid accidentally using it in place of salt to season food. These salt-based mixtures draw out excess liquid; through osmosis, the cells fill with a salty brine. This preserves and protects the meat from decomposition. The term *curing* is also used in cheese making when the loaves or rounds of cheese are rubbed with salt during the aging process. Curing retards spoilage, but low temperature is required for extended storage.

Prague Powder #1

This mixture is mostly salt (93.75 percent) with some sodium nitrite (6.25 percent) and pink dye added. It is used for products that are going to be consumed in a short amount of time, including all types of sausages except for the dried kind. Use 1 ounce per 25 pounds of meat or 1 level teaspoon per 5 pounds of meat.

Prague Powder #2

This mixture is used for dry-cured meats, which require longer curing times in conditions that may be anaerobic. Prague Powder #2 is used for raw products such as prosciutto or Virginia-style hams or any product that does not require smoking, cooking, or refrigerating, such as dry salami. This product is a time-release cure—the sodium nitrate breaks down into sodium nitrite and then, ultimately, into nitric oxide. The standard manufacturer's recommended mixture is 1 ounce of Prague Powder #2 for 25 pounds of meat. This mixture should never be used on any product that will be fried at high temperatures because of the formation of nitrosamines.

Morton® Quick Cure

This product is the brand name of another popular premix. Because the formulas are different, never replace Prague Powder #1 or #2 with this premix, or vice versa, in a recipe. They are not interchangeable.

Sodium or Potassium Nitrate

Nitrates, once known as saltpeter, are no longer used in the curing of meats that are to be smoked or cooked. Nitrates are still allowed in minute quantities in the manufacturing and processing of dry-cured uncooked products.

Kosher salt is the most common salt used in curing mixtures. It is readily available and is a pure salt product. Pickling salt is a finer grade of pure salt and is a little harder to obtain in some areas.

Do not use any other type of salt because the ingredients used to make table salt flow freely, as well as the addition of iodine, are not conducive to the curing process. These minerals can interfere with the pickling or curing process and can lead to off flavors. When preserving, it is important to use pure salt (sodium chloride).

Let us start with a dry-cure rub for fish. This cure will flavor fat-fleshed fish such as salmon and trout. Leave the cure on larger fish for a longer period of time to ensure proper penetration.

dry cure for salmon, sturgeon, or trout   *Yield: 11.5 lbs/enough cure for 4 whole/8 sides of salmon*

Ingredients	Amounts U.S.	Metric	Procedure
Kosher salt	5 lbs	2.27 kg	Mix together all the dry ingredients.
Brown sugar	5 lbs	2.27 kg	To cure fish, cover with 1/2-in layer of this mixture, being sure to cover every section. Cover and place in the refrigerator for 30 minutes to 2 hours.
TCM	2 oz	57 g	
Garlic powder	2 oz	57 g	Rinse the cure off the fish under cold water and pat or blot dry. Let the fish sit uncovered in the refrigerator for an additional half hour to develop a pellicle.
Onion powder	2 oz	57 g	
Allspice, crushed	1 oz	28 g	
Black peppercorns, crushed	2 oz	57 g	Smoke the fish according to the manufacturer's instructions.
Coriander seed, crushed	1 oz	28 g	
Ginger, dried, powdered	1 oz	28 g	
Bay leaf, crushed	4 each	4 each	

NUTRITIONAL INFORMATION PER RECIPE: 9,323 Calories; 12 g Fat (1.1% calories from fat); 29 g Protein; 2,389 g Carbohydrate; 29 g Dietary Fiber; 0 mg Cholesterol; 876,492 mg Sodium. Exchanges: 12 Grain (Starch); 2 Fat; 145 1/2 Other Carbohydrates.

Kosher Salt or Pickling Salt

This recipe is a basic dry cure for bacon. The amount should adequately cover about 12 pounds of pork belly. The pellicle, as mentioned in this recipe, is a slight skin that will form on the outer surface of the meat.

dry cure for bacon   *Yield: Cures 12 lbs (5.5 kg) bacon*

Ingredients	Amounts	
	U.S.	Metric
Kosher salt	1 lb	454 g
Brown sugar	1 lb	454 g
TCM	2 oz	57 g
Black peppercorns, cracked	2 oz	57 g
Pork belly	12 lbs	5.4 kg

Procedure

Mix all the ingredients together. Pack the mixture around the pork belly to coat well. Place the slab in a nonreactive container and cover. Refrigerate for 7 to 10 days, flipping the pork over each day to redistribute the cure.

On the last day, rinse the pork with fresh water and blot dry. Store in a walk-in refrigerator for one day to dry out and develop pellicle.

Cold smoke the bacon with hickory, apple, or other fragrant fruit wood for exceptional flavor. Smoke for 4 to 6 hours, then chill 24 hours to allow flavors to meld and the fat to firm up for ease of slicing.

Slice and cook to serve.

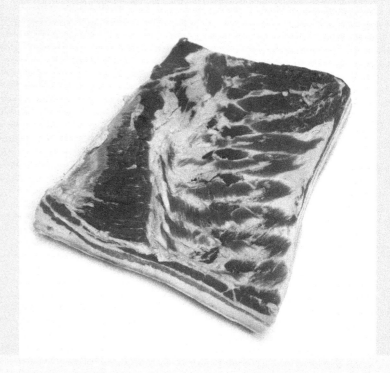

Optional Flavors

Maple sugar or honey	8 oz	227 g

NUTRITIONAL INFORMATION PER RECIPE (FOR THE DRY CURE): 3,344 Calories; 2 g Fat (0.5% calories from fat); 7 g Protein; 871 g Carbohydrate; 15 g Dietary Fiber; 0 mg Cholesterol; 192,916 mg Sodium. Exchanges: 2 1/2 Grain (Starch); 1/2 Fat; 55 Other Carbohydrates.

BENCHMARK RECIPE

Gravlax is a Swedish specialty that has become a popular item on many menus. It consists of salmon that has been cured with a sugar, salt, and dill mixture. Here we present a basic recipe for this delicacy. You can add variety to the flavors by including additional flavoring components such as freshly grated ginger, lemon or lime zest, and different fresh herbs such as cilantro, tarragon, or chervil and other dried spices such as cumin, dried chili flakes, allspice, and other aromatic seeds. Make sure to lightly toast and crush whole spice seeds just before use to release their most potent flavors. An alcohol-based spirit can be sprinkled on the gravlax for additional flavor and preservative qualities. Small salmon fillets weighing about 3 pounds (1.35 kg) each, skin on, fully boned work well for this recipe. Gravlax is often sliced thin and served on rye bread with a mustard sauce.

gravlax
Yield: 5 to 8 lbs of gralvax (2.27 to 3.63 kg)

Ingredient	Amounts U.S.	Metric	Procedure
Kosher salt	8 oz	227 g	Combine the dry ingredients.
Sugar	8 oz	227 g	
Peppercorns, crushed	4 tbsp	57 g	
Coriander seeds, crushed	2 tbsp	28 g	
Whole salmon or two sides of salmon fillet	10 lbs A.P. (As Purchased) or 5 lbs E.P. (Edible Portion)	4.5 kg whole/ 2.27 kg E.P.	Fillet the salmon. Remove the pin bones but leave the skin intact. Press the spice mixture into the flesh.
Dill, fresh, chopped	2 bunches	2 bunches	Sprinkle with the dill. Place each fillet flesh side toward each other. Wrap the fillets carefully in plastic wrap. Refrigerate at least 48 hours. Turn frequently to let the curing mixture penetrate.

When cured, unwrap and rinse gently. Pat dry and rewrap until time for use. Slice very thin and serve with appropriate garnishes. Gravlax is served here on pumpernickel canapes with dill-mustard sauce.

NUTRITIONAL INFORMATION PER RECIPE: 5,317 Calories; 129 g Fat (22.3% calories from fat); 734 g Protein; 282 g Carbohydrate; 20 g Dietary Fiber; 1,889 mg Cholesterol; 87,760 mg Sodium. Exchanges: 3 1/2 Grain (Starch); 101 1/2 Lean Meat; 1/2 Vegetable; 1 Fat; 15 Other Carbohydrates.

Wet Cure (Brine)

Brining, or wet curing, preserves and flavors foods. It can also improve the tenderness of meat. Brining begins with salts and other dry ingredients such as sodium erythorbate, sodium nitrite, and sugar, which are dissolved in water. In the past, salt was dissolved in water until an egg would float on the surface. This was the method used to tell if the brine was at the proper salt to water ratio needed for wet curing. Hydrometers are used today to ensure that the proper ratio of salt to water is used for the brine mixture. This brine can then be used as an injectable mixture and pumped into larger pieces of flesh such as ham. Smaller pieces of meat, poultry, or seafood can be submerged in the brine or cure. *Pickling* refers to cures that have sugar and sometimes vinegar or some other type of acid added. Brine curing is less salty in a flavor profile than a dry- or salt-cured product.

The amount of brining time depends on the cut of meat and the desired results. Below is a chart showing the basic times.

BRINING TIMES

Product	Approximate Brining Times
Boneless chicken or duck breasts, 6 to 8 oz each	2 to 3 hours
2 to 3 lbs whole poultry	4 to 6 hours
3 to 6 lbs whole poultry	8 to 12 hours
Larger poultry up to 12 lbs	24 hours
Larger poultry 12 lbs and up	24 to 48 hours
Pork pieces up to 2 in thick (chops, etc.)	6 to 24 hours
Curing pork chops, pork loin, or larger loin pieces	12 hours to 3 days
Thin fish fillets	1 hour
Whole trout	2 hours

The yield of this recipe depends on the weight and configuration of the product as well as the size of the container. This recipe can cure between 15 and 25 pounds of beef, elk, or other heavy game meat.

brine for beef *Yield: 2 gal (7.6 l)*

Ingredients	Amounts	
	U.S.	Metric
Water	2 gal	7.6 l
Kosher salt	4 lbs	1.8 kg
TCM	1 oz	28 g
Thyme	2 sprigs	2 sprigs
Juniper berries, crushed	2 oz	57 g
Brown sugar	2 lbs	907 g

Procedure

Combine all the ingredients and bring to a boil. Refrigerate at least 24 hours. Strain before use. Submerge the meat in the brine for 24 hours. Meat can remain in the brine for up to a week.

NUTRITIONAL INFORMATION PER RECIPE: 3,470 Calories; 1 g Fat (0.2% calories from fat); 1 g Protein; 897 g Carbohydrate; 5 g Dietary Fiber; 0 mg Cholesterol; 694,394 mg Sodium. Exchanges: 1/2 Grain (Starch); 1/2 Fruit; 0 Fat; 58 Other Carbohydrates.

The following recipe is for two classical deli specials: corned beef and pastrami. Both start out with the same beef brisket or plate meat, but the end result is very different. In the United States, unlike Ireland, corned beef is always associated with St. Patrick's Day celebrations, and pastrami is the favorite of Jewish delicatessens. This batch will cure about 20 to 25 pounds of brisket.

corned beef or pastrami brine   *Yield of brine: 2 gal (7.61 l)*

Ingredients	Amounts		Procedure
	U.S.	Metric	
Water	1 1/2 gal	5.7 l	Combine all the ingredients in a nonreactive pot and bring to a boil. Reduce the temperature and simmer until the salt and sugar dissolve. Cool the brine. Inject into the thickest part of the brisket and submerge in brine to cover.
Kosher salt	3 lbs	1.36 kg	
Sugar	1 lb	454 g	
Brown sugar	6 oz	170 g	
TCM	1 oz	28 g	Let the meat sit in the brine for a minimum of 5 days, then remove from the brine, rinse, and towel dry.
Onion	1 medium	1 medium	
Pickling spices	2 oz	57 g	For corned beef, slow roast it in a 300°F (149°C) oven and roast until the meat is tender, or place in fresh water and simmer for 3 hours until fork tender.
Bay leaves	6 each	6 each	
Garlic, cloves, crushed	8 each	8 each	
Black peppercorns, crushed	2 tsp	10 g	

Hot smoke at 175°F (80°C) until the internal temperature is 150°F (65°C). Chill and slice paper thin for sandwiches.

For Pastrami

Black peppercorns	6 oz	170 g	For pastrami: Coat and rub into the brisket coarsely ground or cracked black pepper and coriander seeds to give it a heavy coat. Amount varies according to taste.
Coriander seeds, lightly seeded	2 oz	57 g	

NUTRITIONAL INFORMATION PER RECIPE (CORNED BEEF): 2,816 Calories; 19 g Fat (5.9% calories from fat); 13 g Protein; 682 g Carbohydrate; 15 g Dietary Fiber; 0 mg Cholesterol; 523,385 mg Sodium. Exchanges: 3 Grain (Starch); 3 Vegetable; 4 Fat; 41 1/2 Other Carbohydrates.

NUTRITIONAL INFORMATION PER RECIPE (PASTRAMI): 3,418 Calories; 35 g Fat (8.3% calories from fat); 39 g Protein; 823 g Carbohydrate; 60 g Dietary Fiber; 0 mg Cholesterol; 523,480 mg Sodium. Exchanges: 12 1/2 Grain (Starch); 3 Vegetable; 7 Fat; 41 1/2 Other Carbohydrates.

Poultry brining is becoming more and more popular because it enhances the flavor, moisture, and tenderness of the finished product. The Madeira in this recipe gives wild poultry a richer taste. This brine is perfect for whole ducks, turkey, or chicken. Once the poultry is brined, it can be smoked, roasted, or grilled for excellent results.

poultry brine *Yield: 1.5 gal (5.7 l)*

Ingredients	Amounts U.S.	Metric	Procedure
Water	1 gal	3.8 l	Combine all the ingredients and simmer until the salt and sugar dissolve. Refrigerate to cool. Strain before use. Once cooled, add the duck, chicken, or other poultry to the brine. Cover the meat completely. Weigh down with a ceramic plate to keep the poultry submerged. Once the poultry is brined, cook or smoke to your desired preference.
Kosher salt	1 lb	454 g	
Sugar	8 oz	227 g	
TCM	1 1/2 oz	43 g	
Maple syrup or honey	6 oz	170 g	
Madeira wine	8 fl oz	237 ml	
Thyme	4 sprigs	4 sprigs	
Juniper berries, crushed	1 oz	28 g	
Bay leaves	2 each	2 each	
Orange zest	1 oz	28 g	

NUTRITIONAL INFORMATION PER RECIPE: 1,653 Calories; 2 g Fat (1.1% calories from fat); 3 g Protein; 365 g Carbohydrate; 8 g Dietary Fiber; 0 mg Cholesterol; 187,340 mg Sodium. Exchanges: 1/2 Grain (Starch); 1/2 Fruit; 0 Fat; 23 Other Carbohydrates.

The following brining mixture will cure two hams. It is also a good brine for other pork parts such as Boston butt, pork loins, pork hocks, and pig's head. You can pump this mixture into the meat or soak the pork in it for full penetration. Pork cured in this manner should be smoked, then steamed or baked to finish the cooking process.

ham brine *Yield: 2 1/4 gal (8.05 l)*

Ingredients	Amounts		Procedure
	U.S.	Metric	
Water, boiling	1 gal	3.8 l	Combine all the dry ingredients with the gallon of boiling water. Stir to dissolve the sugar and salt.
Ice	1 gal	3.8 l	
Kosher salt	2 lbs	907 g	
Brown sugar	1 lb	454 g	
TCM	4 oz	113 g	

Sachet Containing:

Bay leaves	2 each	2 each	Combine all the dry ingredients with the gallon of boiling water, and stir to dissolve the sugar and salt. Add the sachet and let steep for half an hour, then add the ice to cool down quickly.
Thyme, dried	1 tsp	5 g	
Peppercorns, cracked	1 tbsp	15 g	
Juniper berries	2 tsp	10 g	
Ginger, fresh, sliced	2 tsp	10 g	
Sage leaves, fresh, crushed	2 tsp	10 g	

Strain before use.

NUTRITIONAL INFORMATION PER RECIPE: 1,777 Calories; 1 g Fat (0.5% calories from fat); 3 g Protein; 458 g Carbohydrate; 6 g Dietary Fiber; 0 mg Cholesterol; 385,770 mg Sodium. Exchanges: 1 Grain (Starch); 0 Fruit; 0 Fat; 29 Other Carbohydrates.

Brine is first made with warm water to dissolve the salt. Then it should be chilled to 40°F (4°C) or colder before being pumped into the meat. Foods that are brined should be stored in cold, dark places away from the light in refrigeration units. The light can fade the colors.

Using the Brine

Follow these steps to brine a ham.

1. Using a brining needle or pump, inject the brine into the thickest parts of the meat and follow the arterial path, if possible. The meat will swell with the additional 15 to 20 percent of the brine added.
2. Place the meat in a nonreactive, deep container and cover with the remaining brine. Keep the hams or pig's head submerged in the brine for a minimum of 7–10 days, up to 1 month.
3. Check daily for any signs of contamination.
4. Turn the hams and stir the brine at least once a week.
5. Hams can be smoked or cooked after they are fully cured.

>> Smoking

The ancient art of smoking food was born out of necessity to preserve the hunt. The chemicals that form on the surface of the meat from the smoke preserve it from bacterial infestation. The slight drying out of the meat in the process also eliminates moisture from the product, changing the texture as well as adding to the flavor. Smoking for preservation is actually cooking the meat protein, whereas smoking for texture and flavor is usually a cold-smoking process that necessitates the final cooking of the product separately from the smoking process. There are three methods of smoking foods: hot smoking, cold smoking, and using wet-smoking ingredients such as a liquid-based smoke essence.

Rubs are used in the smoking process to give added flavor to the products being smoked. They are dry spice combinations sprinkled over meats and given time to penetrate the products.

HOT SMOKING

Hot smoking is a way to preserve, cure, and/or flavor foods by exposing them to temperatures between 200°F–250°F (95°C–120°C) in a commercial smoker with a gas or electrical unit. The wood chips or coals smolder in the unit and provide enough heat to cook and smoke the product at the same time. Texas-style barbecue is an example of hot smoking (Figure 16-4). A smokehouse is a larger unit or an actual building with a kiln or source of heat for the chips. Meat is racked or stacked up and smoked and cooked at the same time. In most restaurant kitchens, smoking is done on a much smaller scale utilizing portable units or a smoker unit that can be used on the stovetop. In many cases, the smoke-top units consist of deep insert pans or hotel pans that are lined with soaked chips and placed on burners set on

Figure 16-4 Texas-style barbecue brisket is prepared with the hot-smoking method.

"low." A rack is placed over the chips, the food is placed on the rack, and a lid or foil is placed over the food. This smoking process usually takes place over a short period of time, just until the food product is both smoked and cooked through.

COLD SMOKING

Cold smoking is a method used to cure, preserve, and/or flavor food products by exposing them to smoke over a much longer period of time than is required for hot smoking, taking from several hours up to several days. The product is still technically raw as the temperature is never above 90°F (35°C). Lox is prepared with the cold-smoking method (Figure 16-5).

Foods that are cold-smoked are subject to rapid microbial growth. It is important to cold-smoke foods that have been thoroughly salted, cured, or fermented first to prevent bacterial contamination. Sodium nitrate is often used in cold-smoked foods to prevent growth of *Clostridium botulinum, Listeria,* or other dangerous microbes that cause diseases. Cold-smoked meat and poultry products should be cooked to an internal temperature of 165°F (75°C) before they are eaten. The exception to this rule is smoked fish products, such as cold-smoked salmon, that are subject to long cold smoking to maintain their tender texture. In the case of salmon, it is cured, cold-smoked, and eaten in a raw state. Most restaurants and hotels are not set up to do commercial cold smoking, and it is not recommended for the home or professional chef to attempt to cold-smoke without further education on the dangers of this type of smoking. The USDA publishes descriptions and methods for those who are interested in this type of smoking process. Raw seafood or other products that are cold-smoked have the same health risks that other raw foods can contain, so it is advisable to avoid these types of cold-smoked products if you have guests who have immune deficiencies or are elderly, very young, or are expecting.

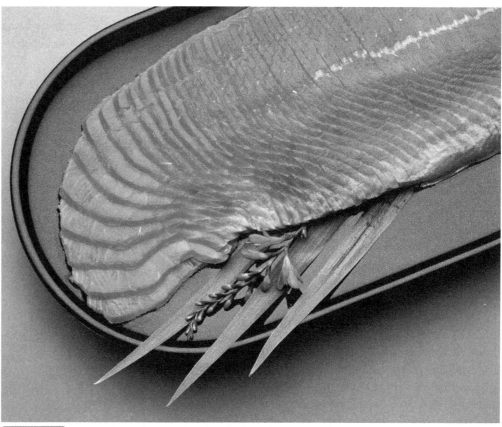

Figure 16-5 Lox is salmon that is brine-cured and cold-smoked.

LIQUID SMOKE/SMOKED SALT

A common practice today is to use a liquid- or salt-based smoke extract to give foods that fresh, out-of-the-smoker flavor. This type of application is not a method of preservation. Instead, it is used to add flavor to food. Liquid hickory or mesquite smoke is a very popular flavoring to add to sauces such as barbeque or teriyaki sauce. Liquid smoke is good for instantly adding the flavor of smoke without the mess, the time involved, or extra equipment and labor. Smoked salts, a relative newcomer to the flavor scene, are a way to deliver both salt and flavor at the same time. By smoking sea or kosher salt over fragrant woods, the salt becomes the carrier of the smokiness. Smoke salt comes in many flavors such as mesquite, chardonnay oak smoked salt, hickory salt, and alderwood or cedar smoked salt.

ITEMS TO SMOKE

Any protein-based food product can be smoked. Meats that are tough or fatty work well with smoking—the long cooking times are perfect for a tougher cut of meat that needs long, slow, moist cooking methods. Following are some examples:

- Beef brisket, plate, round, or chuck, can be smoked. In Texas, what they call barbecue is actually long-smoked and roasted brisket of beef, usually a 12- to 24-hour process. Beef or pork ribs are smoked and then simmered for hours.
- Poultry items such as duck breasts, whole chickens, and turkey are excellent choices for smoking. They are first brined in a flavorful liquid, then hot-smoked. Poultry can be used for appetizers, first courses, and entrées.
- Fish of all types can be used to smoke; however, fatty fish works best for this process. Salmon, shad, and whitefish, which are sometimes referred to as chubb or cisco, and eel are the most common. Sturgeon, sablefish, mackerel, and bluefish are also found on both the West and East coasts. European-style smoked products such as smoked herring from Germany and Holland, as well as smoked haddock (or as it is known, finnen haddie), are also popular as a breakfast or brunch item. Smoked scallops and oysters are used for canapés as well as appetizers. Brine them for a short time and hot-smoke for a taste treat.
- Vegetables and cheese can also be smoked. Traditionally, smoking has been reserved for proteins, but there are many adventurous chefs who are smoking all kinds of other food products, including vegetables and cheese.

STORING SMOKED PRODUCTS

Smoked products are perishable and should always be refrigerated at or below 40°F (5°C). Most smoked products freeze well because of their higher fat content. All smoked products should be stored tightly and wrapped to prevent drying out. Depending on the strength and intensity of the smoke, these products transfer odors to other products stored close by. Keep items such as butter or cheese away from smoked products.

Rubs are not an essential ingredient in food preservation but are often used to impart a unique flavor to smoked meats. They can create an intense flavor in the first few bites. Rubs should enhance the flavor of the meat and not be too powerful to detract from it. Store rubs in an airtight container and use within several months before the flavors lose their potency.

cinnamon spice rub for beef or chicken *Yield: 10 oz (284 g)*

Ingredients	Amounts		Procedure
	U.S.	Metric	
Cinnamon	8 oz	227 g	Mix the items well, rub some peanut oil on the meat prior to roasting, and then sprinkle or rub the meat with the dry mixture.
Kosher salt	1 oz	28 g	
White pepper, ground	1/2 oz	14 g	
Nutmeg, ground	1/4 tsp	1 g	
Cayenne pepper	1 tsp	5 g	
Allspice	1 tsp	5 g	

NUTRITIONAL INFORMATION PER RECIPE: 624 Calories; 8 g Fat (8.1% calories from fat); 10 g Protein; 186 g Carbohydrate; 123 g Dietary Fiber; 0 mg Cholesterol; 10,720 mg Sodium. Exchanges: 12 1/2 Grain (Starch); 1 1/2 Fat.

>> Rubs

The term **jerk** supposedly came from the Spanish word for "dried meat." When we hear the word *jerk* today, we think of foods from the Caribbean Islands, especially those from Jamaica, which have been seasoned with a dry, spicy blend and then cooked over an open fire. Allspice is known as Jamaica pepper in the Caribbean and is used not only as a sweet spice for baked goods, but also in conjunction with other savory spices such as black pepper in mixed spiced blends. Most jerk rubs include garlic, allspice, brown sugar, nutmeg, cinnamon, and black pepper. This recipe works well with pork roast or chops, goat meat, beef, or chicken.

jerk pork rub *Yield: Enough for 5 lbs (2.5 kg) of meat*

Ingredients	Amounts U.S.	Metric	Procedure
Dried minced onions	1 oz	28 g	Mix all the ingredients well. Rub into the meat.
Onion powder	1 tbsp	15 g	Roast, grill, or bake.
Garlic powder	1 tbsp	15 g	
Thyme leaves, dried	1 tbsp	15 g	
Kosher salt	2 tsp	10 g	
Allspice, ground	2 tsp	10 g	
Nutmeg, ground	1/2 tsp	2 g	
Cinnamon, ground	1/2 tsp	2 g	
Black pepper, ground	1 tsp	5 g	
Dark brown sugar	1 tbsp	15 g	
Sugar	1 tbsp	15 g	

NUTRITIONAL INFORMATION PER RECIPE: 293 Calories; 2 g Fat (4.5% calories from fat); 6 g Protein; 69 g Carbohydrate; 7 g Dietary Fiber; 0 mg Cholesterol; 3,784 mg Sodium. Exchanges: 1 1/2 Grain (Starch); 4 1/2 Vegetable; 0 Fat; 1 1/2 Other Carbohydrates.

This is a general, all-purpose meat rub for steaks, chops, and roasts. With the addition of a few drops of liquid smoke, it is good for jerky as well.

zesty garlic rub *Yield: Enough for 5 lbs (2.5 kg) of meat*

Ingredients	Amounts U.S.	Metric	Procedure
Garlic powder	2 oz	57 g	Mix all the ingredients well. Rub into the beef, pork, lamb, or chicken. Roast, grill, or bake.
Onion powder	1 oz	28 g	
Ginger powder	1 tbsp	15 g	
Thyme leaves, dried	1 tbsp	15 g	
Kosher salt	1 oz	28 g	
Black pepper, ground	1 tbsp	15 g	
Sugar	1 tbsp	15 g	

NUTRITIONAL INFORMATION PER RECIPE: 382 Calories; 1 g Fat (3.2% calories from fat); 14 g Protein; 87 g Carbohydrate; 7 g Dietary Fiber; 0 mg Cholesterol; 10,697 mg Sodium. Exchanges: 5 Grain (Starch); 0 Fat; 1 Other Carbohydrates.

LEARNING ACTIVITY 16-1

Making Dry Rubs

Custom-make your own blend of dry rub. Start with 1 ounce of salt, then add a variety of dried herbs and spices, along with other flavoring elements such as lemon or lime zest. Add each ingredient in small increments of 1/4 teaspoon. Try a few different blends. Use them on your favorite cut of meat. Record your favorite blend in the box below.

MY SIGNATURE DRY RUB

Ingredients	Amounts U.S.	Metric	Procedure
Salt	1 oz	28 g	

>> Marinating

Marinades are liquids that typically consist of an acidic ingredient, such as wine and/or vinegar; spices; and oil- or enzyme-based tenderizers such as the protease papain found in papayas. Marinades serve several functions:

- Preservation—the acidity and oil help preserve the meat steeping in the marinade.
- Flavor enhancer—a good example is the North German dish Sauerbraten, which is steeped first and then braised in the marinade.
- Tenderizer—the acidity or enzyme activity in the marinade helps to break down muscle fibers.

Marinating is adapted from an early curing process discovered centuries ago. Before the explorers went to Mexico, the Aztecs were using papaya leaves and other fruits to turn tough meats into tender products. This method utilized the enzymes found in certain plants such as pineapple and papaya. These plant enzymes broke down tough protein and connective tissue. Today we use this same enzyme, papain, in commercial meat tenderizers. Fresh pineapple or papaya juice can also be used as an ingredient in some marinades to tenderize beef or other tough cuts of meat. The down side to this method is that some meats, when over-tenderized, will turn to a mushy texture.

Tenderizing by papain or other protein-dissolving enzymes causes cell walls to break down with resulting moisture loss. Meat dries out. If using this type of marinade, keep the meat in contact with it for only a short amount of time—no more than half an hour. Heat activates the initial tenderization at about 140°F (60°C) and is deactivated at 212°F (100°C). Because tenderizing types of marinades penetrate only to a shallow depth, marinades containing enzymes or acids rely on contact. Meat should be cut into small pieces to allow for the tenderizing effect. When marinating protein, it is best to use pieces that are flat and from 1 to 2 inches thick.

Acid-based marinades are the most common and are used primarily for flavor. Always use nonreactive containers of ceramic, plastics such as lexan, glass, or stainless steel. Do not use aluminum or cast iron—the metal will react to the acids and leach into the foods to give them off flavors and potential health risks. The aluminum container can also darken and become pitted.

There is a health benefit to marinating meats that are cooked over high heat. When meats are cooked by high-heat flame cooking, there is a reaction between the creatine in the muscles and the amino acids. By marinating meats in marinades with a high acid content, there is new research evidence that the suspected cancer-causing agent, HCA (heterocyclic amine), is denatured. According to the American Institute for Cancer Research's pamphlet *Facts About Grilling*, "Studies have shown that even briefly marinating foods is effective in reducing the amount of HCAs—in some cases, as much as 92 to 99 percent. Scientists aren't sure exactly what causes this effect. A marinade may act as a 'barrier,' keeping flames from directly touching the meat. Or the protective powers may lie in the ingredients of a typical marinade. Vinegar, citrus juice, herbs, spices, and olive oil all seem to contribute to the prevention of HCA formation."

Marinades can be divided into two categories:

- Cooked marinades, in which all ingredients are brought to a simmer and poured over the meat while the marinade is still lukewarm. Cooked marinades bring out the flavors of the spices and herbs and can impart better flavor than cold marinades.
- Cold marinades, which have all the components blended while cold and poured over the item to be marinated.

Marinating times vary with the type of product being flavored, and short marinades are often made with prepared condiments and flavorings such as soy sauce, hoisin sauce, and other interesting ingredients. Flavorful, quick marinades can be applied to poultry or fish a few hours before cooking. The term *marinade* is also correctly used for spices, lemon juice, and herbs added to flavor fish and seafood.

Marinated meats must always be stored in the refrigerator in noncorrosive containers and must be covered with the marinade at all times to avoid bacterial contamination. While high acidity can discourage contamination, it is not fool-proof; therefore, always store meats at or below 40°F (5°C). The meat should be tightly packed into the container to minimize the amount of marinade necessary to keep the meat submerged. A heavy ceramic plate placed on top of the meat will keep it submerged. Meat should not be kept longer than 2 or 3 days in the marinade.

Once meat is marinated, it is broiled, roasted, baked, or braised. The marinade can be used as braising liquid and adds flavor to the gravy. A sauce made with bones and the braising liquid usually accompanies marinated roasted meats. Salt is generally not added to marinades because it draws juices out of the meat.

Cooked vegetables can also be marinated to add flavor and to extend shelf-life. A classical preparation is called **à la greque,** French for food prepared "in the Greek style." The term is used to describe a dish of mixed vegetables cooked in olive oil and white wine. The most popular vegetables flavored by this method are leeks, artichokes, and mushrooms.

MARINADE FLAVORINGS

Marinades can be enhanced with the aid of flavorful ingredients. Lemons, limes, oranges, pineapple, papaya, mango, and kiwifruit are examples of fruits that have high acidic content and are full of flavor. Additional acidic ingredients such as apple cider, red wine, white wine, and other flavored vinegars add tartness to the mix. Acidic vegetables such as tomatoes and acidic liquids such as molasses and honey also add sweetness to the marinade.

Sweet fruits such as peaches, pears, and figs add additional sugars to marinades. Pineapple and papaya not only add flavor but also papain, which acts as a tenderizer. Alcohol products such as beer, wine, and spirits can add additional flavors, and the alcohol adds a small amount of bacterial prevention to the marinade. Some dairy products contain lactic acid and act as tenderizers when used as marinades. Buttermilk-soaked chicken, for a tender fried product, is a common marinade ingredient in the Southern part of the United States. Yogurt is used in Indian-style marinades such as tandoori chicken. The lactic acid and yogurt culture adds a nice, tangy flavor profile to the foods marinated by this method.

The following recipes will provide a basic repertoire of marinades.

LEARNING ACTIVITY 16-2

Prepare the Basic Red Wine Meat Marinade. Divide the recipe in half and marinate 2 1/2 pounds of meat for 1 hour before grilling. Marinate the other half of the meat overnight before grilling. What differences in flavor and texture did you detect between the two batches?

Note your observations below:

BASIC RED WINE MEAT MARINADE

Length of marinate	Describe the Texture	Describe the Flavor
One hour marinate		
Overnight marinate		

Our Basic Red Wine Meat Marinade is ideal for use in grilling red meat. It is easy to prepare and provides a delicious flavor. Remember to turn the meat so that all sides are equally exposed to the marinade.

basic red wine meat marinade *Yield: Sufficient for 5 lbs (2.27 kg) meat*

Ingredients	Amounts U.S.	Metric	Procedure
Zesty garlic rub	1 1/2 oz	43 g	Rub the meat with zesty garlic rub seasoning and oil.
Olive oil	12 fl oz	355 ml	
Red onion, sliced	5 oz	142 g	Place in a stainless steel pan or heavy ceramic dish. Cover with vegetables and seasonings. Marinate for a minimum of 1 hour and a maximum of overnight.
Carrots, sliced	3 oz	85 g	
Garlic, crushed	2 cloves	2 cloves	
Mushroom stems, sliced	1 oz	28 g	
Parsley	3 stalks	3 stalks	
Peppercorns, crushed	10 each	10 each	
Cloves	2 each	2 each	
Oregano, fresh	2 sprigs	2 sprigs	
Red wine, strong	1 pt	473 ml	
Merlot vinegar	8 fl oz	237 ml	

NUTRITIONAL INFORMATION PER RECIPE: 3,203 Calories; 328 g Fat (89.2% calories from fat); 6 g Protein; 84 g Carbohydrate; 14 g Dietary Fiber; 0 mg Cholesterol; 2,483 mg Sodium. Exchanges: 3 Grain (Starch); 4 1/2 Vegetable; 65 1/2 Fat; 1 Other Carbohydrates.

This marinade is meant for white meat, from chicken breasts to chicken thighs, to turkey, and pork. It provides a smooth, light flavor.

white meat marinade *Yield: 3 pints (1.4 l)*

Ingredients	Amounts	
	U.S.	**Metric**
Onions, chopped	8 oz	227 g
Carrots, chopped	8 oz	227 g
Olive oil	2 fl oz	59 ml

Procedure

Sauté the onions and carrots in olive oil in a saucepot.

Garlic, sliced	3 cloves	3 cloves
Celery, chopped	2 oz	57 g
Tomatoes, medium, chopped	2 each	2 each
Parsley	3 stalks	3 stalks
Thyme, fresh	2 sprigs	2 sprigs

After browning, add the garlic, then the celery.

Add the tomatoes, parsley, and thyme, and bring to a boil. Simmer for 10 minutes. Cool, strain, and keep refrigerated until used. Marinate meat for up to 12 hours.

NUTRITIONAL INFORMATION PER RECIPE: 710 Calories; 56 g Fat (67.5% calories from fat); 7 g Protein; 53 g Carbohydrate; 15 g Dietary Fiber; 0 mg Cholesterol; 141 mg Sodium. Exchanges: 1/2 Grain (Starch); 9 Vegetable; 11 Fat.

This recipe provides a sweet and tangy marinade to enhance the natural flavor found in raw vegetables. Any assortment of vegetables will work, especially bell peppers, cucumbers, carrots, cabbage, fresh corn, and onions.

sweet and sour vegetable marinade *Yield: 40 fl oz (1.2 l)*

Ingredients	Amounts U.S.	Metric	Procedure
White wine vinegar	1 qt	946 ml	Bring all the ingredients to a boil. Pour the hot liquid over the vegetables. Cool and keep refrigerated for at least 4–6 weeks.
Water	8 fl oz	237 ml	
Brown sugar	8 oz	227 g	
Pickling spice	1 oz	28 g	
Dill seed	1/2 oz	15 g	
Celery seed	1/2 oz	15 g	

NUTRITIONAL INFORMATION PER RECIPE: 933 Calories; 15 g Fat (12.3% calories from fat); 9 g Protein; 230 g Carbohydrate; 9 g Dietary Fiber; 0 mg Cholesterol; 114 mg Sodium. Exchanges: 2 Grain (Starch); 1/2 Lean Meat; 2 1/2 Fat; 13 Other Carbohydrates.

The vegetables for this recipe should be clean and bite sized. Small mushrooms, baby artichokes, and baby winter squash are popular, among many others. Note that green vegetables will turn gray.

marinated vegetables, also called à la greque   Yield: 48 fl oz
(1.4 l) 12 servings 4 oz each

Ingredients	Amounts U.S.	Metric	Procedure
Water	24 fl oz	710 ml	Bring the water and vinegar to a boil.
White wine vinegar	8 fl oz	237 ml	
Fennel seeds	1 tbsp	15 g	Put the spices into a sachet bag or cheesecloth and add to the boiling liquid, reduce the heat, and simmer for 5 minutes.
Coriander seeds	10 each	10 each	
Peppercorns	10 each	10 each	
Bay leaves	2 each	2 each	
Lemons, sliced	2 each	2 each	Add the lemon slices, salt, and onions and simmer for an additional 3 minutes.
Salt	1 tbsp	15 g	
Onions, chopped	6 oz	170 g	
Olive oil	8 fl oz	237 ml	Add the olive oil and stir. Pour the hot liquid over the vegetables. Cool and keep refrigerated for at least 4–6 weeks.

NUTRITIONAL INFORMATION PER RECIPE: 183 Calories; 19 g Fat (86.3% calories from fat); 1 g Protein; 6 g Carbohydrate; 1 g Dietary Fiber; 0 mg Cholesterol; 537 mg Sodium. Exchanges: 0 Grain (Starch); 0 Lean Meat; 0 Vegetable; 0 Fruit; 4 Fat; 0 Other Carbohydrates.

Yogurt marinade is the basis for most chicken tandoori recipes. Chicken should be marinated overnight before it is cooked. The garam masala is available in most Indian ethnic markets or spice suppliers. Powdered food colors are traditional in India and can be obtained from specialty suppliers. This recipe is a traditional tandoori-style marinade.

yogurt marinade *Yield: 16 fl oz (473 ml)*

Ingredients	Amounts U.S.	Metric	Procedure
Onion, chopped	4 fl oz	118 ml	Purée the onion, ginger, and garlic in a blender.
Ginger, fresh	2 tbsp	30 ml	
Garlic, fresh	2 tbsp	30 ml	
Cumin, ground	1 tsp	5 g	Add the cumin, cinnamon, fenugreek, cayenne, garam masala, and red food color.
Cinnamon, ground	1/2 tsp	2 g	
Fenugreek powder	1/2 tsp	2 g	
Cayenne pepper	1/2 tsp	2 g	
Garam masala	2 tbsp	30 g	
Red food color, powder	1/2 tsp	2 g	
Yogurt, plain	8 fl oz	237 ml	Add the yogurt and blend. Remove from the blender and place in a stainless steel bowl.
Red onion, sliced	4 slices	4 slices	Add the onion and lime slices and any meat that you want to marinate. Meat should be marinated for a minimum of 3 hours. For best flavor, marinate overnight.
Lime, sliced	4 slices	4 slices	

NUTRITIONAL INFORMATION PER RECIPE: 313 Calories; 11 g Fat (28.8% calories from fat); 14 g Protein; 46 g Carbohydrate; 9 g Dietary Fiber; 31 mg Cholesterol; 135 mg Sodium. Exchanges: 1/2 Grain (Starch); 0 Lean Meat; 4 Vegetable; 0 Fruit; 1 Nonfat Milk; 2 Fat; 1/2 Other Carbohydrates.

>> Drying

Drying is the act of removing all discernable moisture from food. By removing the moisture, bacterial contamination is avoided and foods can be stored for long periods of time. It is perhaps the oldest form of preservation and the simplest. Put strips of meat out in the hot sun, and within a few hours the meat is bone dry. Of course, this is an oversimplification of the process.

Modern drying is accomplished by dehydrating units. These cabinets have a heat source or lamp to slowly evaporate the moisture from the food product. Rubs and other marinades can add additional flavors to the dehydrated products. Jerky is an example of dried meat, and it comes in many flavors from teriyaki to Cajun spiced. It can be made from beef, game meat, buffalo, turkey, ham, and salmon. The meat is cut into 1/4- to 1/2-inch strips and dried in a dehydrating cabinet or, in a hot and dry climate, out in the sun covered with a bug-proof screen to keep out flies and other bacteria-carrying bugs.

teriyaki jerky   *Yield: About 1 lb (500 g) of finished jerky*

Ingredients	Amounts		Procedure
	U.S.	Metric	
Lean beef chuck or round, venison or buffalo	5 lbs	2.27 kg	Cut the meat into very thin strips 1/4- to 1/2-in thick and pound flat between two pieces of plastic wrap.
Soy sauce	8 fl oz	237 ml	Mix the ingredients together and pour over the meat strips. Mix well so all the meat is covered with the marinade. Marinate for 12 hours.
Pineapple juice	4 fl oz	118 ml	
Mirin	1 fl oz	30 ml	
Brown sugar	2 oz	57 g	
Black pepper, medium cracked	1/2 tsp	2 g	Remove from the marinade and lightly pat dry. Place the strips 1/2-in apart on wire racks and let dry in the refrigerator uncovered to develop a slight skin or pellicle.
Ginger, freshly grated	1 oz	28 g	
Garlic, minced fine	2 cloves	2 cloves	
Pink or curing salt	1/2 tsp	3 g	

Place in a dehydrator or smoker according to manufacturer's instructions.

Dry the meat until it is slightly brittle or leather-like.

NUTRITIONAL INFORMATION PER RECIPE: 5,272 Calories; 356 g Fat (62.2% calories from fat); 373 g Protein; 114 g Carbohydrate; 6 g Dietary Fiber; 1,312 mg Cholesterol; 14,667 mg Sodium. Exchanges: 1 1/2 Grain (Starch); 51 1/2 Lean Meat; 5 Vegetable; 1 Fruit; 38 1/2 Fat; 3 1/2 Other Carbohydrates.

CHEF'S TIP
Small onions are best peeled under hot water—the skins are easier to remove when they are rehydrated. A few minutes in hot water will do this.

>> Pickling

To make spiced pickled onions, select small onions around 1 inch in diameter. Peel and wash, sprinkle with some kosher salt, and leave overnight. Rinse and drain well, pack into jars, and cover with the following onion spice vinegar recipe for up to 3 months.

Pickling is a method of preserving food by using salt, sugar, spices, and acetic acid. In most cases, the acid used is vinegar, and the foods preserved are typically cucumbers, green tomatoes, onions, and peppers. Young cucumbers make a great pickle, but large cucumbers can also be used. Cut large spears or slice. Wash cucumbers well, then sprinkle with kosher salt and leave overnight. Rinse off and dry well. Pack into jars and cover with the pickle liquid. Age the cucumbers for 1 to 3 months under refrigeration. Once the pickles have been aged, continue to store in refrigerator until use.

garlic pickles
Yield: 40 fl oz (1.2 l), enough to cover 5 lbs of pickling cucumbers

Ingredients	Amounts	
	U.S.	Metric
White vinegar	1 qt	946 ml
Champagne vinegar	8 fl oz	237 ml
Garlic, cloves, split	5 each	5 each
Dill seeds	1 tbsp	15 g
Water	8 fl oz	237 ml
Pickling spice	1 1/2 oz	43 g
Red pepper flakes, crushed	1 tbsp	15 g
Kosher salt	1 oz	28 g
Sugar	1 oz	28 g

Procedure

Combine all the ingredients. Bring to a boil. Cool and pour over the cucumbers. Keep refrigerated until use.

NUTRITIONAL INFORMATION PER RECIPE (PICKLE LIQUID ONLY): 554 Calories; 15 g Fat (18.9% calories from fat); 9 g Protein; 136 g Carbohydrate; 9 g Dietary Fiber; 0 mg Cholesterol; 10,707 mg Sodium. Exchanges: 2 Grain (Starch); 0 Lean Meat; 1 Vegetable; 3 Fat; 6 1/2 Other Carbohydrates.

spiced pickled onions
Yield: 40 fl oz (1.2 l), enough to pickle 3–3 1/2 lbs of pickling onions

Ingredients	Amounts	
	U.S.	Metric
Champagne or pear vinegar	1 qt	947 ml
Water	1 pt	473 ml
Pickling spice	1 1/2 oz	43 g
Saffron	1/2 tsp	2 g
Cinnamon stick	1/2 stick	1/2 stick
Cloves	2 each	2 each
Vanilla bean	1/2 bean	1/2 bean
Kosher salt	1 oz	28 g
Sugar	1 oz	28 g

Procedure

Combine all the ingredients and bring to a boil. Keep the pickle liquid refrigerated until use or process correctly in a boiling water canner.

NUTRITIONAL INFORMATION PER RECIPE (PICKLE LIQUID ONLY): 504 Calories; 14 g Fat (20.0% calories from fat); 7 g Protein; 120 g Carbohydrate; 11 g Dietary Fiber; 0 mg Cholesterol; 10,710 mg Sodium. Exchanges: 2 Grain (Starch); 1/2 Vegetable; 3 Fat; 5 1/2 Other Carbohydrates.

The pickling technique can be used to preserve other types of vegetables. This recipe features zucchini squash.

zucchini pickles   *Yield: 10 pints (5.6 l)*

Ingredients	Amounts		Procedure
	U.S.	Metric	
Zucchini, 15 inches long	3 each	3 each	Peel the zucchini. Slice in two and remove the seeds. Cut into cubes. Combine the salt with the ice water. Soak the zucchini in the saltwater brine overnight.
Salt	10 oz	284 g	
Ice water	1 gal	3.8 l	

Onions, diced	4 each	4 each	Add the onions to the brine and soak for 2 hours. Drain both the zucchini and onions.
Green peppers, diced	2 each	2 each	Combine the peppers, sugar, vinegar, and spices. Add the zucchini and onions. Bring the mixture to a boil. Reduce the heat and simmer until the squash is transparent. Keep refrigerated until use.
Red peppers, diced	2 each	2 each	
Sugar	22 oz	624 g	
Vinegar	24 fl oz	710 ml	
Mustard seed	1 1/2 tbsp	22 g	
Celery seed	1 1/2 tbsp	22 g	
Turmeric	1 1/2 tsp	7 g	

NUTRITIONAL INFORMATION PER PINT: 293 Calories; 1 g Fat (2.9% calories from fat); 2 g Protein; 74 g Carbohydrate; 3 g Dietary Fiber; 0 mg Cholesterol; 10,251 mg Sodium. Exchanges: 0 Grain (Starch); 0 Lean Meat; 1 1/2 Vegetable; 0 Fat; 4 1/2 Other Carbohydrates.

Pickle relish is used as a sweet or savory condiment. Relish can be made with fruits or vegetables. This recipe utilizes green tomatoes and mangos. It is a delicious, sweet, and tangy topping for upscale hamburgers or hot dogs. If red mangos are not available, use all green.

green tomato/mango sweet relish *Yield: 12 pints (5.675 l)*

Ingredients	Amounts U.S.	Metric	Procedure
Green tomatoes	12 lbs	5.4 kg	Grind the tomatoes and mangos to a chunky consistency. Drain off any juice. Place the mixture in a large stockpot.
Mangos, red and ripe	3 each	3 each	
Mangos, green	3 each	3 each	
Onions	6 lbs	2.7 kg	
Cider vinegar	40 fl oz	1.18 l	Add the vinegar, sugar, and spices. Bring the mixture to a boil. Reduce the heat and simmer for 15 minutes or until it is cooked to the desired consistency. Keep refrigerated until use.
Sugar	2 1/2 lbs	1.13 kg	
Salt	1 tbsp	15 g	
White mustard seed	4 tsp	20 g	
Celery seed	4 tsp	20 g	

NUTRITIONAL INFORMATION PER PINT: 599 Calories; 2 g Fat (2.8% calories from fat); 9 g Protein; 148 g Carbohydrate; 11 g Dietary Fiber; 0 mg Cholesterol; 603 mg Sodium. Exchanges: 0 Grain (Starch); 0 Lean Meat; 7 1/2 Vegetable; 1 Fruit; 0 Fat; 6 Other Carbohydrates.

Escabeche is a term used to describe a pickled fish dish from Spain. The fish, whole or fillet, is pan-fried or poached and then kept in a marinade. The marinade usually consists of vinegar or citrus juice, onions, and spices. Escabeche is similar to the German dish named *Brathering*.

trout fillets escabeche *Yield: 10 appetizer servings*

Ingredients	Amounts		Procedure
	U.S.	Metric	
Trout fillets, boned, skin on	10 fillets, 4 oz each	10 fillets, 113 g each	Dredge the fish fillets in flour.
Flour	As needed	As needed	

Ingredients	U.S.	Metric	Procedure
Oil	As needed	As needed	Heat the oil in a sauté pan; when the oil is hot, carefully place the fillets in one at a time. Cook until brown on one side, turn carefully, and cook the other side. Remove the fish to a deep platter.
Carrots, sliced	4 oz	113 g	Add the vegetables to the oil; lower the heat. Cook the vegetables for 2 minutes.
Red onions, sliced	4 oz	113 g	
Garlic, chopped	1 tsp	5 g	
Vinegar	4 fl oz	118 ml	Lower the heat again; add the vinegar, peppercorns, coriander, thyme, bay leaf, parsley, and salt. Bring to a boil, reduce the heat, and simmer for 5 minutes. Pour the vegetable mixture over the fish, cool, and refrigerate for 24 hours. Serve the cold fish with lemon slices.
Peppercorns, black	1/2 tbsp	7 g	
Coriander	1 tbsp	15 g	
Thyme	1 sprig	1 sprig	
Bay leaf	1 each	1 each	
Parsley stems	5 sprigs	5 sprigs	
Salt	To taste	To taste	

NUTRITIONAL INFORMATION PER SERVING: 200 Calories; 11 g Fat (49.1% calories from fat); 17 g Protein; 8 g Carbohydrate; 1 g Dietary Fiber; 46 mg Cholesterol; 72 mg Sodium. Exchanges: 1/2 Grain (Starch); 2 1/2 Lean Meat; 1/2 Vegetable; 1 Fat; 0 Other Carbohydrates.

>> Summary

Curing, smoking, marinating, drying, and pickling are methods used to preserve food, particularly proteins. These processes were used in prehistoric times. Many of today's chefs are using the same methods—not so much to preserve food but to impart flavor. As moisture is removed from food products, flavors intensify.

Curing is a method that uses a chemical agent to assist in the preservation. Dry cures or salting removes moisture by osmosis due to the high concentration of salt outside the cell wall. Wet-curing or brining starts with salt and other dry ingredients that are dissolved in a liquid. The food product is either injected with the brine or smoking is done over a fire or heat source. The chemicals that form from the smoke on the food's surface preserve it from bacteria. Hot and cold smoking methods can be used to preserve and flavor foods.

Marinades are liquids that consist of an acidic ingredient coupled with spices and oil. Marinades can preserve, flavor, and tenderize foods. Pickling is a method of preserving food using salt, sugar, spices, and an acid such as vinegar.

>> Review Questions

TRUE/FALSE

1. *Pemmican* is a Spanish word for salt pork.
2. Curing is a method of processing food using a preserving chemical or curing agent.
3. *Jerk* is a Spanish word for dried meat.
4. Marinades are used to cure food products by exposing them to smoke over a long period of time.
5. Pickling is a method of preserving food using salt, sugar, spices, and acids.
6. *Escabeche* is a Spanish dish of pickled, marinated, pan-fried fish fillets.

MATCHING

Match the method of preservation with its description.

_____ 7. marinating
_____ 8. drying
_____ 9. pickling
_____ 10. curing
_____ 11. smoking

a. uses a preserving chemical
b. acidity and oil help preserve the product
c. uses salt, sugar, spices, and acidity
d. removes all discernable moisture from the food
e. cooks the meat protein

MULTIPLE CHOICE

12. Salting is a type of _____.
    a. brine
    b. rub
    c. cure
    d. marination
13. The curing agent needed for prosciutto is
    a. salt.
    b. Prague Powder #1.
    c. Prague Powder #2.
    d. none of the above.
14. Gravlax is
    a. a Spanish word for pork fat.
    b. a type of smoked cheese.
    c. a variety of sea scallops found in the Atlantic Ocean.
    d. a Swedish dish of cured salmon.
15. Corned beef and pastrami are made with which method of preservation?
    a. wet cure/brine
    b. smoke
    c. marination
    d. none of the above

16. Hot smoking exposes food to temperatures between
    a. 50°F–90°F.
    b. 165°F–190°F.
    c. 200°F–250°F.
    d. 325°F–375°F.
17. Marinades are
    a. seasonings that are massaged into meat before it is cooked.
    b. liquids made with an acidic ingredient, spices, and oil.
    c. lightly smoked and air-dried Italian salami.
    d. French compound sauces.
18. The term à la greque is
    a. the French term for pickling vegetables.
    b. food prepared in the Greek style.
    c. a type of bercy butter.
    d. a Greek term meaning "to preserve."
19. Marinades can
    a. preserve.
    b. flavor.
    c. tenderize.
    d. all of the above.

FILL IN THE ANSWERS

20. The two methods of curing are the _____ method and the _____ method.
21. Prague Powder #1 is used for products that are going to be consumed in a _____ of _____.
22. Cold smoking cures foods by exposing them to _____ over a _____ period of time.

23. _____ is known as Jamaica pepper in the Caribbean and is used in most jerk recipes.
24. Papain is a plant enzyme that is found in certain plants such as _____ and _____.
25. Marinated meats must always be stored in the refrigerator in _____-_____ containers.
26. When should you use Prague Powder #2? _____

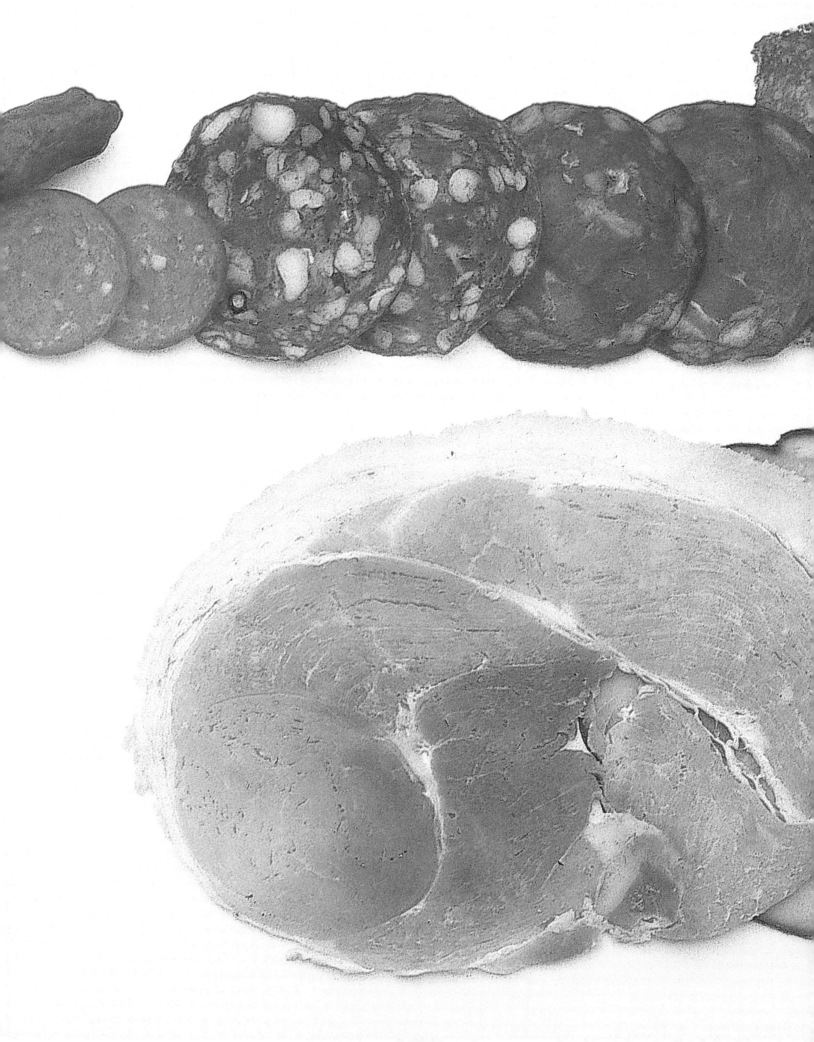

>> Learning Objectives

After you have finished reading this unit, you should be able to:

- Define *forcemeat* and explain its usages.
- Compare fresh, cured, smoked, and dried sausages.
- Describe the sausage-making process.
- Discuss how galatines, ballotines, quenelles, terrines, and rillettes are different.
- Explain the controversy surrounding foie gras.
- Create a variety of basic charcuterie products.
- Prepare a pâté en croûte.

>> Key Terms

aspic	en croûte (in crust)	forcemeats	panadas (*pah-nahd*)
ballotine (*bahl-lo-teen*)	(*ahn-KROOT*)	galantine	quenelles (*kuh-NEHL*)
botulism	fatback	offals (*OWF-fuhl*)	

Charcuterie comes from the French words *chair* and *cuit,* or cooked meat. For centuries, the French have defined all pork products such as sausages, pâtés, terrines, mousseline, and cured pork products as charcuterie. The charcutiers were only allowed to make and sell cooked pork products while the "bouchers" or butchers had the right to butcher and dress the hogs. When the guild system disbanded, the charcutiers were then able to develop their craft into what it is today.

Charcuterie is often used to describe products made from pork, but it can also include those products made from beef, veal, lamb, poultry, game, and seafood. Sausage making, forcemeats of all types, the curing of meats, and even the fine processing of protein into mousselines and pâtés all fall under the description of charcuterie (Figure 17-1).

In small kitchens, the chef performs these tasks with the help of prep cooks or other staff, whereas in large hotel or banquet-style kitchens, the garde-manger chef or cold kitchen department manufactures these special products—in some cases, in special preparation rooms where the temperatures are kept cooler than in the rest of the kitchen.

Figure 17-1 Charcuterie includes sausage making, as well as the production of pâtés, terrines, and similar food products.

In large kitchens, the garde-manger chef also makes products with chopped meats, especially **offals,** including the organs, head meat, tail, and feet, because they are perishable and have to be used as soon as possible. In the past, many chefs worked for nobility or wealthy individuals and were able to add expensive ingredients to their creations. Some of these chefs were very artistic and invented elegant dishes way beyond the necessity of using by-products quickly. Many of these dishes are based on forcemeat.

Because of the nature of forcemeats and other ground products, the potential for cross-contamination is high. We need to pay special attention to the handling of these products. The equipment, work surfaces, and tools used, along with the handling, cooking, and storage of these products, must be guarded under the strictest of sanitation standards (Figure 17-2). It is recommended that all forcemeat products be cooked as soon as they are produced.

>> Forcemeats

Butchers reserved the right to kill animals and sell raw meat. Sausage-making guilds established the criteria and the rights to manufacture sausages and other products made with chopped meats.

Forcemeats are a mixture of finely chopped and seasoned meat, fish, or seafood often containing egg whites and cream. Making forcemeats before machinery was invented required literally much force and physical labor. Meat was chopped by hand as finely as possible, then pounded in a mortar with a pestle, seasoned, and blended. The resulting meat paste still was not fine enough because many fibers got squashed but remained stringy.

Therefore, the paste was forced by hand through a fine-wire-mesh sieve, called a tammis or drum sieve. This required much labor and probably was not a very sanitary process in hot kitchens lacking refrigeration. Knowing how to make forcemeat is still important, and we will be sharing the recipes and processes involved in making various kinds of forcemeats. With modern grinding and processing equipment, these meat products are both safe to make and inexpensive to produce in the kitchen.

There are four basic types of forcemeat: mousse-style, straight method, gratin-style, and campagne or country-style.

MATERIALS AND BINDERS

Forcemeat, also called "farce," is made with sinew-free, lean meat; poultry; fish; or seafood that is first ground, then blended with a filler or an extender. (*Farce* comes from the Latin word *farcire,* meaning "to stuff.") The meat is usually complemented with herbs and spices and not only extends the meat but also binds it with bread, eggs, and milk. One common type of binder is called *panada* (more on panada later).

Figure 17-2 Sanitation is always an important consideration in the professional kitchen but particularly with charcutiere.

MEATS USED IN FORCEMEAT PRODUCTION

Today, we prepare forcemeat by grinding the basic ingredients once or twice through the finest plate of the meat grinder and/or then puréeing the product in the VCM (Vertical Cutting Machine) or Buffalo Chopper for large quantities, and a RobotCoup™ or food processor for medium to small quantities. The product must be very cold before processing, and it is advisable to chill the equipment in the freezer if practical. Some chefs will semi-freeze the ingredients before processing, and others chill it between the processing steps because processing generates heat. Ice is sometimes added to the mix to help chill and emulsify the ingredients.

Forcemeat-based products are used in many different applications and are playing a larger role in today's modern kitchens. Forcemeat is a key ingredient in sausage making and is often used in stuffing or dressings; it can also stand alone as in *quenelles,* the French term for "dumplings." In classical French cooking, forcemeat played a more rigid, codified, and larger role than it does today. The modern chef who learns the techniques for making forcemeats can be more creative, especially by coupling these techniques with the influence of international flavors. Many bold, new dishes consisting of ground or cured meats are finding their way onto today's trend-setting menus. Because the forcemeat is used for so many different applications, the formulas obviously vary.

BINDERS

There are literally hundreds of forcemeat versions, some made with panadas of diced white bread cooked in milk to a thick paste and others made by cooking flour and fat together to a thick paste. Additional recipes call for nonfat dry milk, cereal flours, and soy protein.

Panadas are added as a binding agent to improve the texture of the forcemeat by holding it together. The term *panada* can be traced to *pan*, the Latin word for "bread." Panadas are usually a cooked carbohydrate substance such as bread, rice, or cooked potatoes. They are used with ground meats, along with ground pork fat, butter, cream, or other fats and eggs for consistency. Besides their use in sausage making, panadas are used as the binding or bulking agent in terrines, pâtés, galantines, and ballotines, or they are served alone in quenelles. All of these dishes will be discussed in this unit.

Bread panada is probably the most extensively used and easiest to prepare of the panadas.

bread panada   *Yield: 22 oz (624 g)*

Ingredients	Amounts		Procedure
	U.S.	Metric	
White bread, crust removed	12 oz	340 g	Push the bread through a coarse strainer or chop it rapidly in a food processor.
Milk, cold	10 fl oz	297 ml	Bring the milk to a boil.
Salt	To taste	To taste	Add the bread and salt to the boiling milk. Stir over moderate heat until smooth. Chill, stirring occasionally.

NUTRITIONAL INFORMATION PER RECIPE: 1,518 Calories; 28 g Fat (16.7% calories from fat); 52 g Protein; 260 g Carbohydrate; 8 g Dietary Fiber; 39 mg Cholesterol; 3,338 mg Sodium. Exchanges: 16 1/2 Grain (Starch); 1 Nonfat Milk; 5 Fat.

flour panada 1 *Yield: 1 pint (473 ml)*

Ingredients	Amounts		Procedure
	U.S.	Metric	
Water	12 fl oz	345 ml	Bring the water, butter, and salt to a boil.
Butter	3 oz	85 g	
Salt	To taste	To taste	
Flour, sifted	5 oz	142 g	Add the flour all at once.
			Stir over medium heat until a thick ball forms and no longer clings to the side of the pot. Let simmer to reduce slightly.
			Stir until completely chilled. Store, covered with food wrap, in the refrigerator.

NUTRITIONAL INFORMATION PER RECIPE: 1,126 Calories; 70 g Fat (56.2% calories from fat); 15 g Protein; 108 g Carbohydrate; 4 g Dietary Fiber; 186 mg Cholesterol; 982 mg Sodium. Exchanges: 7 Grain (Starch); 14 Fat.

PANADAS

Flour Panada 2 includes egg yolks and uses hot milk instead of water.

flour panada 2 *Yield: 1 pint (480 ml)*

Ingredients	Amounts		Procedure
	U.S.	Metric	
Flour, sifted	5 oz	142 g	Combine the flour, egg yolks, butter, and salt in a heavy saucepan Stir vigorously.
Egg yolks	5 each	5 each	
Butter, melted	3 1/2 oz	99 g	
Salt	To taste	To taste	

Milk, hot	9 fl oz	266 ml	Add the milk and stir over moderate heat until a thick paste forms. Remove from the heat and stir until cool. Cover with plastic and refrigerate.

NUTRITIONAL INFORMATION PER RECIPE: 1,681 Calories; 116 g Fat (62.1% calories from fat); 38 g Protein; 122 g Carbohydrate; 4 g Dietary Fiber; 1,315 mg Cholesterol; 1,250 mg Sodium. Exchanges: 7 Grain (Starch); 1 1/2 Lean Meat; 1 Nonfat Milk; 21 1/2 Fat.

Potato panada was used classically. Today, most chefs prefer the bread or flour panadas.

potato panada *Yield: 20 fl oz (592 ml)*

Ingredients	Amounts U.S.	Metric	Procedure
Russet potatoes	10 oz	283 g	Peel and slice the potatoes.
Milk	10 fl oz	296 ml	Combine all the remaining ingredients and add the potatoes.
Butter	1 oz	28 g	Simmer until the potatoes are very soft and fall apart. Add more milk, if necessary. Stir occasionally. Cool; when cold, process to fine purée.
Nutmeg	1/4 tsp	1 g	
Salt	To taste	To taste	

NUTRITIONAL INFORMATION PER RECIPE: 604 Calories; 33 g Fat (48.1% calories from fat); 15 g Protein; 64 g Carbohydrate; 5 g Dietary Fiber; 101 mg Cholesterol; 657 mg Sodium. Exchanges: 3 1/2 Grain (Starch); 1 Nonfat Milk; 6 1/2 Fat.

Consider the following tips when preparing forcemeat:

1. Add the salt directly to the meat, fish, or seafood, keeping all the ingredients as cold as possible before grinding. The reaction of the salt on the tissue will start to break down the meat, making it easier to grind.
2. The panada will help to emulsify the fat, so add it before you add the fat.
3. To achieve the best bind, add eggs and fats lasts. (Cream has a high fat content and should be considered a fat.)

This recipe for poultry forcemeat works well with boneless chicken breast, although any chicken meat will do.

Making excellent forcemeat is based on coaxing as much cream as possible into the meat mixture. This is achieved by adding the cream in small increments. It is advisable to place the stainless steel bowl containing the puréed product on ice when adding the cream, although the forcemeat can be processed completely in the food processor. This basic forcemeat can be used to stuff chicken breasts, make quenelles, and used in other applications.

poultry forcemeat *Yield: 36 oz (1 kg)*

Ingredients	Amounts U.S.	Metric	Procedure
Chicken meat	10 oz	283 g	Remove the fat, bones, and sinew from the chicken pieces. Chill the meat until almost frozen and then salt. Grind twice through the fine plate of the meat grinder. Place the bowl inside a larger bowl filled with ice to begin the cool-down process. Chill again.
Salt	To taste	To taste	
Flour panada (recipe 2)	4 fl oz	118 ml	Blend the ground chicken with the panada in small increments, with the remaining ingredients kept over ice.
Egg whites	2 each	2 each	
Heavy cream	10 fl oz	296 ml	Add the egg whites, cream, and pepper. Blend completely. Make a small sample by dropping teaspoon-size forcemeat in simmering water.
Pepper	To taste	To taste	

If too solid, add more cream; if too soft, add a little egg white.

NUTRITIONAL INFORMATION PER RECIPE: 1,830 Calories; 162 g Fat (79.1% calories from fat); 57 g Protein; 39 g Carbohydrate; 1 g Dietary Fiber; 842 mg Cholesterol; 1,105 mg Sodium. Exchanges: 2 Grain (Starch); 6 Lean Meat; 1 Nonfat Milk; 29 Fat.

This forcemeat is made without panada and can be used for stuffed veal birds, stuffed breast of veal, and related products. It is more solid than the poultry forcemeat previously listed. Purchased ground veal would not work in this recipe.

veal forcemeat *Yield: 36 oz (1 kg)*

Ingredients	Amounts		Procedure
	U.S.	Metric	
Veal meat, sinews removed	1 lb	454 g	Chill the meats. Salt and grind twice through the fine plate of a meat grinder.
Chicken meat, deboned, skin and sinews removed	6 oz	170 g	
Salt	To taste	To taste	
Butter, cold	4 oz	113 g	Add the cold butter and blend in a food processor. Chill the mixture again.
Heavy cream	8 fl oz	237 ml	Add the remaining ingredients and process.
Nutmeg	1/4 tsp	1 g	
Pepper	To taste	To taste	
Mace	Dash	Dash	

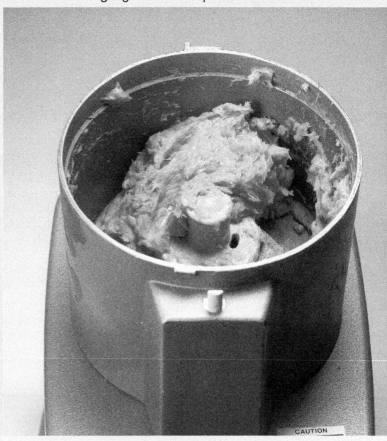

NUTRITIONAL INFORMATION PER RECIPE: 2,376 Calories; 219 g Fat (82.6% calories from fat); 96 g Protein; 7 g Carbohydrate; trace Dietary Fiber; 980 mg Cholesterol; 1,676 mg Sodium. Exchanges: 0 Grain (Starch); 12 1/2 Lean Meat; 1/2 Nonfat Milk; 38 Fat.

Country-style is characterized with its coarse ground pork and distinctive seasonings, usually including onion, garlic, and parsley. Some recipes include juniper berries.

country-style forcemeat   *Yield: 4 1/2 lbs (2.04 kg)*

Ingredients	Amounts		Procedure
	U.S.	Metric	
Lean pork, diced	2 lbs	907 g	Combine the diced pork with the pâté spice, salt, pepper, and brandy; marinate under refrigeration for several hours.
Pâté spice	2 tbsp	30 g	
Salt	1 tbsp	15 g	
Black pepper	To taste	To taste	
Brandy	2 fl oz	59 ml	
Pork liver, cleaned and diced	1 lb	454 g	Grind the liver and force it through a drum sieve. Reserve.

Fatback, diced	1 lb	454 g	Grind the marinated pork and fatback through the grinder's large die.
Onion, diced	3 oz	85 g	Grind half the pork and fatback a second time through the medium die along with the onions, garlic, and parsley.
Garlic, minced	1 tbsp	15 g	
Fresh parsley, chopped	3 tbsp	45 g	
Eggs	4 each	4 each	Working over an ice bath, combine the coarse and medium ground pork with the liver and eggs. Make a small sample by dropping teaspoon-size forcemeat in simmering water. Adjust the seasonings if necessary.
Pistachio nuts	4 oz	113 g	Add the pistachio nuts by folding them into the mixture. Olives, pine nuts, and other garnishment may be added at this time. The forcemeat is now ready to use as desired in the preparation of pâtés, terrines, galantines, and sausages.

NUTRITIONAL INFORMATION PER RECIPE: 6,105 Calories; 437 g Fat (67.1% calories from fat); 439 g Protein; 42 g Carbohydrate; 8 g Dietary Fiber; 3,227 mg Cholesterol; 23,016 mg Sodium. Exchanges: 1 Grain (Starch); 59 1/2 Lean Meat; 1 1/2 Vegetable; 55 Fat; 0 Other Carbohydrates.

This recipe includes heavy cream and nutmeg, giving the stuffing a creamy, luxurious texture. Raw fish, veal, or other poultry can be used in place of the turkey or chicken breast.

forcemeat for stuffing, quenelles, and mousselines
Yield: 3 lbs 8 oz (1.588 kg)

Ingredients	Amounts U.S.	Metric	Procedure
Turkey or chicken breast, raw	2 lbs 4 oz	1 kg	Cube the meat; chill.
White bread	7 oz	199 g	Cube the bread, removing the crust. Soak the bread cubes in egg and 1 cup of the heavy cream to make a panada. (Reserve the rest of the cream for the next step.) Chill.
Egg whites	3 each	3 each	
Heavy cream	16 fl oz	473 ml	
Ice	1 to 2 fl oz	29–60 ml	Add half the ice to the cubed meat and season with salt, pepper, nutmeg, and sage. Purée in a food processor. Add the rest of the ice and the bread panada and purée. Slowly add the rest of the cream while the machine is going. Make a dumpling test to check the consistency and taste. If too tough, add additional heavy cream. If it doesn't hold together, add an additional egg white (one egg white per pound of ingredients).
Salt	To taste	To taste	
White pepper	To taste	To taste	
Nutmeg	To taste	To taste	
Fresh sage, chopped	1 tbsp	15 g	

NUTRITIONAL INFORMATION PER RECIPE: 14,724 Calories; 855 g Fat (53.6% calories from fat); 1,551 g Protein; 114 g Carbohydrate; 5 g Dietary Fiber; 5,304 mg Cholesterol; 6,256 mg Sodium. Exchanges: 6 1/2 Grain (Starch); 219 1/2 Lean Meat; 1 1/2 Nonfat Milk; 37 Fat.

Mousseline forcemeat contains cream and egg yolks. It is light, tender, and airy. If you prefer a firmer mousseline, substitute whole eggs or egg whites for the egg yolks.

mousseline forcemeat *Yield: 4 lbs (1.814 kg)*

Ingredients	Amounts U.S.	Metric	Procedure
Fresh lean fish such as halibut or fresh shellfish such as scallops or shrimp meat	2 lbs	907 g	Grind the fish or seafood through the large die. Further process it in a food processor until smooth.
Egg yolks	6 each	6 each	Add the egg yolks one at a time and pulse the processor until they are incorporated. Scrape down the sides of the processor's bowl.
Salt	1 tbsp	15 g	Add the spices.
White pepper	To taste	To taste	
Nutmeg	To taste	To taste	
Cayenne pepper	To taste	To taste	
Heavy cream	16 fl oz	464 ml	With the machine running, add the cream in a steady stream. Scrape down the bowl again and process the mousseline until it is smooth and well mixed. Do not overprocess.

Remove the mousseline from the machine and hold in an ice bath. If additional smoothness is desired, force the mousseline through a drum sieve in small batches using a plastic scraper or rubber spatula.

Cook a small portion of the forcemeat. Taste and adjust the seasonings and texture as necessary. Make a small sample by dropping teaspoon-size forcemeat in simmering water. Adjust the seasonings, if necessary.

The forcemeat is now ready to use as desired in the preparation of pâtés, terrines, galantines, or sausages.

NUTRITIONAL INFORMATION PER RECIPE (WITH HALIBUT): 4,351 Calories; 373 g Fat (77.0% calories from fat); 222 g Protein; 28 g Carbohydrate; trace Dietary Fiber; 1,596 mg Cholesterol; 7,463 mg Sodium. Exchanges: 0 Grain (Starch); 29 Lean Meat; 3 Nonfat Milk; 70 1/2 Fat.

This recipe calls for game stock but veal or poultry can be substituted, if needed. We provide a basic stock recipe in the Basic Recipe Appendix located at the back of the book.

basic game forcemeat   Yield: 4 lbs 8 oz (2.04 kg)

Ingredients	U.S.	Metric	Procedure
Venison or antelope	1 lb 8 oz	680 g	Combine the venison or antelope and pork with the brandy, salt, pepper, thyme, and quatre epices. Marinate for several hours or overnight.
Pork butt	1 lb	454 g	
Brandy	4 fl oz	118 ml	
Salt	To taste	To taste	
Dried thyme	1 tsp	5 g	
Quatre epices	1/2 oz	15 g	

Pork fatback, cubed	1 lb	454 g	Grind the marinated meat and marinated ingredients in a chilled meat grinder once through a large die and then once through a small die; refrigerate. Grind the fatback once through the small die. Emulsify the fat with the ground meats in the bowl of a cold food processor. This can be done in several batches. Place the forcemeat in a stainless steel bowl over an ice bath.
Eggs	1 each	1 each	Add the eggs, stock, and parsley to the forcemeat in several batches; work them in by hand.
Game stock, cold	16 fl oz	474 ml	
Fresh parsley, chopped	1 oz	28 g	Additional garnishes may be added as desired. The forcemeat can be used to make a variety of pâtés or terrines.

NUTRITIONAL INFORMATION PER RECIPE: 4,855 Calories; 313 g Fat (63.5% calories from fat); 394 g Protein; 12 g Carbohydrate; 2 g Dietary Fiber; 1,478 mg Cholesterol; 24,918 mg Sodium. Exchanges: 0 Grain (Starch); 53 1/2 Lean Meat; 1/2 Vegetable; 40 Fat; 1/2 Other Carbohydrates.

>> Sausage Making

Sausages might just be our first convenience food (Figure 17-3). During the Middle Ages, the medieval working class in Europe produced guilds specializing in curing meats and making sausage and related products using chopped meat. The word *sausage* comes from the Latin word *salsus,* which means "salted" or "preserved." Sausage making answered the problem of preserving meat for long periods of time. Without proper refrigeration or freezing methods, sausage making extended the life span of meat.

Many countries developed sausage specialties such as *Frankfurters,* known to us as hot dogs, and named after Frankfurt, a city in Germany; *wieners* are named after Vienna, the capital of Austria; *kielbasa* from Poland; *mortadella, bologna,* and *salami* from Italy; and *black pudding* from England and Ireland. The list goes on and on, and there is hardly a culture that did not develop distinctive sausage types. In this unit you will have an opportunity to learn about the basic ratio of sausage making, about the stuffing machinery, and how to make basic sausages.

TYPES OF SAUSAGES

Sausages can be classified as fresh, cured or smoked, and dried. Fresh sausages are made from meat that has not been cured. They must be refrigerated and cooked thoroughly before serving. Some manufacturers sell fresh, cooked sausage, which is reheated before eating. Fresh sausages are never smoked because of the possibility of botulism (Figure 17-4).

Cured and smoked sausages have been both cooked and smoked, or in some cases smoke-cooked (Figure 17-5). This type of sausage can be eaten hot or cold. They should be refrigerated until use. All smoked sausages must be cured to prevent the possibility of botulism. (Botulism is discussed later in the Premix section.)

Salami and summer sausage are examples of dried sausages. Due to their low moisture content, they can be eaten hot or cold and will keep a very long time when properly refrigerated. Some types of salami have been cured with fermentation. Wine, vinegar, and other sour liquids are added for tang and flavor. Dried-style salami takes a long time to produce,

Figure 17-3 The ancient art of sausage making continues today.

Figure 17-4 Fresh pork sausage.

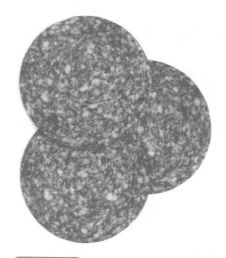

Figure 17-5 Salami is a type of dried sausage.

and without the correct equipment and tools it is hard for the standard kitchen to produce. In addition, the meat used in dried sausage must be certified because the temperatures never reach a high enough, safe temperature to kill trichinosis. Producers must adhere to complex, specific regulations to achieve certification.

We include a recipe for Dried Italian-Style Sausage at the end of this section for those with a more adventuresome spirit.

BASIC INGREDIENTS

Meat

Meat is the basic ingredient of all sausage recipes. Good sausage begins with good meat—always use fresh, clean meat. Keep the meat as cold as possible throughout the entire sausage-making process: 40°F (5°C) or lower. Many experts recommend using partially frozen meat and say it grinds well. Grinding warm meat will cause you to lose the emulsions and many of the meat's natural juices. When meat is kept cold, the juices are sealed in the tissue. It may require that you refrigerate or semi-freeze the meat after you complete each step. When using frozen meat, thaw it in a refrigerator on the lowest shelf to prevent drippings from contaminating other foods.

Whether using beef, pork, lamb, poultry, game, or fish, it is important to focus on the correct lean-to-fat ratios. In earlier times, pâtés, terrines, sausage mixtures, and other forcemeats had a ratio of 2 parts meat to 1 part fat. This evolved over time; today, most pâtés and terrines have a standard ratio of lean meat to fat: 60 percent lean meat to 40 percent fat. The lean meat can be a mixture of 40 percent of the dominant red meat such as beef, venison, elk, or lamb, and 20 percent of pork, as it has a mild, neutral flavor and a texture that blends well in forcemeats. The fat is usually pork **fatback** from the back of the animal. You can also use salt pork or bacon for additional flavor and moisture. Pork fat from the back has a mild flavor, is not too soft or too firm, and produces good emulsification in sausage making. Many sausages have a slightly less fatty ratio of lean to fat—65 percent meat to 35 percent fat—and in some cases, sausages can have as little as 15 percent fat for ultra-lean types. When the chop of the meat or grind of the meat is coarse, the fat content can be lower.

In order to produce a sausage that is juicy, tastes succulent, and binds well, use meat that has a higher fat content. Leaner versions are made but often with a sacrifice to quality and flavor. A number of sausage-makers and individual chefs have been finding success by adding fruits and vegetables, such as apples, cherries, raisins, tofu, artichokes, or even black beans, into their favorite sausage recipes to replace the fat and moisture.

PREFERRED CUTS

Type of Sausage	Recommended Cut
Pork	Boston butt or shoulder
Beef	Round steak, chuck, or blade
Veal	Shoulder
Lamb	Shoulder, leg
Poultry	Thigh and breast meat
Game	Round, shoulder

Herbs and Spices

The sky's the limit as to what combinations of herbs and spices are used to make sausages. Always use high-quality products in your sausage fillings. Just like any other recipe, it is important to use the right amounts of seasoning that not only complement each other but also the meat. It is the herbs and spices that give each type of sausage its unique identity.

Salt is an essential ingredient in sausage. Most sausage is 2 to 3 percent salt. Salt not only adds flavor, it also aids in preserving the sausage and assists in extracting the "soluble" meat protein, which binds the sausage together when it is heated.

CURING INGREDIENTS

Nitrites and Nitrates

Both nitrites and nitrates are used in the curing process and are responsible for giving cured meat its color. More importantly, they guard against the growth of **botulism** and retard rancidity. Nitrites are used for all types of sausages and are the more commonly used of the two. Nitrates are used only with cured, dried sausages.

While these ingredients offer tremendous benefits to the sausage-maker, they are also extremely dangerous if used incorrectly and may even be toxic to humans. Never assume that you can increase the amount of nitrites or nitrates called for in a recipe. It is easier to monitor the amounts when using a commercial premixed cure, which reduces the possibility of mishandling or measuring pure nitrite or nitrate. A good option is to use premix cures, which combine salts and these substances. Replace the salt called for in the recipe with a premixed cure and ignore the listings for nitrites or nitrates. Refer to Unit 16 for a list of curing agents.

SAFETY ALERT

Food-borne botulism is caused by eating foods that contain the botulism toxin. It can be fatal and is considered a medical emergency. It was a deadly problem in the 1800s and was associated with smoked sausages. Botulism occurs when foods are prepared and/or stored in conditions that lack oxygen, have low acidity and high moisture content, and are between 40°F and 140°C (4°C and 60°C). Those conditions are present when smoking sausage. Botulism is especially dangerous because affected food doesn't smell or look contaminated. Symptoms include blurred vision, slurred speech, vomiting, and diarrhea as well as difficulty swallowing and muscle weakness. Affected individuals require immediate medical attention. The best way to prevent botulism in smoked sausages is to use premixes that contain sodium nitrite. Never smoke sausage without using a premix cure.

LEARNING ACTIVITY 17-1

Do research at the library or search the Internet to find some of the typical cures and premixes used in sausage-making. See if you can find one or two other substances that can be used and list them in the blanks provided. Fill in the following chart:

Type	Typical Use	Benefit/Drawback
TCM		
Prague Powder #1		
Prague Powder #2		
Sodium erythorbate		
Morton's Quick Cure		
Sodium ascorbate		

CASINGS

Sausage recipes can be pan-fried in crumbles, formed into patties and fried, oven baked in loaves, or stuffed into casings. Both natural and artificial casings are used in sausage making today. Natural casings are made from the intestines of animals such as lamb or sheep, pigs, and cattle. These types of casings are usually several feet long and come packed in salt.

Synthetic, or artificial, casings are usually made from collagen. They come in similar lengths—several feet. Most commercially prepared sausages are made from synthetic casings because they are more uniform in size than natural casings and have less chance of defects. (As more artisan-style sausages hit the market, there is a trend to go back to the use of natural casings.) Prior to stuffing, most synthetic casings must be soaked in water and pricked with a knife point to eliminate air pockets.

Fibrous casings are used to make dried sausages. They are very strong and will withstand the pressure of this type of tightly packed sausage.

Select the casing that matches the type of sausage you are making. Fresh sausages are best made with smaller casings from sheep or pig. Beef casings work well for smoked sausages. Most recipes describe the best casings to use and the amount you will need. (Generally, it takes 1 pound of meat to stuff 2 feet of medium-size casing.)

Follow these steps to prepare the casings prior to stuffing:

1. Cut the casings into 4- to 6-foot lengths for ease of handling.
2. Rinse the casings with fresh water. Work the casings with your hands to make sure every inch is wet.
3. Soak for an hour in water that is room temperature.
4. Rinse the insides of the casings by placing one end over the faucet, like a rubber hose. Let water flow throughout the length of the casing.
5. Hold the casings in lukewarm water (110°F or 40°C) until stuffed.
6. Return any casings with salt in a container and refrigerate or freeze. (They should last up to a year in the refrigerator and longer in the freezer.)

EQUIPMENT

Grinders

The first step in making sausage is grinding the meat properly. Many different types of meat grinders are available (Figure 17-6).

Most grinders have interchangeable plates that can alter the size of the grind and are available in four standard sizes:

Plate Size	Type of Grind
3/4-inch plate	Coarse grind
3/8-inch plate	Medium-coarse grind
3/16-inch plate	Medium grind
1/8-inch plate	Fine grind

Many recipes will describe the size of grinder plate needed.

LEARNING ACTIVITY 17-2

Describe the parts of a grinder:

A. Housing
B. Worm screw
C. Grinding plates
D. Grinding blade
E. Cylinder ring

Stuffers

Many meat grinders come with a stuffer attachment. There are also stand-alone stuffers available. Stuffers generally come with a variety of sizes of stuffing horns for using different sizes of casings (Figure 17-7).

Figure 17-6 Meat grinder.

Figure 17-7 Stuffer.

Figure 17-8 Smoker.

Figure 17-9 Attach bell housing.

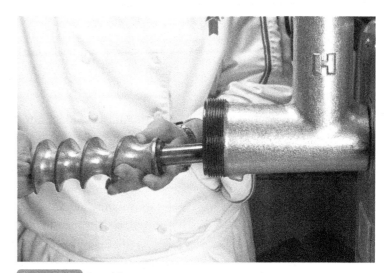

Figure 17-10 Insert the auger.

Smokers

Smokers are necessary for making smoked sausages. A myriad of commercial smoking units are available and come in a variety of sizes and shapes (Figure 17-8).

BASIC SAUSAGE MAKING

The method of filling casings with forcemeat to create sausages hasn't changed much since it first began close to 1,500 years ago. The recipes have become sophisticated, and today sausage making is considered a respected culinary art. The following procedures will work with any of the sausage recipes located later in this unit.

Meat Preparation

The meat must be chilled and ground to a coarse or fine texture. This is done with the aid of a meat grinder.

Prepare the meat grinder by using the following steps:

1. Attach the bell housing to the grinder (Figure 17-9).
2. Insert the auger inside the bell housing (Figure 17-10).

> **CHEF'S TIP**
> All parts of the meat grinder should be chilled in the freezer or refrigerator. This will keep the meat from getting too warm during the grinding process. Avoid setting up the equipment until just prior to grinding, so that each part will still be cold.

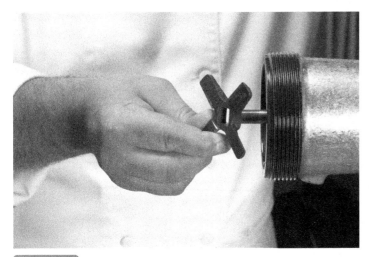

Figure 17-11 Attach the blade.

Figure 17-12 Position the die.

3. Next goes the blade, which looks like the propellers of an airplane (Figure 17-11).
4. The die, which looks like a honeycomb, goes next (Figure 17-12).
5. Screw on the collar (Figure 17-13).
6. Attach the funnel tray (Figure 17-14)

Now that the equipment is ready, it's time to prepare the meat. Follow these simple steps:

1. Pour seasonings into the meat mixture. (Recommended ratio of pork fat to lean pork = 25 percent/75 percent for a leaner sausage and 35 percent/65 percent for a richer, moister sausage) (Figure 17-15).
2. Use your hands to incorporate the seasonings into the meat (Figure 17-16).
3. Prepare a bowl of ice to place under the bowl where the ground meat will be placed. The mixture needs to be kept at or below 40°F (4°C) at all times.
4. Place the mixture into the funnel tray (Figure 17-17). Use the plunger to force the meat mixture into the machine.

Stuffing the Sausage

A sausage stuffer is used for this procedure.

1. Make sure you have followed the procedure given previously in this unit for soaking the casing.

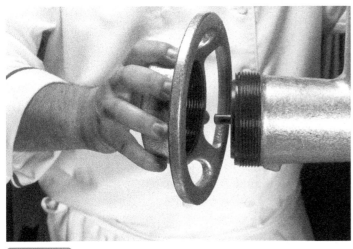

Figure 17-13 Attaching the collar.

Figure 17-14 Add the funnel tray.

Figure 17-15 Add seasonings to the meat.

Figure 17-16 Mixing the mixture.

Figure 17-17 The meat mixture comes through the grinder.

Figure 17-18 Loading the stuffer.

2. Load the meat into the stuffer cylinder and press with the back of your hand to eliminate air pockets (Figure 17-18).
3. Once the cylinder is full of the meat mixture, it should be positioned on the stuffer. Crank the handle until the plunger pushes the meat to the end of the nozzle, which will eliminate any air pockets left in the meat mixture. Turn the handle with one hand and use the other hand to hold the casing (Figure 17-19). Apply a little pressure to the casing.
4. Hold the casing with one hand while the mixture flows into it.
5. Take a soaked casing. Before placing it over the nozzle, open the end of the casing and dip it into the water to create a water bubble, which will lubricate it as it is placed over the nozzle. Place it over the nozzle. Tie the unattached end into a knot, leaving enough casing so that the two ends can be tied together after the casing is full. (Strings can be used if desired; do not use plastic strings with sausages that will be smoked.) (Figure 17-20).
6. Continue to fill the casing to the desired length (Figure 17-21).

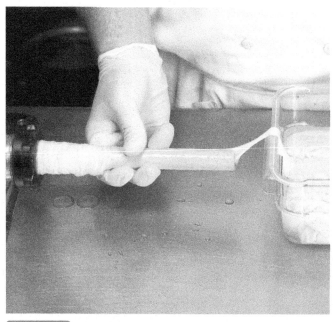
Figure 17-19 Filling the casing with ground meat product.

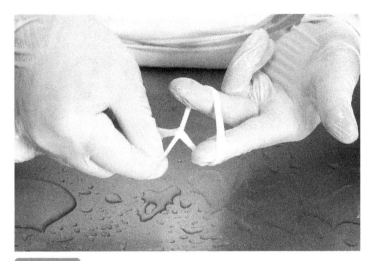

Figure 17-20 Tie the end.

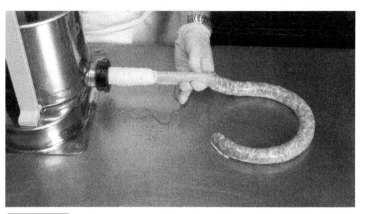

Figure 17-21 Fill to the desired length.

Figure 17-22 Place sausage into a transfer bowl.

7. When the casing is full, stretch it out on a counter and smooth it for even thickness. Cut it with a knife and tie the two ends together.
8. Place the sausage into a bowl or on a sheet pan and transfer it to the walk-in refrigerator (Figure 17-22). Let the sausage hang dry until it is dry to the touch. This may take up to 24 hours. Put a layer of towels or paper to catch the juices that will leak.
9. Keep sausages in the refrigerator until use or freeze.

There are a number of ways to cook sausages. Follow these simple tips:

- Fresh sausage has not been cooked during the sausage-making process and should, therefore, be cooked completely before consumption.
- Fresh sausages can be parboiled by boiling until the sausage is partially cooked and looks grey throughout the center. Parboiled sausages are then fried or grilled. They can also be slow-fried and grilled without parboiling first.
- Smoked/cured and dried sausages have already been cooked during the smoking, curing process and can be eaten cold or steamed. This type of sausage can be baked in casserole dishes, grilled, or pan-fried.

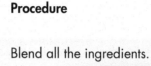

Many chefs prefer to use a favorite seasoning blend to flavor their sausage recipes. Next you will find three favorites.

pork sausage seasoning *Yield: Use 1/2 oz per 1 lb of meat (15 g per 454 g)*

Ingredients	Amounts U.S.	Metric	Procedure
Kosher salt	1 lb	454 g	Blend all the ingredients.
TCM	1/2 oz	15 g	
Red pepper flakes	1 oz	28 g	
Black pepper, ground	1 oz	28 g	
Ground nutmeg	1 oz	28 g	
Ground mace	1 oz	28 g	
Fresh parsley, chopped	2 oz	57 g	
Fennel, coarsely chopped	1 oz	28 g	
Sage, whole dried leaf	2 oz	57 g	

NUTRITIONAL INFORMATION PER RECIPE: 654 Calories; 28 g Fat (33.6% calories from fat); 19 g Protein; 106 g Carbohydrate; 50 g Dietary Fiber; 0 mg Cholesterol; 177,244 mg Sodium. Exchanges: 5 1/2 Grain (Starch); 1/2 Vegetable; 5 1/2 Fat.

Seasoning Blends

Chipolata sausages originated in the United Kingdom and typically include nutmeg and thyme.

chipolata sausage seasoning
Yield: Use 1/2 oz for each pound of meat
(15 g per 454 g)

Ingredients	Amount U.S.	Metric	Procedure
Kosher salt	4 lbs	1.8 kg	Blend all the ingredients together.
White pepper	1/2 lb	227 g	
Coriander, ground	2 oz	57 g	
Red pepper flakes	2 oz	57 g	
Nutmeg, ground	1 oz	28 g	
Thyme, ground	1/2 oz	15 g	
Cayenne pepper	1 oz	28 g	
Chili powder	1/2 oz	15 g	

NUTRITIONAL INFORMATION PER RECIPE: 1,195 Calories; 25 g Fat (16.4% calories from fat); 43 g Protein; 245 g Carbohydrate; 96 g Dietary Fiber; 0 mg Cholesterol; 683,124 mg Sodium. Exchanges: 13 1/2 Grain (Starch); 1/2 Vegetable; 4 1/2 Fat.

Louis Diat once said, "There are five elements: earth, air, fire, water, and garlic." It is true that garlic is truly a wonderful flavoring agent, as featured in the following seasoning mix.

garlic sausage seasoning *Yield: Use 1/2 oz per 1 lb of meat (15 g per 454 g)*

Ingredients	Amounts U.S.	Metric	Procedure
Kosher salt	8 oz	227 g	Blend all the ingredients together.
Crushed red pepper flakes	1/2 oz	15 g	
Black pepper	1/2 oz	15 g	
Garlic, granulated roasted	1 oz	28 g	
Coriander	1/2 oz	15 g	
Sage leaves, dried and crushed	1/2 oz	15 g	

NUTRITIONAL INFORMATION PER RECIPE: 115 Calories; trace Fat (3.4% calories from fat); 6 g Protein; 25 g Carbohydrate; 3 g Dietary Fiber; 0 mg Cholesterol; 85,292 mg Sodium. Exchanges: 1 1/2 Grain (Starch); 0 Vegetable; 0 Fat.

There are more than 250 varieties of sausage sold commercially, and new flavors are being added all the time. Only top-quality meat should be used in sausage making. It is best to use cuts with higher fat content to provide moisture and flavor. The following collection of recipes demonstrates a cross-section of sausage favorites.

pork breakfast sausage
Yield: 25 lbs /11.34 kg 100 each 4 oz (113 g) servings

Ingredients	Amounts		Procedure
	U.S.	**Metric**	
*Pork shoulder or loin with fat	25 lbs	11.3 kg	Bone and trim, cutting into strips 3 to 6 in long.

Some of the back fat can be removed to make these sausages leaner. Weigh the meat and grind through a 3/16-in grinder plate.

Black pepper, ground	1/2 oz	15 g	Mix in the spices thoroughly. Immediately transfer to pans, cool as quickly as possible, and place in a freezer. Sausage may be stuffed when cool.
Sage, ground	1/2 oz	15 g	
Ginger, ground	1/4 oz	8 g	
Nutmeg	1/4 oz	8 g	
Salt	8 oz	227 g	
Cayenne, optional	1/4 oz	8 g	
**Lamb casings			

*Use fatback if fatty meat is unavailable. Fatback is the fresh (unsmoked and unsalted) layer of fat that runs along the animal's back.

**You can use lamb casings (typical for pork sausage), hog casings, cloth casings, or fiberous 3 1/2-in × 24-in casings, or you can make into sausage patties.

NUTRITIONAL INFORMATION PER SERVING: 203 Calories; 15 g Fat (69.8% calories from fat); 15 g Protein; trace Carbohydrate; trace Dietary Fiber; 60 mg Cholesterol; 934 mg Sodium. Exchanges: 0 Grain (Starch); 2 Lean Meat; 2 Fat.

SAUSAGE RECIPES

Scrapple's has been defined in the dictionary as "cornmeal mush made with the meat and broth of pork, seasoned with onions, spices and herbs and shaped into loaves for slicing and frying." Scrapple comes from the odds and ends, or "scraps," of a pig. It is often called Philadelphia Scrapple, but it actually originated with the early Pennsylvania Dutch settlers. Scrapple is commonly found on breakfast menus throughout the Mid-Atlantic states. Pork butt can be substituted for the pork shoulder.

Philadelphia scrapple   *Yield: 8 lbs 32 each 4 oz (113 g) servings*

Ingredients	Amounts		Procedure
	U.S.	Metric	
Boneless pork shoulder	4 lbs	1.8 kg	Chop up the boneless pork shoulder meat into 1-in cubes. Place into a deep stockpot.
Pork hock	2 whole	2 whole	Add the pork hocks, thyme, sage, chicken stock, salt, and cayenne pepper. Simmer for 2 to 3 hours or until the meat falls apart. Drain and reserve the stock. Pull or shred the cooked pork meat and chop with a knife or food processor, being careful not to grind it too fine. Reserve in a large bowl. Measure 10 cups of stock and return it to the pot.
Thyme	1/4 oz	7 g	
Sage	1/3 oz	9 g	
Chicken stock	3 qt	2.84 l	
Salt	1 oz	30 g	
Cayenne pepper	1 tsp	5 g	
Cornmeal, yellow	22 oz	624 g	Bring it to a simmer; add the meat, cornmeal, and pepper. Stir constantly until thick and smoother, about 15 to 30 minutes. Pour 2 lbs of the mixture into each of four loaf pans and refrigerate until completely chilled. To cook and serve, remove from the loaf pan and slice into approximately 2-oz slices. Fry in either lard or clarified butter until golden brown and crisp on both sides.
Black pepper, coarse grind	1 1/2 tbsp	23 g	

NUTRITIONAL INFORMATION PER SERVING: 190 Calories; 9 g Fat (45.8% calories from fat); 11 g Protein; 14 g Carbohydrate; 1 g Dietary Fiber; 37 mg Cholesterol; 1,237 mg Sodium. Exchanges: 1 Grain (Starch); 1 Lean Meat; 1 Fat.

This is a traditional French sausage. As the name indicates, the sausage is white and is poached in milk and water.

Boudin blanc *Yield: 4 lbs (1.81 kg) 16 each 4 oz (113 g) servings*

Ingredients	Amounts		Procedure
	U.S.	Metric	
Sausage casing, medium	4 ft	1.2 m	Soak the casing in cold water and set aside.
Pork fatback, cubed	8 oz	227 g	Process the pork fat until a fine purée.
Onions, sliced	16 oz	453 g	In a heavy saucepan, melt the fatback and add the onions. Cook the onions until transparent without letting them get brown. Set aside to cool.
Milk	8 fl oz	237 ml	Bring the milk to a boil. Add the bread cubes. Cook over moderate heat, stirring continuously to a smooth paste. Set aside.
White bread, crust removed, cubed	6 slices	6 slices	
Turkey breast	1 lb	454 g	Grind the chilled meats twice through the fine plate of a meat grinder. Chill.
Veal, all sinews removed	1 lb	454 g	
Salt	1 tbsp	15 g	Put the meat and spices in a food processor.
Nutmeg	1/2 tsp	2 g	
Allspice	1/2 tsp	2 g	
White pepper, ground	1/2 tsp	2 g	
Eggs	2 each	2 each	Add the onions and bread mixture to the food processor. Add the eggs and the egg whites and process the mixture. Add the herbs last.
Egg whites	2 fl oz	59 ml	
Parsley, chopped	1 tbsp	15 g	
Chives, cut fine	1 tbsp	15 g	
Milk	As needed	As needed	Drain the casings and fill loosely with the above mixture. Tie off 5-in the links.
Water	As needed	As needed	
			Fill a large pot with half milk and half water. Prick the sausage to prevent bursting. Poach for 15 minutes.

NUTRITIONAL INFORMATION PER SERVING: 290 Calories; 16 g Fat (51.6% calories from fat); 24 g Protein; 10 g Carbohydrate; 1 g Dietary Fiber; 107 mg Cholesterol; 989 mg Sodium. Exchanges: 1/2 Grain (Starch); 3 Lean Meat; 1/2 Vegetable; 0 Nonfat Milk; 1 1/2 Fat.

Sausages in Great Britain are often called "bangers." They are traditionally made from pork, as in this recipe.

Irish banger sausages   *Yield: 10 lbs (4.54 kg) 40 each 4 oz (113 g) servings*

Ingredients	Amounts U.S.	Metric	Procedure
Pork butt, 30% fat/70% lean	10 lbs	4.54 kg	Trim the pork and dice into 1/2-in cubes. Chop the meat coarsely, reserving half to chop again to fine chop.
Ginger, ground	2 tsp	10 g	Sprinkle on the spices and salts and mix thoroughly until evenly blended.
Nutmeg, ground	1 tsp	5 g	
Dry sage, whole dried leaves, crumbled	1 tbsp	15 g	Make sure not to blend too smooth.
White pepper, freshly ground	1 tbsp	15 g	
Salt	3 3/4 oz	106 g	
Curing salt	1/2 tsp	2 g	
White bread crumbs	1 lb	454 g	Add the bread crumbs and some of the water, if needed.
Ice water	8 fl oz	237 ml	Pan-fry a small amount in a pan to adjust for taste.
Hog casings			Stuff into hog casings; twist into 3-in links. Poach.

NUTRITIONAL INFORMATION PER SERVING: 281 Calories; 19 g Fat (62.6% calories from fat); 21 g Protein; 4 g Carbohydrate; trace Dietary Fiber; 78 mg Cholesterol; 1,165 mg Sodium. Exchanges: 1/2 Grain (Starch); 3 Lean Meat; 2 Fat.

Chicken sausage has gained popularity in recent years. This recipe combines chicken and veal with Southwestern favorites including green chilies, cilantro, chili powder, and cumin.

new Mexican chicken sausage *Yield: 2 1/2 lbs (1.13 kg)*
10 each 4 oz (113 g) servings

Ingredients	Amounts U.S.	Metric	Procedure
Oil—corn, soy, or canola	1 fl oz	30 ml	Heat the oil and sauté the onion, garlic, and green chilies until the onions are translucent; remove and chill well.
Onion, chopped fine	6 oz	170 g	
Garlic, minced	1 tbsp	28 g	
Green chilies, chopped	2 oz	56 g	
Chicken breast meat	2 lbs	907 g	Trim the chicken meat of fat. Grind the chicken and veal in a cold meat grinder, once through the large die and then through the medium die.
Veal, lean, diced	8 oz	227 g	
Sherry vinegar	1 fl oz	30 ml	Working over an ice bath, combine the meats, vinegar, water, and seasonings. Add the sautéed onions, garlic, and chilies.
Water	4 fl oz	118 ml	
Fresh cilantro, chopped	1 oz	28 g	
White pepper	1/2 tsp	2 g	
Chili powder	1 tsp	5 g	
Cumin, ground	1 tsp	5 g	
Salt	1 tsp	5 g	

Blend well. Cook a small portion to test the flavor and texture. Adjust the seasonings.

Stuff into casings or portion into 2-oz patties and broil.

NUTRITIONAL INFORMATION PER SERVING: 209 Calories; 11 g Fat (49.0% calories from fat); 21 g Protein; 5 g Carbohydrate; 1 g Dietary Fiber; 65 mg Cholesterol; 187 mg Sodium. Exchanges: 0 Grain (Starch); 3 Lean Meat; 1/2 Vegetable; 1/2 Fat; 0 Other Carbohydrates.

Italian sausage is the perfect accompaniment to any pasta dish. Fennel is often associated with this type of sausage.

spicy Italian sausage   *Yield: 5 lbs (2.27 kg) 20 each 4 oz (113 g) servings*

Ingredients	Amounts		Procedure
	U.S.	Metric	
Pork butt, 2/3 lean, 1/3 fat	5 lbs	2.27 kg	Cut the meat into 2-in cubes.
Salt	1 1/2 oz	45 g	Combine the pork with the remaining ingredients except for the water. Grind the meat once through the coarse die of a well-chilled grinder.
Black pepper	1 1/2 tsp	7 g	
Morton's Tender Quick	1 tsp	5 g	
Garlic, chopped	2 oz	59 g	
Fennel seeds	2 tbsp	30 g	
Paprika	1 tbsp	15 g	
Coriander, ground	3/4 tsp	4 g	
Cold water	5 fl oz	148 ml	Add the cold water and mix well. Stuff the sausage into the casings.

NUTRITIONAL INFORMATION PER SERVING: 243 Calories; 20 g Fat (75.3% calories from fat); 13 g Protein; 1 g Carbohydrate; trace Dietary Fiber; 60 mg Cholesterol; 632 mg Sodium. Exchanges: 0 Grain (Starch); 2 Lean Meat; 0 Vegetable; 3 Fat.

Chorizo is associated with Spanish or Mexican food. It includes red pepper flakes and other common Spanish flavorings such as cumin and cayenne pepper. Chorizo sausage adds heat to many recipes featuring this spicy sausage.

chorizo *Yield: 7 1/2 lbs (3.4 kg) 30 each 4 oz (113 g) servings*

Ingredients	Amounts		Procedure
	U.S.	Metric	
Pork, lean	5 lbs	2.27 kg	Cut the pork and fatback in 1-in pieces. Grind the pork once using a medium die. Grind half of the pork a second time together with the fatback through a fine die.
Fatback	2 lbs 8 oz	1.13 kg	
Red pepper flakes	2 tsp	10 g	Combine all the ingredients in the bowl of a mixer using the paddle attachment. The sausage may be used in bulk or formed into links as desired.
Garlic, chopped	2 oz	57 g	
Cumin, ground	1 1/2 oz	45 g	
Cayenne pepper	1 1/2 oz	45 g	
Salt	1 1/2 oz	45 g	
Spanish smoked paprika	2 oz	57 g	
Red wine vinegar	3 fl oz	85 ml	

NUTRITIONAL INFORMATION PER SERVING: 313 Calories; 24 g Fat (70.0% calories from fat); 21 g Protein; 2 g Carbohydrate; 1 g Dietary Fiber; 71 mg Cholesterol; 831 mg Sodium. Exchanges: 0 Grain (Starch); 3 Lean Meat; 0 Vegetable; 3 Fat; 0 Other Carbohydrates.

Lamb is known for its mild flavor, which is detected in this sausage recipe.

lamb sausage *Yield: 3 lbs 12 each 4 oz (113 g) servings*

Ingredients	Amounts		Procedure
	U.S.	Metric	
Lamb shoulder	3 lbs	1.36 kg	Cut lamb into 1-in cubes.

Salt	1 tbsp	15 g	Combine the lamb cubes with the seasonings and wine. Refrigerate for 1 hour. Grind the meat through a medium die directly into the casing. To serve, grill or sauté the sausage links.
Garlic, chopped	2 tsp	10 g	
Smoked Spanish paprika	1 tbsp	15 g	
Cayenne pepper	1/2 tsp	2 g	
Black pepper	1/2 tsp	2 g	
Cumin	1 tbsp	15 g	
Fresh thyme, chopped	2 tbsp	30 g	
Red wine	3 fl oz	85 ml	

NUTRITIONAL INFORMATION PER SERVING: 248 Calories; 19 g Fat (72.6% calories from fat); 15 g Protein; 1 g Carbohydrate; trace Dietary Fiber; 65 mg Cholesterol; 594 mg Sodium. Exchanges: 0 Grain (Starch); 2 Lean Meat; 0 Vegetable; 2 1/2 Fat.

Almost any type of meat or seafood can be used in sausage making. This recipe features salmon, although sole also works well. The lemon juice, fresh tarragon, and wild rice combine to make this a memorable and unusual sausage.

seafood sausage *Yield: 22 oz (624 g) Approximately 5 each 4 oz (113 g) servings*

Ingredients	Amounts U.S.	Metric	Procedure
Sausage casing, medium	3 ft	0.75 m	Soak the casings and set aside.
Salmon or sole fillets	8 oz	227 g	Chill the fish until semi-frozen and grind through the fine plate. Chill again.
Salt	1 tsp	5 g	Put the fish, salt, cayenne pepper, egg, lemon juice, and heavy cream in a food processor and process to a fine paste.
Cayenne pepper	1/4 tsp	1 g	
Egg	1 each	1 each	
Lemon juice	1 tsp	5 ml	
Heavy cream	6 fl oz	177 ml	
Wild rice, cooked	7 oz	198 g	Add the wild rice and tarragon to the fish mixture and pulse to blend.
Fresh tarragon, chopped	1 tsp	5 g	Fill the sausage and poach in court bouillon about 15 minutes.

NUTRITIONAL INFORMATION PER SERVING: 383 Calories; 20 g Fat (46.9% calories from fat); 20 g Protein; 32 g Carbohydrate; 3 g Dietary Fiber; 144 mg Cholesterol; 608 mg Sodium. Exchanges: 2 Grain (Starch); 2 Lean Meat; 0 Fruit; 0 Nonfat Milk; 3 1/2 Fat.

Linguica sausage comes from Portugal. It is also popular in Brazil because of the Portuguese influence. Pork and garlic are two standard ingredients in linguica recipes.

NOTE: USDA regulations classify "linguica" as an uncooked sausage, so it should be thoroughly cooked before serving.

linguica sausage   *Yield: Approximately 11 lbs of meat (4.99 kg)*
44 each 4 oz (113 g) servings

Ingredients	Amounts		Procedure
	U.S.	Metric	
Pork butts, sinew and connective tissue removed	10 lbs	4.54 kg	Dice the pork into 1/2-in pieces and place in a mixer.
Salt	3 oz	85 g	Add all the ingredients to the meat except the water and wine or cider. Mix until all the ingredients are evenly distributed. Place the meat into curing tubs and let stand in a cooler overnight.
Powdered dextrose	1 oz	28 g	
Prague Powder #1	1/3 oz	10 g	
Garlic	6 large cloves	6 large cloves	
Paprika	2 oz	57 g	
Black pepper, ground	1/2 oz	15 g	
Cayenne pepper	1 tsp	5 g	
Marjoram	1 tbsp	15 g	
Soy protein concentrate or nonfat dry milk	6 oz	170 g	
Wine or cider vinegar	1 fl oz	30 ml	The next morning, place the meat into a mixer and add the water and vinegar. Mix the vinegar together with the water very well. Remove to the stuffer.
Ice water	16 fl oz	473 ml	

Hog casings			Stuff into 35- to 38-mm hog casings and hang on smoke sticks. Allow the sausage to air dry before placing in the smokehouse. After the sausage is dry, place into the cool smokehouse overnight at 105°F (40°C). The next morning, raise the temperature to 135°F (60°C) and hold this temperature until the sausage firms up. Remove the sausage from the smokehouse and allow it to hang at room temperature before placing it into a 45°F (10°C) cooler overnight.

NUTRITIONAL INFORMATION PER SERVING: 240 Calories; 14 g Fat (54.6% calories from fat); 25 g Protein; 2 g Carbohydrate; trace Dietary Fiber; 64 mg Cholesterol; 1,301 mg Sodium. Exchanges: 0 Grain (Starch); 3 Lean Meat; 0 Vegetable; 0 Nonfat Milk; 1 Fat; 0 Other Carbohydrates.

Kielbasa is also known as Polish sausage. Typical recipes feature pork and garlic. It is smoked before it is cooked and served.

kielbasa *Yield: Approximately 12 lbs of meat (5.4 kg) 48 each 4 oz (113 g) servings*

Ingredients	Amounts		Procedure
	U.S.	Metric	
Pork meat, 60% lean, 40% fat	8 lbs 13 oz	4 kg	Grind the trimmed meats through a 1/4-in or 3/8-in plate. Mix the seasonings, milk powder, and flour with the pork, trimmed and cut to 1/2-in cubes. Mix the seasonings with the trimmings thoroughly.
Beef or veal	2 lbs 3 oz	1 kg	
Salt	3 oz	85 g	
Milk powder	4 oz	113 g	
Flour	4 oz	113 g	
Sugar	1 oz	28 g	
Mustard seed	1 oz	28 g	
Marjoram	1 oz	28 g	
Black pepper	1 oz	28 g	
White pepper	1/2 oz	15 g	
Paprika	1 oz	28 g	
Curing salt	1 oz	28 g	
Garlic, crushed	5 large cloves	5 large cloves	

Pork casing			Stuff the mixture in natural casings. Smoke until the internal temperature reaches 160°F (70°C).

Steam or bake to serve.

NUTRITIONAL INFORMATION PER SERVING: 272 Calories; 19 g Fat (62.6% calories from fat); 20 g Protein; 5 g Carbohydrate; 1 g Dietary Fiber; 74 mg Cholesterol; 982 mg Sodium. Exchanges: 0 Grain (Starch); 2 1/2 Lean Meat; 0 Vegetable; 0 Nonfat Milk; 2 Fat; 0 Other Carbohydrates.

When an exquisite sausage is needed, try this recipe. It combines duck meat and foie gras with cognac.

duck and foie gras sausage   *Yield: 8 lbs (3.63 kg) 32 each*
4 oz (113 g) servings

Ingredients	Amounts		Procedure
	U.S.	Metric	
Duck meat	5 1/2 lbs	2.5 kg	Remove the skin, bone, and sinews from the duck. Cube the duck into 1/2-in cubes; grind the meat through a 1/4-in dye.
Butter	1 oz	28 g	Sweat the shallots in butter until tender and cool.
Shallots, minced	4 oz	113g	
Foie gras, B grade	1 1/2 lbs	680 g	Dice the foie gras into rough 1/3-in cubes.
TCM	1/4 oz	8 g	Combine the meat and foie gras with the shallots, TCM, and cognac. Grind on the medium die; then grind fine in the food processor.
Cognac	2 fl oz	59 ml	
Egg whites	5 each	5 each	Add the egg whites, heavy cream, salt, white pepper, truffles, and herbs to the forcemeat. Prepare a poach test to check the flavor and consistency.
Heavy cream	24 fl oz	710 ml	
Salt	2 oz	57 g	
White pepper, ground	1/2 tsp	2 g	
Truffles, chopped	2 oz	57 g	
Chives, minced	2 oz	57 g	
Chervil, coarsely chopped	1 oz	28 g	
Sheep casings	30 ft	9.1 m	Stuff into sheep casings and twist off at 2-in intervals. Poach the sausage in 165°F (75°C) water until just firm to the touch; drain and cool. The sausage may be finished by poaching, sautéing, or grilling.

NUTRITIONAL INFORMATION PER SERVING: 348 Calories; 33 g Fat (87.2% calories from fat); 8 g Protein; 3 g Carbohydrate; trace Dietary Fiber; 94 mg Cholesterol; 1,021 mg Sodium. Exchanges: 0 Grain (Starch); 1 Lean Meat; 0 Vegetable; 0 Nonfat Milk; 6 Fat; 0 Other Carbohydrates.

Almost every culture has a favorite sausage recipe. This recipe features Asian ingredients such as soy sauce, Szechuan pepper, Chinese Five Spice, and ginger.

smoked five spice pork sausage   *Yield: 5 lbs (2.27 kg) 20 each*
4 oz (113 g) servings

Ingredients	Amounts		Procedure
	U.S.	Metric	
Pork, 1-in cubes	3 1/2 lbs	1.6 kg	Combine the pork and fatback.
Fatback, 1-in cubes	1 1/2 lbs	680 g	
Salt	1 oz	28 g	Mix the meat mixture with salt, soy sauce, peppers, TCM, brown sugar, Chinese Five Spice, and ginger.
Soy sauce	1 fl oz	30 ml	
Red pepper flakes	1/4 oz	8 g	
Szechuan pepper, ground	1/4 oz	8 g	
TCM	1/2 tsp	3 g	
Brown sugar	3 oz	85 g	
Chinese Five Spice	2 tbsp	30 g	
Fresh ginger, grated	1 oz	28 g	
Garlic, minced	2 oz	57 g	In a separate sauté pan, sweat the garlic and chives in peanut oil until tender; drain off excess fat and cool.
Chinese chives, minced	2 oz	57 g	
Peanut oil	2 fl oz	59 ml	When cool, add to the meat. Grind the meat through a medium plate (1/4 in) of a meat grinder.
Ice water	6 fl oz	177 ml	Mix the forcemeat in a mixer with a paddle attachment on low speed for 1 minute. Gradually add ice water. Mix on medium speed for 15 to 20 seconds until the mixture is sticky to the touch. Prepare a poach test and adjust the seasonings as needed.
Hog casings	12 feet	3.75 m	Stuff the mixture into prepared casings and twist into 5-in links. Refrigerate overnight uncovered on a wire to form a pellicle (a dry skin coating). Cold smoke at 80°F (25°C) for 2 hours. The sausage may be poached, grilled, or sautéed to a finished internal temperature of 165°F (75°C).

NUTRITIONAL INFORMATION PER SERVING: 426 Calories; 33 g Fat (70.2% calories from fat); 25 g Protein; 6 g Carbohydrate; trace Dietary Fiber; 84 mg Cholesterol; 1,683 mg Sodium. Exchanges: 3 1/2 Lean Meat; 1/2 Vegetable; 4 1/2 Fat; 1/2 Other Carbohydrates.

The Spanish paprika in this recipe gives the sausage a beautiful color and a sweet and spicy flavor.

spicy lamb sausage   *Yield: 10 lbs (4.5 kg) 40 each 4 oz (113 g) servings*

Ingredients	Amounts U.S.	Metric	Procedure
Lamb shoulder, 1-in cubes	6 lbs	2.7 kg	Combine the lamb meat, fatback, and bacon. Mix with the remaining ingredients.
Fatback, 1-in cubes	2 lbs	907 g	Grind the meat through a 1/4-in die. Place into a mixing bowl over ice.
Bacon	1 lb	454 g	
Garlic, minced	1 oz	28 g	Mix the forcemeat in a mixer with a paddle attachment on low speed for 1 minute, gradually adding the reserved stock. Mix on medium speed for 15 to 20 seconds until the mixture is sticky to the touch.
Red onion, minced	4 oz	113 g	
Salt	2 oz	57 g	
Black pepper, ground	1 tsp	5 g	Prepare a poach test and adjust the seasonings as necessary.
Crushed red pepper flakes	1 tsp	5 g	
Spanish paprika	1 1/2 tsp	8 g	
Coriander, ground	2 tsp	10 g	
TCM	1 tsp	5 g	
Dextrose	1 oz	30 g	
Fresh thyme, coarsely minced	2 tbsp	30 g	
Fresh sage, chopped	1 tbsp	15 g	
Rosemary, coarsely chopped	1 tsp	5 g	
Ice water	6 fl oz	177 ml	
Hog casings	24 ft	7 1/2 m	Stuff the sausage into the prepared casings and twist into 5-in links.

NUTRITIONAL INFORMATION PER SERVING: 279 Calories; 23 g Fat (74.6% calories from fat); 16 g Protein; 2 g Carbohydrate; trace Dietary Fiber; 58 mg Cholesterol; 998 mg Sodium. Exchanges: 0 Grain (Starch); 2 Lean Meat; 0 Vegetable; 3 Fat; 0 Other Carbohydrates.

Salami is a favorite in Italian cuisine and most delis. It features intense spices.

dried Italian-style salami *Yield: 6.25 lbs (2.8 kg) 25 each*
4 oz (113 g) servings

Ingredients	Amounts U.S.	Metric	Procedure
Pork butt or shoulder	4 lbs	1.8 kg	Cut the meat and fat into 1-in cubes. Freeze the meat and fat until slightly frozen. Grind the fat through the fine plate. Grind the pork and beef through a medium plate. Add the fat to the meat and mix well.
Beef chuck or clod	1 lb	454 g	
Pork backfat	1 lb	454 g	
Dextrose	1 oz	28 g	In a stainless steel bowl, mix together all of the dry ingredients except the lactic acid starter and the red wine vinegar and mix well to combine. Sprinkle the dry spice and salt mix over the meat and fat and toss to mix well.
Salt	1 oz	28 g	
White pepper, ground	2 tsp	10 g	
Cayenne pepper	1 tsp	5 g	
Garlic powder	1 tsp	5 g	
Cloves, ground	1/4 tsp	1 g	
Cinnamon, ground	1/4 tsp	1 g	
Black peppercorns	2 tsp	10 g	
Prague Powder #2	1 tsp	5 g	
Lactic acid culture	1 tsp	5 g	Mix the lactic acid starter with water and sugar.
Water	2 tbsp	30 ml	Add the starter to the meats and mix it well.
Sugar	1 tsp	5 g	
Red wine vinegar	2 tsp	10 ml	Add the red wine vinegar to the mixture and mix in well.
Collagen or protein-lined fibrous casings	8 oz	227 g	Stuff the ground meat mixture into beef or cellulose fiber casings and tie off each link about 10 in. Place the sausage links into a undampered smoker and ferment at 85°F (30°C) and at relative humidity of 90 percent for 24 hours. (Follow the instructions from the starter lactic acid culture manufacturer.) Let salami hang at 55°F (10°C) with a relative humidity of 75 percent for 4 weeks (2 1/2-in in diameter size) until 25 percent of its weight has evaporated away.

NUTRITIONAL INFORMATION PER SERVING: 279 Calories; 22 g Fat (71.0% calories from fat); 18 g Protein; 2 g Carbohydrate; trace Dietary Fiber; 65 mg Cholesterol; 860 mg Sodium. Exchanges: 0 Grain (Starch); 2 1/2 Lean Meat; 0 Nonfat Milk; 3 Fat; 0 Other Carbohydrates.

Figure 17-23   The galantine is poached in an aspic stock.

Figure 17-24   Plated ballotine.

>> Galantin, Ballotine, and Dondine de Canard Production

Whereas sausages are forcemeat stuffed into casings, the **galantine** consists of forcemeat that is stuffed into the skin of boned poultry or fish, shaped into a log or sausage shape, and then poached in a flavorful stock. Often galantines can be pressed into special forms after cooking. Large birds, such as chickens, turkeys, geese, and pheasants, as well as large fish are often used for galantines. Once it is formed, galantine is poached in an aspic stock, chilled, and served sliced as appetizers (Figure 17-23). The word *galantine* comes from the Latin term for *gallianceus,* referring to poultry. Galantines are served chilled.

Ballotines are similar to galantines but are shaped like bundles. In fact, the term *ballotine* comes from the French word *ballot,* which means "bundle" or "to roll around." Unlike galantines, which are always served cold, ballotines are usually served hot (Figure 17-24). They are baked, poached, or braised.

Another form of ballotine is the Dondine de Canard. This is made with a boned duck that is stuffed with forcemeat, rolled and cooked in the same manner as a ballontine. It is often served with a spicy sauce. The technique for making a dondine is the same as that for making a ballontine.

CHICKEN GALANTINE—STEPS IN PREPARATION

Galantines, ballotines, and dondines take time to prepare. A number of steps are involved in the process:

1. The process starts with boning the bird or fish (Figure 17-25). Place the bird breast down and make an incision along the backbone. Cut the skin and flesh through the backbone of the chicken so you are able to remove each breast in one piece.
2. Peel the meat away without piercing the skin (Figure 17-26).
3. Trim up the skin so that you are left with a rectangular piece (Figure 17-27).

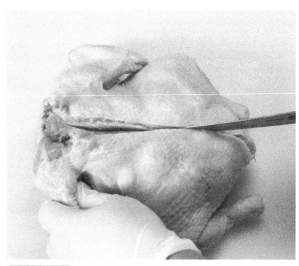

Figure 17-25   Debone the bird.

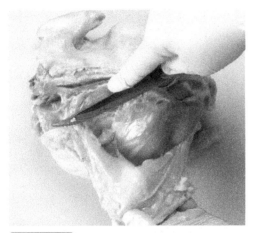

Figure 17-26 Peel the meat from the skin.

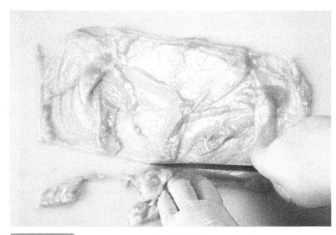

Figure 17-27 Square up the sides of the flesh to create a rectangle.

4. Remove each breast intact (Figure 17-28).
5. Butterfly each breast (Figure 17-29).

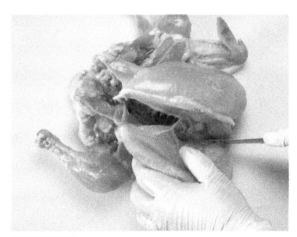

Figure 17-28 Remove the breasts.

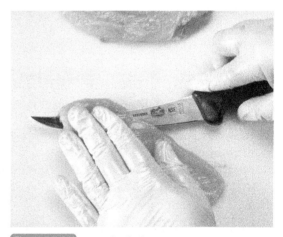

Figure 17-29 Butterfly the breasts.

6. Open up the butterflied breast and slice further, if needed. Don't go through the incision; leave enough flesh intact so that the breast can be opened up (Figure 17-30).
7. Place the butterflied breast between two sheets of plastic wrap and flatten with a meat cleaver (Figure 17-31).

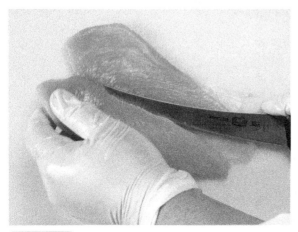

Figure 17-30 Butterflied breasts.

Figure 17-31 Flattened breasts.

8. Spread out the flattened breasts on top of the skin (Figure 17-32).
9. Spread a layer of the forcemeat (made from meat obtained from the rest of the chicken) on top of the breast (Figure 17-33).

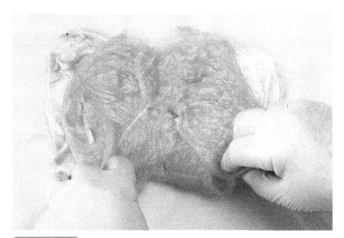

Figure 17-32 Place the flattened breasts on the skin.

Figure 17-33 Spread the forcemeat on the breast.

10. Add garnishes such as julienned strips of ham and pistachios (Figure 17-34).
11. Place the galantine on top of a piece of cheesecloth (Figure 17-35).

Figure 17-34 Add garnishes.

Figure 17-35 Position the galantine on the cheesecloth.

12. Wrap the cheesecloth around the galantine (Figure 17-36).
13. Use a string or twine to tie off both of the ends (Figure 17-37).

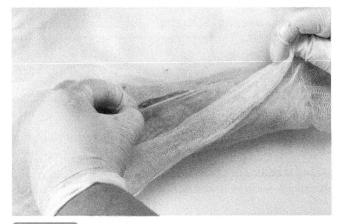

Figure 17-36 Wrap cheesecloth around the galantine.

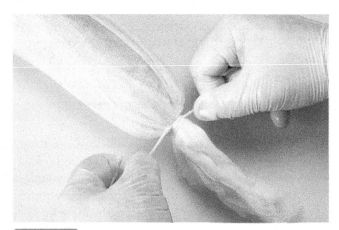

Figure 17-37 Tie off the ends.

14. Wrap the galantine in plastic wrap. Use a flat edge to press tightly to produce a tight seal (Figure 17-38).
15. Hold onto the ends of the plastic wrap and roll the galantine on a hard surface to produce a smooth, round roll (Figure 17-39).

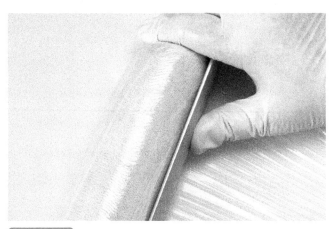

Figure 17-38 Wrap in plastic wrap.

Figure 17-39 Roll to make the galantine smooth.

16. If desired, place in a heat-resistant pouch and seal in a vacuum sealer (Figure 17-40).
17. Poach the galantine, using a traditional stovetop poaching method, or use a circulator made for cooking sous vide and vacuum-packed foods (Figure 17-41). For stovetop, poach in simmering stock until done, about 1 hour. The quality of the stock influences the flavor of the galantine and should be made with bones from the bird and added veal bones, spices, and soup vegetables.

The advantage of using a circulator is that it keeps the water continually moving and cooks the food in a lower-temperature-controlled environment. Using this method, the product stays round; with the consistent, lower temperature and longer cooking time, the product is more tender, cooked fully, and keeps more of its beautiful color.

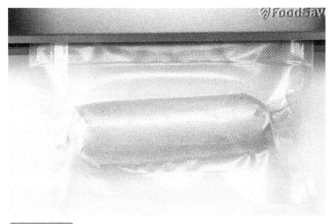

Figure 17-40 Vacuum sealing the galantine.

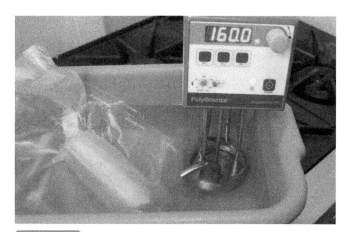

Figure 17-41 Poaching galantine in a circulator.

18. Chill. To serve, remove the plastic wrap and cheesecloth. Keep it cold and slice in thin slices (Figure 17-42).
19. Dip in poultry aspic before plating (Figure 17-43).
20. Plate galantine for service and garnish with cold sauces, relish, or small salad portions, if desired (Figure 17-44).

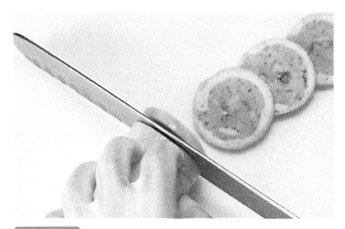

Figure 17-42 Slicing the galantine.

Figure 17-43 Dip the galantine into aspic prior to serving.

Figure 17-44 Plated galantine.

Duck is another popular poultry galantine choice.

duckling galantine   *Yield: 6 lbs (3.29 kg) 15 to 20 slices*

Ingredients	Amount		Procedure
	U.S.	Metric	
Duckling, purchased with giblets	5 lbs	2.27 kg	Bone the duckling as previously described. Save the bones for galantine stock. Add pistachio nuts to forcemeat and proceed as above.
*Poultry forcemeat	1 lb	454 g	
Pistachio nuts	2 oz	57 g	

*Use the Poultry Forcemeat Benchmark Recipe found earlier in this unit.

NUTRITIONAL INFORMATION PER SERVING: 307 Calories; 30 g Fat (87.6% calories from fat); 9 g Protein; 1 g Carbohydrate; trace Dietary Fiber; 53 mg Cholesterol; 198 mg Sodium. Exchanges: 0 Grain (Starch); 1 Lean Meat; 5 Fat.

Figure 17-45 Debone the fish.

Figure 17-46 Remove the skin.

FISH GALANTINE, STEPS IN PREPARATION

1. The process starts, again, with boning the fish. Use a needle-nose pliers to remove the small bones (Figure 17-45).
2. Much time can be saved if the fish is purchased in large fillets, skin on. The resulting galantine will be only 3 inches across, which is a nice size for appetizers.
   Remove the skin, starting at the tail (Figure 17-46).
3. Save the skin and salmon meat. There will be more salmon meat than needed.
4. Square the skin to a rectangle and place on the cheesecloth (Figures 17-47 and 17-48).
5. Square the skin in the other direction so that the skin is squared on all sides.

Figure 17-47 Square the skin in one direction.

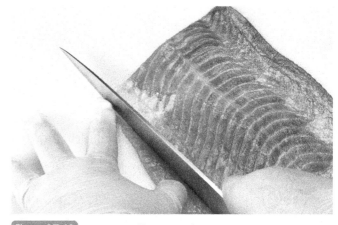

Figure 17-48 Trimming off excessive skin.

6. Spread the filling, roll, and tie together on both ends (Figure 17-49). Add a garnish on top of the filling, if desired (Figure 17-50).
7. Roll the filled skin in cheesecloth to a sausage shape (Figure 17-51). Use the side of a chef's knife to press the filled skin against the cheesecloth to ensure a tight roll (Figure 17-52).
8. Poach in simmering stock until done, about 1 hour. The quality of the stock influences the flavor of the galantine and should be made with fish bones, added veal bones, vinegar, white wine, spices, and soup vegetables without carrots because they contain sugar and would make the resulting stock too sweet.
9. The next step is pressing the galantine. Cool the galantine in its stock until lukewarm. Remove from stock, wrap again in clean cloth because the galantine has shrunk, and then tie and press lightly to maintain the shape and bind all ingredients.
10. Chill. To serve, keep cold and slice in thin slices.

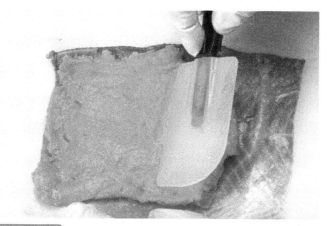

Figure 17-49 Filling being spread onto skin.

Figure 17-50 Add a shrimp garnish.

Figure 17-51 Form a sausage shape by rolling the filled skin in cheesecloth.

Figure 17-52 Use a chef's knife to press the roll tight.

salmon galantine *Yield: 25–30 slices*

Ingredients	Amounts		Procedure
	U.S.	Metric	
Salmon side, fresh	5 lbs	2.27 kg	Process as previously described.
Heavy cream	1 pt	473 ml	Process the salmon meat to forcemeat. Make a sample to ensure the mixture has a pleasant consistency.
Salt	To taste	To taste	
Pepper	To taste	To taste	

Make a fish stock with salmon bones. Fill the skin and process as previously described.

NUTRITIONAL INFORMATION PER SERVING: 72 Calories; 7 g Fat (88.8% calories from fat); 2 g Protein; 1 g Carbohydrate; trace Dietary Fiber; 29 mg Cholesterol; 22 mg Sodium. Exchanges: 0 Grain (Starch); 0 Lean Meat; 0 Nonfat Milk; 1 1/2 Fat.

STUFFED QUAIL GALANTINE

Quail are small birds that can be stuffed, provided they are roasted soon after stuffing. This particular stuffing uses chicken livers, grapes, and chicken mousse. Usually two quails are used for one serving. Very luxurious operations add a dollop of goose liver to the stuffing for each bird.

Follow these steps:

1. Place the quails skin side down on a table. (Use a semi-boned bird with the carcass removed, but ensure the leg bones remain.)
2. Add the mousse with a pastry bag; add two grapes each.
3. Wrap the quails in grape leaves and place in a buttered saucepan.

stuffed quail wrapped in grape leaves *Yield: 10 servings*

Ingredients	Amounts		Procedure
	U.S.	Metric	
Quail, boneless	20 each	20 each	Place the quails, skin side down, on a work surface.
Chicken mousse	20 oz	567 g	Add 1 oz (28 g) mousse and two grapes each.
Grapes, seedless	40 each	40 each	
Grape leaves, parboiled	20 each	20 each	Shape the birds to a natural shape and wrap in grape leaves. Place the seam side down in a suitable roasting pan. Bake at 325°F (160°C) until the internal temperature is 165°F (75°C).

NUTRITIONAL INFORMATION PER SERVING: 560 Calories; 36 g Fat (58.3% calories from fat); 45 g Protein; 12 g Carbohydrate; trace Dietary Fiber; 250 mg Cholesterol; 340 mg Sodium. Exchanges: 6 1/2 Lean Meat; 1/2 Vegetable; 0 Fruit; 3 Fat; 1/2 Other Carbohydrates.

Grape leaves are often sold preserved in brine and can be salty. They should be soaked to remove the excess salt.

CHICKEN LEG BALLOTINE

This item is practical for luncheon dishes served hot with a suitable sauce such as a mushroom sauce or served cold when sliced.

Follow these steps:

1. Bone the legs, without disturbing the skin. The skin will act as the casing.
2. Force the stuffing into the hollowed leg (recipe follows).
3. Shape into little bundles.
4. Place the bundles on wax paper squares, skin up; fold the paper and place tightly in a roasting pan.
5. Season and roast at 350°F (175°C) for 25 minutes.

classic chicken leg ballotine or dondine de canard
Yield: 10 servings

Ingredients	Amounts		Procedure
	U.S.	Metric	
Chicken legs or duck legs	10 each 8–10 oz	10 each 227–280 g	Fold the ham into the forcemeat. Follow the preceding instructions listed, for stuffing the chicken legs with forcemeat.
*Chicken or duck forcemeat	20 oz	567 g	
Ham or smoked cured tongue, diced	5 oz	142 g	

*Refer to the Poultry Forcemeat recipe, which was presented earlier in this unit

NUTRITIONAL INFORMATION PER SERVING: 575 Calories; 45 g Fat (71.3% calories from fat); 39 g Protein; 1 g Carbohydrate; 0 g Dietary Fiber; 185 mg Cholesterol; 697 mg Sodium. Exchanges: 5 1/2 Lean Meat; 5 1/2 Fat.

Figure 17-53 Quenelles are poached in stock.

To make a Dondine de Canard, substitute duck legs for the chicken, and duck forcemeat for the chicken forcemeat. Use smoked, cured tongue for the garniture. Roast and serve.

>> Quenelles

By now you have probably realized how versatile forcemeat can be. We've already used it in a number of applications. Another simple use for forcemeat is the quenelle, which can be made from any kind of forcemeat and bound with eggs. **Quenelle** is the French term for "dumpling," often used for dumplings made with meat or fish. They can be shaped in small balls with an ice cream scoop or with two soup spoons, or forced through a pastry bag onto butchered paper. Quenelles can be poached in water or stock. Alternatively, they can be poached or dressed on a sheet pan and steamed (Figure 17-53). Small quenelles are used as a soup garnish. Large quenelles are served hot with a variety of sauces as a main course. One famous classical French cuisine dish is Quenelles de Brochet, a pike dumpling.

>> Foie Gras

As was discussed in the appetizer unit, *foie gras* is the French term for fattened goose or duckling liver. The French term, literally translated, is "fat liver" and refers to liver from geese or a special duckling breed fattened by a cumbersome process. Allegedly, the Egyptians were the first who realized the delectable flavor of geese just prior to their migrating season. The birds stuffed themselves with grains growing along the Nile River to store enough fat for the migration south. It didn't take the Egyptians long to start force-feeding geese and ducks so that the treat was available at all times. Force-feeding encouraged the liver to grow to a gigantic size and store much excess fat, resulting in livers that were pale yellow rather than red.

The process of producing foie gras is labor intensive and, therefore, the product is very expensive. It is important to know a little about foie gras before deciding where you stand on the issue.

The business of producing commercially raised foie gras started in the Alsace region of France. Foie gras is served without any hesitation in many European countries with champagne or sweet wine and is associated with festive occasions. For many years, the only foie gras available in this country was canned and imported. Fresh foie gras of excellent quality is now being produced here in the United States.

Foie gras is graded and priced by size:

A = 14 oz (400 g) to 22 oz (625 g) each
B = 11 oz (310 g) to 13 oz (360 g) each
C = 7 oz (200 g) to 10 oz (280 g) each

Grade A is the most expensive and is usually served sliced and quickly sautéed. For making mousselines, terrines, and pâté, **en croûte (in crust)** grade C is adequate. Grades B and C often show veins and other imperfections that must be removed and can decrease yield, but they are much less expensive than grade A.

Canned foie gras is available in many shapes, sizes, and price levels. The most expensive are whole livers, and the least expensive is liver pâtés made with pork and other livers with a small percentage of foie gras added.

>> Pâté

Pâté, the French word for "pie," is generally used in connection with pies made with seasoned meats (often liver) from poultry, beef, pork, game, or seafood. There are also vegetable pâtés.

Can you think of any dish that has a patent on it? Chef Louis Jean-Joseph Clause earned a patent in 1784 for his recipe for pâté de foie gras. Not all pâtés are made with foie gras, but those that are command a high price.

Figure 17-54 Pâté en croûte.

The term *pâté* is derived from a pastry or paste that is wrapped around, hence pâté en croute. It refers to forcemeat baked in crust (en croute) (Figure 17-54). The crust could be baked in a special-shaped mold, similar to a spring-form pan, for easy release. The meaning of the term *pâté* has been blurred and is now also used for terrines slowly baked without crust in decorative molds made of china or earthenware. Traditionally, terrines were presented in the molds they were baked in and pâtés were served unmolded and sliced. Both terrines and pâtés are served cold today, but can be served hot.

PÂTÉ SEASONING BLENDS

Use one of the following seasoning blends in recipes that call for seasoning mixes. Quatre Epices is a traditional French four-spice blend that is used in pâtés, terrines, and forcemeat of all kinds. This dry spice blend does not contain salt. It is a recipe from the Classic Larousse Gastronomique.

quatre epices   *Yield: 7 oz (198 g), use about 1 oz (28 g) for 2 1/2 lbs (1.12 kg) forcemeat*

Ingredients	Amounts U.S.	Metric	Procedure
White pepper	4.5 oz	127 g	Mix all the dry spices together and use in pâtés.
Clove, ground	1/3 oz	9 g	
Ginger, ground	1 oz	28 g	
Nutmeg	1 oz	28 g	

NUTRITIONAL INFORMATION PER RECIPE: 655 Calories; 17 g Fat (20.4% calories from fat); 18 g Protein; 127 g Carbohydrate; 46 g Dietary Fiber; 0 mg Cholesterol; 43 mg Sodium. Exchanges: 8 1/2 Grain (Starch); 3 Fat.

Mace comes from the nutmeg tree and is the protective covering for the nutmeg. It tastes similar to nutmeg but is more pungent. It provides a punch to this spice blend.

pâté and terrine spice blend *Yield: 3.25 oz (92 g)*

Ingredients	Amounts		Procedure
	U.S.	Metric	
Black pepper, finely ground	3/4 oz	21 g	Mix and use for an assortment of pâtés, terrines, and sausages.
Coriander, ground	1/2 oz	14 g	
Thyme, ground	1/4 oz	7 g	
Bay leaf, ground	3/4 oz	21 g	
Mace, ground	1/4 oz	7 g	
Marjoram, ground	1/4 oz	7 g	

NUTRITIONAL INFORMATION PER RECIPE: 195 Calories; 4 g Fat (16.3% calories from fat); 5 g Protein; 41 g Carbohydrate; 17 g Dietary Fiber; 0 mg Cholesterol; 33 mg Sodium. Exchanges: 1 1/2 Grain (Starch); 0 Vegetable; 1/2 Fat.

Pâté Dough

When a recipe ends with the phrase *en croûte*, it means that the forcemeat is filled into a mold lined with pie dough and baked. The pie dough must be rather solid and compact to keep its shape when the cold pâté is sliced. During baking, the pâté recedes, leaving an air gap between the crust and the forcemeat. The gap is filled with flavor-corresponding jelly, which is needed to keep the pâté from drying out. **Aspic** is a savory jelly made with meat or fish stick and thickened by gelatin. The English word for jelly is usually associated with sweet, thickened juice, although the word is derived from *gel*, which means to thicken a liquid to a semisolid consistency. The jelly is usually a veal- or poultry-based gel that is laced with a complementary wine such as Madeira, port, or sherry.

pâté dough *Yield: 1 lb 8 oz (670 g)*

Ingredients	Amounts		Procedure
	U.S.	Metric	
All-purpose flour	1 lb	450 g	Place the flour and shortening in a mixer kettle and blend at low speed with a paddle until evenly crumbing.
Shortening	7 oz	200 g	
Salt	7 g	7 g	Combine the salt, water, and egg; add to the flour and shortening mixture.
Water	5 oz	150 ml	
Egg	1 each	1 each	Knead until smooth and refrigerate. The dough will be easier to work if allowed to rest for at least 1 hour.
			Use to encase pâtés in a pastry crust.

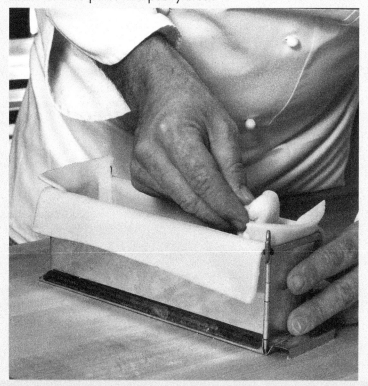

NUTRITIONAL INFORMATION PER RECIPE: 3,481 Calories; 208 g Fat (53.9% calories from fat); 53 g Protein; 347 g Carbohydrate; 12 g Dietary Fiber; 212 mg Cholesterol; 3,281 mg Sodium. Exchanges: 22 1/2 Grain (Starch); 1 Lean Meat; 40 Fat.

To line a pâté mold, it is important to roll out the dough very thin, and to cut the dough to fit the pan with at least a 1/2-inch overlap. Roll the dough out 18 by 24 inches and place on a parchment-lined sheet pan.

Using the pâté mold, cut according to the overall shape. Place the dough in the pan with the excess hanging out. Place forcemeat inside the pan. Then, using the excess dough, encase the meat.

If using a collapsible pan, slide the base off of the pan, and reverse it so that the top is now the bottom of the terrine and the bottom is the top. The seam will be baked on the bottom. This allows for a smooth top with no seams. Cut two steam vents on the top using a knife, cutter, or large piping tip for venting chimneys. Bake the terrine at 425°F (218°C) for the first 15 minutes, turning it down to 375°F (191°C) for the remainder of the bake time. Bake until the internal temperature is 165°F (74°C). Remove from the oven and chill.

Aspic is generally applied to cold foods to keep them moist and fresh. Pâtés en croûte are made with openings on the top to allow filling with semi-liquid aspic when the pâtés are thoroughly chilled.

meat aspic gelee   *Yield: Enough for one standard terrine mold*

Ingredients	Amounts		Procedure
	U.S.	Metric	
*Beef stock	8 fl oz	177 ml	Clarify the stock by reducing it from 8 oz to 6 oz and bring to a simmer.
Granular gelatin	1 oz	28 g	Bloom gelatin by soaking it in cold water for 5 minutes.
Cold water	2 fl oz	59 ml	Thoroughly combine the gelatin with the warm beef stock.

**Madeira	1/2 fl oz	15 ml	Add the Madeira and salt and stir until all the ingredients are dissolved. Place in a bowl in the refrigerator.
Salt	Pinch	Pinch	
			This can be stored for several weeks.

*Chicken stock or water can be substituted for the beef stock.

**Madeira is a semi-sweet fortified wine of Portuguese origin often used in cooking.

NUTRITIONAL INFORMATION PER RECIPE: 138 Calories; trace Fat (1.0% calories from fat); 3 g Protein; 26 g Carbohydrate; 0 g Dietary Fiber; 0 mg Cholesterol; 1,838 mg Sodium. Exchanges: 1 1/2 Other Carbohydrates.

Terrines are baking molds, usually oval, square, or rectangular, and made of oven-proof porcelain, glass, enameled cast iron, or earthenware. Terrines always have lids. When forcemeat is baked in this kind of mold or form, it is called *terrine*. It could also be called a pâté without a crust.

Inventive chefs who make terrines have quite a creative outlet with the use of colorful and intensely flavorful ingredients. The forcemeat is baked in a mold, so it can be chunkier or wetter than forcemeat baked in a pastry crust. The meat in a terrine is held together by the moisture and albumin content of the ingredients.

basic terrine *Yield: 2 1/2 lbs (1.13 kg) 10 each 4 oz (113 g) servings*

Ingredients	Amounts U.S.	Metric	Procedure
Boneless pork meat	1 lb	454 g	Finely grind all the meats. Mix them all together in a bowl or tub set in a larger tub of ice.
Boneless veal	1 lb	454 g	
Eggs, large	2 each	2 each	Add the remaining ingredients and mix well. Fry a small amount of the forcemeat to taste. Adjust the seasonings.
Onion, diced	1/2 oz	14 g	
Fatback, diced small	4 oz	113 g	
Dry white wine	10 fl oz	290 ml	Pack the forcemeat into an oiled terrine or baking mold.
Jellied meat stock	8 fl oz	237 ml	
Salt	To taste	To taste	Bake at 300°F (150°C), in a water bath, for 2 hours or until the terrine has shrunk away from the sides of the mold. Cool; then chill thoroughly. Decorate at will.
Pepper	To taste	To taste	
Quatre epices (recipe above)	1 oz	30 g	Quatre epices is just a spice blend and it is described in the preceding recipe. It should be in in the line just under the salt and pepper as it is a seasoning with them.

NUTRITIONAL INFORMATION PER SERVING: 260 Calories; 17 g Fat (61.4% calories from fat); 22 g Protein; 2 g Carbohydrate; trace Dietary Fiber; 121 mg Cholesterol; 687 mg Sodium. Exchanges: 0 Grain (Starch); 3 Lean Meat; 0 Vegetable; 1 1/2 Fat.

>> Terrines

Duck's distinctive flavor adds to the recipe, making it an attractive alternative to traditional terrines.

duck terrine   *Yield: 4 lbs (1.8 kg) Approximately 16 each*
4 oz (113 g) servings

Ingredients	Amounts		Procedure
	U.S.	Metric	
Duck, 1 whole	5 lbs	2.27 kg	Place the duck on a cutting board and make an incision along the back. Peel off the skin and set aside. De-bone the duck. There should be about 2 lbs (900 g) of meat. Save the liver and add to the liver below.
Chicken and duck liver	8 oz	226 g	Dice the livers, pork, and fatback.
Pork, lean	8 oz	226 g	
Fatback	1 lb	454 g	
Quatre epices	2 oz	57 g	Marinate the duck meat, pork, and fatback with quatre epices the and brandy 4 hours or overnight.
Brandy	2 fl oz	59 ml	In the meantime, coarsely chop duckling bones and roast until light brown.
Chicken stock	24 fl oz	709 ml	Add the chicken stock and wine. Bring to a boil, reduce the heat, and simmer for 2 hours. Strain and chill. There should be about 1 cup of stock.
Muscatel or sweet wine	4 fl oz	118 ml	
Eggs	2 each	2 each	Add the eggs, flour, and salt to the meats and grind though a medium-fine plate.
Flour	1 oz	30 g	
Salt	1 tbsp	15 g	
Pistachios, unshelled	4 oz	113 g	Add the cold stock and pistachio nuts. Blend with a paddle. Line the terrine mold with the saved duckling skin. If there is not enough skin, fill the empty spots with sliced bacon. Fill the terrine with ground meat. Make sure there are no air pockets.
Bacon, sliced	4 each	4 each	Cover the meat with bacon slices. Cover the terrine with aluminum foil, place in a water bath, and bake for about 2 hours at 325°F (163°C).
Aspic	1 pt	473 ml	When completely cooled, slowly fill the terrine with aspic, eliminating any air by tapping on the sides. Top with bay leaves, if desired. Chill for 24 hours before slicing.

NUTRITIONAL INFORMATION PER SERVING: 715 Calories; 61 g Fat (79.0% calories from fat); 29 g Protein; 7 g Carbohydrate; 1g Dietary Fiber; 202 mg Cholesterol; 1,680 mg Sodium. Exchanges: 0 Grain (Starch); 4 Lean Meat; 1/2 Vegetable; 10 Fat.

Traditionally, recipe names that include the words *farmer's wife* contain plenty of fresh ingredients. This terrine includes fresh herbs with a little touch of cognac or brandy.

farmer's wife terrine *Yield: 6 1/2 lbs (2.95 kg) 26 each*
4 oz (113 g) servings

Ingredients	Amounts U.S.	Metric	Procedure
Pork shoulder, boned and cut into 1-in pieces	2 lbs	907 g	Grind the pork, fatback, chicken meat, and liver medium fine.
Fatback, diced	8 oz	227 g	
Chicken breast or thigh, boneless, cut into 1-in pieces	1 lb	454 g	
Chicken liver	1 lb	454 g	
Shallots, chopped	4 oz	113 g	Sauté the shallots and garlic until translucent.
Garlic, chopped	5 cloves	5 cloves	
Salt	1 oz	30 g	Add all the remaining seasoning ingredients except for the caul fat and mix very well (caul fat is the fat that lines the viscera, and is the lacy fat that is used much like sausage skin, to hold and wrap meat).
TCM	1 tsp	5 g	
White pepper	1 tsp	5 g	
Quatre epices (recipe above)	2 oz	57 g	
Fresh thyme leaves, chopped	2 tsp	10 g	
Fresh sage leaves, chopped	1 tsp	5 g	
Eggs	6 each	6 each	
Cognac or brandy	6 fl oz	177 ml	
Lace caul fat	5 oz	142 g	Soak the caul fat to remove the salt. Line the terrine with caul fat.
Bacon or smoked fatback, sliced thin	7 oz	198 g	Fill the lined terrine with the seasoned forcemeat and level off the top of the terrine flat.

Fold over any remaining caul fat and cover the terrine with bacon or smoked fatback.

To bake the terrine, place in a 300°F to 325°F (150°C to 160°C) oven for 2 hours or until the internal temperature reaches 155°F (70°C).

Remove from the oven, chill slightly, then place a weight or foil-covered brick on the terrines. Chill for 12 hours at 38°F (5°C).

Unmold to clean and scrape away any unwanted impurities. Return to the cleaned mold and fill the cavities with aspic jelly. Serve in the mold or sliced. Serve with chutney or relish and cornichons, which are pickled gherkin cucumbers.

NUTRITIONAL INFORMATION PER SERVING: 267 Calories; 17 g Fat (63.6% calories from fat); 19 g Protein; 3 g Carbohydrate; trace Dietary Fiber; 171 mg Cholesterol; 946 mg Sodium. Exchanges: 0 Grain (Starch); 2 1/2 Lean Meat; 0 Vegetable; 2 Fat.

You'll note that this recipe includes TCM, which is often associated with sausage making. It is added here for a couple of reasons. Terrines usually have a long shelf-life. TCM will help to maintain the reddish meat color and it will help to protect the ingredients against botulism. Terrines create a high-fat, low-oxygen environment that can become a breeding ground for bacterial growth.

hunter's terrine *Yield: 6 lbs (2.7 kg) 24 each 4 oz (113 g) servings*

Ingredients	Amounts		Procedure
	U.S.	Metric	
Fatback	8 oz	227 g	Freeze the fatback and then slice on a machine into thin even slices. Put the slices in a basket and dip it briefly in boiling water. Put aside. If fatback is not available, use sliced bacon. It does not require the boiling.
Pork shoulder, boned and sinews removed, cut into 1-in pieces	2 lbs	907 g	Place the meats into a large mixing bowl or bus tub.
Venison shoulder, boned and sinews removed, cut into 1-in pieces	2 lbs	907 g	
Veal shoulder, boned and sinews removed, cut into 1-in pieces	2 lbs	907 g	
Salt	1 tbsp	15 g	Season the meats with spices, herbs, wine, brandy, salt, and TCM. Marinate for 3 hours.
White pepper	2 tsp	2 g	
Garlic, minced	3 cloves	3 cloves	Grind the seasoned meats through the medium plate of a meat grinder. Put the ground meats in a machine kettle and thoroughly blend with a paddle.
Dried juniper berries	1 tsp	5 g	
Dried thyme	1 tsp	5 g	Line the terrines with blanched fatback. Sauté a small amount of the forcemeat and adjust to taste.
Dried marjoram	1 tsp	5 g	
TCM	1 tsp	5 g	Pack the meat mixture into the terrine.
Mace	1/2 tsp	2 g	Cover the filled mold with additional fatback or bacon slices. Place a bay leaf on top of the terrines.
Cinnamon	1/2 tsp	2 g	
Dry white wine	8 fl oz	237 ml	Bake in a water bath in a preheated oven 300°F (150°C) for 3 hours.
Cognac or good brandy	2 fl oz	59 ml	Internal temperature should reach 165°F (75°C).
Whole bay leaves	8 each	8 each	

Cool in the refrigerator with a weight, overnight, or for several hours.

This terrine is best served a few days after the baking to mature and mellow the flavors.

NUTRITIONAL INFORMATION PER SERVING: 216 Calories; 12 g Fat (55.0% calories from fat); 22 g Protein; 1 g Carbohydrate; trace Dietary Fiber; 84 mg Cholesterol; 569 mg Sodium. Exchanges: 0 Grain (Starch); 3 Lean Meat; 0 Vegetable; 0 Fruit; 1 1/2 Fat.

The Swedish specialty dish, gravlax, with its salty, sugary, and dill cure, adds a distinctive flavor to this delicious terrine. Consult Unit 17 for a basic gravlax recipe.

gravlax and herb terrine   *Yield: 4 lbs (1.8 kg) 16 each 4 oz (113 g) servings*

Ingredients	Amounts U.S.	Metric	Procedure
Cream cheese, room temperature	1 lb 12 oz	794 g	Stir the cream cheese until soft and smooth.
Eggs, large	4 each	4 each	Incorporate the eggs.
Heavy cream	16 fl oz	473 ml	Fold in the heavy cream and blend well.
Gravlax, small diced	8 oz	227 g	Incorporate the remainder of the ingredients until well blended. Spoon into buttered, 2 oz (60 ml) or 4 oz (120 ml) ramekins.
Gruyere cheese, finely grated	6 oz	170 g	
Fresh chervil, tarragon, or herbs of your choice, finely minced	2 tbsp	30 g	
Nutmeg, freshly ground	1/4 tsp	1 g	
White pepper, freshly ground	1/2 tsp	2 g	

Place the ramekins in a bain-marie (water bath) and bake in a preheated 325°F (160°C) oven until set, 25–30 minutes. Remove from the water bath and cool to room temperature. The terrines may be served at room temperature or chilled. The terrines may be turned out of the ramekins or served as is. Serve with toast points and a green salad as an appetizer or light lunch.

NUTRITIONAL INFORMATION PER SERVING: 360 Calories; 33 g Fat (82.7% calories from fat); 11 g Protein; 4 g Carbohydrate; trace Dietary Fiber; 166 mg Cholesterol; 488 mg Sodium. Exchanges: 0 Grain (Starch); 1 1/2 Lean Meat; 0 Vegetable; 0 Fruit; 0 Nonfat Milk; 6 Fat; 0 Other Carbohydrates.

>> Mousse

Mousse, according to *Webster's New World Dictionary of Culinary Arts* (2nd edition), is "a soft, creamy food, either sweet or savory, lightened by adding whipped cream, beaten egg whites or both." Mousse can be served hot or cold.

Hot mousse is generally made with meat, fish, shellfish, or vegetables and baked in a water bath. Cold mousse is made by puréeing cooked ingredients such as meat, fish, seafood, or vegetables, blending the purée with a small amount of corresponding sauce made of whipped cream and warm aspic jelly.

Pâté is sometimes changed into a mousse form by puréeing the ingredients until smooth. This process adds air and, therefore, volume to the recipes, producing a lighter texture. Because of this, mousse has a lower fat content compared to pâté.

silky chicken liver pâté *Yield: 4 lbs (1.8 kg) 16 each 4 oz (113 g) servings*

Ingredients	Amounts		Procedure
	U.S.	Metric	
Salted butter	2 lbs	907 g	Melt the butter and begin to cool. Set aside.
Shallots, chopped fine	3 large	3 large	Combine the shallots, garlic, and thyme in a sauté pan with olive oil and cook slowly until soft; then cool.
Garlic, chopped fine	6 cloves	6 cloves	
Fresh thyme, chopped	1 oz	28 g	
Olive oil	1 oz	30 ml	
Chicken livers, trimmed	2 lbs	907 g	Purée the liver and spices in a food processor until smooth.
Black pepper	2 tsp	10 g	
Ground cloves	1/2 tsp	2 g	
Nutmeg	1 tsp	5 g	
Cumin	1 tsp	5 g	
Port wine	4 fl oz	118 ml	Add port to the food processor and room temperature shallot mixture. Purée until smooth again.
			Place on a tamis and push through to remove all bit of herbs and any remaining sinews. The mixture should be very smooth. Place back into a clean food processor bowl.
			When the butter is cooled between 95°F and 105°F (35°C and 40°C), slowly pour it into the running food processor with the liver mixture. Place the mixture in a well-buttered or paper-lined loaf pan. Cover with buttered paper and then foil to seal out water. Bake in a water bath at 275°F (135°C) until the internal temperature is 140°F (60°C). Cool with a weight on top. Slice when completely chilled.

NUTRITIONAL INFORMATION PER SERVING: 515 Calories; 50 g Fat (87.6% calories from fat); 11 g Protein; 5 g Carbohydrate; 1 g Dietary Fiber; 373 mg Cholesterol; 516 mg Sodium. Exchanges: 0 Grain (Starch); 1 1/2 Lean Meat; 0 Vegetable; 9 1/2 Fat.

A velouté is a French sauce made by thickening stock with a roux. This recipe, which goes with the preceding salmon mousse recipe, calls for a fish velouté, which is a rich sauce made with fish stock. The recipe follows the mousse recipe.

salmon mousse *Yield: 1 lb 8 oz (680 g) 6 each 4 oz (113 g) servings*

Ingredients	Amounts U.S.	Metric	Procedure
Salmon, boneless, skinless	12 oz	340 g	Steam the salmon and transfer it to the food processor while still warm.
Fish velouté, warm	8 fl oz	225 ml	Add the warm velouté in a steady stream while the machine is running.
Heavy cream	8 oz	237 ml	Whip the cream to soft peaks and reserve.
Granulated gelatin	1 1/2 oz	45 g	Add the gelatin to the wine and allow it to rest for 5 minutes. Heat the gelatin mixture to a simmer.
White wine	4 oz	118 ml	
Salt	To taste	To taste	Transfer the salmon and velouté to a mixing bowl and stir in the gelatin mixture. Season with salt, pepper, and cayenne.
Black pepper	To taste	To taste	
Cayenne pepper	To taste	To taste	

When the mixture has cooled to near room temperature, fold in the whipped cream with a rubber spatula until just mixed.

The mousse is now ready to be formed into timbales or molded into various shapes as desired.

NUTRITIONAL INFORMATION PER SERVING: 387 Calories; 26 g Fat (61.1% calories from fat); 16 g Protein; 21 g Carbohydrate; trace Dietary Fiber; 82 mg Cholesterol; 1,388 mg Sodium. Exchanges: 1 Grain (Starch); 1 1/2 Lean Meat; 0 Nonfat Milk; 5 Fat; 0 Other Carbohydrates.

fish velouté *Yield: 8 fl oz (237 ml)*

Ingredients	Amounts U.S.	Metric	Procedure
Butter	1/2 oz	14 g	Melt the butter in a saucepot, add the flour, and cook the roux until it is a light cream color, approximately 5 minutes.
Flour	1/2 oz	14 g	
Fish stock	8 oz	237 ml	Add the hot stock and stir to blend. Cook 10 minutes to cook out the raw flour flavor and develop thickness.

NUTRITIONAL INFORMATION PER RECIPE: 255 Calories; 17 g Fat (71.0% calories from fat); 2 g Protein; 14 g Carbohydrate; 1 g Dietary Fiber; 47 mg Cholesterol; 353 mg Sodium. Exchanges: 1/2 Grain (Starch); 2 1/2 Fat; 0 Other Carbohydrates.

Mousses traditionally have three components: the base, the binder, and the aerator. In the following Ham Mousse recipe, the ham is the base, the gelatin is the binder, and the whipped cream is the aerator or volumizer.

ham mousse *Yield: 3 lbs 8 oz (1.58 kg) 28 each 2 oz (56 g) servings*

Ingredients	Amounts		Procedure
	U.S.	Metric	
Ham, cooked	2 lbs	896 g	Chop the ham in a food processor until it is finely minced.
Chicken stock	4 fl oz	116 ml	Bloom the gelatin in the chicken stock and sherry. Warm this mixture to approximately 110°F (43°C). Add the gelatin to the ham mixture above and process until it is incorporated.
Gelatin	2 oz	56 g	
Sherry	4 fl oz	116 ml	
Heavy cream	16 fl oz	464 ml	Whip the heavy cream, seasoning it with salt and cayenne pepper. Place the ham mixture over an ice bath and stir until it is slightly thickened. Fold in the whipped cream and put it into lightly oiled molds or a 2-quart mold. Chill until it is set, preferably overnight. Remove from molds and serve.
Salt	1/2 tsp	3 g	
Cayenne pepper	1/8 tsp	1 g	

NUTRITIONAL INFORMATION PER SERVING: 132 Calories; 10 g Fat (68.8% calories from fat); 6 g Protein; 4 g Carbohydrate; trace Dietary Fiber; 42 mg Cholesterol; 515 mg Sodium. Exchanges: 0 Grain (Starch); 1 Lean Meat; 0 Nonfat Milk; 1 1/2 Fat; 0 Other Carbohydrates.

Any variety of cooked or blanched vegetables can be substituted for the peppers in the following vegetable mousse. Replace the 10 ounces (283 g) of peppers with 10 ounces (283 g) of cooked asparagus purée, broccoli purée, cooked mushroom purée, cooked carrot purée, cooked cauliflower purée, or a vegetable of your choice.

roasted red pepper mousse   *Yield: 1 lb 10 oz (737 g) Approximately*
6 each 4 oz (113 g) servings

Ingredients	Amounts U.S.	Metric	Procedure
Onion, diced small	3 oz	85 g	Sauté the onions and garlic in the olive oil until translucent and tender.
Garlic, chopped	1 tsp	5 g	
Olive oil	1 fl oz	30 ml	
Red bell pepper, fire-roasted, peeled, and diced	10 oz	283 g	Add the fire-roasted red bell pepper, salt and pepper, and chicken stock. Bring to a boil; reduce to a simmer and cook 5 minutes.
Salt	To taste	To taste	
Pepper	To taste	To taste	
Chicken stock	8 oz	237 ml	

Ingredients	Amounts U.S.	Metric	Procedure
Gelatin, granulated	1 oz	30 g	Soften the gelatin in the cold white wine, and then add it to the hot pepper mixture. Purée the mixture in a blender.
Dry white wine	2 fl oz	59 ml	Whip the cream to medium soft peaks.
Heavy whipping cream	6 fl oz	177 ml	Place the pepper mixture over an ice bath and stir until the mixture just starts to thicken. Fold in the whipped cream and pour the mousse into aspic-lined or well-oiled timbale molds or other shaped molds and refrigerate until the mixture is solid—a few hours or overnight. Unmold the mousse and serve as desired.

NUTRITIONAL INFORMATION PER SERVING: 172 Calories; 16 g Fat (84.6% calories from fat); 1 g Protein; 5 g Carbohydrate; 1 g Dietary Fiber; 41 mg Cholesterol; 391 mg Sodium. Exchanges: 0 Grain (Starch); 1/2 Vegetable; 0 Nonfat Milk; 3 Fat; 0 Other Carbohydrates.

The French term *rillette* refers to meat slowly cooked in its own fat until very soft and then shredded. The concept started as a way of preserving meat because the very fatty, spicy meat blend could be stored in earthen jars in cool basements. Another name is *confit*, and a recipe for duck confit follows.

Typically, rillettes are served cold as a spread with toast points or crackers, similar to a pâté.

basic rillette *Yield: 2 lbs (907 g) 8 each 4 oz (113 g) servings*

Ingredients	Amounts		Procedure
	U.S.	**Metric**	
Bone-in pork shoulder	3 lbs	1.36 kg	Cut the meat and fat into large, finger-sized julienne pieces.
Pâté spices	3 oz	85 g	Season with the spice blend and the salt and pepper and bay leaf.
Salt	1 tbsp	15 g	Cook in a heavy Dutch oven with lid for 3 to 4 hours at 250°F (120°) until the meat falls apart.
Black pepper, ground	1 tsp	5 g	Strain off the fat and reserve the fat for later. Remove the bay leaves. With a fork, shred the meat in coarse pieces.
Bay leaves	2 each	2 each	

Press into an earthenware or ceramic bowl or crock.

Blend and cover with the reserved fat, covering completely to seal out any air.

Keep refrigerated up to 6 months.

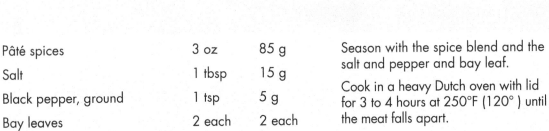

NUTRITIONAL INFORMATION PER SERVING: 302 Calories; 23 g Fat (70.0% calories from fat); 22 g Protein; trace Carbohydrate; trace Dietary Fiber; 91 mg Cholesterol; 882 mg Sodium. Exchanges: 0 Grain (Starch); 3 Lean Meat; 3 Fat.

>> Rillettes

Confit is a French method of preserving meat, and is particularly used with poultry. The following recipe for duck confit is another example of a rillette, but one that is served warm.

duck confit *Yield: 2 lbs (907 g) 8 each 4 oz (113 g) servings*

Ingredients	Amounts		Procedure
	U.S.	Metric	
One whole duck, cut into four pieces	5 lbs	2.27 kg	Rub the duck pieces with the Kosher salt.
Kosher salt	1 tbsp	15 g	
Black pepper, cracked fresh	1 tsp	5 g	Place the skin side down in a roasting pan just large enough to hold the pieces in one layer. Season with the black pepper, crumbled bay leaves, fresh thyme, bruised and crushed garlic. Cover and refrigerate overnight.
Bay leaves	4 each	4 each	
Fresh thyme	6 sprigs	6 sprigs	
Garlic, cloves, crushed	4 each	4 each	
Duck, goose, or chicken fat (use lard or shortening if other fat is unavailable)	2 lbs	907 g	Bake the duck at 325°F (160°C) until brown, approximately 15 to 25 minutes. Add enough melted fat to cover the pieces completely.

Cover the pan and roast or cook at 250°F (150°C) in the oven for approximately 2–3 hours until the duck is very tender, or simmer on the stove for 2 hours.

Remove the duck from the fat and place in a deep hotel pan. Cover the pieces with the fat.

Store this preserved cooked duck for as long as 4 months refrigerated.

To serve, remove from the fat and bake at 350°F (175°C) to crisp the skin and heat through, or use in a traditional cassoulet, a French dish made with beans and sausages.

NUTRITIONAL INFORMATION PER SERVING: 929 Calories; 97 g Fat (94.2% calories from fat); 12 g Protein; 1 g Carbohydrate; 1 g Dietary Fiber; 132 mg Cholesterol; 418 mg Sodium. Exchanges: 0 Grain (Starch); 1 1/2 Lean Meat; 0 Vegetable; 18 1/2 Fat.

TEMPERATURES

It is important to adhere to the cooking times and temperatures when working with pâté. The following chart serves as a general and reliable guide.

TEMPERATURE CHART FOR COOKING PÂTÉ AND TERRINES

Ingredient	Cooking Temps.	Cooking Time	Internal Temps.	Water Bath Temp.
Pâté en croûte	425°F (220°C), then reduce heat to 350°F (175°C)	20–30 minutes, then 45 minutes	155°F (70°C)	None
Pâté de foie gras	270°F (130°C)	35 minutes	140°F (60°C)	175°F (80°C) maximum
Terrines	350°F (175°C)	55–65 minutes	155°F (70°C)	Simmering
Timbales	350°F (175°C)	15 minutes	155°F (70°C)	Simmering

For pâtés or terrines with a solid internal core, the minimal internal temperature should be 140°F (60°C).

>> Summary

Charcuterie refers to products made from ground meats including forcemeats, sausages, pâtés, galantines, ballotines, rillettes, and a host of other tasty and visually stimulating products. Forcemeat is the basis for many of these products. It is the mixture of finely chopped and seasoned meat, fish, and seafood, and often contains egg whites and cream.

Sausages have been a favorite fast food for over 1,500 years. Sausages consist of ground or pounded, highly seasoned meat stuffed into casing. Sausages can be classified as fresh, cured or smoked, and dried.

Galantines consist of forcemeat that is stuffed into poultry or fish skin and then roll shaped. Ballotines are similar but are shaped like bundles. Quenelles are small, delicate dumplings made from meat or fish forcemeat that are boiled or poached.

Pâtés are made with delicately seasoned, finely ground meats, often including livers and fat. Herbs, spices, wines, and liquors are added for flavorings. The high fat content makes for a creamy, melt-in-your-mouth texture. Foie gras (fattened goose or duck liver) is a popular ingredient in pâtés, but not all pâtés contain foie gras. Pâtés are generally baked inside a dough-lined mold. Terrines are baked in a water bath in heavy china, earthenware, or other suitable molds. The name *terrine* has become interchangeable with pâté; hence, canned pâté does not contain baked dough.

Rillette is shredded meat, slowly cooked in its own fat and then mixed with additional fat to form a smooth paste.

>> Review Questions

SHORT ANSWER

1. List four different ingredients that are used as binders in sausage making.
2. Explain the benefit of adding salt directly to the meat, fish, or seafood before grinding.
3. What are the two major types of casings used in sausage-making? Describe the benefits of each type.
4. Write a brief history of foie gras.

MATCHING

Match the ingredient to its description.

5. mixture of finely chopped and seasoned meat
6. wrapped in pastry and baked
7. forcemeat that is shaped into a bundle
8. fattened goose or duck liver
9. delicate meat or fish dumpling
10. cornmeal mush with meat and spices, made into loaves
11. seasoned ground meat that is stuffed into casings
12. binding agent used to improve texture of forcemeat
13. formed pâté
14. puréed food with a lighter texture
15. seasoned with Spanish seasonings
16. shredded meat mixed with fat to form a smooth paste

a. panada
b. scrapple
c. sausage
d. quenelles
e. ballotine
f. forcemeat
g. foie gras
h. chorizo
i. en croûte
j. terrine
k. rillet
l. mousse

Match the foreign term with the English translation.

17. pie
18. bundle
19. cooked meat
20. fattened goose
21. sausage
22. dumpling

a. salsus
b. charcuterie
c. quenelle
d. ballotine
e. foie gras
f. pâté

MULTIPLE CHOICE

23. Another name for farce is
    a. innards.
    b. foie gras.
    c. forcemeat.
    d. pâté.
24. Which cut of pork is preferred for making sausage?
    a. Boston butt
    b. loin
    c. belly
    d. ham

25. The best way to prevent botulism in smoked sausages is to use
    a. Morton's Quick Cure.
    b. sodium nitrite.
    c. potassium nitrite.
    d. Prague Powder #1.
26. What size plate holes should be used on a grinder to obtain a coarse grind?
    a. 3/16-inch plate
    b. 3/4-inch plate
    c. 1-inch plate
    d. 3/8-inch plate

Buffets and Catering

>> Unit 18

Buffets

>> Unit 19

Catering

The backbone of most professional kitchens is often the buffet and catering business. It brings in more revenue than most other streams. The cold kitchen chef is generally actively involved in both buffet preparation, as discussed in Unit 18, and in catering. Unit 19 will cover the logistics of on- and off-premise catering, including mass production, plating, and box lunches.

UNIT 18

Buffets

>> Learning Objectives

After you have finished reading this unit, you should be able to:

- Describe the logistics of buffet service.
- Discuss buffet traffic flow and supply issues.
- Design the menu and food display for a wedding reception.
- Explain ways to safely display ice carvings.
- Describe the basic equipment used in buffet service.
- Demonstrate how to make both inedible and edible table decorations.
- Describe action stations.
- Discuss the basic elements of buffet presentation.

>> Key Terms

action stations	freezer spray	table skirting	Viennese table
carving stations	induction stove	tallow	zones
cooking stations	risers		

This unit discusses the setup and organization of buffets for many types of occasions. The term *buffet* means a table, series of tables, or holding units used to display and self-serve just about any kind of food ranging from breakfast pastries, sandwiches, and salads to the elaborate presentations of cold and hot foods. Guests love buffets because they provide an abundance of choices. They can choose what to eat and how much to eat. Guests with special dietary needs or restrictions can usually find a well-balanced meal within the array of options.

The advantages of serving buffet style are many:

- A simplified menu with a set purchase amount aids in control of food costs.
- Food is produced in greater quantity with fewer staff members.
- Productivity is increased.
- Underutilized products or trimmings can be turned into salads, spreads. and other delectables.
- Foods are easier to provide in alternative settings such as parks, offices, the beach, and large venues.

Figure 18-1 Simple props can add to the effectiveness of the buffet. A simple wooden fan is used as a trivet to showcase the appetizers.

>> Elements of Successful Buffets

One key element of planning a successful buffet is to plan for smaller portion sizes to avoid waste and to encourage guests to choose from a wide variety of foods. Other important factors for successful buffets are balance and attractiveness. Today, buffet setups tend toward less contrived decoration and more natural options such as beautiful ice carvings, as well as nonedible items and inedible props and centerpieces (Figure 18-1). These styles of props can be made from natural materials such as shells, flowers, or rocks, and, when sculpted, tallow, butter, cheese, or chocolate.

Tallow is a classic, nonedible decorative showpiece that is beautiful and challenging to create. It is a blend of sheep or beef fat or suet and paraffin wax (Figure 18-2).

Tallow is often used in candle making. Paraffin wax is a petroleum-based product. The fat is rendered, bleached, and mixed with equal portions of paraffin to give it stability and strength. Learning to work with and master tallow is worth the effort, although it is one of the more arcane of the culinary skills.

> **CHEF'S TIP**
> *Tallow should never be allowed to come into contact with food. Because it is often saved and used from time to time, it is unsanitary.*

Figure 18-2 Decorative showpieces made of tallow can be used time and again and will last for years.

THE MENU

The most important component of any buffet is the food. It should be attractively displayed and delicious to taste. Hot foods should be kept hot and cold foods cold. The amount of food and the variety depend on the event.

Here are a few sample buffet menus.

BREAKFAST BUFFET MENU

Assorted Juices to include Orange, Grapefruit, Tomato, and Cranberry

Fresh Fruits including Melon, Berries, and Citrus in season

Assorted Cold Cereals

French Toast, Pancakes, and Waffles

Scrambled Eggs or Eggs Benedict

Link Sausages or Patties

Canadian Bacon, Ham, or Bacon

Corned Beef Hash

Home Fries

Assorted Muffins, Scones, and Danish Pastries from Our Bakery

Coffee, Decaffeinated Coffee, Regular or Herbal Tea,

Hot Cocoa, or Milk

Sunday Brunch Buffet Menu

Assorted Juices to include Fresh Squeezed Orange Juice, Grapefruit Juice,
Tomato Juice, and Cranberry Juice

Fresh Fruit Mirror to include Pineapple Slices, Melon and Cantaloupe, Seasonal Berries,
and Strawberry Bowl with Sauce Romanoff

Assorted Breakfast Pastries to include Muffins, Scones, and Viennoiserie

Eggs Benedict or Eggs Sardo

Potatoes O'Brien

Bacon, Link Pork Sausage, Turkey Sausage

An assortment of Bagels with Cream Cheese

Lox Mirror with Accompaniments—Capers, Red Onion Brunoise, Sour Cream, and Lemon Wedges

Cold Seafood Bar to include Poached Prawns, Oysters on the Half Shell,
and Cracked Dungeness Crab

Assorted Cold Salads to include Pasta, Potato, and Quinoa Salad

Assorted Garden Greens with your choice of Balsamic Vinaigrette,
Creamy California Herb, or Buttermilk Bleu.

Entrée Items

Grilled Lemon Herb Chicken

Chicken Florentine

Country Fried Buttermilk Chicken

Poached Salmon served with Lemon Caper Tomato Butter

Sea Scallop Sauté with Wild Mushroom and White Wine Butter Sauce

Baked Pineapple Ham

Sautéed Seasonal Vegetables

Rice Pilaf

Steamed Red Creamer Potatoes with Parsley Butter

Dessert Bar

A fabulous assortment of Cakes, Tortes and Gateaux, Tarts, Pies, and Cheesecake

Ice Cream Bar with assorted Toppings

Working Lunch Buffet

Soup, Salad, and Sandwich Buffet
Choice of House-Made Soup of the Day or New England Clam Chowder
Sliced Breads, Yeast Rolls, Lavash Wrap Bread
Assorted Deli Tray (Sliced Turkey, Ham, Roast Beef, and Corned Beef)
Assorted Cheeses
Lettuce, Tomato, Onion Slices, Pickles, Olives, and Condiments
Tuna Salad, Ham Salad, or Egg Salad
Fresh Tossed Salad (with Assorted Dressings) or Caesar Salad
Potato and Pasta Salad
Potato Chips

Dessert Bar with
Brownie, Lemon, and Pecan Bars
Cheesecake with Cherry or Blueberry Topping
Ice Cream with Toppings

Assorted Sodas, Iced and Hot Tea, and Coffee

Dinner Buffet

Fresh Tossed Salad (with choice of dressings) or Caesar Salad

Fresh Vegetables du Jour and Rice, Noodles, Garlic Mashed, or Boiled Red Potato

Rolls and Butter

Entrées

Red Snapper served with Southwest Peppers and Cilantro Pesto

Seafood Tortellini

Grilled Coho Salmon with Lemon Dill Sauce

Chicken Breast with Marsala Sauce

Stir-Fry of Chicken, Beef, or Shrimp with Fresh Vegetables

Beef Burgundy served over Pastry Shells

Sirloin Tips with Mushrooms and Demi-glace

Dessert Bar

Cheesecake with Cherry or Blueberry Topping, Assorted Cookies,

Ice Cream with Toppings

Ballroom Grand Opening

Butler Passed Hors d'oeuvre
Ahi Tuna with Kiwi Relish served on Chinese Spoons
Local Roasted Porcini Mushrooms Bruschetta

Northwest Seafood Bar
Quilcene Bay and Royal Miyagi Oysters on the Half Shell
Black Lip Mussel Mignonette, Large Poached Prawns,
Yellow Gazpacho Shooters with Dungeness Crab

International Cheese and Charcuterie Display
Handcarved Prosciutto, Local and Internationally Crafted Sausages
Cacciatore, Crespone, Felino, Finocchiona Salami
Comte, Mimolette Viella, Chestnut Leaf Sheep Cheeses
Served with Flavored Flat Bread

Braised Short Ribs with Parsnip Purée
With Corn Fried Okra

Northwest Fall Harvest
Roasted Vegetable Crisp and Butternut Squash Bisque
Complimented with Cinnamon Toasted Pumpkin Seeds

Halibut
Northwest Halibut with Saffron Risotto

Desserts
Lavender Crème Brulée, Mini Pear Tarts
Parfaits, Chocolate Hazelnut Flourless Cake

Espresso and Coffees
With Biscotti Dipped in Chocolate, After Dinner Liqueurs

Beer and Wine Sommelier
Offering definitive tastings to pair with Chef's menu

Chocolate Truffles and Departing Gifts

Southwestern Dinner Buffet

Crisp Blue Corn Tortilla Chips
Guacamole and Salsa Fresca
Southwestern Crudite with Roasted Pepper Aioli

Beef and Chicken Fajitas with Grilled Sweet Peppers and Onions
Fresh Flour Tortillas
Green Chili Posole
Carne Asada
Chicken Enchiladas
Tamales
Spanish Rice
Refried Beans
Tossed Green Salad with your choice of
Chipotle Ranch or Orange Chili Vinaigrette

Desserts
Tres Leche Cake
Chocolate Chili Flan
Cinnamon Ice Cream with Caramel and Mango Sauce

The Italian Dinner Buffet

Starters
Hearts of Romaine with Creamy Parmesan Dressing

Antipasto Platter (Slices of Italian Imported Meats and Cheeses, Grilled Vegetables, Marinated
Artichoke Hearts, and Olives)

Tomatoes Layered with Fresh Mozzarella and Basil
Drizzled with Extra Virgin Olive Oil and Aged Balsamic Vinegar

Entrées and Pasta
Chicken and Ricotta Stuffed Manicotti
Pasta Puttanesca with Sun-dried Tomatoes
Eggplant Parmesan
Tricolored Cheese-Filled Tortellini with Pesto Cream
Fettuccini and Scampi Fra Diavolo

Veal Marsala with
Gorgonzola Gnocchi

Served with Seasonal Vegetables

Dessert
Tiramisu
Assorted Cannolis
Assorted Gelato

Review the sample menus and create your own menu. Choose one of the following occasions or themes to serve as your inspiration: New Year's Eve, Asian-Inspired, Tuscan, Wedding, Business Meeting Luncheon, Mother's Day Brunch, All-American Cuisine, or Summer Picnic Buffet. Record your buffet menu in the space provided below:

_____

_____

_____

_____

>> Buffet Equipment

Attractive equipment is the key to successful buffets. No matter how good the food is and how hard the chefs worked to make it attractive, unless it is presented on good-looking service plates, platters, and bowls, it will not be appreciated. Occasionally, economics forces chefs to use old, worn-out platters. The chef has to come up with creative ways to hide the flaws and cover them. Kale or lettuce leaves can hide damaged platters or boards covered with aluminum foil.

Equipment for service is very expensive. Many hotels and catering operations budget for equipment, but smaller operations may only be able to buy one or two pieces a year and make up the difference with inexpensive baskets or plastic ware.

Although not every operation can offer the best equipment, by using a bit of creativity it is possible to make eye-catching displays (Figure 18-3). Whenever possible, purchase what is affordable to build up a stock of buffet equipment. Hardware stores and specialty shops can be treasure troves of decorating ideas.

CHEF'S TIP

Precautions must be taken when using metal platters for service. Use only metal platters that have been approved for foodservice. When in doubt, look for the NSF stamp of approval on the platter. NSF International certifies equipment that should be used. The surface must have a nonreactive coating and be nontoxic, easy to clean, nonabsorbent, and corrosion resistant. Certain metals such as aluminum, silver, and copper can leach into foods. This can cause off flavors, potential food poisoning, and discoloration in the food. Silver trays should have a nonreactive liner between the food and the metal. For platters, create a line between the food and the metal by using a thin layer of aspic, lettuce leaves, or another liner. When using marble or other stone for service, make sure to use a liner—acidic foods such as fresh fruit can etch the marble and damage the surface.

Figure 18-3 A variety of baskets, buckets, and dishes can be used to create an interesting buffet.

Clean, food-safe serving surfaces can be made with large pieces of granite, marble, or tile available from a hardware store. Carving tools and other equipment used for decoration work can be found in tool shops, art stores, and hardware stores as well.

>> Buffet Layout

Every event is different, and there are no general guidelines that specify where buffets should be located or how they should be organized. In most operations, the size and shape of buffets vary depending on the number of guests, the type of food, the client's wishes, and the configuration of the banquet room selected. Buffets must be set up to make it convenient for customers to access food and practical for servers to replenish food.

Years ago, most buffets started with fixed locations for plates and silverware, followed by salads, bread displays, cold food, hot food, and desserts. The modern buffet is organized in clusters and, when possible, is accessible from all sides. The clusters can be identical, such as cluster buffets for desserts and hot and cold beverages, or organized by courses, such as individual buffets for appetizers, cold meats and salads, seafood, and hot serving stations.

Tips for Planning and Setting Up Buffets
- Plan the complete menu well ahead of time so you can schedule the help for production and service.
- Lay out the tables and make any adjustments necessary.
- Plan for centerpieces, ice carvings, tallow sculpture, or any other display pieces.
- Include in the plan any decorations; all food to be served; serving pieces for completed food products such as bowls, trays, and platters or mirrors; and utensils to serve the food.
- Plan for the flow of food and customer access. Lines should be avoided when possible.
- Take into consideration the desired speed of the buffet line. Some buffets are served quickly; for example, on-location catering for the film industry. Meals need to be quick and self-contained. Other buffets are leisurely paced with several back-up platters to cover several hours of service.
- Always plan for the highest sanitation standards when food is potentially at risk.
- Have an ample supply of plates on each buffet or at the dining tables. For separate stations, plates need to be placed at various accessible locations.
- Ensure an adequate supply of napkins, forks, and spoons, and, when needed, knives.
- Provide plates that are smaller than dinner plates to encourage customers to take small samplings and return for other food. For longer sit-down affairs, use dinner plates for service. These can be preset at the table or stacked at the buffet table.
- Plan for separate beverage and dessert stations with accompanying cups, dishes, and serving utensils.
- Preset the table for large sit-down-style meals. The table can be preset with water goblets, wine glasses, silverware, and napkins.
- Work from a budget—cost is a factor that can affect the buffet. The amount of dishes presented and served and the elaborateness of the function may have to be adjusted according to dollars available.
- Preset the appetizers on the table on occasion, and display only main courses on the buffet. For longer dining events, some clients prefer the appetizer and main course to be served at the table and the desserts served from a dessert buffet, often called a **Viennese table.**

CONFIGURATIONS AND ZONES

Buffets can be self-service or assisted. In large rooms, the buffet can be an island configuration, accessible from all sides and with servers placed in the center to assist the customers. Small, attended buffets are sometimes placed near architectural features such as large alcoves,

Figure 18-4 The traffic flow should always be a concern when setting up a buffet.

pillars, and other decorative room elements. Easy access for customers is always a concern (Figure 18-4). It is crucial that no fire exits are blocked.

Buffets are usually placed on portable tables. Buffet tables are available in many sizes and shapes, including half moon and crescent shaped. In some banquet facilities and hotels, the executive chef is involved in choosing the shape and sizes of the buffet tables (Figure 18-5).

Zones for both food preparation areas and setups are commonly used in buffet layout. **Zones** are areas that are specific to a task or a food item. In the kitchen, food is prepared in the cold kitchen or the hot kitchen, depending on the menu item. Each zone has its own specific equipment and needs.

The cold kitchen typically has the following zones:

- Salad or vegetable prep sink with drain board
- Prep tables
- Walk-in or reach-in refrigerators (in large hotels, there might be more than one walk-in designated for the cold kitchen)
- Equipment storage for blenders, mixers, vacuum-sealing machines, blast chillers, and other equipment

In the hot kitchen, ranges, convection ovens, combi-ovens and cook-and-holds are typically located in convenient areas next to the serving areas, along with heat wells, steamers, and hot boxes. The Queen Mary's, which are large, rolling multi-shelved racks for moving large amounts of food, are located in the serving zone. Also in that zone are plate racks, speed or rolling racks, metal tables, conveyor systems, and walk-ins for holding foods for service.

Figure 18-5 Portable banquet tables can be configured in a variety of shapes and sizes, depending on the needs of each event.

Figure 18-6 Pasta stations are just one type of zone that can be used in a buffet line.

In the banquet or buffet area, food zones take over. These zones are areas where foods are arranged in specific food groupings or stations such as stations for pasta, carving, sushi, or desserts and beverages (Figure 18-6). The zones might also include stationary fruit or vegetable displays, surrounded by cut-up vegetables, fruits, salads, and the appropriate sauces. There might be a cheese board with a large variety of assorted types of cheeses to include spreads, dips, chunks, cubes, and slices, along with the appropriate breads, crackers, or chips. Other stationary zones might include an area with large mirrors or platters of sliced meats, smoked or cured fish such as lox, or perhaps a large, ice-filled tray with oysters and clams such as a seafood bar. These zones can be accented and highlighted with an accompanying ice carving, along with the sauces and tools needed for service.

Stations, or zones, help to eliminate the crowding associated with buffets. The guests have room to circulate freely and to choose which foods they want to eat. This method of service eliminates the feeling of mass feeding and gives a more intimate feel to the buffet and banquet. It also helps the staff because servers are assigned to specific zones. There isn't a bottleneck with servers trying to refill a platter on the buffet line just as a fellow server brings in a large chafing dish full of product on the same line.

TABLECLOTH SIZES FOR BANQUET TABLES

Round Tables	
Size	**Tablecloth Size**
2 feet (0.6 m)	72 inches × 72 inches (1.82 m)
2 1/2 feet (0.76 m)	72 inches × 72 inches (1.82 m)
3 feet (0.91 m)	72 inches × 72 inches (1.82 m)
4 1/2 feet (1.36 m)	90 inches × 90 inches
5 feet (1.52 m)	90 inches × 90 inches
5 1/2 feet (1.67 m)	108 inches × 108 inches (2.73 m)
6 feet (1.82 m)	108 inches × 108 inches (2.73 m)
Rectangle	
Size	**Tablecloth Size**
18 inches × 6 feet (0.45 × 1.82 m)	2 each 62 inches × 62 inches (1.57 m)
30 inches × 4 feet (0.76 × 1.21 m)	72 inches × 72 inches (1.82 m)
30 inches × 6 feet (0.76 × 1.82 m)	2 each 72 inches × 72 inches (1.82 m)
3 feet × 6 feet (0.91 × 1.82 m)	2 each 72 inches × 72 inches (1.82 m)
3 feet × 8 feet (0.91 × 2.40 m)	2 each 72 inches × 72 inches (1.82 m)
Crescent	
Size	**Tablecloth Size**
6 × 3 feet (1.82 × 091 m)	20 each 90 inches × 90 inches (1.82 m)

TABLE SKIRTING

Buffet tables should have **table skirting,** which covers the legs of the table (Figure 18-7). It usually attaches around the table and falls within 1 inch of the floor. The material can be solid, pleated, transparent lace, shiny, or dull. Many operations offer their clients a choice of materials and colors for table skirting. There are a number of methods to attach the skirts to the tables such as using the clip style or Velcro strips.

Before ordering table skirting, the type of buffet must be taken into consideration. When the buffet tables are up against the wall or have staff serving from one side, there is no need to skirt the backside of the table. When the guests will surround the table, the skirting must go all the way around the table. This is generally not a consideration when using round tables—they are always skirted all the way around the table.

Use the following formula to calculate the amount of skirting required for round tables:

Diameter of the table (in feet) × 3.14 = the amount of skirting required to go around the table

Always round up to the nearest 6-inch increment.

EXAMPLE:

To determine the amount of skirting needed for a 5-foot table, take

$$5 \times 3.14 = 15.7$$

Round up to 16 feet of table skirting.

Use the following formula to calculate the amount of skirting required for rectangular or square tables. (There are times when this formula will come in handy; generally speaking, however, skirting for rectangular tables is ordered based on the length of the table. For instance, you would just order skirting for an 8-foot table.)

Add the length of the table with the width of the table. (In most cases you'll have to change the length to inches.) Multiply that sum by 2. Round up to the nearest 6-inch increment.

EXAMPLE:

To determine the amount of skirting needed for a 30-inch × 6-foot table, first change the 6 feet into inches (6 × 12 = 72 inches). Add 30 for the width of the table (72 + 30 = 102). Multiply the sum by 2 (102 × 2 = 204). Now change that amount back to feet (divide by 12). That gives you exactly 17 feet. Always round up 6 inches to provide for the overlap. In this case, 17 1/2 feet of skirting is necessary.

LEARNING ACTIVITY 18-2

Scenario 1: You need to order table skirting for a banquet that will be using five 6-foot tables. How much skirting is required?
Scenario 2: You need to or der table skirting for three rectangular tables measuring 18 inches × 6 feet. How much skirting is required?

THE FLOW

When the party starts, each buffet table is at its peak. The food is set up in a flow to ensure that guests can build their meal in a traditional sequence. Most salads, soups, and side dishes are the first items guests encounter, with the heavier, protein-based selections situated toward the later part of the service table. Sauce boats or chaffers should be situated next to each protein item with necessary serviceware such as spoons, ladles, or tongs. There should be plenty of room between items so that the table does not appear overcrowded. The guests must have access to everything on the table, so items should be accessible at all times to avoid crossover. Displays should be attractive without taking over the buffet or causing a hazard. Signs designating the name of each item are often found at buffets or banquets. These signs should be discreet yet readable and should not get in the way of the flow of traffic.

Displays of foods look beautiful for the first 5 minutes; however, after a few guests have picked over the displays, they must be quickly resupplied with fresh food to maintain the appearance of freshness (Figure 18-8). It is not recommended to place all of the food on the table at the same time unless the serving time is very short, such as at a luncheon buffet in a corporate setting. To make resupply efficient yet graceful, the platters should be small, and duplicate platters should be available at all times for backups. The basic concept is that a platter should be removed when it is 1/2 to 3/4 depleted, depending upon company policy. It should be immediately replaced with a fresh platter. This usually involves two servers: one that removes the depleted platter and one standing right there with the new one. There should be no obvious empty spaces at a buffet. Bigger isn't always better. Purchase platters that can be easily handled by one person and change them out often. Back-up platters should be held in the cold kitchen until service, or in the banquet set-up zone. Many

Figure 18-8 There must be constant attention paid to restocking buffet tables. *Sandra Ivany/Jupiter Images-PictureArts Corporation*

hotels and banquet facilities have staging areas in which to hold foods in waiting for service time. These small, ancillary service areas usually have reach-ins in which to hold cold foods and, in many cases, hot boxes or cook-and-hold for hot items.

It is important to stress sanitation in banquet and buffet service. Foods that are cold should not be out of the refrigerator for more than 2 hours. It is advisable to keep just what you need out and replenish often. When this is not possible, the use of chill plates or cold wells is advisable. Conversely, hot foods can be held in chaffers or portable steam table units (Figure 18-9). They need to be held at or above 135°F (57°C). The chef or cook should monitor each station for temperature control to ensure that the food is out of the danger zone at all times.

As the event progresses, platters should be consolidated onto slightly smaller platters in the kitchen. If the buffet is set up into zones, they can be closed out as the number of party guests begins to dwindle. Tables can be cleared of everything except the tablecloth and centerpiece or floral arrangement. The challenge is to provide a reasonable selection on the buffet until all customers are served. Food should never be restocked onto existing platters, particularly in view of guests. Instead, arrange food onto a clean serving tray or bowl out of sight before placing it on the buffet table. Hot food should be replenished with a clean chafing dish insert when possible.

Sanitation and food safety are important issues to take into consideration. In most cases, the food on tables is not refrigerated, and it is possible for the food to become contaminated. Chefs must be very careful to properly chill cold food before it is placed on the buffet tables and to follow time and temperature rules. It is better to err on the

Figure 18-9 Hot foods must be kept in heating units at temperatures above 135°F (57°C).

side of sanitation. The clock is ticking from the moment the food leaves the refrigeration unit. This is often a challenge, specifically in large hotels where the kitchen can be located many floors away from the banquet rooms. When practical, food should be displayed on small platters that can be easily refurbished. Again, when the banquet rooms are far removed from the refrigerators, this can become a logistical problem. Raw bars and other means of chilling such as cold tops and ice troughs can be effective ways to keep cold food cold during a buffet.

There is also concern about contamination by customers. Health departments in many states require sneeze guards to shield food from airborne contamination. If the buffet is a permanent fixture in the restaurant or hotel, sneeze guards are usually required (Figure 18-10). Sneeze guards are usually portable but unfortunately detract from the attractiveness of the food display.

If the buffet is a one-time affair, generally speaking, sneeze guards are not required. Check with local and state health codes for the current rules in specific jurisdictions.

>> Table Decorations

Buffets should be artful displays of attractive food and beverages. The linens and table decorations, along with the food, make up the whole package (Figure 18-11).

Food expectations have changed—years ago, most buffets featured centerpieces of whole fish, large lobsters, stuffed suckling pigs, decorated hams, and similar items. In many cases, the large display pieces were not really edible although they were made of food. Often the centerpieces were at the head of a display table, or up on risers, where they were hard to reach. In most cases, they were more for show than for eating purposes. Often only parts of the items were sliced and the rest left whole as decoration. When the sliced food was gone, customers would be left looking at the remaining whole fish or ham without a way to cut it up and eat it. In today's buffet service, the trend is to have all of the food on the buffet sliced into small portions. Decorations are usually placed adjacent to the food. In many cases there is no need for decorations when attractive platters are used.

Buffets must attract the attention of the guests. One of the best ways to accomplish that is to use a variety of heights and focal points in the buffet. Compare the buffet table to a stage that is dressed and ready for the first act of a play. The staging enhances the production. Varying platter heights can be achieved by using wooden or plastic bases or platforms called **risers**

Figure 18-10 Permanent buffets generally require sneeze guards, depending on local and state health codes.

Figure 18-11 Fruits and vegetables are artfully arranged to enhance the delicious seafood, creating an opulent display.

Figure 18-12 Risers of various heights are used to add interest to this dessert buffet.

(Figure 18-12). Risers can be draped with tablecloths and, many times, with other large pieces of colorful and festive cloth, lace, cellophane, metallic cloth or paper, or even leaves and straw.

FOCAL POINTS

It is also appropriate to have large floral or fruit displays and other props in the center or at the back of the table (Figure 18-13). Large upscale hotels and large banquet houses have massive and sometimes custom-made gold or silver serving or presentation platters and pieces that can be filled with fruits or flowers.

There is no limit to the imagination when it comes to props. In many hotels, catering halls, and other large-scale foodservice operations, the chef and banquet managers have accumulated a treasure trove filled with old crates, barrels, boats, sails, nets, wine racks, and many, many more items (Figure 18-14). The use of these props should be governed by the following considerations:

- Props can look rustic but not dirty or dusty.
- Props should never smell.
- Props must be out of the way and not accessible to guests.
- Props should be in good taste.
- Props must correspond to the theme of the buffet.

LEARNING ACTIVITY 18-3

Design a buffet table for one of the following scenarios:

- Beach theme
- Informal wedding
- Fall harvest theme
- Winter wonderland theme

Select props from your home or school that will enhance the overall look of the table. Remember to use objects with varying heights.

Figure 18-13 A basket of fall leaves and harvested fruits serves as the focal point for a brunch buffet.

Figure 18-14 There is no limit to the types of props that can be used to enhance a buffet.

LIGHTING

The effectiveness and attractiveness of buffets can increase dramatically with proper lighting. There are many ways to light buffets, and banquet houses specializing in buffets frequently have permanently installed spotlights. Smaller operations or those with flexible demands do not enjoy this luxury. Safety must be a primary concern when lighting buffets. Stringing extension wires in front of or in the back of the buffet tables creates tripping hazards. An inexpensive and effective method of lighting is to place small, low-wattage spotlights under the table when the skirting is transparent lace. These lights generate very little heat and have a high visual impact. Again, the distance to electrical outlets dictates whether electric lights can be used. Less light is usually better than too much light. Be aware that colored lights and flowers sometimes clash.

CANDLES AND BUFFETS

We do not recommend using candles on buffets, as burning candles are safety hazards for customers and staff. Wax can drip on the food, and frequently candles burn unevenly from drafts created by the ventilation system. In some cities, a licensed company must fireproof table skirting whenever candles are used. Some counties and states do not permit the use of any open flames with table linens. Please check your local, county, and state fire ordinances for guidance.

TALLOW SCULPTURES

Tallow sculptures are decidedly old school, but with skill and an artistic ability, any chef can still use them for attractive displays. These carvings can attract customers and have many applications (Figure 18-15). Tallow should never be allowed to come in contact with food.

To make a tallow sculpture, you should learn how to make and use armatures, which are made from wire and are supported by a wood or Styrofoam base. The tallow is applied in small layers over the armature and modeled, usually with the aid of a detailed sketch or template.

Considerable artistic skill is needed to create pleasing tallow centerpieces. Some chefs use hard tallow and carve statues and displays, not unlike wood carvers. For less

Figure 18-15 A chef's artistic skills can be used to create tallow centerpieces.

artistically inclined chefs, tallow can be melted and poured into purchased molds. This process is fast and can create beautiful centerpieces without too much effort. Tallow pieces have the advantage that they are usually much lighter than ice carvings and will last a long time. Large banquet houses have tallow pieces stored in a place with ambient temperature and, hopefully, without access by rodents. Tallow can last for many seasons and does not smell.

Tallow can be purchased ready-for-use in various colors, including chocolate brown. If the colors available from the manufacturers are not satisfactory, custom coloring is possible. Various coloring gels are available today in many hues. Tallow comes in 25-pound pails. It is pliable at room temperature, and it is very convenient to use.

Some chefs prefer to prepare carving tallow from scratch.
The following recipe makes a standard carving tallow.

tallow for carving *Yield: 18 lbs*

Ingredients	Amounts		Procedure
	U.S.	Metric	
Beef suet	8 lbs	3.6 kg	Soak the suet overnight in cold water. Grind through the coarse plate of a meat grinder. Put the suet in a heavy, large saucepot, cover with water, and melt over very low heat. Eventually the water will evaporate, and the fat will separate. This is a lengthy process; during separation, the fat will get hot and must be watched carefully. The fat is rendered when clear, and the suet pieces are crisp and light brown. Set aside to cool before straining through a double-layer cheesecloth because the fat is very hot.

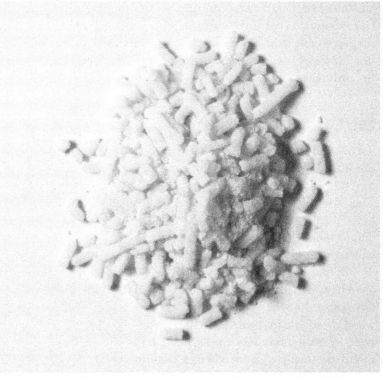

| Beeswax | 5 lbs | 2.26 kg | Blend the strained fat with beeswax and paraffin and melt together in a water bath. Use when solid. |
| Paraffin | 5 lbs | 2.26 kg | |

This recipe for pliable tallow is flammable and should never be melted on the stove or used near candles or other heat sources.

pliable tallow *Yield: 15 lbs (6.78 kg)*

Ingredients	Amounts U.S.	Metric	Procedure
Beeswax	5 lbs	2.26 kg	Combine the ingredients and melt together in a water bath. Use when chilled.
Rendered beef suet	5 lbs	2.26 kg	
Shortening	5 lbs	2.26 kg	

Remember not to put tallow in contact with any food products. It is not sanitary and should be used for display purposes only.

DISPLAYING ICE CARVINGS

Ice carvings can add a touch of class and attract the attention of the guests to any buffet (Figure 18-16). In Unit 20 we will discuss the process of creating simple ice carvings. In this unit, we focus on the display of these pieces. As with all items in the kitchen, safety comes first. Ice carvings are heavy, even when a considerable amount of ice is chipped away from the original 300-pound blocks. Combined pieces can weigh anywhere from 100 pounds up to 500 pounds based on the shape and size of multi-block pieces. Most banquet tables cannot safely support such weight, especially when employees stand, kneel, or have to sit on the table while setting up the ice pieces. It is sensible to make sure that the spot selected on the buffet table can support the weight before the size of the ice piece is decided. Some hotels have custom-built, reinforced tables made to carry the ice display and to match the standard banquet tables in height and width.

There is a possibility of injury when handling heavy items such as ice carvings. Chefs and other employees who handle the ice should be instructed on safe lifting practices. They should wear the appropriate safety gear such as sturdy shoes and, for some, ergonomic back braces designed to be worn when lifting. They should wear gloves or use kitchen towels to prevent slipping when handling finished carvings. Pieces can shift while they are being handled, and it is always helpful to have assistance with setup. Ice carvings should never be grabbed at vulnerable spots, such as necks, legs, handles, stems, and tails. It can be frustrating to have a piece break during setup.

Ice carvings should never be placed in direct sunlight—the infrared rays internally break down the ice structure and make it brittle. They should never be placed near heat sources or hot lights.

Figure 18-16 An ice carving becomes the focal point of any buffet.

Always make preparations for the run-off water that appears as the ice carving melts. Use a drip pan that is deep enough to hold the expected amounts of ice melt, or use a pan that is equipped with a drain and hose that flows to a bucket below the table. Ice carvings should be placed on sturdy wooden slats that fit exactly in the drip pan, and covered with tablecloths or napkins to prevent sliding. The tablecloths or napkins hide the base and can be decorated with ferns or flowers. Ice will not melt evenly—the melting process is influenced by ventilation and heating drafts; heat generated by lights and sunlight; and other factors. This uneven melting process can make the ice pieces unstable.

If the carving is to be illuminated, consideration must be given for the location of the electrical outlets. Electric lights generate heat, which is obviously an enemy of frozen water. Some chefs use cold neon lights to illuminate their carvings. Be aware that electricity and water are a dangerous combination. Purchased ice glows have built-in, low-energy lighting to highlight the ice. These units can come with multi-colored insets so a chef can have an ice sculpture with a blue, red, green, or yellow hue based on the gel or inset used.

Carving Repairs

Ice pieces break occasionally during the carving process and, unfortunately, during the setup in the dining room. Because ice consists of frozen water, it is logical to join frozen pieces together with ice slush, created while carving, and freeze them together in the freezer. The pieces must be held together in the freezer until the broken pieces are frozen together. Ice welding techniques may be used to harden the ice. By using dry ice, the edges can be made ultra-cold and more amendable to welding together. There is also a product called **freezer spray,** which is a canned product that rapidly reduces the temperature of the ice. Some carvers prefer to use it to reattach broken pieces.

>> Calculating Food Quantities for the Buffet

One of the vexing challenges for most chefs is calculating food quantities for buffets. The cardinal rule is that both the first customer and the last customer must have the same fabulous experience and food selection. This can cause problems, because usually the more expensive items are the first things eaten; filler items such as salads and starches are the last. It is important to present the food in stages to pace the dining experience and ensure that there is food at all stages of the service.

Sometimes a buffet may have more than one seating, so staging food in the walk-in is the best way to ensure uniformity throughout the banquet. Some operations place the expensive items at the end of the buffet or at hard-to-reach places, hoping that the customers will first fill up their plates with everything else, leaving less room for the high-ticket items. It is assumed that guests will not take as much food if it is harder to reach.

Food quantities are also determined by selling cost. If a banquet manager sells a relatively inexpensive buffet, yet puts lobsters and shrimp on the menu, the chef has to calculate carefully the quantity of expensive merchandise and how to balance cost with customer satisfaction. This is not always easy. Chefs are under pressure to keep the food cost at a set percentage of revenue, and banquet sales people are under pressure to fill the banquet space with customers. There can be conflict between promises made by the sales staff and kitchen management to manage the food. The bottom line is that overriding policy should be to make the customers happy and never skimp on quality and quantity.

Here are a few rules to remember when determining food amounts:

- Once the estimated number of diners is determined, add enough food for 10 percent more guests (5 percent if the number of guests exceeds 100). The goal is to have an adequate amount of food without too much excess.
- If appetizers are to be served before the buffet, limit them to two to five servings per person so that guests will still have an appetite for the buffet food.

Figure 18-17 Meat is carved in front of the guests at a carving station.

- The more selections that appear on the buffet table, the lower amounts you will need. When faced with lots of options, guests tend to take smaller portions so that they can try more items.
- Guests usually consume a total of 1–4 ounces of salad; 4–8 ounces of meat, poultry, or fish; and 2–4 ounces of starch at a buffet dinner.
- The richer the dessert, the smaller the portions will be.

>> Action Stations

The term **action station** refers to areas in the dining room where chefs prepare or slice food in front of the customers. The concept is relatively new and is thought to have emerged from corporate dining facilities. Customers love action stations because they provide excitement and drama. Both hot and cold food can be prepared at an action station.

Carving stations, where the cook or chef slices meat or fish as ordered, are common types of action stations (Figure 18-17). Other action stations include those where omelets, pastas, or various types of sushi are prepared (Figure 18-18). Employees working at action stations should be dressed in a clean uniform. Chefs should wear clean aprons, cravats, and chefs' toques or caps. Servers should wear comfortable uniforms, usually not incorporating any sort of headgear. Some cooks are shy and nervous when facing customers; others enjoy the interaction with guests.

Consider the following when using a carving station:

- All chefs and foodservice workers should wear gloves.
- The cutting board should be large enough to accommodate comfortably the item to be carved. Additional food supply should be nearby and kept in a sanitary manner—hot foods hot, cold foods cold.

Figure 18-18 Omelets are made to order at the omelet action station.

- A nearby plate or receptacle for scraps is required.
- Plenty of towels or napkins should be provided to keep the station clean and tidy.
- The knife must be sharp. Serrated knives are often preferred because they slice evenly.
- Keep a steel handy for honing any nonserrated knives.
- Stock stacks of plates in front of the carver. To speed up the process, the carver can cut a few portions ahead of time when the traffic at the buffet is heavy.
- All garnishes and sauces should be in easy reach of the customers.
- Flatware and napkins should be readily available.
- Large pieces that require boning and chopping do not belong on the buffet. A large turkey might be awkward to slice. It is better to serve a large, boneless turkey breast.
- The carver should be informed as to what is being carved. If a guest asks what the food is, the carver should know what type of cut, what type of meat, and how it was prepared.
- Carvers should smile and act relaxed.

In the past, tableside cooking was very popular. It often involved dousing the food with strong alcohol and igniting huge flames. Unfortunately, this practice has virtually ceased, partially due to safety concerns. In addition, high rents have basically eliminated tableside cooking because wide aisle space is needed to maneuver the mobile cooking trolleys around the tables. Those concerned with the establishment's bottom line often believe this space could be better served by filling the dining area with more tables.

Today, **cooking stations** on buffets where the finishing touches of a dish are prepared for all guests to see, have become popular. Cooking stations on buffets typically use electrical **induction stoves,** which heat rapidly but don't get hot to the touch as they use a specialized magnetic field to produce heat (Figure 18-19). Small, portable stoves heated with butane gas or sterno are also used in buffet lines. The dishes are usually precooked and only finished at the buffet. These foods include pasta blended with sauces, small pancakes filled with sweet or savory fillings, and related items.

The following pointers should be kept in mind when using cooking stations:

- Avoid strong-smelling ingredients. One chef made a melted cheese dish on the buffet, and the whole banquet floor smelled of pungent cheese.
- Don't use excessive amounts of garlic for the same reason as above.
- Be aware of foods that splatter, which rules out cooking most meat and seafood from scratch.
- Avoid food that takes too long to cook. Customers do not want to wait.

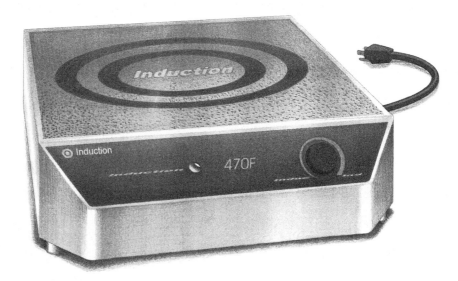

Figure 18-19 Induction cooktops work well for cooking stations. The heat is instantaneous and the stove is not hot to the touch.

Figure 18-20 Wedding buffets offer a creative challenge for the chef.

- Eliminate foods that generate smoke and flames.
- Safety is always the most important consideration.

>> Wedding Receptions

Wedding receptions are unique because they are usually a once-in-a-lifetime occasion (Figure 18-20). Weddings can range from low-key and low-budget events to elaborate affairs consisting of lavish receptions, sit-down dinners, and ceremonies orchestrated by a DJ, bandleader, or master of ceremonies.

Weddings present special challenges for the kitchen. Unlike most other receptions, guests go to the dining room right after the ceremony. The buffets must be organized to avoid long lines, and there must be ample food ready to resupply the buffet. The bride's party normally comes to the dining room after the wedding pictures are taken. It is important that there is fresh food on the buffet table when they arrive.

Weddings are an opportunity to showcase the capability of the kitchen crew and can be the best advertising because many of the guests are prospective brides and their mothers who may be looking for a caterer or a location to host their celebration. It is important for chefs to remember proper food scheduling. Because of the reception line, the wedding photos, opening of presents, and a myriad of other potential events, the food is subordinated to the event schedule.

Wedding cakes can range from the traditional multi-tiered cakes to artistic challenges for the cake artist. When and how the cake is displayed is a decision the bride and groom must make (Figure 18-21). At some weddings, the cake is hidden and wheeled into the room with appropriate pomp at the right moment; at other weddings, the cake is displayed all evening for everybody to admire.

Figure 18-21 The placement of the wedding cake requires careful consideration.

>> Holiday Theme Buffets

Holiday themes, special events, sports events, and corporate-sponsored events open up the possibilities for the buffet and banquet team to shine. Often traditional foods that are associated with the holiday become the focus of the buffet (Figure 18-22). More nonfood décor is generally added to holiday theme buffets.

Figure 18-22 Holiday-inspired foods and décor add a festive touch to the buffet table.

>> Summary

Buffets are generally liked and accepted by most customers but represent challenges to the operator. Buffets should be attractive, yet must meet sanitary requirements and operational objectives. Long lines should be avoided, if possible, by setting up satellite buffets and action stations where cooks prepare hot or cold dishes in front of the customers.

Modern trends shift decorations away from food and toward the attractiveness of equipment and props. Props must be eye-catching and should complement the theme without overshadowing the food. The height on the buffet table is important to make a dramatic statement when customers view the setting. Ice carvings can serve as dramatic and memorable centerpieces, but precautions must be taken when placing them. This unit also covered the resupply issues related to food safety, important pointers for wedding receptions, and safety issues regarding action stations.

>> Review Questions

TRUE/FALSE

1. More staff is required to run a buffet than a sit-down dinner.
2. A buffet is an easier way to provide food in alternate settings such as parks and offices.
3. Tallow is used to create classic, nonedible, decorative showpieces.
4. Buffets should only be used when the meal is to be served at a leisurely pace.
5. In general, plates used on buffets are smaller than dinner plates.
6. Dessert buffets are sometimes called Tuscan Tables.
7. Platters should be removed from the buffet table when they are one-fourth depleted.
8. Ice carvings should always be placed on sturdy wooden slats fitting exactly in the drip pan.
9. Action stations can serve hot or cold food.
10. Strong-smelling ingredients should not be prepared at a buffet cooking station.

MULTIPLE CHOICE

11. Induction stoves are heated by
    a. electricity.
    b. canned fuel.
    c. alcohol.
    d. butane gas.
12. Which of the following is *not* an advantage of serving buffet style?
    a. Food is produced in greater quantity with fewer staff.
    b. Productivity is increased.
    c. Food wastes are high.
    d. Buffets are great sources for underutilized products.
13. What size tablecloth does a 5-foot round table need?
    a. 72 in × 72 in
    b. 90 in × 90 in
    c. 108 in × 108 in
    d. 62 in × 62 in
14. How much table skirting is required to go around a 3-foot table?
    a. 12 ft
    b. 8 ft
    c. 9 ft
    d. 10 1/2 ft
15. The key ingredients in tallow are suet and
    a. shortening.
    b. butter.
    c. glycerin.
    d. paraffin.
16. Paraffin is made from
    a. vegetable oil.
    b. beeswax.
    c. beef suet.
    d. petroleum.

SHORT ANSWER

17. Describe ways that chefs can hide the flaws of older platters.

_____

_____

18. Explain what is meant by "modern buffets are organized in clusters."

_____

_____

19. Why are risers used on a buffet table?

_____

_____

20. Give two ways to deal with the run-off water created from melting ice carvings.

_____

_____

Catering

>> **Learning Objectives**

After you have finished reading this unit, you should be able to:

- List some of the items that should be included in a Banquet Event Order (BEO).
- Describe the basic service methods.
- Discuss some of the considerations that must be made when catering off-site.
- Describe typical ingredients found in boxed lunches.
- Explain the purpose of in-room gifts.

>> **Key Terms**

arm service	buffet	compotier (*KAHM-*	tray service
Banquet Event Orders	butler service	*poht-tee-ay*)	
(BEO)			

atering is a movable feast. As chefs and culinarians, we "cater" or supply food and service. Catering is different from other forms of foodservice in that it is usually a one-time meal, the customer base is guaranteed, the menu is set, and the major segment of the bill is pre-paid so much of the financial risk is removed. Much catering occurs off-site, away from the production kitchen. Many foodservice operations, such as restaurants, country clubs, and hotels, have catering departments that specialize in the one-time meal. A lot of these same places would not be profitable without the catering revenue. The cold kitchen assists with many of the functions of the catering department.

Catering can be on-premise or off-site. Most banquet halls supply food as well as facilities. Catering companies do not usually have a location for serving, but transport food and equipment to a location for many types of parties or foodservice. They may supply fosod, service, beverage, linen, cake, and a myriad of services to the customer.

In large hotels, as an example, the catering or banquet department books the parties, rents the rooms, and handles all aspects of the room setup, from table arrangement and decorations to breaking down the tables and even establishing dance floors. In some cases, the catering department is responsible for renting space and booking parties in large operations such as country clubs and banquet halls. In smaller operations such as restaurants or small hotels, the general manager or restaurant manager does the booking. When a potential client plans to have a special event such as a wedding, anniversary or birthday party, or one of the many types of festive or business gatherings, one of the first things a catering manager does is check the availability of the banquet room or facility. The manager then discusses the arrangements with the client to ascertain the amount of guests that will be present at the function, the menu choices, any dietary special needs or restrictions, the beverage service, the room setup, and, if necessary, flowers, photographer, and music arrangements. Many times, the chef is included in these early discussions, and a tasting menu is scheduled. In some facilities, the menu is a standardized banquet menu with choices based on cost. Some banquet facilities have three-tiered menu structures to accommodate a range of prices.

Other facilities custom-design each menu so that every occasion is, indeed, unique. Off-site catering means that the event takes place away from the home-base facility. There are expenses incurred for off-site events. While off-site catering can be potentially more profitable than parties booked on-premise, it is important to realize that with off-site catering, there is the additional expense of needing a vehicle for transport, equipment for transporting the food, the rental of equipment, tables and chairs, and other expenses, both seen and unseen.

In this unit you will be introduced to the basic paperwork and information regarding catered events. You will learn the service terminology used in a typical catering department. Boxed lunches will be discussed, because they are made in the pantry and often ordered in country clubs, hotels, and conference centers for catered events. Amenity baskets and plates are also discussed. These goodies are usually edible gifts sent by management to VIPs. They can be cold or hot and sometimes come with a tasty beverage such as champagne.

>> Banquet Event Order (BEO)

Whenever a catering function or special event is booked, confirmed, and, when required, a deposit made, the manager or sales representative generates a "BEO." This is known as the **Banquet Event Order,** which is a complete instruction sheet giving all the details of the event (Figure 19-1). A copy of the BEO is sent to all departments that have anything to do with the function.

Simple parties require only a single sheet listing some of the following details:

- Day and date of the event
- Count, or how many will be served
- Time and type of service
- Selected menu and beverage items

Elaborate parties might require many pages of additional information including the following:

- Decorations
- Floral arrangements
- Linens and chair treatments
- Placement of musicians
- Service instructions
- Beverage service
- Servers' uniforms

In large operations, the BEO is sent to many departments such as the front office, security, laundry, and valet parking service. Copies of the BEO are sent to the kitchen to keep the executive chef informed about banquet room occupancy, even when no food is ordered for the event. The executive chef is responsible for the distribution of the BEO requiring food to the pertinent departments such as the pantry, butcher shop, pastry department, and banquet

BANQUET EVENT ORDER (BEO) FORM

UMBC Department: _____

Contact Person: _____

Date: _____

Phone #: _____

E-mail: _____

Event Name: _____

Location of Event: _____

Estimated number of Guests: _____

Type of Event:
_____ Breakfast
_____ Lunch
_____ Dinner
_____ Reception
_____ Other: _____

Set-up Time: _____
Event Start Time: _____
Event End Time: _____

List Menus Items:

_____   _____
_____   _____
_____   _____
_____   _____
_____   _____

List Beverages:

_____   _____
_____   _____
_____   _____

List Equipment Needed:

_____   _____
_____   _____
_____   _____
_____   _____

List Miscellaneous Services Needed:

_____   _____
_____   _____

Figure 19-1 The BEO is an important document that keeps all departments informed of the pending event.

sous chefs. The BEO is posted so that all cooks, not just the station chefs, read the BEO every day and note changes. Besides the guest count and menu items, the most important point to remember is the day, date, and serving time. Many hotels and banquet halls have contracts that are time specific. If a contracted meal is late, the guest may not have to pay the entire amount, and in a few high-end resorts, a late party could result in the guest having a free banquet meal. The results could be the loss of several thousand dollars' worth of revenue, so it is vitally crucial to be on time. Catering is a one-shot meal, and when the guests arrive, they cannot be kept waiting. One of the many challenges with catering is the fluctuation of the counts. In most hotels, the kitchen is given a 48-hour advance notice. With catering, the final count is usually 72 hours in advance. The changing customer count increases or decreases the amount of food that must be prepared. The chef must be prepared for such occurrences.

Unlike restaurants, which are open daily and have a steady flow of customers, catering can generate large swings of activities. Some days might be slow and other days incredibly busy. This is normal in the hospitality industry, and, as such, work schedules need to be adjusted frequently.

>> Terminology of Service

Understanding the basic terminology used on the typical BEO is important. The first items to note are the main service methods. The type of service is important because the food is plated or served accordingly.

Figure 19-2 The butler style of service.

Figure 19-3 The desserts are plated and set on a tray to be delivered to each guest.

Many events use a combination of service methods:

- **Butler or Passed Service**

The term **butler service** goes back to the time when private households employed butlers. Butlers served food and drinks from platters, and family members helped themselves. In the hospitality industry, the term means that food and beverages are put on platters or small trays (Figure 19-2), carried by servers around the room, and the customers take what they like. The common phrase in addition to butler service is "passed."

- **Tray Service**

Tray service is used for delivering food at large banquets or small sit-down dinners. Each plate is dished up, covered, and set on a tray to be delivered to the guest (Figure 19-3). Usually, a server will take enough plates to service one full table. Experienced waitstaff can handle up to 10 plates worth of food. Tray service is also used to serve food in restaurants. It is an efficient method to deliver many dishes at once.

- **Arm Service**

Arm service is the term given to hand-carried plate service. The waitstaff can safely carry up to three plates of food with their hands and arms, which is where this type of service got its name (Figure 19-4).

- **Buffet**

The term **buffet** is used when food is placed on stationary tables (Figure 19-5). Serving equipment such as chaffers, portable steam tables, or bain-maries are used to keep the food hot. Ice glows, ice bowls, or tubs are used to keep the cold items chilled, such as those used for a seafood bar. Salads and other dishes are served on large trays or in large bowls. The serviceware and plateware may be at the tables or on the buffet tables, depending upon the guests' requests. We will discuss more buffet information in Unit 20.

- **Cocktail Party**

Figure 19-4 Experienced waitstaff can carry multiple plates using the arm service method.

The term *cocktail party* is used for a gathering of people for the sole purpose of socializing (Figure 19-6). Cocktail parties are customarily associated with the openings of shows, charitable events, museum openings, as the icebreaker at

Figure 19-5 Guests at a buffet serve themselves from the offerings available.

conventions and meetings, and the start of sit-down dinners and many other occasions. Sometimes wedding celebrations consist of cocktail parties rather than sit-down dinners. An event that is identified as a *cocktail party* usually is an indication that no food will be served after the party. It is common to serve food at cocktail parties. Depending upon the time or the type of function, the food can range from light fare to heavy hors d'oeuvre that make up a meal; from simple cubed cheese and fruits to elaborate buffets.

Figure 19-6 Cocktail parties give guests the opportunity to socialize.

Despite the name of this type of party, beverages served at cocktail parties often do not include a full selection of cocktails. Typically, wine by the glass, beer, and a few standard cocktails are served along with soft drinks and mineral water.

• **Receptions**

Many gatherings that provide a dinner often also have a reception beforehand (Figure 19-7). This serves as an opportunity for the guests to get acquainted and also for the practical purpose of extending the arrival time of guests. It is not realistic to expect that people invited to an event arrive exactly at the same time. The term *reception* implies that after the initial gathering period, food will be served. The foodservice can be a sit-down dinner, a buffet, or even a food event at another location.

Many catering departments use the French term *hors d'oeuvre* for hot reception food.

>> Off-Site Catering

When you cater off-site, every contingency must be considered. You are away from your home base, and anything can happen and frequently does (Figure 19-8). From equipment malfunction, swarms of bees, rain and tornados, and strong winds blowing through the tent, many things can happen to throw off the party. The first thing to do when a party is booked is to check out the location of the event. A site visit is critical for the success of the party. This preliminary visit will help you design the layout of the portable kitchen and service areas. The following questions should be answered:

• Are the transporting vehicles in good working order?
• Do all members of the staff have adequate directions to the site?
• Is the area that you will be cooking in or serving in covered or out in the air?
• Is the location well lit or will you need to bring in lighting?

Figure 19-7 Receptions often provide a buffet with snacks on tables.

Figure 19-8 Off-site catering is done away from the home base and requires transporting food and goods.

- Is the electrical supply adequate?
- Are there any fuel needs?
- Will cooking be in eyesight of the guests or will there be an area with shelter?
- Is the unloading and loading of equipment close to the catering site?
- What sanitation and safety concerns are there?
- Will the cold food be held at the correct temperatures? Is the refrigeration at the site working?
- What type of transporting, cooking, holding, and storage equipment will be needed?
- Do we have a back-up plan in case of breakdowns, accidents, or anything else that could happen?

The location dictates the needs. Catering off-site can occur in many locations. Following is a list of some of the more typical locations:

- Home kitchens are great for smaller parties but pose problems for larger functions as the stove, oven, and refrigeration are usually not adequate. There are also legal ramifications; depending on local laws, it may not be legal for a caterer to prepare food in a home kitchen. In most cases, chefs merely serve from the home kitchen. Catering chefs must bring equipment such as portable burners or stoves and additional refrigeration or cold storage units. Smaller sheet pans are in order as professional-sized pans may not fit in the oven. Small wares such as tongs and ladles need to be brought to the party to make the location work.
- Large buildings such as garages, carports, and work sheds or barns work well for catered functions. Portable stoves may be used, but any highly flammable type of fueled equipment must be located outside of the building.
- Outdoor tenting works well for parties that are scheduled for outside venues. They can be used for cooking and serving. Tents with or without sidewalls are ideal for protecting the guests and the food from inclement weather. When renting tents, it is wise to rent a tent one size larger than you think you will need, so you have room to cook, dish up, and clean up.
- Boats, yachts, docks, and other waterside dining locations have their own special challenges. Small galley kitchens, rolling and rocking decks and kitchens, wind, and sun can give the catering chef many challenges. For a caterer, seeing the special salad or the wedding cake fall off the transom of a boat is a very sobering situation.

Equipment Needs
- Power sources—Plenty of fuel, an adequate number of extension cords, and lots of lighting. Clamp-on or stand-type flood lights are a must for night-time functions. Make sure that the electric sources are grounded and safety tested.
- Vans, trucks, and transportation vehicles—Transportation to bring food and equipment to and from the event.
- Refrigeration—As simple as ice chests or as large and elaborate as refrigerated trucks for storage.
- Tables—Banquet tables in various sizes used for preparation as well as service. To make them work for double duty, leg extensions can be used to elevate them. Wooden blocks specially drilled out, bricks, and leg extenders are used for this purpose.
- Kitchen equipment—Coffee makers, water cans, warming cabinets, and all the standard pieces of equipment needed to produce the menu.
- Safety equipment—First aid kit, bug bite kit, and fire extinguishers round out the list of important pieces of equipment to keep the staff and guests safe.
- Bug prevention—Methods and products to keep bugs and bees away. Yellow jackets love proteins and sweets, and the honey pot type of bug attracter works well. A little known trick is placing pieces of bacon around the perimeter of a picnic site to lure yellow jackets away from the food. Fly zappers require electricity but can save a party from a serious health hazard. Before the party, ant and fly spray can be used on the legs of the equipment or tables to keep these bugs at bay.

LEARNING ACTIVITY 19-1

Create a detailed BEO for the following scenarios.

Situation #1

You are catering a garden party on the estate of Mr. and Mrs. Jonathon Pringle III. There will be 135 guests. Mrs. Pringle wants the party to be in the south rose garden. She would like to bring in a string quartet and a portable dance floor. She has approved a menu for a light supper. Create a BEO based on the information that you have received.

Situation #2

You are the food and beverage manager at a large hotel. A large corporation is having a 2-day managers' meeting on your premises. On the first night, the company will be hosting a reception in one of the hotel's smaller ballrooms prior to transporting the managers to a restaurant across town for dinner. Create a BEO for the reception.

>> Service Equipment

The beauty and functionality of service utensils is important. Listed and illustrated next is serviceware for passed canapés, appetizers, and simple buffets. Elaborate service utensils used on elegant buffets will be explained in Unit 20, Buffets.

BASKETS

Baskets are inexpensive and useful for serving any kind of solid food. Flat baskets are often used for bread and roll service or for serving canapés butler style. Large baskets are used for fruits and raw vegetables.

BOWLS

Bowls are available in many sizes for salads, seafood, dips, and condiments. They should be sturdy, but not heavy, and dishwasher safe. They can be made from ceramic, glass, and other nonreactive materials.

CHEESE TRAYS

Traditionally, cheeses are served on trays, mirrors, woven mats, and, for elegant displays, on marble slabs. Marble is a type of soft limestone polished to a mirror finish and is somewhat fragile. Harsh acids or grit can easily scratch marble; therefore, only soft cheeses or cubed cheese should be served on it. In many banquet presentations, cheeses are served or displayed on a wooden board. The boards should be at least 1-inch thick so they do not warp after washing. Cheeses passed butler style should be cubed. Toothpicks should be supplied, along with small paper napkins. A method should be in place for getting rid of the used napkins and picks.

COMPOTIERS

A **compotier** is a stand made of glass, china, or metal, usually with a center post to serve dainty sandwiches, candies, and assorted cold tidbits.

MATS

Many caterers use bamboo, artificial straw, and other mats on trays for canapé service. Canapés do not slide, the mats add to the attractiveness, and they can be changed when trays are brought back to the kitchen for refills.

PAPER PASTRY CUPS

Pastry cups are available in many sizes, colors, and textures. They are used in catering to hold small baked items or candies.

PLATTERS

Platters are made from many types of food-friendly materials and can range in cost from inexpensive disposable plastic or aluminum to expensive heavy silver, china, or crystal trays. The key to platter use is practicality. Off-premise caterers rely on disposable trays. Today's caterer has an array of attractive trays to select from for butler-style service. Trays should not be heavy or too large because the servers must be able to carry them as they walk through crowds. Trays with two handles should never be used for butler service because the servers need both hands to carry them.

SERVICE UTENSILS

Most simple buffets are self-service where the guests are able to easily serve themselves. For this reason, guests must be able to get the food on the plate efficiently. Tongs, ladles, and appropriate-sized serving spoons or forks aid the guests in retrieving their food neatly. Service utensils are usually found next to the chaffers and salad bowls. Small plates should be placed next to each main item on the buffet. These serve as clean resting places for the serving utensils.

>> Canapés Service

Canapés for large catered parties can cost hundreds, if not thousands, of dollars. It is important for the cold kitchen staff to have an understanding of what amounts are necessary for each specific party or function. Typically, a BEO calls for three to five pieces per person for a light cocktail party. Using this as a guide, a banquet for 100 guests would need at least 500 canapés. When working with amounts this high or even much higher, good planning, workspace management, and refrigeration space are required.

When possible, components and even completed canapés can be made ahead of time and stored until needed. For large parties, the catering department should make an effort to sell canapés that can be mass produced ahead of time. The finished canapés are placed on sheet pans, each variety on a separate pan, covered with plastic film, and refrigerated or frozen. However, they should be frozen only for a short time, as freezing can damage the quality of the end product (Figure 19-9). For additional information about canapé production, consult Unit 7.

Figure 19-9 Frozen canapés are removed prior to service.

Figure 19-10 The first step in making canapés is to create the base.

Figure 19-11 The second step is to add a flavored spread on top of the base.

Banquet canapés are made assembly line fashion in the following steps:

1. Lay out the base pieces (Figure 19-10).
2. Add the flavor spread (Figure 19-11).
3. Add the first layer (Figure 19-12).
4. Add the decorations (Figure 19-13).
5. Add the finishing touches (Figure 19-14).

Canapés can be preserved by spraying them with a very fine layer of aspic jelly (Figure 19-15). The layer must be very thin and the aspic flavor compatible with the main ingredient. Aspic jelly can also be brushed on, but this method is labor intensive and may result in a thick coating that lacks flavor appeal.

Banquet rooms tend to be located far away from the kitchen and sometimes it is not practical to send the canapés ready to serve on platters. The standard practice is to send one cook to the banquet pantry kitchen or side station closest to the banquet room and plate the

Figure 19-12 Next goes the first layer.

Figure 19-13 Add any decorations.

Figure 19-14 The canapé is ready for service.

Figure 19-15 Spraying finished canapés with aspic.

canapés as needed. These small side kitchens usually have a refrigerator and some counters but usually no cooking equipment.
As servers return with trays for replenishing, the cook in charge
is responsible for cleaning, replating, and arranging the trays so
they are presentable. Whether the canapés are served butler style
(passed) or placed on buffet trays or tables, they must look attractive and appetizing and should scream, "Eat me, eat me!"
(Figure 19-16).

The service platters and trays can be varied to match the size
and type of food. Trays on buffets should be large enough to hold
many canapés in as many varieties as possible because buffet trays
are hard to refurbish; at the same time, very large trays will look
half empty and unsightly after a while. Always replenish trays before they look too picked over. Remember that the last guest in
line deserves the same excitement as the first guest, so keep the
trays full until the very end of the service period. Many banquet
chefs start to downsize the amount of trays toward the end of a
party. If tables are set up as individual stations, table sections can
be closed off as the number of guests dwindles. This helps to
keep the available trays full looking but also helps the kitchen at
the ultimate end of the party—clean-up.

Figure 19-16 Beautifully displayed canapés
entice the guests' appetites.

Trays passed butler style should be relatively small to allow the servers to pass through
the crowd. The trays should not be too heavy for the server to carry in one hand, because
they need the other hand to carry napkins.

Whimsical trays and platters are fun. Many parties have themes; in keeping with
seasonal or special theme parties, canapés and other foods can be presented on flat baskets,
wooden boards, china, silver, composite material, theme items such as clam shells, bamboo mats, or whatever the imagination might suggest. This is an area where caterers can
get creative.

Servers must be instructed to return to the kitchen frequently to get trays refilled. Trays
must look clean and neat coming out of the kitchen. If possible, backup, reserved canapés
should be refrigerated until needed. Canapés exposed for a long time to people in a crowded
banquet room should be discarded because they may become contaminated. For this reason,

it is advisable to send food on smaller platters so it can be replenished frequently. The person refilling the tray should use gloves and clean spatulas.

Canapé trays and platters should be decorated to look attractive and interesting. The decorations may consist of live flowers, ribbons, folded napkins, vegetable carvings, and more.

Decorations should:

- Not overwhelm or hide the food; they should highlight and accent the food.
- Not smell; strong-smelling flowers can detract from the food.
- Be securely anchored because the servers or guests may accidentally knock them over and damage the display.
- Not impede access to the food. If canapés are hard to reach, people will not eat them.
- Look fresh and clean every time they are sent to the dining room.

A NOTE ON ALLERGIES: Some customers have allergy concerns, and the cold kitchen chefs and servers should be informed about the ingredients and components used in both the food and the decorations. Certain flowers and nut products can result in serious complications for someone who has an allergy to these materials.

LEARNING ACTIVITY 19-2

Design a buffet table where a variety of canapés will be served. Your client has asked that you select the colors, linens, serving pieces, and decorations to complement an upscale, tropical paradise theme.

> **CHEF'S TIP**
> *Always include a warning notice with boxed lunches to keep lunches in a cooler, out of the sun, or to consume them within a certain period of time.*

Figure 19-17 Boxed lunches generally contain everything needed for the meal including the drink, food, napkins, and cutlery.

>> Boxed Lunches

Boxed lunches are a mainstay of many catering departments. These portable meals are served away from the establishment and should be totally self-contained (Figure 19-17). They should look as attractive as possible. This starts with the design and shape of the box, the matching paper napkins, and disposable flatware and cup. The food should be the type that does not spoil easily. Once boxed lunches are out of refrigeration, there is a short window of time to maintain food safety.

The food must be selected to match the event. If it is a fancy picnic lunch for an event in the wine country, for example, cheeses, nuts, and selected fresh fruit might be inside the box. Food that is prone to spoil should not be included in boxed lunches that will be out of refrigeration for more than 4 hours. Boxed lunches are usually eaten at awkward locations such as in an airplane, on a bus, in a car while traveling, on a golf course, during a business meeting, or as a picnic in the field. All foods contained in the boxed lunch should be easily accessible and require a minimum of cutting and slicing. For example, some whole fruits are hard to eat, and juicy items might be messy. Keeping this in mind, here is a list of typical ingredients found in boxed lunches:

- One or two half sandwiches containing meat and/or cheese, dry, with packaged condiments such as mayonnaise or mustard
- One-quarter freshly roasted or fried chicken, partially or completely boned
- One hard-boiled egg, peeled, with salt/pepper packets
- One small serving of salad greens with packaged dressing
- One small portion of pasta, potato, or other starch-based salad (only if served within a short period of time from refrigeration)
- One small dessert or cookie
- One soft roll (hard rolls can be crumbly)

- Fresh fruit in slices or chunks in plastic cup or whole apple, pear, banana, or orange
- Napkins (two), plasticware, wet nap, and toothpick
- Bottled water or canned soda

Boxed lunches are usually preordered days or weeks before the event. Boxed lunches are easily put together, and for quick or last-minute orders, they are the saving grace for most cold kitchens. They should be treated like all catering orders, and a BEO should be written for them.

>> Room Service and Amenities

In many hotels, management sends gifts or amenities to certain customers—VIPs, frequent guests, or guests who are dissatisfied with their room or unhappy with the service. In convention hotels, the convention host might send gifts or amenities to the attendees to make them feel welcome.

Figure 19-18 Customer gifts may include a fruit and cheese basket with wine.

Typically, hotels have three levels of room gifts:

- Basic—Basket with fruits and cheeses
- Upgraded—Fruits and cheeses with chocolate or candies, or perhaps a flight of cheese, nuts, and wine (Figure 19-18).
- Deluxe—If it is a spa style of resort or hotel, for example, the gift basket or tray might have bath products, gift bathrobe, and toiletries. If it is a food basket, it might contain a high-end wine, a bottle of high-quality champagne or brandy, fruits, a selection of cheeses, pâté breads or crackers, and perhaps a chocolate bag or box filled with truffles and other candies; or if themed, it might contain sports-oriented products, magazines, spritzers, and other products. The chef and management make the decisions on what is contained in these special-amenities baskets.

In-room gifts are prepared either in the room-service kitchen or side room or in the cold kitchen pantry and delivered by room service. When the order is intended to placate an unhappy guest, it will arrive at the pantry unexpectedly and must be filled as soon as possible. For this reason, experienced cold kitchen chefs should maintain an inventory of fruits, individual portion-sized cheese, crackers, and other amenity items at all times.

The usual procedure is as follows:

1. Room service will deliver the order slip. It must state the name and room number of the recipient, the time when to deliver, and the type of gift.
2. Room service will pick up the order. If the order includes chocolate, candies, or wine, room service will add it.

Keep in mind that the order is a gift and should make the recipient happy!

- Baskets must be clean; napkins and doily papers must be fresh.
- Fruits must be unblemished and ripe.
- Fruits must be washed and dry.
- Packaged cheese must be clean with the label visible.
- Fresh cheese must be wrapped carefully in plastic wrap to prevent drying out. Cheeses that minimize strong odors in a room should be selected unless the guest requests a specific type of cheese.
- These orders must be given priority. The order must be ready when requested. Sometimes the delivery time window is very short.

>> Summary

Catering is a profitable segment in most operations and can be best described as providing many meals at the same time to a group of customers. It is essential that the right amount of food is ready at the prescribed time, so all kitchen employees must read the BEO carefully and keep the requirements in mind.

This unit detailed the different service styles important for catered events. It also covers boxed lunches and hotel or club amenity baskets and room service needs.

>> Review Questions

MATCHING

Match the term with its definition.

1. _____ reception
2. _____ butler service
3. _____ cocktail parties
4. _____ tray service
5. _____ arm service
6. _____ buffet

a. Servers carry food around the room and the customers take what they like.
b. Servers carry up to three plates of food at once.
c. A gathering of people who want to socialize.
d. A gathering that takes place before dinner.
e. Food is placed on stationary tables.
f. Food is delivered to the guest.

MULTIPLE CHOICE

7. BEO is the abbreviation for
   a. Bound Executive Order.
   b. Banquet Error Oversight.
   c. Banquet Event Order.
   d. Beverage Event Order.
8. When a party is booked, off-site caterers should first
   a. check out the location of the event.
   b. plan the menu.
   c. get a guest count.
   d. determine the number of employees required to execute the party.
9. A compotier is
   a. a silver tray.
   b. stewed fruits.
   c. a service stand made of glass, china, or metal.
   d. computer software used in catering.

10. BEO typically calls for _____ canapés per person for a light cocktail party.
    a. 2 to 4
    b. 3 to 5
    c. 4 to 6
    d. 5 to 7
11. Canapés can be preserved by spraying them with a very fine layer of _____ _____.
    a. cold water
    b. warm water
    c. edible starch
    d. aspic jelly

SHORT ANSWER

12. List at least four questions that should be asked when catering off-site.
13. In a large operation, who should be sent a copy of the BEO?
14. What types of cheeses can be served on marble?

15. Describe the three levels of gifts found in typical hotels.
    Basic:
    Upgraded:
    Deluxe:

The Craft

>> Unit 20

Decorating Work—The Heart of the Garde Manger

>> Unit 21

Preparing for Culinary Competitions

The previous units were dedicated to teaching the foundation of cold kitchen work. Our final two units focus on decorating work and culinary competitions. Unit 20 discusses the history of garde-manger decorating and teaches basic decorating techniques including platter design, aspic work, and vegetable and ice carving. The new art of molecular gastronomy is also introduced in this unit. Decorating is where a chef's artistic talents can be utilized to prepare beautiful showpieces.

Unit 21 provides an introduction to culinary competitions and includes practical information that can be used to organize and run a successful team.

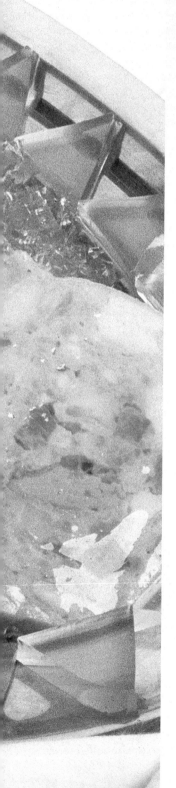

Decorating Work—
The Heart of the Garde Manger

>> Learning Objectives

After you have finished reading this unit, you should be able to:

- Describe how to make aspic jelly from scratch.
- Explain what *chaud froid* is and how it is used.
- Demonstrate how to make several simple vegetable carvings.
- Explain how to make a watermelon basket and melon carving.
- Explain the steps used in creating a simple ice carving.
- Discuss *fruit caviar*—how it is made and its uses.
- Describe gelled products.

>> Key Terms

bouquet garni	gelatinous	molecular gastronomy	spherification
dead dough	Madeira wine	pH level	templates

We learned in Unit 1 that the Egyptians and Romans encouraged their chefs to decorate food for special times and for feasting. Garlands of bay laurel leaves, sprigs of herbs, fur, and feathers all had their places in early feasts. The ancients talked of eating food with the eyes first, and this saying is still true today (Figure 20-1). Lifestyles change, fashions change, and what constitutes beauty changes and is reflected in how we as chefs present food. The perception of beauty is very subjective. In this unit we will study both timeless and contemporary basic decorating ingredients and techniques including the use of aspic jelly and its derivative, chaud froid.

Current foodservice trends lean toward serving food without elaborate decorations. Today's dining guests enjoy many styles of cooking presented with natural, clean lines. Many of the newest trends, like the subtle and artistic use of gelatins, aspics, and chaud froid, are grounded in the classics of yesterday.

Buffets that once sported cooked lobsters garishly painted deep red and playing the fiddle; whole, poached fish covered with cucumber scales; and hams sculptured with mashed, sweet potatoes into heads of Indian chiefs now serve that same lobster, fish, and ham in their natural beauty. These center-of-the-table items are highlighted and surrounded by foods that complement

Figure 20-1   This fifteenth-century Egyptian fresco shows an elaborate table.

Figure 20-2   Cruise lines provide elaborate buffets that utilize the chef's decorating skills.

Figure 20-3   Chefs create beautiful centerpieces with fruit and vegetable carvings.

them, without the contrived garnishment of the past. The work and talents of the chefs of yesteryear should be admired, and their techniques adapted to the modern service and trends. There is still a place for ornate platters and set pieces. In high-end hotels, country clubs, and on many cruise ships, the sumptuous buffets are headlined with amazing platter work (Figure 20-2). The skill of the garde manger is demonstrated in such examples as the midnight, end-of-voyage buffets on most cruise liners, consisting of many large show platters. These show platters still draw large admiring crowds.

Some of the newest decorative foods come from the commercial application of food science. Trendsetting items now finding their way onto menus are fruit caviars, gels, and agar agar-based items. These items are used to add excitement to foods. By mastering the science side of cooking, by applying new techniques with classical food items, and stirring in some artisitic ability, the garde-manger chef is the trendsetter in the kitchen.

Many of today's naturalistic styles of buffet decoration and platters or baskets are enhanced by carved fruits and vegetables (Figure 20-3). Many of the best vegetable carvings are inspired by the artisan chefs of Asia. They have led the way to some of the most beautiful styles of vegetable carving, and have developed the tools to skillfully enable anyone to do this type of work. In this unit, you will learn how to make a traditional watermelon basket and a not-so-traditional melon carving. We will also cover basic ice carving in this unit as well.

>> The Past, Present, and Future of Food Decorations

In the past, gastronomy was directly connected with wealth. For centuries, talented cooks worked for clerical or lay nobility before jobs in fine hotels and restaurants became available. Depending on the affluence of the host, elaborately decorated foods were used to demonstrate power, influence, and, at times, arrogance. Cooks labored for days creating towering, usually inedible, centerpieces of tallow, sugar, and pastries (Figure 20-4). As recently as the late nineteenth century, cold food was still served on pedestals, also called *socles*.

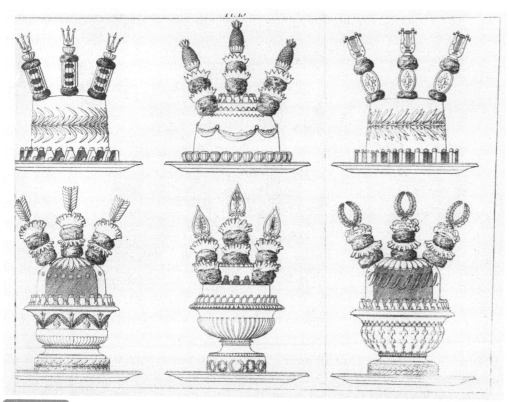

Figure 20-4 This page from *Le Cuisinier parisien'* by Antoine Careme, published in 1842, shows designs for elaborate food decoration.

They were made with rice, bread, gelatin, and other foodstuffs, which were thrown away after use—an appalling practice when so many employees in the kitchens went to bed hungry.

Making these decorations required many hours of tedious work, often performed by underpaid kitchen workers. Chef's magazines published in the early 1900s still devoted many pages to instructions on how to make carefully chiseled towers out of bread loaves and sculptures with suet and wax.

The famed French chef, Auguste Escoffier, realized at the turn of the nineteenth century, along with other contemporary chefs of the time, that food presentation should be simplified. However, he himself became interested in making wax flowers and was quite famous for his wax flower bouquets exhibited at many culinary shows.

The Edwardian age of excess and opulence, from the late 1800s to the first decade of the twentieth century, gave way to the deprivations brought on by the demise of the aristocracy during World War I. The watershed years from 1914 through 1918 saw the elimination of large segments of the European aristocracy and their wealth. The death of the Hapsburgs, the family that had ruled Austria for six centuries, and the demise of the Russian Tzar and Tzarina marked the end of the era.

In the United States during the late 1800s, large hotels were built and going out for dinner became socially acceptable. The very wealthy were "putting on the ritz." Hotels such as the Palace in San Francisco, the Palmer House in Chicago, and the Ansonia in New York City hired only the best chefs from Europe. Many of the chefs came to the states to escape the tragedies in Europe. They brought with them a high level of culinary skills.

As times changed, so did food presentations. They became more simplified, pedestals and socles were rarely used, and wax flowers became a curiosity displayed at food shows. The worldwide depression, starting with the 1929 stock market crash and the resulting economic upheaval, made a further dent in the scope of decorations and food presentation was further simplified. So many had lost fortunes, and what was once considered festive was now thought of as excess.

Figure 20-5 A chef carves a sculpture out of a block of ice in front of guests.

Elaborately decorated food lost customer appeal, and management could not financially justify its costs.

During World War II, many GIs had their first taste of European cuisine. They came back after the war with a new appreciation for old-world styles and foods. After the war, as fortunes picked up, stylish food returned to the hotels and dining halls.

Fine dining never goes out of fashion; however, trends change to reflect current fiscal health. No matter what the pocketbook says, many customers still enjoy expertly decorated cold dishes. Many chefs pride themselves on the ability to make cold dishes and the various techniques involved with the cold kitchen. Today, we have seen resurgence in this style of cuisine. Many cruise lines offer elaborate buffets, with ice carvings, large fruit displays, and platters laden and overflowing with amazing food displays (Figure 20-5). Many chefs get enthusiastic to make a decorated cold platter and are willing to put in the time and effort needed. Their effort must be applauded and admired.

One pioneer in modernizing cold food presentation was the Swiss chef Adelrich Furrer. His work was much admired from the 1920s to the 1950s. Over the years, his style has been copied and imitated. He pioneered the presentation of cold food in portion sizes on minimally decorated trays. He spent his last working years as chef traiteur (caterer) in Zurich, Switzerland.

>> Work Environment—A Basic Decorating Principle

Cold foods, especially decorated cold foods, can be made only in lower-temperature-controlled environments. Those trying to decorate cold food in makeshift locations frequently end up frustrated. The area should be air conditioned and squeaky clean due to the nature of handling food that will be served cold without further cooking. Again, sanitation must always be given the utmost consideration when working with cold foods. Ample stainless steel counters with floor space around the tables must be available. It is difficult to create elaborate decoration when there is high traffic around the workspace from other chefs and servers. Decorating foods require frequent trips to the walk-in coolers to keep the food chilled at safe temperatures. An ideal workspace is adjacent to the coolers. Space in the refrigerator must be ample and decorated pieces in progress should not have to balance precariously on crates and boxes. Sanitation standards must remain high.

Even large display pieces must be edible and, therefore, should be handled with respect and an eye toward taste. Flavor balance is important and should never be sacrificed for the sake of aesthetics. The famous New York chef, George Waldner, was an early modern pioneer of garde manger. His showpieces were legendary and he made a point that all of the showpieces he created were properly seasoned, even when he knew that they would not be consumed. Foodservice personnel should wear latex or vinyl gloves because much of the food is not cooked further (Figure 20-6). Many local and state health departments require workers to wear these gloves. Getting the finished trays and platters to and from the banquet and dining room also has to be taken into consideration.

Transporting large platters can be a challenge. In some hotels, the platters are finished at the table before the party. Banquet halls and dining rooms are usually located on a different floor or a large distance from the kitchens. Large transport racks called "Queen Marys" are used in many hotels. Size matters—what looks nice in the kitchen could look monstrous on a table in the dining room. Keep in mind also that within 5 minutes of service, the platter looks picked over, so having backup platters is essential.

Decorated food is still in demand and will continue to be (Figure 20-7) at brunch buffets, holiday events, wedding buffets, and for advertising purposes and culinary shows.

Keep the following tips in mind when you are designing decorated food displays:

- The food must look beautiful, real, edible, and inviting.
- The food must look clean and be wholesome.
- The items must be recognizable.
- The food must look fresh.
- The food should not look handled.
- The food must be accessible without guests having to dig through layers of decorations.
- All decorations must be edible and relate to the dish.

Figure 20-6 Sanitation is a prime concern when doing decorating work. Chefs should wear gloves when handling foods that won't be cooked further.

Figure 20-7 There is still a place for beautifully decorated food.

Figure 20-8 A chef spooning the aspic jelly over slices of chilled pâtè.

>> Aspic Jelly

Aspic jelly is meat- or fish-flavored jelly used as a garnish, decorating glaze, and as a flavor component. As a glaze, aspic is used to coat and protect foods, like a varnish (Figure 20-8). Taste is secondary to the function of the aspic as a protecting cover. It is also used to fill the cavities in terrines and pâtès. In this unit, we discuss aspic as a major decorating element. Aspic jelly can be made from scratch or purchased as a fully seasoned commercial product that requires only blending with hot water. Commercially produced instant aspic is used in many operations as a time saver or when the equipment for making aspic jelly is not available. While handy, it lacks the wonderful flavor that only scratch cooking can produce.

Taking the time and effort to make flavorful aspic from scratch will result in a great-tasting product that complements cold food. Aspic should have a pleasant aroma and be well flavored because only a small amount is eaten.

The following points should be considered when using aspic:

- The flavor should match the dish for which it is intended and complement it without overpowering.
- The color should be pale amber to dark gold and match the base ingredient.
- The aspic should be completely transparent.
- Fish aspic should be slightly lighter in color than meat aspic, but still completely clear.
- A good jelly coats and holds the food but is a delicate texture.
- Meat aspic is often flavored with **Madeira wine,** a sweet wine from Portugal.
- Dry, clear white wine is often added to fish aspic as a flavor component.

Aspic jelly is made with a **gelatinous** stock, the sticky protein derived from veal knuckles, pork feet or pork skin, or in the case of fish stock, by adding gelatin (Figure 20-9). These products add collagen for body, as well as flavor to stocks. When the stock does not contain enough gelatin to jell sufficiently, commercial gelatin must be added. It is not the same as commercial aspic powder, which is made with salt, flavoring, and gelatin. Plain gelatin is available in sheets or powder. Both work equally well; however, sheet gelatin is slightly more expensive.

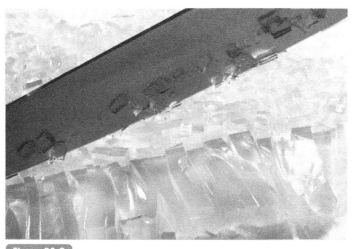

Figure 20-9 Aspic has a gelatinous texture.

To bloom the gelatin, you must first soak the sheets in cold water to soften. They will dissolve immediately when added to hot stock. Gelatin powder must first be blended with a little amount of cold water to bloom. Allow the powdered gelatin to sit for up to 30 minutes to fully bloom. This step will keep the gelatin from lumping when added to the hot stock.

The amount of added gelatin obviously depends on the natural gelatin content in the stock. Chefs should always make a test by putting a few drops on a chilled plate to check its stability. Too much added gelatin gives too stiff a texture and a rubbery, gluey taste. As a general guideline, 1 ounce (28 g) of gelatin is sufficient for 1 pint (480 ml) of stock. Additional gelatin might be needed in hot weather or if the stock itself has a larger amount of acid from wine or vinegar.

>> Working with Dry Gelatin Products

Powdered gelatin and sheet gelatin are interchangeable. Generally, there are 12 to 14 sheets per ounce of dry gelatin. The less gelatin used, the more fragile the matrix, so ideally you should use small quantities for gelled soups and more for a mirror coating.

Use the following chart to determine the amount of gelatin you will need for the specific job at hand.

Amount per Quart	Amount per Cup	Strength of Gel	Usage
1/2 ounce	1/8 ounce	Light	Clear soups such as consommé
1 ounce	1/4 ounce	Medium light	Coating and edible chaud froid
2 ounces	1/2 ounce	Medium	Braun and headcheese, topping terrines, and pâté en croûte
3 ounces	3/4 ounce	Firm gel	Mirror and platter coating for competition
4 ounces	1 ounce	Extra-firm gel	Use when cream is used as in cream cheese, pastry cream, and mousselines

CLARIFICATION PROCESS

Meat and fish stock are usually cloudy, even when made very carefully. Adding some acid such as wine and vinegar to the stock will help to clarify it. Aspic, as a rule, is usually clarified as described in Unit 10, the section about cold consommé. The recipe listed on the next page does not use the standard, clear meat process. Instead, it depends entirely on slow simmering, skimming the surface, and occasionally wiping the inside rim of the pot with a moist towel.

Low-sodium canned broth can be used as the chicken broth in the following recipe. **Bouquet garni** is a collection of herbs and vegetables tied together in a bundle. Typical ingredients include celery, thyme, parsley, carrots, and leeks. To skim or degrease, use a ladle and carefully remove the fat and impurities (raft) that float on top of the stocks. Avoid stirring, which will incorporate the fat back into the stock.

classic meat aspic   *Yield: 1 qt (960 ml)*

Ingredients	Amounts		Procedure
	U.S.	Metric	
Veal knuckle	2 lbs	907 g	Lightly roast the bones without browning.
Calves feet, boned and blanched	1 each	1 each	
Pork feet, cleaned and blanched	1 each	1 each	
Cold beef, veal, or chicken broth	1 1/2 qt	1.42 l	Place the bones in a stockpot and add the broth. Bring it to a slow boil. Skim carefully and wipe the side of the pot with a clean cloth to remove any scum. Simmer for 3 hours, skimming frequently and keeping the sides clean.
Onions, chopped	2 oz	57 g	Add the remaining ingredients. Simmer for an hour. Strain through a double layer of cheesecloth. Test its consistency by placing a small amount on a chilled plate or on ice. If need be, strengthen the mixture by adding a small amount of additional gelatin bloomed in cold water and heated. Then add to aspic.
Carrots, chopped	2 oz	57 g	
Bouquet garni	As desired	As desired	
Sea salt	1/2 oz	14 g	
Tomatoes, crushed, canned	8 fl oz	237 ml	

NUTRITIONAL INFORMATION PER RECIPE: 2,383 Calories; 108 g Fat (42.3% calories from fat); 307 g Protein; 26 g Carbohydrate; 5 g Dietary Fiber; 1,111 mg Cholesterol; 11,093 mg Sodium. Exchanges: 42 Lean Meat; 3 1/2 Vegetable; 7 1/2 Fat.

When a quick aspic is needed for an application in the garde manger, this modern adaptation of aspic works well.

modern aspic *Yield: 1 qt (960 ml)*

Ingredients	Amounts		Procedure
	U.S.	Metric	
Cold beef, veal, or chicken consommé	1 1/2 qt	1.42 l	Place the consommé in a pot and heat to reduce to 1 quart. Remove from heat and cool to 110°F (43°C).

Ingredients	Amounts		Procedure
Gelatin sheets or powder	3 oz	85 g	Bloom the gelatin in 4 oz cold water. When softened, add to the consommé in the pot and melt the gelatin.
Cold water	4 fl oz	116 ml	
Sea salt	1 tsp	5 g	Add salt for flavor and use for glazing or for chaud froid.

NUTRITIONAL INFORMATION PER SERVING: 678 Calories; 0 g Fat (0.0% calories from fat); 71 g Protein; 98 g Carbohydrate; 0 g Dietary Fiber; 0 mg Cholesterol; 9,775 mg Sodium. Exchanges: 7 1/2 Lean Meat; 5 Other Carbohydrates.

There are times when fish aspic is needed. This is a basic recipe that can be used with a multitude of dishes. You'll know when the egg whites coagulate when they change from a liquid state into a solid. Use the Fish Stock recipe provided below.

fish aspic   *Yield: 1 qt (946 ml)*

Ingredients	Amounts		Procedure
	U.S.	**Metric**	
Fish stock, warm	36 fl oz	1. 08 l	Combine all the ingredients and stir well to distribute the egg whites. Heat the stock until the egg whites start to coagulate, which will happen when the temperature is approximately 170°F (80°C). When the raft starts to form, stop stirring. Do not disturb the raft floating on top. Simmer 15 minutes. Cool down. Carefully ladle the stock through a double cheesecloth-lined sieve. The stock should be clear and free of particles. Test for consistency. Add more gelatin if necessary.
Egg whites	2–3 each	2–3 each	
Saffron	1 pinch	1 pinch	
Parsley sprigs	3 each	3 each	
Bay leaf	1/2 each	1/2 each	
Tarragon, fresh	1 sprig	1 sprig	
White peppercorns, crushed	3 each	3 each	
Gelatin, powdered	2 oz	56 g	
Vinegar, white	1/4 cup	59 ml	
Salt	To taste	To taste	

NUTRITIONAL INFORMATION PER RECIPE: 747 Calories; 26 g Fat (39.5% calories from fat); 19 g Protein; 72 g Carbohydrate; 4 g Dietary Fiber; 72 mg Cholesterol; 1,642 mg Sodium. Exchanges: 0 Grain (Starch); 1 1/2 Lean Meat; 0 Vegetable; 1 Fat; 4 1/2 Other Carbohydrates.

Any firm, white-fleshed fish, such as flounder, sole, halibut, or bass, should work in the following recipe. The white vinegar can be replaced with 1/2 cup of dry white wine.

fish stock *Yield: 32 fl oz (946 ml)*

Ingredients	Amounts		Procedure
	U.S.	Metric	
Fish bones, from nonfatty white fish	2 lbs	907 g	Wash the bones thoroughly in cold water.
Onions, diced	4 oz	113 g	Place all the ingredients in a stockpot and cover with water. Bring to a slow boil and reduce to a simmer. Simmer for 20 minutes. Strain through cheesecloth.
Parsley stems	5 each	5 each	
Mushroom trimmings	4 oz	113 g	
White peppercorns	1/2 tsp	2 g	
White vinegar	1 fl oz	30 ml	
Water, cold	2 1/2 pt	1.18 l	

NUTRITIONAL INFORMATION PER RECIPE: 92 Calories; 1 g Fat (5.4% calories from fat); 4 g Protein; 21 g Carbohydrate; 5 g Dietary Fiber; 0 mg Cholesterol; 48 mg Sodium. Exchanges: 0 Grain (Starch); 3 Vegetable; 0 Fat; 0 Other Carbohydrates.

The fish stock can be used as the key ingredient in the following recipe for Rich Fish Aspic. This recipe can also be made with any firm, white-fleshed fish in place of the scallops for guests who may be allergic to bivalves.

rich fish aspic *Yield: 1 qt (946 ml)*

Ingredients	Amounts		Procedure
	U.S.	Metric	
Fish stock	1 qt	960 ml	Warm the fish stock.
Gelatin	2 1/2 oz	71 g	Dissolve the gelatin in wine and add it to the stock.
White wine, dry	4 fl oz	118 ml	

Scallops or white-fleshed fish	2 oz	56 g	Combine the remaining ingredients in a food processor and purée. Stir the purée vigorously into the warm stock. Bring to a slow simmer, stirring occasionally until a raft forms. Simmer 30 minutes. Strain through double layers of cheesecloth.
Egg whites	2 each	2 each	
Sole trimmings	2 oz	56 g	

NUTRITIONAL INFORMATION PER RECIPE: 891 Calories; 24 g Fat (32.3% calories from fat); 35 g Protein; 79 g Carbohydrate; 3 g Dietary Fiber; 110 mg Cholesterol; 1,377 mg Sodium. Exchanges: 4 Lean Meat; 1 Fat; 5 Other Carbohydrates.

A roast turkey, goose, or hen breast can be enhanced when covered with aspic and garnishes. The following recipe is standard poultry aspic and can be used with any type of poultry.

poultry aspic *Yield: 1 qt (946 ml)*

Ingredients	Amounts		Procedure
	U.S.	Metric	
Chicken bones, necks and backs, browned	1 lb	454 g	Combine the chicken bones, stock, and gelatin in a heavy saucepot. Allow for the gelatin to bloom. Then heat to warm.
Chicken stock, good quality	36 fl oz	1.06 l	
Gelatin	2 oz	57 g	
Chicken trimmings, raw	8 oz	226 g	Dice the carrots, onions, and celery.
Carrots	2 oz	57 g	
Onions	4 oz	113 g	
Celery	2 oz	57 g	
Egg whites	2 each	2 each	
Salt	To taste	To taste	

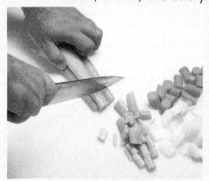

Process the remaining ingredients in a food processor.

Stir the puréed ingredients into the warm chicken stock. Bring to a slow simmer. Simmer for 1 1/2 hours. Strain through cheesecloth. Check the flavor and add salt, if needed.

NUTRITIONAL INFORMATION PER RECIPE: 1,546 Calories; 100 g Fat (60.8% calories from fat); 80 g Protein; 64 g Carbohydrate; 2 g Dietary Fiber; 350 mg Cholesterol; 10,498 mg Sodium. Exchanges: 10 Lean Meat; 1 1/2 Vegetable; 14 1/2 Fat; 3 1/2 Other Carbohydrates.

Tomato aspic is used as a garnish as well as a chilled "salad" served on a bed of lettuce with a slice of lime. It is low calorie and will especially complement caviar or cold fish dishes. Cut into diamonds or squares, it adds a blast of vibrant color to platters and individual coupe. More gelatin is needed with tomato aspic, due to the acid content of the tomatoes.

tomato aspic *Yield: 1 pt (472 ml)*

Ingredients	Amounts		Procedure
	U.S.	Metric	
Tomato juice	16 fl oz	472 ml	Combine all the ingredients. Make sure the gelatin is evenly dissolved. Slowly heat to approximately 110°F (45°C), stirring gently. Cool and fill in a suitable mold.
Sugar	1 tbsp	14 g	
Gelatin	3/4 oz	21 g	
Vinegar	1 fl oz	30 ml	
Celery salt	1 tsp	5 g	
Lemon juice	1/2 oz	14 ml	
White pepper	Dash	Dash	

NUTRITIONAL INFORMATION PER RECIPE: 227 Calories; 1 g Fat (2.4% calories from fat); 6 g Protein; 56 g Carbohydrate; 6 g Dietary Fiber; 0 mg Cholesterol; 3,400 mg Sodium. Exchanges: 0 Grain (Starch); 3 1/2 Vegetable; 0 Fruit; 0 Fat; 2 Other Carbohydrates.

In the realm of showpieces, there are times when it is truly just for show. Therefore, we are including a recipe for mock aspic. It is edible, but would not be palatable due to the lack of any flavoring ingredients or salt. This type of coating is used for display pieces that are not intended for consumption or for the final coating of an edible display where a thin layer of "shine" is required.

coating or display aspic   *Yield: 2 qt (1.9 l)*

Ingredients	Amounts		Procedure
	U.S.	Metric	
Cold water	1/2 gallon	1.9 l	Place the cold water in a stainless steel bowl. Sprinkle or place the gelatin granules or sheets into the cold water. Let soak or bloom for 5 minutes to absorb. Heat gently over a bain-marie until the temperature reaches 100°F–105°F (38°C–40°C) and is thoroughly dissolved.
Gelatin	5 oz	141 g	

To use as a final coating over chaud froid or other foods for shine, cool to 80°F–90°F (27°C–32°C).

NUTRITIONAL INFORMATION PER RECIPE: 540 Calories; 0 g Fat (0.0% calories from fat); 11 g Protein; 128 g Carbohydrate; 0 g Dietary Fiber; 0 mg Cholesterol; 417 mg Sodium. Exchanges: 8 1/2 Other Carbohydrates.

>> Chaud Froid Sauce

For centuries, food that was served from elaborately decorated buffets or from large platters had to travel a great distance from the kitchen to the diner. By the time it reached the table, the food was no longer hot. Many of the dishes were covered with rich sauces or pan drippings that congealed when they got cold. These were prepared hot and served cold. Though this sounds disgusting, it was discovered that these dishes were tasty, and the term *chaud froid* (hot cold) was coined. Eventually chefs started putting decorations on the congealed sauces because they provided a suitable medium for their artistic creations.

The next evolution came when the chefs started to make chaud froid sauces separately from the underlying dish and concentrated more and more on using chaud froid sauces as a decorating medium. Natural colorants such as paprika, tomato, truffles, and saffron were added to the sauces and were poured as a thin coating layer on the platter. When cold, these colorful chaud froids were cut into many shapes. They were then used to create patterns and designs in contrasting colors that were applied to the food covered with a base chaud froid sauce. The completed pattern was then coated in thin, clear aspic, giving it a shiny exterior, somewhat like varnish.

The practice reached its zenith about 80 years ago and is still somewhat in fashion today. The skill required to cover poultry, meat, or whole fish evenly with sauce and decorate it with a complicated pattern became the yardstick by which chefs were judged. Thin pieces of truffle, thin slices of colored aspic, and blanched thin slices of vegetables were used to make mosaic-type pictures on top of the large pieces of meat. These pieces were used as the centerpiece of a platter presentation for large buffets.

Chaud froid can be poured over cold dishes, or the food itself can be dipped into the sauce and placed in the refrigerator to solidify (Figure 20-10). This practice takes much skill and time and has almost become a dying art.

In the past, large hotels employed a garde-manger chef to do all of the chaud froid decorations. These cooks had the artistic skill and experience required to handle these tasks. The decorator or garde-manger chef would create amazing pictures and designs using the cold sauce chaud froid as base. Not all cooks are gifted decorators and not all culinary artists are good cooks. It is, however, within the realm of all culinarians to be able to do the simple chaud froid work. When just starting out, it is important to keep the designs minimal until the cook or chef gets enough experience to do the more complicated and ornate design work. Unless a cook is truly gifted and has the resources and experience, decorations should be kept at a minimum. Stressing the natural world is ideal.

While it might seem outdated to cover food with cold, gelatinized sauce, fashions change and what was once "outré" now finds itself in fashion. Timeless techniques and old skills have found a rebirth in today's contemporary kitchens. Gels, starches, and other thick ingredients are becoming the basis for many of the more innovative items found in the kitchen today.

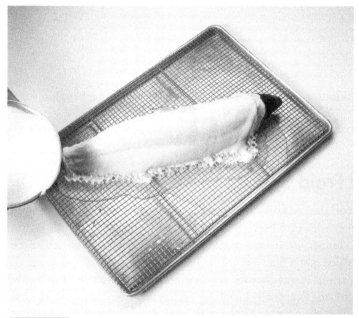

Figure 20-10 A fish is glazed with the chaud froid before going into the refrigerator to congeal.

To add to your arsenal of cooking techniques, it is important that you learn how to make and how to utilize chaud froid sauces. The following recipe is a traditional, basic chaud froid. It is made with chicken velouté, a thick sauce based on chicken stock, flour, and butter. Use the Poultry Aspic recipe previously given in this unit. To make a fish chaud froid sauce, simply use the White Chaud Froid Sauce Benchmark recipe below and substitute fish velouté and fish aspic.

white chaud froid sauce *Yield: 1 qt (946 ml)*

Ingredients	Amounts		Procedure
	U.S.	Metric	
Chicken velouté	1 qt	946 ml	Carefully warm the velouté and aspic jelly.
Poultry aspic	16 fl oz	473 ml	
Gelatin, powdered	2 oz	57 g	Dissolve the gelatin in cold cream. Warm the cream and add it to the sauce. Bring it to a boil, reduce to a simmer, and add cream. Stir very carefully to avoid scorching and excessive bubbles.
Heavy cream, cold	8 fl oz	237 ml	
Salt	To taste	To taste	Season to taste. Strain through cheesecloth. Cool, stirring occasionally. Use after it has cooled to 75°F–80°F (24°C–27°C).
Pepper	To taste	To taste	

NUTRITIONAL INFORMATION PER RECIPE: 1,565 Calories; 109 g Fat (60.4% calories from fat); 33 g Protein; 129 g Carbohydrate; 4 g Dietary Fiber; 327 mg Cholesterol; 4,825 mg Sodium. Exchanges: 2 1/2 Grain (Starch); 6 Vegetable; 1/2 Nonfat Milk; 22 Fat; 3 1/2 Other Carbohydrates.

This Benchmark Recipe for Brown Chaud Froid Sauce is made with demi glace sauce, which is a brown sauce made with bones and thickened with flour. The veal stock is made with bones and is not thickened. Truffle juice is available canned and can be ordered from a specialty food supplier. Use the Poultry Aspic recipe previously given in this unit. A sweet, nonalcoholic wine can be substituted in schools for the Madeira wine, if required.

brown chaud froid sauce *Yield: 3 1/2 pt (1.7 l)*

Ingredients	Amounts		Procedure
	U.S.	Metric	
Demi glace sauce	1 qt	946 ml	Combine the sauce, stock, and truffle juice. Bring to a slow simmer.
Veal stock	8 fl oz	237 ml	
Truffle juice—if available, optional	1 1/2 fl oz	44 ml	
Poultry aspic	16 oz	473 g	Warm the aspic, add the gelatin, and dissolve. Add to the sauce.
Gelatin, powdered	2 oz	57 6	
Madeira wine	8 fl oz	237 ml	Add the wine. Bring to a boil, reduce to a simmer for 3 minutes, and test for taste and consistency. Strain through a double layer of cheesecloth.

NUTRITIONAL INFORMATION PER RECIPE: 1,254 Calories; 16 g Fat (21.3% calories from fat); 26 g Protein; 110 g Carbohydrate; 5 g Dietary Fiber; 23 mg Cholesterol; 7,750 mg Sodium. Exchanges: 6 Vegetable; 3 Fat; 4 1/2 Other Carbohydrates.

CHAUD FROID SAUCES IN DIFFERENT COLORS

Natural pigments can be used to color chaud froid. Using commercial food colors is never recommended because the colors are artificial and make the food look unnatural. Commercial food colorants also bleed and stain other foods around them. Using commercial food colors is a totally unacceptable practice in competitions.

In the next recipe, Green Chaud Froid Sauce is colored with spinach and parsley. Use the White Chaud Froid Sauce recipe as a basis for the colored sauce.

green chaud froid sauce *Yield: 1 qt (946 ml)*

Ingredients	Amounts U.S.	Metric	Procedure
Spinach	1 bunch	1 bunch	Remove the leaves from the spinach and the stems from the parsley. Wash well to remove any sand. Blanch and shock the spinach and parsley.
Parsley	1 large bunch	1 large bunch	

Water	2 fl oz	60 ml	Put the spinach and parsley with water into a food processor and process to a fine purée. Line a strainer with a double layer of cheesecloth and strain. Press out as much liquid as possible. Reserve the green juice.
White chaud froid sauce	1 qt	946 ml	Warm the sauce and add the natural green color until the desired shade is obtained.

NUTRITIONAL INFORMATION PER RECIPE: 1,649 Calories; 111 g Fat (57.4% calories from fat); 42 g Protein; 143 g Carbohydrate; 13 g Dietary Fiber; 327 mg Cholesterol; 508 mg Sodium. Exchanges: 2 1/2 Grain (Starch); 8 1/2 Vegetable; 1/2 Nonfat Milk; 22 Fat; 3 1/2 Other Carbohydrates.

Saffron is a powerful coloring agent. It only takes a miniscule amount to give the sauce a bright yellow color. Steep the saffron in a hot liquid before combining it with other ingredients. Use the White Chaud Froid Sauce as the base for the yellow sauce. Use any of the aspic jelly recipes from earlier and dissolve it by heating to 85°F to 90°F (30°C–32°C) to melt.

yellow chaud froid sauce   *Yield: 1 qt (946 ml)*

Ingredients	Amounts		Procedure
	U.S.	Metric	
Saffron	1/2 tsp	2 g	Steep the saffron in hot aspic jelly for approximately 30 minutes. Strain and retain the yellow liquid.
Aspic jelly, dissolved	8 fl oz	237 ml	

White chaud froid sauce	1 qt	946 ml	Warm the sauce and blend with the yellow liquid until the desired shade is obtained.

NUTRITIONAL INFORMATION PER RECIPE: 1,646 Calories; 110 g Fat (57.2% calories from fat); 40 g Protein; 145 g Carbohydrate; 6 g Dietary Fiber; 327 mg Cholesterol; 5,640 mg Sodium. Exchanges: 2 1/2 Grain (Starch); 8 1/2 Vegetable; 1/2 Nonfat Milk; 22 Fat; 3 1/2 Other Carbohydrates.

Puréed pimentos can be used to change a white chaud froid sauce (use recipe below) into a pink sauce.

pink chaud froid sauce   *Yield: 1 qt (946 ml)*

Ingredients	Amounts		Procedure
	U.S.	**Metric**	
Red pimento, canned and drained	8 fl oz	237 ml	Purée the pimento in a food processor. Strain the purée through cheesecloth.

Ingredients	Amounts		Procedure
White chaud froid sauce	1 qt	946 ml	Warm the sauce and blend with the pimento purée to achieve the desired hue.

NUTRITIONAL INFORMATION PER RECIPE: 1,392 Calories; 110 g Fat (67.8% calories from fat); 29 g Protein; 88 g Carbohydrate; 4 g Dietary Fiber; 327 mg Cholesterol; 4,711 mg Sodium. Exchanges: 2 1/2 Grain (Starch); 6 1/2 Vegetable; 1/2 Nonfat Milk; 22 Fat; 1/2 Other Carbohydrates.

Some may be tempted to dye the sauce with beet juice because of its beautiful color, but the coloring will be so strong that it can stain other foods in the vicinity and wouldn't work for platter design. Use any of the aspic recipes from above, dissolved by heating to 85°F to 90°F (30°C–32°C) to melt.

red chaud froid sauce   *Yield: 1 qt (946 ml)*

Ingredients	Amounts		Procedure
	U.S.	Metric	
Tomato paste	8 fl oz	237 ml	Blend the paste with aspic as smoothly as possible.
Aspic, dissolved	8 fl oz	237 ml	

White chaud froid sauce	16 fl oz	473 ml	Warm the chaud froid sauce and blend with the tomato mixture.

NUTRITIONAL INFORMATION PER RECIPE: 1,712 Calories; 110 g Fat (55.0% calories from fat); 41 g Protein; 162 g Carbohydrate; 10 g Dietary Fiber; 327 mg Cholesterol; 6,267 mg Sodium. Exchanges: 2 1/2 Grain (Starch); 12 Vegetable; 1/2 Nonfat Milk; 22 Fat; 3 1/2 Other Carbohydrates.

One quick way to make chaud froid sauce is to blend it with mayonnaise and aspic jelly. This next recipe is only for quick application and should be used immediately. It will separate when stored in the refrigerator. The oil in the mayonnaise appears as small drops on the surface, which is why we suggest that you only make the amount that you will need and don't try to save any for future applications.

quick chaud froid sauce (french mayonnaise collée)   *Yield: 24 fl oz (710 ml)*

Ingredients	Amounts		Procedure
	U.S.	Metric	
Mayonnaise	16 fl oz	473 m	Combine the ingredients to make a smooth sauce.
Aspic jelly, warm	8 fl oz	237 ml	

NUTRITIONAL INFORMATION PER RECIPE: 3,235 Calories; 374 g Fat (96.8% calories from fat); 12 g Protein; 16 g Carbohydrate; 2 g Dietary Fiber; 154 mg Cholesterol; 3,316 mg Sodium. Exchanges: 3 Vegetable; 31 1/2 Fat.

Mock chaud froid is used for practice and as a covering for foods for dummy displays or displays where the food will not be eaten.

mock chaud froid *Yield: 24 fl oz (710 ml)*

Ingredients	Amounts		Procedure
	U.S.	Metric	
Aspic (clear or display)	8 fl oz	237 ml	Warm the aspic to 100°F (40°C).
Mayonnaise	8 fl oz	237 ml	Combine the aspic and mayonnaise, stirring carefully to avoid large amounts of bubbles. When blended smoothly and ready for use, place over an ice bath until it just starts to set. Pour, dip, or brush chaud froid on the product and chill until the coating is firm and set.

NUTRITIONAL INFORMATION PER RECIPE: 1,689 Calories; 193 g Fat (95.5% calories from fat); 8 g Protein; 12 g Carbohydrate; 1 g Dietary Fiber; 79 mg Cholesterol; 1,928 mg Sodium. Exchanges: 2 1/2 Vegetable; 16 1/2 Fat.

>> Decorating Techniques and Skills

APPLYING CHAUD FROID SAUCE

The concept in using chaud froid sauce is to cover a large piece of meat, fish, or poultry with sauce and, when congealed, apply decorations that are glued on with aspic jelly. Consider the following basic pointers when working with chaud froid sauce:

- The item to be covered must be very cold and dry. It should be placed on a rack to catch the overflowing sauce. Remove any grease or residual fat from chicken or other pieces of cold meat that you plan on coating.
- The sauce should be at 70°F–80°F (20°C–27°C).
- The sauce should be stirred gently to avoid air bubbles.
- The sauce is applied with a ladle in one smooth move, covering, if possible, the whole piece at once.
- Small items can also be dipped in sauce.
- When dip coating, carefully wipe the dipping tool by dragging it over a towel before placing the dipped piece on a rack or sheet pan.
- It is better to apply a thin layer and, if necessary, apply a second layer. The thickness of the layer is governed by the temperature of the sauce; as the sauce cools it will get thicker.
- The chaud froid sauce should be cooled gradually. Cooling the sauce quickly over ice could make it lumpy because the sauce closest to the bottom will solidify before the rest.
- Carefully trim any "legs," or dripping chaud froid, from the piece you are coating with a small scissors or knife.

The piece or pieces covered with chaud froid sauce look attractive plain, but the artistic flare comes out when you are able to use some additional decorations. Decorations may consist of thinly shaved and blanched vegetables, paper-thin slices of truffles or mushrooms, meat slices, egg paste or seafood, and colored chaud froid sauce.

Consider the following pointers when adding decorations:

- Before beginning, have a plan and a general outline.
- Practice first on plain 9-inch dinner plates to get comfortable with the technique.
- All decorations must be edible.
- Decorations should be cooked or par-boiled to adhere better.
- All decorations must be dry with no oil or fat.
- The piece to be decorated must be completely cold and the environment must be cold.
- Decorations can be first built on a plate or flat piece of plastic or a half sheet pan and then trimmed and transferred to the finished piece.

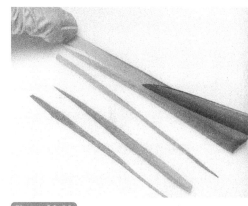

Figure 20-11 Cutting decoration pieces.

EXAMPLE: Decorating a Chicken/Turkey Breast

1. Cut the decoration pieces into the desired shape (Figure 20-11).
2. Dip the pieces, one by one, into liquid lukewarm aspic jelly (Figure 20-12). Place on a rack to drain into a parchment-lined baking pan.
3. Apply the decoration (Figure 20-13). The pieces should stick.
   The trend is for natural foods to be sliced in convenient portion sizes. Large pieces of meat are often sliced and then the slices are attractively arranged on top of the frame or carcass.
4. Refrigerate.
5. After the piece is decorated and completely chilled, it should be covered with a thin layer of aspic jelly (Figure 20-14). This can be poured, brushed on, or sprayed on.

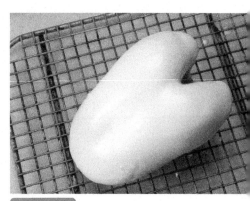

Figure 20-12 Dipping decoration in aspic.

Figure 20-13 Applying decoration.

Figure 20-14 Adding additional coating for shine.

CHEF'S TIP
Cold mousse made with the same basic components is often used to smooth out cavities.

USING COLORED CHAUD FROID SAUCE

When colored chaud froid sauce is used for decorative purposes, it should be warmed and poured about 1/4-inch thick onto a perfectly level pan or platter. It is recommended to place the platter in the walk-in refrigerator, check the pan or platter with a level to assure that it is in perfectly plumb, and then ladle the sauce on the platter. It will congeal in about 1 hour. The cold sauce can then be cut into different shapes such as diamonds, squares, and other shapes. One of the more challenging patterns is the Harlequin pattern, which is comprised of three or four colors in diamond- or lozenge-shaped pieces.

EXAMPLE: **Decorating a Filled Ham with Ham Slices:**
1. Carve the ham as detailed in this unit.
2. Place ham mousse (recipe is in Unit 17) around the ham and shape attractively.
3. Arrange the ham slices attractively over the chilled mousse.

Good-quality aspic jelly can be poured into a thin sheet pan and then diced fine when set. It can be chopped or cut into different shapes and makes a flavorful, edible accoutrement that also looks nice. Finely chopped aspic jelly can be moistened with a few drops of cold water to make it slippery and then piped with a dressing bag. The finished piece will have the look of dark brown jewels or diamonds.

>> Principles of Platter Design

Platter design is very much dependent on the equipment available as well as on the personal taste of the chef. In many cases, concepts and function dictate form and design. There may be times when a large buffet is booked and the table space is limited. In this case, and the chef has no choice but to put as much food as possible on the platters. On the flip side, there may be times when the number of anticipated guests dwindles and the chef is faced with the challenge of filling a large buffet table with little food. Both scenarios are commonplace in catered buffet events, so a chef must be prepared to adjust to the customers' needs.

Consider the following tips when designing platters:

- The platter size must make sense. A huge platter filled with a few morsels looks ridiculous and will be grazed clear in minutes (Figure 20-15).
- The portion sizes must make sense. Buffets are meant to provide choices; therefore, the individual portions must be small, but not miniature (Figure 20-16).

Figure 20-15 The amount of food should match the size of the platter without looking too sparse or too cramped.

Figure 20-16 The size of the portion is a big consideration in the design of a platter.

- Food must be easy to access. Food that requires a struggle to get to is not guest friendly.
- Decorations must never get in the way of food and should be kept at a sensible distance.
- The portions and their garnishes must correspond whether they are placed on the same platter or in different containers. It does not make sense to provide heaps of shrimp and a small bowl of cocktail sauce.
- Put like items together; for example, place bread with spread; put dip with crudités (Figure 20-17). Placing a bread basket on the same platter as the crudités does not make sense.
- Platters with decorated large pieces present a guest dilemma: "Should the piece be eaten and therefore, be accessible, or is it just a decoration?" If it should be eaten, a slice should be cut out to show the inside and serviceware should be placed next to it (Figure 20-18).

Figure 20-17 Like ingredients are served together, as in the tray of crudités and dip.

Figure 20-18 The focal point on this tray is the decorated fruit centerpiece, which is fully edible.

Figure 20-19 Fruit and vegetable carvings can add an interesting touch to any buffet.

Figure 20-20 Food carving is considered to be an art form in most of Asia.

>> Vegetable Carving

Vegetable carving is a way to enhance plates, platters, and buffet presentations (Figure 20-19). From the simplest of scallion brushes to ornate dragons and fish carved from large squash or melons, these bright additions of colorful vegetables make for appetizing displays. While most chefs have some experience with vegetable carving, it is the chefs from Asia who have taken this artistic skill to a new level. The vegetable and fruit carvings from Singapore, China, and especially Thailand are unrivaled (Figure 20-20). The Thai Royal Family sponsored culinary schools that encouraged students and the public to learn vegetable carving, which is considered an art form in Thailand. From a spiritual as well as an aesthetic side, food is not just about taste. All of the senses are required to fully enjoy the meal. Visual beauty in the intricate vegetable carvings enriches the overall dining experience. In Japan, not only is food looked upon in a visual way, but the art of flower arrangement also goes hand in hand with food. In China, culinary schools have for decades taught the art of making ornate, several-feet-long, dragon-shaped tallow carvings and ornate vegetable carvings.

In world cooking competitions, the Thais and Japanese have been formidable in their beautiful presentations. The use of hard squashes and melons coupled with simple small carving knives and penknives are the hallmark of this type of carving. The Japanese won the Coupe Du Monde in 2002, with their intricate floral presentations done completely in decorative dead dough.

There are several publications currently on the market that highlight some of the more difficult and challenging carving techniques. For our purposes, we will present a number of garnishes, vegetable flowers, and a squash carving that are easy to master and can make a simple platter more attractive.

Figure 20-21 Scallion brushes add a festive decoration to the platter of Chinese pork spare ribs.

EXAMPLE: **Scallion Brush**

Scallion brushes are some of the easiest of garnishes to make and are very useful for vegetable crudités, or meat platters. The result is a little fluffy scallion that resembles a flower or brush.

1. Trim the scallion by cutting off the root ends and the green parts, leaving about 3 inches of the scallion.
2. Use a paring knife and make a 1/2-inch cut from the white end. Repeat the scoring until there are five to seven cuts around the circumference of each stalk (Figure 20-21). If a double tassel is desired, make the same length incision from the ends leaving at least 1 inch of solid scallion in the center.
3. Place the scallion in ice water until both ends curl (approximately 15 minutes).

EXAMPLE: **Tomato or Citrus Rose**

The tomato or citrus rose is another example of a simple garnish that is a favorite of caterers for meat or seafood platters.

1. Use a sharp paring knife and begin peeling the tomato from the top down. The width of the peel should be around 1 inch. Try to make one long, continuous piece of peeling that is very thin with little flesh attached.
2. Lay the long continuous piece of peel flesh side up on a work surface. Begin at one end and roll it up so that it resembles a rose (Figure 20-22).
3. For an added touch use mint leaves placed under the blossom, if desired.

Figure 20-22 Three tomato roses.

EXAMPLE: **Carrot Daisy**

Carrot daisies add a touch of vibrant orange to any platter. They can also be used in soups or salads or stir-fried vegetable dishes. The key to making a carrot daisy is to have a large, firm carrot and a sharp paring knife.

1. Wash and peel a large carrot.
2. Slice the carrot into even disks that are approximately 1/4-inch thick (Figure 20-23).

Figure 20-23 Slice carrots into even disks.

3. Make indentations all around the disk so that it looks like the points of each petal. Small, flower-shaped cookie cutters can also be used for this step. If using a cutter, create the shape first and then slice the carrot (Figure 20-24).
4. Use the paring knife and score a circle in the center of the flower to resemble the center of a daisy. If desired, make a crisscross pattern in the center circle, by scoring lines into the carrot.
5. Create 8 to 10 petals by scoring the carrot from the outside rim into the center circle.

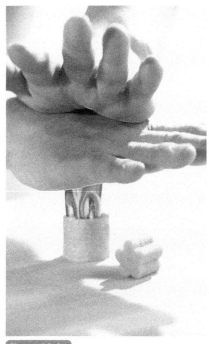

Figure 20-24 Using a cutter is an easy way to create a carrot flower.

Figure 20-25 Making a radish rose garnish.

EXAMPLE: **Radish Flower**

Radish flowers can be made from red or white radishes (Figure 20-25). They are used to decorate platters or sandwich plates, Asian entrées, or as a crudite with dip. The radish rose or flower has been around for a long time; we include it here as it is a good way to help students develop the knife manipulation skills they will need with more difficult carvings.

1. Cut off the radish top and trim off the root end (medium-size, round radishes work best).
2. Use a paring knife and make a circular-shaped slit from the tip of the radish down to the stem end, but don't cut through the base. Do this all the way around the radish.
3. Move in 1/8 inch and make slits around the radish. If there's room, do one more set of slits spaced about 1/8 inch inside the last slits. Avoid making the cuts too thin—the petals might break (Figure 20-26).
4. Place in a bowl filled with ice water. (Soak for an hour until the petals curl like roses.) The petals will open and the radish will look like a rose.
5. An optional method is to use a paring knife to cut a zigzag pattern around the radish (Figure 20-27). Discard the top.

Figure 20-26 Radish roses are quick and easy to make.

Figure 20-27 Zigzag radish rose serves as a garnish for salmon steaks.

>> Fruit Baskets

Fruit carving is also useful for fruit platters and displays (Figure 20-28). A simple carved pineapple can enhance a fruit tray. A more ornate watermelon basket or honeydew bowl adds charm and grace to any fruit display.

Figure 20-28 A display of carved fruits.

WATERMELON BASKET

The watermelon basket is the mainstay and workhorse of many a fruit display. It is always popular and much in demand. Use the watermelon basket as a serving dish for any salad. It works especially well with fruit salads (Figure 20-29).

To carve a watermelon bowl, follow these steps:

1. Lay the melon on its side to prevent it from rolling. Use a chef's knife and slice off a thin slice of the side of the melon to produce a flat side. Tip the watermelon on its side on this flat surface.
2. Use a pencil to draw the handle. It should be located in the top half of the melon and run down the center. The handle should be 2–2 1/2 inches wide.
3. Cut along the lines of the handle and then cut around the ends of the melon to form a basket.
4. Carefully remove the excess watermelon pieces located on each side of the handles.
5. Remove the fruit from inside the basket with a large spoon, leaving the shell and handle.
6. Give the edge of the basket and the handle a zig zag, or scalloped cut, if desired. Or carve a pattern into the handle (Figure 20-30). The white layer located directly under the thick skin can be used to create stunning designs. Repeat the pattern all of the way around the melon.

Most melons and pineapples can be carved into either a basket or a bowl and used as a functional and artistic serving piece (Figure 20-31).

Figure 20-29 A watermelon of any size can be used as a basket or serving bowl, depending on the size of the salad.

Figure 20-30 Any design can be carved into the handle of the watermelon basket.

Figure 20-31 Fruit carving.

>> Dough Carving

Similar to other decorative pieces, cracker, bread, and salt dough represent yet another medium in which to impress the guest with visual enticements. Containers made from these materials are used to hold or support many food items. They are useful as woven baskets, trays, stands, and art pieces that decorate buffet tables and food displays (Figure 20-32). The dough is easy to make and easy to use. Materials are inexpensive and, with planning and

practice, the cold kitchen chef can make many beautiful displays that can last for up to a year when properly baked and sealed.

CRACKER AND COOKIE DOUGH

Crackers and cookies have multiple uses in the cold kitchen. We use edible crackers with dips and salads, as a soup garnish, and as a platform for cheese and other canapés. When rolled out and cut using a **template,** which is a pattern, mold, or free form, cookies and crackers can be used as an exciting and edible garnish with many styles of dishes and desserts. Cracker and cookie dough can be rolled out, shaped, and baked into baskets, spoons, fish, cactus, leaves, and any creative shape that you want. They can also be used for barquettes and eaten.

herbed cracker dough

Yield: Approx. 46 oz

Servings 92, 1/2 oz crackers

Ingredients	Amounts		Procedure
	U.S.	Metric	
All-purpose flour	28 oz	793 grams	Sift the flour, thyme, sugar, baking soda, salt, and cayenne pepper together. Place the sifted ingredients into a bowl.
Thyme leaves or dill weed, chopped fine	2 oz	57 grams	
Sugar	2 oz	57 grams	
Baking soda	1 1/2 tbsp	21 grams	
Salt	2 tbsp	28 grams	
Cayenne pepper	1/4 tsp	2 grams	
Unsalted butter	4 oz	113 grams	Use a pastry cutter to cut in the butter.
Sour cream	6 oz	170 grams	Beat in the sour cream and tomato paste. Let the dough rest for 20 minutes covered and refrigerated.
Tomato paste	1 oz	28 grams	

Roll the dough to 1/8 in or thinner for decorative cracker pieces. If possible, use a pasta roller for thinner pieces. Cut into desired shapes or, for plain crackers, cut into 1 1/2 in squares or circles. Bake on Silpat® liners for 6 to 7 minutes at 400°F (204°C). Store in a dry environment until used.

NUTRITIONAL INFORMATION PER PIECE: 49 Calories; 2 g Fat (28% calories from fat); 1g Protein, 8 g Carbohydrate; Trace Dietary Fiber: 4 mg Cholesterol; 215 mg Sodium. Exchanges: 1/2 Grain (Starch); 1/2 Fat.

The following recipe works very well for stencil work and garnishments. Curry powder, cracked pink peppercorns, paprika, or any other dried herb or spice can be substituted for the cracked pepper.

decorative savory tuiles cookies

Yield: 14 oz (397 g)   *Approximately 28 1/2 oz cookies*

Ingredients	Amounts		Procedure
	U.S.	Metric	
Pastry flour	5 oz	140 g	Mix to a batter. Heat oven to 350°F (177°C). Using a stencil on a Silpat® or greased sheet pan, spread a thin layer and bake until golden brown. Remove from the sheet pan and shape while still warm. Use tuile as garnish for savory dishes.
Egg whites	4 each	4 each	
Clarified butter	3 1/2 oz	100 g	
Sea salt	1 tsp	5 g	
Cracked black pepper	1–2 tsp	5–10 g	

NUTRITIONAL INFORMATION PER PIECE: 52 Calories; 4 g Fat; 9 mg Cholesterol; 84 mg Sodium; 1 g Protein, 4 g Carbohydrates; Trace, Fiber; Exchange: 1/2 Fat.

This Cheese Cracker recipe calls for cheddar cheese but other types of cheeses can be used, including Gorgonzola, stilton, and gouda. Ground almonds, pecans, and pistachios can be substituted for the walnuts. Serve the crackers with fruit and cheese.

cheese crackers

Yield: 3 lbs (1.36 kg)   *Approximately 48 1 oz crackers*

Ingredients	Amounts		Procedure
	U.S.	Metric	
Butter, room temperature	4 oz	112 g	Cream the butter and cream cheese together.
Cream cheese	4 oz	112 g	
Sharp cheddar cheese, finely grated	16 oz	448 g	Blend in the remaining ingredients. Roll into thin logs approximately 1 1/2 in in diameter. Chill for 30 minutes or longer. Use within several days or freeze until needed. Slice into 1/4-in thin disks and place on parchment or Silpat® and bake at 350°F (177°C) until slightly golden in color and crisp.
All-purpose flour	16 oz	448 g	
Salt	2 tsp	10 g	
Cayenne pepper	1/4 tsp	1 g	
Walnuts, chopped fine	8 oz	224 g	

NUTRITIONAL INFORMATION PER PIECE: 9 g Fat (61.6% calories from fat); 4 g Protein; 8 g Carbohydrate; trace Dietary Fiber; 18 mg Cholesterol; 175 mg Sodium. Exchanges: 1/2 Grain (Starch); 1/2 Lean Meat; 1 1/2 Fat.

DEAD (SCULPTURE) DOUGH

Dead dough gets its name from the fact that this dough does not contain yeast or any active ingredients. There is no chance of it rising. It is also called sculpture dough and it is great dough for pressing into forms, molding into shapes, forming around armatures, cutting, or braiding (Figure 20-33).

When baked at a low temperature to dry out, this dough produces finished pieces that can last for a year or more. It is best to sculpt the dough the day it is made; however, it can be kept under refrigeration for up to 2 days. Always cover the unbaked dough before refrigerating. Remove it 2 hours before use to warm the dough to room temperature.

The following Dead Dough recipe is made with sugar syrup. The syrup will keep for up to 2 weeks in the refrigerator before use.

Figure 20-33 Dead dough was used to create a Noah's Ark, complete with animals.

simple sugar syrup (large batch) *Yield: 23 1/2 lbs 10.7 kg*

Ingredients	Amounts		Procedure
	U.S.	Metric	
Sugar	10 lbs	4.7 kg	Place the sugar, corn syrup, and water in a stainless steel pot. Stir to blend, then heat the mixture until the sugar crystals dissolve completely. Remove from the stove and cool to room temperature. May be stored for one month.
Corn syrup	3 lbs 10 oz	1.72 l	
Water	9 lbs, 11 oz	4.56 ml	

NUTRITIONAL INFORMATION PER RECIPE: 22,207 Calories; 0 g Fat (0.0% calories from fat); 0 g Protein; 5,795 g Carbohydrate; 0 g Dietary Fiber; 0 mg Cholesterol; 2,171 mg Sodium. Exchanges: 388 Other Carbohydrates.

Use the Simple Syrup recipe just given to make this Basic Dead Dough recipe.

basic dead (sculpture) dough *Yield: 5 lbs (2.27 kg)*

Ingredients	Amounts		Procedure
	U.S.	Metric	
White or rye flour	4 lbs	1.8 kg	Use the paddle attachment and place the flour in the mixing bowl. Pour the sugar syrup into a mixing bowl and mix at low speed. Mix until the ingredients are combined and not sticky. If the mixture is too dry, add a small amount of syrup. Wrap in plastic wrap until used. It can be sculpted into any type of finished piece.
Simple sugar syrup	2 lbs 9 oz	917 ml	

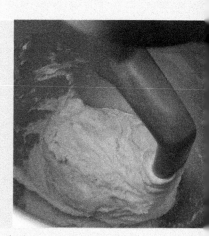

NUTRITIONAL INFORMATION PER RECIPE: 9,888 Calories; 18 g Fat (1.6% calories from fat); 188 g Protein; 2,276 g Carbohydrate; 60 g Dietary Fiber; 0 mg Cholesterol; 1,443 mg Sodium. Exchanges: 91 Grain (Starch); 59 1/2 Other Carbohydrates.

Many natural colors can be obtained by adding spices to the dough. Adjust the Basic Dead Dough recipe as follows.

colored doughs

Desired Dough Color	Spice to Be Added	Amounts U.S.	Metric	Substitution
Red	Paprika	4 oz	113 g	Substitue paprika for 4 oz of flour.
Yellow	Turmeric	2 oz	57 g	Substitute turmeric for 2 oz of flour.
Brown	Coffee extract or powdered espresso	2 oz	57 g	Substitute coffee for 2 oz of the syrup or flour depending on whether you are using extract or dry powder.
Black	Dark or black cocoa	3 oz	85 g	Substitute cocoa for 3 oz of flour.

> **CHEF'S TIP**
> *To avoid cracking the dough, dry the sculpture at low temperatures. If the oven is too hot, the skin will keep all of the moisture from passing out.*

Using Dead Dough

1. Roll out the dough to 1/4- to 1/8-inch thickness.
2. Following a stencil or mold, cut out the dough into the desired shape. (Royal icing can be used to glue pieces together; recipe follows.)
3. Let air-dry for 24 hours.
4. To completely harden for long-term display, bake at a low temperature such as 150°F to 175°F (65°C to 80°C) until the piece is dried out.
5. Apply an egg wash before it is baked, if a shiny exterior is needed.
6. Let the dough sculpture dry overnight or at least a couple of hours to help the water inside migrate out.
7. Continue drying in a very low-temperature oven, no more than 200°F (90°C).
8. Spray the dried sculpture with an art fixative or shellac to keep it for a year or more.

Using Royal Icing

In competitions where only food-grade materials can be used, royal icing is the best "glue" to attach pieces together in a permanent fashion. If permanence is the main requirement, and the seams are unseen, a hot glue gun can also be used to assemble the pieces. Place the icing into a piping bag and use it to attach pieces of dried dough together. Air-dry to set.

royal icing *Yield: 2 lbs (907 g)*

Ingredients	Amounts		Procedure
	U.S.	Metric	
Confectioner's or icing sugar	2 lbs	907 g	Place the egg whites into a stainless steel bowl. Slowly sieve the icing sugar over the whites and blend in a mixer until smooth.
Egg whites (large)	4 each	4 each	

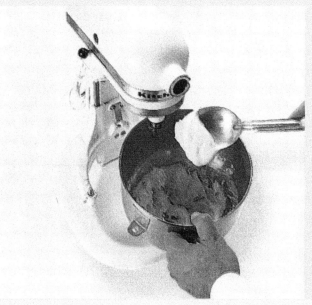

NUTRITIONAL INFORMATION PER RECIPE: 599 Calories; 1 g Fat (0.2% calories from fat); 14 g Protein; 905 g Carbohydrate; 0 g Dietary Fiber; 0 mg Cholesterol; 228 mg Sodium. Exchanges: 2 Lean Meat; 61 Other Carbohydrates.

Salt Dough

Salt dough is useful for display work, especially for those pieces that require a more rustic appearance. It is similar to tallow in that you carve it, once it is thick and set. This medium can be carved or grated to make shapes or figurines. The shapes can be painted with food coloring for colorful displays and shellacked or varnished to keep them shiny and sturdy through numerous displays.

The salt dough can also be tinted with spices for natural-looking, colored dough. Try using chili powder, turmeric, ginger, and dried parsley. Grind the spices in a spice grinder and mix with the salt dough.

basic salt dough *Yield: 7 1/2 lbs (3.4 kg)*

Ingredients	Amounts		Procedure
	U.S.	Metric	
Cornstarch	1 1/2 lbs	680 g	Mix the cornstarch into cold water and blend thoroughly. Heat to boiling while stirring gently to keep the starch from scorching.
Water, cold	2 pt	946 ml	
Fine salt	4 lbs	1.8 kg	When it is a thick paste, blend in the salt and mix thoroughly. Store the dough in a plastic-lined pan until needed. Dough can be carved or sculpted into various shapes.

NUTRITIONAL INFORMATION PER RECIPE: 2,595 Calories; trace Fat (0.1% calories from fat); 2 g Protein; 622 g Carbohydrate; 6 g Dietary Fiber; 0 mg Cholesterol; 703,935 mg Sodium. Exchanges: 41 Grain (Starch).

>> Ice Carving

Glittering ice carvings as exquisite decoration pieces have attracted banquet guests for centuries (Figure 20-34). Ice carvers from just about every country that has long, cold winters and access to frozen river or lake ice developed the ability to carve ice into animals or symbols to enliven winter festivals. St. Petersburg, the imperial capital of Russia, celebrated winter festivities with large ice buildings and statues. The ice carnival in Montreal, Canada, dates back to 1883 and was inaugurated with a huge ice castle, including corner towers complete with electric illumination. Other ice carnivals followed in Canada and in the United States (Figure 20-35).

Figure 20-34 Any subject can be carved into ice. This sculpture depicts a client's favorite friend, his Labrador retriever.

Figure 20-35 This ice palace was made for a winter festival in Quebec, Canada.

Japan is the leading country in creating modern artistic ice displays. Many Japanese hotels employ ice carvers and attendance in ice carving schools is high. The annual winter festival in Sapporo has been held every February since it was started in 1950 and is considered to be the leading exhibit of artistic ice carvings in the world.

Around 1850, mechanical ice machines were invented. These machines depended on ammonia as a freezing medium, and although they were less efficient than today's modern freezers, they made year-round use of ice possible. In 1964, Virgil Clinebell made available sculpture ice equipment that produces a crystal clear, flawless, carving ice. Carving ice is usually purchased in 300-pound blocks measuring 10 inches by 20 inches at the base and about 40 to 42 inches standing up. These blocks can be purchased in most cities and are used by most ice carvers.

ICE-CARVING TOOLS

Ice carving requires several types of tools, including the following:

- Ice tongs are used to move the ice pieces around. The points should be sharp to hold on to the ice securely.
- Ice chippers are hand tools that usually have four to six prongs (Figure 20-36). They are used to chip ice into the desired form. Ice chippers are available with short or long handles. Both types are needed to work efficiently.
- Ice picks are sharp steel needles that measure about 6 to 8 inches long and have a wooden handle (Figure 20-37). They are used to separate or cut blocks into smaller pieces, as well as score designs on the ice.

Figure 20-36 Ice chipper.

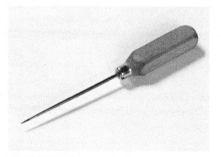

Figure 20-37 Ice pick.

- Measuring tools include a steel T square, with the dimensions of 18 inches by 24 inches. The T square is essential when squaring off the ice block before carving. A level also helps to make sure the block is square and level. Simple yardsticks for checking the progress of work are handy and work better than a cloth tape measure, which can slip or wrinkle. Calipers and dividers are useful for measuring the thickness of the piece. A large circle is very useful when making ice bowls and platters. Using templates can help with shapes as well.
- Hand saws come in two basic shapes. One large tooth saw has a blade of about 12 inches in lenth (Figure 20-38). It is used to cut blocks into basic shapes, thereby speeding the process considerably. The other saw has a curved handle, is smaller, and is used to fine-cut small openings.
- Ice chisels are used to shave ice into the desired shape. These are tempered for use specifically with ice. The steel is less likely to shatter or chip, unlike chisels made for wood carving. They come in a variety of shapes for each type of carving purpose: V-, U-, and flat blades (Figure 20-39). Flat-bladed chisels with long handles remove large sections; narrow, bladed, rounded, U-shaped chisels and V-shaped chisels create special effects, such as grooves and curves. These are especially good for making diamond-grooved shapes or "flash."

Figure 20-38 Ice saw.

Figure 20-39 Ice chisel.

Advanced and Electric Ice-Carving Tools

Modern ice carving has advanced with the advent of electrically powered carving tools. These tools are very efficient, but can be dangerous if misused. Proper training of all safety measures is very important. All electrical ice-carving tools such as chain saws and ice routers must be grounded when used in a wet environment (Figures 20-40 and 20-41). It is imper-

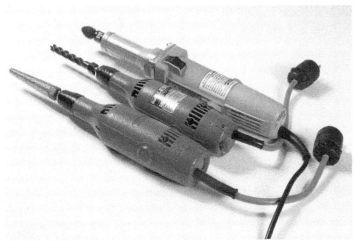

Figure 20-40 Ice routers with various bits.

Figure 20-41 Many advanced carvers rely heavily on the chain saw.

ative that the tools are plugged into a Ground Fault Circuit Interrupter (GFCI). Use only chain saws and routers that have been specifically designed for ice carving and use in wet environments.

POPULAR SUBJECTS USED IN ICE CARVING

Popular and easy-to-execute subjects can be made ahead of time, ready to use, and are appropriate for many events or settings (Figure 20-42).

- Horns of plenty are suitable for New Years, Thanksgiving, Sunday brunch, and many other occasions in which abundance can be represented.
- Hearts and lovebirds are popular for wedding showers and wedding parties, as well as for wedding anniversaries and Valentine's Day.
- Letters and numbers are suitable for many occasions and easy to make and store.
- Swans are always attractive, and the swan is a universal symbol of tranquility and grace.
- Boats made of one block lying flat filled with seafood are always popular.
- Baskets are always popular, especially when filled with flowers or fruits.
- Pineapples are the universal symbol for hospitality and work well with most any occasion.
- Company logos on a flat piece of ice engraved from the back with the help of a stencil are easy to make and are always perfect for a business-sponsored or charity event.
- Trays and bowls can be made by splitting a standard block of ice into two pieces and carving each piece flat.

Figure 20-42 This ice carving depicts a stack of dice and face cards and would be perfect in a casino buffet line.

TEMPLATES FOR ICE CARVING

Templates are patterns used for outlining a subject. Templates are a great help and time saver for less-experienced ice carvers. They are made of thin cardboard, paper, or thin particleboard. Specific templates for ice carving can be purchased from a number of sources. Some designs are copyright protected. In most cases, templates for simple shapes and sculptures can be made inexpensively, even by those who are artistically challenged. Ideas can be found in advertising, artist sketchbooks, wildlife and nature books, and many other sources. Many shapes such as geometrical designs, hearts, swans, boats, and platters are not copyrighted. With modern copy machines, templates can be easily duplicated from a drawing or design.

If the carver has some drawing ability, templates can be made freehand. Use a scale model drawing if possible. All ice sculptures must have a base for stability that is at least 5 inches high, covering the width and length of the basic block. Balance must be taken into consideration when choosing a design. Top-heavy pieces can tip over during setup or during a function. Ice is heavy and can cause physical harm if it falls on a guest, employee, or student.

LEARNING ACTIVITY 20-1

Before attempting to work with ice, follow these steps:

1. A good way for a beginner to get comfortable carving is to first carve a small model with a large russet potato. First shape the potato into a rectangle to approximate the shape of the block of ice. Then carve the design on the potato block. This gets you thinking in three dimensions.
2. At this point, make a model out of a large block of Styrofoam. The material is inexpensive and can be cut with a sharp knife and shaped with a coarse rasp. The basic sheets come in various sizes and shapes and can be held together with wood picks or special Styrofoam glue. The Styrofoam models are a great help and can be used many times. When you are comfortable, move on to a block of ice.

Figure 20-43 When carving outdoors, make sure that the platform is arranged in an area that is shaded and out of direct sunlight.

Figure 20-44 The ice block is secured to the hand truck with a large rubber band.

Figure 20-45 Carvers should periodically step back and take a look at the sculpture during the carving process.

LOGISTICS OF ICE CARVING

Ice carving is usually done in the kitchen or on the loading dock (Figure 20-43). It is imperative that the location is shaded and a floor drain is nearby, as large quantities of shaved ice accumulate and melt. For comfort and safety, the carver should wear sturdy, waterproof boots, a waterproof apron (if possible), waterproof coveralls or pants, and waterproof gloves, not mittens. When power tools are used, the carver should also wear safety goggles and ear plugs for noise protection. Ice taken directly out of the freezer is too brittle and should be tempered in the walk-in cooler for at least 4 to 6 hours. The block will soften a little, obviously depending on the temperature of the walk-in cooler. The ice is ready for carving when there is no visible frost on the block.

Transporting the Ice

Getting the heavy ice block from the walk-in cooler to the desired location is a challenge and requires the use of a hand truck, a furniture dolly, or an insulated ice block bag (Figure 20-44). When ice needs to be lifted into place for display, it is best moved with the help of ice tongs and recycled table linens or tablecloths draped around the ice.

Carving the Ice

Tools should be kept razor sharp. They need to be laid out in a well-organized manner. A small portable table or cart is suggested for laying out the tools. The table should be covered with two layers of towels to absorb moisture. Tools should never be left on the floor, as they can get lost in the wet shavings, or worse.

Ice should never be carved on stainless steel kitchen tables or on kitchen carts, which are not strong enough to safely support the ice. In addition, the table or cart top will vibrate, and the ice can slide off. Also, metal conducts heat and will melt the base at a faster rate than will occur on other surfaces. It is best to carve ice on wooden platforms or pallets. Carving is started from the top, cutting first the general outline. All delicate parts such as handles, legs, necks, and tails should be left slightly thicker than originally planned. Ice will melt, and excessive ice can be removed later, even at the buffet table. Once ice is melted, it cannot be built up again. Scoring the piece to enhance details is important and a challenge to any carver. Stepping back and looking at the sculpture creates a temptation to remove just a little more ice here and there, to add a little more detail, or to chip away a little more (Figure 20-45). Make your ice template, follow it, and enjoy the finished work.

The finished piece must be stored in the walk-in freezer to harden it. If space permits, it should be stored on a kitchen cart so it can be wheeled directly to the display table when needed. The piece should be placed on a bath towel or double-folded tablecloth to prevent it from sliding off during transportation. It will freeze to the material but will come off easily.

Repairs

When the ice breaks during set-up in the dining room, it is difficult to repair on site. Ideally, you can remove the piece and repair it in the kitchen. If this is not possible, planning for a modified piece can be effective. By cleaning up the jagged edges and having a chipper or chisel handy, the ice piece can be repaired on-site. One remedy is to sprinkle a little salt on the surface of the pieces to be joined. The salt will lower the ice temperature, and the two pieces are able to stick together. Salt lowers the temperature of brine. Keep in mind that too much salt will lower the temperature but will also melt the piece. The salt method should be used with caution, and the mended crack should be splashed with ice-cold water to wash the salt away. For more information, see the section on ice sculpture repairs in Unit 18.

OTHER ICE DISPLAY OPTIONS

While a beautifully and professionally carved ice sculpture is hard to beat, creative chefs have come up with other alternatives. Buffet centerpieces can also be made by filling purchased plastic, latex, or rubber molds with clear or colored water (Figure 20-46). Most molds can be used only once because they have to be cut open and peeled away to remove the ice piece.

Inexpensive ice decorations can be made by filling kitchen utensils with water and freezing. Almost any kind of pot or pan can be filled with water and placed in the freezer. A large cake mold filled with water and a few leaves or colorful flowers make a nice base for cold desserts or salads. Ring molds can be purchased in many sizes and make nice pedestals for seafood and fruit salads. The molds must be filled gradually in layers with small amounts of water to prevent white spots and hazing of the ice. The goal is to have clear, clean ice for presentation. The bowl or mold must sit on a perfectly level base, which is usually the freezer floor. It should be checked with a leveling tool to make sure the ice freezes level. To minimize tensions during the freezing process, we suggest that you use tap water and dissolve ice cubes in it to clarify and chill the water for the molds. The water can be colored, but many customers balk at ice in unnatural hues. As a rule, homemade ice is difficult to carve because it is more brittle and lacks the purity of ice-carving blocks. It should be used as is without any further handling. Leaves and flowers can be frozen into the mold in any of the layers. Delicate flowers might not survive freezing, but firmer plants such as ferns, lemon leaves, and galax leaves freeze well and are attractive. As always, when working with food, any flower or leaf product that you use must be nonpoisonous and should not be treated with pesticides.

Attach leaves and flowers to the ice with a small amount of water. This method will give you control to create your own pattern. Ice will melt at room temperature and become slippery. All platters or bowls placed on ice sculptures should be set on wet cloth napkins to prevent them from sliding off.

Figure 20-46 Water is poured into this "horn of plenty" plastic mold.

ICE CARVING COMPETITIONS

There are ice carving competitions sponsored by the American Culinary Federation and the National Ice Carving Association (NICA). The NICA is good source for ice carving information and competitions. Its website is www.nica.org.

>> Modern Trends in Decoration

Molecular gastronomy has been popularized by the media and, depending on who you ask, either embraced or vilified by the culinary establishment. Chefs who understand the molecular breakdown of proteins, fats, carbohydrates, sugars, and water and manipulate these macronutrients into breakout food concepts and trends are practicing **molecular gastronomy.** The term itself was coined by the late Nicholas Kurti, a Hungarian physicist, and Hervé This, a French scientist who runs the "gastronomie moléculaire" at the College de France in Paris.

Early scientific study in the 1800s by Justus von Liebig and Antoin Lavoisier explored the properties of stocks, gelatin, proteins, and fats. As the gap widened between the kitchen and the science lab, cooks lost sight of the whys and hows of food ingredients. It was in the research lab of food chemists that many of the new trends we see today were first developed.

Meat glue is a term used to describe transglutaminase, a product developed in Japan and widely used in manufactured foods such as pork and chicken nuggets. Today, chefs are using transglutaminase to bond proteins together; for example, this technology is being used today to "glue" together, cook, and serve two or three kinds of fish. The combinations are endless, and this type of food science opens up the door to many different and beautiful combinations.

Another type of food science is **spherification,** which is accomplished by mixing fruit or vegetable juices and purées with sodium alginate, then immersing this mixture in a water and calcium chloride bath. The result is the formation of perfect, round spheres. A thin skin is formed on the outside of the sphere, and, when eaten, the membrane crunches and releases an intensively flavored liquid. These fruit "caviars" and "worms" or strings have become popular as a garnish for desserts; in some cases, they have become the main dessert component itself.

ADDITIONAL TRENDS

What was once the domain of the research kitchen has now become a new avenue of creativity for many of today's top chefs. Working with new methods and new ingredients to fuse and flex food into unique shapes, textures, and tastes challenges the cold kitchen chef to learn the language and methods of science.

Tapioca maltodextrin is another product that is being used with interesting results. When it is mixed at high speeds with oil-based products, an edible powder results. Imagine eating a cold salad or dish topped with a garnish of toasted sesame seed oil powder or some other flavored oil that has been turned into a powdered garnish.

Dehydration has also become a popular means to add additional flavor layers to foods. Vegetables, fruits, and even meat products are first dehydrated, then pulverized into a fine powder with a spice or coffee grinder. Diners can bite into a flavorful salad that has been topped with a spark of pancetta or prosciutto dust.

Firming foods with gelatin has been performed for years. Gelling and thickening foods with sodium lactate, calcium chloride, sodium alginate, carrageenan, pectin, locust bean, xanthan gum, agar agar, and other colloidials and biopolymers is enabling chefs to create new taste sensations and create other foods such as fruit angel hair and other interesting shapes. Finding fruit pasta floating in a fresh fruit consommé is an example of ways these new products are being used.

Considerations

As with all new methods, there are certain important points to remember:

- Follow the recipes precisely. These methods, unlike those used in standard cooking, are based on scientific methods and accurate measurement of ingredients is needed for the chemical transformations to occur properly.
- Learn metric measures. Like most scientifically based formulas, the formulas used in these new cooking methods are in metric measures to accommodate the minute quantities of some of the chemicals needed to do the job right.
- Use only food-grade chemicals in these recipes.

The following recipes cover some of the more common of these new techniques.

All of the recipes in this section are based on chemical reactions. It is important that the proper pH levels are maintained. **pH level** is a measure of the acidity or alkalinity of a solution. Solutions with a pH less than 7 are considered acidic, whereas those with a pH greater than 7 are considered basic (alkaline). pH test kits can be obtained from most restaurant supply stores or pharmacies.

Fruit caviar can be used as a delicious garnish for chilled soups, palate refreshers, salads, first courses, or amuse-bouche. They can be refrigerated in simple syrup or equal amounts of water to sugar. Mango, raspberry, or cassis fruit purée work especially well in the following recipe. In a nutshell, the caviar is based on the following formula: 2 percent by weight purée of calcium lactate and your choice of flavor, dipped into 1 percent by weight solution of sodium alginate bath to form caviar.

fruit "caviar" *Yield: 10 oz (284 g)*

This amount can make approximately 300 individual, small "caviar" droplets.

Ingredient	Amounts		Procedure
	U.S.	Metric	
Fruit purée	10 1/2 oz	300 g	In a stainless steel or nonreactive container, mix thoroughly the purée and calcium lactate with an immersion blender. Let the mixture sit for 1 hour. Test the pH.
Calcium lactate	1/5 oz	6 g	

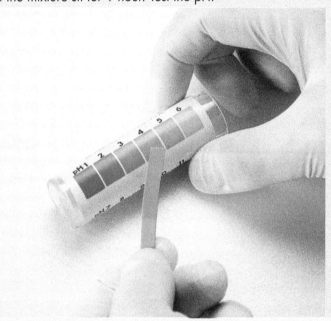

Ingredient	Amounts		Procedure
Sodium citrate or lemon juice, if needed	1/4 tsp	to 2 g	The pH of the mixture needs to be around 4. If it is higher, add a very small amount of sodium citrate or lemon juice to lower it. Test again with a pH test strip.
Water	34 1/2 fl oz	1,000 g	Sprinkle the sodium alginate into the water. Blend thoroughly with an immersion blender. Refrigerate for 1 hour. When the alginate mixture is clear, you can make the fruit caviar or raviolis.
Sodium alginate	1/3 oz	10 g	

NUTRITIONAL INFORMATION PER RECIPE: 182 Calories; 0 g Fat (0.0% calories from fat); 1 g Protein; 49 g Carbohydrate; 4 g Dietary Fiber; 0 mg Cholesterol; 3,720 mg Sodium. Exchanges: 3 Fruit; 0 Other Carbohydrates.

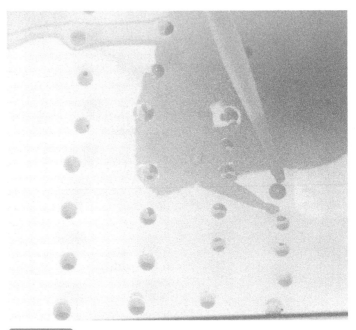

Figure 20-47 Drop the caviar-sized balls from the syringe into the lactate mixture.

Steps for Making "Caviar"

1. Use an eyedropper or food-grade syringe. Draw up some of the fruit purée and lactate mixture.
2. Squirt a steady stream of this mixture into the sodium alginate mixture in small to medium, caviar-size balls (Figure 20-47).
3. Splash a little of the sodium alginate mixture over each ball (Figure 20-48). Within a minute, a firm shell will form around each drop. The inside of the shell will form a liquid center. Let these "fruit caviars" sit in the mixture for about 5 minutes.
4. Carefully remove the "fruit caviar" balls with a fine sieve and rinse carefully in cool water (Figure 20-49).

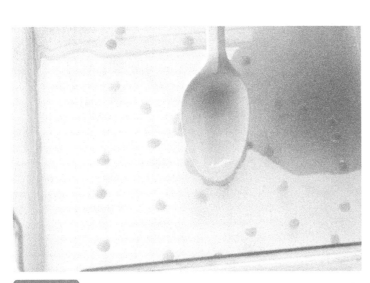

Figure 20-48 Use the spoon to make sure that each ball is covered with the mixture.

Figure 20-49 Rinse the balls in a sieve with cool water.

Figure 20-50 "Fruit caviar" is served as an amuse-bouche.

Figure 20-51 Mango "fruit caviar" tops a bowl of apple consommé.

5. Any unused products can be stored in the refrigerator in simple syrup made with equal parts water and sugar.

6. The uses for this product are endless and limited only by the chef's imagination. For example, try serving the "fruit caviar" in a decorative spoon as an amuse-bouche or as a garnish in a chilled soup (Figures 20-50 and 20-51).

HI-TECH RAVIOLI

This type of ravioli is a spherical-shaped ball of flavor made from any savory vegetable puréed and blended with sodium alginate, which is then dropped into a light solution of calcium chloride and water. These spheres, or "raviolis," can be served as a first course or amuse-bouche. The carrot "raviolis" can be garnished with a fine brunoise of candied ginger or gari. Minced tarragon works well with the pea "ravioli." Other garnishes for this dish could be tarragon oil or carrot chips.

Use the "raviolis" as an amuse-bouche or in conjunction with another appetizer.

carrot "ravioli"

Yield: 20 oz (567 g)   *20 each 1 oz (28 g) pieces*

Ingredient	Amounts		Procedure
	U.S.	Metric	
Soak:			
Water	52 oz	1,500 g	Sprinkle the sodium alginate into the water. Blend thoroughly with an immersion blender. Refrigerate for 1 hour. When the alginate mixture is clear, you can make the fruit caviar or raviolis.
Food-grade sodium alginate	1/2 oz	15 g	
Ravioli:			
Water	11 oz	325 g	While waiting for the mixture to cool, prepare the ravioli mixtures. Combine the water and the sodium alginate. Use a stick blender and blend until the mixture is smooth and the dry ingredient is dissolved. The resting liquid will be quite viscous.
Food-grade calcium lactate	2 tsp	12 g	
Carrot juice, fresh	9 oz	260 g	Meanwhile, prepare the carrot mixture; blend the juices with the calcium mixture and blend until it thoroughly combines. Chill for 1 hour.
Lemon juice	1 tsp	5 g	
Ginger juice	1 tsp	5 g	

NUTRITIONAL INFORMATION PER RAVIOLI: 6 Calories; trace Fat (2.9% calories from fat); trace Protein; 1 g Carbohydrate; trace Dietary Fiber; 0 mg Cholesterol; 281 mg Sodium. Exchanges: 0 Vegetable; 0 Fruit; 0 Other Carbohydrates.

The baby peas give the next recipe a vibrant color and fresh taste.

spring pea "ravioli"

Yield: 21 oz (600 g)   21 each 1 oz (28 g) servings

Ingredient	Amounts		Procedure
	U.S.	Metric	
Soak:			
Water	52 fl oz	1,500 g	Sprinkle the sodium alginate into the water. Blend thoroughly with an immersion blender. Refrigerate for 1 hour. When the alginate mixture is clear, you can make the fruit caviar or raviolis.
Food-grade sodium alginate	1/2 oz	15 g	
Ravioli:			
Water	11 1/2 oz	325 g	While waiting for the mixture to cool, prepare the ravioli mixtures. Combine the water and the calcium lactate. Use a stick blender and blend until the mixture is smooth and the dry ingredient is dissolved. The resting liquid will be quite viscous.
Food-grade calcium lactate	2 tsp	12 g	
Frozen baby peas	9 1/4 oz	260 g	Blanch the peas for a couple of minutes and add the tarragon leaves for the last 3 or 4 seconds. Shock by placing the peas and leaves in an ice bath to cool. Remove and place in a blender or container with a stick blender. Blend until a smooth purée. Add to the calcium lactate mixture and blend. Strain. Check the pH. If needed, add a small amount of lemon juice. (The pH should register around 4.)
Tarragon leaves, fresh	10 each	10 each	

NUTRITIONAL INFORMATION PER RAVIOLI: 14 Calories; trace Fat (8.4% calories from fat); 1 g Protein; 2 g Carbohydrate; 1 g Dietary Fiber; 0 mg Cholesterol; 469 mg Sodium. Exchanges: 0 Grain (Starch); 0 Lean Meat; 469 mg Sodium. Exchanges: 0 Grain (Starch); 0 Lean Meat.

Making the "Raviolis"

1. Take the cold calcium chloride mixture out of the refrigerator.
2. Pour the mixture into a silicon mold (small and round). Place in the freezer until solid.
3. Remove from the freezer and unmold each "ravioli." Drop into the sodium alginate bath (Figure 20-52). Don't allow individual "raviolis" to touch.
4. Move the bath around the pieces to completely submerge each one. Once they are set up, they will sink. Keep submerged for 1 minute.
5. Carefully remove and place in a container of cold water to rinse.

Most any purée will work with the above recipes (Figure 20-53).

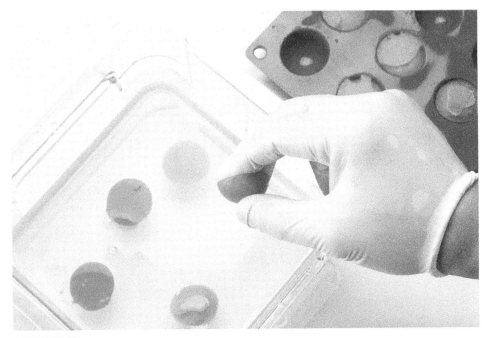

Figure 20-52 Pop out of the mold and drop into a sodium alginate bath. Make sure to leave space around each "ravioli" so that they don't touch.

Figure 20-53 Mango "ravioli" with a strawberry mango sauce is served as an amuse-bouche.

>> Summary

Food decorating techniques have been around for many centuries. Some of the methods are rather old-fashioned, such as covering food with jellied sauces, but they are important to know and understand. Other decorative techniques from Asia are growing in popularity, such as intricate melon, fruit, and vegetable carvings. Ice sculptures have become very popular. This unit gives you the basic understanding of how to carve ice.

>> Review Questions

TRUE/FALSE

1. Cold food, especially decorated cold food, can be made only in lower-temperature-controlled environments.
2. In a commercial kitchen, a *Queen Mary* refers to a large transport rack.
3. Display aspic is not intended for consumption.
4. Aspic isn't always transparent.
5. Bouquet garni are flowers used as garnishes on banquet platters.
6. Basic chaud froid is made with chicken velouté, flour, and butter.
7. Finished sculptures made of dead dough must be refrigerated.
8. It is best to carve ice on wooden platforms or pallets.

MULTIPLE CHOICE

9. Raft is
   a. fat and impurities.
   b. poultry.
   c. consommé.
   d. a ball of herbs.
10. French mayonnaise collée is
    a. aspic.
    b. mock chaud froid.
    c. quick chaud froid.
    d. hot cream sauce.
11. Which of these statements is *not* true in regard to plate design?
    a. The decorations should never get in the way of the food.
    b. The food must be accessible.
    c. The amount of food should correspond to the size of the platter.
    d. The larger the portion, the better.
12. Which type of dough is also called sculpture dough?
    a. dead dough
    b. modeling dough
    c. salt dough
    d. cracker dough
13. Blocks of ice used for ice carving usually weigh
    a. 300 lbs.
    b. 250 lbs.
    c. 350 lbs.
    d. 100 lbs.
14. Which of the following is *not* a type of chisel used in ice carving?
    a. V
    b. U
    c. barrel
    d. flat
15. Meat glue is
    a. aspic.
    b. transglutaminase.
    c. sodium alginate.
    d. calcium lactate.

SHORT ANSWER

16. What influence did World War I have on food presentation?
17. Describe the ideal work environment for decorating cold foods.
18. Discuss the uses of aspic.
19. Describe molecular gastronomy and explain how it is used in the cold kitchen.
20. What is spherification and how is it used in culinary arts?

Preparing for Culinary Competitions

>> Learning Objectives

After you have finished reading this unit, you should be able to:

- Describe a Culinary Salon.
- Understand the long history of culinary competitions.
- List the names of the two culinary competition pioneering chefs.
- Describe how culinary teams are selected.
- Know the basic rules regarding how entries are judged.
- Name the competition categories.
- Be familiar with competition guidelines and know where to get the information about competitions.
- Learn about teamwork and team spirit.
- Describe the international rules governing judging.
- Discuss the future directions that culinary shows could take.

>> Key Terms

ACF Competition Rules   Culinary Salon   IKAHOGA   Société Culinaire
culinary judge   Philanthropique

"**N**inety seconds to go. Come on, hurry! Put the ice on the fish. Four seconds, three seconds, two seconds, one second, whew done! On time, yeah! Okay, let's clean up and get ready for the next section—the cook off."

Hands that were once shaking are now steady. The team's focus is needle sharp. The adrenaline is pumping. The team is working as one smooth unit, set on the goal of getting the plate-up perfect, just like in practice, only this time there are floor judges scrutinizing every cut and every move. The food is about ready to plate, the clock is ticking, and now the pressure is on. Every plate must look the same, all the textures must complement each other, and the flavors must be dead on and sexy.

"WOW!" the lead judge utters as he looks at the plates. That is a good sign! He evaluates every plate, notes every flaw, and uses every teachable moment to share his experience. His great suggestions and advice flow like water, filling the team member's heads with new techniques and ideas for improving the procedure. As he tastes the last dessert, he asks the team what that incredible flavor is in the pastry. At that moment, the team knows that the day is theirs and they will move on to the next level. They have won their state competition and now begin the arduous task of taking it all the way.

This unit provides an overview of competing in culinary exhibitions, often called the Culinary Salon. Much of the work called for in culinary competitions begins with skills honed in the cold kitchen. Successful competitors must have masterful knife skills, and be able to work with aspic, decorate food, and design platters.

As has been discussed previously in this book, food presentation is important for customer satisfaction. Great food and cooking is often referred to as *culinary art,* and culinary competitions utilize the visual aspect of cooking, the refined development of flavors, and the technical hand skills.

Cooking is a reflection of lifestyles, so cooking techniques and trends are continually changing and evolving. Trendsetters influence customer expectations and the media encourage experimentation.

International exhibitions attract national teams from all over the world, with teams organized by chef's associations, gourmet societies, branches of the military, hotel companies, and exhibitors representing individual hotels and restaurants. It is an awesome and inspiring sight when national teams march into the exhibition hall to line up on the stage at the beginning of the salon and at the end of the show when the grand prize winners are announced. There is fierce competition, but also a spirit of sportsmanship and camaraderie. Lifelong friendships are forged. For many years, the ACF has actively supported culinary exhibitions as an educational tool and has established local, regional, and national competitions. The ACF also sends teams to the most prestigious international competitions such as the Culinary World Cup and the IKAHOGA, or Culinary Olympics.

There are many components in putting together a culinary team, including the following:

- Team and judge selection process
- Judges' training
- Team practice sessions, aiming for perfection
- Teamwork
- Financing
- Rules and guidelines for culinary exhibition
- Equipment used in competitions

At the international, national, and even some regional shows, a hot food cooking competition component has been added to address the real nature of cooking under time pressure. Just like on live TV or a real restaurant line, teams and individuals work in show kitchens in front of an audience, the dishes are judged for flavor and visual harmony, and, in some cases, the food is sold to the public at the show's restaurant. International teams have to produce 100 servings of a set menu, consisting of appetizer, main course, and dessert. Two or more international teams compete at the same time and a bell goes off announcing the first team that sells all 100 covers.

>> Why Compete?

In the grandeur of this moment, at the pinnacle of competition, lies the small seed of that first culinary competition, that first baby step of putting yourself out there, taking the risks, spending the hours to hone your skills, developing your eye, learning new methods, and becoming the culinarian you want to be. A wise chef once said, "The day you stop learning is the day that you die." By competing, you will exponentially learn more about cooking, and yourself, than at almost any other time throughout the rest of your career. As a team practices repetitive speed training, which is called "culinary wind sprints," you will watch your-self improve with each session (Figure 21-1). By developing a game plan and a time line, you will develop skills that are directly transferable to the day-to-day line-cooking pressures that chefs face every day. By working with others as a unit, you will learn teamwork and team spirit.

Figure 21-1 A culinary team participates in culinary wind sprints in preparation for an upcoming competition.

>> History of Culinary Competition

SOCIÉTÉ CULINAIRE PHILANTHROPIQUE

The oldest **Culinary Salon** was organized by the **Société Culinaire Philanthropique** in New York City and has been held annually since 1869. According to the event's website, "The annual event is not only a friendly competitive display of knowledge and skilled workmanship but a progressive inspiration to the profession."

ACF CULINARY COMPETITIONS

Some competitions are single events taking place at ACF chapters. Other student and professional competitions include individual and team events. Competitors engage in a rigorous qualifying process that begins at the local ACF chapter level, advances to the AFC Regional Conferences, and culminates with the finals at the ACF National Convention. Regardless of the level, the purpose is the same—to continually raise the standards of culinary excellence in the United States while promoting camaraderie and educational opportunities among culinary professionals. See the ACF website at www.acfchefs.org for more information.

IKAHOGA/CULINARY OLYMPICS

Before the turn of the twentieth century, culinary shows were held in many large European cities, with the foremost in London, Basel, Vienna, Berlin, and Paris. Frankfurt, Germany, was the host of the 1878 culinary show; since 1892, Germany has been the host to the Internationale Kochkunstaustellung, also known as **IKAHOGA,** or the Culinary Olympics. This is the most prestigious Culinary Salon in the world. It has been named the Culinary Olympics because it always takes place at the same time as the Olympics, but has no official connection with the athletic competitions.

U.S. Involvement in the Culinary Olympics

According to www.unichef.com, "The United States culinary teams have competed in IKAHOGA since 1956 when they were clearly the underdogs. But the Americans soon established themselves as world class cooks. The 1960 team, headed up by Paul Laesecke, captured the world championship on a menu of Maryland Fried Chicken, Prime Rib, and Stuffed Baked Potato cooked in aluminum foil. By 1988, the American team had won the prestigious hot food competition three times in a row, and still holds the record for the most consecutive wins.

The ACF actively supports education and has made participation at culinary shows part of its program of education. The selection of team members is done by a rigorous nation-wide selection process based on winning local, state, and regional competitions and making the champions compete with each other until the very best emerge.

U.S. Team History

The following chefs have served as team managers for the U.S. team:

1956, Fred Wohlkopf, team manager
1960, Paul Laesecke, team manager
1964, John Monbaron, team manager

1968 and 1972, Jack Sullivan, team manager
1976, Richard Bosnjak, team manager with Ferdinand Metz as team captain
1980, Ferdinand Metz, team manager
1984, Ferdinand Metz, team manager
1988, Ferdinand Metz, team manager
1992, Keith Keoh, CEC, team manager
1996, Keith Keoh, CEC, team manager
2000, Edward G. Leonard, CMC, team manager
2004, Edward G. Leonard, CMC, team manager
2008, Edward G. Leonard, CMC, team manager

Metz instituted practice sessions and attention to detail; each exhibit was produced over and over, judged by ACF judges, then adjusted and tweaked until the hot and cold entrées were considered perfect. this huge effort paid off in 1980, when the U.S. team won 21 gold medals and placed first in Hot Foods and second in Cold Foods.

In the 1980s, women were finding places on the teams for the first time, thus opening up the competitions to everyone. Lyde Buchtenkirch, CMC of Rhinebeck, New York, was the first woman on the U.S. team and the only female certified master chef.

In 1984, the U.S. Team garnered the seemingly impossible—the first prize in *both* the Hot and Cold Food competitions against dozens of international competitors. In 1988, the ACF National Team to the Salon of Culinary Arts, now called the Culinary Olympics, achieved third place against stiff competition in overall international ranking. Under the direction of Edward Leonard, the U.S. team won the first prize in Hot Foods and the second prize in Cold Foods in 2004.

>> Chef Heroes

There are too many outstanding chefs who have contributed to the advancement of the culinary arts to mention them all. Some have become famous household names in culinary circles. Others have remained anonymous, never having reached name recognition, but nonetheless have worked tirelessly to promote gastronomy and culinary arts. Some chefs are gifted visual artists capable of creating culinary masterpieces in food, chocolate, or ice. Some are great culinarians who can cook like angels, but are not endowed with the ability to create stunning food displays. Many work behind the scenes to coach and encourage talented culinarians, both young and old, and give them the tools to exhibit and compete. A few rare chefs are exceptions to the rule, and can do multiple tasks on a championship level. The following are some early pioneers who could do both.

AUGUSTE ESCOFFIER

Escoffier, a famous chef and reformer, was also a gifted artist who specialized in making wax flowers. He updated and simplified traditional French cooking methods, and worked tirelessly to elevate the status of chef to a respected profession.

ADELRICH FURRER

In Zürich, Switzerland, from the 1930s to the 1950s, Adelrich Furrer was the leading garde-manger chef in Europe. He pioneered the modern, clean look.

Before Chef Furrer's time, cold food was usually presented as one big item. A whole fish, fowl, or roast might be elaborately decorated with feathers and fur intact, and was often put on an inedible base to elevate the food. Chef Furrer did away with that method by presenting cold food in portion sizes with minimal decoration, highlighting one small, unsliced piece for dramatic effect.

HERMANN G. RUSCH

Hermann Rusch, a Swiss chef, became the executive chef at the New York World's Fair in 1939. He exhibited a magnificent buffet at the Salon of Culinary Arts and won the "Grand Prix de Cuisine" of the show. Rusch stayed in the United States and spent many years as executive chef and food and beverage director for the famed Greenbrier Resort, White Sulphur Springs, West Virginia, where he established an apprenticeship program. He was an advisor to the 1984 U.S. ACF National Culinary Team. Rusch's motto holds true even today: "Dedication, Endurance and Achievement." The ACF has created an achievement award that is named in honor of Hermann G. Rusch and recognizes other top chefs.

>> The Future of Culinary Exhibitions

Culinary art is constantly evolving. All of us eat, and all of us have likes and dislikes. Some segments of the food industry and the public question the need to display artistically decorated food when there is still hunger in the world. Some people disdain the idea of food as an art form, and would rather have a good, solid, well-seasoned, and prepared meal. The trend toward emphasizing cooking skills by preparing hot food in front of an audience and letting the audience purchase the food in a restaurant setting diffuses these arguments. There is validity to this approach because we are, after all, cooks and our mission is to prepare wholesome food for our customers to eat.

Preparing artistically presented cold foods has many benefits, often hidden but still real. They are:

- **Opportunity to practice skills.** In preparing for a competition, the repetitive nature of practice increases hand-to-eye coordination and timing, which is essential to real-world cooking (Figure 21-2). Knife skills are honed, timing is improved, and plating skills are enhanced. These are all transferable skills that are required to perform kitchen work, day after day. By perfecting these skills, cooks can exhibit their hidden skills and talents.
- **Building confidence and fostering self-esteem.** Cooks working behind the scenes seldom get praise or get out of their confined environment. By participating at culinary competitions and salons, they can demonstrate that every job in the kitchen is important.
- **Learning about trends and sharing new ideas.** Culinarians work the odd hours when others have time away from work to dine out. Many cooks seldom have the opportunity to visit other restaurants and, as a result, become isolated from new foods. Participation in and visits to culinary shows help these individuals to keep current with trends, flavors, and new techniques.

Figure 21-2 Culinary competitions teach skills that can be used on the job.

- **Interaction with other chefs.** Often, even at the local or state level competitions, you will find chefs from all over the world. You will meet certified master chefs, executive chefs, and foodservice movers and shakers. By getting your face out there, by competing, you become a known quantity. The benefits of networking cannot be stressed enough. You get to meet the greats of the industry as colleagues and fellow professionals. International chefs bring to the table the dishes and flavors that until recently were considered esoteric. These new flavor trends of today are becoming tomorrow's mainstream dishes. You get to experience them firsthand.

Participation at culinary shows can require tremendous personal sacrifice from the participants. Entering culinary shows can be expensive and puts a heavy burden on individuals and on their employers. Practice sessions take time. If you are a student, you may also have the additional burden of school and work responsibilities. If you have family responsibilities, you have to learn to balance your school, work, and home life during competition time, and if you are the chef in charge, or an employee, you have to balance your workload so that your operation or job can continue uninterrupted.

Participation at a culinary show or salon, despite widespread popularity, does not always ensure that management understands the benefits. A hotel manager once asked a famous executive chef, "Tell me how many additional rooms I will sell because you are exhibiting!" Sometimes, the management looks at the short-term bottom line and not the long-term gain of skills and prestige for the property. School administration can also be short-sighted. It isn't just about the winning of medals and trophies for the school's display case. Everyone benefits from the experience of participating in culinary competitions—students gain knowledge and experience and receive carryover support from other students, and the reputation of the participating school is enhanced.

These are some of the pitfalls that you need to work through in order to compete. By showing the management or administration new ideas or skills you have learned, you are helping to build the necessary support. Bottom line? Competitions and salons can only benefit the operation.

>> Team Selection

Putting together a team starts like a small trickle at the local ACF chapter that sponsors competitions. These small competitions are where you get the necessary experience to compete at a higher level. The scoring is based on the set ACF standards. Points are accrued and medals awarded based on the total number of points. This means that everyone might win a medal, whether it is bronze, silver, or gold, or no one wins medals. Best of show is, again, based on the highest number of points. Whether a local team or the national team, selection is based on this point system. For Junior ACF or school teams, the chapter or schools have open try-outs. Other schools base their teams on points earned through participation, grade point average, and timed try-outs. For professional teams, the competitions at state and regional levels determine who is on or off the team. For national-level competitions, regional winners compete, usually at large venues such as the national ACF convention held each summer, or at the National Restaurant Association convention held in May. Other competitions such as the Bocuse d' Or held in Lyon, France, and the Culinary Classic held at the NRA show in Chicago every 3 years are just some of the exciting venues available to all chefs willing to put in the hours of training and sacrifice to become the best in their fields.

Some teams are formed in culinary schools, whereas others are formed by individuals who come together to form teams. Others compete on an individual level. In the end, an ACF

chapter sponsors the state championship, and the winner for the Junior ACF team for that state, as an example, heads to the regional competitions (Figure 21-3). At the regional level, the stakes get higher. At this competition, held at the ACF regional conventions in the spring of each year, the level of competence is elevated and each team must produce and demonstrate its artistic side. Each Junior ACF state team must produce a cold platter as well as demonstrate their culinary skill sets and cooking abilities. Each region then sends the winning team to the national competition. At the national level, each Junior ACF team has the new challenge of cooking a four-course meal for 25 people in 4 hours. The team has 30 minutes to set up, followed by 3 hours and 20 minutes for cooking, and 40 minutes to dish up. Team members then have 30 minutes to clean up. At the end of this quest, the team with the most points wins. Some of these team members go on to compete at the international level with the U.S. team or as the Junior U.S. team.

Figure 21-3 Junior team prepares to participate at a regional competition.

In 2004, as an example, there were 32 national teams, 12 pastry teams, 16 student teams, 12 military teams, and over 30 regional teams from 16 different countries participating in the Culinary Olympics. Along with the teams, there were several individuals from all around the world who competed.

As you can see, the sky is the limit when it comes to competing. You are only limited by your imagination. If you have the passion for it, you should try it. You may never win a medal, but you will benefit by honing your skills and improving your craft. You will learn from others, meet other chefs, exchange ideas, and enrich your life. There are chefs who have competed for years and never quite captured a medal and there are also gold medal master chefs. It seems that both types of competitors say the same thing: "I learned so much from the process. It was a great experience and I would do it again."

TEAM MEMBERS

Teams consist of the following:

- Team manager
- Team captain
- Team members (four members plus an alternate)
- Support personnel such as a team secretary or treasurer (The secretary handles correspondence and takes notes during practice judging. The treasurer oversees the money and the budget. Often one or more apprentices are assigned to the team to handle these auxiliary tasks.)

FINANCING A TEAM

In many cases, the decision to send a team starts with developing a budget. National teams are often sponsored by food companies and financed by their national chef's association. Regional, state, local, and school/junior teams must raise money through dinners, donations, and other ways.

The budget should include:

- Travel costs to practice sessions and to the event. These costs must include lodging, meals, van rental, shipping expenses, air fares, taxis, and so on.
- Cost of all food and materials for practice sessions and for the main event.
- Uniforms, usually consisting of a dress uniform for official events and whites for the cooking sessions. It is expected that the uniforms have the team and event logo.
- Equipment including those items used for cooking, storing, and transporting.
- China, silver, glassware, and other display items.
- Pins and small gifts given to officials and friends.
- Funds for receptions and social affairs.
- Logo design, stationary, business cards, and contingency funds for any office work or printing required.
- Petty cash for last-minute purchases.

>> Preparing for Competition

EQUIPMENT USED IN COMPETITIONS

The size and quality of plates and platters enhance the displays. For some teams, much time is spent selecting the tableware and fitting it to the theme and budget. Equipment companies constantly offer new designs, often in conjunction with celebrity chefs. These new designs often inspire a team to create new dishes. Usually, equipment companies lend new equipment to national teams to showcase their products, but are not allowed to place advertising at the competition table. In some cases, well-financed teams order custom platters.

Again, regional, state, and local teams need to purchase their own equipment. A good source can be local equipment companies. As with the national teams, local teams can use the competition to enhance the reputation of the purveyor's wares. Everyone wins in this situation.

TRANSPORTATION AND LOGISTICS

There are a number of logistical issues to consider when a team travels to another city to compete. They include the following:

- **Equipment and materials.** Packing the equipment and, if permitted, food components is a logistical challenge. The responsibility rests with the team manager to pack and ship all equipment and supplies. In rare cases, airlines offer free or reduced rates when a team's travel arrangements are made. In some cases, teams have been known to purchase extra seats to accommodate very delicate pastry showpieces, which are diligently watched over by the team members who are seated nearby.
- **Lodging.** Team members share rooms when possible. The team manager or captain requires a larger room or suite to hold meetings and, in some cases, to work on showpieces. During large shows or conventions, hotel accommodations can be scarce, requiring team members to be housed at off-site and inconvenient locations.
- **Meal policy.** All team members, including apprentices, must be fed. The issues to be resolved prior to travel include the type of meals, whether team members have room charge privileges, whether they must eat together, whether they can spend free time in the host city, and who will pay for the expenses.
- **Workspace.** The team must be able to set up its products and equipment and have a place to do pre-prep work. In most host cities, workspace is at a premium during culinary shows. Local hotels and restaurants usually allow teams to work in their kitchens, but workspace is tight. There have been cases when competitors at international shows worked in school kitchens, hospitals, food factories, and even in hotel rooms. It is essential that one team member, usually the team manager or the team captain, takes a trip to the host city to survey in detail the available workspace and to make final arrangements. When this option is not possible, it is helpful to utilize the Internet for information, and to call the host chapter or location of the competition. Professionals at the host chapter are usually more than willing to share information with the team manager on the types of equipment available: how many burners, what type of refrigeration, and any problems or issues that might arise based on the location itself. There have been cases when expected equipment was not available or out of order, when refrigeration space became too crowded to work efficiently, and when too many people were scheduled to use the cooking equipment at the same time.

  Since teams usually work overnight, sometimes the night cleaning service at the location may be working and can get in the way. In some cases, the exhibition hall provides setup space to finish the platters with fully prepared components. It is important to always ask about available electrical service, and to communicate to the organizers what types of electrical or other power sources the team will need. Portable heating devices to warm aspic jelly must be brought in. In some areas, portable gas equipment is not allowed due to fire codes. All of these issues must be identified and dealt with prior to the competition.

  Additional considerations include the following:

- **Transportation to and from the workspace.** Usually one or more vans must be rented. Designated drivers must make at least one dry run to become familiar with the route. Knowledge of the local language is very helpful. During most international shows, the platters must be set up precisely at the designated time and removed on time. At large shows, that could entail waiting a considerable amount of time at check-in.
- **Table setup.** In many shows, the exhibition company supplies the number and size of tables ordered beforehand. The exhibitors are responsible for covering and skirting the

table and for adding inedible decorations, such as centerpieces, flowers, tableware, or anything else that will enhance the theme of the exhibit. This task usually falls on the team manager.

- **Signs and labels.** Most shows require teams to display signs indicating the names of the dishes and their components. During the judging process, no signage is allowed on the table to maintain the impartiality of the judges. When judging is over, signs are allowed to identify the team and team members. The signs are an integral part of the overall table look and theme.

Despite the best-laid plans and detailed arrangements, unexpected problems will inevitably pop up. When that happens, the team must be flexible and remain calm. Team members might be tired and edgy after having worked all night. When conflicts do arise, it is up to the team manager, together with the team captain, to resolve the issues. Their word is final. Team spirit and submission to the decisions made are essential. The group must operate as a team and personal ambitions must be set aside. There is no "I" in the word *team*. Coming together as a team is essential if you want your team to be winners.

In most cases, there is a spirit of cooperation among competing teams. Chefs from all over the state, region, or even the world usually help each other when there is a need. Fairness and sportsmanship prevail in most cases and collegial, lifelong friendships are often forged during culinary shows.

PRACTICE SESSIONS

The process starts with developing concepts or themes. All team members are encouraged and required to contribute ideas. Often the ideas reflect personal expertise.

Keep in mind the nature of the food that you are using. Make each dish or platter concept reflect the real nature of the food—make it all as real and natural looking as possible. For example, when using trout (freshwater fish) on a mirror, use crayfish (another freshwater food) as the shellfish. Watercress grows around streams, thus adding another good choice for the platter, as it follows the natural surroundings of the foods that are the highlight of this particular platter design.

The theme chosen should highlight the food's genuine colors and flavors. Everything on the platter has to have a reason to be there—it all has to make sense. The team manager and team captain must sort through the ideas and develop with the team a cohesive plan. These sessions usually involve sketching out plate or platter diagrams, possible table layouts, and centerpieces.

When the basic ideas are firmed up, the plates and platters must be selected. They could be borrowed, purchased, or, in some rare cases, custom-made. Each team member is required to make a template for each platter indicating, in scale, each component.

The next step is making actual food. Often it is discovered that ideas that work well as concepts do not work in reality. Concepts are frequently tossed out, and new ideas are developed. It can take dozens of attempts at a concept to finally achieve one that you know is just right. At this stage, experienced judges and colleagues are invited to judge the dishes or platters and offer advice (Figure 21-4). Equipment is often changed at this point—a certain concept might work better on a different plate, platter, or bowl. The judge's comments are recorded by the team secretary or team members, discussed, and kept on file.

The team takes photos of each stage to show the progression. A digital camera is an essential piece of equipment to develop the look of the plate (Figure 21-5). Seeing the dish or platter displayed on a large overhead screen or on a TV screen can really reveal the flaws of a dish.

Figure 21-4 An advisor offers advice on platter design.

Figure 21-5 Up-close shots of plates should be studied by team members and changes made to the dish, if needed.

Critique at this stage may be painful, but it is essential to achieve perfection. The hot dishes go through the same appraisal process.

THE RULES

It is important to learn the rules of each skills-type competition. There are several sources of good information about the rules, but the number one source for **ACF Competition Rules** is the ACF website. Just go to www.acfchefs.org for all the information needed to compete in any local, state, regional, and national competition. For international competition, here are a couple of sites that will get you started:

- For the IKA or Culinary Olympics, go to www.culinary-olympics .com. This competition is held every 4 years.
- The Scothot rotates every 2 years and features a senior and a junior class. For information, go to http://site.org.uk/scothot/.

There are other international culinary competitions such as the World Cup, the Singapore Cup, and the Culinary Master's in Switzerland.

Rules for various competitions vary, so it is vitally important to learn the rules for each competition. Read, read, and read again the rules. Have all members of the team learn the rules as well. It takes just one small error to disqualify a team or severely compromise the points in a competition.

TIMING

Timing is essential to any competition success. In the Junior ACF competition, the first part of the competition usually is a skills-type test. In the past, each team member was required to break down and fabricate chicken and fish and complete a series of vegetable cuts. Currently, each team member is picked to randomly do one of four skill sets in a relay fashion: chicken fabrication, fish fabrication, vegetable cuts, or dessert segment, including making a pastry cream and segmenting out an orange. In the future, some other skill may be highlighted. The important thing to remember is that this first section highlights the hand skills required of the culinarian—knife skills are the first skills a chef should learn. Therefore, this first skill set is essential in setting the bar higher for a young cook or chef to master.

"CULINARY WIND SPRINTS"

Setting a time line or spreadsheet to track these skills is essential for practice. Each team member must master every skill required—the random selection by the judges makes this very clear. Coaches should set up timed trials or, to borrow from the world of sports, "culinary wind sprints." By cutting the practice time down by 2 minutes each section, each member of the team works faster as well as cleaner, which is key to scoring high in this category. By practicing the same techniques over and over and over again, the motions become second nature, and the automatic movements become natural (Figure 21-6). Based on the very real nature of working on a restaurant line, every line cook has to do repetitive motions. Therefore, this segment of the competition has real-world applications for the contestant.

Team members must stay focused on the sanitation of the product. Make sure that the food is iced down or kept under refrigeration. Keep food covered and properly labeled. Many teams use zip-lock bags to keep the product iced, both from the top and the bottom. Having containers labeled assists each team member in keeping foods separated and sanitary. Each member of the team should have a timer to keep him- or herself on track during practice. The times should be recorded and each day's efforts tracked to show the progress or the weak spots needed to work on.

Figure 21-6 Repetitive practice can give a competitive edge to a chef.

Every member of the team should keep a log or journal. This aids in the learning aspect. Brainstorming, conceptualizing, and making notes on every detail aids in remembering necessary changes or new tricks. These training logs serve as a great way to save ideas that can be used again in the real-world applications of a professional chef. Sauces, plate designs, and ideas can be recycled in the work kitchen and environment. Ideas borrowed and shared by other chefs can also be used. This is the core of the learning process in competition, which includes the sharing and practicing of skills.

The second part of the Junior ACF competition is the cook-off. Currently, the entrée section of this competition is drawn from the classics. This demonstrates knowledge of the foundations of our craft. Escoffier, the father of modern cooking techniques, taught that going back to the basics enhances the overall skill of the cook. Each culinarian, whether a new student just starting out or an experienced chef heading up an international team, must view the basics as the very foundation upon which professionals build their skills. Whether you succeed or fail always goes back to the foundation. By understanding the basic nature of food's components—proteins, carbohydrates, sugars, fats, and water—and by applying those foundational skills brought forth by the masters of an earlier time, such as Escoffier, or in more modern times by chefs like Ferdinand Metz and Fritz Sonnenschmidt, you become a champion.

The remaining courses are used to showcase the talents of the cooks by demonstrating menu conception and execution. Each team has to produce an appetizer course, a salad or soup course, the predetermined entrée, and the dessert course. Each course should demonstrate at least three to four culinary skill competencies, such as poaching at the correct temperature to achieve the right texture of the finished dish, or roasting or pan-searing a piece of fish or poultry to achieve the crisp, golden brown crust. Does the salad have the right balance of acid and oil in the vinaigrette, or is it drowned in a puddle of vinegary goo? Are the vegetables cooked al dente, not undercooked or overcooked? Is the sauce used on the entrée shiny and flavorful or dull and flat? Is the dessert fabulous with many components, creamy smooth with crunchy notes, sweet and sour, and the chocolate sauce smooth and rich, not stiff? Can the team demonstrate utilization of the products? By utilizing and not wasting the products that were first fabricated in the skills segment, the competitors show they know how to avoid excessive waste. By using up the ingredients in creative and imaginative ways and by demonstrating proper technique for each course, the team enhances its chances of winning.

Complete practice run-throughs of the cooking segment of the competition are essential. Teams should practice complete time trials at least a dozen times or more. Some teams practice biweekly; others practice five times a week. The manager, coach, and team members need to determine practice times.

The team should have someone judge its work as well, such as a chapter mentor or officer, and, if available, an ACF judge or certified executive chef. This gives the team valuable feedback and can help get the menu concepts the critical appraisal necessary for development of a strong presentation.

When the team is working on cold platter presentations, the initial design should be evaluated with the same critical viewpoint. Does it look like real food? The tasting plate should be tasty; the food should be the starting point of the platter, not the other way around. Unlike in earlier platter work with a huge central showpiece, the modern platter should scream reality. Start with the taste and color of the food. Each component of the platter should be able to be a stand-alone item. It should have great flavor and balance. Then it should complement the overall dish. The colors should be real, not altered. Caution must be taken when using products such as beets, as they can bleed into surrounding foods. If using saltwater fish, use saltwater shellfish and other items from the area. If using trout or fresh fish such as pike, keep to the freshwater theme—don't combine saltwater products with freshwater products. Keep it real!

Think of the greenery or vegetable products that will go with the protein item on the tray. An example might be watercress sauce with rainbow trout or pike. Make sure the

Figure 21-7 Aspic should be thinly applied to create a lustrous glaze.

aspic is shiny and not too thick on the portions, which will make them inedible (Figure 21-7). When the aspic is over-gelled, the product takes on the look of plastic food. Keep it real! Slices should be placed an equal distance from each other, slightly overlapping or closely spaced. There should be equal amounts of proteins, starches, and vegetable servings on the platter.

There are different requirements for each competition category, so be sure to check the official competition rules. Again, you can find this on the ACF website or at the sponsoring agency if it's not an ACF-sponsored event. Check the rules for the current requirements before designing your platters.

When you have the dishes and platters finalized and you are satisfied with the results, display your platter on a table mock setup (Figure 21-8). This will help you to determine the location of your platter in relationship to any table decorations or settings that you might need. This is an essential exercise. The table should not be too big and have too much empty space; on the other hand, it has happened in competition that a table was too small and the platters were crowded or, in the worst-case scenario, did not fit. Again, during the mock table session, it sometimes becomes necessary to make painful decisions about platter sizes. When this happens, the components of the platter must be reconfigured.

When the dishes are finalized, the ingredients list is developed. The list must be as complete as possible and must have built-in redundancy to compensate for unforeseen difficulties. The ingredients list must take into consideration the amount and type of food that can be taken to the show and what must be purchased locally. Many counties and states have differing health regulations. If competing internationally, many countries have stringent health regulations concerning importation of food; and, in most cases,

Figure 21-8 Moving a platter to a mock table gives the team the opportunity to scrutinize it from a different viewpoint.

anything edible will be confiscated at the customs gate or border. It is essential that teams consider these regulations when they are drawing up the ingredient list. It is also helpful to become familiar with local conditions. Most European countries have well-stocked supermarkets offering a wide choice of food, but local specifications and prices vary.

>> Competition Formulas

Unlike the formulas found in Unit 17, Basic Charcuterie, the aspic formula for competition is based more on a gelled consommé. It has to be crystal clear.

There are differing levels of strengths of aspic for specific jobs on a mirror or platter display. Some aspics should be very tender and light while others need to withstand the bright lights and drying environment of a convention hall or auditorium. The following recipes are for an assortment of applications. Gelatin comes in powdered or sheet form. There are several brands that are used in competition. Many teams rely on Grayslake while others prefer Haco. Some teams work with commercial Knox while others use the sheet variety from Germany. If bloomed correctly and used in the proper ratio with the liquid, all types of gelatin produce acceptable and winning results.

Some chefs recommend using water with gelatin for the glazing process. While this is an acceptable practice and the formula is included, it is more classical to use a clarified stock, both from the skills set side of things as well as the taste. Using parsley water in the aspic to give it a natural pale green color on a tray is an electrifying technique to give foods a natural and elegant light.

fish or poultry aspic for general glazing *Yield: 1 gal (3.79 l)*

Ingredients	Amounts		Procedure
	U.S.	Metric	
Pike, trout, sole, or poultry consommé	1 gal	3.79 l	Place the cold consommé in a stainless steel bowl or bain-marie.
Gelatin	16 oz	454 g	Sprinkle powdered gelatin on the surface while slowly stirring or add the sheets to the cold liquid. Let the gelatin bloom for half an hour. Over a pot of warm water, heat until the gelatin melts in the liquid between 95°F and 110°F (35°C and 43°C). Do not let it get above 135°F (57°C) or the gelatin will break down.
			Remove from heat and cool slightly, holding the aspic at 85°F to 95°F (29°C to 35°C).

NUTRITIONAL INFORMATION PER RECIPE (FISH): 1,891 Calories; 93 g Fat (62.2% calories from fat); 15 g Protein; 112 g Carbohydrate; 11 g Dietary Fiber; 256 mg Cholesterol; 3,966 mg Sodium. Exchanges: 3 1/2 Fat; 7 1/2 Other Carbohydrates.

Parsley is used to color the aspic green in the following recipe. Use the Parsley Water recipe listed after the Green Aspic recipe.

green aspic for general glazing *Yield: 1 1/2 qt (1.39 l)*

Ingredients	Amounts		Procedure
	U.S.	Metric	
Fish or poultry consommé	1 qt	946 ml	Place the cold consommé and parsley water in a stainless steel bowl or bain-marie.
Parsley water	2 fl oz	59 ml	
Gelatin	16 oz	454 g	Sprinkle powdered gelatin on the surface while slowly stirring or add the sheets to the cold liquid. Let the gelatin bloom for half an hour. Over a pot of warm water, heat until the gelatin melts in the liquid, 95°F to 110°F (35°C to 43°C). Do not let it get above 135°F (57°C) or the gelatin will break down.
			Remove from heat and cool slightly, holding the aspic at 85°F to 95°F (29°C to 35°C).

NUTRITIONAL INFORMATION PER RECIPE: 383 Calories; 0 g Fat (0.0% calories from fat); 27 g Protein; 71 g Carbohydrate; 0 g Dietary Fiber; 0 mg Cholesterol; 2,737 mg Sodium. Exchanges: 3 Lean Meat; 4 Other Carbohydrates.

parsley water   *Yield: 2 oz (60 ml)*

Ingredients	Amounts		Procedure
	U.S.	Metric	
Parsley leaves, no stems	3 oz	85 g	Chop the fresh parsley very fine. Place in a linen napkin or cheesecloth and run under cold water. Squeeze the parsley to remove the liquid. Save 2 oz of this dark green parsley juice or water for your aspic. Add to the aspic for a natural light-green colorant.

NUTRITIONAL INFORMATION PER RECIPE: 31 Calories; 1 g Fat (16.0% calories from fat); 3 g Protein; 5 g Carbohydrate; 3 g Dietary Fiber; 0 mg Cholesterol; 48 mg Sodium. Exchanges: 1 Vegetable.

The following aspic recipe is to be used for showpieces where flavor is not an issue.

plain aspic for general glazing *Yield: 144 fl oz (4.32 l)*

Ingredients	Amounts		Procedure
	U.S.	Metric	
Cold water	1 gal	3.79 l	Place cold water in a stainless steel bowl or bain-marie.
Gelatin	16 oz	454 g	Sprinkle powdered gelatin on the surface while slowly stirring or add the sheets to the cold liquid. Let the gelatin bloom for half an hour. Over a pot of warm water, heat until the gelatin melts in the liquid, 95°F to 110°F (35°C to 43°C). Do not let it get above 135°F (57°C) or the gelatin will break down.
			Remove from heat and cool slightly, holding the aspic at 85°F to 95°F (29°C to 35°C).

NUTRITIONAL INFORMATION PER RECIPE: 268 Calories; 0 g Fat (0.0% calories from fat); 5 g Protein; 64 g Carbohydrate; 0 g Dietary Fiber; 0 mg Cholesterol; 304 mg Sodium. Exchanges: 4 Other Carbohydrates.

This fruit glaze is useful for sweet fruit platters and displays. Using clear fruit juices and gelatin can give not only a beautiful look to a platter but add to the flavor as well. Apple, cranberry, or other nonparticulate juice will work well in this fruit glaze.

fruit glaze *Yield: 1 gal (3.79 l)*

Ingredients	Amounts		Procedure
	U.S.	Metric	
Clear fruit juice	1 gal	3.79 l	Place cold juice in a stainless steel bowl or bain-marie.
Gelatin	16 oz	454 g	Sprinkle powdered gelatin on the surface while slowly stirring or add the sheets to the cold liquid. Let the gelatin bloom for half an hour. Over a pot of warm water, heat until the gelatin melts in the liquid, 95°F to 110°F (35°C to 43°C). Do not let it get above 135°F (57°C) or the gelatin will break down.
			Remove from heat and cool slightly, holding the fruit gel at 85°F to 95°F (29°C to 35°C).

NUTRITIONAL INFORMATION PER RECIPE (USING APPLE JUICE): 2,133 Calories; 4 g Fat (1.8% calories from fat); 8 g Protein; 527 g Carbohydrate; 4 g Dietary Fiber; 0 mg Cholesterol; 310 mg Sodium. Exchanges: 27 1/2 Fruit; 4 Other Carbohydrates.

For aspic with medium consistency, adjust the amount of gelatin used. Lower it to 12 ounces per gallon of liquid. This is a good consistency for items that will be eaten. It gives a lighter coat to the food and looks shinier without the risk of making the food look plastic (Figure 21-9).

For highly skilled competitors, a solution of 8 to 10 ounces of gelatin per gallon of liquid is used when a very clear and tender coating is desired and the location of the food display will be in a colder environment.

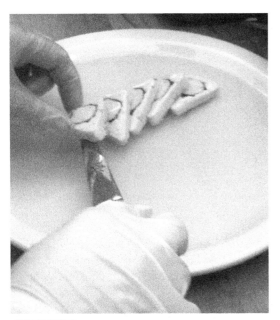

Figure 21-9 Aspic should make the food look shiny and appetizing.

>> Categories of Competition

According to the ACF, there are 10 traditional categories in which chefs and culinarians can compete. There are other non-ACF competitions as well; if you are interested in competing in any of these, research the rules. All competitions share similarities, but many have slight variations, so make sure that you thoroughly read through the rules for each competition. Never assume that you know the rules unless you have read them at least three times or more. It takes just one time to miss an instruction to lose critical points or, worse, to be disqualified. To lose this way is a shame, so do the homework—study the rules!

The ACF has identified the categories by the letters A through H, K, P, and W, with many of them split into differing subcategories, which are then tagged with an additional number. An example would be Category A-2 Cold Platter of Fish and/or Shellfish. Each category presents its own set of challenges. The hot food competition, for instance, requires more commitment of time, staffing, food materials, serviceware, and equipment than most of the other categories.

The following is a list of ACF categories and a description of what each represents. For a more detailed list, go to Competition Rules on the ACF website, www.acfchefs.org. This list is subject to change.

Category	Title	Description	Subcategories
A	Cooking (Professional and Student)	Show platters must serve a minimum of eight portions on the platter and one portion of each item on a show plate. It must contain two proteins; two garnishes; one salad; one sauce that goes with the theme or items.	A-1 Cold platter of meat, beef, veal, lamb, or pork A-2 Cold platter of fish and/or shellfish A-3 Cold platter of poultry A-4 Cold platter of game A-5 Cold hors d' oeuvre selection with a minimum of eight varieties, appropriate garniture, and sauces A-6 Eight varieties of tapas or finger foods, hot or cold, or combination of hot and cold—must be presented cold
B	Cooking (Professional Individual)	Hot food presented cold. This is based on special gastronomic menu, based on the special occasion or degustation menu. A central theme is carried throughout the presentation.	B-1 Six different cold appetizer plates B-2 Six different hot appetizers plated and presented cold B-3 One five-course menu gastronomique for one person prepared hot and presented cold, with two appetizers, one consommé, one salad, and one entrée, all within the size of a contemporary tasting menu B-4 One nine-course degustation tasting menu (A degustation menu is a fine-dining tasting menu.)
C	Patisserie/Confectionary (Professional and Student)	All requirements must be displayed, and these displays must be made of edible materials.	C-1 Single-tier, decorated celebration cake—sugar paste, rolled fondant, royal icing, chocolate, marzipan, or sugar. • Minimum of three techniques displayed. • Can be any shape with a maximum display area of 15" × 15". • No dummy cakes are permitted. C-2 One buffet platter of fancy cookies, chocolates, or petit fours (platter must be made up of five varieties, six portions each) with one presentation plate. C-3 Six different individual hot or cold desserts served as individual plates and all shown cold. C-4 Wedding cake: Three tiers with maximum display area of 36" × 36". No blank dummy cakes, only real cake allowed. No C-5 category.

Category	Title	Description	Subcategories
D	Showpieces		Acceptable mediums are: ice, vegetables, fruits, tallow, saltillage, pastillage, chocolate, marzipan, and cooked sugar. No external supports are allowed. • Showpieces are eligible to be entered in only one ACF competition.
E	Live Action Showpieces, Professional, Individual	A team prepares a buffet that has a maximum display of 12 ft × 10 ft that must include six different appetizers, one portion each; a plated seven-course meal for one; one show platter of either meat, poultry, or game; one show platter of fish or seafood. Additional information about the descriptions and sub-categories can be found on the ACFChefs.org website. These categories and descriptions are subject to change.	**E-1 Fruit/Vegetable Carving Mystery Basket** • Theme announced in advance by show chair. • Three hours to create and display showpiece. • All competitors receive identical basket of fruits and vegetables. • All items in mystery basket must be utilized in final showpiece. • Base cannot exceed 30″ × 30″, height is unrestricted. **E-2 Cake Decoration** • Theme announced in advance by show chair. • Competitor has three hours to decorate and display cake. • Cake is to be three-tier and base cannot exceed 30″ × 30″. • Competitor will bring in filled cake of any shape, but without any final finish. • Competitors will finish the cake with glaze, buttercream, rolled fondant, chocolate, and so on, and decorate it to fit the theme. • Decorations cannot be brought in, only the raw materials necessary to make them (i.e., marzipan, chocolate, sugar, etc.). • Cakes may be sliced for inspection to ensure that only edible cakes are used; however, cakes will not be tasted. • All decoration must be edible. • Competitors may bring in an air brush. **E-3 Decorative Centerpiece** • Competitors have three hours to create a decorative centerpiece of any medium or a composite of mediums, such as chocolate, sugar, marzipan, pastillage, modeling chocolate, rolled fondant, gum paste, nougat, and so on. • Base cannot exceed 30″ × 30″, height is unrestricted. • A simple, generic base of poured sugar, pastillage, chocolate, nougat, and so on, in simple shapes, may be brought in. • Any decorating of the base must be done on-site. • Competitors can bring cooked sugar of their choice; pre-cooked sugars and pistoles are allowed only for the purpose of pulling and blowing. • Chocolate can be brought in chopped or in pistoles. • Pastillage and gum paste can be premade and brought in, but must be kept white. Any coloring must be done during the competition. • Competitors are responsible for bringing their own tools, marble slabs, sugar equipment, measuring scale, warming lamp, and hair dryer (for cooling). • Competitors may bring in decorative platters to display the assignment. • Competitors may bring in a household-size (small) microwave. • Prewarming the sugar and/or chocolate tempering in the staging area is permitted.

(continued)

Category	Title	Description	Subcategories
			E-4 Sugar Centerpiece • Competitors have four hours to create a decorative sugar centerpiece. • Base cannot exceed 30" × 30", height is unrestricted. • Competitors can bring cooked sugar of their choice; pre-cooked sugars and pistoles are allowed, only for the purpose of pulling and blowing. • All pulling and blowing must be done on-site. • Pastillage and gum paste can be premade and brought in, but must be kept white. Any coloring must be done during the competition. • Competitors are responsible for bringing their own tools, marble slabs, sugar equipment, measuring scale, warming lamp, and hair dryer (for cooling). • Competitors may bring in decorative platters to display the assignment. • Competitors may bring in a household-size (small) microwave. • Prewarming the sugar in the staging area is permitted.
F	Hot Food Competition	This competition demonstrates foods that not only have to look great, but taste great as well.	**F-1 Mystery Basket, Professional, Individual** • Competitors will prepare four servings of a four-course menu of their choice. (Dessert course is optional.) • Total time for competition is four hours, not including set-up and clean-up. • Menu must be submitted/picked up within first 30 minutes. Cooking may begin immediately upon submission of menu. • Service window opens at 3 hours and 20 minutes. • All items in the mystery basket must be utilized in the menu. No substitutions of the mystery basket items are permitted. • Of the four portions prepared, three are for judges, tasting, and one is for display/critique. **F-2 Mystery Basket, Professional, Two-Man Team** • Teams will prepare eight servings of a four-course menu of their choice. (Dessert course is optional.) • Total time for competition is four hours, not including set-up and clean-up. • Menu must be submitted/picked up within first 30 minutes. Cooking may begin immediately upon submission of menu. • Service window opens at 3 hours, 20 minutes. • All items in the mystery basket must be utilized in the menu. No substitutions of mystery basket items are permitted. • Of the eight portions prepared, three are for judges, tasting, one is for display/critique, and the remaining four may be used for tasting. **F-3 Regional Tastes/Custom Competition** These are based on the ACF-approved guidelines and highlight regions' dishes or materials. Each of these must be approved by the ACF. **F-4 Nutritional Hot Food Challenge** This unique competition format is ideal for strengthening the established alliance with a registered dietician. • Competitors will prepare four servings of a four-course meal (hot appetizer/soup, salad, entrée and dessert). • Competitors have 3 hours cooking time, with an additional 40 minutes for plating.

Category Title	Description	Subcategories

- The total caloric value of the meal should not exceed 1,000 kcal. The balance should be 15–20 percent protein, 45–60 percent carbohydrates, and 25–30 percent fat.
- Competitors will submit the menu with recipes, pictures, and nutritional analysis for each course.
- Nutritional analysis must be confirmed and completed by a registered dietician. Confirmation must be presented in the form of a "letter" stating that the meal plan was evaluated for overall nutritional adequacy and meets the nutritional guidelines required for the competition. Also, indicate which software program was used for the analysis.
- All ingredients, except proteins, may be pre-scaled and will be checked on-site.
- Proteins may be brought in market form, but some fabrication must take place during the cooking phase.
- Of the four portions prepared, three are for judges, tasting, and one is for display/critique.

F-5 Pastry Mystery Basket, Professional, Individual

- Competitors will prepare one 8" decorated torte/cake, any shape, and four portions each of one hot and one cold dessert.
- Total time for competition is 4 hours, not including set-up and clean-up.
- Menu must be submitted/picked up within first 30 minutes. Cooking may begin immediately upon submission of menu.
- Service window opens at 3 hours, 20 minutes.
- All items in the mystery basket must be utilized in the menu. No substitutions of mystery basket items are permitted.
- The torte/cake should be presented whole.
- Of the four portions prepared of the hot and cold desserts, three are for judges, tasting and one is for display/critique.

F-6 Pastry Mystery Basket, Professional, Two-Man Team

- Teams will prepare one 8" decorated torte/cake, any shape, a decorative showpiece to display the torte/cake, and four portions each of one hot and one cold dessert.
- Total time for competition is 4 hours, not including set-up and clean-up.
- The menu must be submitted/picked-up within first 30 minutes. Cooking may begin immediately upon submission of menu.
- The service window opens at 3 hours and 20 minutes.
- All items in the mystery basket must be utilized in the menu. No substitutions of mystery-basket items are permitted.
- The torte/cake should be presented with the showpiece, with one slice removed for tasting. The slice should be 1/8" of the cake and presented on a dessert plate for tasting.
- The minimum height of the showpiece is 24" and must incorporate a stand to display the cake.
- The cake and showpiece should be in harmony.
- Of the four portions prepared of the hot and cold desserts, three are for judges, tasting and one is for display/critique.
- The decorative centerpiece can be of any medium or a composite of mediums, such as chocolate, sugar, marzipan, modeling chocolate, rolled fondant, nougat, and so on.
- Competitors can bring cooked sugar of their choice. Pre-cooked sugars and pistoles are allowed only for the purpose of pulling and blowing.

(continued)

Category	Title	Description	Subcategories
			• Chocolate can be brought in chopped or in pistoles.
			• Competitors are responsible for bringing their own tools, marble slabs, sugar equipment, measuring scale, warming lamp, and hair dryer (for cooling).
			• Teams may bring in decorative platters to display the assignment.
			• Teams may bring in a household-size (small) microwave.
			• Prewarming the sugar and/or chocolate tempering in the staging area is permitted.
G	Edible Cold Food	This competition highlights foods that are prepared and served cold. The sanitation standards for this competition are high. All food must be maintained at 41°F (5°C) or colder during the entire competition. (This is one of the more challenging competitions to compete in due to the nature of the food and the time involved; it takes two 8-hour days.)	**Cooking**—One cold buffet or hors d'oeuvre platter for eight to ten portions. The hors d'oeuvre must consist of a minimum of six varieties. The platter must also present the appropriate salads and garnitures. **Pastry**—One buffet platter, eight to ten portions of each variety with confectionery or desserts with theme. The platter must consist of a minimum of six varieties.
H	Ice Carving	Ice carving is one of the more spectacular skills that a chef or culinarian can acquire. Huge blocks of ice are turned into graceful and awe-inspiring sculpture. Fragile as glass, and just as sparkling as diamonds, it takes an artistic flair to carve ice. It is also dangerous and safety cannot be stressed enough. Chain saws, ice routers, and sharp saws can spell disaster in a split second of inattention. In judging, a safety violation can lead to a loss of points and even disqualification. In competitions, all carving is done on-site and within a time limit. Multi-block carvings take more time and in some cases are team carved.	H-1 Single 300-lb block individual freestyle, 3-hour time limit. H-2 Two-person team, three blocks, 3 hours. H-3 Three-person team, five blocks, 3 hours. H-4 Two- or three-person team, 15 to 20 blocks, exhibition carving, 48-hour time limit, outdoors.
K	Practical and Contemporary Hot Food Cooking	This category highlights the individual competitor's fabrication and cooking skills. Each competitor must prepare four portions in 60 minutes including the fabrication and cooking. An additional 5 minutes is allocated to plate the dish.	K-1 Rock Cornish game hen, chicken, or duck K-2 Bone-in pork loin K-3 Bone-in veal loin or rack K-4 Bone-in lamb loin or rack K-5 Game birds, pheasant, quail, squab, or guinea fowl K-6 Bone-in game (venison or antelope) racks or loin K-7 Whole rabbit K-8 Live lobster (kill and fabricate, cook to specifications) K-9 Fish fabrication, flat or round fish and cook to specifications

Category	Title	Description	Subcategories
P	Practical and Contemporary Patisserie	Competitors demonstrate their pastry and baking skills in the five subcategories of patisserie.	P-1 Hot/Warm desserts: Pastry chefs will have 60 minutes to prepare a hot or warm dessert of their choice, with 5 minutes to serve. P-2 Composed Cold Dessert: Pastry chefs will have 90 minutes to prepare the dessert of their choice, with 5 minutes to serve.
W	Customized Wildcard Category	Chapters wishing to host hot-food competitions that do not follow the standard category formats must apply for approval. Any changes or exceptions to standardized categories must have the approval of the Culinary Competition Committee chair prior to the competition and before ACF medals and CEH are awarded. The standard application must be supplemented with a detailed description of the proposed competition, and must be submitted a full four months before the competition. The description must include the following information: • Indicate whether an individual or team category; if a team category, indicate how many team members • Number of portions • Number of courses • Time frame • Use of any special or required ingredients **Note:**.	For a customized individual category, competitors are required to prepare at least four portions of a four-course menu. For a customized team category, teams must prepare a minimum of eight portions of a four-course menu

JUDGING CRITERIA

A **culinary judge** scores platters by using score sheets. The points given by all judges are added up and then divided by the number of judges. Judging art is always subjective; therefore, in competitions there will be winners and those who don't win. The judges are trained, well experienced, and as impartial as possible. All have preferences, likes, and dislikes. This is part of the game and must be expected and respected.

The judges consider the following basic points:

• Is the food edible? Exhibitors are not allowed to cheat in order to make the food look better, such as undercooking food and putting food on top of inedible material.
• How does the food taste? The judges will probe and try to taste whether the food is seasoned. One of the greatest cold kitchen chefs in New York during the 1950s and 1960s was Chef Waldner. He always seasoned his dishes carefully, even when he knew that they would be for display only and would not be eaten.

Figure 21-10 Competitions require careful attention to all aspects of plating and should entice the customer.

- What is the level of craftsmanship? Judges determine how precisely the food is cut, how well it is glazed, whether there are any fingerprints on the platters, and how perfectly each component is executed.
- Do the colors balance? Judges determine if the platter is pleasing to the eye and if there is harmony.
- Is there nutritional balance? Judges decide if the dish meets nutritional expectations and if it contains proteins, starch, and vegetables.
- Is the portion size appropriate? Judges look for harmony between the main object and the garnishes. To promote awareness of portion size, exhibitors of large platters are required to present, in addition, one individual plate with the same components as those on the large platter. Judges decide if that plate will satisfy potential customers (Figure 21-10).
- Is there a numerical match of garnishes and main components?
- Is the dish practical? Judges decide if the food is too complicated or intimidating to customers. Is it too artsy? Is it too far out there?
- Is the food harmonious? Judges determine if the components complement the flavor profile of the dish, or if they are fighting each other.

>> Summary

This unit has been an overview of some of the more typical competition options available to the chef or culinarian with the desire to enhance and improve his or her skills. From the first-time competitor to the seasoned veteran of the Culinary Olympics, the motivation for competition is for chefs to learn more about their craft and themselves. Education is of the greatest importance when it comes to competing. Winning medals is the icing on the cake.

We learned how a team is picked and what is involved in training a team to go all the way to the top. Menu development, planning, time lines, and practice guidelines were some concepts introduced to you. We learned what the judges are looking for when they evaluate our efforts in the competition arena as well as the future of culinary competition with the focus on dietary needs and contemporary cuisine.

>> Review Questions

TRUE/FALSE

1. Escoffier is the father of modern cooking techniques.
2. Alice Waters was the first U.S. female culinary Olympian.
3. The oldest Culinary Salon was in Philadelphia.
4. New York City is the home of the Culinary Olympics.
5. Ferdinand Metz managed the U.S. team in 1980 with the team winning 21 gold medals.

MULTIPLE CHOICE

6. The IKAHOGA is also known as the
   a. World Cup.
   b. Culinary Master's.
   c. Culinary Olympics.
   d. International Salon of Culinary Arts.
7. Which greenery would be most acceptable on a protein plate with trout?
   a. watercress
   b. cilantro
   c. seaweed
   d. lettuce
8. Which of the following is *not* a brand of gelatin?
   a. Knox®
   b. Grayslake®
   c. Haco®
   d. Bridgers®
9. The main purpose for using parsley water in aspic is to
   a. add a fresh taste.
   b. give it a natural pale green color.
   c. give it a pleasant smell.
   d. aid in thickening the liquid.
10. In what category of ACF competition would you find competitors making a cooked sugar piece?
    a. C-2
    b. D-6
    c. B-4
    d. F-5
11. What category of ACF competition is a hot food competition that has a focus on nutrition?
    a. F-4
    b. K-7
    c. P-1
    d. B-4
12. Which is *not* one of the criteria judges look for when scoring a platter on its craftsmanship?
    a. precise cuts
    b. ease of preparation
    c. how perfectly each component is executed
    d. practicality

>> **Food Safety Review**

This is a list of possible food safety hazards and remedies that chefs might face on a common basis. These are general suggestions. Some food items will require a different remedy.

Hazards	Remedies
Holding cold food on buffet lines	Chefs or employees should use a hand-held, insta-read thermometer and check the temperature on a regular basis every 30 minutes to 1 hour.
Food displays	Food displays should include sneeze guards, which provide a protective barrier between the customer and the food.
Pre-set banquet main-course salads	Avoid pre-setting this type of salad. If it must be done, ensure that the food is out of the refrigerator no more than half an hour before guests consume it.
Presentation dessert trays	Use dummy trays and keep the real dessert tray under refrigeration at all times.
Canapé trays	This type of tray can sit out at room temperature for up to 2 hours. Keep back-up trays in the refrigerator. Only replenish from these trays. Discard any canapés that have been sitting out for longer than 2 hours.
Flatware storage	To avoid dust and dirt, keep all flatware and dishes in covered conditions until needed for service.
Glassware storage	To prevent dust, smoke, fumes, and germs, avoid storing in overhead racks; instead, keep all glassware in covered conditions until needed for service.
Food holding	Hold cold food at 41°F (5°C) or below and hot food at 135°F (57°C) or above.
Service utensils	Always use clean serving utensils or handle with clean gloves.
Food storage	Always store food in clean and sanitized containers that are in good repair. Containers with pits, scratches, and chips should be discarded. Only store food in proper refrigeration units or dry storage areas that are free from any vector contamination. Do routine temperature checks on all refrigeration and freezer units. Never store food in a malfunctioning unit.
Storing chemicals	Store chemicals away from any food service activity.
Mixing of foods	Never mix previously cooked or leftover foods into newly cooked or raw foods.
Sick employees	Ill workers should stay home until they are well.

>> Basic First Aid

Injury	Action to Take
Minor cut	Clean with soap and hot water. Apply antibiotic cream (if your employer permits it) and a bandage. Use a finger cot and glove for finger cuts. Keep the cut or wound clean and dry.
Serious cut	Call 911. Apply pressure to the wound with a thick, clean cloth. Elevate it above the victim's heart. Get immediate medical help.
Minor burn	Run cool water over the burn area or use indirect application of ice. Wash with mild soap; apply antibiotic cream. Never use grease, ointment, or butter.
Serious burn	Call 911. Wrap the injured area in large, wet, clean towels. Get immediate medical help.
Poisoning	Call local poison control and be prepared to describe the product and the amount that was swallowed.
Electrical shock	Look but don't touch. The current may pass to you. Turn off any electrical power if possible. Otherwise, move the source away from the victim with an object made of wood, plastic, or cardboard. Look for signs of breathing. Call 911 if the victim is experiencing heart rhythm problems, respiratory failure, muscle pain and contractions, seizures, numbness and tingling, or unconsciousness.
Falls	Never try to move someone who has fallen unless the victim is certain that there are no breaks. If serious, call 911.

>> Safety Tips When Using Foodservice Equipment

- Always keep your eyes on your work. Do not be distracted.
- Always unplug a machine when cleaning, maintaining, or servicing.
- Never use a machine without the required safety guards in place.
- When applicable, use safety glasses.
- Make sure blades are sharp and the tension is adjusted properly.
- Operate electrical equipment with dry hands to avoid shocks or slipping. Wear protective gloves when necessary.
- Be conscious of loose clothing that could get caught on or in a machine.
- Unplug and zero out slicer blades to protect your hands from accidental slicing when cleaning. (When the dial is turned to zero, the blade fits snugly against the machine in a safe position.)
- Disassemble the machine under supervision. Most machine parts can be cleaned in the dishwasher but not the electric motor and cable. Wash, rinse, and sanitize each part of the machine.
- For machines with a stationary base, use a soap and sanitizer on the machine itself. Use the raising device on most machines to lift up and clean under the machine where food particles can be found.
- Reassemble the machine when parts have been properly cleaned and sanitized.

>> Metric Conversion Chart

In this book we used the following metric conversion chart and did not round up.

LIQUIDS

U.S. Measurements	Metric Equivalents
1 tsp	5 ml
1 tbsp	15 ml
1 fl oz	29.57 ml
8 fl oz	237 ml
16 fl oz or 1 pt	473 ml
32 fl oz or 1 qt	946 ml

DRY WEIGHT

U.S. Measurements	Metric Equivalents
1 oz	28.35 g
16 oz or 1 lb	454 g
2.2 lbs	1 kg

>> Scoop Sizes

The following chart gives the size of common scoops.

Type of Scoop	Amount It Holds
#12	2.7 fl oz
#16	2 fl oz
#20	1.6 fl oz
#30	1.1 fl oz

>> Meat Grinder Plates

Most grinders have interchangeable plates that can alter the size of the grind and are available in four standard sizes:

Plate Size	Type of Grind
3/4-in plate	Coarse grind
3/8-in plate	Medium-coarse grind
3/16-in plate	Medium grind
1/8-in plate	Fine grind

>> Tablecloth Sizes for Banquet Tables

ROUND TABLES

Size	Tablecloth Size
2 ft (0.6 m)	72 in × 72 in (1.82 m)
2 1/2 ft (0.76 m)	72 in × 72 in (1.82 m)
3 ft (0.91 m)	72 in × 72 in (1.82 m)
4 1/2 ft (1.36 m)	90 in × 90 in
5 ft (1.52 m)	90 in × 90 in
5 1/2 ft (1.67 m)	108 in × 108 in (2.73 m)
6 ft (1.82 m)	108 in × 108 in (2.73 m)

RECTANGLE

Size	Tablecloth Size
18 in × 6 ft (0.45 × 1.82 m)	2 each 62 in × 62 in (1.57 m)
30 in × 4 ft (0.76 × 1.21 m)	72 in × 72 in (1.82 m)
30 in × 6 ft (0.76 × 1.82 m)	2 each 72 in × 72 in (1.82 m)
3 ft × 6 ft (0.76 × 1.82 m)	2 each 72 in × 72 in (1.82 m)
3 ft × 8 ft (0.91 × 2.40 m)	2 each 72 in × 72 in (1.82 m)

CRESCENT

Size	Tablecloth Size
6 × 3 ft (1.82 × 0.91 m)	20 each 90 in × 90 in (1.82 m)

>> Bad Fats Versus Good Fats

Information provided by Healthcastle.com, "Which cooking oil is the best?"
(Written by Gloria Tsang, RD)

	The Bad Fats
Saturated fats	Saturated fats raise total blood cholesterol as well as LDL cholesterol (the bad cholesterol). Saturated fats are mainly found in animal products such as meat, dairy, eggs, and seafood. Some plant foods are also high in saturated fats, such as coconut, palm oil, and palm kernel oil.
Trans fats	Trans fats were invented as scientists began to "hydrogenate" liquid oils so that they could withstand better in food production processes and provide a better shelf-life. As a result of hydrogenation, trans-fatty acids are formed. Trans-fatty acids are found in many commercially packaged goods such as cookies and crackers, commercially fried food such as French fries from some fast-food chains, other packaged snacks such as microwave popcorn, as well as in vegetable shortening and hard stick margarine.
	The Good Fats
Monounsaturated fats	Monounsaturated fats lower total cholesterol and LDL cholesterol (the bad cholesterol) and increase the HDL cholesterol (the good cholesterol). Nut, canola, and olive oils are high in monounsaturated fats.
Polyunsaturated fats	Polyunsaturated fats also lower total cholesterol and LDL cholesterol. Seafoods like salmon and fish oil, as well as corn, soy, safflower, and sunflower oils, are high in polyunsaturated fats. Omega-3 fatty acids belong to this group.

>> Aging of Cheddar Cheese

The following chart explains the characterization of cheddar depending on the length of time it is aged.

Length of Time Aged	Description
Newly processed, aged for 30 days	Mild
1 to 3 months	Mild
3 to 6 months	Medium
6 to 9 months	Sharp
9 months to 2 years or more	Extra sharp

>> Categories of Lobsters and Their Weights

Name	Weight
Chicken	1 pound
Quarters	1 1/4 pounds
Selects	1 1/2 pounds on up to 2 1/4 pounds
Jumbos	2 1/4 pounds

>> Salmon Comparisons

Name	Species	Characteristics	Size	Culinary Applications
Chinook/King	Oncorhynchus tshawytscha	Oil rich, scarlet flesh, succulent flavor	18–20 lbs, 18 to 20 in long	Grilling, broiling, sautéing, baking, poaching, steaming, and smoking
Sockeye	Oncorhynchus nerka	Brilliant red, firm and rich flavor	6 lbs	Poaching, steaming, smoking, curing, grilling, baking, and sautéing
Silver/Coho	Oncorhynchus kisutch	Orange red flesh, firm flesh, and moderately oily texture	12 lbs, 20 to 35 in long	Cured and smoked
Pink	Oncorhynchus gorbuscha	Lower in fat than most other species, high in protein; light rosy pink flesh, tender texture, and delicate flavor	1–4 lbs	Canned, baked, and sautéed
Keta/chum/silverbright	Oncorhynchus keta	Orange pink color; firm texture, lower fat content; mild flavor	18–15 lbs	Curing, smoking, and grilling
Atlantic salmon	Salmo salar	Mild and oily flavor; flesh is softer due to the higher fat content; bright orange flesh	4–20 lbs	Fattier species good for grilling, broiling, and baking. If poaching, use a low of 160°F (71°C)

>> Tuna Steaks

Name	Species	Characteristics	Culinary Applications
Albacore	Thunnus alalunga	White meat; fresh is fattier than most other species; high in omega-3s	Canned and used for salads, sandwiches, and other cooking applications; fresh grilled (rare), broiled, or sautéed
Ahi/Yellowfin	Thunnus albacares	Bright yellow side markings; average size is 7–20 lbs; mild, meaty taste and a firm texture; bright red meat when raw (turns grayish tan when cooked)	Sashimi, grilled, broiled, sautéed, baked, and smoked
Bluefin	Thunnus thynnus	Largest commercially viable tuna (some weigh over a ton with a length of 12 ft); most are between 200 and 400 lbs; available in three grades based on fat content and color	Sashimi, grilling

>> Number of Slices per Loaf of Bread

The following chart shows the number of slices available from a 2-pound (900 g) loaf, depending on the thickness of each slice.

Type of Slice	Size of Slices	Yield
Average	1/2-in	32 slices
Thin	1/3-in	34 slices
Extra thin	1/4-in	40 slices

>> Salad Cultivation Seasons

This is a listing of greens and salad herbs arranged by their cultivation season. Obviously, there are some climates with longer growing seasons. This list provides a general time frame for most greens and herbs.

Spring	Summer	Autumn	Winter
Sorrel	Iceberg	Bok choy	Escarole
Watercress	Bronze leaf lettuce	Swiss chard	Kale
Beet greens	Basil	Beet greens	Cabbage
Chard	Thyme	Fennel	Savoy cabbage
Chervil	Borage	Garlic	Celery root
Dandelion greens	Sage blossoms		Chicories
Frisee	Garlic		Endive
Arugula			Collard
Mustard greens			Mache (lamb's lettuce)
Nettles			
Lettuces			Radicchio
Fiddlehead ferns			Mizuna
Garlic scapes			Shiso leaves

>> Brining Times

Product	Approximate Brining Times
Boneless chicken or duck breasts, 6 to 8 oz each	2 to 3 hours
2 to 3 lbs whole poultry	4 to 6 hours
3 to 6 lbs whole poultry	8 to 12 hours
Larger poultry up to 12 lbs	24 hours
Larger poultry 12 lbs and up	24 to 48 hours
Pork pieces up to 2 in thick (chops, etc.)	6 to 24 hours
Curing pork chops, pork loin, or larger loin pieces	12 hours to 3 days
Thin fish filets	1 hour
Whole trout	2 hours

>> Preferred Cuts for Making Sausage

Types of Sausage	Recommended Cut
Pork	Boston butt or shoulder
Beef	Round steak, chuck, or blade
Veal	Shoulder
Lamb	Shoulder, leg
Poultry	Thigh and breast meat
Game	Round, shoulder

>> Gelatin Usage Chart

Use the following chart to determine the amount of gelatin you will need for the specific job at hand.

Amount per Quart	Amount per Cup	Strength of Gel	Usage
1/2 oz	1/8 oz	Light	Clear soups such as consommé
1 oz	1/4 oz	Medium light	Coating and edible chaud froid
2 oz	1/2 oz	Medium	Braun and head cheese, topping terrines, and pâté en croûte
3 oz	3/4 oz	Firm gel	Mirror and platter coating for competition
4 oz	1 oz	Extra firm gel	Use when cream is used as in cream cheese, pastry cream, and mousselines

Primal Cuts

Beef:

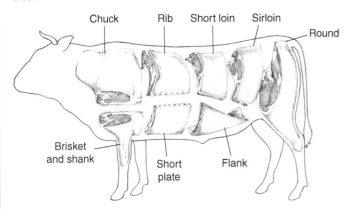

Pork:

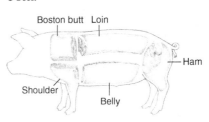

Veal:

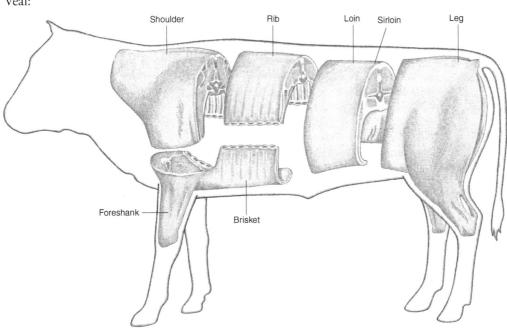

Lamb:

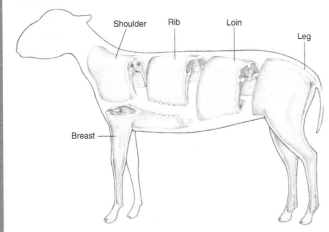

Appendix D

>> ACF Competition Categories

The following is a list of ACF categories and a description of what each represents. For a more detailed list, go to Competition Rules on the website www.acfchefs.org. This list is subject to change.

Category	Title	Description	Subcategories
A	Cooking (Professional and Student)	Show platters must serve a minimum of eight portions on the platter and one portion of each item on a show plate. It must contain two proteins; two garnishes; one salad; one sauce that goes with the theme or items.	A-1 Cold platter of meat, beef, veal, lamb, or pork A-2 Cold platter of fish and/or shellfish A-3 Cold platter of poultry A-4 Cold platter of game A-5 Cold hors d'oeuvre selection with a minimum of eight varieties, appropriate garniture, and sauces
B	Cooking (Professional and Student)	Hot food presented cold. This is based on a special gastronomic menu based on a the special occasion or degustation menu. A central theme is carried throughout the presentation.	B-1 Six different cold appetizer plates B-2 Six different hot appetizers plated and presented cold B-3 One five-course tasting menu for one person prepared hot and presented cold, with two appetizers, one consommé, one salad, and one entrée, all within the size of a contemporary tasting menu. B-4 One restaurant platter for four persons prepared hot and displayed cold and one vegetarian platter for two prepared hot but displayed cold.
C	Patisserie/Confectionary (Professional and Student)	All requirements must be displayed, and these displays must be made of edible materials.	C-1 Decorated special occasion cake; decoration must be of sugar paste, rolled fondant, or royal icing with a maximum display area of 15 in × 15 in. No blank cakes allowed. It must be made with a real cake base. C-2 One buffet platter of fancy cookies, chocolates, or petit fours (platter must be made up of five varieties, six portions each) with one presentation plate, plus a tasting plate with all the varieties represented. C-3 Six different individual hot or cold desserts served as individual plates and all shown cold. C-4 Wedding cake: Three tiers with maximum display area of 36 in × 36 in. No blank dummy cakes, only real cake allowed. C-5 Novelty cake: An imaginative and original creation in design and shape with all components, such as cake, icing and garniture, edible

Category	Title	Description	Subcategories
D	Showpieces		D-1 Tallow, fruit, and vegetables; cheese; butter for carving: 30 in × 30 in maximum display area with no external supports allowed.
			D-2 Salt dough or carving: 30 in × 30 in maximum display area with no external supports allowed.
			D-3 Pastillage or gum paste: 30 in × 30 in maximum display area with no external supports allowed.
			D-4 Chocolate showpiece: 30 in × 30 in maximum display area with no external supports allowed.
			D-5 Marzipan: 24 in × 24 in maximum display area with no supports allowed.
			D-6 Cooked Sugar: 30 in × 30 in maximum display area with no supports allowed.
E	Live Action Showpieces, Professional, Individual		• All work must be done on-site by the competitor.
			• All work must be displayed on an acceptable food surface.
			E-1 Fruit/Vegetable Carving Mystery Basket
			• Theme announced in advance by show chair.
			• Three hours to create and display showpiece.
			• All competitors receive identical basket of fruits and vegetables.
			• All items in mystery basket must be utilized in final showpiece.
			• Base can not exceed 30" x 30", height is unrestricted.
			E-2 Cake Decoration
			• Theme announced in advance by show chair.
			• Competitor has three hours to decorate and display cake.
			• Cake is to be 3-tier and base can not exceed 30" x 30".
			• Competitor will bring in filled cake of any shape, but without any final finish.
			• Competitors will finish the cake with glaze, buttercream, rolled fondant, chocolate, etc., and decorate it to fit the theme.
			• Decorations can not be brought in, only the raw materials necessary to make them. (i.e., marzipan, chocolate, sugar, etc.)
			• Cakes may be sliced for inspection to ensure that only edible cakes are used; however, cakes will not be tasted.
			• All decoration must be edible.
			• Competitors may bring in an air brush.
			E-3 Decorative Centerpiece
			• Competitors have three hours to create a decorative centerpiece of any medium or a composite of mediums, such as chocolate, sugar, marzipan, pastillage, modeling chocolate, rolled fondant, gum paste, nougat, etc.

Category	Title	Description	Subcategories
			• Base can not exceed 30" x 30", height is unrestricted.
			• A simple, generic base of poured sugar, pastillage, chocolate, nougat, etc., in simple shapes, may be brought in.
			• Any decorating of the base must be done on-site.
			• Competitors can bring cooked sugar of their choice, pre-cooked sugars and pistoles are allowed only for the purpose of pulling and blowing.
			• Chocolate can be brought in chopped or in pistoles.
			• Pastillage and gum paste can be premade and brought in, but must be kept white. Any coloring must be done during the competition.
			• Competitors are responsible for bringing their own tools, marble slabs, sugar equipment, measuring scale, warming lamp and hair dryer (for cooling).
			• Competitors may bring in decorative platters to display the assignment.
			• Competitors may bring in a household-size (small) microwave.
			• Pre-warming the sugar and/or chocolate tempering in the staging area is permitted.

E-4 Sugar Centerpiece

- Competitors have four hours to create a decorative sugar centerpiece.

- Base can not exceed 30" x 30", height is unrestricted.

- Competitors can bring cooked sugar of their choice, pre-cooked sugars and pistoles are allowed, only for the purpose of pulling and blowing.

- All pulling and blowing must be done on-site.

- Pastillage and gum paste can be premade and brought in, but must be kept white. Any coloring must be done during the competition.

- Competitors are responsible for bringing their own tools, marble slabs, sugar equipment, measuring scale, warming lamp and hair dryer (for cooling).

- Competitors may bring in decorative platters to display the assignment.

- Competitors may bring in a household-size (small) microwave.

- Pre-warming the sugar in the staging area is permitted.

Category	Title	Description	Subcategories
F	Hot Food Competition	This competition demonstrates foods that not only have to look great, but taste great as well.	F-1 Professional: Each competitor has four hours to prepare 10 servings of a four-course meal. Three plates are for judging, one for display, and the remaining six for individual plated service. F-2 Student: Each competitor has four hours to prepare 10 servings of a three-course menu consisting of a starter, entrée, and dessert. It should demonstrate knowledge of basic culinary skills such as knife skills and cooking techniques. Three plates are for judging, one for display, and the remaining six for individual plated service. F-3 Regional Tastes/Custom Competition: These are based on the ACF-approved guidelines and highlight regions' dishes or materials. Each of these must by the ACF. F-4 Nutritional Hot Food Challenge: This competition is a hot food competition that has a focus on nutrition. Each menu item must be selected in conjunction with the guidelines set forth by the USDA and the Department of Health and Human Resources. F-5 Pastry Mystery Basket: Each competitor has three hours to prepare 10 servings of three plated desserts: three plates for judging, one for display, and the remaining six for individual plated service.
G	Edible Cold Food	This competition highlights foods that are prepared and served cold. The sanitation standards for this competition are high. All food must be maintained at 41°F (5°C) or colder during the entire competition. (This is one of the more challenging competitions to compete in due to the nature of the food and the time involved—two 8-hour days.)	Cooking: One cold buffet or hors d'oeuvre platter with 8 to 10 portions. Pastry: One buffet platter with 8 to 10 portions of each variety of confectionery or dessert with theme.
H	Ice Carving	Ice carving is one of the more spectacular skills that a chef or culinarian can acquire. Huge blocks of ice are turned into graceful and awe-inspiring sculpture. Fragile as glass, and just as sparkling as diamonds, it takes an artistic flair to carve ice. It is also dangerous, and safety cannot be stressed enough. Chain saws, ice routers, and sharp saws can spell disaster in a split second of inattention. In judging, a safety violation can lead to a loss of points and even disqualification. In competitions, all carving is done on site and within a time limit. Multi-block carvings take more time and in some cases are team carved.	H-1 Single 300-lb block individual freestyle, 3-hour time limit. H-2 Two-person team, three blocks, 3 hours. H-3 Three-person team, five blocks, 3 hours. H-4 Two- or three-person team, 15 to 20 blocks, exhibition carving, 48-hour time limit, outdoors.

Category	Title	Description	Subcategories
K	Practical and Contemporary Hot Food Cooking	This category highlights the individual competitor's fabrication and cooking skills. Each competitor must prepare four portions in 60 minutes including the fabrication and cooking. An additional five minutes is allocated to plate the dish.	K-1 Rock Cornish game hen, chicken, or duck K-2 Bone-in pork loin K-3 Bone-in veal loin or rack K-4 Bone-in lamb loin or rack K-5 Game birds, pheasant, quail, squab, or guinea fowl K-6 Bone-in game (venison or antelope) racks or loin K-7 Whole rabbit K-8 Live lobster (kill and fabricate, cook to specifications) K-9 Fish fabrication, flat or round fish and cook to specifications K-10 Customized ACF chapters can sponsor a contemporary hot food competition that is sponsor- or product-driven. This competition must be approved by the ACF for sanctioned points.
P	Practical and Contemporary Patisserie	Competitors demonstrate their pastry and baking skills in the five subcategories of patisserie.	P-1 Hot/Warm desserts: Pastry chefs will have 60 minutes to prepare a hot or warm dessert of their choice, with 5 minutes to serve. P-2 Composed Cold Dessert: Pastry chefs will have 90 minutes to prepare the dessert of their choice, with 5 minutes to serve. P-3 Cake decoration: This competition demonstrates cake decorating. A theme is chosen by the judges at random, and the pastry chef has 60 minutes to prepare and decorate the cake to specifications. P-4 Marzipan Modeling: Competitors have 60 minutes to produce eight pieces total. The pieces must consist of two different sizes of figurines. Four of each size must be completed for the judges in the allotted time. P-5 Decorative Centerpiece: Sugar, chocolate, marzipan, pastillage, and many other sugar-based products are turned into sculpture. The pastry chef has 90 minutes to produce a decorative centerpiece.
S	Skill Sets Practical	This category is usually incorporated into other formats. The Junior ACF has this component added to demonstrate practical knife cuts such as tourney, brunoise, paysanne, rondelle, julienne, and other cuts.	S-1 Vegetables: 20 minutes to complete three randomly chosen knife cuts.

For molecular gastronomy ingredients, the following sources are available online:

>> *Agar Agar, Calcium Lactate, and Sodium Alginate*

Terra Spice Company
P.O. Box 26
605 Roosevelt Road
Walkerton, Indiana 46574
574.586.2600 (Phone)
574.586.2646 (Fax)
info@terraspicecompany.com

Chef Rubber
6627 Schuster St.
Las Vegas, NV 89118
(702) 614-9350
info@chefrubber.com
http://www.chefrubber.com/

Ajinomoto Foods
For wholesale purchase, "meat glue," dried glutamates, and transglutaminase:
http://www.ajiusafood.com/

For spices and herbs the following are good sources.

The Spice House
http://www.thespicehouse.com/
A great source for dried spices, herbs, and blends in Chicago and the Midwest; also available through mail order

Penzeys
http://www.penzeys.com/cgi-bin/penzeys/shophome.html
Excellent source of mail order spices, herbs, and oils

For fine chef's tools for cooking, baking, and serving:

J.B. Prince
(800) 473-0577 or fax us at anytime at (212) 683-4488
www.jbprince.com

>> Bibliography

101 Cookbooks One Recipe at a Time. 23 June 2007. http://www.101cookbooks.com/.

A La Cuisine. http://www.alacuisine.org/.

Ajinomoto Foods. 1 November 2007. http://www.ajiusafood .com/.

America, The Culinary Institute of. *Garde Manger.* New York: John Wiley & Sons Inc., 2004.

Artusi, Pellegrino. *Science in the Kitchen and the Art of Eating Well.* Toronto: University of Toronto Press, 2003.

Assorted Authors. *The Seafood Chef.* Salt Lake City. http://www.acrllc.com/index.php.

Bertolli, Paul. *Cooking by Hand.* New York: Clarkson Potter/Publishers, 2003.

Bertolli, Paul with Alice Waters. *Chez Panisse Cooking.* New York: Random House, 1990.

Brown, Amy. *Understanding Food, Principles and Preparation.* University of Hawaii at Manoa: Thomson Wadsworth, 2004.

Brown, Helen Evans. *West Coast Cook Book.* Pasadena, CA: Little Brown and Company Publishers, 1952.

Casas, Penelope. *Tapas, The Little Dishes of Spain.* New York: Knopf, 1987.

Culinary Institute of America. *The Professional Chef.* New York: John Wiley & Sons, 2002.

Danforth, Randi, Peter Feierabend, and Gary Chassman. *Culinaria, The United States.* New York: Konemann Publishers, 1998.

Davidson, Alan. *The Oxford Companion to Food.* Oxford: Oxford University Press, 1999.

Derrien, Marcel. *Buffets Sales L'Ecole Lenotre.* Les Lilas, France: Editions Jerome Villette, 1997.

Ducasse, Alain. *Grand Livre de Cuisine.* Paris: La Martiniere Groups/Aubin Printers, 2004.

Folse, John D., CEC AAC. *The Encyclopedia of Cajun and Creole Cuisine.* Gonzales, LA: John Folse and Company, Publishers, 2006.

Fortin, Francois, Editorial Director. *The Visual Food Encyclopedia.* Montreal: John Wiley & Sons, 1996.

Gastronomic Committee/Prosper Montagne. *Larousse Gastronomique.* New York: Random House, 2001.

Geddes, Bruce. *World Food Mexico.* Victoria, Australia: Lonely Planet Publications, 2000.

Gibbons, David, and Max McCalman. *The Cheese Plate.* New York: Clarkson Potter/Publishers, 2002.

Gisslen, Wayne. *Professional Cooking.* 6th ed. New York: John Wiley & Sons, 2007.

Greer, Anne Lindsay. *Cuisine of the American Southwest.* Greenwich, CT: Harper and Row, 1983.

Harbutt, Juliet. *The World Encyclopedia of Cheese.* New York: Lorenz Books, 1998.

Hasegawa, Hideo. *Ice Carving.* Carlsbad, CA: Continental Publications, 1974.

Heil, Andreas. *Creative Compositions.* Stuttgart, Germany: Matthaes Verlag GmbH, 2003.

Jenkins, Steven. *Cheese Primer.* New York: Workman Publishing, 1996.

Jones, Evan. *American Food.* New York: Random House, 1981.

Kilayke, Anton, and Christophe Megel. *An Asian Tapas.* Berkeley, CA: Periplus Editions, 2004.

Kinsella, John, and David T. Harvey. *Professional Charcuterie.* Cincinnati, OH: John Wiley & Sons, 1996.

Kiple, Kenneth F., and Kriemhild Conee Ornelas. *The Cambridge World History of Food Volumes One and Two.* Cambridge: Cambridge University Press, 2000.

Kotschevar, Lendal H., Ph.D. *Standards, Principles and Techniques in Quantity Food Production.* New York: Maple Press Company, 1975.

Kutas, Rytek. *Great Sausage Recipes.* Buffalo, NY: The Sausage Maker Inc., Self Published, 1984.

Labensky, Sarah R., and Alan M. Hause. O*n Cooking*, 4th Edition. New York: Pearson Prentice Hall, 2006.

Lersch, Martin. *Molecular Gastronomy.* 2007. http://khymos .org/.

Loken, Joan, CFE. *The HACCP Food Safety Manual.* New York: John Wiley & Sons, 1995.

Many Authors. *E-Gullet Society for Culinary Arts and Letters.* 2006/2007. http://forums.egullet.org/index.php?act=home.

Mariani, John F. *The Encyclopedia of American Food and Drink.* New York: Lebhar Friedman Books, 1999.

Matsuo, Yukio. *Ice Sculpture:Secrets of a Japanese Maste.* New York: John Wiley & Sons, 1992.

McGee, Harold. *On Food and Cooking.* New York: Scribner, 2004.

Mitterhauser, Klaus, and George K.Waldner. *The Professional Chef's Book of Buffets.* Boston: CBI Publishing Company, 1971.

Multiple Authors. *Epicurious, for People Who Love to Eat.* 2006/2007. http://www.epicurious.com/.

National Restaurant Association Educational Foundation. *ServSafe Essentials.* Chicago: National Restaurant Association Educational Foundation, 2006.

Norman, Jill. *Herbs and Spices: The Cook's Reference.* London: DK Publishing, 2002.

———. *The Cooks Book.* n.d.

North American Meat Processors Association. *The Meat Buyers Guide.* Reston, VA: John Wiley & Sons, May, 2003.

Paul, Pauline C., and Helen H. Palmer. *Food Theory and Applications.* New York: John Wiley & Sons, 1972.

Pauli, Eugen. *Classical Cooking the Modern Way.* Zurich: CBI Publishing Company, Inc., 1979.

Petersen, James. *Sauces: Classic and Contemporary Sauce Making.* New York, Wiley & Sons, Third edition 2009.

———. *Essentials of Cooking.* New York: Artisan Publishing, 1999.

Romans, John R., and William Costello. *The Meat We Eat.* Prentice Hall Publishers, 2000.

Ruffel, Denis. *The Professional Caterer Series.* Paris: Cicem/Van Nostrand Reinhold, 1990.

Sokolov, Raymond A. *The Saucier's Apprentice: A Modern Guide to Classic French Sauces for the Home.* n.d.

Sonnenschmidt, Frederic H., and Jean F. Nicolas. *Art of Garde Manger.* New York: CBI Publishing, 1982.

Stein, Stu. *The Sustainable Kitchen.* Portland, OR: New Society Publishers, 2004.

Stobart, Tom. *Herbs, Spices and Flavorings.* Woodstock: England Overlook Press, 2000.

Sylvestre, J., and J. Planche. *Fundamentals of French Cookery.* Paris: Jacques Lanore Publisher, 1969.

Talbot, Chefs Aki Kamozawa and H. Alexander. *Ideas in Food.* 2006/2007. http://ideasinfood.typepad.com/.

Tannahill, Reay. *Food in History.* New York: Three Rivers Press, 1988.

Terra Spice Company. *Industrial Spice and Herbs.* http://www.terraspicecompany.com/industrial.htm.

Terrell, Margaret E., and Dorothea B. Headlund. *Large Quantity Recipes.* New York: Van Nostrad Reinhold, 1989.

The Society for Food Science and Technology. *Institute of Food Technologists.* 2006/2007. http://www.ift.org/cms/.

This, Herve. *Molecular Gastronomy.* New York: Columbia University Press, 2006.

Villette, Jerome. *Les Buffets Sucres de L'Ecole Lenotre.* Les Lilas: France Editions Jerome Villette, 1997.

Walsh, Michael. *Food and Beverage International.* 2006/2007. http://fbworld.com/.

Wenzel, George L. *Wenzel's Menu Maker.* New York: CBI Books, imprint of Van Nostrand Reinhold Company, 1979.

Wolke, Robert L. *What Einstein Told His Cook.* New York: W.W. Norton and Company, 2002.

Yepsen, Roger B. *Home Food Systems.* Emmaus, PA: Rodale Press, 1981.

>> Glossary

à la greque (*ah-lah-GREHK*)—French meaning food prepared "in the Greek style." The term is used to describe a dish of mixed vegetables cooked in olive oil and white wine.

à la minute—"to the minute," meaning to cook food quickly to order. sautéing a chicken breast to order would be an example of á la minute cooking.

ACF competition rules—the information needed to compete in any local, state, regional, and national competition sanctioned by the American Culinary Federation.

acid—a material or substance with a pH lower than 7. Acids have a tart, sour flavor. Many foods are acidic and give different acid profiles to foods. Some examples are citric acid derived from lemons, acetic acid from wine and grapes, and malic acid from apple cider or apple products.

acidification—lowering the pH of a liquid by adding acid; for example, adding tartaric acid to milk to produce cheese.

action stations—areas where cooks prepare hot or cold dishes in front of the customers.

aerobic bacteria—microorganisms that live in the presence of oxygen.

aesthetic garnishes—garnishes used to heighten the visual appeal of a dish using vibrant colors, designs, clean lines, and neat appearances.

agar agar—vegetarian substance used to gel or thicken liquids. It is extracted from red seaweed *Gelidium amansii* and is used in place of animal-based gelatin.

agliata—garlic and walnut emulsion-based sauce.

aioli (*ay-OH-lee*)—a garlic mayonnaise from France that is used as a sauce and a condiment. Was originally thickened with cooked potatoes and garlic that were first pounded to a paste in a mortar; olive oil was streamed in and mixed to form a thick, potent sauce.

albacore—species of tuna known for its white meat; has a dry texture and a taste that resembles the taste of chicken meat.

albumin—egg-white protein used as a binder in forcemeat preparations.

al dente—"to the tooth"; tender yet with a bite.

alginates—alginates are cell-wall constituents of brown algae (Phaeophyceae). Alginates are used in combination with calcium substances to form foods into spheres, fluid gels, and other thickening and gelification processes.

alkali—a material or substance with a pH higher than 7. Baking soda is an example of an alkaline substance.

allium—perennial bulbous plants related to lily and iris, indigenous to northern temperate climates. Onions, shallots, leeks, and herbs such as garlic and chives are the edible members of the allium family and provide important flavor components to recipes.

allumette—potatoes cut into fine julienne or matchstick, 1/8 by 1/8 by 2 inches in length.

amuse-bouche (*ah-muz-boosh*)—little samples or bites of food to amuse the mouth, invigorate the palate, and whet the appetite. Usually served as a free amusement for guests while they wait for their meal to start.

anaerobic bacteria—microorganisms that live in an oxygen-free environment; for example, *Clostridium botulinum*.

andouille—French pork sausage that is highly spicy and redolent with garlic; is often thought of as a Cajun specialty.

antioxidant—compound that inhibits oxidation, enzymic browning of fruit, and rancidity.

antipasto—meat, cheese, pickled vegetables, and olives served together as an appetizer or hors d'oeuvre. It means "before the pasta" in Italian.

Apicius—Roman gourmand of incredible wealth. He or one of his ancestors named Apicus left recipes and is credited with writing the first cookbook. His notes were compiled and published about three centuries later.

appetizer—food or drink served before a meal to stimulate the appetite, which is often found on menus as a first course.

arm service—the term given to hand-carried plate service. The waitstaff can safely carry up to three plates of food with their hands and arms, which is where this type of service got its name.

aromatics—highly scented and flavored herbs, spices, and vegetables used to bring out and heighten the flavors of foods.

aspic—clear savory jelly made from meat, fish, vegetable stock, or fruit juice and gelatin.

aspic jelly—meat- or fish-flavored jelly used as a garnish, decorating glaze, and flavor component. As a glaze, aspic is used to coat and protect foods, like a varnish.

bacteria—microscopic organisms that can cause benefit or harm depending upon the type. Beneficial bacteria are responsible for fermentation and flavors in cheese, meat, wine, and bread. Harmful bacteria can cause food-borne illness.

bain-marie—water bath used to heat or cook foods in a gentle heat, or hold foods for service at a safe temperature; also known as a double boiler.

ballotine (*bahl-lo-teen*)—from the French word *ballot,* which means bundle or to roll around. Unlike galantines, which are always served cold, ballotines are usually served hot. Ballotines are usually boned and stuffed poultry leg and thigh.

Banquet Event Order (BEO)—complete instruction sheet giving all the details of an event.

barding—tying thin sheets of pork fat back or bacon over lean meats to keep the meat moist and tender during roasting and baking.

barquette (*bahr-KEHT*)—oval, boat-shaped, small baked dough shells that are filled and topped with a garnish.

base—the platform or vehicle upon which a canapé is traditionally built. These consist of traditional breads or updated versions consisting of pita wedges; rye or oat crackers; potato crisps; small, boiled, creamer potatoes; vegetable chips such as beet chips; apple or pear crisps; corn and flour tortillas; chapattis; lavash; wonton; and rice paper.

batonette—small bat- or stick-shaped vegetable cut, 1/4 by 1/4 by 2 inches in length.

bechamel—white or cream sauce made with a white roux and milk, flavored with an onion pique. Considered one of the grand, or mother, sauces of classical French cooking, it originated in Italy and is used for chaud froid and as a base for savory soufflés.

bercy butter (*bair-SEE*)—French compound butter blended with white wine, parsley, lemon, shallots, salt, and pepper.

binder—a protein- or carbohydrate-based substance that is used to hold ingredients together, such as a rice or bread panade, nonfat milk powder, or egg albumin.

binding agent—canapé spread, usually fat-based, that is used to coat and seal bread to keep it from getting soggy and to prevent the toppings from sliding off of a canapé.

biological contaminants—types of contaminants that include molds, fungi, bacteria, viruses, parasites, certain plant and mushroom products that contain poisons and alkaloids, as well as seafoods that contain neurotoxins.

blanch—to plunge food into boiling water or oil to par-cook or set the color.

blast chiller—also known as a blast shocker, blast chillers are freezer/chillers that use convection cold air to reduce the temperature of food in a few minutes by using fans to circulate chilled air.

blender stick—stick or immersion blender; consists of a long handle with a small propeller at the end, turning at several thousand revolutions per minute. When the stick is placed in the bottom of a container, it will blend, purée, or pulverize material in a very short time.

blini—small buckwheat griddle cakes that are the traditional accompaniment with caviar.

bloom—(n) fuzzy white growth of mold commonly found on rind-ripened cheese such as brie. (v) to soften gelatin in cold water before dissolving with heat.

blue-veined cheese—a pungent cheese produced from sheep and cows' milk. Sometimes referred to as "bleu"; has veins of greenish-blue, edible penicillin mold. Blues are some of the oldest styles of cheese around.

borscht—beet-based soup found in Russia and Eastern European cuisine. May be made with beef or pork, or vegetarian. Traditionally garnished with sour cream.

botulism—usually fatal infection caused by *Clostridium botulinum,* an anaerobic bacterium that does not grow well in refrigeration. It is found in produce associated with soil such as potatoes, onions, garlic, and other root vegetables. It was common in early sausages due to their high fat content and lack of oxygen, but with the addition of sodium nitrates and sodium nitrites, this threat was reduced.

boudain noir (boudin) in Louisiana (*BOO-danh*)—blood sausage made with liquid blood, rice, and diced fat.

bouquet garni—a collection of herbs and aromatic vegetables tied together in a bundle; typical ingredients include celery, thyme, parsley, carrots, and leeks.

brassica—any of several cruciferous plants of the genus *Brassica.* The brassica family is comprised of a large variety of leafy or flowering plants ranging from mustard and cabbage, grown for their edible foliage, to cauliflower and broccoli, grown for their edible flower stalks.

bresaola (*brehsh-ay-OH-lah add*)—dried, salted beef filet.

brine—water, salt, and sugar mixture used to cure and flavor protein-based foods.

brining—process for wet-curing preserves and flavoring foods; can improve the tenderness of meat. Brining begins with salts and other dry ingredients such as sodium erythorbate, sodium nitrite, and sugar, which are dissolved in water.

brunoise—1/8th by 1/8th by 1/8th inch square dice.

brunoisette—smaller version of brunoise, 1/16th by 1/16th by 1/16th inch.

buffalo chopper—food chopper considered the workhorse machine in medium to large kitchens; used to chop foods to a uniform size or grind meats or other foods to a medium to fine paste; useful when making large quantities of forcemeats, breadcrumbs, or chopped vegetables. This machine consists of a side motor with an attached rotating bowl and a vertical knife rotating under a protective cowling or cover; the bowl turns when the machine is in use.

buffet—term used when food is placed on stationary tables. Serving equipment such as chaffers, portable steam tables, or bain-maries are used to keep the food hot; ice glows, ice bowls, or tubs are used to keep the cold items chilled.

butler service—method in which food and beverages are put on platters or small trays, carried by servers around the room, and the customers take what they like; the common phrase in addition to butler service is "passed."

C

canapé—small, one to two bite hors d'oeuvre, consisting of a base of bread or other pastry or flour product, topped with flavorful foods such as cheese spreads, anchovies, ham, and other savory foods.

Carême, Marie-Antoine (1783–1833)—the most famous author and culinary artist of his time; he was known for his complex architectural centerpieces. He is considered "the father of haute or grand cuisine," and instituted the practice of using elegant and beautifully designed buffet tables that continues on in our time.

carving stations—area in a buffet where the cook or chef slices meat or fish as ordered and serves the guest.

casein—milk protein found in dairy products that, when acidified, clumps up and curdles to form curds.

casing—the intestinal lining or a synthetic, collagen-based tubing used to encase ground forcemeat.

caul fat—lacy fat membrane from the pig or sheep that is used to wrap or bard meat, pâté, ballotines, and other forcemeat products.

celeriac—also known as knob celery, a specially adapted variety of celery, grown for its large root; is the size of a small potato and is used cooked as well as fresh. Root vegetables are perfect for autumn and winter salads.

cephalopod—a class of mollusks with soft bodies; a thin, cartilage-like internal structure; a hard-shelled beak; long, sucker-laden arms; and the ability to swim rapidly through the water to great depths. Calamari, giant squid, and octopus are in this group.

cereal grains—plants that yield an edible grain such as wheat, rye, oats, rice, or corn.

chalaeza—the protein filament that holds and anchors the yolk to the albumin and shell inside of an egg.

charcuterie (*shahr-coo-tuhr-EE*)—term used to describe products made from pork; can also include products made from beef, veal, lamb, poultry, game, and seafood, as well as the production of sausages, pâté, terrines, galatines, and other similar foods.

chaud froid (*shoh-FRWAH*)—dishes prepared hot and served cold.

cheesecloth—cotton muslin or fine-meshed cloth used originally to strain curds in the cheesemaking process; has many additional uses such as straining stocks and sauces, and as a sachet bag for aromatic herbs and spices.

chef garde manger—the cook or chef in charge of the cold kitchen.

chefs de partie—chef responsible for a section in a kitchen, third in line behind the Sous Chef and Executive Chef. This chef is frequently a banquet chef responsible for a small crew or a lead line.

chemical contaminants—chemical contaminants that include heavy metal, alkaloids, acids, insecticides, bactericides, herbicides, cleaning materials, and petroleum-based products along with cookware that can leach poisonous minerals into the food such as lead, copper sulfate, and, in some cases, radioactive material from some glazed pottery serving dishes.

chermoula (*chair-moo-lah*)—Moroccan marinade made with a variety of herbs and spices; usually used to flavor fish, but it can be used with vegetables or various meats.

chiffonade—leafy vegetables and herbs cut into fine threads; used primarily as a garnish.

chinoise—fine-mesh wire china cap for straining sauces.

chop—to chop or dice roughly into pieces of approximately the same dimensions.

chow chow—relish made with green tomatoes, onions, and other typical garden vegetables; comes from the Southern United States and is still a popular chunky condiment with beans or cooked greens.

chutney—from the Sanskrit word *chatni,* meaning "to lick"; in India today, the word simply means "mixture." Chutney can be fresh or cooked but is generally made from fruit, vinegar, sugar, and spices.

clarification—to remove scum or foam from a liquid or to use a protein-based substance to remove particles from stock.

cleaning—removing food or various types of soil from surfaces such as equipment, cookware, and dishware by using hot water, soap, or detergent and physical agitation or action.

clearmeat—a mixture of poultry or lean meat, egg whites, mirepoix, aromatics, and an acid-based product such as tomatoes, ground fine and added to stock to clarify for consomme.

coagulate—to clump, clot, or become semi-solid by heating or treating protein compounds with an acid.

coagulation—precipitation or clumping of proteins in a liquid into a semi-solid material such as cheese curds.

cold sauces—the basic cold sauce is the egg-based mayonnaise; many other ingredients including tomatoes, mustard, and whipped cream are used to change flavor and consistency.

cold smoking—method of curing that preserves and/or flavors food products by exposing them to smoke over a much longer period of time than is required for hot smoking, taking from several hours up to several days. The product is still technically raw as the temperature is never above 90°F (35°C).

collagen—fibrous protein that supports the muscles and is the primary protein found in connective tissue.

collagen casings—manufactured casings used for sausage making. Made from the hides and hooves of animals; they come in dried tubes that ensure uniformity and ease of storage.

compote—dried and fresh fruit chopped and cooked in a simple syrup with spices.

compotier (*KAHM-poht-tee-ay*)—a stand made of glass, china, or metal, usually with a center post, to serve dainty sandwiches, candies, and assorted cold tidbits.

compound butter—softened whole butter with aromatic materials mixed in, such as herbs, spices, wines, vinegars, or flavorful vegetables added for flavor and color; used on cooked foods for additional flavors and moisture.

concassé—blanched, shocked, peeled, seeded, and coarsely chopped tomatoes.

condiment—savory or aromatic mixture such as ketchup, relishes, chutneys, and other sauces used to flavor, enhance, and accompany foods.

confit—a French method of preserving meat, particularly duck or goose. The leg sections are salted to first cure, then cooked at a low simmer for several hours in rendered duck or goose fat; the whole pieces are cooled and stored submerged in the fat until needed.

consommé—fortified and clarified stock used as a soup, or in the making of aspic.

cook component garnishes—garnish used as a component of the dish, such as a carved rose, orange segments, or melon balls.

cooked dressings—dressings that contain a variety of ingredients that are cooked before being served; the dressing can be served hot or cold, depending on the recipe.

cooking stations—an area in a buffet where foods are cooked to finish, such as an omelet station or pasta station; typically, electrical or butane stoves and portable steam tables or chaffers are used for cooking.

corning—method of curing named after the "corns" or grains of salt used in earlier times to cure beef and pork in a salty brine.

coulis—puréed fruit or vegetables used for sauces; originally comes from puréed proteins such as shellfish or meat juices.

court bouillon—"short broth" made from water, an acid such as wine or vinegar, aromatic vegetables, and herbs; used for poaching fish and other tender proteins.

cream dressings—dressings made with dairy as a base ingredient.

crème fraiche—cultured cream with a thick consistency used in an assortment of sauces; it resists curdling when heated.

crissini—long, thin bread sticks use for hors d'oeuvre.

critical control points—each step in the total process of making food, from the purchasing, cooking, chilling, heating, storing, and serving, where contamination might occur.

croquette (*kroh-keht*)—cooked ingredients such as meats or vegetables thickened with sauce, shaped when cold, breaded, and fried.

cross-contamination—the transfer of disease-carrying microorganisms from one source to another through direct physical contact.

croustade—French term for containers that can be filled with a variety of filling; the most common is hollowed out bread slices, fried or baked pastries, and even crisped potato skins.

crouton—bread that has been cut into cubes or slices, and then lightly oiled, seasoned, and baked off to a crisp; used as a crisp garnish to soups and salads.

crudité—raw vegetables cut into manageable pieces and used as hors d'oeuvre; often served with a dip.

crustaceans—animals with a segmented shell and joined legs; shrimp, crab, lobster, and crayfish are some of the more common examples.

cucurbitaceae—plant family commonly known as *gourds* or *cucurbits;* includes cucumbers, squashes, pumpkins, melons, and watermelons.

culinary judge—trained and experienced chef who has won competitions and has met criteria set forth by the governing body that certifies the competition; required to be as impartial as possible.

Culinary Salon—culinary competition or show in which competitions take place.

curd—the thickened or coagulated protein that remains from milk treated with acids and heat.

curing—method of processing foods to stop them from spoiling. To preserve foods, specifically meat, poultry, and seafood proteins, a preserving chemical or curing agent must be used. Salt, nitrate or nitrite, sugar, and other chemical compounds are used to preserve the flesh, as well as enhance or protect the color and flavor.

curry—from the Indian word *kari* or sauce; a mixture of many aromatic vegetables such as onions, garlic, and ginger, sautéed with whole spices and used as the basis for innumerable Indian sauces; usually finished with garam masala.

curry powder—spice blend invented by the English that contains fenugreek, cumin, chilies, cardamom, fennel seed, and a host of other aromatic spices; is reminiscent of India.

D

dariole—small, oval-shaped mold used to make custard or mousseline-based products.

dead dough—dough that does not contain yeast or any active ingredients, so there is no chance of it rising; also called *sculpture dough.*

dehydrator—a new device that is cropping up in cold kitchens that uses ancient technology. In the quest for new ideas, innovative chefs have happened on the idea of concentrating flavors through dehydration. Dehydrators are used to dehydrate fruits and vegetables to concentrate flavors, develop new textures in old standbys, and expand flavors in foods by circulating warm or hot air.

depurations—a process in which caught shellfish are placed in a treated water solution and allowed to purge sand, excrement, and other impurities. This treatment assures a higher standard of sanitation and a longer shelf-life in oysters, clams, and mussels. With the health concerns of contaminated seafood, this is a good way to ensure a safer product for dining customers.

dice—to cut ingredients into precise, even pieces; 1/4 by 1/4 by 1/4 inch diameter for small dice, 1/2 by 1/2 by 1/2 for medium dice, or 3/4 by 3/4 by 3/4 for large dice.

dim sum—tea time, small menu items individually served from carts; has come to mean small Chinese appetizers and hors d'oeuvre.

dip—thick condiments that are usually made with a sour cream, mayonnaise, cream cheese base, and purée vegetables; served with crudities, crackers, chips, and appetizers.

dondine—a boned duck that is stuffed with forcemeat, rolled, and cooked in the same manner as a ballontine.

drawn fish—a whole fish with head, fins, and tails intact, with scales and viscera removed.

dressed—fish that has been gutted with head, fins, and tail removed, or poultry with viscera, head, feet, and feathers removed, ready for cooking.

drupes—also called *stone fruits,* have a single large seed encased in a hard shell; the shell is called the pit or stone. The fleshy part of the fruit totally surrounds the pit.

dry cure—salt, TCM, spices, and sometimes sugar mixture used to draw out moisture of protein products, usually before smoking.

dry-rind cheeses—semi-soft cheeses that develop a dry rind during the ripening process. They do not receive any washing down, so the skin dehydrates and protects the interior. Because stronger-flavored bacteria do not attach themselves to the rind, these cheeses tend to be much less pungent. Most have a buttery flavor and a slightly firm but tender texture.

E

egg wash—eggs, water, and salt mixture used to coat pastry dough before baking to give a shine to the product, and produce a somewhat water-resistant surface.

emincer—to cut into fine, thin strips.

emulsified dressings—dressings that consist of mayonnaise, egg yolks, or other emulsifying or thickening agents, herbs, spices, and flavorful ingredients.

emulsifiers—ingredients that contain both hydrophobic and hydrophilic properties that enable two immiscible liquids to join together, such as oil and vinegar; some common emulsifiers used in the cold kitchen are egg yolks, dry mustard, paprika, and lecithin.

emulsion—liquid dispersed in another liquid in which it is usually incapable of being mixed, such as oil and water.

en croûte (*ahm-KROOT*)—forcemeat baked in crust.

Escoffier, Auguste (1846–1935)—chef who organized kitchens into clearly defined stations. Under this system refined by Escoffier, the chef saucier made all sauces and sauté dishes, the chef rôtisseur made all roasts, and the chef poissonier cooked all poached fish dishes. Escoffier is considered the "Father of modern French Cuisine,"and his pioneering work is considered the foundation of much of our modern technique and terminology.

extenders—inexpensive ingredients, usually starch-based, added to meat, poultry, and seafood forcemeats.

F

fabricated cuts—roasts, steaks, chops, cutlets, stewing meats, ground meat, etc., as set forth by the IMPS/NAMPS specifications, and even smaller cuts used for foodservice.

farce—*farci* means "stuffed," so a farce is a forcemeat or stuffing mixture.

FAT TOM—an easy way to remember how to keep bacteria away: F = food; A = acidity; T = temperature; T = time; O = oxygen; and M = moisture.

fatback—snow-white pork fat from the top of the pig; used in sheets or cut into long strips for barding and larding meats.

fermentation—process of yeast acting upon the sugars and starches in foods to break them down into alcohol, carbon dioxide, and organic acids for preservation and flavor.

FIFO—first in, first out.

filet or fillet—boneless cut of fish, poultry, or meat.

fines herbes—"fine herbs" in French, this mixture is usually parsley, tarragon, chervil, and chives, finely chopped to the consistency of fine sand, used as a flavoring element or as a garnish.

flatfish—fish with uneven, flattened bodies, both eyes on the top of their head, a light sandy to dark camouflaged top skin to match the environment, and a snow-white bottom side; they swim horizontally and are generally found in deep ocean waters.

fleur de sel—French term for "Flowers of Salt." It is the salt that is collected by hand from the salt marshes near the village of Guerande in Brittany during the months of July and August. These salt crystals resemble flowers, hence the name fleur or flower of salt.

flushing—nitrogen gas used to flush seafood in the process of vacuum packaging to enhance the red color by avoiding the oxidation of the myoglobin; also a process to remove excess salt from cured products by rinsing.

focaccia (*foh-CAH-chee-ah*)—Italian style flat breads made with flour, water, salt, yeast, and olive oil.

foie gras—true foie gras is the fattened liver of geese, but the term has come to mean fattened duck liver as well. Duck or geese are fattened by the process known as gavage, or force feeding, so that the liver grows to three times the normal size.

forcemeat—a mixture of finely chopped and seasoned meat, fish, or seafood often containing egg whites and cream.

freezer spray—a canned product that rapidly reduces the temperature of ice. Some ice carvers prefer to use it to reattach broken pieces.

french—to clean the sinew and tissue off of the rib bones of chops and drumsticks for presentation.

fresh cheese—cheese that has not been aged. Shortly after these cheeses are made, they are ready to be consumed; they rely solely on some type of acidification for their character.

fruit—botanically the developed ovary of a seed plant with its contents and accessory parts, like the pea pod, nut, tomato, pineapple, etc., or the edible part of a plant developed from a flower with any accessory tissues, like the peach, mulberry, banana, etc.

fumet—poaching liquid consisting of water, an acid such as wine or lemon juice, and aromatic vegetables and herbs.

G

galangal root—a rhizome that is closely related to ginger; native to Southeast Asia; has a peppery ginger-like flavor and texture, with a slightly pink color.

galantine—forcemeat that is stuffed into the skin of boned poultry or fish, shaped into a log or sausage shape, and then poached in a flavorful stock. The word *galantine* comes from the Latin term *gallianceus,* referring to poultry.

garde manger (*gahr mohn-zahj*)—most commonly, "to protect or guard" the "manger," a place where the animals were kept in ancient times; it literally translates to "guarding or keeping edibles." Modern, large production kitchens refer to this area as the pantry section, cold kitchen, or garde manger. This is the area in the kitchen where all cold foods are prepared and stored. The task of producing items from the cold kitchen is also called garde manger, so the term *garde manger* is both a noun and a verb, depending on how it is used.

garnish—edible decoration to accompany foods.

gazpacho—cold soup often thought of as a liquid soup, originating in Andalusia, Spain. This soup always contains stale bread, chopped vegetables, garlic, vinegar, water, and olive oil. There are many varieties of gazpacho today, some containing grapes and almonds.

gelatin—the sticky, collagen-based protein derived from veal knuckles, pork feet, or pork skin, or in the case of fish stock, by adding gelatin.

gelatinization—process that occurs when starch is heated and the molecules swell and break to form a matrix to trap free water or moisture; used to thicken sauces and other mixtures.

gelatinous—referring to a texture that is slightly firm and gummy, not quite a liquid. "Gelatinous" liquid that has been thickened or gelled with gelatin, starch, agar agar, or other types of gel-producing substances.

glace—to reduce a liquid to a semi-solid, viscose state.

glace de vinade (*glahs duh vee-AHND*)—reduced brown stock that is similar to syrup in consistency.

glaze—to coat food with a shiny substance such as aspic, sauce, or glace to enhance the appearance and flavor of the food.

goujon—cutting fish filets into small strips or steaks.

grana cheese—sheep and cows' milk in origin, grana, or grating cheese, is extra dry with a crumbly, granular interior and firm dry texture; hence the name. Used as a grating cheese in blends or as an accompaniment with fruit and wine for an appetizer.

gratiné—forcemeat that has a large part of the main meat ingredient browned or seared first and cooled for extra flavor and texture; can also refer to top browning of product under a broiler or salamander.

gravlax (*GRAHV-lahks*)—Swedish specialty that has become a popular item on many menus; consists of salmon that has been cured with a sugar, salt, and dill mixture.

green peppercorns—pepper berries that are picked before they are ripe and either air-dried, freeze dried, or pickled in a brine to prevent fermentation.

grinder—machines used to grind foods into smaller pieces such as a meat grinder, spice grinder, or grain grinder; an auger bit pushes the food into a blade or against a stone to grind or smash the food into smaller pieces or particles.

guilds—associations formed during the Middle Ages to protect and promote specific trades and products.

gyro—Greek sandwich made from formed beef and/or lamb that is shaped into a large cylinder and grilled, from which slices of meat are carved off and served on a toasted pita with tzatziki, grilled onions, and tomatoes.

H

HACCP—acronym for Hazard Analysis Critical Control Point. The program was developed by the Pillsbury Company for the NASA space program and defined over the years by the federal government through a national advisory committee. It has since been adopted for use in foodservice operations around the country. This system uses a scientific approach that follows the flow of food through the foodservice operation and identifies each step in the process, known as critical control points, where contamination might occur.

hard cheese—cheese made from goat, sheep, and cows' milk; has a firm, slightly crumbly interior texture; most well-known varieties are cheddar and Swiss.

head cheese—also known as *Braun,* gelled meat product made from the cured and cooked head of pork containing the chopped cheek meat and tongue, along with the gelled stock; flavored with vinegar, red peppers, and black pepper.

Heimlich maneuver—developed by Henry J. Heimlich, the approved method of helping choking victims by using a series of under-the-diaphragm abdominal thrusts to dislodge any foreign object in the windpipe of the victim.

herb—the leaves of herbaceous plants (plants with stalks that are soft and green compared to plants with woody stems) used to add flavor to foods; usually associated with savory foods.

Herbes de Provence (*AIRBS duh proh-VAWNS*)—herb blend originating in the Provence region of France; consists of dried marjoram, thyme, sage, basil, rosemary, summer savory, fennel seeds, and lavender.

hock—ankle of the pig, lamb, or cow; a good source of collagen in stock making.

hog casings—casing or wrapping made from the cleaned and bleached small and middle intestines of hogs.

hot-smoking—way to preserve, cure, and/or flavor foods by exposing them to temperatures between 200–250°F (95–120°C) in a commercial smoker with a gas or electrical unit; the wood chips or coals smolder in the unit and provide enough heat to cook and smoke the product at the same time.

hummus—dip made from an exotic blend of ground chickpeas, lemon, tahini, and spices.

hydroponic—plants grown without soil in a special growing medium, and fed liquid nutrients.

I

IKAHOGA—acronym for Internationale Kochkunstaustellung, also known as Culinary Olympics; the most prestigious Culinary Salon in the world.

immersion circulator—also called *water bath machine;* machines that maintain the temperature of the water surrounding sealed foods; capable of circulating and holding temperatures at precise increments.

induction stove—stove that heats rapidly using a specialized magnetic field top with a steel pan; the pan gets hot but the stove stays cool to the touch.

infused oils—oils combined with aromatic ingredients such as fresh herbs, peppers, chilies, and other aromatics for flavor.

intermezzo—traditionally a short and inexpensive course used to refresh the palate; is usually a cold, acidic sorbet or granite used to clear the palate after heavier courses in preparation for the entrée to come.

IQF—acronym for individually quick frozen.

J

jerk—term that supposedly came from the Spanish word for "dried meat"; most commonly now refers to highly spiced and seasoned meat from Jamaica.

julienne—vegetables cut into small thin strips, 1/8 by 1/8 by 2 inches; fine julienne is 1/16 by 1/16 by 2 inches.

jus—juice.

jus Lie—meat juice thickened slightly by first reducing, then adding, a small amount of arrowroot.

K

kaltschale—German style cold sweet soup traditionally made from fruit, cider, beer, and dairy products.

L

lard—purified pork fat used for frying and for some pie crusts; *larding* means to thread strips of fat through lean muscle meat for added juiciness and flavor, before roasting or braising.

lardon—strip of pork fat or bacon used to lard or when cooked used as a garnish.

lecithin—a lipid material composed of choline and inositol; is found in all living cells as a major component of cell membranes. It is used as an emulsifying agent and is found in egg yolks and soy beans. Most lecithin used in foodservice is extracted from soy beans.

legume—the edible fruit from the legume family, including beans and peas, lentils, and peanuts. Legumes have an outer shell pod or legume covering the internal seed; the pod splits open into two sections to reveal the seeds inside.

liaison—mixture of cream and egg yolks used to enrich a sauce or soup; added after the cooking to avoid curdling.

link—segmenting of sausages by twisting at equidistant intervals.

liquid smoke—distillate of smoke used as a flavoring ingredient only.

low-fat dressings—dressings that are made with little to no fat and thickened with starch or other nonfat compound such as xanthan gum.

lox—salt- and sugar-cured salmon.

M

Madeira wine—sweet fortified wine from Portugal.

magret—duck breasts taken from the ducks that produce the liver for foie gras.

maillard reaction—browning as a result of the interaction of carbohydrates and proteins during the cooking or searing process; enhances the flavors of meat and baked goods.

mandoline—cutting tool for making gaufrettes, julienne, and batonnet vegetables, and for shredding and slicing vegetables and potatoes.

Marie-Antoine Carême (1783–1833)—the most famous author and culinary artist of his time; he was known for his complex architectural centerpieces. He is considered "the father of haute or grand cuisine," and instituted the practice of using elegant and beautifully designed buffet tables that continues on in our time.

marinades—liquids that typically consist of an acidic ingredient such as wine and/or vinegar, spices, and oil-or enzyme-based tenderizers such as the protease papain found in papayas.

mayonnaise—cold egg-based emulsion sauce with vinegar, lemon juice, salt, mustard, and oil.

mesophile—bacteria that live within the middle range temperature of 60°F to 100°F (15 1/2° C to 38°C); a bacterial starter in cheese making.

mezze—Mediterranean term for hors d'oeuvre or "before the meal snack."

microgreens—baby sprouts of lettuce, broccoli, and other green vegetables used as garnishment salads.

mimosa—hard-cooked eggs finely sieved used as a garnish for salads and other cold dishes; the garnish of chopped eggs resembling mimosa tree blossoms.

mince—to dice or chop into ultrafine pieces.

mirepoix—diced or chopped aromatic vegetables, 50 percent onions, 25 percent carrots, and 25 percent celery, used to flavor stocks, sauces, soups, and any other liquid-based cooking medium.

mise en place—a place for everything and everything in its place; the general term for having one's station prep set and ready to go up to the point of cooking the meal.

molecular gastronomy—the study of the molecular breakdown of proteins, fats, carbohydrates, sugars, and water and the manipulation of ingredients to apply these macronutrients into breakout food concepts and trends. Term coined by the late Nicholas Kurti, a Hungarian physicist, and Hervé This, a French scientist who runs the "gastronomie moléculaire" at the College de France in Paris.

mollusk—soft sea animals with unsegmented bodies living within a singular or pair of calcified, hard, hinged shells.

monounsaturated fats—in nutrition, fatty acids having a single double bond present in the fatty acid chain, with all of the carbons in the chain single-bonded carbons; this is in contrast to polyunsaturated fatty acids, which have more than one double bond. Monounsaturated fats are found in natural foods like nuts and avocados, and are the main component of olive oil; also found in grapeseed oil, peanut oil, canola oil, sesame oil, and corn oil.

mousse—a foamy dessert or savory dish made from a flavorful base that has been stabilized with gelatin and lightened with egg foam and whipped cream.

mousseline—a smooth, light forcemeat made from puréed protein lightened with egg and cream and gently seasoned; a sauce based upon Hollandaise and whipped cream.

MSDS—acronym for Material Safety Data Sheets; the book that contains all of the information on chemical products that an establishment is using.

MSDS book—Material Safety Data Sheets bound in a book and located where all staff can access them, usually near where chemicals and cleaners are stored.

N

nappe—to coat with a sauce, or to thicken a sauce to the nappe stage; demonstrated by coating the back of a spoon.

natural casing—casing used in sausage from a natural source such as a lamb or pig intestine.

nitrate—a food additive used to stabilize the color of meats in the curing and smoking process. It is found in plant substances and is used in the form of sodium nitrate and potassium nitrate in the preservation of food; is also an antioxidant.

nitrite—the chemical that is converted from nitrates; is derived from fruit and vegetative matter and is used in the process of curing meats that are smoked. It is one of the only chemicals that can stop botulism from forming in cured meats and is used for this purpose in dried sausages and other cured products as well as color enhancement of the myoglobin, which ensures a bright red or pink color.

NSF—acronym for National Sanitation Federation; the organization that gives the seal of approval to products that pass a high level of safety and sanitation.

O

offals (*OWF-fuhlz*)—edible internal organ meats, including liver, kidneys, and other variety meat; comes from the meat industry's early history of describing internal organs as "off falling" from the carcass.

onion pique—whole peeled onion with a bay leaf and a clove nail inserted into it to give flavor to béchamel and some cream soups.

orange supreme—from the orange, use a paring knife to completely remove the skin and the pith. Carefully cut the orange into segments or supremes by cutting next to the segment layer, removing the meat between each membrane, being careful to remove all skin and seeds.

oxidation—enzymic browning caused by exposure to air and oxygen.

P

pain de mie—basic white pan bread.

panadas (*pah-nahd*)—a binding agent that improves the texture of forcemeat by holding it together; from *pan,* the Latin word for bread; usually a cooked carbohydrate substance such as bread, rice, or cooked potatoes.

panini—plural for "panino" sandwiches that originated in Italy but are very popular in the United States. Panini sandwiches consist of ciabatta bread, assorted meats, and cheeses, which are then heated in a Panini press.

pantry—derived from *paneterie,* "bread room," a storage place for bread and condiments and for tableware between the kitchen and the dining room. In restaurant kitchens, pantries became service stations that prepare to order a wide array of cold dishes, sandwiches, hot beverages, and often desserts.

panzanella—utilization salad made from leftover bread, onions, tomatoes, and vinaigrette.

parcook—to blanch or partially cook an item.

pasta filata—literally means "spun curds" or "spun paste." There are many different types of pasta filata-style cheese. After the initial curds are developed, the curds are then placed in hot water, slightly melting them, whereas the cheesemaker takes them from the hot water and stretches or spins them until the desired shape and texture is achieved.

pasteurization—process of heating a liquid to a high temperature to kill dangerous organisms, usually 160°F (71°C) or higher, for a minimum of 15 seconds.

pâté— the French word for "pie"; generally used in connection with pies made with seasoned meats (often liver) from poultry, beef, pork, game, or seafood. There are also vegetable pâtés.

pâté de campagna—"country style" forcemeat that is coarse in texture and made from chopped pork products, pork liver, pork fat, spices, and garnishments.

paysanne—a vegetable cut in which the product is cut into triangles, squares, or small circles no more than 1/8 inch thick and 1/2 inch in diameter.

pellicle—a scab-like skin that forms on protein after curing and drying, or air drying, in preparation for smoking; keeps the smoke on the surface of the product during the smoking process.

pemmican—a mixture of fatty game or buffalo meat pounded into a paste and flavored with dried wild berries.

pH level—test for determining the acid or alkaline content or level of a liquid or semi-liquid.

phyllo (Filo)—tissue-paper-thin pastry sheets layered with melted butter to form several assorted flaky, savory, and sweet pastry items; used as a dessert pastry for baklava and spanikopita, a Greek spinach and feta cheese pastry.

physical contaminants—any physical object that gets lost into food products, such as shards of glass, staples from lettuce boxes, dirt, bugs, bandages, jewelry, fingernails, bones, and hair.

piccalilli—sauce that traditionally consists of vegetables, including green tomatoes that are finely diced; is made of vinegar, spices, and mustard. In this case, the mustard flavor comes from the mustard seeds.

pickling—cures that have sugar and sometimes vinegar or some other type of acid added.

pièces montées—elaborate edible buffet and table centerpieces.

pink peppercorn—expensive little berries that are cousins to the ragweed and cashew families and are not considered a true pepper. They are bright pink to red in color and are used for their added color.

polyunsaturated fats (polyunsaturated fatty acids)—a fatty acid in which more than one double bond exists within the representative molecule; they come from corn, soy, sunflower, and safflower. This type of fat may lower your blood cholesterol level when you use it in place of saturated and trans fats.

pomes—fruits with small seeds or pits that are found in the center of the fruit; when the fruit is sliced horizontally, the seeds form a star configuration.

prague powder #1—mixture used for products that are going to be consumed in a short amount of time including all types of sausages except for the dried kind; is mostly salt (93.75 percent) with some sodium nitrite added (6.25 percent) and pink dye.

prague powder #2—mixture used for dry-cured meats, which require longer curing times in conditions that may be anaerobic; used for raw products such as prosciutto or Virginia-style hams or any product not requiring smoking, cooking, or refrigerating such as dry salami. A time-release cure; the sodium nitrate breaks down into sodium nitrite then ultimately into nitric oxide.

primal cuts—the wholesale cuts that are cut to industry standards. A system was devised by the meat industry to standardize all meats sold in the United States. The NAMPS guidelines codified all meat primals, subprimals, and fabricated cuts so that a steak that is sold in Kansas City has the same configuration and quality grading system in New York or in California. Primal cuts are the primary divisions of the quarter cuts.

produce—general term for farm-produced goods, generally fruits and vegetables.

profiteroles (*pro-FEHT-uh-rohls*)—small baked puffs of éclair dough the size of a quarter; used extensively in handheld hors d'oeuvre.

prosciutto—dry-cured Italian ham from Parma, Italy.

pulse—another name for legumes such as beans, peas, and lentils.

Q

qalat daqqa—also known as *Tunisian Five Spice;* a spicy blend of freshly ground black pepper, grains of paradise, nutmeg, cinnamon, and cloves ground together for a fragrant combination; used for lamb and poultry dishes and in marinades.

quatre epices—a French term meaning "four spices." The basic blend centers around pepper, usually white, and a number of different spices; there is no set recipe but this spice blend often includes nutmeg, ginger, cloves, cinnamon, and/or allspice along with the pepper.

quenelles (*kuh-NEH*)—a finely ground forcemeat mixture, lightened with egg whites and cream, then shaped with two spoons into a slightly oval football shape; is usually poached like a dumpling and served as a garnish.

quinoa (*KEEN-wah*)—considered the mother grain of the Andean plateau cultures of the Incas, who called it *chisaya mam,* or the mother of all grains. It is not a true grain, as it is not a grass plant; it is, however, a sustaining seed used as a grain. It is a complete protein and is gluten free. It has a pleasing, nutty flavor and an attractive shape, making it a natural for cold salads.

R

raft—protein mix of lean meat, egg whites, and mirepoix, ground and then added to cold stock. When heated, a thick layer or "raft" forms on the top of the stock, clarifying out sediment. Used in the process of clarification for consommé making.

ratite—flightless birds with strong legs and small wings; the meat resembles red meat in both structure and flavor; popular ratites include ostrich, emu, and the rhea.

ravigote—from the French *ravigoter,* which means "to add a new figure." In culinary arts, a ravigote is a cold, French vinegar-based sauce that contains capers, onions, and herbs; used as a dressing for salad.

relish—cooked or pickled sauce of vinegar and sugar made of vegetables or fruits.

rennet—enzyme found in the fourth lining of calves' stomachs; contains rennin to trigger the clumping up or curding action.

rhizome—a horizontal underground stem that can send out both shoots and roots; sometimes have thickened areas that store starch; ginger, galangal, and turmeric are culinary examples of rhizome.

rillette—meat slowly cooked in its own fat until very soft and then shredded.

rind—the outer skin of cheese or citrus fruit.

ripening—the process in which starches are converted to sugars in the growing cycle of fruits and vegetables; also a term used in cheese making to describe the development of organic acids and textural changes in cheese.

risers—wooden or plastic bases or platforms used to give height to a buffet display. In many facilities, dish racks and milk crates are used for this purpose; linens are used to cover and disguise the riser.

roe—the eggs of fish. Only true sturgeon roe is called caviar; roe from other species must be identified with the name of the fish preceding the word *caviar,* such as salmon caviar or whitefish caviar.

romescu—Spanish sauce made from sweet red peppers, tomatoes, olive oil, vinegar, and almonds or hazelnuts.

roquette—type of greens also known as "Rocket" or Arugula. Peppery flavor and sturdy green leaves.

rouille (*roo-EE*)—paste made with hot chilies, garlic, olive oil, stock, and breadcrumbs.

roulade—a portion of meat, poultry, or fish that is stuffed or layered and rolled before cooking.

round fish—fish with symmetrical round or oval bodies and eyes on either side of the head; they swim in an upright position and are found in all types of environments. Some round fish are hot blooded, such as those from the tuna or thon family.

S

sachet d'epices—bag of spice usually containing aromatic herbs and spices such as black peppercorns, parsley stems, dried thyme leaves, and a bay leaf.

salad—from the Roman term *herba salta* for "salted herb or lettuce"; common usage now means any small dish or course served with a dressing.

salé—salted.

salsa—Mexican type of raw cold sauce, made with chopped chunky tomatoes, chilies, and spices.

salt—sodium chloride; used to season and preserve foods.

sandwich—a meal item usually made with sliced bread or some type of flour-based vehicle, meat, or some sort of hearty protein-based filling, a spread or dressing, and a garnish. It is easily eaten out of hand.

sanitizing—reducing the number of microorganisms to safe levels on surfaces or equipment by using heat or chemical sanitizers.

sashimi—Japanese food that consists of sliced, raw fish served with side condiments such as soy sauce, pickled ginger, and wasabi.

saturated fat—fat that consists of triglycerides containing only saturated fatty acids, which have no double bonds between the carbon atoms of the fatty acid chain; hence, they are fully saturated with hydrogen atoms. Common saturated fats are animal-based, such as butter and meat products and plant fats such as palm and coconut fat.

sauce Andalouse (*ahn-dah-LOOZ*)—a French mayonnaise made with tomato pureé and pimento

sauce verte (*vehrt*)—cold sauce made with green herbs such as chives, tarragon, and chervil, and oil and other piquant ingredients.

sausage—from the Latin word *salsus,* which means "salted" or "preserved"; highly seasoned and salted ground meat stuffed into casings.

sel gris de guerande—"moist" and unrefined salt that comes in coarse or stone ground fine grain. It is light grey to light purple in color because of the color of clay from the salt flats where it is collected in the Celtic Sea.

semi-soft cheese—cheese with a semi-soft texture that can be rind-washed, brined, brushed, or rubbed with salt and sprayed or wiped with an acidic product such as wine or cider.

smoking—applying smoke to a food product for flavor and preservation; one of the oldest forms of preserving foods.

sneeze guard—clear plastic or lexan cover used with salad bars and self-serve food stations to protect food from sneezing patrons.

Société Culinaire Philanthropique—the oldest culinary society in the United States founded in 1865. This organization founded the oldest culinary salon in New York City and it has been held annually since 1869.

socle—a solid, trimmed loaf of bread that is deep fried to make firm and sturdy; used as a bolster or riser under food or used as a base on a cold platter.

sodium nitrate—nitrate-based salt used to preserve and protect foods against harmful microorganisms and loss of color and flavor; used for meats that will not be cooked or smoked.

sodium nitrite—nitrite-based salt used to preserve and protect foods that will be cooked or smoked; protects against harmful microorganisms.

soft-ripened cheese—similar to fresh cheese; are soft in nature but allowed to mature and ripen under controlled environments to produce cheeses that have complex flavors and soft to almost liquid textures.

sous vide (*soo-VEED*)—French word for "under vacuum"; a process that cooks food in a vacuum environment; a method of cooking foods for long periods of time at low temperatures under a vacuum seal.

spherification—accomplished by mixing fruit or vegetable juices and purée with sodium alginate, then immersing this mixture in a water and calcium chloride bath; the result forms perfect round spheres. A thin skin or membrane is formed on the outside of the sphere and, when eaten, the membrane crunches and an intensively flavored liquid is released.

spice—aromatic vegetable product obtained from the roots, flowers, seeds, pods, or bark of the plant.

spreads—thicker sauces and paste-like ingredients such as softened cheeses, flavored butters, and mayonnaise-based products used to coat breads to keep the water moisture from making the breads soggy and to flavor the sandwiches.

stabilizer—an ingredient used to stabilize a protein, fat, or carbohydrate food product to keep it from separating or breaking during the mixing and cooking process.

subprimal cuts—meat cut from a primal down to a more manageable size.

succotash—name derived from the Narraganset, Rhode Island, Indians; a dish that traditionally includes lima beans and corn; can be served either cold or hot.

supreme—a section of an orange with the skin removed and all of the pith and connective membrane removed with a knife. Just the actual orange sacs are intact in one even slice.

surface-ripened cheese—cheese ripened from the surface in.

surimi—ground fish protein-based seafood product that mimics real crab, lobster, and shrimp. Used as an inexpensive substitute for the real product.

sushi—Japanese menu item of cooked rice, seasoned with vinegar, salt, sugar, and saki, chilled down, shaped into one- to two-bite morsels, and topped or filled and rolled in nori or dried seaweed, with raw fish, pickled and raw vegetables, and simple condiments such as soy sauce and gari or pickled ginger.

T

table mock setup—practice table for setting up a platter in a practice session; it should mirror what will be present in competition.

table skirting—linen that covers the legs of the table; usually attaches around the table and falls within 1 inch of the floor.

tallow—a blend of bleached and purified sheep or beef fat or suet and paraffin wax; used to make a classic, beautiful, nonedible showpiece.

tamis—a wooden or metal hoop with a fine screen stretched taut against it; used to sift fine crumbs or push puréed product through to remove bones and bits of fiber; also known as a *drum sieve*.

tandoori—a waist-high, clay oven heated by charcoal that originated in India. Tandoori chicken is a popular oven-roasted dish cooked in a tandoori oven.

tapas—Spanish term that means "to cover" or "top" the glass to keep the fruit flies out of the wine. It has come to mean any small plate or appetizing item to serve with the sherry or wine as an appetizer course; is usually very savory or salty.

tapenade (*ta-pen-AHD*)—traditional French-Italian dish made with olives and anchovies and then seasoned with spices and lemon juice.

tartar sauce—mayonnaise-based sauce with chopped sour dill pickles, lemon, and onion. Used traditionally with fried or grilled seafood.

tartare—chopped raw beef topped with condiments such as anchovy paste, Dijon, and Worchestershire sauce along with raw egg. The term comes from the Tartars, who were reputed to eat their meat raw. In modern usage, it is often used to refer to any chopped raw meat or fish dish. As with all raw products, the utmost care in sanitation is the most important consideration.

tartelette—round, sometimes scalloped, small baked dough shells that are filled and topped with garnish.

TCM—acronym for Tinted Curing Mixture, which is 94 percent salt, 6 percent sodium nitrite, and some red food coloring, which adds a pink tinge so that it cannot be mistaken for regular table salt.

teff—one of the smallest grass-based grains originating in Africa. Complete protein useful in gluten-free dishes that is high in complex carbohydrates and protein, and low in fat.

temperature danger zone—zone between 41°F (5°C) and 135°F (57°C) where bacteria grow rapidly in a short amount of time.

tempering—process of incorporating hot liquid into cold liquid by way of a liaison to gradually raise the temperature; also refers to the slow raising of the temperature of a block of ice in the walk-in to avoid thermal shock of the ice.

templates—patterns made of thin cardboard, paper, or thin particle board; used for outlining a subject. Templates are a great help and timesaver for less experienced carvers.

tenderize—to treat protein with an enzyme that breaks down the muscle fibers, or to physically or mechanically break down the fibrous muscle tissue by cutting or pounding.

terrine—a forcemeat in the shape of a loaf or one that is baked in a terracotta or earthenware mold lined with fatback.

thermal shock—rapid change in temperature that brings on negative changes in ice and other foods to cause breakage and damage.

thermophilic starter—microorganism used in the processing of cheese made at higher temperatures of 110°F to 170°F (71°C to 77°C).

timbale—small, round mold used to shape or cook a custard-based or mousseline-based forcemeat in a water bath; is also the name of the product poached in a timbale.

tomalley—liver of the lobster that is bright green when raw, but turns a dark scarlett red when cooked; used to flavor lobster butter.

total utilization—from the squeek to the eek! Utilizing every possible part of the product in order to reduce waste and improve profits.

tourné—vegetable or potato carved into a seven-sided, football-shaped object, 3/4 inches in diameter and 2 inches in length, with blunted ends.

trans fats—common name for a type of unsaturated fat with trans-isomer fatty acids. Trans fats can be monounsaturated or polyunsaturated. Most trans fats consumed today are created in a commercial manufacturing plant and consist of partially hydrogenating plant oils, a process developed in the early 1900s. These are considered to have a negative impact on coronary heart health.

tray service—type of service used for delivering food at large banquets or small sitdown dinners; each plate is dished up, covered, and set on a tray to be delivered to the guest.

trenchour—wooden boards used as plates that were originally used to sop up the juices and sauces from dripping meats; these were eventually replaced by large loaves of bread in rectangular shapes.

tripe—honeycomb-shaped edible lining of a cow's stomach; used in stocks and stews.

truss—to tie up meat and poultry with string or netting to improve cooking by compacting the meat; ensures a more even cooking process and a more pleasing appearance.

tuber—a swollen, fleshy, usually underground stem of a plant, such as the potato and sunchoke, bearing buds from which new plant shoots arise.

U

ultraviolet light (UVL)—light used in curing and meat processing rooms to help kill bacteria on the surface.

unripened—fruit or cheese that has not reached its prime.

V

variety meats—less-offensive marketing term for the offals or parts of meat that are nontraditional such as testicles, kidneys, and hearts.

VCM or **vertical cutting machine**—piece of equipment used for large-quantity sauces or chopping jobs in the cold kitchen. It consists of a large bowl that can hold several gallons of food. Each unit has an S-shaped blade in the base. A VCM is useful for making gallons of salad dressings, salsas, and chopped fruits and vegetables.

veal—meat from any male calf of dairy cows that is slaughtered between the ages of 8 to 16 weeks of age.

vegetable—any herbaceous (nonwoody) plant or plant part that is eaten with the main course rather than as a dessert; usually has a bland taste.

veloute—one of the mother sauces; made with roux, white stock, and the appropriate aromatics; is also the name for soups made in this manner.

venison—meat from deer or other large game animals.

vichyssoise—cold potato, leek, and cream-based soup invented by the French chef, Louis Diat, at the Ritz Carlton, NY, in 1950.

Viennese table—dessert station at a buffet with whole desserts as well as individually portioned items.

vinaigrette (vihn-uh-GREHT)—simple dressing consisting of two to three parts of oil and one part of an acidic ingredient such as white wine vinegar or lemon juice, aromatics, and spices.

vitello tonnato (*vee-TEL-loa toan-NAA-toa*)—Italian specialty sauce made with tuna; is served over cold roasted veal, but can be served independently as a dip.

W

washed rind cheeses—cheeses that are mainly soft to semi-soft in texture; they are washed in the curing stage with salt brine, acidic liquids such as wine, alcoholic beverages such as beer, hard apple cider, and brandy, or rubbed with aromatic oils during the ripening period.

waxed rind cheeses—semi-soft cheeses that are sealed in wax prior to the aging process; Gouda and edam are the most famous of these cheeses.

whey—dairy product that consists of water, slight amounts of sugar, and residual liquid protein.

whip—to incorporate a large amount of air into a product; the tool that is used to incorporate air.

wilted salads—salads usually made with a hot dressing to get a slightly wilted effect. Some examples are spinach salad with hot bacon dressing.

X

xanthan gum—gum used as a thickener for fat replacement in dressings and sauces.

Y

yeast—friendly fungus-based microorganism that imparts flavor, aids in the development of fermentation, and helps in the formation of bread and cheese.

yogurt—dairy-based cultured liquid with a slight thick texture and tart flavor.

Z

zakuski—Russian for "piece" or "morsel."

zampone (*dzahm-POH-nay*)—sausage made of pork, seasoned with nutmeg, cloves, and pepper.

zest—thin outer layer of the citrus that contains the color and the volatile flavoring oils such as lime or lemon oil used in sauces, flavorings, and baking.

zones—areas that are specific to the task or the food item. In the kitchen, food is prepared in the cold kitchen or the hot kitchen, depending on the menu item; each zone has its own specific equipment and needs.

>> Index

Note: Recipe titles are bolded throughout.

>> Credits

UNIT 1

Unit 1 Opener: Eric Futran/FoodPix/Getty Images, Inc.; 1-1: Harper Collins Publishers/Picture Desk, Inc./Kobal Collection; 1-2: Ancient Art & Architecture/DanitaDelimont .com; 1-3: The Art Archive/Dagli Orti; 1-4: Dagli Orti/Picture Desk, Inc./Kobal Collection; 1-5: Art Resource, N.Y.; 1-6: Muzeum Narodowe, Poznan, Poland/The Bridgeman Art Library; 1-7: Susan Van Etten/PhotoEdit Inc.; 1-8: Andrew Holligan © Dorling Kindersley; 1-9: Robert Fried/robertfriedphotography.com; 1-10: Danny Lehman/CORBIS- NY; 1-11: Alaska Division of Tourism; 1-12: Chateau de Compiegne, Oise, France/The Bridgeman Art Library; 1-13: G Huntington/Pearson Education Corporate Digital Archive; 1-14: Getty Images Inc. - Hulton Archive Photos; 1-15: Hulton Archive/Getty Images; 1-16: Alistair Cotton/Shutterstock.

UNIT 2

Unit 2 Opener: Vincent P. Walter/Pearson Education/PH College; 2-1: michaeljung/ Shutterstock; 2-2: Vincent P. Walter/Pearson Education/PH College; 2-3: Vincent P. Walter/Pearson Education/PH College; 2-4: Vincent P. Walter/Pearson Education/PH College; 2-5: Brady/Pearson Education/PH College; 2-6: Richard Embery; 2-7: © Dorling Kindersley; 2-8: © Culinary Institute of America; 2-9: Vincent P. Walter/Pearson Education/PH College; 2-10: Vincent P. Walter/Pearson Education/PH College; 2-11: Dorling Kindersley Media Library; 2-12: Vincent P. Walter/Pearson Education/PH College; 2-13: Vincent P. Walter/Pearson Education/PH College; 2-14: Vincent P. Walter/Pearson Education/PH College; 2-15: Tischenko Irina/Shutterstock; 2-16: Santje/Shutterstock; 2-17: Andy Crawford © Dorling Kindersley; 2-18: Gary Gaugler/Photo Researchers; 2-19: Janulla/Shutterstock; 2-20: Dr. Jeremy Burgess/Photo Researchers, Inc.; 2-21: Richard Embery; 2-22: Ingram Publishing/Superstock; 2-23: U.S. Department of Labor; 2-24: Vincent P. Walter/Pearson Education/PH College; 2-25: Richard Embery/Pearson Education/PH College; 2-26: Vincent P. Walter/ Pearson Education/PH College; 2-27: Richard Embery/Pearson Education/ PH College; 2-28: Vincent P. Walter/Pearson Education/PH College; 2-29: Vincent P. Walter/Pearson Education/PH College; 2-30: Susanna Price © Dorling Kindersley; 2-31: Vincent P. Walter/Pearson Education/PH College; 2-32: Pearson Education/PH College.

UNIT 3

Unit 3 Opener: Vincent P. Walter/Pearson Education/PH College; 3-1: Richard Embery; 3-2: Richard Embery; 3-3: Richard Embery; 3-4: Vincent P. Walter/Pearson Education/PH College; 3-5: Richard Embery; 3-6: Brady/Pearson Education/ PH College; 3-7: Gary Ombler © Dorling Kindersley; 3-8: Richard Embery/ Pearson Education/PH College; 3-9: Richard Embery/Pearson Education/ PH College; 3-10: © Culinary Institute of America; 3-11: Richard Embery/ Pearson Education/PH College; 3-12: Vincent P. Walter/Pearson Education/ PH College; 3-13: © Culinary Institute of America; 3-14: Richard Embery/ Pearson Education/PH College; 3-15: Dave King © Dorling Kindersley; 3-16: © Culinary Institute of America; 3-17: Vincent P. Walter/Pearson Education/ PH College; 3-18: Slater King © Dorling Kindersley; 3-19: Ian O'Leary © Dorling Kindersley; 3-20: Richard Embery/Pearson Education/PH College; 3-21: Rob Crandall/Stock Connection; 3-22: Vincent P. Walter/Pearson Education/ PH College; 3-23: Richard Embery; 3-24: Richard Embery/Pearson Education/ PH College; 3-25: David Murray © Dorling Kindersley; 3-26: Richard Embery/ Pearson Education/PH College; 3-27: Dave King © Dorling Kindersley; 3-28: Richard Embery/Pearson Education/PH College; 3-29: Richard Embery/ Pearson Education/PH College; 3-30: © Dorling Kindersley; 3-31: Richard Embery/Pearson Education/PH College; 3-32: © Bon Appetit/Alamy.

UNIT 4

Unit 4 Opener: BP/Getty; 4-1: Matthew Ward © Dorling Kindersley; 4-2: Krzysztof Slusarczyk/Shutterstock; 4-3: Steve Gorton © Dorling Kindersley; 4-4: Dave King © Dorling Kindersley; 4-5: © Dorling Kindersley; 4-6: Neil Fletcher and Matthew Ward © Dorling Kindersley; 4-7: Dave King © Dorling Kindersley; 4-8: Richard Embery/Pearson Education/PH College; 4-9: Ian O'Leary © Dorling Kindersley; 4-10: Ian O'Leary © Dorling Kindersley; 4-11: Richard Embery/Pearson Education/PH College; 4-12: Dave King © Dorling Kindersley; 4-13: Dave King © Dorling Kindersley; 4-14: Clive Streeter © Dorling Kindersley; 4-15: Dave King © Dorling Kindersley; 4-16: Alix/Photo Researchers; 4-17: David Murray © Dorling Kindersley; 4-18: Alix/Photo Researchers; 4-19: © Dorling Kindersley; 4-20: Richard Embery/Pearson Education/

PH College; 4-21: Roger Phillips © Dorling Kindersley; 4-22: Richard Embery/ Pearson Education/PH College; 4-23: Neil Fletcher and Matthew Ward © Dorling Kindersley; 4-24: Richard Embery/Pearson Education/PH College; 4-25: Roger Phillips © Dorling Kindersley; 4-26: Philip Dowell © Dorling Kindersley; 4-27: David Murray © Dorling Kindersley; 4-28: Craig Knowles © Dorling Kindersley; 4-29: Richard Embery/Pearson Education/PH College; 4-30: George Mattei/ Envision Stock Photography; 4-31: Martin Norris © Dorling Kindersley; 4-32: Richard Embery/Pearson Education/PH College; 4-33: Richard Embery/Pearson Education/PH College; 4-34: Richard Embery/Pearson Education/PH College; 4-35: Richard Embery/Pearson Education/PH College; 4-36: Richard Embery/ Pearson Education/PH College; 4-37: Dave King © Dorling Kindersley; 4-38: Philip Dowell © Dorling Kindersley; 4-39: Martin Norris © Dorling Kindersley; 4-40: Margrit Kropp/Shutterstock; 4-41: Richard Embery/Pearson Education/PH College; 4-42: Geoff Simpson/Nature Picture Library; 4-43: Philip Dowell © Dorling Kindersley; 4-44: Philip Dowell © Dorling Kindersley; 4-45: Martin Cameron © Dorling Kindersley; 4-46: Philip Dowell © Dorling Kindersley; 4-47: Dave King © Dorling Kindersley; 4-48: Richard Embery/Pearson Education/PH College; 4-49: Roger Phillips © Dorling Kindersley; 4-50: dabjola/Shutterstock; 4-51: Neil Fletcher and Matthew Ward © Dorling Kindersley; 4-52: John Leil/Omni-Photo Communication, Inc.; 4-53: Martin Norris © Dorling Kindersley; 4-54: Peter Chadwick © Dorling Kindersley, Courtesy of the Natural History Museum, London; 4-55: Philip Dowell © Dorling Kindersley; 4-56: Fribus Ekaterina/Shutterstock; 4-57: Richard Embery/Pearson Education/PH College; 4-58: Philip Dowell © Dorling Kindersley; 4-59: Richard Embery/Pearson Education/PH College; 4-60: © Dorling Kindersley; 4-61: Richard Embery; 4-62: Richard Embery/Pearson Education/PH College; 4-63: Martin Norris © Dorling Kindersley; 4-64: Dave King © Dorling Kindersley; 4-65: Richard Embery; 4-66: David Murray © Dorling Kindersley; 4-67: Brian Chase/Shutterstock; 4-68: Aaron Amat/Shutterstock; 4-69: Scott Waldron/Shutterstock; 4-70: Ian O'Leary © Dorling Kindersley; 4-71: Richard Embery/Pearson Education/PH College; 4-72: Richard Embery/Pearson Education/PH College; 4-73: David Murray © Dorling Kindersley; 4-74: © Culinary Institute of America; 4-75: Dusan Zidar/Shutterstock; 4-76: Simon Smith © Dorling Kindersley; 4-77: Richard Embery/Pearson Education/PH College; 4-78: Rachel Epstein/PhotoEdit, Inc.; 4-79: Howard Shooter © Dorling Kindersley; 4-80: Richard Embery; 4-81: Richard Embery; 4-82: Tim Ridley © Dorling Kindersley; 4-83: Richard Embery; 4-84: Clive Streeter and Patrick McLeavy © Dorling Kindersley; 4-85: Richard Embery; 4-86: Richard Embery; 4-87: Neil Mersh © Dorling Kindersley; 4-88: Philip Dowell © Dorling Kindersley; 4-89: © Dorling Kindersley; 4-90: David Murray © Dorling Kindersley; 4-91: © Dorling Kindersley; 4-92: Clive Streeter © Dorling Kindersley; 4-93: Ian O'Leary © Dorling Kindersley; 4-94: Dave King © Dorling Kindersley; 4-95: Dave King © Dorling Kindersley; 4-96: Ian O'Leary © Dorling Kindersley; 4-97: © Dorling Kindersley; 4-98: Clive Streeter and Patrick McLeavy © Dorling Kindersley; 4-99: Clive Streeter and Patrick McLeavy © Dorling Kindersley; 4-100: Paul Williams © Dorling Kindersley; 4-101: David Murray © Dorling Kindersley; 4-102: David Murray © Dorling Kindersley; 4-103: Clive Streeter and Patrick McLeavy © Dorling Kindersley; 4-104: Richard Embery/Pearson Education/ PH College; 4-105: © Dorling Kindersley; 4-106: Paul Williams © Dorling Kindersley; 4-107: Clive Streeter and Patrick McLeavy © Dorling Kindersley; 4-108.

UNIT 5

Unit 5 Opener: Nancy Richmond/The Image Works; 5-1: Andrew Leyerle © Dorling Kindersley 5-2: © Dorling Kindersley; 5-3: DJM-photo/Shutterstock; 5-4: Ian O'Leary © Dorling Kindersley; 5-5: David Murray © Dorling Kindersley; 5-6: Roger Phillips © Dorling Kindersley; 5-7: Dave King © Dorling Kindersley; 5-8: Andreas Von Einsiedel © Dorling Kindersley; 5-9: Andreas Von Einsiedel © Dorling Kindersley; 5-10: © Dorling Kindersley; 5-11: Peter Anderson © Dorling Kindersley; 5-12: Richard Embery/Pearson Education/PH College; 5-13: Roger Phillips © Dorling Kindersley; 5-14: Stephen Oliver © Dorling Kindersley; 5-15: Vuk Adzic/Shutterstock; 5-16: Voisin/Photo Researchers, Inc.; 5-17: Richard Embery/Pearson Education/PH College; 5-18: Jess Koppel/Getty Images, Inc. – Stone Allstock; 5-19: Richard Embery/Pearson Education/PH College; 5-20: Dorling Kindersley Media Library; 5-21: Roger Phillips © Dorling Kindersley; 5-22: Roger Phillips © Dorling Kindersley; 5-23: Chris Bence/Shutterstock; 5-24: Courtesy of United Fresh Fruit & Vegetable Association, Alexandria, Va.; 5-25: Richard Embery; 5-26: John Davis © Dorling Kindersley; 5-27: Richard Embery/Pearson Education/PH College; 5-28: Richard Embery/Pearson Education/PH College; 5-29: Roger Phillips © Dorling Kindersley; 5-30: Richard Embery/Pearson Education/PH College; 5-31: Demetrio Carrasco © Rough Guides; 5-32: © Dorling Kindersley; 5-33: Getty Images, Inc.- Photodisc/Royalty Free; 5-34: Anthony Johnson © Dorling Kindersley; 5-35: Richard Embery/Pearson Education/PH College; 5-36: Dave King © Dorling Kindersley; 5-37: David Murray © Dorling Kindersley; 5-38: Ian O'Leary © Dorling Kindersley; 5-39: David Murray © Dorling

Kindersley; 5-40: Matthew Ward © Dorling Kindersley; 5-41: Philip Dowell © Dorling Kindersley; 5-42: Simon Brown © Dorling Kindersley; 5-43: Ian O'Leary © Dorling Kindersley; 5-44: Ramiro Salazar/Shutterstock; 5-45: Getty Images, Inc.; 5-46: Philip Dowell © Dorling Kindersley; 5-47: Dave King © Dorling Kindersley; 5-48: © Dorling Kindersley; 5-49: Clive Streeter and Patrick McLeavy © Dorling Kindersley; 5-50: Dave King © Dorling Kindersley; 5-51: Matthew Ward © Dorling Kindersley; 5-52: Neil Fletcher and Matthew Ward © Dorling Kindersley; 5-53: Ian O'Leary © Dorling Kindersley; 5-54: Ian O'Leary © Dorling Kindersley; 5-55: Ian O'Leary © Dorling Kindersley; 5-56: Ian O'Leary © Dorling Kindersley; 5-57: Ian O'Leary © Dorling Kindersley; 5-58: Geoff Dann © Dorling Kindersley; 5-59: Dave King © Dorling Kindersley; 5-60: Dave King © Dorling Kindersley; 5-61: Martin Norris © Dorling Kindersley; 5-62: Derek Hall © Dorling Kindersley; 5-63: KEREN SU/DanitaDelimont.com; 5-64: Ken Buschner/Creative Eye/MIRA .com; 5-65: Courtesy of United Fresh Fruit & Vegetable Association, Alexandria, Va.; 5-66: Steve Teague © Dorling Kindersley; 5-67: Dave King © Dorling Kindersley; 5-68: Peter Anderson © Dorling Kindersley; 5-69: Ian O'Leary © Dorling Kindersley; 5-70: Steve Gorton © Dorling Kindersley; 5-71: © Dorling Kindersley; 5-72: Tim Ridley © Dorling Kindersley; 5-73: Maximilian Stock Ltd./Photo Researchers, Inc.; 5-74: Richard Embery/Pearson Education/ PH College; 5-75: Roger Phillips © Dorling Kindersley; 5-76: Roger Phillips © Dorling Kindersley; 5-77: Roger Phillips © Dorling Kindersley; 5-78: Ian O'Leary © Dorling Kindersley; 5-79: Andi Berger/Shutterstock; 5-80: Dwight Smith/Shutterstock; 5-81: Richard Embery; 5-82: Sian Irvine © Dorling Kindersley; 5-83: Roger Phillips © Dorling Kindersley; 5-84: Richard Embery/Pearson Education/PH College; 5-85: Richard Embery/Pearson Education/PH College; 5-86: Richard Embery/Pearson Education/PH College; 5-87: Richard Embery/Pearson Education/PH College; 5-88: © Dorling Kindersley; 5-89: © Dorling Kindersley; 5-90: © David Cavagnaro/Peter Arnold, Inc.; 5-91: Andy Crawford © Dorling Kindersley; 5-92: Philip Dowell © Dorling Kindersley; 5-93: Roger Phillips © Dorling Kindersley; 5-94: © Dorling Kindersley Media Library; 5-95: Richard Embery/Pearson Education/PH College; 5-96: Getty Images - Digital Vision; 5-97: Roger Phillips © Dorling Kindersley; 5-98: Richard Embery/Pearson Education/PH College; 5-99: Richard Embery/ Pearson Education/PH College; 5-100: Richard Embery/Pearson Education/PH College; 5-101: David Murray © Dorling Kindersley; 5-102: © Dorling Kindersley; 5-103: © Dorling Kindersley; 5-104: Richard Embery/Pearson Education/ PH College; 5-105: Stephen Oliver © Dorling Kindersley; 5-106: Richard Embery/Pearson Education/PH College; 5-107: Steve Gorton © Dorling Kindersley; 5-108: Steven Wooster © Dorling Kindersley; 5-109: Richard Embery/Pearson Education/PH College; 5-110: David Murray © Dorling Kindersley; 5-111: Steve Gorton © Dorling Kindersley; 5-112: Getty Images - Stockbyte, Royalty Free; 5-113: John Heseltine © Dorling Kindersley; 5-114: Richard Embery/Pearson Education/PH College; 5-115: Richard Embery/ Pearson Education/PH College; 5-116: Richard Embery/Pearson Education/ PH College; 5-117: Richard Embery/Pearson Education/PH College; 5-118: Dorling Kindersley Media Library; 5-119: Paul Bricknell © Dorling Kindersley; 5-120: David Murray © Dorling Kindersley; 5-121: David Toase/Getty Images, Inc.- Photodisc/Royalty Free; 5-122: Dave King © Dorling Kindersley; 5-123: Dave King © Dorling Kindersley; 5-124: Richard Embery/Pearson Education/PH College; 5-125: Dave King © Dorling Kindersley; 5-126: Clive Streeter © Dorling Kindersley; 5-127: Dave King © Dorling Kindersley; 5-128: Norman Hollands © Dorling Kindersley; 5-129: David Murray © Dorling Kindersley; 5-130: Richard Embery/Pearson Education/PH College; 5-131: Steve Gorton © Dorling Kindersley; 5-132: uni/Dorling Kindersley Media Library; 5-133: Richard Embery/Pearson Education/PH College; 5-134: David Murray © Dorling Kindersley; 5-135: Stephen Oliver © Dorling Kindersley; 5-136: Philip Dowell © Dorling Kindersley; 5-137: © Mugdha Sethi; 5-138: Getty Images, Inc.- Photodisc/Royalty Free; 5-139: Phil Crabbe © Dorling Kindersley; 5-140: S. Meltzer/ Getty Images, Inc.- Photodisc; 5-141: Richard Embery/Pearson Education/ PH College; 5-142: Geoff Brightling © Dorling Kindersley; 5-143: Santokh Kochar/Getty Images, Inc.- Photodisc/Royalty Free; 5-144: Colin Walton © Dorling Kindersley; 5-145: Paul Williams © Dorling Kindersley; 5-146: Ian O'Leary © Dorling Kindersley; 5-147: Roger Phillips © Dorling Kindersley; 5-148: Andy Crawford © Dorling Kindersley; 5-149: Richard Embery/Pearson Education/PH College; 5-150: Roger Phillips © Dorling Kindersley; 5-151: Richard Embery/Pearson Education/PH College; 5-152: © Dorling Kindersley; 5-153: Getty Images, Inc.- Photodisc/Royalty Free; 5-154: Getty Images, Inc.- Photodisc/Royalty Free; 5-155: Howard Shooрer/Dorling Kindersley; 5-156: Roger Dixon © Dorling Kindersley; 5-157: Roger Phillips © Dorling Kindersley; 5-158: David Murray © Dorling Kindersley; 5-159: Richard Embery/Pearson Education/PH College; 5-160: Roger Phillips © Dorling Kindersley; 5-161: Roger Phillips © Dorling Kindersley; 5-162: Richard Embery/Pearson Education/PH College; 5-163: Philip Dowell © Dorling Kindersley; 5-164: David Murray © Dorling Kindersley; 5-165: Roger Phillips © Dorling Kindersley; 5-166: © Dorling Kindersley; 5-167: Neil Fletcher © Dorling Kindersley; 5-169: C Squared Studios/Getty Images, Inc.- Photodisc/Royalty Free; 5-170: Dave King © Dorling Kindersley; 5-171: C Squared Studios/Getty Images, Inc.- Photodisc/ Royalty Free; 5-172: Ian O'Leary © Dorling Kindersley; 5-173: Derek Hall © Dorling Kindersley; 5-174: Craig Knowles © Dorling Kindersley; 5-175: Richard Embery/Pearson Education/PH College; 5-176: Richard Embery/Pearson Education/PH College; 5-177: © Dorling Kindersley; 5-178: Derek Hall © Dorling Kindersley; 5-179: Jonathan Buckley © Dorling Kindersley; 5-180:

Richard Embery/Pearson Education/PH College; 5-181: © Dorling Kindersley; 5-182: Shutterstock/Boris 15; 5-183: Richard Embery/Pearson Education/PH College; 5-184: Richard Embery/Pearson Education/PH College; 5-185: © Dorling Kindersley; 5-186: Sarah Ashun © Dorling Kindersley; 5-187: Philip Dowell © Dorling Kindersley; 5-188: Richard Embery/Pearson Education/ PH College; 5-189: Richard Embery/Pearson Education/PH College; page 163, top left: Roger Phillips © Dorling Kindersley; page 163, middle left: Richard Embery/Pearson Education/PH College; page 163, bottom left: David Murray © Dorling Kindersley; page 163, top right: Richard Embery/Pearson Education/PH College; page 163, bottom right: David Murray © Dorling Kindersley.

UNIT 6

Unit 6 Opener: © Dorling Kindersley; 6-1: © Paul Carter/Alamy; 6-3: Mark Nicholls © The British Museum; 6-4: Dagli Orti/Picture Desk, Inc./Kobal Collection; 6-5: Dave King © Dorling Kindersley; 6-6: © Dorling Kindersley; 6-7: Clive Streeter © Dorling Kindersley; 6-8: Dave King © Dorling Kindersley; 6-9: David Murray © Dorling Kindersley; 6-10: David Murray © Dorling Kindersley; 6-11: Richard Embery/Pearson Education/PH College; 6-12: Simon Smith © Dorling Kindersley; 6-13: Richard Embery/Pearson Education/PH College; 6-14: Neil Mersh © Dorling Kindersley; 6-15: Roger Phillips © Dorling Kindersley; 6-16: C Squared Studios/ Getty Images, Inc.- Photodisc/Royalty Free; 6-17: © Dorling Kindersley; 6-19: Roger Phillips © Dorling Kindersley; 6-20: Richard Embery/ Pearson Education/PH College; 6-21: Philip Dowell © Dorling Kindersley; 6-22: © Dorling Kindersley; 6-23: David Murray © Dorling Kindersley; 6-24: Russ Lappa/Prentice Hall School Division; 6-25: David Murray © Dorling Kindersley; 6-26: Roger Phillips © Dorling Kindersley; 6-27: Richard Embery/Pearson Education/PH College; 6-28: Philip Dowell © Dorling Kindersley; 6-29: Roger Phillips © Dorling Kindersley; 6-30: Dave King © Dorling Kindersley; 6-31: Dave King © Dorling Kindersley; 6-32: Clive Streeter © Dorling Kindersley; 6-33: Stephen Oliver © Dorling Kindersley; 6-34: Philip Dowell © Dorling Kindersley; 6-35: Dave King © Dorling Kindersley; 6-36: Richard Embery/Pearson Education/PH College; 6-37: Dave King © Dorling Kindersley; 6-38: Philip Dowell © Dorling Kindersley; 6-39: Philip Dowell © Dorling Kindersley; 6-40: © Dorling Kindersley; 6-41: Steve Gorton © Dorling Kindersley; 6-42: © Dorling Kindersley; 6-43: © Dorling Kindersley; 6-44: Richard Embery/Pearson Education/PH College; 6-45: Andy Crawford © Dorling Kindersley; 6-46: Martin Brigdale © Dorling Kindersley; 6-47: © Culinary Institute of America; 6-48: David Murray © Dorling Kindersley; 6-49: © Dorling Kindersley; 6-50: Scott Pitts © Dorling Kindersley; 6-51: © Dorling Kindersley; 6-52: Richard Embery/Pearson Education/PH College; 6-53: Pearson Education/PH College; 6-54: © Culinary Institute of America; 6-55: Richard Embery/Pearson Education/PH College; 6-56: Richard Embery/Pearson Education/PH College; 6-57: Pearson Education/PH College; 6-58: Richard Embery/Pearson Education/PH College; 6-59: Andy Crawford © Dorling Kindersley; 6-60: Richard Embery/Pearson Education/PH College; 6-61: David Murray © Dorling Kindersley; 6-62: David Murray © Dorling Kindersley; 6-63: Philip Dowell © Dorling Kindersley; 6-64: © Dorling Kindersley; 6-65: Stephen Hayward © Dorling Kindersley; 6-66: Andrew McKinney © Dorling Kindersley; 6-67: Clive Streeter/Patrick McLeary © Dorling Kindersley; 6-68: © Dorling Kindersley; 6-69: Roger Phillips © Dorling Kindersley; 6-70: © Culinary Institute of America; 6-71: Richard Embery/Pearson Education/PH College; 6-72: Richard Embery/Pearson Education/PH College; 6-73: Colin Newman © Dorling Kindersley; 6-74: Richard Embery/Pearson Education/PH College; 6-75: © Dorling Kindersley; 6-76: Dave King © Dorling Kindersley; 6-77: Philip Dowell © Dorling Kindersley; 6-78: Geoff Dann © Dorling Kindersley; 6-79: Roger Phillips © Dorling Kindersley; 6-80: Richard Embery/Pearson Education/PH College; 6-81: Roger Phillips © Dorling Kindersley; 6-82: Richard Embery/Pearson Education/PH College; 6-83: Jon Milnes/Shutterstock; 6-84: © Dorling Kindersley; 6-85: © Culinary Institute of America; 6-86: David Murray © Dorling Kindersley; 6-87: © Dorling Kindersley; 6-88: Ian O'Leary © Dorling Kindersley; 6-89: Richard Embery/Pearson Education/PH College; 6-90: © Culinary Institute of America; 6-91: spaxiax/Shutterstock; 6-92: Janet Faye Hastings/Shutterstock; 6-93: Pearson Education/PH College; 6-94: Pearson Education/PH College; 6-95: © Culinary Institute of America; 6-96: Richard Embery/Pearson Education/PH College; 6-97: Roger Phillips © Dorling Kindersley; 6-98: Roger Phillips © Dorling Kindersley; 6-99: Richard Embery/Pearson Education/PH College; 6-100: Richard Embery/ Pearson Education/PH College; 6-101: U.S. Department of Agriculture; 6-102: Pearson Education/PH College; 6-103: Pearson Education/PH College; 6-104: Pearson Education/PH College; 6-105: Pearson Education/PH College; 6-106: Pearson Education/PH College; page 171: © Dorling Kindersley; page 172: Jerry Young © Dorling Kindersley; page 173: Jules Selmes and Debi Treloar © Dorling Kindersley; page 174: David Murray and Jules Selmes © Dorling Kindersley; page 175: Clive Streeter © Dorling Kindersley; page 226: Pearson Education/PH College.

UNIT 7

Unit 7 Opener: Sian Irvine © Dorling Kindersley; 7-1: Ian O'Leary © Dorling Kindersley; 7-2: Richard Embery/Pearson Education/PH College; 7-3: Jerry Young © Dorling Kindersley; 7-4: Richard Embery/Pearson Education/PH College; 7-5: David Murray and Jules Selmes © Dorling Kindersley; page 234: Richard Embery; page 235, top: Richard Embery; page 235, 2nd from top: Richard Embery;

page 235, 3rd from top: Richard Embery; page 235, 4th from top: Richard Embery; page 235, bottom: Richard Embery; page 236, top: Richard Embery; page 236, bottom: Richard Embery; page 237, top: Richard Embery; page 237, bottom: © Dorling Kindersley; page 238, top: © Dorling Kindersley; page 238, bottom: Dave King © Dorling Kindersley; page 239: Richard Embery; page 240, top: Richard Embery; page 240, elena moiseeva/Shutterstock; page 241: Philip Dowell © Dorling Kindersley; page 241, bottom: Richard Embery; page 242: David Murray and Jules Selmes © Dorling Kindersley; page 243: Erik Svensson and Jeppe Wikstrom © Dorling Kindersley; page 244: Richard Embery; page 245: Richard Embery; page 246, top: © Culinary Institute of America; page 246, bottom: Richard Embery; page 247, top: Richard Embery/Pearson Education/PH College; page 247, bottom: Richard Embery; page 248: Richard Embery; page 249: Dave King © Dorling Kindersley; page 250, top: David Murray and Jules Selmes © Dorling Kindersley; page 250, bottom: © Culinary Institute of America.

UNIT 8

Unit 8 Opener: Sian Irvine © Dorling Kindersley; 8-1: James Braund/Photolibrary.com; 8-2: Sian Irvine © Dorling Kindersley; 8-3: dusko/Shutterstock; 8-4: © Dorling Kindersley; 8-5: Neil Mersh © Dorling Kindersley; 8-6: © Neil Mersh/Dorling Kindersley; 8-7: © Dorling Kindersley; 8-8: Clive Streeter © Dorling Kindersley; 8-9: David Murray and Jules Selmes © Dorling Kindersley; 8-10: Ildi Papp/Shutterstock; 8-11: Neil Mersh © Dorling Kindersley; 8-12: Shelli Jensen/Shutterstock; 8-13: Sian Irvine © Dorling Kindersley; 8-14: Richard Embery/Pearson Education/PH College; 8-15: Sian Irvine © Dorling Kindersley; 8-16: © Dorling Kindersley; 8-17: Richard Embery/Pearson Education/PH College; 8-18: Richard Embery; 8-19: © Dorling Kindersley; 8-20: Clive Streeter © Dorling Kindersley; 8-21: Getty Images, Inc.- Photodisc; 8-22: Philip Dowell © Dorling Kindersley; 8-23: Ian O'Leary © Dorling Kindersley; 8-24: Christel Rosenfeld/Getty Images Inc. - Stone Allstock; 8-25: © Culinary Institute of America; 8-26: Ian O'Leary © Dorling Kindersley; 8-27: Richard Embery; 8-28: Richard Embery; 8-29: C Squared Studios/Getty Images, Inc.- Photodisc/Royalty Free; 8-30: David Murray and Jules Selmes © Dorling Kindersley; 8-31: Philip Dowell © Dorling Kindersley; 8-32: Clive Streeter © Dorling Kindersley; 8-33: Clive Streeter © Dorling Kindersley; 8-34: Clive Streeter © Dorling Kindersley; page 264: David Murray and Jules Selmes © Dorling Kindersley; page 265: Dave King © Dorling Kindersley; page 266: Richard Embery; page 267: Richard Embery; page 272: David Murray and Jules Selmes © Dorling Kindersley; page 273, top right: David Murray © Dorling Kindersley; page 273, 2nd from top: © Dorling Kindersley; page 273, bottom left: Jerry Young © Dorling Kindersley; page 273, bottom center: David Murray and Jules Selmes © Dorling Kindersley; page 273, bottom right: David Murray and Jules Selmes © Dorling Kindersley; page 274: Ian O'Leary © Dorling Kindersley; page 276, top: David Murray and Jules Selmes © Dorling Kindersley; page 276, middle left: © Culinary Institute of America; page 276, middle right: David Murray and Jules Selmes © Dorling Kindersley; page 276, bottom: Richard Embery; page 277, left: Richard Embery; page 277, top middle: Richard Embery; page 277, bottom middle: Richard Embery; page 277, top right: Richard Embery; page 277, 2nd from top: Richard Embery; page 277, 3rd from top: Richard Embery; page 277, 4th from top: Richard Embery; page 278, top: Richard Embery; page 278, bottom: Richard Embery; page 279: Richard Embery; page 280: Richard Embery; page 282: Clive Streeter © Dorling Kindersley; page 284: Ian O'Leary © Dorling Kindersley; page 285: © Dorling Kindersley; page 286, top: Richard Embery/Pearson Education/PH College; page 286, bottom: © Dorling Kindersley; page 287, top: Richard Embery; page 287, bottom: Ian O'Leary © Dorling Kindersley; page 288: Richard Embery; page 289: David Murray and Jules Selmes © Dorling Kindersley; page 290: Diana Miller © Dorling Kindersley; page 291, top: © Dorling Kindersley; page 291, bottom: © Culinary Institute of America; page 292: Dave King © Dorling Kindersley; page 293: Richard Embery; page 294: Richard Embery/Pearson Education/PH College; page 295: Richard Embery/Pearson Education/PH College; page 296, top: David Murray and Jules Selmes © Dorling Kindersley; page 296, bottom: Ian O'Leary © Dorling Kindersley; page 297: © Dorling Kindersley; page 298: Ian O'Leary © Dorling Kindersley; page 299: Neil Mersh © Dorling Kindersley; page 300: Richard Embery/Pearson Education/PH College; page 301: © Dorling Kindersley; page 302: David Murray and Jules Selmes © Dorling Kindersley; page 303, top: Richard Embery/Pearson Education/PH College; page 303, bottom: Richard Embery/Pearson Education/PH College; page 304: Richard Embery; page 305, top: Richard Embery/Pearson Education/PH College; page 305, bottom: Richard Embery; page 306: David Murray and Jules Selmes © Dorling Kindersley; page 307: Simon Smith © Dorling Kindersley; page 308: Dave King © Dorling Kindersley; page 309: Richard Embery/Pearson Education/PH College; page 310, top: David Murray © Dorling Kindersley; page 310, bottom: Richard Embery/Pearson Education/PH College; page 311: Richard Embery/Pearson Education/PH College; page 313: Ian O'Leary © Dorling Kindersley; page 314: © Culinary Institute of America; page 315: © Dorling Kindersley; page 316: Ian O'Leary © Dorling Kindersley; page 317: Howard Shooter © Dorling Kindersley; page 318: Richard Embery/Pearson Education/PH College; page 319: Richard Embery/Pearson Education/PH College; page 320: Ian O'Leary © Dorling Kindersley; page 321: David Murray and Jules Selmes © Dorling Kindersley.

UNIT 9

Unit 9 Opener: Richard Embery; 9-1: Tatiana Belova/Shutterstock; 9-2: © Dorling Kindersley; 9-3: Nayashkova Olga/Shutterstock; 9-4: Neil Setchfield © Rough Guides; page 329: Stephen VanHorn/Shutterstock; page 330: Richard Embery/Pearson Education/PH College; page 331: Richard Embery; page 332: Pearson Education Corporate Digital Archive; page 333, top: Richard Embery; page 333, bottom: Pearson Education Corporate Digital Archive; page 334: Richard Embery/Pearson Education/PH College; page 335, top: Richard Embery/Pearson Education/PH College, bottom: Dave King © Dorling Kindersley; page 336, top: Dorling Kindersley Media Library; page 336, bottom: Robyn Mackenzie/Shutterstock; page 337: Nayashkova Olga/Shutterstock; page 338: Richard Embery/Pearson Education/PH College; page 339: Richard Embery; page 340: © Dorling Kindersley; page 341, top: Liewluck/Shutterstock; page 341, middle: © Dorling Kindersley; page 341, bottom: © Dorling Kindersley; page 342: Richard Embery; page 343: Greg Ward © Rough Guides; page 344: Richard Embery/ Pearson Education/PH College; page 345: Philip Wilkins © Dorling Kindersley; page 346: © Culinary Institute of America; page 347: Roger Phillips © Dorling Kindersley; page 348: Ian O'Leary © Dorling Kindersley; page 349: Richard Embery; page 350: Richard Embery; page 351, left: Richard Embery; page 351, right: Richard Embery; page 352: Richard Embery/Pearson Education/PH College; page 353, top: Richard Embery/Pearson Education/PH College; page 353, bottom: Richard Embery; page 354: Dave King © Dorling Kindersley; page 355: Richard Embery; page 356: David Murray and Jules Selmes © Dorling Kindersley.

UNIT 10

Unit 10 Opener: Diana Miller © Dorling Kindersley; 10-1: Richard Embery; 10-2: Richard Embery; 10-3: Richard Embery; 10-4: Richard Embery; 10-5: Richard Embery; 10-6: Richard Embery; 10-7: © Culinary Institute of America; page 364: Richard Embery; page 365, top: Richard Embery; page 365, bottom: Richard Embery; page 366: David Murray and Jules Selmes © Dorling Kindersley; page 367: © Dorling Kindersley; page 368: Richard Embery; page 369, top: Richard Embery; page 369, 2nd from top: Richard Embery; page 369, 3rd from top: Richard Embery; page 369, 4th from top: Richard Embery; page 369, bottom: Richard Embery/Pearson Education/PH College; page 370: Howard Shooter © Dorling Kindersley; page 371: Richard Embery; page 372: David Murray and Jules Selmes © Dorling Kindersley; page 373, left: David Murray and Jules Selmes © Dorling Kindersley; page 373, top: Richard Embery; page 373, middle: Richard Embery; page 373, bottom: Richard Embery; page 374: David Murray and Jules Selmes © Dorling Kindersley; page 375, top: David Murray © Dorling Kindersley; page 375, bottom: © Dorling Kindersley; page 376: Richard Embery/Pearson Education/PH College; page 377, top: Howard Shooter © Dorling Kindersley; page 377, bottom: Richard Embery; page 378: Clive Streeter © Dorling Kindersley; page 379, top: Richard Embery/Pearson Education/PH College; page 379, bottom: Clive Streeter © Dorling Kindersley; page 380: Richard Embery; page 381: Richard Embery; page 382: Diana Miller © Dorling Kindersley; page 383: 108/Getty Images/Digital Vision; page 384: Richard Embery; page 385, top: Richard Embery; page 386, bottom: Richard Embery; page 387, top: Richard Embery/Pearson Education/PH College; page 387, bottom: David Murray and Jules Selmes © Dorling Kindersley; page 388: Clive Streeter and Patrick McLeavy © Dorling Kindersley; page 389: Richard Embery/Pearson Education/PH College.

UNIT 11

Unit 11 Opener: Dave King © Dorling Kindersley; 11-1: Richard Embery/Pearson Education/PH College; 11-2: Richard Embery/Pearson Education/PH College; 11-3: Howard Shooter © Dorling Kindersley; 11-4: © Dorling Kindersley; 11-5: Ian O'Leary © Dorling Kindersley; 11-6: © Dorling Kindersley; 11-7: Sian Irvine © Dorling Kindersley; 11-8: Richard Embery/Pearson Education/PH College; 11-9: David Murray © Dorling Kindersley; 11-10: Dave King © Dorling Kindersley; 11-11: Courtesy of The Beef Checkoff; 11-12: John A. Rizzo/Getty Images, Inc.- Photodisc/Royalty Free; 11-13: Howard Shooter © Dorling Kindersley; 11-14: Richard Embery; 11-15: Richard Embery; 11-16: Richard Embery; 11-17: Richard Embery; 11-18: © Culinary Institute of America; 11-19: Richard Embery/Pearson Education/PH College; 11-20: © Culinary Institute of America; 11-21: © Culinary Institute of America; 11-22: paytai/Shutterstock; 11-23: Richard Embery/Pearson Education/PH College; 11-24: Richard Embery; 11-25: Richard Embery; 11-26: Jerry Young © Dorling Kindersley; 11-27: David Murray and Jules Selmes © Dorling Kindersley; 11-28: David Murray and Jules Selmes © Dorling Kindersley; 11-29: Clive Streeter © Dorling Kindersley; 11-30: © Dorling Kindersley; 11-31: David Murray © Dorling Kindersley; 11-32: James Stevenson © Dorling Kindersley; 11-33: Richard Embery; 11-34: Richard Embery; 11-35: Richard Embery; 11-36: Richard Embery; 11-37: Richard Embery; 11-38: Richard Embery; 11-39: Richard Embery; 11-40: Clive Streeter © Dorling Kindersley; 11-41: Dave King © Dorling Kindersley; 11-42: Dave King © Dorling Kindersley; 11-43: David Murray and Jules Selmes © Dorling Kindersley; 11-44: © Dorling Kindersley; 11-45: Richard Embery; 11-46: Richard Embery; 11-47: Richard Embery/Pearson Education/PH College; 11-48: David Murray and Jules Selmes © Dorling

Kindersley; 11-49: Corbis RF; 11-50: Richard Embery; 11-51: cloki/Shutterstock; 11-52: jcpjr/Shutterstock; 11-53: Richard Embery/Pearson Education/PH College; page 407, top: Richard Embery; page 407, bottom: Richard Embery; page 408: Ian O'Leary © Dorling Kindersley; page 409: Roger Phillips © Dorling Kindersley; page 410: David Murray and Jules Selmes © Dorling Kindersley; page 412: David Murray and Jules Selmes © Dorling Kindersley; page 413: David Murray © Dorling Kindersley; page 415: Ian O'Leary © Dorling Kindersley; page 424: Richard Embery; page 425, top: © Dorling Kindersley; page 425, bottom: Richard Embery; page 426: David Murray and Jules Selmes © Dorling Kindersley; page 427: Richard Embery; page 428: Richard Embery; page 429, top: Richard Embery; page 429, bottom: Sian Irvine © Dorling Kindersley; page 430: Ian O'Leary © Dorling Kindersley; page 431: Ian O'Leary © Dorling Kindersley; page 432: Richard Embery; page 433, top: Richard Embery/Pearson Education/PH College; page 433, bottom: Richard Embery; page 434: Dave King © Dorling Kindersley; page 435: Richard Embery; page 436: Richard Embery/Pearson Education/PH College; page 437, top: Richard Embery; page 437, 2nd from top: Richard Embery; page 437, 3rd from top: Richard Embery; page 437, bottom: Richard Embery; page 438: © Dorling Kindersley; page 439: Dave King © Dorling Kindersley; page 440: © Dorling Kindersley.

UNIT 12

Unit 12 Opener: Dorling Kindersely © Dorling Kindersley; 12-1: EyeWire Collection/Getty Images - Photodisc/Royalty Free; 12-2: Ian O'Leary © Dorling Kindersley; 12-3: Ian O'Leary © Dorling Kindersley; 12-4: © Dorling Kindersley; 12-5: Stanley L. Rowin/Creative Eye/MIRA.com; 12-6: Vincent P. Walter/Pearson Education/PH College; 12-7: Vincent P. Walter/Pearson Education/PH College; page 445, top: Richard Embery; page 445, middle: Richard Embery; page 445, bottom: Richard Embery; page 446: Richard Embery/Pearson Education/PH College; page 447: © Dorling Kindersley; page 448: Richard Embery; page 449: Corbis RF; page 450: Colin Walton © Dorling Kindersley; page 451: Martin Norris © Dorling Kindersley; page 452: Richard Embery/Pearson Education/PH College; page 453: Richard Embery/Pearson Education/PH College; page 454: Richard Embery; page 455, top: Richard Embery; page 455, bottom: Richard Embery; page 456: Richard Embery; page 457: Dave King © Dorling Kindersley; page 458: © Dorling Kindersley; page 459, top: Richard Embery; page 459, bottom: Pearson Education Corporate Digital Archive; page 460: David Murray and Jules Selmes © Dorling Kindersley; page 461: Richard Embery/Pearson Education/PH College; page 462: © Dorling Kindersley; page 463: David Murray and Jules Selmes © Dorling Kindersley; page 464: © Dorling Kindersley; page 465: © Dorling Kindersley; page 466: © Dorling Kindersley; page 467: Richard Embery/Pearson Education/PH College; page 468: Richard Embery; page 469: Richard Embery/Pearson Education/PH College; page 470: Richard Embery/Pearson Education/PH College.

UNIT 13

Unit 13 Opener: Andrew Russetti/Creative Eye/MIRA.com; 13-1: Felicia Martinez/PhotoEdit Inc.; 13-2: Robert Koropp/Stock Connection; page 478: Richard Embery; page 479, top: Richard Embery; page 479, bottom: Richard Embery; page 480: Richard Embery; page 481: Richard Embery; page 482: Dave King © Dorling Kindersley; page 483: Richard Embery; page 484: Richard Embery; page 485: Felicia Martinez/PhotoEdit Inc.; page 486: Dave King © Dorling Kindersley; page 487: Richard Embery/Pearson Education/PH College; page 488: Dave King © Dorling Kindersley; page 489: David Murray and Jules Selmes © Dorling Kindersley; page 490: Richard Embery/Pearson Education/PH College; page 491: Richard Embery/Pearson Education/PH College; page 492: Dave King © Dorling Kindersley; page 493: Richard Embery; page 494: David Murray and Jules Selmes © Dorling Kindersley; page 495, top: Richard Embery; page 495, 2nd from top: Richard Embery; page 495, 3rd from top: Richard Embery; page 495, 4th from top: Richard Embery; page 495, bottom: Richard Embery; page 496: © Culinary Institute of America; page 497: Richard Embery; page 498: Barrie Watts © Dorling Kindersley; page 499: Richard Embery/Pearson Education/PH College; page 500: Dave King © Dorling Kindersley.

UNIT 14

Unit 14 Opener: K Sanchez/Getty Images, Inc.- Photodisc/Royalty Free; 14-1: © Culinary Institute of America; 14-2: Richard Haynes\Prentice Hall School Division; 14-3: David Murray and Jules Selmes © Dorling Kindersley; 14-4: Ian O'Leary © Dorling Kindersley; 14-5: © Dorling Kindersley; 14-6: Steve Gorton © Dorling Kindersley; page 507, top: Richard Embery; page 507, bottom: Richard Embery; page 508, top: Clive Streeter © Dorling Kindersley; page 508, bottom: David Murray © Dorling Kindersley; page 509: Richard Embery/Pearson Education/PH College; page 510: Richard Embery; page 511: Daisuke Morita/Getty Images, Inc.- Photodisc/Royalty Free; page 512: Clive Streeter and Patrick McLeavy © Dorling Kindersley; page 513: Ian O'Leary © Dorling Kindersley; page 514: Mark Stout Photography/Shutterstock; page 515: Richard Embery/Pearson Education/PH College; page 516: Dave King © Dorling Kindersley; page 517: Martin Cameron © Dorling Kindersley; page 518: Richard Embery/Pearson Education/PH College; page 519: Richard Embery/Pearson Education/PH College; page 520: Richard Embery; page 521, top: Richard Embery; page 521, bottom: Elena Schweitzer/Shutterstock; page 522: Skowron/Shutterstock; page 523: Richard Embery; page 524: Dave King © Dorling Kindersley; page 525: David Murray and Jules Selmes © Dorling Kindersley; page 527, top: Richard Embery; page 527, bottom: Richard Embery; page 528, top: Richard Embery; page 528, bottom: Richard Embery/Pearson Education/PH College; page 529, top: Dave King © Dorling Kindersley; page 529, middle: Dave King © Dorling Kindersley; page 529, bottom: Dave King © Dorling Kindersley; page 531: Richard Embery/Pearson Education/PH College; page 532: Richard Embery; page 533: David Murray and Jules Selmes © Dorling Kindersley; page 534: Richard Embery; page 535: Russell Illig/Getty Images, Inc.- Photodisc/Royalty Free; page 536: Richard Embery; page 537: Andy Crawford © Dorling Kindersley; page 538: gosphotodesign\Shutterstock; page 539: selfnouveau/Shutterstock; page 540: David Murray and Jules Selmes © Dorling Kindersley; page 542, top: Richard Embery; page 542, bottom: Richard Embery; page 543, top: Clive Streeter © Dorling Kindersley; page 543, bottom: Richard Embery/Pearson Education/PH College; page 544: Richard Embery; page 545, top: Richard Embery; page 545, bottom: David Murray © Dorling Kindersley; page 546: David Murray © Dorling Kindersley; page 547: Richard Embery; page 549, top: Richard Embery; page 549, middle: Dave King © Dorling Kindersley; page 549, bottom: Richard Embery; page 550: Richard Embery; page 551: Clive Streeter © Dorling Kindersley; page 553: David Murray © Dorling Kindersley; page 554, top: Richard Embery; page 554, bottom: Richard Embery; page 555: Dave King © Dorling Kindersley; page 556: Richard Embery/Pearson Education/PH College; page 557: Martin Brigdale © Dorling Kindersley; page 558: Richard Embery; page 559: © Dorling Kindersley; page 560: Richard Embery.

UNIT 15

Unit 15 Opener: Martin Brigdale © Dorling Kindersley; 15-1: Jerry Young © Dorling Kindersley; 15-2: Mark Burnside/Getty Images Inc. - Stone Allstock; 15-3: Ian O'Leary © Dorling Kindersley; 15-4: Nancy R. Cohen/Getty Images, Inc.- Photodisc/Royalty Free; 15-5: Clive Streeter © Dorling Kindersley; page 565: Getty Images, Inc.- Photodisc; page 566: Richard Embery; page 567, top: Richard Embery; page 567, middle: Richard Embery; page 567, bottom: Richard Embery; page 568: Shutterstock; page 569: © Dorling Kindersley; page 570: David Murray and Jules Selmes © Dorling Kindersley; page 571: David Murray © Dorling Kindersley; page 572: Richard Embery; page 573, top: Ian O'Leary © Dorling Kindersley; page 573, bottom: Ian O'Leary © Dorling Kindersley; page 574, top: Richard Embery; page 574, bottom: Ian O'Leary © Dorling Kindersley; page 575: Ian O'Leary © Dorling Kindersley; page 576: Ian O'Leary © Dorling Kindersley; page 577: David Murray and Jules Selmes © Dorling Kindersley; page 578: David Murray and Jules Selmes © Dorling Kindersley; page 579: © Dorling Kindersley; page 579: Richard Embery/Pearson Education/PH College; page 581: David Murray © Dorling Kindersley; page 582: Dave King © Dorling Kindersley; page 583, top: Richard Embery; page 583, bottom: Ledo/Shutterstock; page 585: Howard Shooter © Dorling Kindersley; page 586: David Murray © Dorling Kindersley; page 587, top: Richard Embery; page 587, bottom: Ian O'Leary © Dorling Kindersley; page 588: © Dorling Kindersley; page 589: © Dorling Kindersley; page 590: Richard Embery/Pearson Education/PH College; page 591: Richard Embery; page 592: David Murray © Dorling Kindersley; page 593: Martin Norris © Dorling Kindersley; page 594: Richard Embery; page 595: David Murray and Jules Selmes © Dorling Kindersley; page 596: Richard Embery; page 597: Martin Norris © Dorling Kindersley; page 599, top: Richard Embery; page 599, middle: Richard Embery; page 599, bottom: Richard Embery; page 600: David Murray © Dorling Kindersley; page 601: Howard Shooter © Dorling Kindersley; page 602: Richard Embery; page 604: W. Atlee Burpee & Co.; page 605: Richard Embery; page 606: Richard Embery/Pearson Education/PH College; page 607, top: Richard Embery; page 607, bottom: Richard Embery/Pearson Education/PH College; page 608: Richard Embery/Pearson Education/PH College; page 610: © Dorling Kindersley; page 611: Dave King © Dorling Kindersley; page 612: Ian O'Leary © Dorling Kindersley; page 613: Richard Embery; page 614: Richard Embery; page 615, top: David Murray and Jules Selmes © Dorling Kindersley; page 615, bottom: James Merrell © Dorling Kindersley; page 616: Richard Embery; page 617: Richard Embery; page 618: Richard Embery.

UNIT 16

Unit 16 Opener: Clive Streeter © Dorling Kindersley; 16-1: Danny Lehman/CORBIS-NY; 16-2: Max Alexander © Dorling Kindersley; 16-3: Roger Phillips © Dorling Kindersley; 16-4: Richard Nowitz/National Geographic Image Collection; 16-5: C Squared Studios/Getty Images, Inc.- Photodisc/Royalty Free; page 627: Dave King © Dorling Kindersley; page 628: © Culinary Institute of America; page 629: Ian O'Leary © Dorling Kindersley; page 631: © Dorling Kindersley; page 632: © Dorling Kindersley; page 633: Ian O'Leary © Dorling Kindersley; page 634: Richard Embery/Pearson Education/PH College; page 638: Richard Embery/Pearson Education/PH College; page 639: Richard Embery; page 640: Dave King © Dorling Kindersley; page 643: Paul Williams © Dorling Kindersley; page 644: David Murray and Jules Selmes © Dorling Kindersley;

page 645: Richard Embery/Pearson Education/PH College; page 646: UNI/Dorling Kindersley Media Library; page 647: Dave King © Dorling Kindersley; page 648: Richard Embery; page 649: David Murray © Dorling Kindersley; page 650: David Murray and Jules Selmes © Dorling Kindersley; page 651: SGM/Stock Connection; page 652: Ian O'Leary © Dorling Kindersley; page 653: David Murray © Dorling Kindersley.

UNIT 17

Unit 17 Opener: Dave King © Dorling Kindersley; 17-1: Richard Embery/Pearson Education/PH College; 17-2: Richard Embery; 17-3: Roger Phillips © Dorling Kindersley; 17-4: Roger Phillips © Dorling Kindersley; 17-5: © Dorling Kindersley; 17-6: Richard Embery; 17-7: Richard Embery/Pearson Education/PH College; 17-8: Richard Embery; 17-9: Richard Embery; 17-10: Richard Embery; 17-11: Richard Embery; 17-12: Richard Embery; 17-13: Richard Embery; 17-14: Richard Embery; 17-15: Richard Embery; 17-16: Richard Embery; 17-17: Richard Embery; 17-18: Richard Embery; 17-19: Richard Embery; 17-20: Richard Embery; 17-21: Richard Embery; 17-22: Richard Embery; 17-23 © Culinary Institute of America; 17-24: Richard Embery; 17-25: Richard Embery; 17-26: Richard Embery; 17-27: Richard Embery; 17-28: Richard Embery; 17-29: Richard Embery; 17-30: Richard Embery; 17-31: Richard Embery; 17-32: Richard Embery; 17-33: Richard Embery; 17-34: Richard Embery; 17-35: Richard Embery; 17-36: Richard Embery; 17-37: Richard Embery; 17-38: Richard Embery; 17-39: Richard Embery; 17-40: Richard Embery; 17-41: Richard Embery; 17-42: Richard Embery; 17-43: Richard Embery; 17-44: Richard Embery; 17-45: © Culinary Institute of America; 17-46: David Murray and Jules Selmes © Dorling Kindersley; 17-47: Richard Embery; 17-48: Richard Embery; 17-49: Richard Embery; 17-50: Richard Embery; 17-51: Richard Embery; 17-52: Richard Embery; 17-53: David Murray and Jules Selmes © Dorling Kindersley; 17-54: Richard Embery; page 660, top: Dave King © Dorling Kindersley; page 660, middle: David Murray © Dorling Kindersley; page 660, bottom: David Murray and Jules Selmes © Dorling Kindersley; page 661, top: Diana Miller © Dorling Kindersley; page 661, middle: Diana Miller © Dorling Kindersley; page 661, bottom: Dave King © Dorling Kindersley; page 662: David Murray and Jules Selmes © Dorling Kindersley; page 663: David Murray and Jules Selmes © Dorling Kindersley; page 664, top: Richard Embery/Pearson Education/PH College; page 664, middle: Richard Embery/Pearson Education/PH College; page 664, bottom: Richard Embery/Pearson Education/PH College; page 665: Richard Embery/Pearson Education/PH College; page 666: Richard Embery/Pearson Education/PH College; page 667: David Murray and Jules Selmes © Dorling Kindersley; page 668: © Culinary Institute of America; page 669: Richard Embery/Pearson Education/PH College; page 679: David Murray and Jules Selmes © Dorling Kindersley; page 680: Dave King © Dorling Kindersley; page 681: Andy Crawford and Steve Gorton © Dorling Kindersley; page 682, top left: Richard Embery/Pearson Education/PH College; page 682, top right: Ian O'Leary © Dorling Kindersley; page 682, bottom: Richard Embery; page 683: © Culinary Institute of America; page 684: Roger Phillips © Dorling Kindersley; page 685: Philip Dowell © Dorling Kindersley; page 686: Ian O'Leary © Dorling Kindersley; page 687: David Murray © Dorling Kindersley; page 688: David Murray © Dorling Kindersley; page 689: Ian O'Leary © Dorling Kindersley; page 690: Jerry Young © Dorling Kindersley; page 691: Richard Embery; page 692: Richard Embery; page 693: © Dorling Kindersley; page 694: Richard Embery; page 695: Richard Embery/Pearson Education/PH College; page 696: Ian O'Leary © Dorling Kindersley; page 701: Philip Dowell © Dorling Kindersley; page 703: Richard Embery; page 704: Richard Embery; page 705: David Murray and Jules Selmes © Dorling Kindersley; page 707: Martin Norris © Dorling Kindersley; page 708: Dave King © Dorling Kindersley; page 709: © Culinary Institute of America; page 710: Richard Embery/Pearson Education/PH College; page 711, top: Richard Embery; page 711, bottom: Richard Embery; page 712: David Murray and Jules Selmes © Dorling Kindersley; page 713: Richard Embery/Pearson Education/PH College; page 714: Richard Embery/Pearson Education/PH College; page 715: David Murray and Jules Selmes © Dorling Kindersley; page 716: David Murray and Jules Selmes © Dorling Kindersley; page 717, top: Ian O'Leary © Dorling Kindersley; page 717, bottom: © Culinary Institute of America; page 718: David Murray and Jules Selmes © Dorling Kindersley; page 719: Ian O'Leary © Dorling Kindersley; page 720, left: Richard Embery; page 720, middle: Richard Embery; page 720, top: Richard Embery; page 720, 2nd from top: Richard Embery; page 720, 3rd from top: Richard Embery; page 721: Richard Embery/Pearson Education/PH College.

UNIT 18

Unit 18 Opener: Richard Embery/Pearson Education/PH College; 18-1: Diana Miller © Dorling Kindersley; 18-2: Richard Embery; 18-3: Stephen Hayward © Dorling Kindersley; 18-4: Belinda Banks/Getty Images Inc. - Stone Allstock; 18-5: Silva, Juan/Getty Images Inc. - Image Bank; 18-6: Richard Embery/Pearson Education/PH College; 18-7: Artex International, Ltd.; 18-8: Sandra Ivany/Jupiter Images - PictureArts Corporation; 18-9: G Huntington/Pearson Education Corporate Digital Archive; 18-10: Robert Fried/robertfriedphotography.com; 18-11: © PAUL THOMPSON/DanitaDelimont.com; 18-12: Greg Ward © Rough Guides; 18-13: Richard Embery/Pearson Education/PH College; 18-14: Richard Embery/Pearson Education/PH College; 18-15: Richard Embery; 18-16: Gary Ombler © Dorling Kindersley; 18-17: Richard Embery/Pearson Education/PH College; 18-18: © Culinary Institute of America; 18-19: Pearson Education/PH College; 18-20: Stephen Hayward/Dorling Kindersley Media Library; 18-21: Cleve Bryant/PhotoEdit Inc.; 18-22: Chad Ehlers/Stock Connection; page 742: Roger Phillips © Dorling Kindersley; page 743: Fundamental Photographs, NYC.

UNIT 19

Unit 19 Opener: Cindy Charles/PhotoEdit Inc.; 19-2: Christopher Elwell/Shutterstock; 19-3: fotozotti/Shutterstock; 19-4: Richard Embery; 19-5: Goygel-Sokol Dmitry/Shutterstock; 19-6: Denkou Images/Fotolia, LLC; 19-7: Goygel-Sokol Dmitry/Shutterstock; 19-8: Vincent P. Walter/Pearson Education/PH College; 19-9: Richard Embery/Pearson Education/PH College; 19-10: Richard Embery; 19-11: Richard Embery; 19-12: Richard Embery; 19-13: Richard Embery; 19-14: Richard Embery; 19-15: Richard Embery; 19-16: Sian Irvine © Dorling Kindersley; 19-17: Vincent P. Walter/Pearson Education/PH College; 19-18: Richard Embery.

UNIT 20

Unit 20 Opener: Martin Brigdale © Dorling Kindersley; 20-1: ANCIENT ART & ARCHITECTURE/DanitaDelimont.com; 20-2: Jeff Greenberg/PhotoEdit Inc.; 20-3: Gary Conner/PhotoEdit Inc.; 20-4: Bibliotheque des Arts Decoratifs, Paris, France/The Bridgeman Art Library; 20-5: Dennis MacDonald/PhotoEdit Inc.; 20-6: Vincent P. Walter/Pearson Education/PH College; 20-7: SGM/Stock Connection; 20-8: Richard Embery/Pearson Education/PH College; 20-9: Jerry Young © Dorling Kindersley; 20-10: Richard Embery/Pearson Education/PH College; 20-11: Richard Embery; 20-12: Richard Embery; 20-13: Richard Embery; 20-14: Richard Embery; 20-15: Clive Streeter © Dorling Kindersley; 20-16: David Murray and Jules Selmes © Dorling Kindersley; 20-17: Richard Embery/Pearson Education/PH College; 20-18: Richard Embery/Pearson Education/PH College; 20-19: Getty Images, Inc. – Photodisc; 20-20: David Murray and Jules Selmes © Dorling Kindersley; 20-21: David Murray and Jules Selmes © Dorling Kindersley; 20-22: David Murray and Jules Selmes © Dorling Kindersley; 20-23: Clive Streeter © Dorling Kindersley; 20-24: Ian O'Leary © Dorling Kindersley; 20-25: Allen Polansky/Stock Connection; 20-26: © Dorling Kindersley; 20-27: © Dorling Kindersley; 20-28: Letizia Spanò/Shutterstock; 20-29: David Murray © Dorling Kindersley; 20-30: Jerry Young © Dorling Kindersley; 20-31: Diana Miller © Dorling Kindersley; 20-33: Richard Embery; 20-34: Richard Embery; 20-35: Viesti Associates, Inc.; 20-36: Richard Embery; 20-37: Richard Embery; 20-38: Richard Embery; 20-39: Richard Embery; 20-40: Richard Embery; 20-41: Richard Embery; 20-42: Richard Embery; 20-44: Richard Embery; 20-46: Carlisle FoodService Products; 20-47: Richard Embery; 20-48: Richard Embery; 20-49: Richard Embery; 20-50: Richard Embery; 20-51: Richard Embery; 20-51: Richard Embery; 20-52: Richard Embery; 20-53: Richard Embery; page 774: Culinary Institute of America; page 775: Dave King © Dorling Kindersley; page 776: David Murray © Dorling Kindersley; page 777: Richard Embery/Pearson Education/PH College; page 778: © Dorling Kindersley; page 779, top: Richard Embery/Pearson Education/PH College; page 779, bottom: Ian O'Leary/Dorling Kindersley Media Library; page 780: © Dorling Kindersley; page 781: Richard Embery/Pearson Education/PH College; page 783, top: Jerry Young © Dorling Kindersley; page 783, middle: © Culinary Institute of America; page 783, bottom: Richard Embery/Pearson Education/PH College; page 784, top: Richard Embery/Pearson Education/PH College; page 784, middle: Jerry Young © Dorling Kindersley; page 784, bottom left: Ian O'Leary © Dorling Kindersley; page 785: Shutterstock/Nordling; page 786: Richard Embery; page 787: Clive Streeter © Dorling Kindersley; page 788: Richard Embery; page 789: Jerry Young © Dorling Kindersley; page 790: Richard Embery/Pearson Education/PH College; page 799: Jerry Young © Dorling Kindersley; page 800: Richard Embery/Pearson Education/PH College; page 801: David Murray and Jules Selmes © Dorling Kindersley; page 803, top: Richard Embery; page 803, bottom: Richard Embery/Pearson Education/PH College; page 805: Richard Embery/Pearson Education/PH College; page 806: Steve Gorton © Dorling Kindersley; page 813: Richard Embery; page 816: Richard Embery; page 817: Richard Embery.

UNIT 21

Unit 21 Opener: Tina Powers; 21-1: Tina Powers; 21-2: Tina Powers; 21-3: Tina Powers; 21-4: Tina Powers; 21-5: Tina Powers; 21-6: Tina Powers; 21-7: Tina Powers; 21-8: Tina Powers; 21-9: Tina Powers; 21-10: Tina Powers; Page 833: © Culinary Institute of America; page 834: Richard Embery/Pearson Education/PH College; page 835: Richard Embery/Pearson Education/PH College; page 836: Jerry Young © Dorling Kindersley; page 837: Richard Embery.